CHRISTIAN
ROMAN EMPIRE
SERIES

Vol. 10

THE

COMPLETE WORKS

OF

SAINT CYPRIAN

OF CARTHAGE

edited by

Phillip Campbell

introduction by

Ryan Grant

Evolution Publishing
Merchantville NJ
2013

Translation of St. Cyprian's works
originally published as part of
The Ante-Nicene Fathers:
The Writings of the Fathers down to AD 325,
Volume 5
1885

This edition © 2013 by Evolution Publishing
Merchantville, New Jersey.

Printed in the United States of America

ISBN 978-1-935228-11-0

Library of Congress Cataloging-in-Publication Data

Cyprian, Saint, Bishop of Carthage.
 [Works. English. 2013]
 The complete works of Saint Cyprian of Carthage / edited by Phillip Campbell ;
introduction by Ryan Grant.
     pages cm. -- (Christian Roman empire series ; vol. 10)
 "Translation of St. Cyprian's works originally published as part of The Ante-
Nicene Fathers: The Writings of the Fathers down to AD 325, Volume 5, 1885."
 Includes bibliographical references and index.
 ISBN 978-1-935228-11-0 (alk. paper)
 1. Theology--Early works to 1800. I. Title.
 BR65.C8E5 2013
 230'.13--dc23
                            2013009135

TABLE OF CONTENTS

INTRODUCTION

"It is superfluous to weave together the sign of his genius, since his works are brighter than the sun."[1]

These words of St. Jerome on the merits of St. Cyprian are no exaggeration. Among the Fathers of the Christian Church, few stand out as brilliantly as St. Cyprian of Carthage. Cyprian was one of the first of the Latin Fathers, and his importance in the development of Latin Christianity cannot easily be overstated. His fearless advocacy for the unity of the Church and contributions in the field of ecclesiology made him a pillar and inspiration for the universal Church of later centuries. In the course of his writings he appropriated a number of classical Latin terms and imbued them with a Catholic meaning, developing the foundations of what would become a standard theological Latin vocabulary in the west. The conflicts over the *lapsi* and the rebaptism controversy at the end of his episcopate gave the Church the impetus to further develop its theology of penance, indulgences, and sacraments; Cyprian was at the core of all these discussions. His maxims, like "No salvation outside the Church," and "He cannot have God as his Father who will not have the Church as his Mother," are still as potent today as they were in the third century. Between Tertullian in the second century and Augustine in the fourth, the African Church produced no greater luminary than St. Cyprian.

Thascus Caecilius Cyprianus was born around the year 200. His deacon Pontius wrote a treatise of his life that has survived to our day and is included in this work (although it treats mainly of the details of Cyprian's martyrdom). Cyprian was born to pagan parents and trained as a jurist, orator and lawyer known for his eloquence.

His conversion came about by a priest named Caecilianus, with whom Cyprian went to live when he became a catechumen. In his zeal Cyprian sold his worldly goods and his estates with their many gardens and distributed them to the poor. He was baptized in approximately 246 and began to write shortly thereafter. His first Christian work was the monologue *Ad Donatum*, where Cyprian compares the worldly life of Roman society and juxtaposes it with Christian virtue, which alone gives one the ability to conquer vice.

He went on to write twelve treatises and over eighty letters whose blunt and forceful exposition of the Catholic Faith made him renowned even in his own day. Unlike other ealry Fathers (St. Justin Martyr or St. Clement of Alexandria), Cyprian was neither a philosopher nor a theologian. Despite his eloquence, his mind was not philosophical or abstract, but rather legal and administrative, and it is as administrator of the sprawling Church of Carthage that he is at his best.

This is the great irony of Cyprian's episcopate; though he made monumental contributions to the Church's theology, he was not a theologian but rather a pastor at heart. His theological contributions were ancillary to real pastoral concerns.

It seems that Cyprian decided early on to pursue the priesthood. His official biography suggests that he had been married as a pagan but that his wife opposed his conversion.[2] What became of her is not known, but he was in fact ordained to the priesthood shortly after his baptism. He made rapid progress in holiness and was soon chosen to be the bishop of Carthage. Not everyone in Carthage was happy with his election, as he had been a Christian a very short time and many considered Cyprian too inexperienced for the episcopate. Others saw his elevation as a sign of God's approval. Pontius tells us: "For the proof of his good works I think that this one thing is enough—that by the judgement of God and the favor of the people, he was chosen to the office of the priesthood and the degree of the episcopate while still a neophyte, and, as it was, considered a novice."[3] Upon election he immediately set to putting his administrative skills to work reforming his diocese and enforcing ecclesiastical discipline.

Even as St. Cyprian was busy bringing order and discipline to the Church of Carthage, the order of the Roman world at large was breaking down. The Roman empire in the mid 3rd century was in a state of anarchy commonly called the "Crisis of the Third Century." The historical background that led up to the crisis is too great to be treated here, but it suffices to say that the power, efficiency and civil virtue that had once characterized the Roman government had long since waned and given way to administrative ineptitude and internal dissention. Since the reign of Septimius Severus (193-211) the empire had been dominated by a series of military dictatorships. Rival generals vied for power and civil war engulfed the empire. From 235 to 285, Rome saw over twenty-five rulers ascend to the purple with an average reign of two years; almost every emperor during this period began and ended their reign in blood. The situation was made worse by monetary inflation, the beginning of the barbarian invasions, natural disasters and even an outbreak of the plague. Rome seemed on the road to collapse.

Historians continue to debate the causes for Rome's sudden decline in the mid-3rd century, and the question is far from settled. What is certain is that this inner decay exacerbated the political problems within the structure of the empire; specifically problematic was the issue of imperial succession, which had always been a tricky business in ancient Rome. From the time of Augustus, the first emperor, Rome had no stable policy of succession. Sometimes succession was dynastic, as in the case of the Julio-Claudians; sometimes emperors appointed their successors, as with the much-praised Antonines; sometimes a general simply killed and replaced an emperor, as usually happened in the latter empire. With the continual rise of usurpers from the death of Marcus Aurelius through the remainder of the life of the Roman Empire, the army spent more time fighting itself than foreign enemies. Meanwhile, foreign powers, such as Persia, cut away Roman territory on the empire's periphery. If we had to isolate one factor that ensured Rome's fall more than anything else, the lack of any tradition of succession would probably be it.

The pagans of the day, however, blamed their woes on Roman society's loss of the classical virtue of *pietas*, which meant for the Romans not piety, but reverence for one's forefathers, country and patriotic gods. The reverent practice of *pietas* brought about the *pax deorum*, the peace of the gods, whereby the public veneration of the fatherland and its gods secured the blessings of peace and stability. Thus, when the new Roman Emperor Decius ascended to the imperial purple in 249, one of his goals was to restore the ancient public virtues linked with the ancient patriarchal gods of the Roman people, which would again bring down the blessing of the gods upon the empire. The problem was deceivingly simple: the *pax deorum* had been disrupted, and to restore stability it must be restored.

Though many religious movements struggled for supremacy in third century Rome, it was against the Christians that Decius turned with special fury, for it was well known that they steadfastly refused to worship the state gods of the empire. Not only did they refuse to practice Roman *pietas*, but they went so far as to claim that the gods of Rome were in fact demons. The Jews, also, refused to participate in the state worship, but the Romans were not as alarmed by this because the Jewish practice was to keep to themselves and have no intermingling with common pagans. Due to the prevailing Pharisaic interpretation of the Covenant at the time, the Jews were not driven by an evangelical impulse. The great antiquity of the Jewish religion also earned them some respect from the Romans, who valued tradition and antiquity.

This was not the case with Christianity, which seemed a dangerous and treasonous novelty. Christians not only refused to worship the gods of Rome but sought to teach every man to do likewise. This was severely problematic, especially in the tumultuous climate of the mid-third century, where the Christian "threat" appeared particularly sinister.

At the time Decius ascended to the throne, North Africa had enjoyed many years of peace and very little persecution. Many in the Church had been given to worldly living, especially among the clergy. This would change violently in January of 250 when Decius issued an edict demanding that every free Roman was to offer sacrifice to the ancestral gods within the space of a year, to be witnessed by a government official. Christians had been put in this dilemma before, but Decius' edict represents the first universal, empire-wide persecution of the Church.

When Christians refused to offer sacrifice to the gods, they were imprisoned or executed. In North Africa, some of the Carthaginian clergy fled. Among them was Cyprian and he directed the affairs of his see from hiding. Some of the clergy at Rome and Carthage criticized him for this, for which afterward he would make account of himself at the Council of Carthage of 251.[4] During this period Cyprian also wrote elegant accounts of numerous martyrdoms. While it is debatable whether Cyprian's flight was motivated by fear or prudence, it is certain that it preserved his life. Cyprian's fellow bishop Pope Fabian chose to remain in Rome and suffered martyrdom. Matters were in such disarray that it took the Roman Church a year to elect another pope.

Though the persecution swiftly came to an end with the death of Decius in 251, it had revealed a real lack of fortitude among many Christians. An embarrassing number of believers had apostasized during the persecution. Those who apostasized and sacrificed to the pagan gods were known as the *lapsi* (the lapsed, or fallen); these were further subdivided into those who merely pinched incense (*thurificati*) and those who actually offered a sacrifice (*sacrifitici*). Still worse, some had avoided the difficulty by bribing magistrates to obtain a certificate stating that they had sacrificed; these were called the *libellatici*, the "certificate-takers."

How to reconcile those *lapsi* who sought readmission to the Church posed a serious problem. On the one hand, the Church had an undeniable mission to forgive the sinner and restore the brother who had fallen and sought reconciliation with tears. On the other hand, a reconciliation of the *laspi* that was too quick or too easy would be a grave offense against the martyrs, many of whom had suffered horrible torments rather than deny the Faith. This was St. Cyprian's first pastoral dilemma as he returned from hiding at the close of the persecution.

One popular method was to have the *lapsi* ask forgiveness from other confessors and martyrs as they were going to their death. The grant of forgiveness by the martyrs served as a kind of indulgence, commuting the penance of the *lapsi* and allowing them a swift reconciliation. Cyprian, while not denying the validity of this practice, had serious concerns about the liberality with which these letters of indulgence (*libelli*) were being granted and he insisted that each case be evaluated individually and sufficient penances be imposed.[5] Some thought Cyprian's approach too lenient while others believed it was too strict.

The various reactions to reconciliation of the lapsed produced a number of schisms, both among those who thought no one should be reconciled, and those who thought everyone should be reconciled with no penance. The first work Cyprian composed upon returning from hiding was *De Lapsis* ("On the Lapsed"), which preaches the reconciliation of the lapsed provided that they confess their faults and endure public penance. Due to the schisms which had developed, he also at this time composed his classic work *De Unitate Ecclesiae* ("On the Unity of the Church") which contains the immortal words: "*Habere non potest Deum patrem, qui non habet ecclesiam matrem*".[6] *De Unitate* is the centerpiece of the Cyprianic corpus and most perfectly and succinctly summarizes his ecclesiology.

Decius died in battle on the Rhine in June of 251, which allowed Church life to regain some normality. The Roman Church elected a new pope, Cornelius, for whom Cyprian would form such an affinity that they are always mentioned together in the Roman canon.

As things recovered, several of the clergy in Rome wrote a letter criticizing Cyprian for his flight during the persecution. As noted, Cyprian's purpose was to continue directing the affairs of the Church rather than save his own skin. He called a council to defend himself, and also wrote several letters explaining his activities to the Roman clergy who had written inquiring about his conduct. He also read to the Carthaginian bishops an account of the election of Cornelius as pope in Rome, although it was accompanied by a contentious letter from a certain priest named Novatian, who would become a thorn in Cyprian's flesh.

Just as a schismatic party developed in Carthage who had thought St. Cyprian was too severe in imposing penance, so Novatian became the head of a rigorist party at Rome who thought Pope Cornelius was too mild in even reconciling the *lapsi* at all. This Novatian obtained episcopal consecration and set himself up as an anti-pope. Cyprian passed over Novatian's letter condemning Cornelius in the council, but sent Bishops to Rome to investigate. After ascertaining the facts of Cornelius' election, the North African Church unanimously communicated with Pope Cornelius—a sign of the importance of papal elections at that time. The Church of Carthage remained faithful to the pope.

Meanwhile, Novatian sent priests to the major cities of the Christian world, as Dionysius of Alexandria says, to Antioch, Jerusalem, Tyre, Alexandria, Syria, etc. This is a fascinating witness to the supremacy the Papacy enjoyed in the third century, that an anti-Pope would presume to demand that every Church communicate with him. Cyprian wrote to the pope and also sent him copies of his *De Lapsis* and *De Unitate* along with some letters which caused several who had followed Novatian to return to the cause of Pope Cornelius. Confusion reigned for several months, but at last the true story of Cornelius' election became known and all churches again communicated with the legitimate claimant of the papal throne. The Novatian schism ended, in large part due to the vehement defense of Cornelius's cause by St. Cyprian. Cyprian's language in *De Unitate* is a clear witness to what Catholics believed and still believe concerning the chair of Peter. Cyprian's style and language, however, are not of a brilliant theologian, but of a practical man with practical applications of the Tradition, applied in much the style that he is described to have conducted all affairs as a bishop.

Cyprian became powerfully attached to Pope Cornelius during the schism, but the friendship was prematurely ended when Cornelius was martyred in 253 under the renewed persecution of the emperors Gallus and Volusianus. He was succeeded by St. Lucius, who was quickly exiled, and died shortly thereafter. Following a pause in the persecution after the death of Gallus, Stephen, the archdeacon of Pope Lucius, ascended the Chair of Peter as Pope Stephen I. The election of Pope Stephen set the stage for Cyprian's dramatic conflict with the papacy.

Once again, the issue would be reconciliation, but this time the individuals in question were not *lapsi*, but penitent heretics. The presence of schisms originating from heresy raised the question of what to do about those who converted from heretical sects such as the Montanists and the Marcionites and had received baptism in those sects. One custom was to re-baptize those who had been baptized by heretics, arguing on various grounds that their baptism was invalid. This was prevalent in Africa, and in certain parts of the East. Other churches, however, observed the Roman custom of simply laying hands on the penitent heretics before readmitting them to the Church. This practice implicitly recognized the validity of baptisms performed outside of the institutional Church and was directly at odds with the North African custom. Cyprian, when consulted, strongly affirmed the North African practice of re-baptizing, as evidently he considered it a matter of discipline, not doctrine. He called a council at Carthage in 255 and affirmed the practice. He also began writing letters to other bishops, arguing against the Roman custom with increasing forcefulness and advocating the African custom of re-baptism.

At this point Pope Stephen decided to intervene. The pope wrote a rather severe letter addressed to St. Cyprian and the African Church declaring, "If any might come to you from any heresy, nothing should be innovated except that which was handed down, namely that the hand is imposed over them in penance."[7] He even went so far as to threaten St. Cyprian with excommunication should the Bishop of Carthage not comply.

It is interesting to note the context in which each side placed their argument. Cyprian for his own part seemed to regard it as a matter of discipline, and continued to resist the pope (though the Seventh Council of Carthage, convened to address this issue, would offer many theological explanations to back up the North African discipline). The pope also seemed to regard the matter as a disciplinary affair and demanded unquestioning obedience of Carthage to the Roman custom. The polemics between Rome and Carthage grew more and more heated.

The dispute could have erupted into a full-blown schism had the problem not resolved itself in 257 with the death of Stephen and the election Pope Sixtus II, who was more diplomatic than the his contentious predecessor. The new pontiff was cautious in handling the situation; given that many in the east held to the same practice as the North Africans, Sixtus seemed think it best to let the issue quitely drop rather than risk open schism with a large number of churches. We can also see in this the hand of God, for had a major schism erupted, Cyprian's place in the annals of Church history would undoubtdely be greatly diminished. Instead of an ardent supporter of Church unity, he might be remembered as a fomentor of schism.

As subsequent developments in doctrine would uphold the Roman pratice, it is without question that Cyprian was in error in the rebaptism controversy. Yet, it seems clear that his error was in theory, not in any motivation or stubborn denial of papal authority or desire to break bonds with the See of Rome. Neither Cyprian nor the pope wanted schism. It is interesting that no one, including Pope Stephen, seems to have thought of the teaching later furnished by St. Augustine: that Christ Himself is the minister of the sacraments, not the priest or bishop, and that the validity of a sacrament depends not upon the merits of the one who administers it. Cyprian clearly believed that the validity of baptism was at least related to the standing of the minister, though he did not work out this theory too far beyond this fundamental point. One could obviously cite pastoral concerns for this position: if the regenerating waters of life were available from the hands of heretics, to what purpose need anyone join the Church? Yet Cyprian might have had another motivation behind his vehement support of rebaptism. Cyprian tended to follow his fellow North African Tertullian in many things prior to the latter's falling into the Montanist sect. We learn from St. Jerome that Cyprian read Tertullian's writings every day.[8] In fact, it appears that Tertullian was Cyprian's only major source for Christian doctrine other than the Scriptures. Rebaptism of heretics was a particular teaching of Tertullian which he would carry out even as a Montanist, and Cyprian appears to have felt that this teaching was handed down from Tradition.[9]

In 257 the new Emperor Valerian renewed the persecution against the Church. The persecution was savage but short. Valerian's edict ordered bishops, priests and deacons to be apprehended and put to death. Pope Sixtus was put to death in the catacombs. That same year Cyprian was exiled by the proconsul to Curubis, a village on the coast near Carthage where Cyprian maintained a villa. Cyprian remained there for a year directing and guiding the affairs of the Church, as well as providing for the poor and needy. His last letters are a flurry of correspondance with several bishops whom had been exiled to the mines. He was finally summoned again to the proconsul and asked to sacrifice. Cyprian refused and was subsequently blindfolded and beheaded in the yard of his villa, the first bishop-martyr of the Carthaginian church. Pontius the Deacon says the whole village turned out to watch the beheading with people climbing up into the trees to get a better view.[10] With characteristic charity, Cyprian commanded that a sum of money be provided to the executioner in payment for his service. His martyrdom occurred on September 14, 258. The saint's body was hung up for public view for a time but was taken and interred by the faithful near the place of his execution shortly afterward. Churches marked the spots of his martyrdom and villa until destroyed by the Vandals in the 5th century.

Moving from the life of the saint to his writings, Cyprian's works are divided properly into treatises and letters. As mentioned previously, he was dependent upon Tertullian for much of his thought, yet his writing style is clearly his own and differs widely from that of Tertullian. His diction is free, pleasant and as Lactantius and St. Jerome describe, like a transparent and tranquil stream.[11] Since the themes of his writings vary tremendously it is probably best to consider his works chronologically.

Ad Donatum, ("To Donatus," composed sometime between 246 and 248) was his first known work and takes the form of a monologue composed to an unknown friend on how the virtues of Christianity alone allowed him to conquer the vices of the world.

Next comes his treatise *De Habitu Virginum* ("On the Dress of Virgins") which was essentially a pastoral letter to women and was Cyprian's first work as the Bishop of Carthage. It warns the women of his flock particularly to avoid vanity in dress, which was as much a problem at that time as it is today. He refers to women, particularly women devoted to God's service, as "the blossoms on the tree of the Church."[12] Many scholars have noted that it resembles Tertullian's work *De Cultu Feminarum*, from which Cyprian drew heavily.

The saint wrote little during the Decian persecution. Towards its end, we see an exchange of letters with the Roman Church justifying his flight into hiding. Following the conclusion of the persecution in 251, Cyprian composed *De Lapsis* ("On the Lapsed") where he laments the apostasy of so many Christians and lays down a strict program of penance as a condition for their reconciliation; this treatise was coupled with several pastoral letters to other bishops on the manner in which the *lapsi* were to be reconciled. Cyprian's doctrine is an important point in the development of patristic sacramental teaching on penance. As would be the case in the medieval Church, a public penance was required for grave sins, and so the *lapsi* were required to make a good confession and have a penance that corresponded to their degree of fault.

In the same year belongs his immortal work *De Catholicae Ecclesiae Unitate* ("On the Unity of th Church"), a formidable defense of the Church against the Novatian schismatics. Cyprian states that Christ founded His Church on one, namely Peter. The unity of the foundation guarantees the unity of the edifice, while schism and heresy are used by the devil to undermine it. One of his most famous phrases, *habere non potest Deum patrem, qui ecclesiam non habet matrem*,[13] shows his understanding of the catholicity of the Church, its universality: every man must belong to it without exception, and those who claim to be faithful to the revelation of Jesus Christ but refuse obedience to the one Catholic Church are hypocrites. Though Cyprian did not invent the phrase "catholicity" he certainly enunciated the principle more than any father before him when faced with schism and heresy both in Carthage and abroad. Properly speaking, St. Cyprian is the first theorist of catholicity, yet his thinking is still imperfect and has sometimes been given to misinterpretation.

He believes power is shared by bishops equally as a whole and individually.[14] Cyprian clearly believes that bishops have a certain autonomy, yet not an absolute autonomy. There must be a consensus of the faithful, centered upon the one Rock upon which the Church was founded. Yet, as we saw, his formulation of this doctrine of universality did not stop him from vehemently opposing the pope's teaching later in his episcopate. While Cyprian pioneers thought on the question of universality, he seems to not have fully understood all that is entailed by the privileges of Peter. Clearly this doctrine of papal authority, though present incipently in patristic teaching, was not fully developed in Cyprian's time, or if it were, Cyprian had not yet worked out its implications. This could be attributed to the rapidity of his conversion, entrance to the priesthood and elevation to the episcopacy. Cyprian did not know any Greek and thus the corpus of the eastern fathers was inaccesible to him.

Chronologically, the next work is his treatise *De Dominica Oratione* ("On the Lord's Prayer"), written around 252, which became a commonly read exposition of the Our Father in antiquity. Here Cyprian shows himself as concerned with practical morality as a pastor leading his flock to salvation. The particular virtue which he puts before his flock is charity, which cuts envy at the root and is an essential for a life of prayer, as well as grace which draws the newly baptized away from the stale atmosphere of paganism.

Between 252 and 254 he composed the treatise *De Mortalitate* ("On Mortality"), commenting on the pestilence that raged throughout Carthage and the whole Roman Empire. It offers consolation and reminds Christians that the plague carried off the faithful as well as the heathens because all Christians must eventually suffer trial and adversity. In this attempt to offer an explanation for the suffering of the good along with the evil, it anticipates the arguments of St. Augustine in *City of God.* To the same period belongs *De Opere et Elemosynis*, ("On Works and Almsgiving"), reminding Christians of the grace which is to be obtained to atone for our post-baptismal faults.

De Bono Patientiae ("On the Advantage of Patience") was written during the summer of 256 in the midst of the rebaptism controversy in order to encourage peace among the churches of North Africa. Likewise *De Zelo et Livore* ("On Jealousy") was a work depicting a reconciling arbiter and a deciding judge. Envy and jealousy are portrayed as poisonous shoots which strike at the heart of the soil of the Church, which bring about their fruits, schism and heresy.

In *Ad Fortunatum* ("Exhortation to Martyrdom"), written in 257, Cyprian collected passages from the Scripture and arranged them to give solace to the faithful during persecution. This work has particular value in arranging the verses of the old Italian Latin translation of the Bible, which precedes St. Jerome's Vulgate and has been indispensable for scholars to reconstruct its contents. In this work Cyprian sets up thirteen theses relative to the trials of this world, confirming each by quotations from the Scriptures.

To the same year belongs *Ad Quirinum* ("Three Books of Testimonies Against the Jews") which is an apologetical work showing the Jewish rejection of the Messiah and the vocation of Christians, as well as a sketch on Christology (Book 2) and virtues (Book 3), where he especially emphasizes the Theological Virtues. Like *Ad Fortunatum* they are filled with scriptural quotations to reenforce his arguments.

Cyprian's letters all date from the time of his episcopacy, from 248–258. These vividly paint for us the life of the Church in North Africa, as well as many of the facts of the life of the great Bishop of Carthage. They provide doctrinal teaching and illuminate the motivations of the characters involved in some of the controversies of Cyprian's day, such as Novatian and Pope Stephen. Cyprian's letters clearly and forcefully express his theology and many have an apologetical value for modern Catholics, such as Letter 63 which confirms the traditional Catholic doctrine on the sacrificial character of the Holy Eucharist.

Cyprian's authority and fame were so great that soon spurious works would be attributed to him, such as *De Laude Martyrii; Adversus Judaeos; De Montibus Sina et Sion; De Spectaculis; De Bono Pudicitiae, Ad Novatianum* and *De Aleatoribus*. Scholars universally reject their Cyprianic authorship and consequently they do not appear in this volume. Yet, that so many works should be attributed to Cyprian shows how universally he was admired in the early Church. Cyprian's deacon Pontius declares: "...the memory of his worthy name survives; and although the profuse fertility of his eloquence and of God's grace so expands itself in the exuberance and richness of his discourse, that he will probably never cease to speak even to the end of the world."[15] Augustine makes use of Cyprian in a reply to a Donatist: "If the authority of St. Cyprian delights you...why are you not delighted because the unity of the world and of all nations he kept by zeal and defended by disputation?"[16] St. Jerome's statement, which appears at the heading of this introduction, is worth repeating: "It is superfluous to weave together the sign of his genius, since his works are brighter than the sun."[17]

In so many ways Cyprian is a model for us not only in adversity, but in virtue, in charity and in his theological methodology. His faults, as we mentioned, appear to have more to do with his rapid entry into the faith than any fault in virtue. To the end he is a stirring witness of the life of grace fertilizing generations of seeds planted in the earth by the Apostles, blossoming in the fertile ground of the Holy Church. Prudentius perhaps provides the best tribute we can render of St. Cyprian:

Punica terra tulit quo splendeat omne quidquid usquam est,
inde domo Cyprianum, sed decus orbis et magistrum.
Est proprius patriæ martyr, sed amore et ore noster;
incubat in Libya sanguis, sed ubique lingua pollet,
sola superstes agit de corpore, sola obire nescit,
dum genus esse hominum Christus sinet et vigere mundum.
Dum liber ullus erit, dum scrinia sacra litterarum,
te leget omnis amans Christum, tua, Cypriane, discet.
Spiritus ille Dei, qui fluxerat auctor in prophetas,
fontibus eloquii te cælitus actus irrigavit.[18]

The Punic land brought forth one by whom everything
    wherever it may be should be brightened,
for though [Carthage] was Cyprian's home, indeed he
    was a glorious teacher of the world.
Though a martyr of his country, he is ours by love and
    prayer,
Libya keeps a watch over his blood, but the power of
    his tongue is everywhere,
which alone outlives his body, it alone knows not
    death,
provided Christ shall permit the race of men and the
    world to flourish,
While there should be any book or any holy library
    entrusted with his books,
everyone who loves Christ and reads them shall learn
    by you, O Cyprian.

That spirit of God, that author which flowed into the
    prophets,
it was a heavenly deed that watered you by fonts of
    eloquence.

—Ryan Grant

31 July, 2012

Feast of St. Ignatius Loyola

NOTES

1. St. Jerome, *De Viris Illustribus*, LXVII
2. *Life and Passion of Cyprian*, 3.
3. Ibid., 5.
4. See Letters 2 and 3.
5. See Letters 8-12.
6. "He cannot have God as Father who will not have the Church as Mother."
7. See Letter 74.
8. Letter 84:2.
9. Many of Cyprian's works mimic earlier works of Tertullian. *On the Dress of Virgins* is a good example.
10. Pontius, *Life and Passion of Cyprian*, 18.
11. Lactantius *Div. Inst. v. 1, 25;* Jerome *Epistle 58, 10.*
12. Cyprian, *On the Dress of Virgins*, 3
13. "One cannot have God as father, who does not have the Church as mother." *On the Unity of the Church*, 6.
14. "Episcopatus unus est, cujus a singulis in solidum pars tenetur." *On the Unity of Church*, 4.
15. Pontius, *Life and Passion of Cyprian*, 1.
16. St. Augustine, Ep. 93:36.
17. St. Jerome, *De Viris Illustribus*, LXVII
18. Prudentius, *Peristephanon liber, poema* 13. Literally, the "Crown of Martyrdom," composed in the 5th century.

BIBLIOGRAPHY
AND FURTHER READING

Arbesmann, Rudolph, Sr. Emily Joseph Daly and Edwin A Quain (transl.) 1959. *Tertullian: Disciplinary, Moral and Ascetical Works.* Fathers of the Church series, Vol. 40. Fathers of the Church: New York.

Bakker, Henk, Paul van Geest and Hans van Loon 2010. *Cyprian of Carthage: Studies in His Life, Language, and Thought.* Peeters: Leuven, Belgium.

Bévenot, Maurice (transl.) 1971. *De Lapsis and De Ecclesiae Catholicae Unitate.* Clarendon Press: Oxford.

Brent, Allen 2010. Cyprian and Roman Carthage. Cambridge University Press: Cambridge, UK.

Burns, J. Patout 2002. *Cyprian the Bishop.* Routledge: London.

Catholic Church 2003. *Catechism of the Catholic Church: With Modifications from the Editio Typica.* Doubleday: New York.

Charles, R. H. (transl.) 1917. *The Book of Enoch.* Society for Promoting Christian Knowledge: London.

Daniel, Robin 2010. *This Holy Seed: Faith, Hope and Love in the Early Churches of North Africa.* Tamarisk Publications: Chester.

Deferrari, Roy J. (transl.) 1958. *Saint Cyprian: Letters,* Fathers of the Church series, Vol. 51. Fathers of the Church: New York.

DeSimone, Russell J. 1972. *Novatian.* Catholic University of America: Washington, DC.

Donna, Sr. Rose Bernard (transl.) 1958. *Saint Cyprian: Treatises,* Fathers of the Church series, Vol. 36. Fathers of the Church: New York.

Dunn, Geoffrey D. 2007. *Cyprian and the Bishops of Rome.* St. Paul's Publications: Strathfield, New South Wales, Australia.

Fahey, Michael Andrew, S.J. 1971. *Cyprian and the Bible: A Study in Third Century Exegesis.* (Beiträge zur Geschichte der biblischen Hermeneutik, 9) J. C. B. Mohr: Tübingen.

Fichter, Joseph H. 1942. *Saint Cecil Cyprian, Early Defender of the Faith.* B. Herder Book Co.: London.

Greer, Rowan A. 1979. *Origen: An Exhortation to Martyrdom, Prayer and Selected Works.* Paulist Press: New York.

Halton, Thomas P. (transl.) 1999. *Saint Jerome: On Illustrious Men.* Fathers of the Church series, Vol. 100. Fathers of the Church: New York.

Healy, Rev. Patrick J. 1905. *The Valerian Persecution.* Houghton Mifflin: Boston.

Herbermann, Charles G., et al. 1913. The Catholic Encyclopedia: An International Work of Reference on teh Constitution, Doctrine, Discipline, and Hisotry of the Catholic Church. The Encyclopedia Press: New York. Electronic edition available at: http://www.newadvent.org/cathen/

Newman, Rev. John Henry 1846. *An Essay on the Development of Christian Doctrine.* James Toovey: London.

Sage, Michael M. 1975. *Cyprian.* Philadelphia Patristics Foundation: Philadelphia, PA.

Schaff, Philip (ed.) 1994. *A Select Library of Nicene and Post-Nicene Fathers of the Christian Church, First Series, Volume 2: St. Augustin: City of God and Christian Doctrine.* Hendrickson Publishers: Peabody, MA.

Schaff, Philip (ed.) 1994. *A Select Library of Nicene and Post-Nicene Fathers of the Christian Church, First Series, Volume 4: St. Augustin: The Writings against the Manichaeans and against the Donatists.* Hendrickson Publishers: Peabody, MA.

Schaff, Philip (ed.) 1994. *A Select Library of Nicene and Post-Nicene Fathers of the Christian Church, First Series, Volume 3: St. Augustin: On the Holy Trinity, Doctrinal Treatises, Moral Treatises.* Hendrickson Publishers: Peabody, MA.

Schaff, Philip and Henry Wace (eds.) 1994. *A Select Library of Nicene and Post-Nicene Fathers of the Christian Church, Second Series, Volume 6: The Principle Works of Saint Jerome.* Hendrickson Publishers: Peabody, MA.

Sullivan, Rev. Daniel David 1933. *The Life of the North Africans as Revealed in the Works of Saint Cyprian.* Catholic University of America: Washington, DC.

Thaninayagam, Fr. Xavier Stanislaus 1947. *The Carthaginian Clergy during the Episcopate of Saint Cyprian.* Ceylon Printers: Colombo, India.

Tilley, Maureen A. 1996. *Donatist Martyr Stories: The Church in Conflict in North Africa.* Liverpool University Press: Liverpool, UK.

Waterworth, James 1898. *The Canons and Decrees of the Sacred and Oecumenical Council of Trent.* C. Dolman: London.

PART I:
THE TREATISES OF CYPRIAN

THE LIFE AND PASSION OF CYPRIAN
BY PONTIUS THE DEACON

1. Although Cyprian, the devout priest and glorious witness of God, composed many writings whereby the memory of his worthy name survives; and although the profuse fertility of his eloquence and of God's grace so expands itself in the exuberance and richness of his discourse, that he will probably never cease to speak even to the end of the world; yet, since to his works and deserts it is justly due that his example should be recorded in writing, I have thought it well to prepare this brief and compendious narrative. Not that the life of so great a man can be unknown to any even of the heathen nations, but that to our posterity also this incomparable and lofty pattern may be prolonged into immortal remembrance. It would assuredly be hard that, when our fathers have given such honor even to lay-people and catechumens who have obtained martyrdom, for reverence of their very martyrdom, as to record many, or I had nearly said, well near all, of the circumstances of their sufferings, so that they might be brought to our knowledge also who as yet were not born, the passion of such a priest and such a martyr as Cyprian should be passed over, who, independently of his martyrdom, had much to teach, and that what he did while he lived should be hidden from the world. And, indeed, these doings of his were such, and so great, and so admirable, that I am deterred by the contemplation of their greatness, and confess myself incompetent to discourse in a way that shall be worthy of the honor of his deserts, and unable to relate such noble deeds in such a way that they may appear as great as in fact they are, except that the multitude of his glories is itself sufficient for itself, and needs no other heraldry. It enhances my difficulty, that you also are anxious to hear very much, or if it be possible every thing, about him, longing with eager warmth at least to become acquainted with his deeds, although now his living words are silent. And in this behalf, if I should say that the powers of eloquence fail me, I should say too little. For eloquence itself fails of suitable powers fully to satisfy your desire. And thus I am sorely pressed on both sides, since he burdens me with his virtues, and you press me hard with your entreaties.

2. At what point, then, shall I begin—from what direction shall I approach the description of his goodness, except from the beginning of his faith and from his heavenly birth? Inasmuch as the doings of a man of God should not be reckoned from any point except from the time that he was born of God. He may have had pursuits previously, and liberal arts may have imbued his mind while engaged therein; but these things I pass over; for as yet they had nothing to do with anything but his secular advantage. But when he had learned sacred knowledge, and breaking through the clouds of this world had emerged into the light of spiritual wisdom, if I was with him in any of his doings, if I have discerned any of his more illustrious labors, I will speak of them; only asking meanwhile for this indulgence, that whatever I shall say too little (for too little I must needs say) may rather be attributed to my ignorance than subtracted from his glory. While his faith was in its first rudiments, he believed that before God nothing was worthy in comparison of the observance of continency. For he thought that the heart might then become what it ought to be, and the mind attain to the full capacity of truth, if he trod under foot the lust of the flesh with the robust and healthy vigor of holiness. Who has ever recorded such a marvel? His second birth had not yet enlightened the new man with the entire splendor of the divine light, yet he was already overcoming the ancient and pristine darkness by the mere dawning of the light. Then—what is even greater—when he had learned from the reading of Scripture certain things not according to the condition of his novitiate, but in proportion to the earliness of his faith, he immediately laid hold of what he had discovered, for his own advantage in deserving well of God. By distributing his means for the relief of the indigence of the poor, by dispensing the purchase-money of entire estates, he at once realized two benefits—the contempt of this world's ambition, than which nothing is more pernicious, and the observance of that mercy which God has preferred even to His sacrifices, and which even he did not maintain who said that he had kept all the commandments of the law; whereby with premature swiftness of piety he almost began to be perfect before he had learned the way to be perfect. Who of the ancients, I pray, has done this? Who of the most celebrated veterans in the faith, whose hearts and ears have throbbed to the divine words for many years, has attempted any such thing, as this man—of faith yet unskilled, and whom, perhaps, as yet nobody trusted—surpassing the age of antiquity, accomplished by his glorious and admirable labors? No one reaps immediately upon his sowing; no one presses out the vintage harvest from the trenches just formed; no one ever yet sought for ripened fruit from newly planted slips. But in him all incredible things concurred. In him the threshing preceded (if it may be said, for the thing is beyond belief)—preceded the sowing, the vintage the shoots, the fruit the root.[1]

3. The apostle's epistle says that novices should be passed over, lest by the stupor of heathenism that yet clings to their unconfirmed minds, their untaught inexperience should in any respect sin against God.[2] He first, and I think he alone, furnished an illustration that greater progress is made by faith than by time. For although in the Acts of the Apostles the eunuch is described as at once baptized by Philip, because he believed with his whole heart, this is not a fair parallel. For he was a Jew, and as he came from the temple of the Lord he was reading the prophet Isaiah, and he hoped in Christ, although as yet he did not believe that He had come; while the other, coming from the ignorant heathens, began with a faith as mature as that with which few perhaps have finished their course. In short, in respect of God's grace, there was no delay, no postponement—I have said but little—he immediately received the presbyterate and the priesthood.[3] For who is there that would not entrust every grade of honor to one who believed with such a disposition? There are many things which he did while still a layman, and many things which now as a presbyter he did—many things which, after the examples of righteous men of old, and following them with a close imitation, he accomplished with the obedience of entire consecration—that deserved well of the Lord. For his discourse concerning this was usually, that if he had read of any one being set forth with the praise of God, he would persuade us to inquire on account of what doings he had pleased God. If Job, glorious by God's testimony, was called a true worshipper of God, and one to whom there was none upon earth to be compared, he taught that we should do whatever Job had previously done, so that while we are doing like things we may call forth a similar testimony of God for ourselves. He, contemning the loss of his estate, gained such advantage by his virtue thus tried, that he had no perception of the temporal losses even of his affection. Neither poverty nor pain broke him down; the persuasion of his wife[4] did not influence him; the dreadful suffering of his own body did not shake his firmness. His virtue remained established in its own home, and his devotion, founded upon deep roots, gave way under no onset of the devil tempting him to abstain from blessing his God with a grateful faith even in his adversity. His house was open to every comer. No widow returned from him with an empty lap; no blind man was unguided by him as a companion; none faltering in step was unsupported by him for a staff; none stripped of help by the hand of the mighty was not protected by him as a defender. Such things ought they to do, he was accustomed to say, who desire to please God. And thus running through the examples of all good men, by always imitating those who were better than others he made himself also worthy of imitation.

4. He had a close association among us with a just man, and of praiseworthy memory, by name Caecilius, and in age as well as in honor a presbyter, who had converted him from his worldly errors to the acknowledgment of the true divinity.[5] This man he loved with entire honor and all observance, regarding him with an obedient veneration, not only as the friend and comrade of his soul, but as the parent of his new life. And at length he, influenced by his attentions, was, as well he might be, stimulated to such a pitch of excessive love, that when he was departing from this world, and his summons was at hand, he commended to him his wife and children; so that him whom he had made a partner in the fellowship of his way of life, he afterwards made the heir of his affection.[6]

5. It would be tedious to go through individual circumstances; it would be laborious to enumerate all his doings. For the proof of his good works I think that this one thing is enough, that by the judgment of God and the favor of the people, he was chosen to the office of the priesthood and the degree of the episcopate while still a neophyte, and, as it was considered, a novice. Although still in the early days of his faith, and in the untaught season of his spiritual life, a generous disposition so shone forth in him, that although not yet resplendent with the glitter of office, but only of hope, he gave promise of entire trustworthiness for the priesthood that was coming upon him. Moreover, I will not pass over that remarkable fact, of the way in which, when the entire people by God's inspiration leapt forward in his love and honor, he humbly withdrew, giving place to men of older standing, and thinking himself unworthy of a claim to so great honor, so that he thus became more worthy. For he is made more worthy who dispenses with what he deserves. And with this excitement were the eager people at that time inflamed, desiring with a spiritual longing, as the event proved, not only a bishop—for in him whom then with a latent foreboding of divinity they were in such wise demanding, they were seeking not only a priest—but moreover a future martyr.[7] A crowded fraternity was besieging the doors of the house, and throughout all the avenues of access an anxious love was circulating. Possibly that apostolic experience might then have happened to him, as he desired, of being let down through a window, had he also been equal to the apostle in the honor of ordination. It was plain to be seen that all the rest were expecting his coming with an anxious spirit of suspense, and received him when he came with excessive joy. I speak unwillingly, but I must needs speak. Some resisted him, even that he might overcome them; yet with what gentleness, how patiently, how benevolently he gave them indulgence! How mercifully he forgave them, reckoning them afterwards, to the astonishment of many, among his closest and, most intimate friends! For who would not be amazed at the forgetfulness of a mind so retentive?

6. Henceforth who is sufficient to relate the manner in which he bore himself?— what pity was his? What vigor? How great his mercy? How great his strictness? So much sanctity and grace beamed from his face that it confounded the minds of the beholders. His countenance was grave and joyous. Neither was his severity gloomy, nor his affability excessive, but a mingled tempering of both; so that it might be doubted whether he most deserved to be revered or to be loved, except that he deserved both to be revered and to be loved. And his dress was not out of harmony with his countenance, being itself also subdued to a fitting mean. The pride of the world did not inflame him, nor yet did an excessively affected penury make him sordid, because this latter kind of attire arises no less from boastfulness, than does such an ambitious frugality from ostentation. But what did he as bishop in respect of the poor, whom as a catechumen he had loved? Let the priests of piety consider, or those whom the teaching of their very rank has trained to the duty of good works, or those whom the common obligation of the Sacrament has bound to the duty of manifesting love. The bishop's cathedra received Cyprian such as he had been before—it did not make him so.[8]

7. And therefore for such merits he at once obtained the glory of proscription also. For nothing else was proper than that he who in the secret recesses of his conscience was rich in the full honor of religion and faith, should moreover be renowned in the publicly diffused report of the Gentiles. He might, indeed, at that time, in accordance with the rapidity wherewith he always attained everything, have hastened to the crown of martyrdom appointed for him, especially when with repeated calls he was frequently demanded for the lions, had it not been needful for him to pass through all the grades of glory, and thus to arrive at the highest, and had not the impending desolation needed the aid of so fertile a mind. For conceive of him as being at that time taken away by the dignity of martyrdom. Who was there to show the advantage of grace, advancing by faith? Who was there to restrain virgins to the fitting discipline of modesty and a dress worthy of holiness, as if with a kind of bridle of the lessons of the Lord? Who was there to teach penitence to the lapsed, truth to heretics, unity to schismatics, peacefulness and the law of evangelical prayer to the sons of God? By whom were the blaspheming Gentiles to be overcome by retorting upon themselves the accusations which they heap upon us? By whom were Christians of too tender an affection, or, what is of more importance, of a too feeble faith in respect of the loss of their friends, to be consoled with the hope of futurity? Whence should we so learn mercy? Whence patience? Who was there to restrain the ill blood arising from the envenomed malignity of envy, with the sweetness of a wholesome remedy? Who was there to raise up such great martyrs by the exhortation of his divine discourse? Who was there, in short, to animate so many confessors sealed with a second inscription on their distinguished brows, and reserved alive for an example of martyrdom, kindling their ardor with a heavenly trumpet?[9] Fortunately, it occurred then, and truly by the Spirit's direction, that the man who was needed for so many and so excellent purposes was withheld from the consummation of martyrdom. Do you wish to be assured that the cause of his withdrawal was not fear? To allege nothing else, he did suffer subsequently, and this suffering he assuredly would have evaded as usual, if he had evaded it before. It was indeed that fear—and rightly so—that fear which would dread to offend the Lord—that fear which prefers to obey God's commands rather than to be crowned in disobedience. For a mind dedicated in all things to God, and thus enslaved to the divine admonitions, believed that even in suffering itself it would sin, unless it had obeyed the Lord, who then bade him seek the place of concealment.[10]

8. Moreover, I think that something may here be said about the benefit of the delay, although I have already touched slightly on the matter. By what appears subsequently to have occurred, it follows that we may prove that that withdrawal was not conceived by human pusillanimity, but, as indeed is the case, was truly divine. The unusual and violent rage of a cruel persecution had laid waste God's people; and since the artful enemy could not deceive all by one fraud, wherever the incautious soldier laid bare his side, there in various manifestations of rage he had destroyed individuals with different kinds of overthrow. There needed some one who could, when men were wounded and hurt by the various arts of the attacking enemy, use the remedy of the celestial medicine according to the nature of the wound, either for cutting or for cherishing them. Thus was preserved a man of an intelligence, besides other excellences, also spiritually trained, who between the resounding waves of the opposing schisms could steer the middle course of the Church in a steady path. Are not such plans, I ask, divine? Could this have been done without God? Let them consider who think that such things as these can happen by chance. To them the Church replies with clear voice, saying, I do not allow and do not believe that such needful then are reserved without the decree of God.

9. Still, if it seem well, let me glance at the rest. Afterwards there broke out a dreadful plague, and excessive destruction of a hateful disease invaded every house in succession of the trembling populace, carrying off day by day with abrupt attack numberless people, every one from his own house. All were shuddering, fleeing, shunning the contagion, impiously exposing their own friends, as if with the exclusion of the person who was sure to die of the plague, one could exclude death itself also. There lay about the meanwhile, over the whole city, no longer bodies, but the carcasses of many, and, by the contemplation of a lot which in their turn would be theirs, demanded the pity of the passers-by for themselves. No one regarded anything besides his cruel gains. No one trembled at the remembrance of a similar event. No one did to another what he himself wished to experience. In these circumstances, it would be a wrong to pass over what the pontiff of Christ did, who excelled the pontiffs of the world as much in kindly affection as he did in truth of religion.[11] On the people assembled together in one place he first of all urged the benefits of mercy, teaching by examples from divine lessons, how greatly the duties of benevolence avail to deserve well of God. Then afterwards he subjoined, that there was nothing wonderful in our cherishing our own people only with the needed attentions of love, but that he might become perfect who would do something more than the publican or the heathen, who, overcoming evil with good, and practicing a clemency which was like the divine clemency, loved even his enemies, who would pray for the salvation of those that persecute him, as the Lord admonishes and exhorts. God continually makes His sun to rise, and from time to time gives showers to nourish the seed, exhibiting all these kindnesses not only to His people, but to aliens also. And if a man professes to be a son of God, why does not he imitate the example of his Father? "It becomes us," said he, "to answer to our birth; and it is not fitting that those who are evidently born of God should be degenerate, but rather that the propagation of a good Father should be proved in His offspring by the emulation of His goodness."

10. I omit many other matters, and, indeed, many important ones, which the necessity of a limited space does not permit to be detailed in more lengthened discourse, and concerning which this much is sufficient to have been said. But if the Gentiles could have heard these things as they stood before the rostrum,[12] they would probably at once have believed. What, then, should a Christian people do, whose very name proceeds from faith? Thus the ministrations are constantly distributed according to the quality of the men and their degrees. Many who, by the straitness of poverty, were unable to manifest the kindness of wealth, manifested more than wealth, making up by their own labor a service dearer than all riches. And under such a teacher, who would not press forward to be found in some part of such a warfare, whereby he might please both God the Father, and Christ the Judge, and for the present so excellent a priest? Thus what is good was done in the liberality of overflowing works to all men, not to those only who are of the household of faith. Something more was done than is recorded of the incomparable benevolence of Tobias. He must forgive, and forgive again, and frequently forgive; or, to speak more truly, he must of right concede that, although very much might be done before Christ, yet that something more might be done after Christ, since to His times all fullness is attributed. Tobias collected together those who were slain by the king and cast out, of his own race only.[13]

11. Banishment followed these actions, so good and so benevolent. For impiety always makes this return, that it repays the better with the worse. And what God's priest replied to the interrogation of the proconsul, there are Acts which relate.[14] In the meantime, he is excluded from the city who had done some good for the city's safety; he who had striven that the eyes of the living should not suffer the horrors of the infernal abode; he, I say, who, vigilant in the watches of benevolence, had provided—oh wickedness! with unacknowledged goodness—that when all were forsaking the desolate appearance of the city, a destitute state and a deserted country should not perceive its many exiles. But let the world look to this, which accounts banishment a penalty. To them, their country is too dear, and they have the same name as their parents; but we abhor even our parents themselves if they would persuade us against God. To them, it is a severe punishment to live outside their own city; to the Christian, the whole of this world is one home. Wherefore, though he were banished into a hidden and secret place, yet, associated with the affairs of his God, he cannot regard it as an exile. In addition, while honestly serving God, he is a stranger even in his own city. For while the continency of the Holy Spirit restrains him from carnal desires, he lays aside the conversation of the former man, and even among his fellow citizens, or, I might almost say, among the parents themselves of his earthly life, he is a stranger. Besides, although this might otherwise appear to be a punishment, yet in causes and sentences of this kind, which we suffer for the trial of the proof of our virtue, it is not a punishment, because it is a glory. But, indeed, suppose banishment not to be a punishment to us, yet the witness of their own conscience may still attribute the last and worst wickedness to those who can lay upon the innocent what they think to be a punishment. I will not now describe a charming place; and, for the present, I pass over the addition of all possible delights. Let us conceive of the place, filthy in situation, squalid in appearance, having no wholesome water, no pleasantness of verdure, no neighboring shore, but vast wooded rocks between the inhospitable jaws of a totally deserted solitude, far removed in the pathless regions of the world. Such a place might have borne the name of exile, if Cyprian, the priest of God, had come there; although to him, if the ministrations of men had been wanting, either birds, as in the case of Elias, or angels, as in that of Daniel, would have ministered. Away, away with the belief that anything would be wanting to the least of us, so long as he stands for the confession of the name. So far was God's pontiff, who had always been urgent in merciful works, from needing the assistance of all these things.

12. And now let us return with thankfulness to what I had suggested in the second place, that for the soul of such a man there was divinely provided a sunny and suitable spot, a dwelling, secret as he wished, and all that has before been promised to be added to those who seek the kingdom and righteousness of God. And, not to mention the number of the brethren who visited him, and then the kindness of the citizens themselves, which supplied to him everything whereof he appeared to be deprived, I will not pass over God's wonderful visitation, whereby

He wished His priest in exile to be so certain of his passion that was to follow, that in his full confidence of the threatening martyrdom, Curubis[15] possessed not only an exile, but a martyr too. For on that day whereon we first abode in the place of banishment (for the condescension of his love had chosen me among his household companions to a voluntary exile: would that he could also have chosen me to share his passion!), "There appeared to me," said he, "ere yet I was sunk in the repose of slumber, a young man of unusual stature, who, as it were, led me to the praetorium, where I seemed to myself to be led before the tribunal of the proconsul, then sitting. When he looked upon me, he began at once to note down a sentence on his tablet, which I knew not, for he had asked nothing of me with the accustomed interrogation. But the youth, who was standing at his back, very anxiously read what had been noted down. And because he could not then declare it in words, he showed me by an intelligible sign what was contained in the writing of that tablet. For, with hand expanded and flattened like a blade, he imitated the stroke of the accustomed punishment, and expressed what he wished to be understood as clearly as by speech—I understood the future sentence of my passion. I began to ask and to beg immediately that a delay of at least one day should be accorded me, until I should have arranged my property in some reasonable order. And when I had urgently repeated my entreaty, he began again to note down, I know not what, on his tablet. But I perceived from the calmness of his countenance that the judge's mind was moved by my petition, as being a just one. Moreover, that youth, who already had disclosed to me the intelligence of my passion by gesture rather than by words, hastened to signify repeatedly by secret signal that the delay was granted which had been asked for until the morrow, twisting his fingers one behind the other. And I, although the sentence had not been read, although I rejoiced with very glad heart with joy at the delay accorded, yet trembled so with fear of the uncertainty of the interpretation, that the remains of fear still set my exulting heart beating with excessive agitation."

13. What could be more plain than this revelation? What could be more blessed than this condescension? Everything was foretold to him beforehand which subsequently followed. Nothing was diminished of the words of God, nothing was mutilated of so sacred a promise. Carefully consider each particular in accordance with its announcement. He asks for delay till the morrow, when the sentence of his passion was under deliberation, begging that he might arrange his affairs on the day which he had thus obtained. This one day signified a year, which he was about to pass in the world after his vision. For, to speak more plainly, after the year was expired, he was crowned, on that day on which, at the commencement of the year, the fact had been announced to him. For although we do not read of the day of the Lord as a year in sacred Scripture, yet we regard that space of time as due in making promise of future things.[16] Whence is it of no consequence if, in this case, under the ordinary expression of a day, it is only a year that in this place is implied, because that which is the greater ought to be fuller in meaning. Moreover, that it was explained rather by signs than by speech, was because the utterance of speech was reserved for the manifestation of the time itself. For anything is usually set forth in words, whenever what is set forth is accomplished. For, indeed, no one knew why this had been shown to him, until afterwards, when, on the very day on which he had seen it, he was crowned. Nevertheless, in the meantime, his impending suffering was certainly known by all, but the exact day of his passion was not spoken of by any of the same, just as if they were ignorant of it. And, indeed, I find something similar in the Scriptures. For Zacharias the priest, because he did not believe the promise of a son, made to him by the angel, became dumb; so that he asked for tablets by a sign, being about to write his son's name rather than utter it.[17] With reason, also in this case, where God's messenger declared the impending passion of His priest rather by signs, he both admonished his faith and fortified His priest. Moreover, the ground of asking for delay arose out of his wish to arrange his affairs and settle his will. Yet what affairs or what will had he to arrange, except ecclesiastical concerns? And thus that last delay was received, in order that whatever had to be disposed of by his final decision concerning the care of cherishing the poor might be arranged. And I think that for no other reason, and indeed for this reason only, indulgence was granted to him even by those very persons who had ejected and were about to slay him, that, being at hand, he might relieve the poor also who were before him with the final or, to speak more accurately, with the entire outlay of his last stewardship. And therefore, having so benevolently ordered matters, and so arranged them according to his will, the morrow drew near.

14. Now also a messenger came to him from the city from Xistus, the good and peace-making priest, and on that account most blessed martyr.[18] The coming executioner was instantly looked for who should strike through that devoted neck of the most sacred victim; and thus, in the daily expectation of dying, every day was to him as if the crown might be attributed to each. In the meantime, there assembled to him many eminent people, and people of most illustrious rank and family, and noble with the world's distinctions, who, on account of ancient friendship with him, repeatedly urged his withdrawal; and, that their urgency might not be in some sort hollow, they also offered places to which he might retire. But he had now set the world aside, having his mind suspended upon heaven, and did not consent to their tempting persuasions. He would perhaps even then have done what was asked for by so many and faithful friends, if it had been bidden him by divine command. But that lofty glory of so great a man must not be passed over without announcement, that now, when the world was swelling, and of its trust in its princes breathing out hatred of the name, he was instructing God's servants, as opportunity was given, in the exhortations of the Lord, and was animating them to tread under foot the sufferings of this present time by the contemplation of a glory to come hereafter. Indeed, such was his love of sacred discourse, that he wished that his prayers in regard to his suffering might be so answered, that he would be put to death in the very act of speaking about God.

15. And these were the daily acts of a priest destined for a pleasing sacrifice to God, when, behold, at the bidding of the proconsul, the officer with his soldiers on a sudden came unexpectedly on him—or rather, to speak more truly, thought that he had come unexpectedly on him, at his gardens—at his gardens, I say, which at the beginning of his faith he had sold, and which, being restored by God's mercy, he would assuredly have sold again for the use of the poor, if he had not wished to avoid ill-will from the persecutors.[19] But when could a mind ever prepared be taken unawares, as if by an unforeseen attack? Therefore now he went forward, certain that what had been long delayed would be settled. He went forward with a lofty and elevated mien, manifesting cheerfulness in his look and courage in his heart. But being delayed to the morrow, he returned from the praetorium to the officer's house, when on a sudden a scattered rumor prevailed throughout all Carthage, that now Thascius[20] was brought forward, whom there was nobody who did not know as well for his illustrious fame in the honorable opinion of all, as on account of the recollection of his most renowned work. On all sides all men were flocking together to a spectacle, to us glorious from the devotion of faith, and to be mourned over even by the Gentiles. A gentle custody, however, had him in charge when taken and placed for one night in the officer's house; so that we, his associates and friends, were as usual in his company. The whole people in the meantime, in anxiety that nothing should be done throughout the night without their knowledge, kept watch before the officer's door. The goodness of God granted him at that time, so truly worthy of it, that even God's people should watch on the passion of the priest. Yet, perhaps, some one may ask what was the reason of his returning from the praetorium to the officer. And some think that this arose from the fact, that for his own part the proconsul was then unwilling. Far be it from me to complain, in matters divinely ordered, of slothfulness or aversion in the proconsul. Far be it from me to admit such an evil into the consciousness of a religious mind, as that the fancy of man should decide the fate of so blessed a martyr. But the morrow, which a year before the divine condescension had foretold, required to be literally the morrow.

16. At last that other day dawned—that destined, that promised, that divine day— which, if even the tyrant himself had wished to put off, he would not have had any power to do so; the day rejoicing at the consciousness of the future martyr; and, the clouds being scattered throughout the circuit of the world, the day shone upon them with a brilliant sun. He went out from the house of the officer, though he was the officer of Christ and God, and was walled in on all sides by the ranks of a mingled multitude. And such a numberless army hung upon his company, as if they had come with an assembled troop to assault death itself. Now, as he went, he had to pass by the race-course. And rightly, and as if it had been contrived on purpose, he had to pass by the place of a corresponding struggle, who, having finished his contest, was running to the crown of righteousness. But when he had come to the praetorium, as the proconsul had not yet come forth, a place of retirement was accorded him. There, as he sat moistened after his long journey with excessive perspiration (the seat was by chance covered with linen, so that even in the very moment of his passion he might enjoy the honor of the episcopate),[21] one of the officers (Tesserarius), who had formerly been a Christian, offered him his clothes, as if he might wish to change his moistened garments for drier ones; and he doubtless coveted nothing further in respect of his proffered kindness than to possess the now blood-stained sweat of the martyr going to God. He made reply to him, and said, "We apply medicines to annoyances which probably today will no longer exist." Is it any wonder that he despised suffering in body who had despised death in soul? Why should we say more? He was suddenly announced to the proconsul; he is brought forward; he is placed before him; he is interrogated as to his name. He answers who he is, and nothing more.

17. And thus, therefore, the judge reads from his tablet the sentence which lately in the vision he had not read—a spiritual sentence, not rashly to be spoken—a sentence worthy of such a bishop and such a witness; a glorious sentence, wherein he was called a standard-bearer of the sect, and an enemy of the gods, and one who was to be an example to his people; and that with his blood discipline would begin to be established. Nothing could be more complete, nothing more true, than this sentence. For all the things which were said, although said by a heathen, are divine. Nor is it indeed to be wondered at, since priests are accustomed to prophesy of the passion. He had been a standard-bearer, who was accustomed to teach concerning the bearing of Christ's standard; he had been an enemy of the gods, who commanded the idols to be destroyed. Moreover, he gave example to his friends, since, when many were about to follow in a similar manner, he was the first in the province to consecrate the first-fruits of martyrdom. And by his blood discipline began to be established; but it was the discipline of martyrs, who, emulating their teacher, in the imitation of a glory like his own, themselves also gave a confirmation to discipline by the very blood of their own example.

18. And when he left the doors of the praetorium, a crowd of soldiery accompanied him; and that nothing might be wanting in his passion, centurions and tribunes guarded his side. Now the place itself where he was about to suffer is level, so that it affords a noble spectacle, with its trees thickly planted on all sides. But as, by the extent of the space beyond, the view was not attainable to the confused crowd, persons who favored him had climbed up into the branches of the trees, that there might not even be wanting to him (what happened in the case of Zacchaeus), that he was gazed upon from the trees. And now, having with his own hands bound his eyes, he tried to hasten the slowness of the executioner, whose office was to wield the sword, and who with difficulty clasped the blade in his failing right hand with trembling fingers, until the mature hour of glorification strengthened the hand of the centurion with power granted from above to accomplish the death of the excellent man, and at length supplied him with the permitted strength. O blessed people of the Church, who as well in sight as in feeling, and, what is more, in outspoken words, suffered with such a bishop as theirs; and, as they had ever heard him in his own discourses, were crowned by God the Judge! For although that which the general wish desired could not occur, viz. that the entire congregation should suffer at once in the fellowship of a like glory, yet whoever under the eyes of Christ beholding, and in the hearing of the priest, eagerly desired to suffer, by the sufficient testimony of that desire did in some sort send a missive to God, as his ambassador.

19. His passion being thus accomplished, it resulted that Cyprian, who had been an example to all good men, was also the first who in Africa imbued his priestly crown with blood of martyrdom, because he was the first who began to be such after the apostles. For from the time at which the episcopal order is enumerated at Carthage, not one is ever recorded, even of good men and priests, to have come to suffering. Although devotion surrendered to God is always in consecrated men reckoned instead of martyrdom; yet Cyprian attained even to the perfect crown by the consummation of the Lord; so that in that very city in which he had in such wise lived, and in which he had been the first to do many noble deeds, he also was the first to decorate the insignia of his heavenly priesthood with glorious gore. What shall I do now? Between joy at his passion, and grief at still remaining, my mind is divided in different directions, and twofold affections are burdening a heart too limited for them. Shall I grieve that I was not his associate? But yet I must triumph in his victory. Shall I triumph at his victory? Still I grieve that I am not his companion. Yet still to you I must in simplicity confess, what you also are aware of, that it was my intention to be his companion. Much and excessively I exult at his glory; but still more do I grieve that I remained behind.[22]

NOTES

1. Pontius emphasizes the uncommonly quick progress Cyprian made in the spiritual life; indeed, it is believed that Cyprian was baptized at Easter, 246 and made Bishop of Carthage in 248 or 249. This fact alone attests to the holiness of his character, his zeal for the faith and his intellectual prowess.

2. 1 Tim. 3:6: "Not a neophyte: lest, being puffed up with pride, he fall into the judgment of the devil."

3. The word "priesthood" used with reference to the episcopacy, since in the bishop is found the fullness of priestly power. The 1913 Catholic Encylcopedia says in the entry for "Priest": "This priesthood has two degrees: the first, total and complete, the second an incomplete participation of the first. The first belongs to the bishop. The bishop is truly a priest (*sacerdos*), and even a high-priest; he has chief control of the Divine worship (*sacrorum antistes*), is the president of liturgical meetings; he has the fullness of the priesthood, and administers all the sacraments. The second degree belongs to the priest (presbyter), who is also a *sacerdos*, but of the second rank (*secundi sacerdotes*); by his priestly ordination he receives the power to offer sacrifice (i.e. to celebrate the Eucharist), to forgive sins, to bless, to preach, to sanctify, and in a word to fulfil the non-reserved liturgical duties or priestly functions. In the exercise of these functions, however, he is subject to the authority of the bishop to whom he has promised canonical obedience; in certain cases even he requires not only authorization, but real jurisdiction, particularly to forgive sins and to take care of souls." We could also cite the *Catechism of the Catholic Church*, which calls the bishop "the steward of the grace of the supreme priesthood" (CCC 893).

4. Since St. Cyprian does not mention any wife in his exile letters or in any of his other writings, and since Pontius states that Cyprian was a pagan before his conversion, it is probable that Cyprian dissolved his union with his wife, making use of what is called the Pauline Privilege, after the instructions of St. Paul: "To the married, however, I give this instruction (not I, but the Lord): a wife should not separate from her husband—and if she does separate she must either remain single or become reconciled to her husband—and a husband should not divorce his wife. To the rest I say (not the Lord): if any brother has a wife who is an unbeliever, and she is willing to go on living with him, he should not divorce her; and if any woman has a husband who is an unbeliever, and he is willing to go on living with her, she should not divorce her husband. For the unbelieving husband is made holy through his wife, and the unbelieving wife is made holy through the brother. Otherwise your children would be unclean, whereas in fact they are holy. If the unbeliever separates, however, let him separate. The brother or sister is not bound in such cases; God has called you to peace. For how do you know, wife, whether you will save your husband; or how do you know, husband, whether you will save your wife?" (1 Cor. 7:10-16) This permits a pagan who converts to Christianity to leave his pagan spouse if the spouse refuses to "go on living" with the Christian spouse in peace. Since Pontius tell us that Cyprian's wife actively opposed his zeal for the Faith, we may presume that this natural marriage was dissolved on the basis of St. Paul's admonition, though it is also possible that she died around the time of his conversion, a state of affairs that is not uncommon in the lives of the saints.

5. This Caecilius may have been a relative of Cyrpian, since Cyprian also is part of the gens *Caecilii,* his full name being Thaschus *Caecilius* Cyprianus. The *Caecilii* were a very ancient and notable family in Republican Rome who managed to maintain their prestigious position

under the empire.

6. In other words, Caecilius commended the care of his family to Cyprian.

7. Following an apostolic custom, Cyprian was elected bishop by acclamation, that is, by the popular will of the local church. Because of the potential for corruption and politicization, this practice was abandoned after the patristic era, but remnants of it remain in the eastern churches, where after the ordination of a priest, the people assembled will cry, "Axios!" ("He is worthy!").

8. A testimony to the existence of the episcopal *cathedra*, or throne, in the mid-3rd century. It has been common in secular accounts of Church history to designate the adoption of the *cathedra* by the bishops as after the time of Constantine, a case of the Church adopting imperial trappings and insignia. This comment from Pontius clearly disproves this theory; an actual catehdra used by St. Hippolytus (c. 222) is still in existence.

9. The first "inscription" on the brow is the *sphragis*, the sign associated with baptism and confirmation (conferred together in the early Church) that marks one out as belonging to Jesus Christ. The second "inscription" is the special seal given to the martyrs, perhaps associated with the "new name" mentioned in Revelation 3:12 that is promised to those victors who overcome, which in the early Church, always referred to the martyrs.

10. Pontius here attempts to give a defense to those who accused St. Cyprian of cowardice when he withdrew from Carthage during the Decian Persecution in early 250.

11. In ancient Latin, a pontiff (*pontifex*) was a high priest, specifically of one of the official Roman pagan priestly colleges. Pontius' use of the word here with reference to Cyprian demonstrates that the early Church viewed the bishops as high priests of the New Covenant. In analogy with the Aaronic priesthood, the Christian presbyterate was referred to as the *priesthood* and the deacons often referred to as *Levites*. The use of the word pontifex with reference to a bishop became more common in the late 3rd and early 4th centuries. The use of the term *Pontifex Maximus* ("Supreme Pontiff") with reference to the Bishop of Rome dates from the time of Pope Damasus (366-384), though some say it originated later, during the 5th century.

12. In ancient Rome, the *rostrum* was the elevated platform or podium from where public speeches were made, the most famous of which was the rostrum of the Roman forum. In early Christian churches, this word was applied to the elevated platform from which the Gospel was proclaimed (preaching, at least when done by bishops, was usually done from the bishop's *cathedra* in the seated position, though Pontius seems to suggest here that Cyprian was also accustomed to preaching from the rostrum). The rostrum would later develop into the *ambo*, commonly called the *pulpit*.

13. Tob. 1:18

14. Cyprian was brought before the proconsul Aspasius Paternus on August 30th, 257 and was sentenced to exile in the town of Curubis. He spent a year in exile prior to his martyrdom on September 16th, 258.

15. Curubis: modern Korba, Tunisia, on the eastern shore of Cape Bon.

16. The interpretation of a day as a year is extremely common in the Fathers and among the medieval theologians.

17. Luke 1:59-63

18. Pope St. Sixtus II (257–258). The pontificate of Sixtus followed the divisive pontificate of St. Stephen, under whom the African and Asian churches almost ruptured with the Roman church over the issue of rebaptism of heretics. Sixtus was a conciliatory pope who reached out to Cyprian by writing him a letter of condolence in his exile, mentioned above by Pontius (though the pope still continued to uphold the Roman teaching on rebaptism). St. Sixtus was martyred on August 6th, 258 during the same persecution as Cyprian. The Roman Martyrology for that day reads: "At Rome, on the Appian Way, in the cemetery of Callistus, the birthday of blessed Sixtus II, pope and martyr, who received the crown of martyrdom in the persecution of Valerian by being put to the sword."

19. These gardens, mentioned by Cyprian in Letter 1 to Donatus, were one of his favorite places to pray and contemplate heavenly things. He says of these gardens: "[T]he vintage festival invites the mind to unbend in repose, and to enjoy the annual and appointed respite of the declining year. Moreover, the place is in accord with the season, and the pleasant aspect of the gardens harmonizes with the gentle breezes of a mild autumn in soothing and cheering the senses. In such a place as this it is delightful to pass the day in discourse, and, by the study of the sacred parables, to train the conscience of the breast to the apprehension of the divine precepts...The neighboring thickets ensure us solitude, and the vagrant trailings of the vine branches creeping in pendent mazes among the reeds that support them have made for us a porch of vines and a leafy shelter. Pleasantly here we clothe our thoughts in words; and while we gratify our eyes with the agreeable outlook upon trees and vines, the mind is at once instructed by what we hear, and nourished by what we see..." (Letter 1:1).

20. In other words, Cyprian. Thascius, or Thaschus, was Cyprian's first name, his *praenomen*, which would have only been used by persons with whom he was very familiar.

21. A testimony that in Cyprian's time the bishops were distinguished from other clergy by the use of linen vestments.

22. Calling to mind the words of St. Paul, "To live is Christ and to die is gain," and "I long to depart this life and be with Christ, for that is much better" (Php. 1:21, 23).

ON THE UNITY OF THE CHURCH

1. Since the Lord warns us, saying, you are the salt of the earth,[1] and since He bids us to be simple to harmlessness, and yet with our simplicity to be prudent,[2] what else, beloved brethren, befits us than to use foresight and watching with an anxious heart, both to perceive and to beware of the wiles of the crafty foe, that we, who have put on Christ the wisdom of God the Father,[3] may not seem to be wanting in wisdom in the matter of providing for our salvation? For it is not persecution alone that is to be feared; nor those things which advance by open attack to overwhelm and cast down the servants of God. Caution is more easy where danger is manifest, and the mind is prepared beforehand for the contest when the adversary avows himself. The enemy is more to be feared and to be guarded against, when he creeps on us secretly; when, deceiving by the appearance of peace, he steals forward by hidden approaches, whence also he has received the name of the Serpent. That is always his subtlety; that is his dark and stealthy artifice for circumventing man. Thus from the very beginning of the world he deceived; and flattering with lying words, he misled inexperienced souls by an incautious credulity. Thus he endeavored to tempt the Lord Himself: he secretly approached Him, as if he would creep on Him again, and deceive; yet he was understood, and beaten back, and therefore prostrated, because he was recognized and detected.

2. From which an example is given us to avoid the way of the old man, to stand in the footsteps of a conquering Christ, that we may not again be incautiously turned back into the nets of death, but, foreseeing our danger, may possess the immortality that we have received. But how can we possess immortality, unless we keep those commands of Christ whereby death is driven out and overcome, when He Himself warns us, and says, "If you will enter into life, keep the commandments"?[4] And again: "If you do the things that I command you, henceforth I call you not servants, but friends."[5] Finally, these persons He calls strong and steadfast; these He declares to be founded in robust security upon the rock, established with immovable and unshaken firmness, in opposition to all the tempests and hurricanes of the world. "Whosoever," says He, "hears my words, and does them, I will liken him unto a wise man, that built his house upon a rock: the rain descended, the floods came, the winds blew, and beat upon that house; and it fell not: for it was founded upon a rock."[6] We ought therefore to stand fast on His words, to learn and do whatever He both taught and did.[7] But how can a man say that he believes in Christ, who does not do what Christ commanded him to do? Or whence shall he attain to the reward of faith, who will not keep the faith of the commandment? He must of necessity waver and wander, and, caught away by a spirit of error, like dust which is shaken by the wind, be blown about; and he will make no advance in his walk towards salvation, because he does not keep the truth of the way of salvation.[8]

3. But, beloved brethren, not only must we beware of what is open and manifest, but also of what deceives by the craft of subtle fraud. And what can be more crafty, or what more subtle, than for this enemy, detected and cast down by the advent of Christ, after light has come to the nations, and saving rays have shone for the preservation of men, that the deaf might receive the hearing of spiritual grace, the blind might open their eyes to God, the weak might grow strong again with eternal health, the lame might run to the Church, the dumb might pray with clear voices and prayers—seeing his idols forsaken, and his lanes and his temples deserted by the numerous concourse of believers[9]—to devise a new fraud, and under the very title of the Christian name to deceive the incautious? He has invented heresies and schisms, whereby he might subvert the faith, might corrupt the truth, might divide the unity. Those whom he cannot keep in the darkness of the old way, he circumvents and deceives by the error of a new way. He snatches men from the Church itself; and while they seem to themselves to have already approached to the light, and to have escaped the night of the world, he pours over them again, in their unconsciousness, new darkness; so that, although they do not stand firm with the Gospel of Christ, and with the observation and law of Christ, they still call themselves Christians, and, walking in darkness, they think that they have the light, while the adversary is flattering and deceiving, who, according to the apostle's word, transforms himself into an angel of light,[10] and equips his ministers as if they were the ministers of righteousness, who maintain night instead of day, death for salvation, despair under the offer of hope, perfidy under the pretext of faith, antichrist under the name of Christ; so that, while they feign things like the truth, they make void the truth by their subtlety. This happens, beloved brethren, so long as we do not return to the source of truth, as we do not seek the head nor keep the teaching of the heavenly Master.

4.[11] If any one consider and examine these things, there is no need for lengthened discussion and arguments. There is easy proof for faith in a short summary of the truth. The Lord speaks to Peter, saying, "I say unto you, that you are Peter; and upon this rock I will build my Church, and the gates of hell shall not prevail against it. And I will give unto you the keys of the kingdom of heaven; and whatsoever you shall bind on earth shall be bound also in heaven, and whatsoever you shall loose on earth shall be loosed in heaven."[12] [Upon one He builds His Church, and to the same He says after His resurrection, 'feed My sheep'. And though to all His Apostles He gave an equal power yet did He set up one chair, and disposed the origin and manner of unity by his authority. The other Apostles were indeed what Peter was, but the primacy is given to Peter, and the Church and the chair is shown to be one. And all are pastors, but the flock is shown to be one, which is fed by all the Apostles with one mind and heart. He that holds not this unity of the Church, does he think that he holds the faith? He who deserts the chair of Peter, upon whom the Church is founded, is he confident that he is in the Church?] And again to the same He says, after His resurrection, "Feed my sheep."[13] And although to all the apostles, after His resurrection, He gives an equal power, and says, "As the Father has sent me, even so send I you: Receive the Holy Ghost: Whose soever sins you remit, they shall be remitted unto him; and whose soever sins you retain, they shall be retained;"[14] yet, that He might set forth unity, He arranged by His authority the origin of that unity, as beginning from one. Assuredly the rest of the apostles were also the same as was Peter, endowed with a like partnership both of honor and power; but the beginning proceeds from unity. Which one Church, also, the Holy Spirit in the Song of Songs designated in the person of our Lord, and says, "My dove, my spotless one, is but one. She is the only one of her mother, elect of her that bare her."[15] Does he who does not hold this unity of the Church think that he holds the faith? Does he who strives against and resists the Church trust that he is in the Church, when moreover the blessed Apostle Paul teaches the same thing, and sets forth the sacrament of unity, saying, "There is one body and one spirit, one hope of your calling, one Lord, one faith, one baptism, one God?"[16]

5. And this unity we ought firmly to hold and assert, especially those of us that are bishops who preside in the Church, that we may also prove the episcopate itself to be one and undivided. Let no one deceive the brotherhood by a falsehood: let no one corrupt the truth of the faith by perfidious prevarication. The episcopate is one, each part of which is held by each one for the whole. The Church also is one, which is spread abroad far and wide into a multitude by an increase of fruitfulness. As there are many rays of the sun, but one light; and many branches of a tree, but one strength based in its tenacious root; and since from one spring flow many streams, although the multiplicity seems diffused in the liberality of an overflowing abundance, yet the unity is still preserved in the source. Separate a ray of the sun from its body of light, its unity does not allow a division of light; break a branch from a tree—when broken, it will not be able to bud; cut off the stream from its fountain, and that which is cut off dries up. Thus also the Church, shone over with the light of the Lord, sheds forth her rays over the whole world, yet it is one light which is everywhere diffused, nor is the unity of the body separated. Her fruitful abundance spreads her branches over the whole world.

She broadly expands her rivers, liberally flowing, yet her head is one, her source one; and she is one mother, plentiful in the results of fruitfulness: from her womb we are born, by her milk we are nourished, by her spirit we are animated.

6. The spouse of Christ cannot be adulterous; she is uncorrupted and pure. She knows one home; she guards with chaste modesty the sanctity of one couch. She keeps us for God. She appoints the sons whom she has born for the kingdom.[17] Whoever is separated from the Church and is joined to an adulteress, is separated from the promises of the Church; nor can he who forsakes the Church of Christ attain to the rewards of Christ. He is a stranger; he is profane; he is an enemy. He can no longer have God for his Father, who has not the Church for his mother. If any one could escape who was outside the ark of Noah, then he also may escape who shall be outside of the Church. The Lord warns, saying, "He who is not with me is against me, and he who gathers not with me scatters."[18] He who breaks the peace and the concord of Christ, does so in opposition to Christ; he who gathers elsewhere than in the Church, scatters the Church of Christ. The Lord says, "I and the Father are one,"[19] and again it is written of the Father, and of the Son, and of the Holy Spirit, "And these three are one."[20] And does any one believe that this unity which thus comes from the divine strength and coheres in celestial sacraments, can be divided in the Church, and can be separated by the parting asunder of opposing wills? He who does not hold this unity does not hold God's law, does not hold the faith of the Father and the Son, does not hold life and salvation.[21]

7. This sacrament of unity, this bond of a concord inseparably cohering, is set forth where in the Gospel the coat of the Lord Jesus Christ is not at all divided nor cut, but is received as an entire garment, and is possessed as an uninjured and undivided robe by those who cast lots concerning Christ's garment, who should rather put on Christ. Holy Scripture speaks, saying, "But of the coat, because it was not sewed, but woven from the top throughout, they said one to another, 'Let us not rend it, but cast lots whose it shall be.'"[22] That coat bore with it an unity that came down from the top, that is, that came from heaven and the Father, which was not to be at all rent by the receiver and the possessor, but without separation we obtain a whole and substantial entirety. He cannot possess the garment of Christ who parts and divides the Church of Christ. On the other hand, again, when at Solomon's death his kingdom and people were divided, Abijah the prophet, meeting Jeroboam the king in the field, divided his garment into twelve sections, saying, "Take you ten pieces; for thus says the Lord, Behold, I will rend the kingdom out of the hand of Solomon, and I will give ten scepters unto you; and two scepters shall be unto him for my servant David's sake, and for Jerusalem, the city which I have chosen to place my name there."[23] As the twelve tribes of Israel were divided, the prophet Abijah rent his garment. But because Christ's people cannot be rent, His robe, woven and united throughout, is not divided by those who possess it; undivided, united, connected, it shows the coherent concord of our people who put on Christ. By the sacrament and sign of His garment, He has declared the unity of the Church.

8. Who, then, is so wicked and faithless, who is so insane with the madness of discord, that either he should believe that the unity of God can be divided, or should dare to rend it—the garment of the Lord—the Church of Christ? He Himself in His Gospel warns us, and teaches, saying, "And there shall be one flock and one shepherd."[24] And does any one believe that in one place there can be either many shepherds or many flocks? The Apostle Paul, moreover, urging upon us this same unity, beseeches and exhorts, saving, "I beseech you, brethren, by the name of our Lord Jesus Christ, that you all speak the same thing, and that there be no schisms among you; but that you be joined together in the same mind and in the same judgment."[25] And again, he says, "Forbearing one another in love, endeavoring to keep the unity of the Spirit in the bond of peace."[26] Do you think that you can stand and live if you withdraw from the Church, building for yourself other homes and a different dwelling, when it is said to Rahab, in whom was prefigured the Church, "Your father, and your mother, and your brethren, and all the house of your father, you shall gather unto you into your house; and it shall come to pass, whosoever shall go abroad beyond the door of your house, his blood shall be upon his own head"?[27] Also, the sacrament of the passover contains nothing else in the law of the Exodus than that the lamb which is slain in the figure of Christ should be eaten in one house. God speaks, saying, "In one house shall you eat it; you shall not send its flesh abroad from the house."[28] The flesh of Christ, and the holy of the Lord, cannot be sent abroad, nor is there any other home to believers but the one Church. This home, this household of unanimity, the Holy Spirit designates and points out in the Psalms, saying, God, who makes men to dwell with one mind in a house, in the house of God, in the Church of Christ, men dwell with one mind, and continue in concord and simplicity.

9. Therefore also the Holy Spirit came as a dove, a simple and joyous creature, not bitter with gall, not cruel in its bite, not violent with the rending of its claws, loving human dwellings, knowing the association of one home; when they have young, bringing forth their young together; when they fly abroad, remaining in their flights by the side of one another, spending their life in mutual intercourse, acknowledging the concord of peace with the kiss of the beak, in all things fulfilling the law of unanimity. This is the simplicity that ought to be known in the Church, this is the charity that ought to be attained, that so the love of the brotherhood may imitate the cloves, that their gentleness and meekness may be like the lambs and sheep. What does the fierceness of wolves do in the Christian breast? What the savageness of dogs, and the deadly venom of serpents, and the sanguinary cruelty of wild beasts? We are to be congratulated when such as these are separated from the Church, lest they should lay waste the doves and sheep of Christ with their cruel and envenomed contagion. Bitterness cannot consist and be associated with sweetness, darkness with light, rain with clearness, battle with peace, barrenness with fertility, drought with springs, storm with tranquility. Let none think that the good can depart from the Church. The wind does not carry away the wheat, nor does the hurricane uproot the tree that is based on a solid root. The light straws are tossed about by the tempest, the feeble trees are overthrown by the onset of the whirlwind. The Apostle John execrates and severely assails these, when he says, "They went forth from us, but they were not of us; for if they had been of us, surely they would have continued with us."[29]

10. Hence heresies not only have frequently been originated, but continue to be so; while the perverted mind has no peace—while a discordant faithlessness does not maintain unity. But the Lord permits and suffers these things to be, while the choice of one's own liberty remains, so that while the discrimination of truth is testing our hearts and our minds, the sound faith of those that are approved may shine forth with manifest light.[30] The Holy Spirit forewarns and says by the apostle, "It is needful also that there should be heresies, that they which are approved may be made manifest among you."[31] Thus the faithful are approved, thus the perfidious are detected; thus even here, before the day of judgment, the souls of the righteous and of the unrighteous are already divided, and the chaff is separated from the wheat. These are they who of their own accord, without any divine arrangement, set themselves to preside among the daring strangers assembled, who appoint themselves prelates without any law of ordination, who assume to themselves the name of bishop, although no one gives them the episcopate; whom the Holy Spirit points out in the Psalms as sitting in the seat of pestilence, plagues, and spots of the faith, deceiving with serpent's tongue, and artful in corrupting the truth, vomiting forth deadly poisons from pestilential tongues; whose speech does creep like a cancer, whose discourse forms a deadly poison in the heart and breast of every one.

11. Against people of this kind the Lord cries; from these He restrains and recalls His erring people, saying, "Hearken not unto the words of the false prophets; for the visions of their hearts deceive them. They speak, but not out of the mouth of the Lord. They say to those who cast away the word of God, 'You shall have peace, and every one that walks after his own will. Every one who walks in the error of his heart, no evil shall come upon him.' I have not spoken to them, yet they prophesied. If they had stood on my foundation,[32] and had heard my words, and taught my people, I would have turned them from their evil thoughts."[33] Again, the Lord points out and designates these same, saying, "They have forsaken me, the fountain of living waters, and have hewed them out broken cisterns which can hold no water."[34] Although there can be no other baptism but one, they think that they can baptize; although they forsake the fountain of life, they promise the grace of living and saving water. Men are not washed among them, but rather are made foul; nor are sins purged away, but are even accumulated. Such a nativity does not generate sons to God, but to the devil. By a falsehood they are born, and they do not receive the promises of truth. Begotten of perfidy, they lose the grace of faith. They cannot attain to the reward of peace, since they have broken the Lord's peace with the madness of discord.[35]

12. Nor let any deceive themselves by a futile interpretation, in respect of the Lord having said, "Wheresoever two or three are gathered together in my name, there am I in the midst of them."[36] Corrupters and false interpreters of the Gospel quote the last words, and lay aside the former ones, remembering part, and craftily suppressing part: as they themselves are separated from the Church, so they cut off the substance of one section. For the Lord, when He would urge unanimity and peace upon His disciples, said, "I say unto you, That if two of you shall agree on earth touching anything that you shall ask, it shall be given you by my Father which is in heaven. For wheresoever two or three are gathered together in my name, I am with them;" showing that most is given, not to the multitude, but to the unanimity of those that pray. If, He says, "two of you shall agree on earth:" He placed agreement first; He has made the concord of peace a prerequisite; He taught that we should agree firmly and faithfully. But how can he agree with any one who does not agree with the body of the Church itself, and with the universal brotherhood? How can two or three be assembled together in Christ's name, who, it is evident, are separated from Christ and from His Gospel? For we have not withdrawn from them, but they from us; and since heresies and schisms have risen subsequently, from their establishment for themselves of diverse places of worship, they have forsaken the Head and Source of the truth. But the Lord speaks concerning His Church, and to those also who are in the Church He speaks, that if they are in agreement, if according to what He commanded and admonished, although only two or three gathered together with unanimity should pray—though they be only two or three—they may obtain from the majesty of God what they ask. Wheresoever two or three are gathered together in my name, I, says He, am with them; that is, with the simple and peaceable—with those who fear God and keep God's commandments. With these, although only two or three, He said that He was, in the same manner as He was with the three youths in the fiery furnace; and because they abode towards God in simplicity, and in unanimity among themselves, He animated them, in the midst of the surrounding flames, with the breath of dew: in the way in which, with the two apostles shut up in prison, because they were simple-minded and of one mind, He Himself was present; He Himself, having loosed the bolts of the dungeon, placed them again in the market-place, that they might declare to the multitude the word which they faithfully preached. When, therefore, in His commandments He lays it down, and says, "Where two or three are gathered together in my name, I am with them," He does not divide men from the Church, seeing that He Himself ordained and made the Church; but rebuking the faithless for their discord, and commending peace by His word to the faithful, He shows that He is rather with two or three who pray with one mind, than with a great many who differ, and that more can be obtained by the discordant prayer of a few, than by the discordant supplication of many.

13. Thus, also, when He gave the law of prayer, He added, saying, "And when you stand praying, forgive, if you have ought against any; that your Father also which is in heaven may forgive you your trespasses."[37] And He calls back from the altar one who comes to the sacrifice in strife, and bids him first agree with his brother, and then return with peace and offer his gift to God: for God had not respect unto Cain's offerings; for he could not have God at peace with him, who through envious discord had not peace with his brother. What peace, then, do the enemies of the brethren promise to themselves? What sacrifices do those who are rivals of the priests think that they celebrate? Do they deem that they have Christ with them when they are collected together, who are gathered together outside the Church of Christ?

14. Even if such men were slain in confession of the Name, that stain is not even washed away by blood: the inexpiable and grave fault of discord is not even purged by suffering. He cannot be a martyr who is not in the Church; he cannot attain unto the kingdom who forsakes that which shall reign there. Christ gave us peace; He bade us be in agreement, and of one mind. He charged the bonds of love and charity to be kept uncorrupted and inviolate; he cannot show himself a martyr who has not maintained brotherly love. Paul the apostle teaches this, and testifies, saying, "And though I have faith, so that I can remove mountains, and have not charity, I am nothing. And though I give all my goods to feed the poor, and though I give my body to be burned, and have not charity, it profits me nothing. Charity is magnanimous; charity is kind; charity envies not; charity acts not vainly, is not puffed up, is not easily provoked, thinks no evil; loves all things, believes all things, hopes all things, endures all things Charity never fails."[38] Charity, says he, never fails. For she will ever be in the kingdom, she will endure for ever in the unity of a brotherhood linked to herself. Discord cannot attain to the kingdom of heaven; to the rewards of Christ, who said, "This is my commandment that you love one another even as I have loved you."[39] He cannot attain who has violated the love of Christ by faithless dissension. He who has not charity has not God. The word of the blessed Apostle John is: "God, says he, is love; and he that dwells in love dwells in God, and God dwells in him."[40] They cannot dwell with God who would not be of one mind in God's Church. Although they burn, given up to flames and fires, or lay down their lives, thrown to the wild beasts, that will not be the crown of faith, but the punishment of perfidy; nor will it be the glorious ending of religious valor, but the destruction of despair. Such a one may be slain; crowned he cannot be. He professes himself to be a Christian in such a way as the devil often feigns himself to be Christ, as the Lord Himself forewarns us, and says, "Many shall come in my name, saying, I am Christ, and shall deceive many."[41] As he is not Christ, although he deceives in respect of the name; so neither can he appear as a Christian who does not abide in the truth of His Gospel and of faith.

15. For both to prophesy and to cast out devils, and to do great acts upon the earth is certainly a sublime and an admirable thing; but one does not attain the kingdom of heaven although he is found in all these things, unless he walks in the observance of the right and just way.[42] The Lord denounces, and says, "Many shall say to me in that day, 'Lord, Lord, have we not prophesied in Your name, and in Your name have cast out devils, and in Your name done many wonderful works?' And then will I profess unto them, 'I never knew you: depart from me, you that work iniquity.'"[43] There is need of righteousness, that one may deserve well of God the Judge; we must obey His precepts and warnings, that our merits may receive their reward. The Lord in His Gospel, when He would direct the way of our hope and faith in a brief summary, said, "The Lord your God is one God: and you shall love the Lord your God with all your heart, and with all your soul, and with all your strength. This is the first commandment; land the second is like it: You shall love your neighbor as yourself. On these two commandments hang all the law and the prophets."[44] He taught, at the same time, love and unity by His instruction. He has included all the prophets and the law in two precepts. But what unity does he keep, what love does he maintain or consider, who, savage with the madness of discord, divides the Church, destroys the faith, disturbs the peace, dissipates charity, profanes the sacrament?

16. This evil, most faithful brethren, had long ago begun, but now the mischievous destruction of the same evil has increased, and the envenomed plague of heretical perversity and schisms has begun to spring forth and shoot anew; because even thus it must be in the decline of the world, since the Holy Spirit foretells and forewarns us by the apostle, saying, "In the last days," says he, "perilous times shall come, and men shall be lovers of their own selves, proud, boasters, covetous, blasphemers, disobedient to parents, unthankful, unholy, without natural affection, truce-breakers, false accusers, incontinent, fierce, hating the good, traitors, heady, high-minded, lovers of pleasures more than lovers of God, having a sort of form of religion, but denying the power thereof. Of this sort are they who creep into houses, and lead captive silly women laden with sins, which are led away with various lusts; ever learning, and never coming to the knowledge of the truth. And as Jannes and Jambres withstood Moses, so do these also resist the truth; but they shall proceed no further, for their folly shall be manifest unto all men, even as theirs also was."[45] Whatever things were predicted are fulfilled; and as the end of the world is approaching, they have come for the probation as well of the men as of the times. Error deceives as the adversary rages more and more; senselessness lifts up, envy inflames, covetousness makes blind, impiety depraves, pride puffs up, discord exasperates, anger hurries headlong.

17. Yet let not the excessive and headlong faithlessness of many move or disturb us, but rather strengthen our faith in the truthfulness which has foretold the matter. As some have become such, because these things were predicted beforehand, so let other brethren beware of matters of a like kind, because these also were predicted beforehand, even as the Lord instructs us, and says, "But take heed: behold, I have told you all things."[46] Avoid, I beseech you, brethren, men of this kind, and drive away from your side and from your ears, as if it were the contagion of death, their mischievous conversation; as it is written, "Hedge your ears about with thorns, and refuse to hear a wicked tongue."[47] And again, "Evil communications corrupt good manners."[48] The Lord teaches and warns us to depart from such. He says, "They are blind leaders of the blind; and if the blind lead the blind, they shall both fall into the ditch."[49] Such a one is to be turned away from and avoided, whosoever he may be, that is separated from the Church. Such a one is perverted and sins, and is condemned of his own self. Does he think that he has Christ, who acts in opposition to Christ's priests, who separates himself from the company of His clergy and people? He bears arms against the Church, he contends against God's appointment. An enemy of the altar, a rebel against Christ's sacrifice, for the faith faithless, for religion profane, a disobedient servant, an impious son, a hostile brother, despising the bishops, and forsaking God's priests, he dares to set up another altar, to make another prayer with unauthorized words,[50] to profane the truth of the Lord's offering by false sacrifices, and not to know that he who strives against the appointment of God, is punished on account of the daring of his temerity by divine visitation.

18. Thus Korah, Dathan, and Abiram, who endeavored to claim to themselves the power of sacrificing in opposition to Moses and Aaron the priest, underwent immediate punishment for their attempts. The earth, breaking its fastenings, gaped open into a deep gulf, and the cleft of the receding ground swallowed up the men standing and living.[51] Nor did the anger of the indignant God strike only those who had been the movers (of the sedition); but two hundred and fifty sharers and associates of that madness besides, who had been mingled with them in that boldness, the fire that went out from the Lord consumed with a hasty revenge; doubtless to admonish and show that whatever those wicked men had endeavored, in order by human will to overthrow God's appointment, had been done in opposition to God. Thus also Uzziah the king—when he bare the censer and violently claimed to himself to sacrifice against God's law, and when Azariah the priest withstood him, would not be obedient and yield—was confounded by the divine indignation, and was polluted upon his forehead by the spot of leprosy: he was marked by an offended Lord in that part of his body where they are signed who deserve well of the Lord.[52] And the sons of Aaron, who placed strange fire upon the altar, which the Lord had not commanded, were at once extinguished in the presence of an avenging Lord.[53]

19. These, doubtless, they imitate and follow, who, despising God's tradition, seek after strange doctrines, and bring in teachings of human appointment, whom the Lord rebukes and reproves in His Gospel, saying, "You reject the commandment of God, that you may keep your own tradition."[54] This is a worse crime than that which the lapsed seem to have fallen into, who nevertheless, standing as penitents for their crime, beseech God with full satisfactions. In this case, the Church is sought after and entreated; in that case, the Church is resisted: here it is possible that there has been necessity; there the will is engaged in the wickedness: on the one hand, he who has lapsed has only injured himself; on the other, he who has endeavored to cause a heresy or a schism has deceived many by drawing them with him. In the former, it is the loss of one soul; in the latter, the risk of many. Certainly the one both understands that he has sinned, and laments and bewails it; the other, puffed up in his heart, and pleasing himself in his very crimes, separates sons from their Mother, entices sheep from their shepherd, disturbs the sacraments of God; and while the lapsed has sinned but once, he sins daily. Finally, the lapsed, who has subsequently attained to martyrdom, may receive the promises of the kingdom; while the other, if he have been slain without the Church, cannot attain to the rewards of the Church.

20. Nor let any one marvel, beloved brethren, that even some of the confessors[55] advance to these lengths, and thence also that some others sin thus wickedly, thus grievously. For neither does confession make a man free from the snares of the devil, nor does it defend a man who is still placed in the world, with a perpetual security from temptations, and dangers, and onsets, and attacks of the world; otherwise we should never see in confessors those subsequent frauds, and fornications, and adulteries, which now with groans and sorrow we witness in some. Whosoever that confessor is, he is not greater, or better, or dearer to God than Solomon, who, although so long as he walked in God's ways, retained that grace which he had received from the Lord, yet after he forsook the Lord's way he lost also then Lord's grace. And therefore it is written, "Hold fast that which you have, lest another take your crown."[56] But assuredly the Lord would not threaten that the crown of righteousness might be taken away, werc it not that, when righteousness departs, the crown must also depart.

21. Confession is the beginning of glory, not the full desert of the crown; nor does it perfect our praise, but it initiates our dignity; and since it is written, "He that endures to the end, the same shall be saved;"[57] whatever has been before the end is a step by which we ascend to the summit of salvation, not a terminus wherein the full result of the ascent is already gained. He is a confessor; but after confession his peril is greater, because the adversary is more provoked. He is a confessor; for this cause he ought the more to stand on the side of the Lord's Gospel, since he has by the Gospel attained glory from the Lord. For the Lord says, "To whom much is given, of him much shall be required; and to whom more dignity is ascribed, of him more service is exacted."[58] Let no one perish by the example of a confessor; let no one learn injustice, let no one learn arrogance, let no one learn treachery, from the manners of a confessor. He is a confessor, let him be lowly and quiet; let him be in his doings modest with discipline, so that he who is called a confessor of Christ may imitate Christ whom he confesses. For since He says, "Whosoever exalts himself shall be abased, and he who humbles himself shall be exalted;"[59] and since He Himself has been exalted by the Father, because as the Word, and the strength, and the wisdom of God the Father, He humbled Himself upon earth, how can He love arrogance, who even by His own law enjoined upon us humility, and Himself received the highest name from the Father as the reward of His humility? He is a confessor of Christ, but only so if the majesty and dignity of Christ be not afterwards blasphemed by him. Let not the tongue which has confessed Christ be evil-speaking; let it not be turbulent, let it not be heard jarring with reproaches and quarrels, let it not after words of praise, dart forth serpents' venom against the brethren and God's priests. But if one shall have subsequently been blameworthy and obnoxious; if he shall have wasted his confession by evil conversation; if he shall have stained his life by disgraceful foulness; if, finally, forsaking the Church in which he has become a confessor, and severing the concord of unity, he shall have exchanged his first faith for a subsequent unbelief, he may not flatter himself on account of his confession that he is elected to the reward of glory, when from this very fact his deserving of punishment has become the greater.

22. For the Lord chose Judas also among the apostles, and yet afterwards Judas betrayed the Lord. Yet not on that account did the faith and firmness of the apostles fail, because the traitor Judas failed from their fellowship; so also in the case in question the holiness and dignity of confessors is not immediately diminished, because the faith of some of them is broken. The blessed Apostle Paul in his epistle speaks in this manner: "For what if some of them fall away from the faith, shall their unbelief make the faith of God without effect? God forbid: for God is true, though every man be a liar."[60] The greater and better part of the confessors stand firm in the strength of their faith, and in the truth of the law and discipline of the Lord; neither do they depart from the peace of the Church, who remember that they have obtained grace in the Church by the condescension of God; and by this very thing they obtain a higher praise of their faith, that they have separated from the faithlessness of those who have been associated with them in the fellowship of confession, and withdrawn from the contagion of crime. Illuminated by the true light of the Gospel, shone upon with the Lord's pure and white brightness, they are as praiseworthy in maintaining the peace of Christ, as they have been victorious in their combat with the devil.[61]

23. I indeed desire, beloved brethren, and I equally endeavor and exhort, that if it be possible, none of the brethren should perish, and that our rejoicing Mother may enclose in her bosom the one body of a people at agreement. Yet if wholesome counsel cannot recall to the way of salvation certain leaders of schisms and originators of dissensions, who abide in blind and obstinate madness, yet do you others, if either taken in simplicity, or induced by error, or deceived by some craftiness of misleading cunning, loose yourselves from the nets of deceit, free your wandering steps from errors, acknowledge the straight way of the heavenly road. The word of the witnessing apostle is: "We command you," says he, "in the name of our Lord Jesus Christ, that you withdraw yourselves from all brethren that walk disorderly, and not after the tradition that they have received from us."[62] And again he says, "Let no man deceive you with vain words; for because of these things comes the wrath of God upon the children of disobedience. Be not therefore partakers with them."[63] We must withdraw, nay rather must flee, from those who fall away, lest, while any one is associated with those who walk wickedly, and goes on in ways of error and of sin, he himself also, wandering away from the path of the true road, should be found in like guilt. God is one, and Christ is one, and His Church is one, and the faith is one, and the people is joined into a substantial unity of body by the cement of concord. Unity cannot be severed; nor can one body be separated by a division of its structure, nor torn into pieces, with its entrails wrenched asunder by laceration. Whatever has proceeded from the womb cannot live and breathe in its detached condition, but loses the substance of health.

24. The Holy Spirit warns us, and says, "What man is he that desires to live, and would fain see good days? Refrain your tongue from evil, and your lips that they speak no guile. Eschew evil, and do good; seek peace, and ensue it."[64] The son of peace ought to seek peace and ensue it. He who knows and loves the bond of charity, ought to refrain his tongue from the evil of dissension. Among His divine commands and salutary teachings, the Lord, when He was now very near to His passion, added this one, saying, "Peace I leave with you, my peace I give unto you."[65] He gave this to us as an heritage; He promised all the gifts and rewards of which He spoke through the preservation of peace. If we are fellow-heirs with Christ, let us abide in the peace of Christ; if we are sons of God, we ought to be peacemakers. "Blessed," says He, "are the peacemakers; for they shall be called the sons of God."[66] It behooves the sons of God to be peacemakers, gentle in heart, simple in speech, agreeing in affection, faithfully linked to one another in the bonds of unanimity.

25. This unanimity formerly prevailed among the apostles; and thus the new assembly of believers, keeping the Lord's commandments, maintained its charity. Divine Scripture proves this, when it says, "But the multitude of them which believed were of one heart and of one soul." And again: "These all continued with one mind in prayer with the women, and Mary the mother of Jesus, and with His brethren."[67] And thus they prayed with effectual prayers; thus they were able with confidence to obtain whatever they asked from the Lord's mercy.

26. But in us unanimity is diminished in proportion as liberality of working is decayed. Then they used to give for sale houses and estates; and that they might lay up for themselves treasures in heaven, presented to the apostles the price of them, to be distributed for the use of the poor. But now we do not even give the tenths from our patrimony; and while our Lord bids us sell, we rather buy and

increase our store.[68] Thus has the vigor of faith dwindled away among us; thus has the strength of believers grown weak. And therefore the Lord, looking to our days, says in His Gospel, "When the Son of man comes, think you that He shall find faith on the earth?"[69] We see that what He foretold has come to pass. There is no faith in the fear of God, in the law of righteousness, in love, in labor; none considers the fear of futurity, and none takes to heart the day of the Lord, and the wrath of God, and the punishments to come upon unbelievers, and the eternal torments decreed for the faithless. That which our conscience would fear if it believed, it fears not because it does not at all believe. But if it believed, it would also take heed; and if it took heed, it would escape.

27. Let us, beloved brethren, arouse ourselves as much as we can; and breaking the slumber of our ancient listlessness, let us be watchful to observe and to do the Lord's precepts. Let us be such as He Himself has bidden us to be, saying, "Let your loins be girt, and your lamps burning; and you yourselves like men that wait for their Lord, when He shall come from the wedding, that when He comes and knocks, they may open to Him. Blessed are those servants whom their Lord, when He comes, shall find watching."[70] We ought to be girt about, lest, when the day of setting forth comes, it should find us burdened and entangled. Let our light shine in good works, and glow in such wise as to lead us from the night of this world to the daylight of eternal brightness. Let us always with solicitude and caution wait for the sudden coming of the Lord, that when He shall knock, our faith may be on the watch, and receive from the Lord the reward of our vigilance. If these commands be observed, if these warnings and precepts be kept, we cannot be overtaken in slumber by the deceit of the devil; but we shall reign with Christ in His kingdom as servants that watch.

NOTES

1. Matt. 5:13.
2. An allusion to Matt. 10:16.
3. 1 Cor. 1:24.
4. Matt. 19:17.
5. John 14:15.
6. Matt. 7:24.
7. Note that Cyprian sees Christ's whole Person as revelatory; not only what He taught, but also what He did is a revelation. Christ's whole life is revelation, not just His spoken words. "His deeds, miracles and words all revealed that 'in him the whole fullness of deity dwells bodily.' His humanity appeared as "sacrament," that is, the sign and instrument, of his divinity and of the salvation he brings: what was visible in his earthly life leads to the invisible mystery of his divine sonship and redemptive mission" (*Catechism of the Catholic Church* § 515).
8. Orthodoxy and orthopraxy go hand in hand. Cyprian does not seem to consider the possibility, put forward by the modernists, that a man who is in error but sincerely following his conscience can be pleasing to God. The error itself is problematic, regardless of its consequences. Belief and action are closely aligned. "Religious error is in itself of an immoral

nature...that it is enough if we sincerely hold what we profess...—this is the principle of philosophies of heresies, which is very weakness" (Bl. John Henry Cardinal Newman, *An Essay on the Development of Christian Doctrine,* Chap. VIII. Sect. I§1).

9. "For many persons of every age, every rank, and also of both sexes are and will be endangered. For the contagion of this superstition has spread not only to the cities but also to the villages and farms. But it seems possible to check and cure it. It is certainly quite clear that the temples...had been almost deserted" (Pliny to Trajan, Letter 10:96-97).

10. 2 Cor. 11:14.

11. There is some controversy on this chapter. Apparently, Cyprian issued two editions of the treatise, one for general circulation, and an amended version that he sent to the confessors at Rome, praising the authority of the Chair of Peter. The amended, "Roman" version contains the following additions, inserted after the quote from Matt. 16:18-19 and bracketed in the text above: "Upon one He builds His Church, and to the same He says after His resurrection, 'feed My sheep'. And though to all His Apostles He gave an equal power yet did He set up one chair, and disposed the origin and manner of unity by his authority. The other Apostles were indeed what Peter was, but the primacy is given to Peter, and the Church and the chair is shown to be one. And all are pastors, but the flock is shown to be one, which is fed by all the Apostles with one mind and heart. He that holds not this unity of the Church, does he think that he holds the faith? He who deserts the chair of Peter, upon whom the Church is founded, is he confident that he is in the Church?" Protestants have tried to assert that this passage is spurious, a later Roman interpolation. It was, however, known of in the time of Pope Gelasius (492-496) and even by St. Jerome (340-420). Both versions are found in early manuscripts and are sometimes given together; critical examination of the language of the text support a Cyprianic authorship and Cyprian's authorship of the passage is now generally admitted. See the notes for Letter 50:4 for more on this issue.

12. Matt. 16:18-19.

13. John 21:17.

14. John 20:21.

15. Song of Songs 6:9.

16. Eph. 4:4. Note that Cyprian interprets St. Paul's exhortation to unity to refer to a unity that is manifested corporally in a visible structure, not in an ethereal "invisible Church."

17. Perhaps an allusion to Psalm 45:17: "The throne of your fathers your sons will have; you shall make them princes through all the land. I will make your name renowned through all generations; thus nations shall praise you forever," spoken with reference to the "princess arrayed in Ophir's gold."

18. Matt. 12:30.

19. John 10:30.

20. 1 John 5:7.

21. The physical and spiritual unity of the Church, which is exemplified in the union of the heavenly and the earthly that emerges in the sacraments, is itself based on the unity of the Three Persons of the Trinity. Hence, to be in union with the Church is to be incorporated into the union of the Trinity, which is life-giving. Contrariwise, to be outside the Church is to be cut off from the unity of the Trinity, and this to be devoid of "life and salvation."

22. John 19:23-24.

23. 1 Kings 11:31.

24. John 10:16.

25. 1 Cor. 1:10.

26. Eph. 4:3.

27. Jos. 2:19.

28. Ex. 12:46.

29. 1 John 2:19.

30. The principle behind the idea later enunciated by Newman that it was the challenge posed by

heresy that moved the early Church to make concrete dogmatic definitions."No doctrine is defined until it is violated" (Bl. John Henry Cardinal Newman, *An Essay on the Development of Christian Doctrine,* Chap. IV, Sect. III§4).

31. 1 Cor. 11:19.
32. *substantia,* ὑποοτα.
33. Jer. 23:16-21.
34. Jer. 2:13.
35. Cyrpian's position, that baptism of heretics is always invalid, was corrected by Pope Stephen I, who in 256 ordered the rebaptism of heretics to cease (providing they were baptized with proper form) and ordered that the Roman tradition of merely laying hands on converted heretics in sign of absolution must be everywhere observed on pain of excommunication. For more on the rebaptism controversy, see Letters 69, 70, 71, 72 and 73.
36. Matt. 18:20.
37. Mark 11:25.
38. 1 Cor. 13:2-7.
39. John 15:12.
40. 1 John 4:16.
41. Mark 13:6.
42. Cyprian, while denying the validity of heretical baptism, seems to imply that the charismatic gifts of the Church could be (and at times were) operative outside of her physical confines, though he refutes the argument as it applies to the question of the legitimacy of the Novatian schism. This must have been an argument made by the Novatian schismatics on behalf of the validity of their heresy, otherwise Cyprian would not have had to refute it.
43. Matt. 7:22.
44. Mark 19:29-31.
45. 2 Tim. 3:1-5.
46. Mark 13:23.
47. A Latin mistranslation of the Greek text of Sirach 28:24, which reads, "Hedge in thy ears with thorns, hear not a wicked tongue, and make doors and bars to thy mouth."
48. 1 Cor. 15:33.
49. Matt. 15:14.
50. Cyprian's condemnation of prayers made in "unauthorized words" suggests that one hallmark of schismatic conventicles was innovation in liturgical texts.
51. Num. 16.
52. As told in 2 Chr. 26:19-21, King Uzziah was struck with leprosy for trying to offer incense in the Jerusalem temple. The leprosy broke out "on his forehead" (Vulgate: *in fronte eius coram*). The head, according to St. Paul, is the crown of man and the symbol of the glory of God (1 Cor. 11). Thus, those receiving the sacrament of Confirmation are claimed for Christ by the marking of the sign (*sphragis*) of the Lord upon their foreheads.
53. Lev. 10:1.
54. Mark 7:9.
55. The term "confessor" in Cyprian's time was sometimes applied loosely to all martyrs, but more properly to those who, having suffered persecution and torture for the faith, were afterwards released and allowed to die in peace. Cyprian is here referring to persons who at one point made a heroic defense of the faith but have since lapsed into sin.
56. Rev. 3:11.
57. Matt. 10:22.
58. Luke 12:48.
59. Luke 18:14.
60. Rom. 3:3.
61. The preceding sections on the faith of confessors suggests that at least some of those who suffered in the Decian persecution (251-253) afterwards went on to become leaders in the

Novatian schism,which Cyprian says is doubly reprehensible by virtue of the sufferings these confessors had once endured. Thus, the glory confessors merited by their sufferings becomes "wasted" and their "punishment becomes greater."

62. 2 Thess. 3:6.
63. Eph. 5:6.
64. 1 Pet. 3:10-11.
65. John 14:27.
66. Matt. 5:9.
67. Acts 4:32, 1:14.
68. Cyprian's lament that the Christians of his age were too engaged in amassing in worldly goods suggests that the intense eschatological expectation that characterized the Church of the 1st and 2nd centuries had by his day begun to fade, though earlier in the treatise (16) Cyprian states his belief that the increase of heresies in his own day were a sign of the imminent end of the world.
69. Luke 18:8.
70. Luke 12:35.

ON THE DRESS OF VIRGINS[1]

1. Discipline, the safeguard of hope, the bond of faith, the guide of the way of salvation, the stimulus and nourishment of good dispositions, the teacher of virtue, causes us to abide always in Christ, and to live continually for God, and to attain to the heavenly promises and to the divine rewards. To follow her is wholesome, and to turn away from her and neglect her is deadly. The Holy Spirit says in the Psalms, "Keep discipline, lest perchance the Lord be angry, and you perish from the right way,"[2] when His wrath is quickly kindled against you. And again: "But unto the ungodly says God, 'Why do you preach my laws, and takest my covenant into your mouth? Whereas you hate discipline, and hast cast my words behind you.'"[3] And again we read: "He that casts away discipline is miserable."[4] And from Solomon we have received the mandates of wisdom, warning us: "My son, despise not the discipline of the Lord, nor faint when you are rebuked of Him: for whom the Lord loves He corrects."[5] But if God rebukes whom He loves, and rebukes him for the very purpose of amending him, brethren also, and especially priests, do not hate, but love those whom they rebuke, that they may mend them; since God also before predicted by Jeremiah, and pointed to our times, when he said, "And I will give you shepherds according to my heart: and they shall feed you with the food of discipline."[6]

2. But if in Holy Scripture discipline is frequently and everywhere prescribed, and the whole foundation of religion and of faith proceeds from obedience and fear, what is more fitting for us urgently to desire, what more to wish for and to hold fast, than to stand with roots strongly fixed, and with our houses based with solid mass upon the rock unshaken by the storms and whirlwinds of the world, so that we may come by the divine precepts to the rewards of God? Considering as well as knowing that our members, when purged from all the filth of the old contagion by the sanctification of the layer of life, are God's temples, and must not be violated nor polluted, since he who does violence to them is himself injured. We are the worshippers and priests of those temples; let us obey Him whose we have already begun to be. Paul tells us in his epistles, in which he has formed us to a course of living by divine teaching, "You are not your own, for you are bought with a great price; glorify and bear God in your body."[7] Let us glorify and bear God in a pure and chaste body, and with a more complete obedience; and since we have been redeemed by the blood of Christ, let us obey and give furtherance to the empire of our Redeemer by all the obedience of service, that nothing impure or profane may be brought into the temple of God, lest He should be offended, and forsake the temple which He inhabits. The words of the Lord giving health and teaching, as well curing as warning, are: "Behold, you are made whole: sin no more, lest a worse thing come unto you."[8] He gives the course of life, He gives the law of innocency after He has conferred health, nor suffers the man afterwards to wander with free and unchecked reins, but more severely threatens him who is again enslaved by those same things of which he had been healed, because it is doubtless a smaller fault to have sinned before, while as yet you had not known God's discipline; but there is no further pardon for sinning after you have begun to know God.[9] And, indeed, let as well men as women, as well boys as girls; let each sex and every age observe this, and take care in this respect, according to the religion and faith which they owe to God, that what is received holy and pure from the condescension of the Lord be preserved with a no less anxious fear.

3. My address is now to virgins, whose glory, as it is more eminent, excites the greater interest.[10] This is the flower of the ecclesiastical seed, the grace and ornament of spiritual endowment, a joyous disposition, the wholesome and uncorrupted work of praise and honor, God's image answering to the holiness of the Lord, the more illustrious portion of Christ's flock. The glorious fruitfulness of Mother Church rejoices by their means, and in them abundantly flourishes; and in proportion as a copious virginity is added to her number, so much the more it increases the joy of the Mother. To these I speak, these I exhort with affection rather than with power; not that I would claim—last and least, and very conscious of my lowliness as I am—any right to censure, but because, being unceasingly careful even to solicitude, I fear more from the onset of Satan.

4. For that is not an empty carefulness nor a vain fear, which takes counsel for the way of salvation, which guards the commandments of the Lord and of life; so that they who have dedicated themselves to Christ, and who depart from carnal concupiscence, and have vowed themselves to God as well in the flesh as in the spirit, may consummate their work, destined as it is to a great reward, and may not study any longer to be adorned or to please anybody but their Lord, from whom also they expect the reward of virginity; as He Himself says: "All men cannot receive this word, but they to whom it is given. For there are some eunuchs, which were so born from their mother's womb; and there are some eunuchs, which were made eunuchs of men; and there are eunuchs which have made themselves eunuchs for the kingdom of heaven's sake."[11] Again, also by this word of the angel the gift of continency is set forth, and virginity is preached: "These are they which have not defiled themselves with women, for they have remained virgins; these are they which follow the Lamb wherever He goes."[12] For not only thus does the Lord promise the grace of continency to men, and pass over women; but since the woman is a portion of the man, and is taken and formed from him, God in Scripture almost always speaks to the *Protoplast*, the first formed, because they are two in one flesh, and in the male is at the same time signified the woman also.[13]

5. But if continency follows Christ, and virginity is destined for the kingdom of God, what have they to do with earthly dress, and with ornaments, wherewith while they are striving to please men they offend God? Not considering that it is declared, "They who please men are put to confusion, because God has despised them;" and that Paul also has gloriously and sublimely uttered, "If I yet pleased men, I should not be the servant of Christ."[14] But continence and modesty consist not alone in purity of the flesh, but also in seemliness, as well as in modesty of dress and adornment; so that, according to the apostle, she who is unmarried may be holy both in body and in spirit. Paul instructs and teaches us, saying, "He that is unmarried cares for the things of the Lord, how he may please God: but he who has contracted marriage cares for the things which are of this world, how he may please his wife."[15] So both the virgin and the unmarried woman consider those things which are the Lord's, that they may be holy both in body and spirit. A virgin ought not only to be so, but also to be perceived and believed to be so: no one on seeing a virgin should be in any doubt as to whether she is one. Perfectness should show itself equal in all things; nor should the dress of the body discredit the good of the mind. Why should she walk out adorned? Why with dressed hair, as if she either had or sought for a husband? Rather let her dread to please if she is a virgin; and let her not invite her own risk, if she is keeping herself for better and divine things. They who have not a husband whom they profess that they please, should persevere, sound and pure not only in body, but also in spirit. For it is not right that a virgin should have her hair braided for the appearance of her beauty, or boast of her flesh and of its beauty, when she has no struggle greater than that against her flesh, and no contest more obstinate than that of conquering and subduing the body.

6. Paul proclaims in a loud and lofty voice, "But God forbid that I should glory, save in the cross of our Lord Jesus Christ, by whom the world is crucified unto me, and I unto the world."[16] And yet a virgin in the Church glories concerning her fleshly appearance and the beauty of her body! Paul adds, and says, "For they that are Christ's have crucified their flesh, with its faults and lusts."[17] And she who professes to have renounced the lusts and vices of the flesh, is found in the midst of those very things which she has renounced! Virgin, you are taken, you are exposed, you boast one thing and affect another. You sprinkle yourself with the stains of carnal concupiscence, although you are a candidate of purity and modesty. "Cry," says the Lord to Isaiah, "All flesh is grass, and all the glory of it as the flower of the grass: the grass withers, and the flower fades; but the word of the Lord endures for ever."[18] It is becoming for no Christian, and especially it is not becoming for a virgin, to regard any glory and honor of the flesh, but only to desire the word of God, to embrace benefits which shall endure for ever. Or, if she must glory in the flesh, then assuredly let her glory when she is tortured in confession of the name; when a woman is found to be stronger than the tortures; when she suffers fire, or the cross, or the sword, or the wild beasts, that she may be crowned. These are the precious jewels of the flesh, these are the better ornaments of the body.

7. But there are some rich women, and wealthy in the fertility of means, who prefer their own wealth, and contend that they ought to use these blessings. Let them know first of all that she is rich who is rich in God; that she is wealthy who is wealthy in Christ; that those are blessings which are spiritual, divine, heavenly, which lead us to God, which abide with us in perpetual possession with God. But whatever things are earthly, and have been received in this world, and will remain here with the world, ought so to be condemned even as the world itself is condemned, whose pomps and delights we have already renounced when by a blessed passage we came to God. John stimulates and exhorts us, witnessing with a spiritual and heavenly voice. "Love not the world," says he, "neither the things that are in the world. If any man love the world, the love of the Father is not in him. For all that is in the world, is lust of the flesh, and the lust of the eyes, and the pride of life, which is not from the Father, but is of the lust of the world. And the world passes away, and the lust thereof: but he that does the will of God abides for ever, even as God also abides for ever."[19] Therefore eternal and divine things are to be followed, and all things must be done after the will of God, that we may follow the divine footsteps and teachings of our Lord, who warned us, and said, "I came down from heaven, not to do my own will, but the will of Him that sent me."[20] But if the servant is not greater than his lord, and he that is freed owes obedience to his deliverer, we who desire to be Christians ought to imitate what Christ said and did. It is written, and it is read and heard, and is celebrated for our example by the Church's mouth, "He that says he abides in Christ ought himself also so to walk even as He walked."[21] Therefore we must walk with equal steps; we must strive with emulous[22] walk. Then the following of truth answers to the faith of our name, and a reward is given to the believer, if what is believed is also done.

8. You call yourself wealthy and rich; but Paul meets your riches, and with his own voice prescribes for the moderating of your dress and ornament within a just limit. "Let women, said he, adorn themselves with shamefacedness and sobriety, not with broidered hair, nor gold, nor pearls, nor costly array, but as becomes women professing chastity, with a good conversation."[23] Also Peter consents to these same precepts, and says, "Let there be in the woman not the outward adorning of array, or gold, or apparel, but the adorning of the heart."[24] But if these also warn us that the women who are accustomed to make an excuse for their dress by reference to their husband, should be restrained and limited by religious observance to the Church's discipline, how much more is it right that the virgin should keep that observance, who has no excuse for adorning herself, nor can the deceitfulness of her fault be laid upon another, but she herself remains in its guilt!

9. You say that you are wealthy and rich. But not everything that can be done ought also to be done; nor ought the broad desires that arise out of the pride of the world to be extended beyond the honor and modesty of virginity; since it is written, "All things are lawful, but all things are not expedient: all things are lawful, but all things edify not."[25] For the rest, if you dress your hair sumptuously, and walk so as to draw attention in public, and attract the eyes of youth upon you, and draw the sighs of young men after you, nourish the lust of concupiscence, and inflame the fuel of sighs, so that, although you yourself perish not, yet you cause others to perish, and offer yourself, as it were, a sword or poison to the spectators; you cannot be excused on the pretence that you are chaste and modest in mind. Your shameful dress and immodest ornament accuse you; nor can you be counted now among Christ's maidens and virgins, since you live in such a manner as to make yourselves objects of desire.[26]

10. You say that you are wealthy and rich; but it becomes not a virgin to boast of her riches, since Holy Scripture says, "What has pride profited us? Or what benefit has the vaunting of riches conferred upon us? And all these things have passed away like a shadow."[27] And the apostle again warns us, and says, "And they that buy, as though they bought not; and they that possess, as though they possessed not; and they that use this world, as though they used it not. For the fashion of this world passes away."[28] Peter also, to whom the Lord commends His sheep to be fed and guarded, on whom He placed and founded the Church, says indeed that he has no silver and gold, but says that he is rich in the grace of Christ—that he is wealthy in his faith and virtue—wherewith he performed many great works with miracle, wherewith he abounded in spiritual blessings to the grace of glory. These riches, this wealth, she cannot possess, who had rather be rich to this world than to Christ.[29]

11. You say that you are wealthy and rich, and you think that you should use those things which God has willed you to possess. Use them, certainly, but for the things of salvation; use them, but for good purposes; use them, but for those things which God has commanded, and which the Lord has set forth. Let the poor feel that you are wealthy; let the needy feel that you are rich. Lend your estate to God; give food to Christ. Move Him by the prayers of many to grant you to carry out the glory of virginity, and to succeed in coming to the Lord's rewards. There entrust your treasures, where no thief digs through, where no insidious plunderer breaks in. Prepare for yourself possessions; but let them rather be heavenly ones, where neither rust wears out, nor hail bruises, nor sun burns, nor rain spoils your fruits constant and perennial, and free from all contact of worldly injury. For in this very matter you are sinning against God, if you think that riches were given you by Him for this purpose, to enjoy them thoroughly, without a view to salvation.[30] For God gave man also a voice; and yet love-songs and indecent things are not on that account to be sung. And God willed iron to be for the culture of the earth, but not on that account must murders be committed. Or because God ordained incense, and wine, and fire, are we thence to sacrifice to idols? Or because the flocks of cattle abound in your fields, ought you to immolate victims and offerings to the gods? Otherwise a large estate is a temptation, unless the wealth minister to good uses; so that every man, in proportion to his wealth, ought by his patrimony rather to redeem his transgressions than to increase them.

12. The characteristics of ornaments, and of garments, and the allurements of beauty, are not fitting for any but prostitutes and immodest women; and the dress of none is more precious than of those whose modesty is lowly. Thus in the Holy Scriptures, by which the Lord wished us to be both instructed and admonished, the harlot city is described more beautifully arrayed and adorned, and with her ornaments; and the rather on account of those very ornaments about to perish. "And there came," it is said, "one of the seven angels, which had the seven phials, and talked with me, saying, 'Come hither, I will show you the judgment of the great whore, that sits upon many waters, with whom the kings of the earth have committed fornication.' And he carried me away in spirit; and I saw a woman sit upon a beast, and that woman was arrayed in a purple and scarlet mantle, and was adorned with gold, and precious stones, and pearls, having a golden cup in her hand, full of curses, and filthiness, and fornication of the whole earth."[31] Let chaste and modest virgins avoid the dress of the unchaste, the manners of the immodest, the ensigns of brothels, the ornaments of harlots.

13. Moreover Isaiah, full of the Holy Spirit, cries out and chides the daughters of Sion, corrupted with gold, and silver, and raiment, and rebukes them, affluent as they were in pernicious wealth, and departing from God for the sake of the world's delights. "The daughters of Sion," says he, "are haughty, and walk with stretched-out neck and beckoning of the eyes, trailing their gowns as they go, and mincing with their feet. And God will humble the princely daughters of Sion, and the Lord will unveil their dress; and the Lord will take away the glory of their apparel, and their ornaments, and their hair, and their curls, and their round tires like the moon, and their crisping-pins, and their bracelets, and their clusters of pearls, and their armlets and rings, and earrings, and silks woven with gold and hyacinth. And instead of a sweet smell there shall be dust; and you shall be girt with a rope instead of with a girdle; and for a golden ornament of your head you shall have baldness."[32] This God blames, this He marks out: hence He declares that virgins are corrupted; hence, that they have departed from the true and divine worship. Lifted up, they have fallen; with their heads adorned, they merited dishonor and disgrace. Having put on silk and purple, they cannot put on Christ; adorned with gold, and pearls, and necklaces, they have lost the ornaments of the heart and spirit. Who would not execrate and avoid that which has been the destruction of another? Who would desire and take up that which has served as the sword and weapon for the death of another? If he who had drunk should die by draining the cup, you would know that what he had drunk was poison; if, on taking food, he who had taken it were to perish, you would know that what, when taken could kill, was deadly; nor would you eat or drink of that whence you had before seen that others had perished. Now what ignorance of truth is it, what madness of mind, to wish for that which both has hurt and always will hurt and to think that you yourself will not perish by those means whereby you know that others have perished!

14. For God neither made the sheep scarlet or purple, nor taught the juices of herbs and shell-fish to dye and color wool, nor arranged necklaces with stones set in gold, and with pearls distributed in a woven series or numerous cluster, wherewith you would hide the neck which He made; that what God formed in man may be covered, and that may be seen upon it which the devil has invented in addition. Has God willed that wounds should be made in the ears, wherewith infancy, as yet innocent, and unconscious of worldly evil, may be put to pain, that subsequently from the scars and holes of the ears precious beads may hang, heavy, if not by their weight, still by the amount of their cost? All which things sinning and apostate angels put forth by their arts, when, lowered to the contagions of earth, they forsook their heavenly vigor. They taught them also to paint the eyes with blackness drawn round them in a circle, and to stain the cheeks with a deceitful red, and to change the hair with false colors, and to drive out all truth, both of face and head, by the assault of their own corruption.[33]

15. And indeed in that very matter, for the sake of the fear which faith suggests to me, for the sake of the love which brotherhood requires, I think that not virgins only and widows, but married women also, and all of the sex alike, should be admonished, that the work of God and His fashioning and formation ought in no manner to be adulterated, either with the application of yellow color, or with black dust or rouge, or with any kind of medicament which can corrupt the native lineaments. God says, "Let us make man in our image and likeness"[34]; and does any one dare to alter and to change what God has made? They are laying hands on God when they try to re-form that which He formed, and to transfigure it, not knowing that everything which comes into being is God's work, everything that is changed is the devil's. If any artist, in painting, were to delineate in envious coloring the countenance and likeness and bodily appearance of any one; and the likeness being now painted and completed, another person were to lay hands on it, as if, when it was already formed and already painted, he, being more skilled, could amend it, a serious wrong and a just cause of indignation would seem natural to the former artist. And do you think yourself likely with impunity to commit a boldness of such wicked temerity, an offense to God the artificer? For although you may not be immodest among men, and are not unchaste with your seducing dyes, yet when those things which belong to God are corrupted and violated, you are engaged in a worse adultery. That you think yourself to be adorned, that you think your hair to be dressed, is an assault upon the divine work, is a prevarication of the truth.

16. The voice of the warning apostle is, "Purge out the old leaven, that you may be a new lump, as you are unleavened; for even Christ our passover is sacrificed. Therefore let us keep the feast, not with old leaven, neither with the leaven of malice and wickedness, but with the unleavened bread of sincerity and truth."[35] But are sincerity and truth preserved when what is sincere is polluted by adulterous colors, and what is true is changed into a lie by the deceitful dyes of medicaments? Your Lord says, "You can not make one hair white or black;"[36] and you, in order to overcome the word of your Lord, will be more mighty than He, and stain your hair with a daring endeavor and with profane contempt. With evil presage of the future, you make a beginning to yourself already of flame-colored hair; and sin (oh, wickedness!) with your head—that is, with the nobler part of your body! And although it is written of the Lord, "His head and His hair were white like wool or snow"[37], you curse that whiteness and hate that hoariness which is like to the Lord's head.

17. Are you not afraid, I entreat you, being such as you are, that when the day of resurrection comes, your Maker may not recognize you again, and may turn you away when you come to His rewards and promises, and may exclude you, rebuking you with the vigor of a Censor and Judge, and say: "This is not my work, nor is this our image." You have polluted your skin with a false medicament, you have changed your hair with an adulterous color, your face is violently taken possession of by a lie, your figure is corrupted, your countenance is another's. You cannot see God, since your eyes are not those which God made, but those which the devil has spoiled. You have followed him, you have imitated the red and painted eyes of the serpent. As you are adorned in the fashion of your enemy, with him also you shall burn by and by. Are not these, I beg, matters to be reflected on by God's servants? Are they not always to be dreaded day and night? Let married women see to it, in what respect they are flattering themselves concerning the solace of their husbands with the desire of pleasing them, and while they put them forward indeed as their excuse, they make them partners in the association of guilty, consent. Virgins, assuredly, to whom this address is intended to appeal, who have adorned themselves with arts of this kind, I should think ought not to be counted among virgins, but, like infected sheep and diseased cattle, to be driven from the holy and pure flock of virginity, lest by living together they should pollute the rest with their contagion; lest they ruin others even as they have perished themselves.

18. And since we are seeking the advantage of continency, let us also avoid everything that is pernicious and hostile to it. And I will not pass over those things, which while by negligence they come into use, have made for themselves a usurped licence, contrary to modest and sober manners. Some are not ashamed to be present at marriage parties, and in that freedom of lascivious discourse to mingle in unchaste conversation, to hear what is not becoming, to say what is not lawful, to expose themselves, to be present in the midst of disgraceful words and drunken banquets, by which the ardor of lust is kindled, and the bride is animated to bear, and the bridegroom to dare lewdness. What place is there at weddings for her whose mind is not towards marriage? Or what can there be pleasant or joyous in those engagements for her, where both desires and wishes are different from her own? What is learned there—what is seen? How greatly a virgin falls short of her resolution, when she who had come there modest goes away immodest! Although she may remain a virgin in body and mind, yet in eyes, in ears, in tongue, she has diminished the virtues that she possessed.

19. But what of those who frequent promiscuous baths, who prostitute to eyes that are curious to lust, bodies that are dedicated to chastity and modesty?[38] They who disgracefully behold naked men, and are seen naked by men, do they not themselves afford enticement to vice, do they not solicit and invite the desires of those present to their own corruption and wrong? Let every one, say you, look to the disposition with which he comes there: my care is only that of refreshing and washing my poor body. That kind of defense does not clear you, nor does it excuse the crime of lasciviousness and wantonness. Such a washing defiles; it does not purify nor cleanse the limbs, but stains them. You behold no one immodestly, but you yourself are gazed upon immodestly. You do not pollute your eyes with disgraceful delight, but in delighting others you yourself are polluted. You make a show of the bathing-place; the places where you assemble are fouler than a theatre. There all modesty is put; off together with the clothing of garments, the honor and modesty of the body is laid aside; virginity is exposed, to be pointed at and to be handled.[39] And now, then, consider whether when you are clothed you are modest among men, when the boldness of nakedness has conduced to immodesty.

20. For this reason, therefore, the Church frequently mourns over her virgins; hence she groans at their scandalous and detestable stories; hence the flower of her virgins is extinguished, the honor and modesty of continency are injured, and all its glory and dignity are profaned. Thus the hostile besieger insinuates himself by his arts; thus by snares that deceive, by secret ways, the devil creeps in. Thus, while virgins wish to be more carefully adorned, and to wander with more liberty, they cease to be virgins, corrupted by a furtive dishonor; widows before they are married, adulterous, not to their husband, but to Christ. In proportion as they had been as virgins destined to great rewards, so will they experience great punishments for the loss of their virginity.

21. Therefore hear me, O virgins, as a parent; hear, I beseech you, one who fears while he warns; hear one who is faithfully consulting for your advantage and your profit. Be such as God the Creator made you; be such as the hand of your Father ordained you. Let your countenance remain in you incorrupt, your neck unadorned, your figure simple; let not wounds be made in your ears, nor let the precious chain of bracelets and necklaces circle your arms or your neck; let your feet be free from golden bands, your hair stained with no dye, your eyes worthy of beholding God. Let your baths be performed with women, among whom your bathing is modest. Let the shameless feasts and lascivious banquets of marriages be avoided, the contagion of which is perilous. Overcome dress, since you are a virgin; overcome gold, since you overcome the flesh and the world. It is not consistent to be unable to be conquered by the greater, and to be found no match for the less. Strait and narrow is the way which leads to life; hard and difficult is the track which tends to glory. By this pathway the martyrs progress, the virgins pass, the just of all kinds advance. Avoid the broad and roomy ways. There are deadly snares and death-bringing pleasures; there the devil flatters, that he may deceive; smiles, that he may do mischief; entices, that he may slay. The first fruit for the martyrs is a hundred-fold; the second is yours, sixty-fold.[40] As with the martyrs there is no thought of the flesh and of the world, no small, and trifling, and delicate encounter; so also in you, whose reward is second in grace, let there be the strength in endurance next to theirs. The ascent to great things is not easy. What toil we suffer, what labor, when we endeavor to ascend the hills and the tops of mountains! What, then, that we may ascend to heaven? If you look to the reward of the promise, your labor is less. Immortality is given to the persevering, eternal life is set before them; the Lord promises a kingdom.

22. Hold fast, O virgins! Hold fast what you have begun to be; hold fast what you shall be. A great reward awaits you, a great recompense of virtue, the immense advantage of chastity. Do you wish to know what ill the virtue of continence avoids, what good it possesses? "I will multiply," says God to the woman, "your sorrows and your groanings; and in sorrow shall you bring forth children; and your desire shall be to your husband, and he shall rule over you."[41] You are free from this sentence. You do not fear the sorrows and the groans of women. You have no fear of child-bearing; nor is your husband lord over you; but your Lord and Head is Christ, after the likeness and in the place of the man; with that of men your lot and your condition is equal. It is the word of the Lord which says, "The children of this world beget and are begotten; but they who are counted worthy of that world, and of the resurrection from the dead, neither marry nor are given in marriage: neither shall they die any more: for they are equal to the angels of God, being the children of the resurrection."[42] That which we shall be, you have already begun to be. You possess already in this world the glory of the resurrection. You pass through the world without the contagion of the world; in that you continue chaste and virgins, you are equal to the angels of God. Only let your virginity remain and endure substantial and uninjured; and as it began bravely, let it persevere continuously, and not seek the ornaments of necklaces nor garments, but of conduct. Let it look towards God and heaven, and not lower to the lust of the flesh and of the world, the eyes uplifted to things above, or set them upon earthly things.

23. The first decree commanded to increase and to multiply; the second enjoined continency. While the world is still rough and void, we are propagated by the fruitful begetting of numbers, and we increase to the enlargement of the human race. Now, when the world is filled and the earth supplied, they who can receive continency, living after the manner of eunuchs, are made eunuchs unto the kingdom. Nor does the Lord command this, but He exhorts it; nor does

He impose the yoke of necessity, since the free choice of the will is left. But when He says that in His Father's house are many mansions, He points out the dwellings of the better habitation. Those better habitations you are seeking; cutting away the desires of the flesh, you obtain the reward of a greater grace in the heavenly home. All indeed who attain to the divine gift and inheritance by the sanctification of baptism, therein put off the old man by the grace of the saving laver, and, renewed by the Holy Spirit from the filth of the old contagion, are purged by a second nativity. But the greater holiness and truth of that repeated birth belongs to you, who have no longer any desires of the flesh and of the body. Only the things which belong to virtue and the Spirit have remained in you to glory. It is the apostle's word whom the Lord called His chosen vessel, whom God sent to proclaim the heavenly command: "The first man," says he, "is from the earth, of earth; the second man is from heaven. Such as is the earthy, such are they also who are earthy; and such as is the heavenly, such also are the heavenly. As we have borne the image of him who is earthy, let us also bear the image of Him who is heavenly."[43] Virginity bears this image, integrity bears it, holiness bears it, and truth. Disciplines which are mindful of God bear it, retaining righteousness with religion, steadfast in faith, humble in fear, brave to all suffering, meek to sustain wrong, easy to show mercy, of one mind and one heart in fraternal peace.

24. Every one of which things, O good virgins, you ought to observe, to love, to fulfill, who, giving yourselves to God and Christ, are advancing in both the higher and better part to the Lord, to whom you have dedicated yourselves. You that are advanced in years, suggest a teaching to the younger. You that are younger, give a stimulus to your coevals. Stir one another up with mutual exhortations; provoke to glory by rival proofs of virtue. Endure bravely, go on spiritually, attain happily. Only remember us at that time, when virginity shall begin to be rewarded in you.

NOTES

1. In this treatise St. Cyprian exhorts widows, virgins and married women called by the name of Christ to avoid the physcial adornment of the world, such as hair dyes, suggestive clothing, jewelry and ornamentation. Some of Cyprian's condemnations may seem particularly harsh to modern ears (15–18), but it must be remembered that in Cyprian's day excessive adornments were closely associated with prostitution and the theatre, which was a place of excessive immorality. Though we might find some of Cyprian's opinions a little outlandish (such as his assertion that on the day of judgment God will not be able to recognize a person who has dyed their hair), this treatise nevertheless makes the very valid point that those who live for Christ, especially virgins, ought not to concern themselves with making their bodies beautiful for the sake of the world. Such is nothing other than vanity.
2. A paraphrase of Psalm 2:12, "Kiss the son, lest he be angry and you perish in the way."
3. Ps. 50:16-17.

4. Wisdom 3:11.
5. Prov. 3:11.
6. Jer. 3:15.
7. 1 Cor. 6:14.
8. John 5:14.
9. St. Cyprian is here calling to mind Hebrews 6:4-6: "For it is impossible for those who were once illuminated, have tasted also the heavenly gift and were made partakers of the Holy Ghost, have moreover tasted the good word of God and the powers of the world to come, and are fallen away to be renewed again to penance, crucifying again to themselves the Son of God and making him a mockery." Given Cyprian's opposition to the antipope Novatian, who held that readmission to the Church of lapsed Christians was impossible, we ought not to see Cyprian as denying the possibility of repentance for those who fall into sin in an absolute sense, though he was notably strict with regards to the *lapsi*. He is here not making a theological assertion about salvation but giving an exhortation to men and women to remain pure, warning them of the penalties of disobedience and appealing to holy fear to aid them in their resolve.
10. In this paragraph St. Cyprian lauds the glories of virginity, which is superior to the married state. This is a constant tradition in the Church. "If any one saith, that the marriage state is to be placed above the state of virginity, or of celibacy, and that it is not better and more blessed to remain in virginity, or in celibacy, than to be united in matrimony; let him be anathema" (Council of Trent, Session XXIV, Can. X); "Virginity for the sake of the kingdom of heaven is an unfolding of baptismal grace, a powerful sign of the supremacy of the bond with Christ and of the ardent expectation of his return, a sign which also recalls that marriage is a reality of this present age which is passing away" (*Catechism of the Catholic Church*, 1619).
11. Matt. 19:11.
12. Rev. 14:4.
13. When Scripture speaks of things generically applying to men, women are implied as well, since woman, as coming from man, is implied in the term "man."
14. Gal. 1:10.
15. 1 Cor. 7:14.
16. Gal. 6:14.
17. Gal. 5:24.
18. Isa. 40:6.
19. 1 John 2:15-17.
20. John 6:38.
21. A paraphrase of 1 John 2:6, "He that saith he abideth in him ought himself also to walk even as he walked."
22. Emulous; that is, eager to imitate.
23. 1 Tim. 2:9-10.
24. 1 Pet. 3:3-4.
25. 1 Cor. 10:23.
26. St. Cyprian here gives an example of the concept in Catholic moral theology of the possibility of being guilty of the sin of another by enabling the other in their sin.
27. Wis. 5:8. Note that Cyrpian here refers to the Book of Wisdom as "Holy Scripture," as opposed to the opinions of certain Protestants who hold that the deuterocanonical books were not accepted by the early Church.
28. 1 Cor. 7:30-31.
29. John 21:15-17; Matt. 16:17-19; Acts 3:6.
30. "In the beginning God entrusted the earth and its resources to the common stewardship of mankind to take care of them, master them by labor, and enjoy their fruits. The goods of creation are destined for the whole human race. However, the earth is divided up among men to assure the security of their lives, endangered by poverty and threatened by violence. The

appropriation of property is legitimate for guaranteeing the freedom and dignity of persons and for helping each of them to meet his basic needs and the needs of those in his charge. It should allow for a natural solidarity to develop between men. The *right to private property*, acquired or received in a just way, does not do away with the original gift of the earth to the whole of mankind. The *universal destination of goods* remains primordial, even if the promotion of the common good requires respect for the right to private property and its exercise" (*Catechism of the Catholic Church*, 2402-2403).

31. Rev. 17:1.
32. Isa. 3:16.
33. This idea of the fallen angels as responsible for introducing the arts of jewelry and adornment to the human race is also found in Tertullian (*On the Apparel of Women*, Book 1:2) and is based on the apocryphal Book of Enoch, Chapter 8: "And Azâzêl taught men to make swords, and knives, and shields, and breastplates, and made known to them the metals [of the earth] and the art of working them, and bracelets, and ornaments, and the use of antimony, and the beautifying of the eyelids, and all kinds of costly stones, and all coloring tinctures."
34. Gen. 1:26.
35. 1 Cor. 5:7.
36. Matt. 5:36.
37. Rev. 1:14.
38. A reference to the large public baths that were common in ancient Rome. Many of these baths were gender segregated, although some, as Cyrpian points out, were not.
39. "Handled"—a reference to the practice at the baths of the bather having themselves rubbed with oil by slaves at the conclusion of the bath.
40. A reference to the parable of the sower in Matt, 13:8 and Mark 4:8. This interpretation of the hundred-fold reward going to the martyrs, the sixty-fold to the virgins and the thirty-fold to the faithful of the married state was common among the Fathers, with some variations. See, for example, St. Augstine *On Holy Virginity*, 46; St. Jerome Letter XLVIII:2; Origen *Exhortation to Martyrdom*, 14.
41. Gen. 3:16.
42. Luke 20:35-36.
43. 1 Cor. 15:47.

ON THE LAPSED[1]

1. Behold, beloved brethren, peace is restored to the Church; and although it lately seemed to incredulous people difficult, and to traitors impossible, our security is by divine aid and retribution re-established. Our minds return to gladness; and the season of affliction and the cloud being dispersed, tranquillity and serenity have shone forth once more. Praises must be given to God, and His benefits and gifts must be celebrated with giving of thanks, although even in the time of persecution our voice has not ceased to give thanks. For not even an enemy has so much power as to prevent us, who love the Lord with our whole heart, and life, and strength, from declaring His blessings and praises always and everywhere with glory. The day earnestly desired, by the prayers of all has come; and after the dreadful and loathsome darkness of a long night, the world has shone forth irradiated by the light of the Lord.

2. We look with glad countenances upon confessors illustrious with the heraldry of a good name, and glorious with the praises of virtue and of faith; clinging to them with holy kisses, we embrace them long desired with insatiable eagerness. The white-robed cohort of Christ's soldiers is here, who in the fierce conflict have broken the ferocious turbulence of an urgent persecution, having been prepared for the suffering of the dungeon, armed for the endurance of death. Bravely you have resisted the world: you have afforded a glorious spectacle in the sight of God; you have been an example to your brethren that shall follow you. That religious voice has named the name of Christ, in whom it has once confessed that it believed; those illustrious hands, which had only been accustomed to divine works, have resisted the sacrilegious sacrifices; those lips, sanctified by heavenly food after the body and blood of the Lord, have rejected the profane contacts and the leavings of the idols. Your head has remained free from the impious and wicked veil with which the captive heads of those who sacrificed were there veiled; your brow, pure with the sign of God, could not bear the crown of the devil, but reserved itself for the Lord's crown. How joyously does your Mother Church receive you in her bosom, as you return from the battle! How blissfully, how gladly, does she open her gates, that in united bands you may enter, bearing the trophies from a prostrate enemy! With the triumphing men come women also, who, while contending with the world, have also overcome their sex; and virgins also come with the double glory of their warfare, and boys transcending their years with their virtues. Moreover, also, the rest of the multitude of those who stand fast follow your glory, and accompany your footsteps with the insignia of praise, very near to, and almost joined with, your own. In them also is the same sincerity of heart, the same soundness of a tenacious faith. Resting on the unshaken roots of the heavenly precepts, and strengthened by the evangelical traditions, the prescribed banishment, the destined tortures, the loss of property, the bodily punishments, have not terrified them. The days for proving their faith were limited beforehand; but he who remembers that he has renounced the world knows no day of worldly appointment, neither does he who hopes for eternity from God calculate the seasons of earth any more.

3. Let none, my beloved brethren, let none depreciate this glory; let none by malignant dispraise detract from the uncorrupted steadfastness of those who have stood. When the day appointed for denying had gone by, every one who had not professed within that time not to be a Christian, confessed that he was a Christian. It is the first title to victory to confess the Lord under the violence of the hands of the Gentiles. It is the second step to glory to be withdrawn by a cautious retirement, and to be reserved for the Lord.[2] The former is a public, the latter is a private confession. The former overcomes the judge of this world; the latter, content with God as its judge, keeps a pure conscience in integrity of heart. In the former case there is a readier fortitude; in the latter, solicitude is more secure. The former, as his hour approached, was already found mature; the latter perhaps was delayed, who, leaving his estate, withdrew for a while, because he would not deny, but would certainly confess if he too had been apprehended.

4. One cause of grief saddens these heavenly crowns of martyrs, these glorious spiritual confessions, these very great and illustrious virtues of the brethren who stand; which is, that the hostile violence has torn away a part of our own bowels, and thrown it away in the destructiveness of its own cruelty. What shall I do in this matter, beloved brethren? Wavering in the various tide of feeling, what or how shall I speak? I need tears rather than words to express the sorrow with which the wound of our body should be bewailed, with which the manifold loss of a people once numerous should be lamented. For whose heart is so hard or cruel, who is so unmindful of brotherly love, as, among the varied ruins of his friends, and the mournful relics disfigured with all degradation, to be able to stand and to keep dry eyes, and not in the breaking out of his grief to express his groanings rather with tears than with words? I grieve, brethren, I grieve with you; nor does my own integrity and my personal soundness beguile me to the soothing of my griefs, since it is the shepherd that is chiefly wounded in the wound of his flock. I join my breast with each one, and I share in the grievous burden of sorrow and mourning. I wail with the wailing, I weep with the weeping, I regard myself as prostrated with those that are prostrate. My limbs are at the same time stricken with those darts of the raging enemy; their cruel swords have pierced through my bowels; my mind could not remain untouched and free from the inroad of persecution among my downfallen brethren; sympathy has cast me down also.

5. Yet, beloved brethren, the cause of truth is to be had in view; nor ought the gloomy darkness of the terrible persecution so to have blinded the mind and feeling, that there should remain no light and illumination whence the divine precepts may be beheld. If the cause of disaster is recognized, there is at once found a remedy for the wound. The Lord has desired His family to be proved; and because a long peace had corrupted the discipline that had been divinely delivered to us, the heavenly rebuke has aroused our faith, which was giving way, and I had almost said slumbering; and although we deserved more for our sins, yet the most merciful Lord has so moderated all things, that all which has happened has rather seemed a trial than a persecution.[3]

6. Each one was desirous of increasing his estate; and forgetful of what believers had either done before in the times of the apostles, or always ought to do, they, with the insatiable ardor of covetousness, devoted themselves to the increase of their property. Among the priests there was no devotedness of religion; among the ministers there was no sound faith: in their works there was no mercy; in their manners there was no discipline. In men, their beards were defaced; in women, their complexion was dyed: the eyes were falsified from what God's hand had made them; their hair was stained with a falsehood.[4] Crafty frauds were used to deceive the hearts of the simple, subtle meanings for circumventing the brethren. They united in the bond of marriage with unbelievers; they prostituted the members of Christ to the Gentiles. They would swear not only rashly, but even more, would swear falsely; would despise those set over them with haughty swelling, would speak evil of one another with envenomed tongue, would quarrel with one another with obstinate hatred. Not a few bishops who ought to furnish both exhortation and example to others, despising their divine charge, became agents in secular business, forsook their throne, deserted their people, wandered about over foreign provinces, hunted the markets for gainful merchandise, while brethren were starving in the Church. They sought to possess money in hoards, they seized estates by crafty deceits, they increased their gains by multiplying usuries. What do not such as we deserve to suffer for sins of this kind, when even already the divine rebuke has forewarned us, and said, "If they shall forsake my law, and walk not in my judgments; if they shall profane my statutes, and shall not observe my precepts, I will visit their offenses with a rod, and their sins with scourges?"[5]

7. These things were before declared to us, and predicted. But we, forgetful of the law and obedience required of us, have so acted by our sins, that while we despise the Lord's commandments, we have come by severer remedies to the correction of our sin and probation of our faith. Nor indeed have we at last been converted to the fear of the Lord, so as to undergo patiently and courageously this our correction and divine reproof. Immediately at the first words of the threatening foe, the greatest number of the brethren betrayed their faith, and were cast down, not by the onset of persecution, but cast themselves down by voluntary lapse. What unheard of thing, I beg of you, what new thing had happened, that, as if on the occurrence of things unknown and unexpected, the obligation to Christ should be dissolved with headlong rashness? Have not prophets aforetime, and subsequently apostles, told of these things? Have not they, full of the Holy Spirit, predicted the afflictions of the righteous, and always the injuries of the heathens? Does not the sacred Scripture, which ever arms our faith and strengthens with a voice from heaven the servants of God, say, "You shall worship the Lord your God, and Him only shall you serve?"[6] Does it not again show the anger of the divine indignation, and warn of the fear of punishment beforehand, when it says, "They worshipped them whom their fingers have made; and the mean man bows down, and the great man humbles himself, and I will forgive them not?"[7] And again, God speaks, and says, "He that sacrifices unto any gods, save unto the Lord only, shall be destroyed."[8] In the Gospel also subsequently, the Lord, who instructs by His words and fulfils by His deeds, teaching what should be done, and doing whatever He had taught, did He not before admonish us of whatever is now done and shall be done? Did He not before ordain both for those who deny Him eternal punishments, and for those that confess Him saving rewards?

8. From some—ah, misery!—all these things have fallen away, and have passed from memory. They indeed did not wait to be apprehended ere they ascended, or to be interrogated ere they denied. Many were conquered before the battle, prostrated before the attack. Nor did they even leave it to be said for them, that they seemed to sacrifice to idols unwillingly. They ran to the market-place of their own accord; freely they hastened to death, as if they had formerly wished it, as if they would embrace an opportunity now given which they had always desired. How many were put off by the magistrates at that time, when evening was coming on; how many even asked that their destruction might not be delayed! What violence can such a one plead as an excuse? How can he purge his crime, when it was he himself who rather used force to bring about his own ruin? When they came voluntarily to the Capitol—when they freely approached to the obedience of the terrible wickedness—did not their tread falter? Did not their sight darken, their heart tremble, their arms fall helplessly down? Did not their senses fail, their tongue cleave to their mouth, their speech grow weak? Could the servant of God stand there, and speak and renounce Christ, when he had already renounced the devil and the world? Was not that altar, whither he drew near to perish, to him a funeral pile? Ought he not to shudder at and flee from the devil's altar, which he had seen to smoke, and to be redolent of a foul foetor, as if it were the funeral and sepulchre of his life? Why bring with you, O wretched man, a sacrifice? Why immolate a victim? You yourself have come to the altar an offering; you yourself have come a victim: there you have immolated your salvation, your hope; there you have burnt up your faith in those deadly fires.

9. But to many their own destruction was not sufficient. With mutual exhortations, people were urged to their ruin; death was pledged by turns in the deadly cup. And that nothing might be wanting to aggravate the crime, infants also, in the arms of their parents, either carried or conducted, lost, while yet little ones, what in the very first beginning of their nativity they had gained. Will not they, when the day of judgment comes, say, "We have done nothing; nor have we forsaken the Lord's bread and cup to hasten freely to a profane contact; the faithlessness of others has ruined us. We have found our parents our murderers; they have denied to us the Church as a Mother; they have denied God as a Father: so that, while we were little, and unforeseeing, and unconscious of such a crime, we were associated by others to the partnership of wickedness, and we were snared by the deceit of others?"

10. Nor is there, alas, any just and weighty reason which excuses such a crime. One's country was to be left, and loss of one's estate was to be suffered. Yet to whom that is born and dies is there not a necessity at some time to leave his country, and to suffer the loss of his estate? But let not Christ be forsaken, so that the loss of salvation and of an eternal home should be feared. Behold, the Holy Spirit cries by the prophet, "Depart, depart, get out of there, touch not the unclean thing; get out of her midst, and be separate, you who bear the vessels of the Lord."[9] Yet those who are the vessels of the Lord and the temple of God do not go out from the midst, nor depart, that they may not be compelled to touch the unclean thing, and to be polluted and corrupted with deadly food. Elsewhere also a voice is heard from heaven, forewarning what is becoming for the servants of God to do, saying, "Come out of her, my people, that you be not partakers of her sins, and that you receive not of her plagues."[10] He who goes out and departs does not become a partaker of the guilt; but he will be wounded with the plagues who is found a companion in the crime. And therefore the Lord commanded us in the persecution to depart and to flee; and both taught that this should be done, and Himself did it. For as the crown is given of the condescension of God, and cannot be received unless the hour comes for accepting it, whosoever abiding in Christ departs for a while does not deny his faith, but waits for the time; but he who has fallen, after refusing to depart, remained to deny it.

11. The truth, brethren, must not be disguised; nor must the matter and cause of our wound be concealed. A blind love of one's own property has deceived many; nor could they be prepared for, or at ease in, departing when their wealth fettered them like a chain. Those were the chains to them that remained—those were the bonds by which both virtue was retarded, and faith burdened, and the spirit bound, and the soul hindered; so that they who were involved in earthly things might become a booty and food for the serpent, which, according to God's sentence, feeds upon earth. And therefore the Lord the teacher of good things, forewarning for the future time, says, "If you will be perfect, go, sell all that you have, and give to the poor, and you shall have treasure in heaven: and come and follow me."[11] If rich men did this, they would not perish by their riches; if they laid up treasure in heaven, they would not now have a domestic enemy and assailant. Heart and mind and feeling would be in heaven, if the treasure were in heaven; nor could he be overcome by the world who had nothing in the world whereby he could be overcome. He would follow the Lord loosed and free, as did the apostles, and many in the times of the apostles, and many who forsook both their means and their relatives, and clave to Christ with undivided ties.

12. But how can they follow Christ, who are held back by the chain of their wealth? Or how can they seek heaven, and climb to sublime and lofty heights, who are weighed down by earthly desires? They think that they possess, when they are rather possessed; as slaves of their profit, and not lords with respect to their own money, but rather the bond-slaves of their money. These times and these men are indicated by the apostle, when he says, "But they that will be rich, fall into temptation, and a snare, and into many foolish and hurtful lusts, which drown men in destruction and in perdition. For the root of all evil is the love of money, which, while some have coveted, they have erred from the faith, and pierced themselves through with many sorrows."[12] But with what rewards does the Lord invite us to contempt of worldly wealth? With what compensations does He atone for the small and trifling losses of this present time? "There is no man," says He, "that leaves house, or land, or parents, or brethren, or wife, or children, for the kingdom of God's sake, but he shall receive seven fold even in this time, but in the world to come life everlasting."[13] If we know these things, and have found them out from the truth of the Lord who promises, not only is not loss of this kind to be feared, but even to be desired; as the Lord Himself again announces and warns us, "Blessed are you when men shall persecute you, and when they shall separate you from their company, and shall cast you out, and shall speak of your name as evil, for the Son of man's sake! Rejoice on that day, and leap for joy; for, behold, your reward is great in heaven."[14]

13. But (say they) subsequently tortures had come, and severe sufferings were threatening those who resisted. He may complain of tortures who has been overcome by tortures; he may offer the excuse of suffering who has been vanquished in suffering. Such a one may ask, and say, "I wished indeed to strive bravely, and, remembering my oath, I took up the arms of devotion and faith; but as I was struggling in the encounter, varied tortures and long-continued sufferings overcame me. My mind stood firm, and my faith was strong, and my soul struggled long, unshaken with the torturing pains; but when, with the renewed barbarity of the most cruel judge, wearied out as I was, the scourges were now tearing me, the clubs bruised me, the rack strained me, the claw dug into me, the fire roasted me; my flesh deserted me in the struggle, the weakness of my bodily frame gave way—not my mind, but my body, yielded in the suffering." Such a plea may readily avail to forgiveness; an apology of that kind may excite compassion.[15] Thus at one time the Lord forgave Castus and Aemilius[16]; thus, overcome in the first encounter, they were made victors in the second battle. So that they who had formerly given way to the fires became stronger than the fires, and in that in which they had been vanquished they were conquerors. They entreated not for pity of their tears, but of their wounds; nor with a lamentable voice alone, but with laceration and suffering of body. Blood flowed instead of weeping; and instead of tears, gore poured forth from their half-scorched entrails.

14. But now, what wounds can those who are overcome show? What gashes of gaping entrails, what tortures of the limbs, in cases where it was not faith that fell in the encounter, but faithlessness that anticipated the struggle? Nor does the necessity of the crime excuse the person compelled, where the crime is committed of free will. Nor do I say this in such a way as that I would burden the cases of the brethren, but that I may rather instigate the brethren to a prayer of atonement. For, as it is written, "They who call you happy cause you to err, and destroy the paths of your feet,"[17] he who soothes the sinner with flattering blandishments furnishes the stimulus to sin; nor does he repress, but nourishes wrong-doing. But he who, with braver counsels, rebukes at the same time that he instructs a brother, urges him onward to salvation. "As many as I love," says the Lord, "I rebuke and chasten."[18] And thus also it behooves the Lord's priest not to mislead by deceiving concessions, but to provide with salutary remedies. He is an unskillful physician who handles the swelling edges of wounds with a tender hand, and, by retaining the poison shut up in the deep recesses of the body, increases it. The wound, must be opened, and cut, and healed by the stronger remedy of cutting out the corrupting parts. The sick man may cry out, may vociferate, and may complain, in impatience of the pain; but he will afterwards give thanks when he has felt that he is cured.

15. Moreover, beloved brethren, a new kind of devastation has appeared; and, as if the storm of persecution had raged too little, there has been added to the heap, under the title of mercy, a deceiving mischief and a fair-seeming calamity. Contrary to the vigor of the Gospel, contrary to the law of the Lord and God, by the temerity of some, communion is relaxed to heedless persons—a vain and false peace, dangerous to those who grant it, and likely to avail nothing to those who receive it. They do not seek for the patience necessary to health nor the true medicine derived from atonement. Penitence is driven forth from their breasts, and the memory of their very grave and extreme sin is taken away. The wounds of the dying are covered over, and the deadly blow that is planted in the deep and secret entrails is concealed by a dissimulated suffering. Returning from the altars of the devil, they draw near to the holy place of the Lord, with hands filthy and reeking with smell, still almost breathing of the plague-bearing idol-meats; and even with jaws still exhaling their crime, and reeking with the fatal contact, they intrude on the body of the Lord, although the sacred Scripture stands in their way, and cries, saying, "Every one that is clean shall eat of the flesh; and whatever soul eats of the flesh of the saving sacrifice, which is the Lord's, having his uncleanness upon him, that soul shall be cut off from his people."[19] Also, the apostle testifies, and says, "You cannot drink the cup of the Lord and the cup of devils; you cannot be partakers of the Lord's table and of the table of devils."[20] He threatens, moreover, the stubborn and froward, and denounces them, saying, "Whosoever eats the bread or drinks the cup of the Lord unworthily, is guilty of the body and blood of the Lord."[21]

16. All these warnings being scorned and condemned—before their sin is expiated, before confession has been made of their crime, before their conscience has been purged by sacrifice and by the hand of the priest,[22] before the offense of an angry and threatening Lord has been appeased, violence is done to His body and blood; and they sin now against their Lord more with their hand and mouth than when they denied their Lord. They think that that is peace which some with deceiving words are blazoning forth: that is not peace, but war; and he is not joined to the Church who is separated from the Gospel. Why do they call an injury a kindness? Why do they call impiety by the name of piety? Why do they hinder those who ought to weep continually and to entreat their Lord, from the sorrowing of repentance, and pretend to receive them to communion? This is the same kind of thing to the lapsed as hail to the harvests; as the stormy star to the trees; as the destruction of pestilence to the herds; as the raging tempest to shipping. They take away the consolation of eternal hope; they overturn the tree from the roots; they creep on to a deadly contagion with their pestilent words; they dash the ship on the rocks, so that it may not reach to the harbor. Such a facility does not grant peace, but takes it away; nor does it give communion, but it hinders from salvation. This is another persecution, and another temptation, by which the crafty enemy still further assaults the lapsed; attacking them by a secret corruption, that their lamentation may be hushed, that their grief may be silent, that the memory of their sin may pass away, that the groaning of their heart may be repressed, that the weeping of their eyes may be quenched; nor long and full penitence deprecate the Lord so grievously offended, although it is written, "Remember from whence you are fallen, and repent."[23]

17. Let no one cheat himself, let no one deceive himself. The Lord alone can have mercy. He alone can bestow pardon for sins which have been committed against Himself, who bare our sins, who sorrowed for us, whom God delivered up for our sins. Man cannot be greater than God, nor can a servant remit or forego by his indulgence what has been committed by a greater crime against the Lord, lest to the person lapsed this be moreover added to his sin, if he be ignorant that it is declared, "Cursed is the man that puts his hope in man."[24] The Lord must be besought. The Lord must be appeased by our atonement, who has said, that him that denies Him, He will deny, who alone has received all judgment from His Father.[25] We believe, indeed, that the merits of martyrs and the works of the righteous are of great avail with the Judge; but that will be when the day of judgment shall come; when, after the conclusion of this life and the world, His people shall stand before the tribunal of Christ.[26]

18. But if any one, by an overhurried haste, rashly thinks that he can give remission of sins to all, or dares to rescind the Lord's precepts, not only does it in no respect advantage the lapsed, but it does them harm. Not to have observed His judgment is to have provoked His wrath, and to think that the mercy of God must not first of all be entreated, and, despising the Lord, to presume on His power. Under the altar of God the souls of the slain martyrs cry with a loud voice, saying, "How long, O Lord, holy and true, do You not judge and avenge our blood upon those who dwell on the earth?"[27] And they are bidden to rest, and still to keep patience. And does any one think that, in opposition to the Judge, a man can become of avail for the general remission and pardon of sins, or that he can shield others before he himself is vindicated? The martyrs order something to be done; but only if this thing be just and lawful, if it can be done without opposing the Lord Himself by God's priest,[28] if the consent of the obeying party be easy and yielding, if the moderation of the asking party be religious. The martyrs order something to be done; but if what they order be not written in the law of the Lord, we must first know that they have obtained what they ask from God, and then do what they command. For that may not always appear to be immediately conceded by the divine majesty, which has been promised by man's undertaking.[29]

19. For Moses also besought for the sins of the people; and yet, when he had sought pardon for these sinners, he did not receive it. "I pray You," said he, "O Lord, this people have sinned a great sin, and have made them gods of gold. Yet now, if You will forgive their sin, forgive it; but if not, blot me out of the book which You have written. And the Lord said unto Moses, 'Whosoever has sinned against me, him will I blot out of my book.'"[30] He, the friend of God; he who had often spoken face to face with the Lord, could not obtain what he asked, nor could appease the wrath of an indignant God by his entreaty. God praises Jeremiah, and announces, saying, "Before I formed you in the womb, I knew you; and before you were born I sanctified you, and I ordained you a prophet unto the nations."[31] And to the same man He says, when he often entreated and prayed for the sins of the people, "Pray not for this people, neither lift up cry nor prayer for them; for I will not hear them in the time wherein they call on me, in the time of their affliction."[32] But who was more righteous than Noah, who, when the earth was filled with sins, was alone found righteous on the earth? Who more glorious than Daniel? Who more strong for suffering martyrdom in firmness of faith, more happy in God's condescension, who so many times, both when he was in conflict conquered, and, when he had conquered, lived on? Was any more ready in good works than Job, braver in temptations, more patient in sufferings, more submissive in his fear, more true in his faith? And yet God said that He would not grant to them if they were to seek. When the prophet Ezekiel entreated for the sin of the people, "Whatsoever land," said He, "shall sin against me by trespassing grievously, I will stretch out mine hand upon it, and will break the staff of bread thereof, and will send famine upon it, and will cut off man and beast from it. Though these three men, Noah, Daniel, and Job, were in it, they should deliver neither sons nor daughters; but they only should be delivered themselves."[33] Thus, not everything that is asked is in the pre-judgment of the asker, but in the free will of the giver; neither can human judgment claim to itself or usurp anything, unless the divine pleasure approve.

20. In the Gospel the Lord speaks, and says, "Whosoever shall confess me before men, him will I also confess before my Father which is in heaven: but he that denies me, him will I also deny."[34] If He does not deny him that denies, neither does He confess him that confesses; the Gospel cannot be sound in one part and waver in another. Either both must stand firm, or both must lose the force of truth. If they who deny shall not be guilty of a crime, neither shall they who confess receive the reward of a virtue.[35] Again, if faith which has conquered be crowned, it is of necessity that faithlessness which is conquered should be punished. Thus the martyrs can either do nothing if the Gospel may be broken; or if the Gospel cannot be broken, they can do nothing against the Gospel, since they become martyrs on account of the Gospel. Let no one, beloved brethren, let no one decry the dignity of martyrs, let no one degrade their glories and their crowns. The strength of their uncorrupted faith abides sound; nor can he either say or do anything against Christ, whose hope, and faith, and virtue, and glory, are all in Christ: those cannot be the authority for the bishops doing anything against God's command, who themselves have done God's command. Is any one greater than God, or more merciful than God's goodness, that he should either wish that undone which God has suffered to be done, or, as if God had too little power to protect His Church, should think that we could be preserved by his help?

21. Unless, perchance, these things have been done without God's knowledge, or all these things have happened without His permission; although Holy Scripture teaches the indocile, and admonishes the unmindful, where it speaks, saying, "Who gave Jacob for a spoil, and Israel to those who made a booty of him? Did not the Lord against whom they sinned, and would not walk in His ways, neither were obedient unto His law? And He has poured upon them the fury of His anger."[36] And elsewhere it testifies and says, "Is the Lord's hand shortened, that it cannot save; or His ear heavy, that it cannot hear? But your iniquities separate between you and your God; and because of your sins He has hid His face from you, that He may not have mercy."[37] Let us rather consider our offenses, revolving our doings and the secrets of our mind; let us weigh the deserts of our conscience; let it come back upon our heart that we have not walked in the Lord's ways, and have cast away God's law, and have never been willing to keep His precepts and saving counsels.

22. What good can you think of him, what fear can you suppose to have been with him, or what faith, whom neither fear could correct nor persecution itself could reform? His high and rigid neck, even when it has fallen, is unbent; his swelling and haughty soul is not broken, even when it is conquered. Prostrate, he threatens those who stand; and wounded, the sound. And because he may not at once receive the body of the Lord in his polluted hands, the sacrilegious one is angry with the priests. And—oh your excessive madness, O frantic one—you are angry with him who endeavors to avert the anger of God from you; you threaten him who beseeches the divine mercy on your behalf, who feels your wound which you yourself do not feel, who sheds tears for you, which perhaps you never shed yourself. You are still aggravating and. enhancing your crime; and while you yourself are implacable against the ministers and priests of God, do you think that the Lord can be appeased concerning you?

23. Receive rather, and admit what we say. Why do your deaf ears not hear the salutary precepts with which we warn you? Why do your blind eyes not see the way of repentance which we point out? Why does your stricken and alienated mind not perceive the lively remedies which we both learn and teach from the heavenly Scriptures? Or if some unbelievers have little faith in future events, let them be terrified with present ones. Lo, what punishments do we behold of those who have denied! What sad deaths of theirs do we bewail! Not even here can they be without punishment, although the day of punishment has not yet arrived. Some are punished in the meantime, that others may be corrected. The torments of a few are the examples of all.[38]

24. One of those who of his own will ascended the Capitol to make denial, after he had denied Christ, became dumb. The punishment began from that point whence the crime also began; so that now he could not ask, since he had no words for entreating mercy.[39] Another, who was in the baths, (for this was wanting to her crime and to her misfortunes, that she even went at once to the baths, when she had lost the grace of the laver of life); there, unclean as she was, was seized by an unclean spirit, and tore with her teeth the tongue with which she had either impiously eaten or spoken. After the wicked food had been taken, the madness of the mouth was armed to its own destruction. She herself was her own executioner, nor did she long continue to live afterwards: tortured with pangs of the belly and bowels, she expired.

25. Learn what occurred when I myself was present and a witness: Some parents who by chance were escaping, being little careful on account of their terror, left a little daughter under the care of a wet-nurse. The nurse gave up the forsaken child to the magistrates. They gave it, in the presence of an idol whither the people flocked (because it was not yet able to eat flesh on account of its years), bread mingled with wine, which however itself was the remainder of what had been used in the immolation of those that had perished. Subsequently the mother recovered her child. But the girl was no more able to speak, or to indicate the crime that had been committed, than she had before been able to understand or to prevent it. Therefore it happened unawares in their ignorance, that when we were sacrificing, the mother brought it in with her.[40] Moreover, the girl mingled with the saints, became impatient of our prayer and supplications, and was at one moment shaken with weeping, and at another tossed about like a wave of the sea by the violent excitement of her mind; as if by the compulsion of a torturer the soul of that still tender child confessed a consciousness of the fact with such signs as it could. When, however, the solemnities were finished, and the deacon began to offer the cup to those present, and when, as the rest received it, its turn approached, the little child, by the instinct of the divine majesty, turned away its face, compressed its mouth with resisting lips, and refused the cup. Still the deacon persisted, and, although against her efforts, forced on her some of the sacrament of the cup. Then there followed a sobbing and vomiting. In a profane body and mouth the Eucharist could not remain; the draught sanctified in the blood of the Lord burst forth from the polluted stomach. So great is the Lord's power, so great is His majesty. The secrets of darkness were disclosed under His light, and not even hidden crimes deceived God's priest.

26. This much about an infant, which was not yet of an age to speak of the crime committed by others in respect of herself. But the woman who in advanced life and of more mature age secretly crept in among us when we were sacrificing, received not food, but a sword for herself; and as if taking some deadly poison into her jaws and body, began presently to be tortured, and to become stiffened with frenzy; and suffering the misery no longer of persecution, but of her crime, shivering and trembling, she fell down. The crime of her dissimulated conscience was not long unpunished or concealed. She who had deceived man felt that God was taking vengeance. And another woman, when she tried with unworthy hands to open her box, in which was the holy [Body] of the Lord, was deterred by fire rising from it from daring to touch it. And when one, who himself was defiled, dared with the rest to receive secretly a part of the sacrifice celebrated by the priest; he could not eat nor handle the holy of the Lord, but found in his hands when opened that he had a cinder. Thus by the experience of one it was shown that the Lord withdraws when He is denied; nor does that which is received benefit the undeserving for salvation, since saving grace is changed by the departure of the sanctity into a cinder. How many there are daily who do not repent nor make confession of the consciousness of their crime, who are filled with unclean spirits! How many are shaken even to unsoundness of mind and idiocy by the raging of madness! Nor is there any need to go through the deaths of individuals, since through the manifold lapses occurring in the world the punishment of their sins is as varied as the multitude of sinners is abundant. Let each one consider not what another has suffered, but what he himself deserves to suffer; nor think that he has escaped if his punishment delay for a time, since he ought to fear it the more that the wrath of God the judge has reserved it for Himself.[41]

27. Nor let those persons flatter themselves that they need repent the less, who, although they have not polluted their hands with abominable sacrifices, yet have defiled their conscience with certificates.[42] That profession of one who denies is the testimony of a Christian disowning what he had been. He says that he has not done what another has actually committed; and although it is written,

"You cannot serve two masters,"[43] he has served an earthly master in that he has obeyed his edict; he has been more obedient to human authority than to God. It matters not whether he has published what he has done with less either of disgrace or of guilt among men. Be that as it may, he will not be able to escape and avoid God his judge, seeing that the Holy Spirit says in the Psalms, "Your eyes saw my substance, that it was imperfect, and in Your book shall all men be written."[44] And again: "Man sees the outward appearance, but God sees the heart."[45] The Lord Himself also forewarns and prepares us, saying, "And all the churches shall know that I am He which searches the reins and the heart."[46] He looks into the hidden and secret things, and considers those things which are concealed; nor can any one evade the eyes of the Lord, who says, "I am a God at hand, and not a God afar off. If a man be hidden in secret places, shall not I therefore see him? Do not I fill heaven and earth?"[47] He sees the heart and mind of every person; and He will judge not alone of our deeds, but even of our words and thoughts. He looks into the minds, and the wills, and conceptions of all men, in the very lurking-places of the heart that is still closed up.

28. Moreover, how much are they both greater in faith and better in their fear, who, although bound by no crime of sacrifice to idols or of certificate, yet, since they have even thought of such things, with grief and simplicity confess this very thing to God's priests,[48] and make the conscientious avowal, put off from them the load of their minds, and seek out the salutary medicine even for slight and moderate wounds, knowing that it is written, "God is not mocked."[49] God cannot be mocked, nor deceived, nor deluded by any deceptive cunning. Yea, he sins the more, who, thinking that God is like man, believes that he evades the penalty of his crime if he has not openly admitted his crime. Christ says in His precepts, "Whosoever shall be ashamed of me, of him shall the Son of man be ashamed."[50] And does he think that he is a Christian, who is either ashamed or afraid to be a Christian? How can he be one with Christ, who either blushes or fears to belong to Christ? He will certainly have sinned less, by not seeing the idols, and not profaning the sanctity of the faith under the eyes of a people standing round and insulting, and not polluting his hands by the deadly sacrifices, nor defiling his lips with the wicked food. This is advantageous to this extent, that the fault is less, not that the conscience is guiltless. He can more easily attain to pardon of his crime, yet he is not free from crime; and let him not cease to carry out his repentance, and to entreat the Lord's mercy, lest what seems to be less in the quality of his fault, should be increased by his neglect of atonement.[51]

29. I entreat you, beloved brethren, that each one should confess his own sin, while he who has sinned is still in this world, while his confession may be received, while the satisfaction and remission made by the priests are pleasing to the Lord. Let us turn to the Lord with our whole heart, and, expressing our repentance for our sin with true grief, let us entreat God's mercy. Let our soul lie low before Him. Let our mourning atone to Him. Let all our hope lean upon Him. He Himself tells us in what manner we ought to ask. "Turn to me," He says, "with all your heart, and at the same time with fasting, and with weeping, and with mourning; and rend your hearts, and not your garments."[52] Let us return to the Lord with our whole heart. Let us appease His wrath and indignation with fastings, with weeping, with mourning, as He Himself admonishes us.

30. Do we believe that a man is lamenting with his whole heart, that he is entreating the Lord with fasting, and with weeping, and with mourning, who from the first day of his sin daily frequents the bathing-places with women; who, feeding at rich banquets, and puffed out with fuller dainties, belches forth on the next day his indigestions, and does not dispense of his meat and drink so as to aid the necessity of the poor? How does he who walks with joyous and glad step mourn for his death? And although it is written, "You shall not mar the figure of your beard,"[53] he plucks out his beard, and dresses his hair; and does he now study to please any one who displeases God? Or does she groan and lament who has time to put on the clothing of precious apparel, and not to consider the robe of Christ which she has lost; to receive valuable ornaments and richly wrought necklaces, and not to bewail the loss of divine and heavenly ornament? Although you clothe yourself in foreign garments and silken robes, you are naked; although you adorn yourself to excess both in pearls, and gems, and gold, yet without the adornment of Christ you are unsightly. And you who stain your hair, now at least cease in the midst of sorrows; and you who paint the edges of your eyes with a line drawn around them of black powder, now at least wash your eyes with tears. If you had lost any dear one of your friends by the death incident to mortality, you would groan grievously, and weep with disordered countenance, with changed dress, with neglected hair, with clouded face, with dejected appearance, you would show the signs of grief. Miserable creature, you have lost your soul; spiritually dead here, you are continuing to live to yourself, and although yourself walking about, you have begun to carry your own death with you. And do you not bitterly moan; do you not continually groan; do you not hide yourself, either for shame of your sin or for continuance of your lamentation? Behold, these are still worse wounds of sinning; behold, these are greater crimes—to have sinned, and not to make atonement—to have committed crimes, and not to bewail your crimes.

31. Ananias, Azarias, and Misael, the illustrious and noble youths, even amid the flames and the ardors of a raging furnace, did not desist from making public confession to God. Although possessed of a good conscience, and having often deserved well of the Lord by obedience of faith and fear, yet they did not cease from maintaining their humility, and from making atonement to the Lord, even amid the glorious martyrdoms of their virtues. The sacred Scripture speaks, saying, "Azarias stood up and prayed, and, opening his mouth, made confession before God together with his companions in the midst of the fire."[54] Daniel also, after the manifold grace of his faith and innocency, after the condescension of the Lord often repeated in respect of his virtues and praises, strives by fastings still further to deserve well of God, wraps himself in sackcloth and ashes, sorrowfully making confession, and saying, "O Lord God, great, and strong, and dreadful, keeping Your covenant and mercy for them that love You and keep Your commandments, we have sinned, we have committed iniquity, and have done wickedly: we have transgressed, and departed from Your precepts, and from Your judgments; neither have we hearkened to the words of Your servants the prophets, which they spoke in Your name to our kings, and to all the nations, and to all the earth. O Lord, righteousness belongs unto You, but unto us confusion."[55]

32. These things were done by men, meek, simple, innocent, in deserving well of the majesty of God; and now those who have denied the Lord refuse to make atonement to the Lord, and to entreat Him. I beg you, brethren, acquiesce in wholesome remedies, obey better counsels, associate your tears with our tears, join your groans with ours; we beseech you in order that we may beseech God for you: we turn our very prayers to you first; our prayers with which we pray God for you that He would pity you. Repent abundantly, prove the sorrow of a grieving and lamenting mind.

33. Neither let that imprudent error or vain stupor of some move you, who, although they are involved in so grave a crime, are struck with blindness of mind, so that they neither understand nor lament their sins. This is the greater visitation of an angry God; as it is written, "And God gave them the spirit of deadness."[56] And again: "They received not the love of the truth, that they might be saved. And for this cause God shall send them the working of error, that they should believe a lie; that they all might be damned who believed not the truth, but had pleasure in unrighteousness."[57] Unrighteously pleasing themselves, and mad with the alienation of a hardened mind, they despise the Lord's precepts, neglect the medicine for their wound, and will not repent. Thoughtless before their sin was acknowledged, after their sin they are obstinate; neither steadfast before, nor suppliant afterwards: when they ought to have stood fast, they fell; when they ought to fall and prostrate themselves to God, they think they stand fast. They have taken peace for themselves of their own accord when nobody granted it; seduced by false promises, and linked with apostates and unbelievers, they take hold of error instead of truth: they regard a communion as valid with those who are not communicants; they believe men against God, although they have not believed God against men.

34. Flee from such men as much as you can; avoid with a wholesome caution those who adhere to their mischievous contact. Their word does eat as does a cancer; their conversation advances like a contagion; their noxious and envenomed persuasion kills worse than persecution itself. In such a case there remains only penitence which can make atonement.[58] But they who take away repentance for a crime, close the way of atonement. Thus it happens that, while by the rashness of some a false safety is either promised or trusted, the hope of true safety is taken away.

35. But you, beloved brethren, whose fear is ready towards God, and whose mind, although it is placed in the midst of lapse, is mindful of its misery, do you in repentance and grief look into your sins; acknowledge the very grave sin of your conscience; open the eyes of your heart to the understanding of your sin, neither despairing of the Lord's mercy nor yet at once claiming His pardon. God, in proportion as with the affection of a Father He is always indulgent and good, in the same proportion is to be dreaded with the majesty of a judge. Even as we have sinned greatly, so let us greatly lament. To a deep wound let there not be wanting a long and careful treatment; let not the repentance be less than the sin. Think you that the Lord can be quickly appeased, whom with faithless words you have denied, to whom you have rather preferred your worldly estate, whose temple you have violated with a sacrilegious contact? Think you that He will easily have mercy upon you whom you have declared not to be your God? You must pray more eagerly and entreat; you must spend the day in grief; wear out nights in watchings and weepings; occupy all your time in wailful lamentations; lying stretched on the ground, you must cling close to the ashes, be surrounded with sackcloth and filth; after losing the raiment of Christ, you must be willing now to have no clothing; after the devil's meat, you must prefer fasting; be earnest in righteous works, whereby sins may be purged; frequently apply yourself to almsgiving, whereby souls are freed from death. What the adversary took from you, let Christ receive; nor ought your estate now either to be held or loved, by which you have been both deceived and conquered. Wealth must be avoided as an enemy; must be fled from as a robber; must be dreaded by its possessors as a sword and as poison. To this end only so much as remains should be of service, that by it the crime and the fault may be redeemed. Let good works be done without delay, and largely; let all your estate be laid out for the healing of your wound; let us lend of our wealth and our means to the Lord, who shall judge concerning us. Thus faith flourished in the time of the apostles; thus the first people of believers kept Christ's commands: they were prompt, they were liberal, they gave their all to be distributed by the apostles; and yet they were not redeeming sins of such a character as these.

36. If a man make prayer with his whole heart, if he groan with the true lamentations and tears of repentance, if be incline the Lord to pardon of his sin by righteous and continual works, he who expressed His mercy in these words may pity such men: "When you turn and lament, then shall you be saved, and shall know where you have been."[59] And again: "I have no pleasure in the death of him that dies, says the Lord, hut that he should return and live."[60] And Joel the prophet declares the mercy of the Lord in the Lord's own admonition, when he says: "Turn to the Lord your God, for He is merciful and gracious, and patient, and of great mercy, and repents Him with respect to the evil that He has inflicted."[61] He can show mercy; He can turn back His judgment. He can mercifully pardon the repenting, the labouring, the beseeching sinner. He can regard as effectual whatever, in behalf of such as these, either martyrs have besought or priests have done.[62] Or if any one move Him still more by his own atonement, if he appease His anger, if he appease the wrath of an indignant God by righteous entreaty, He gives arms again whereby the vanquished may be armed; He restores and confirms the strength whereby the refreshed faith may be invigorated. The soldier will seek his contest anew; he will repeat the fight, he will provoke the enemy, and indeed by his very suffering he is made braver for the battle. He who has thus made atonement to God; he who by repentance for his deed, who by shame for his sin, has conceived more both of virtue and of faith from the very grief of his fall, heard and aided by the Lord, shall make the Church which he had lately saddened glad, and shall now deserve of the Lord not only pardon, but a crown.

NOTES

1. This treatise was written in 251 after the cessation of the Decian Persecution. Here St. Cyprian praises the constancy of the martyrs, reproaches the inconstancy of the lapsed and warns the faithful against the emerging schism of Novatian.
2. Cyprian himself fell into this latter category who, when the persecution was declared in January 250, retired from Carthage to safe place of concealment, an act for which his opponents accused him of cowardice.
3. Here Cyprian refers to the brevity of the persecution, which only lasted for about ten months, despite being very fierce, especially in April 250.
4. For St. Cyprian's views on ornamentation and hair dye, see *On the Dress of Virgins*, especially 15-18.

5. Ps. 89:30-33.
6. Deut. 6:13.
7. Isa. 2:8-9.
8. Ex. 22:20.
9. Isa. 52:11.
10. Rev. 18:4.
11. Matt. 19:21.
12. 1 Tim. 6:9.
13. Mark 10:29.
14. Luke 6:22.
15. Note that Cyprian is not condemning all those who apostasized, but those who apostasized voluntarily and without the coersion of torture.
16. Mentioned in the Roman Martyrology on May 22nd: "In Africa, the holy martyrs Castus and Aemilius, who met their martyrdom by fire, St. Cyprian says that they were overcome by the first trial, but that in the second God made them victorious, so that those who had first weakened in the face of the fire were made mightier than the flames." Rev. Butler places their martyrdom at the outbreak of the persecution in 250; Cyprian assumes his readers have already heard the tale.
17. Isa. 3:12.
18. Rev. 3:19.
19. Lev. 7:20.
20. 1 Cor. 10:21.
21. 1 Cor. 11:27.
22. A testimony to the importance of Holy Communion and formal absolution by a priest when it came to reconciliation in the early Church.
23. Rev. 2:5.
24. Jer. 17:5.
25. Matt. 10:33.
26. "[T]he merits of the martyrs and the works of the righteous;" a reference to the practice, cited by Tertullian as well as Cyprian, of lapsed Christians obtaining letters of indulgence (*libelli pacis*) from the confessors, petitioning that their own merits should be applied to the excommunicated, and procure them a remission of the temporal punishment due to their defection (*Ad Martyras* 1; *On Modesty*, 22). In this is found the germ of the Catholic doctrine of indulgences. See also St. Cyprian's letters 15 and 34. Letter 16 provides and example of one of these *libelli pacis* from a confessor called Lucian.
27. Rev. 6:10.
28. "God's priest" acts with the authority of Christ Himself, and thus to oppose them is to oppose "the Lord Himself."
29. St. Cyprian is here writing against the practice of *libelli pacis* being given out too liberally by confessors and without the consent of the local pastors. He apparently proposes an arrangement where the lapsed penitent must first obtain the permission of the local bishop or priest before approaching a confessor for a *libelli pacis*. In such cases where indulgence is obtained illicitly and without other demonstrations of penance, the penitent should not presume upon God's mercy, as Cyprian goes on to state in the following section. A related discussion about reconciliation with the lapsi being given out too liberally is found in Cyprian's Letter 9.
30. Ex. 32:31.
31. Jer. 1:5.
32. Jer. 7:16.
33. Ezk. 14:13.
34. Luke 12:8.
35. Cyprian here draws upon the Catholic belief, strong in the early Church, that the martyrs

went immediately to heaven, in order to establish the argument that the apostates stood condemned. Just as certain as confession of Christ and martyrdom brought the sure glories of heaven, so apostasy and sacrifice to idols brought certain condemnation, not unforgiveable by God, but perhaps outside the power of the Church to reconcile without extraordinary demonstrations of penitence.

36. Isa. 13:24.
37. Isa. 59:1.
38. Cyprian here relates contemporary stories from abroad of persons who had apostasized during the persecution endruing all sorts of supernatural judgments.
39. A testimony to the practice of auricular confession in the early Church; Cyprian states that "he could not ask" for mercy since he "had no words," signifying that mercy and forgiveness were sought auricularly.
40. The child had inadvertently been given bread and wine offered to demons in her parents' absence; when the parents returned, they brought the child to Mass and gave her the Blood of Christ to drink, at which point she vomited up the sacred species. Note how the Eucharist is here referred to as a "sacrifice," and again in 26.
41. These accounts call to mind the warnings by St. Paul against unworthy reception of the Eucharist in 1 Cor. 11.
42. Cyprian here refers to the *libellatici*, those who, while not apostasizing, made use of bribery or some other underhanded means to obtain certificates of sacrifice from the pagan magistrates so as to avoid the dilemma of having to apostasize or be martyred.
43. Matt. 6:24.
44. A paraphrase of Psalm 139:16: "Thy eyes did see my imperfect being, and in thy book all shall be written."
45. 1 Sam. 16:7.
46. Rev. 2:23.
47. Jer. 23:23.
48. Another example of auricular confession in the early Church.
49. Gal. 6:7.
50. Luke 9:26.
51. Atonement is not complete unless accompanied by sufficient penance on the part of the penitent, against those who would assert that the concept of penance was an invention of the Middle Ages.
52. Joel 2:12.
53. Lev. 9:27-28. The full verse reads, "You shall not round the edge of your head, nor shall you destroy the edge of your beard. And you shall not make a cutting for the dead in your flesh, nor shall you make a written tattoo upon you; I am the Lord." The verse prohibits four distinct actions: (1) Cutting the head or hair (2) Cutting the face or beard (3) Cutting the flesh (4) Inscribing writing on the flesh. Cyprian misinterprets the verse to apply to shaving or grooming the beard in an absolute sense, whereas the context of this verse is actually referring to practices of mourning forbidden to the ancient Israelites, as they were common among the pagans. The Law never prohibited grooming the beard in an absolute sense; indeed, sometimes shaving the beard was an act of purification (see Lev. 14:9, Num. 8:7). Leviticus only prohibits it as an act of mourning. Even had the verse meant grooming in an absolute sense, it is doubtful whether this Levitical prohibition would have applied to Christians in the New Covenant.
54. This seems to be a sloppy paraphrase of Daniel 3:25-26, "Then Azarias standing up, prayed in this manner, and opening his mouth in the midst of the fire, he said: 'Blessed art thou, O Lord, the God of our fathers, and thy name is worthy of praise, and glorious for ever.'" At any rate, it is a testimony to the acceptance of the additions to the Book of Daniel by the African Christians of the mid-3rd century.
55. Dan. 9:4.

56. Rom. 11:8. The word "deadness" here is often translated as "stupor" or "slumber" in modern translations, a kind of spiritual sleep that makes one insensible to the movements of grace. The Vulgate strangely translates this word as *conpunctionis*, meaning "pricking" or "remorse." The Greek word is κατανυξις (katanyxis), which denotes insensibility, especially of the kind when a limb has "fallen asleep." Perhaps the "pricking" or tingling attendant upon a limb that has gone numb was the reason why St. Jerome chose the Latin word *compunctionis*. The Douay-Rheims more accurately translates the word as "insensibility."
57. 2 Thess. 2:10.
58. By refusing to admit that they have sinned, the lapsed cannot be admitted to the order of penitents and obtain pardon.
59. Isa. 30:51.
60. Ezk. 33:11.
61. Joel 2:13.
62. The *libelli pacis* of the martyrs or the sacrifice of the Eucharist offered by the priests are both effectual in atoning for the penalties due to sin.

ON THE LORD'S PRAYER[1]

1. The evangelical precepts, beloved brethren, are nothing else than divine teachings—foundations on which hope is to be built, supports to strengthen faith, nourishments for cheering the heart, rudders for guiding our way, guards for obtaining salvation—which, while they instruct the docile minds of believers on the earth, lead them to heavenly kingdoms. God, moreover, willed many things to be said and to be heard by means of the prophets His servants; but how much greater are those which the Son speaks, which the Word of God who was in the prophets testifies with His own voice; not now bidding to prepare the way for His coming, but Himself coming and opening and showing to us the way, so that we who have before been wandering in the darkness of death, without forethought and blind, being enlightened by the light of grace, might keep the way of life, with the Lord for our ruler and guide![2]

2. He, among the rest of His salutary admonitions and divine precepts wherewith He counsels His people for their salvation, Himself also gave a form of praying—Himself advised and instructed us what we should pray for. He who made us to live, taught us also to pray, with that same benignity, to wit, wherewith He has condescended to give and confer all things else; in order that while we speak to the Father in that prayer and supplication which the Son has taught us, we may be the more easily heard. Already He had foretold that the hour was coming when the true worshippers should worship the Father in spirit and in truth;[3] and He thus fulfilled what He before promised, so that we who by His sanctification have received the Spirit and truth, may also by His teaching worship truly and spiritually. For what can be a more spiritual prayer than that which was given to us by Christ, by whom also the Holy Spirit was given to us? What praying to the Father can be more truthful than that which was delivered to us by the Son who is the Truth, out of His own mouth? So that to pray otherwise than He taught is not ignorance alone, but also sin; since He Himself has established, and said, You reject the commandments of God, that you may keep your own traditions.

3. Let us therefore, brethren beloved, pray as God our Teacher has taught us. It is a loving and friendly prayer to beseech God with His own word, to come up to His ears in the prayer of Christ. Let the Father acknowledge the words of His Son when we make our prayer, and let Him also who dwells within in our breast Himself dwell in our voice. And since we have Him as an Advocate with the Father for our sins, let us, when as sinners we petition on behalf of our sins, put forward the words of our Advocate. For since He says, that whatsoever we shall ask of the Father in His name, He will give us,[4] how much more effectually do we obtain what we ask in Christ's name, if we ask for it in His own prayer!

4. But let our speech and petition when we pray be under discipline, observing quietness and modesty. Let us consider that we are standing in God's sight. We must please the divine eyes both with the habit of body and with the measure of voice. For as it is characteristic of a shameless man to be noisy with his cries, so, on the other hand, it is fitting to the modest man to pray with moderated petitions. Moreover, in His teaching the Lord has bidden us to pray in secret—in hidden and remote places, in our very bed-chambers—which is best suited to faith, that we may know that God is everywhere present, and hears and sees all, and in the plenitude of His majesty penetrates even into hidden and secret places, as it is written, "I am a God at hand, and not a God afar off. If a man shall hide himself in secret places, shall I not then see him? Do not I fill heaven and earth?"[5] And again: "The eyes of the Lord are in every place, beholding the evil and the good."[6] And when we meet together with the brethren in one place, and celebrate divine sacrifices with God's priest, we ought to be mindful of modesty and discipline—not to throw abroad our prayers indiscriminately, with unsubdued voices, nor to cast to God with tumultuous wordiness a petition that ought to be commended to God by modesty; for God is the hearer, not of the voice, but of the heart. Nor need He be clamorously reminded, since He sees men's thoughts, as the Lord proves to us when He says, "Why do you think evil in your hearts?"[7] And in another place: "And all the churches shall know that I am He that searches the hearts and reins."[8]

5. And this Hannah in the first book of Kings,[9] who was a type of the Church, maintains and observes, in that she prayed to God not with clamorous petition, but silently and modestly, within the very recesses of her heart. She spoke with hidden prayer, but with manifest faith. She spoke not with her voice, but with her heart, because she knew that thus God hears; and she effectually obtained what she sought, because she asked it with belief. Divine Scripture asserts this, when it says, "She spoke in her heart, and her lips moved, and her voice was not heard; and God did hear her."[10] We read also in the Psalms, "Speak in your hearts, and in your beds, and be pierced."[11] The Holy Spirit, moreover, suggests these same things by Jeremiah, and teaches, saying, "But in the heart ought God to be adored by you."[12]

6. And let not the worshipper, beloved brethren, be ignorant in what manner the publican prayed with the Pharisee in the temple. Not with eyes lifted up boldly to heaven, nor with hands proudly raised; but beating his breast, and testifying to the sins shut up within, he implored the help of the divine mercy. And while the Pharisee was pleased with himself, this man who thus asked, the rather deserved to be sanctified, since he placed the hope of salvation not in the confidence of his innocence, because there is none who is innocent; but confessing his sinfulness he humbly prayed, and He who pardons the humble heard the petitioner. And these things the Lord records in His Gospel, saying, "Two men went up into the temple to pray; the one a Pharisee, and the other a publican. The Pharisee stood, and prayed thus with himself: God, I thank You that I am not as other men are, unjust, extortioners, adulterers, even as this publican. I fast twice in the week, I give tithes of all that I possess. But the publican stood afar off, and would not so much as lift up his eyes unto heaven, but smote upon his breast, saying, God, be merciful to me a sinner. I say unto you, this man went down to his house justified rather than the Pharisee: for every one that exalts himself shall be abased; and whosoever humbles himself shall be exalted."[13]

7. These things, beloved brethren, when we have learned from the sacred reading, and have gathered in what way we ought to approach to prayer, let us know also from the Lord's teaching what we should pray. Thus, says He, pray: —"Our Father, who art in heaven, Hallowed be Your name. Your kingdom come. Your will be done, as in heaven so in earth. Give us this day our daily bread. And forgive us our debts, as we forgive our debtors. And suffer us not to be led into temptation; but deliver us from evil. Amen."[14]

8. Before all things, the Teacher of peace and the Master of unity would not have prayer to be made singly and individually, as for one who prays to pray for himself alone. For we say not 'My Father, which art in heaven,' nor 'Give me this day my daily bread;' nor does each one ask that only his own debt should be forgiven him; nor does he request for himself alone that he may not be led into temptation, and delivered from evil. Our prayer is public and common; and when we pray, we pray not for one, but for the whole people, because we the whole people are one.[15] The God of peace and the Teacher of concord, who taught unity, willed that one should thus pray for all, even as He Himself bore us all in one. This law of prayer the three children observed when they were shut up in the fiery furnace, speaking together in prayer, and being of one heart in the agreement of the spirit; and this the faith of the Sacred Scripture assures us, and in telling us how such as these prayed, gives an example which we ought to follow in our prayers, in order that we may be such as they were: "Then these three," it says, "as if from one mouth sang an hymn, and blessed the Lord."[16] They spoke as if from one mouth, although Christ had not yet taught them how to pray. And therefore, as they prayed, their speech was availing and effectual, because a peaceful, and sincere, and spiritual prayer deserved well of the Lord. Thus also we find that the apostles, with the disciples, prayed after the Lord's ascension: "They all," says the Scripture, "continued with one accord in prayer, with the women, and Mary who was the mother of Jesus, and with His brethren."[17] They continued with one accord in prayer, declaring both by the urgency and by the agreement of their praying, that God, who makes men to dwell of one mind in a house, only admits into the divine and eternal home those among whom prayer is unanimous.

9. But what matters of deep moment are contained in the Lord's prayer! How many and how great, briefly collected in the words, but spiritually abundant in virtue, so that there is absolutely nothing passed over that is not comprehended in these our prayers and petitions, as in a compendium of heavenly doctrine. "After this manner," says He, pray: "Our Father, which art in heaven." The new man, born again and restored to his God by His grace, says 'Father,' in the first place because he has now begun to be a son. "He came," He says, "to His own, and His own received Him not. But as many as received Him, to them gave He power to become the sons of God, even to them that believe in His name."[18] The man, therefore, who has believed in His name, and has become God's son, ought from this point to begin both to give thanks and to profess himself God's son, by declaring that God is his Father in heaven; and also to bear witness, among the very first words of his new birth, that he has renounced an earthly and carnal father, and that he has begun to know as well as to have as a father Him only who is in heaven, as it is written: "They who say unto their father and their mother, 'I have not known you,' and who have not acknowledged their own children these have observed Your precepts and have kept Your covenant."[19] Also the Lord in His Gospel has bidden us to call no man our father upon earth, because there is to us one Father, who is in heaven.[20] And to the disciple who had made mention of his dead father, He replied, "Let the dead bury their dead;"[21] for he had said that his father was dead, while the Father of believers is living.

10. Nor ought we, beloved brethren, only to observe and understand that we should call Him Father who is in heaven; but we add to it, and say our Father, that is, the Father of those who believe—of those who, being sanctified by Him, and restored by the nativity of spiritual grace, have begun to be sons of God. This is a word, moreover, which rebukes and condemns the Jews, who not only unbelievingly despised Christ, who had been announced to them by the prophets, and sent first to them, but also cruelly put Him to death; and these cannot now call God their Father, since the Lord confounds and confutes them, saying, "You are born of your father the devil, and the lusts of your father you will do. For he was a murderer from the beginning, and abode not in the truth, because there is no truth in him."[22] And by Isaiah the prophet God cries in wrath, "I have begotten and brought up children; but they have despised me. The ox knows his owner, and the ass his master's crib; but Israel has not known me, and my people has not understood me. Ah sinful nation, a people laden with sins, a wicked seed, corrupt children! You have forsaken the Lord; you have provoked the Holy One of Israel to anger."[23] In repudiation of these, we Christians, when we pray, say 'Our Father;' because He has begun to be ours, and has ceased to be the Father of the Jews, who have forsaken Him. Nor can a sinful people be a son; but the name of sons is attributed to those to whom remission of sins is granted, and to them immortality is promised anew, in the words of our Lord Himself: "Whosoever commits sin is the servant of sin. And the servant abides not in the house for ever, but the son abides ever."[24]

11. But how great is the Lord's indulgence! How great His condescension and plenteousness of goodness towards us, seeing that He has wished us to pray in the sight of God in such a way as to call God Father, and to call ourselves sons of God, even as Christ is the Son of God, a name which none of us would dare to venture on in prayer, unless He Himself had allowed us thus to pray! We ought then, beloved brethren, to remember and to know, that when we call God Father, we ought to act as God's children; so that in the measure in which we find pleasure in considering God as a Father, He might also be able to find pleasure in us. Let us converse as temples of God, that it may be plain that God dwells in us. Let not our doings be degenerate from the Spirit; so that we who have begun to be heavenly and spiritual, may consider and do nothing but spiritual and heavenly things; since the Lord God Himself has said, "Them that honor me I will honor; and he that despises me shall be despised."[25] The blessed apostle also has laid down in his epistle: "You are not your own; for you are bought with a great price. Glorify and bear about God in your body."[26]

12. After this we say, "Hallowed be Your name;" not that we wish for God that He may be hallowed by our prayers, but that we beseech of Him that His name may be hallowed in us. But by whom is God sanctified, since He Himself sanctifies? Well, because He says, "Be holy, even as I am holy,"[27] we ask and entreat, that we who were sanctified in baptism may continue in that which we have begun to be. And this we daily pray for; for we have need of daily sanctification, that we who daily fall away may wash out our sins by continual sanctification. And what the sanctification is which is conferred upon us by the condescension of God, the apostle declares, when he says, "neither fornicators, nor idolaters, nor adulterers, nor effeminate, nor abusers of themselves with mankind, nor thieves, nor deceivers, nor drunkards, nor revilers, nor extortioners, shall inherit the kingdom of God. And such indeed were you; but you are washed; but you are justified; but you are sanctified in the name of our Lord Jesus Christ, and by the Spirit of our God."[28] He says that we are sanctified in the name of our Lord Jesus Christ, and by the Spirit of our God. We pray that this sanctification may abide in us and because our Lord and Judge warns the man that was healed and quickened by Him, to sin no more lest a worse thing happen unto him,[29] we make this supplication in our constant prayers, we ask this day and night, that the sanctification and quickening which is received from the grace of God may be preserved by His protection.[30]

13. There follows in the prayer, "Your kingdom come." We ask that the kingdom of God may be set forth to us, even as we also ask that His name may be sanctified in us. For when does God not reign, or when does that begin with Him which both always has been, and never ceases to be? We pray that our kingdom, which has been promised us by God, may come, which was acquired by the blood and passion of Christ; that we who first are His subjects in the world, may hereafter reign with Christ when He reigns, as He Himself promises and says, "Come, you blessed of my Father, receive the kingdom which has been prepared for you from the beginning of the world."[31] Christ Himself, dearest brethren, however, may be the kingdom of God, whom we day by day desire to come, whose advent we crave to be quickly manifested to us. For since He is Himself the Resurrection, since in Him we rise again, so also the kingdom of God may be understood to be Himself, since in Him we shall reign. But we do well in seeking the kingdom of God, that is, the heavenly kingdom, because there is also an earthly kingdom. But he who has already renounced the world, is moreover greater than its honors and its kingdom. And therefore he who dedicates himself to God and Christ, desires not earthly, but heavenly kingdoms. But there is need of continual prayer and supplication, that we fall not away from the heavenly kingdom, as the Jews, to whom this promise had first been given, fell away; even as the Lord sets forth and proves: "Many," says He, "shall come from the east and from the west, and shall recline with Abraham, and Isaac, and Jacob in the kingdom of heaven. But the children of the kingdom shall be cast out into outer darkness: there shall be weeping and gnashing of teeth."[32] He shows that the Jews were previously children of the kingdom, so long as they continued also to be children of God; but after the name of Father ceased to be recognized among them, the kingdom also ceased; and therefore we Christians, who in our prayer begin to call God our Father, pray also that God's kingdom may come to us.

14. We add, also, and say, "Your will be done, as in heaven so in earth;" not that God should do what He wills, but that we may be able to do what God wills. For who resists God, that He may not do what He wills? But since we are hindered by the devil from obeying with our thought and deed God's will in all things, we pray and ask that God's will may be done in us; and that it may be done in us we have need of God's good will, that is, of His help and protection, since no one is strong in his own strength, but he is safe by the grace and mercy of God. And further, the Lord, setting forth the infirmity of the humanity which He bore, says, "Father, if it be possible, let this cup pass from me" and affording an example to His disciples that they should do not their own will, but God's, He went on to say, "Nevertheless not as I will, but as You will."[33] And in another place He says, "I came down from heaven not to do my own will, but the will of Him that sent me."[34] Now if the Son was obedient to do His Father's will, how much more should the servant be obedient to do his Master's will! As in his epistle John also exhorts and instructs us to do the will of God, saying, "Love not the world, neither the things that are in the world. If any man love the world, the love of the Father is not in him. For all that is in the world is the lust of the flesh, and the lust of the eyes, and the ambition of life, which is not of the Father, but of the lust of the world. And the world shall pass away, and the lust thereof: but he that does the will of God abides for ever, even as God also abides for ever."[35] We who desire to abide for ever should do the will of God, who is everlasting.

15. Now that is the will of God which Christ both did and taught. Humility in conversation; steadfastness in faith; modesty in words; justice in deeds; mercifulness in works; discipline in morals; to be unable to do a wrong, and to be able to bear a wrong when done; to keep peace with the brethren; to love God with all one's heart; to love Him in that He is a Father; to fear Him in that He is God; to prefer nothing whatever to Christ, because He did not prefer anything to us; to adhere inseparably to His love; to stand by His cross bravely and faithfully; when there is any contest on behalf of His name and honor, to exhibit in discourse that constancy wherewith we make confession; in torture, that confidence wherewith we do battle; in death, that patience whereby we are crowned—this is to desire to be fellow heirs with Christ; this is to do the commandment of God; this is to fulfill the will of the Father.[36]

16. Moreover, we ask that the will of God may be done both in heaven and in earth, each of which things pertains to the fulfillment of our safety and salvation. For since we possess the body from the earth and the spirit from heaven, we ourselves are earth and heaven; and in both—that is, both in body and spirit—we pray that God's will may be done. For between the flesh and spirit there is a struggle; and there is a daily strife as they disagree one with the other, so that we cannot do those very things that we would, in that the spirit seeks heavenly and divine things, while the flesh lusts after earthly and temporal things; and therefore we ask that, by the help and assistance of God, agreement may be made between these two natures, so that while the will of God is done both in the spirit and in the flesh, the soul which is new-born by Him may be preserved. This is what the Apostle Paul openly and manifestly declares by his words: "The flesh," says he, "lusts against the spirit, and the spirit against the flesh: for these are contrary the one to the other; so that you cannot do the things that you would. Now the works of the flesh are manifest, which are these; adulteries, fornications, uncleanness, lasciviousness, idolatry, witchcraft, murders, hatred, variance, emulations, wraths, strife, seditions, dissensions, heresies, envyings, drunkenness, revellings, and such like: of the which I tell you before, as I have also told you in times past, that they which do such things shall not inherit the kingdom of God. But the fruit of the spirit is love, joy, peace, magnanimity, goodness, faith, gentleness, continence, chastity."[37] And therefore we make it our prayer in daily, yea, in continual supplications, that the will of God concerning us should be done both in heaven and in earth; because this is the will of God, that earthly things should give place to heavenly, and that spiritual and divine things should prevail.

17. And it may be thus understood, beloved brethren, that since the Lord commands and admonishes us even to love our enemies, and to pray even for those who persecute us, we should ask, moreover, for those who are still earth, and have not yet begun to be heavenly, that even in respect of these God's will should be done, which Christ accomplished in preserving and renewing humanity. For since the disciples are not now called by Him earth, but the salt of the earth, and the apostle designates the first man as being from the dust of the earth, but the second from heaven, we reasonably, who ought to be like God our Father, who makes His sun to rise upon the good and bad, and sends rain upon the just and the unjust, so pray and ask by the admonition of Christ as to make our prayer for the salvation of all men; that as in heaven—that is, in us by our faith—the will of God has been done, so that we might be of heaven; so also in earth—that is, in those who believe not—God's will may be done, that they who as yet are by their first birth of earth, may, being born of water and of the Spirit, begin to be of heaven.[38]

18. As the prayer goes forward, we ask and say, "Give us this day our daily bread." And this may be understood both spiritually and literally, because either way of understanding it is rich in divine usefulness to our salvation. For Christ is the bread of life; and this bread does not belong to all men, but it is ours. And according as we say, "Our Father," because He is the Father of those who understand and believe; so also we call it our bread, because Christ is the bread of those who are in union with His body. And we ask that this bread should be given to us daily, that we who are in Christ, and daily receive the Eucharist for the food of salvation, may not, by the interposition of some heinous sin, by being prevented, as withheld and not communicating, from partaking of the heavenly bread, be separated from Christ's body, as He Himself predicts, and warns, "I am the bread of life which came down from heaven. If any man eat of my bread, he shall live for ever: and the bread which I will give is my flesh, for the life of the world."[39] When, therefore, He says, that whoever shall eat of His bread shall live for ever; as it is manifest that those who partake of His body and receive the Eucharist by the right of communion are living, so, on the other hand, we must fear and pray lest any one who, being withheld from communion, is separate from Christ's body should remain at a distance from salvation; as He Himself threatens, and says, "Unless you eat the flesh of the Son of man, and drink His blood, you shall have no life in you."[40] And therefore we ask that our bread—that is, Christ—may be given to us daily, that we who abide and live in Christ may not depart from His sanctification and body.

19. But it may also be thus understood, that we who have renounced the world, and have cast away its riches and pomps in the faith of spiritual grace, should only ask for ourselves food and support, since the Lord instructs us, and says, "Whosoever forsakes not all that he has, cannot be my disciple."[41] But he who has begun to be Christ's disciple, renouncing all things according to the word of his Master, ought to ask for his daily food, and not to extend the desires of his petition to a long period, as the Lord again prescribes, and says, "Take no thought for the morrow, for the morrow itself shall take thought for itself. Sufficient for the day is the evil thereof."[42] With reason, then, does Christ's disciple ask food for himself for the day, since he is prohibited from thinking of the morrow; because it becomes a contradiction and a repugnant thing for us to seek to live long in this world, since we ask that the kingdom of God should come quickly. Thus also the blessed apostle admonishes us, giving substance and strength to the steadfastness of our hope and faith: "We brought nothing," says he, "into this world, nor indeed can we carry anything out. Having therefore food and raiment, let us be herewith content. But they that will be rich fall into temptation and a snare, and into many and hurtful lusts, which drown men in perdition and destruction. For the love of money is the root of all evil; which while some coveted after, they have made shipwreck from the faith, and have pierced themselves through with many sorrows."[43]

20. He teaches us that riches are not only to be condemned, but that they are also full of peril; that in them is the root of seducing evils, that deceive the blindness of the human mind by a hidden deception. Whence also God rebukes the rich fool, who thinks of his earthly wealth, and boasts himself in the abundance of his overflowing harvests, saying, "You fool, this night your soul shall be required of you; then whose shall those things be which you have provided?"[44] The fool who was to die that very night was rejoicing in his stores, and he to whom life already was failing was thinking of the abundance of his food. But, on the other hand, the Lord tells us that he becomes perfect and complete who sells all his goods, and distributes them for the use of the poor, and so lays up for himself treasure in heaven.[45] He says that that man is able to follow Him, and to imitate the glory of the Lord's passion, who, free from hindrance, and with his loins girded, is involved in no entanglements of worldly estate, but, at large and free himself, accompanies his possessions, which before have been sent to God. For which result, that every one of us may be able to prepare himself, let him thus learn to pray, and know, from the character of the prayer, what he ought to be.

21. For daily bread cannot be wanting to the righteous man, since it is written, "The Lord will not slay the soul of the righteous by hunger;"[46] and again "I have been young and now am old, yet have I not seen the righteous forsaken, nor his seed begging their bread."[47] And the Lord moreover promises and says, "Take no thought, saying, 'What shall we eat, or what shall we drink, or wherewithal shall we be clothed?' For after all these things do the nations seek. And your Father knows that you have need of all these things. Seek first the kingdom of God and His righteousness, and all these things shall be added unto you."[48] To those who seek God's kingdom and righteousness, He promises that all things shall be added. For since all things are God's, nothing will be wanting to him who possesses God, if God Himself be not wanting to him. Thus a meal was divinely provided for Daniel: when he was shut up by the king's command in the den of lions, and in the midst of wild beasts who were hungry, and yet spared him, the man of God was fed.[49] Thus Elijah in his flight was nourished both by ravens ministering to him in his solitude, and by birds bringing him food in his persecution. And—oh detestable cruelty of the malice of man!—the wild beasts spare, the birds feed, while men lay snares, and rage![50]

22. After this we also entreat for our sins, saying, "And forgive us our debts, as we also forgive our debtors." After the supply of food, pardon of sin is also asked for, that he who is fed by God may live in God, and that not only the present and temporal life may be provided for, but the eternal also, to which we may come if our sins are forgiven; and these the Lord calls debts, as He says in His Gospel, "I forgave you all that debt, because you desired me."[51] And how necessarily, how providently and salutarily, are we admonished that we are sinners, since we are compelled to entreat for our sins, and while pardon is asked for from God, the soul recalls its own consciousness of sin! Lest any one should flatter himself that he is innocent, and by exalting himself should more deeply perish, he is instructed and taught that he sins daily, in that he is bidden to entreat daily for his sins. Thus, moreover, John also in his epistle warns us, and says, "If we say that we have no sin, we deceive ourselves, and the truth is not in us; but if we confess our sins, the Lord is faithful and just to forgive us our sins."[52] In his epistle he has combined both, that we should entreat for our sins, and that we should obtain pardon when we ask. Therefore he said that the Lord was faithful to forgive sins, keeping the faith of His promise; because He who taught us to pray for our debts and sins, has promised that His fatherly mercy and pardon shall follow.

23. He has clearly joined herewith and added the law, and has bound us by a certain condition and engagement, that we should ask that our debts be forgiven us in such a manner as we ourselves forgive our debtors, knowing that that which we seek for our sins cannot be obtained unless we ourselves have acted in a similar way in respect of our debtors. Therefore also He says in another place, "With what measure you mete, it shall be measured to you again." And the servant who, after having had all his debt forgiven him by his master, would not forgive his fellow-servant, is cast back into prison; because he would not forgive his fellow-servant, he lost the indulgence that had been shown to himself by his lord.[53] And these things Christ still more urgently sets forth in His precepts with yet greater power of His rebuke. 'When you stand praying," says He, "forgive if you have anything against any, that your Father which is in heaven may forgive you your trespasses. But if you do not forgive, neither will your Father which is in heaven forgive you your trespasses."[54] There remains no ground of excuse in the day of judgment, when you will be judged according to your own sentence; and whatever you have done, that you also will suffer. For God commands us to be peacemakers, and in agreement, and of one mind in His house; and such as He makes us by a second birth, such He wishes us when new-born to continue, that we who have begun to be sons of God may abide in God's peace, and that, having one spirit, we should also have one heart and one mind. Thus God does not receive the sacrifice of a person who is in disagreement, but commands him to go back from the altar and first be reconciled to his brother, that so God also may be appeased by the prayers of a peace-maker. Our peace and brotherly agreement is the greater sacrifice to God—and a people united in one in the unity of the Father, and of the Son, and of the Holy Spirit.

24. For even in the sacrifices which Abel and Cain first offered, God looked not at their gifts, but at their hearts, so that he was acceptable in his gift who was acceptable in his heart. Abel, peaceable and righteous in sacrificing in innocence to God, taught others also, when they bring their gift to the altar, thus to come with the fear of God, with a simple heart, with the law of righteousness, with the peace of concord. With reason did he, who was such in respect of God's sacrifice, become subsequently himself a sacrifice to God; so that he who first set forth martyrdom, and initiated[55] the Lord's passion by the glory of his blood, had both the Lord's righteousness and His peace. Finally, such are crowned by the Lord, such will be avenged with the Lord in the day of judgment; but the quarrelsome and disunited, and he who has not peace with his brethren, in accordance with what the blessed apostle and the Holy Scripture testifies, even if he have been slain for the name of Christ, shall not be able to escape the crime of fraternal dissension, because, as it is written, "He who hates his brother is a murderer"[56] and no murderer attains to the kingdom of heaven, nor does he live with God. He cannot be with Christ, who had rather be an imitator of Judas than of Christ. How great is the sin which cannot even be washed away by a baptism of blood[57]—how heinous the crime which cannot be expiated by martyrdom!

25. Moreover, the Lord of necessity admonishes us to say in prayer, "And suffer us not to be led into temptation." In these words it is shown that the adversary can do nothing against us except God shall have previously permitted it; so that all our fear, and devotion, and obedience may be turned towards God, since in our temptations nothing is permitted to evil unless power is given from Him. This is proved by divine Scripture, which says, "Nebuchadnezzar king of Babylon came to Jerusalem, and besieged it; and the Lord delivered it into his hand."[58] But power is given to evil against us according to our sins, as it is written, "Who gave Jacob for a spoil, and Israel to those who make a prey of Him? Did not the Lord, against whom they sinned, and would not walk in His ways, nor hear His law? And He has brought upon them the anger of His wrath."[59] And again, when Solomon sinned, and departed from the Lord's commandments and ways, it is recorded, "And the Lord stirred up Satan against Solomon himself."[60]

26. Now power is given against us in two modes: either for punishment when we sin, or for glory when we are proved, as we see was done with respect to Job; as God Himself sets forth, saying, "Behold, all that he has I give unto your hands; but be careful not to touch himself."[61] And the Lord in His Gospel says, in the time of His passion, "You could have no power against me unless it were given you from above."[62] But when we ask that we may not come into temptation, we are reminded of our infirmity and weakness in that we thus ask, lest any should insolently vaunt himself, lest any should proudly and arrogantly assume anything to himself, lest any should take to himself the glory either of confession or of suffering as his own, when the Lord Himself, teaching humility, said, "Watch and pray, that you enter not into temptation; the spirit indeed is willing, but the flesh is weak"[63]; so that while a humble and submissive confession comes first, and all is attributed to God, whatever is sought for suppliantly with fear and honor of God, may be granted by His own loving-kindness.

27. After all these things, in the conclusion of the prayer comes a brief clause, which shortly and comprehensively sums up all our petitions and our prayers. For we conclude by saying, "But deliver us from evil," comprehending all adverse things which the enemy attempts against us in this world, from which there may be a faithful and sure protection if God deliver us, if He afford His help to us who pray for and implore it. And when we say, "Deliver us from evil," there remains nothing further which ought to be asked. When we have once asked for God's protection against evil, and have obtained it, then against everything which the devil and the world work against us we stand secure and safe. For what fear is there in this life, to the man whose guardian in this life is God?

28. What wonder is it, beloved brethren, if such is the prayer which God taught, seeing that He condensed in His teaching all our prayer in one saving sentence? This had already been before foretold by Isaiah the prophet, when, being filled with the Holy Spirit, he spoke of the majesty and loving-kindness of God, consummating and shortening His word, He says, "in righteousness, because a shortened word will the Lord make in the whole earth."[64] For when the Word of God, our Lord Jesus Christ, came unto all, and gathering alike the learned and unlearned, published to every sex and every age the precepts of salvation He made a large compendium of His precepts, that the memory of the scholars might not be burdened in the celestial learning, but might quickly learn what was necessary to a simple faith. Thus, when He taught what is life eternal, He embraced the sacrament of life in a large and divine brevity, saying, "And this is life eternal, that they might know You, the only and true God, and Jesus Christ, whom You have sent."[65] Also, when He would gather from the law and the prophets the first and greatest commandments, He said, "Hear, O Israel; the Lord your God is one God: and you shall love the Lord your God with all your heart, and with all your mind, and with all your strength. This is the first commandment. And the second is like it, You shall love your neighbor as yourself. On these two commandments hang all the law and the prophets."[66] And again: "Whatsoever good things you would have men do to you, do even so to them. For this is the law and the prophets."[67]

29. Nor was it only in words, but in deeds also, that the Lord taught us to pray, Himself praying frequently and beseeching, and thus showing us, by the testimony of His example, what it behooved us to do, as it is written, "But Himself departed into a solitary place, and there prayed."[68] And again: "He went out into a mountain to pray, and continued all night in prayer to God."[69] But if He prayed who was without sin, how much more ought sinners to pray; and if He prayed continually, watching through the whole night in uninterrupted petitions, how much more ought we to watch nightly in constantly repeated prayer!

30. But the Lord prayed and besought not for Himself—for why should He who was guiltless pray on His own behalf?—but for our sins, as He Himself declared, when He said to Peter, "Behold, Satan has desired that he might sift you as wheat. But I have prayed for you, that your faith fail not."[70] And subsequently He beseeches the Father for all, saying, "Neither pray I for these alone, but for them also which shall believe in me through their word; that they all may be one; as You, Father, art in me, and I in You, that they also may be one in us."[71] The Lord's loving-kindness, no less than His mercy, is great in respect of our salvation, in that, not content to redeem us with His blood, He in addition also prayed for us. Behold now what was the desire of His petition, that like as the Father and Son are one, so also we should abide in absolute unity; so that from this it may be understood how greatly he sins who divides unity and peace, since for this same thing even the Lord besought, desirous doubtless that His people should thus be saved and live in peace, since He knew that discord cannot come into the kingdom of God.

31. Moreover, when we stand praying, beloved brethren, we ought to be watchful and earnest with our whole heart, intent on our prayers. Let all carnal and worldly thoughts pass away, nor let the soul at that time think on anything but the object only of its prayer. For this reason also the priest, by way of preface before his prayer, prepares the minds of the brethren by saying, "Lift up your hearts," that so upon the people's response, "We lift them up unto the Lord,"[72] he may be reminded that he himself ought to think of nothing but the Lord. Let the breast be closed against the adversary, and be open to God alone; nor let it suffer God's enemy to approach to it at the time of prayer. For frequently he steals upon us, and penetrates within, and by crafty deceit calls away our prayers from God, that we may have one thing in our heart and another in our voice, when not the sound of the voice, but the soul and mind, ought to be praying to the Lord with a simple intention. But what carelessness it is, to be distracted and carried away by foolish and profane thoughts when you are praying to the Lord, as if there were anything which you should rather be thinking of than that you are speaking with God! How can you ask to be heard of God, when you yourself do not hear yourself? Do you wish that God should remember you when you ask, if you yourself do not remember yourself? This is absolutely to take no precaution against the enemy; this is, when you pray to God, to offend the majesty of God by the carelessness of your prayer; this is to be watchful with your eyes, and to be asleep with your heart, while the Christian, even though he is asleep with his eyes, ought to be awake with his heart, as it is written in the person of the Church speaking in the Song of Songs, "I sleep, yet my heart wakes."[73] Wherefore the apostle anxiously and carefully warns us, saying, "Continue in prayer, and watch in the same;"[74] teaching, that is, and showing that those are able to obtain from God what they ask, whom God sees to be watchful in their prayer.

32. Moreover, those who pray should not come to God with fruitless or naked prayers. Petition is ineffectual when it is a barren entreaty that beseeches God. For as every tree that brings not forth fruit is cut down and cast into the fire, assuredly also, words that do not bear fruit cannot deserve anything of God, because they are fruitful in no result. And thus Holy Scripture instructs us, saying, "Prayer is good with fasting and almsgiving."[75] For He who will give us in the day of judgment a reward for our labors and alms, is even in this life a merciful hearer of one who comes to Him in prayer associated with good works. Thus, for instance, Cornelius the centurion, when he prayed, had a claim to be heard. For he was in the habit of doing many almsdeeds towards the people, and of ever praying to God. To this man, when he prayed about the ninth hour, appeared an angel bearing testimony to his labors, and saying, "Cornelius, your prayers and your alms are gone up in remembrance before God."[76]

33. Those prayers quickly ascend to God which the merits of our labors urge upon God. Thus also Raphael the angel was a witness to the constant prayer and the constant good works of Tobias, saying, "It is honorable to reveal and confess the works of God. For when you prayed, and Sarah, I did bring the remembrance of your prayers before the holiness of God. And when you buried the dead in simplicity, and because you did not delay to rise up and to leave your dinner, but went out and covered the dead, I was sent to prove you; and again God has sent me to heal you, and Sarah your daughter-in-law. For I am Raphael, one of the seven holy angels which stand and go in and out before the glory of God."[77] By Isaiah also the Lord reminds us, and teaches similar things, saying, "Loosen every knot of iniquity, release the oppressions of contracts which have no power, let the troubled go into peace, and break every unjust engagement. Break your bread to the hungry, and bring the poor that are without shelter into your house. When you see the naked, clothe him; and despise not those of the same family and race as yourself. Then shall your light break forth in season, and your raiment shall spring forth speedily; and righteousness shall go before you, and the glory of God shall surround you. Then shall you call, and God shall hear you; and while you shall yet speak, He shall say, 'Here I am.'"[78] He promises that He will be at hand, and says that He will hear and protect those who, loosening the knots of unrighteousness from their heart, and giving alms among the members of God's household according to His commands, even in hearing what God commands to be done, do themselves also deserve to be heard by God. The blessed Apostle Paul, when aided in the necessity of affliction by his brethren, said that good works which are performed are sacrifices to God. "I am full," says he, "having received of Epaphroditus the things which were sent from you, an odor of a sweet smell, a sacrifice acceptable, well pleasing to God."[79] For when one has pity on the poor, he lends to God; and he who gives to the least gives to God—sacrifices spiritually to God an odor of a sweet smell.

34. And in discharging the duties of prayer, we find that the three children with Daniel, being strong in faith and victorious in captivity, observed the third, sixth, and ninth hour, as it were, for a sacrament[80] of the Trinity, which in the last times had to be manifested. For both the first hour in its progress to the third shows forth the consummated number of the Trinity, and also the fourth proceeding to the sixth declares another Trinity; and when from the seventh the ninth is completed, the perfect Trinity is numbered every three hours, which spaces of hours the worshippers of God in time past having spiritually decided on, made use of for determined and lawful times for prayer. And subsequently the thing was manifested, that these things were of old sacraments, in that anciently righteous men prayed in this manner. For upon the disciples at the third hour the Holy Spirit descended, who fulfilled the grace of the Lord's promise. Moreover, at the sixth hour, Peter, going up unto the house-top, was instructed as well by the sign as by the word of God admonishing him to receive all to the grace of salvation, whereas he was previously doubtful of the receiving of the Gentiles to baptism. And from the sixth hour to the ninth, the Lord, being crucified, washed away our sins by His blood; and that He might redeem and quicken us, He then accomplished His victory by His passion.[81]

35. But for us, beloved brethren, besides the hours of prayer observed of old, both the times and the sacraments have now increased in number. For we must also pray in the morning, that the Lord's resurrection may be celebrated by morning prayer. And this formerly the Holy Spirit pointed out in the Psalms, saying, "My King, and my God, because unto You will I cry; O Lord, in the morning shall You hear my voice; in the morning will I stand before You, and will look up to You."[82] And again, the Lord speaks by the mouth of the prophet: "Early in the morning shall they watch for me, saying, Let us go, and return unto the Lord our God."[83]

Also at the sunsetting and at the decline of day, of necessity we must pray again. For since Christ is the true sun and the true day, as the worldly sun and worldly day depart, when we pray and ask that light may return to us again, we pray for the advent of Christ, which shall give us the grace of everlasting light. Moreover, the Holy Spirit in the Psalms manifests that Christ is called the day. "The stone," says He, "which the builders rejected, has become the head of the corner. This is the Lord's doing; and it is marvellous in our eyes. This is the day which the Lord has made; let us walk and rejoice in it."[84] Also the prophet Malachi testifies that He is called the Sun, when he says, "But to you that fear the name of the Lord shall the Sun of righteousness arise, and there is healing in His wings."[85] But if in the Holy Scriptures the true sun and the true day is Christ, there is no hour excepted for Christians wherein God ought not frequently and always to be worshipped; so that we who are in Christ—that is, in the true Sun and the true Day—should be instant throughout the entire day in petitions, and should pray; and when, by the law of the world, the revolving night, recurring in its alternate changes, succeeds, there can be no harm arising from the darkness of night to those who pray, because the children of light have the day even in the night. For when is he without light who has light in his heart? Or when has not he the sun and the day, whose Sun and Day is Christ?[86]

36. Let not us, then, who are in Christ—that is, always in the lights cease from praying even during night. Thus the widow Anna, without intermission praying and watching, persevered in deserving well of God, as it is written in the Gospel: "She departed not, it says, from the temple, serving with fastings and prayers night and day."[87] Let the Gentiles look to this, who are not yet enlightened, or the Jews who have remained in darkness by having forsaken the light. Let us, beloved brethren, who are always in the light of the Lord, who remember and hold fast what by grace received we have begun to be, reckon night for day; let us believe that we always walk in the light, and let us not be hindered by the darkness which we have escaped. Let there be no failure of prayers in the hours of night—no idle and reckless waste of the occasions of prayer. New-created and newborn of the Spirit by the mercy of God, let us imitate what we shall one day be. Since in the kingdom we shall possess day alone, without intervention of night, let us so watch in the night as if in the daylight. Since we are to pray and give thanks to God for ever, let us not cease in this life also to pray and give thanks.

NOTES

1. This treatise very closely mimics Tertullian's *On Prayer* in its structure and argumentation.
2. "God, who, at sundry times and in divers manners, spoke in times past to the fathers by the prophets, last of all, in these days, hath spoken to us by his Son, whom he hath appointed heir

of all things, by whom also he made the world" (Heb. 1:1-2).

3. John 4:23.
4. John 16:23.
5. Jer. 23:23-24.
6. Prov. 15:3.
7. Matt. 9:4.
8. Rev. 2:23.
9. Cyprian is referring to 1 Samuel, known as 1 Kings in the Vulgate.
10. 1 Sam. 1:13.
11. An obscure paraphrase of Psalm 4:5, "Be ye angry, and sin not: the things you say in your hearts, be sorry for them upon your beds." The RSV has this as Psalm 4:4 and has it rendered, "Be angry, but sin not; commune with your own hearts on your beds, and be silent." Cyprian's quote is probably based off the Septuagint translation for Psalm 4:4, which reads, "Be ye angry, and sin not; feel compunction upon your beds for what ye say in your hearts." Cyrpian must have been using a Latin translation of the Psalms, since as far as we know, he had no working knowledge of Greek.
12. A paraphrase of Baruch 6:5, "Say you in your hearts: Thou oughtest to be adored, O Lord." This is further evidence of the acceptance of the deuterocanonical books as Scripture by the Fathers, since St. Cyprian not only cites Baruch but says its words are inspired by the Holy Spirit.
13. Luke 18:10-14.
14. Matt. 6:9.
15. "Our prayer in public and common," signifying the liturgical use of the Lord's Prayer.
16. Daniel 3:51, from the "Song of the Three Children."
17. Acts 1:14.
18. John 1:11.
19. Deut. 33:9.
20. Matt. 23:9. Cyprian here insists that Christians should seek their identity and patrimony in God alone; he does not mean to deny the pious custom of referring to spiritual leaders within the Church as "fathers." Cyprian himself is addressed as "father" in Letter 16; see also Philemon 10, 1 Cor. 4:14-15, 1 John 2:13-14, Phil. 2:22.
21. Matt. 8:22.
22. John 8:44.
23. Isa. 1:3.
24. John 8:34.
25. 1 Sam. 2:30.
26. 1 Cor. 6:20.
27. Lev. 20:7.
28. 1 Cor. 6:9.
29. John 5:14.
30. Cyprian's language in this paragraph demonstrates that he did not believe in eternal security ("once saved, always saved"). Christians are in "need of daily sanctification, that we who daily fall away may wash out our sins by continual sanctification;" nor can Christians rest entirely secure in this sanctification, but must be constantly vigilant in its defense, "that the sanctification and quickening which is received from the grace of God may be preserved by His protection."
31. Matt. 25:34.
32. Matt. 8:11.
33. Matt. 26:39.
34. John 6:38.
35. 1 John 2:15-17.

36. Sanctification and holiness consist in the transformation of the Christian into an image of Christ (*imago dei*).
37. Gal. 5:17-22.
38. Rom. 12:14; Matt. 5:13, 5:45.
39. John 6:58.
40. John 6:53.
41. Luke 14:33.
42. Matt. 6:34.
43. 1 Tim. 6:7.
44. Luke 12:20.
45. Matt. 6:19-20.
46. Prov. 10:3.
47. Ps. 37:25.
48. Matt. 6:31.
49. Daniel 6 mentions nothing about Daniel being fed miraculously. It is uncertain what Cyprian is referring to here.
50. 1 Kings 17:2-5.
51. Matt. 18:32.
52. 1 John 1:8.
53. Matt. 18:33.
54. Mark 11:26.
55. In other words, prefigured.
56. 1 John 3:15.
57. An important testimony to belief in the possibility of "baptism of blood" in the early Church.
58. 2 Kings 24:11.
59. Isa. 13:24.
60. 1 Kings 11:14.
61. Job 1:12.
62. John 19:11.
63. Mark 14:38.
64. Isa. 10:22.
65. John 17:3.
66. Matt. 22:40.
67. Matt. 7:12.
68. Luke 5:16.
69. Luke 6:12.
70. Luke 13:31.
71. John 17:20-21.
72. A remarkable testament to the presence of the *sursum corda* prayer in the Mass of the mid-third century. The *sursum corda* is the preface to the *anaphora*, or Eucharistic Prayer of the Mass. It signifies the transition from the first part of the Mass (Mass of the Catechumens/Liturgy of the Word) from the second part (Mass of the Presanctified/Liturgy of the Eucharist). "In the preface, the Church gives thanks to the Father, through Christ, in the Holy Spirit, for all his works: creation, redemption, and sanctification. The whole community thus joins in the unending praise that the Church in heaven, the angels and all the saints, sing to the thrice-holy God" (*Catechism of the Catholic Church* § 1352).
73. Song of Songs 5:2.
74. Col. 1:2.
75. Tobit 12:8. Another reference ot a deuterocanonical book as "Holy Scripture."
76. Acts 10:4.
77. Tobit 12:12-15.

78. Isa. 58:6-9.
79. Phil. 4:18.
80. Cyprian does not use the word *sacrament* here in the more theologically refined definition of an outward sign of inward grace, instituted by Christ for our sanctification; he uses it in the more general sense of a mystery that reveals something—a prefiguration—recalling the original Greek word *mysterion*, of which the Latin *sacramentum* is a translation. Thus the three hours of prayer kept by the three children are said to be sacraments of the Trinity because they mystically prefigure or point to the Trinity.
81. Acts 2:14-15, 10:10-16; Mark 15:33.
82. Ps. 5:3.
83. Hos. 6:1.
84. Ps. 118:22-24.
85. Mal. 4:2.
86. We see here the genesis of the Divine Office. The Apostles followed the Jewish custom of praying during the third, sixth and ninth hours, as well as at midnight (see Acts 10:3, 9; 16:25). This custom was retained by the early Christian churches, though the practice of frequenting the Temple soon stopped as Christianity diverged from Judaism and the Temple was subsequently destroyed. Other appropriate prayers were eventually added, until by the 5th century the Divine Office had taken its final form, the form that would be perfected and popularized by St. Benedict of Nursia.
87. Luke 2:37.

AN ADDRESS TO DEMETRIANUS[1]

1. I had frequently, Demetrianus, treated with contempt your railing and noisy clamor with sacrilegious mouth and impious words against the one and true God, thinking it more modest and better, silently to scorn the ignorance of a mistaken man, than by speaking to provoke the fury of a senseless one. Neither did I do this without the authority of the divine teaching, since it is written, "Speak not in the ears of a fool, lest when he hear you he should despise the wisdom of your words;"[2] and again, "Answer not a fool according to his folly, lest you also be like him."[3] And we are, moreover, bidden to keep what is holy within our own knowledge, and not expose it to be trodden down by swine and dogs, since the Lord speaks, saying, "Give not that which is holy unto the dogs, neither cast your pearls before swine, lest they trample them under their feet, and turn again and rend you."[4] For when you used often to come to me with the desire of contradicting rather than with the wish to learn, and preferred impudently to insist on your own views, which you shouted with noisy words, to patiently listening to mine, it seemed to me foolish to contend with you; since it would be an easier and slighter thing to restrain the angry waves of a turbulent sea with shouts than to check your madness by arguments. Assuredly it would be both a vain and ineffectual labor to offer light to a blind man, discourse to a deaf one, or wisdom to a brute; since neither can a brute apprehend, nor can a blind man admit the light, nor can a deaf man hear.

2. In consideration of this, I have frequently held my tongue, and overcome an impatient man with patience; since I could neither teach an unteachable man, nor check an impious one with religion, nor restrain a frantic man with gentleness. But yet, when you say that very many are complaining that to us it is ascribed that wars arise more frequently, that plague, that famines rage, and that long droughts are suspending the showers and rains, it is not fitting that I should be silent any longer, lest my silence should begin to be attributed to mistrust rather than to modesty;[5] and while I am treating the false charges with contempt, I may seem to be acknowledging the crime. I reply, therefore, as well to you, Demetrianus, as to others whom perhaps you have stirred up, and many of whom, by sowing hatred against us with malicious words, you have made your own partisans, from the budding forth of your own root and origin, who, however, I believe, will admit the reasonableness of my discourse; for he who is moved to evil by the deception of a lie, will much more easily be moved to good by the cogency of truth.

3. You have said that all these things are caused by us, and that to us ought to be attributed the misfortunes wherewith the world is now shaken and distressed, because your gods are not worshipped by us. And in this behalf, since you are ignorant of divine knowledge, and a stranger to the truth, you must in the first place know this, that the world has now grown old, and does not abide in that strength in which it formerly stood; nor has it that vigor and force which it formerly possessed. This, even were we silent, and if we alleged no proofs from the Sacred Scriptures and from the divine declarations, the world itself is now announcing, and, bearing witness to its decline by the testimony of its failing estate. In the winter there is not such an abundance of showers for nourishing the seeds; in the summer the sun has not so much heat for cherishing the harvest; nor in the spring season are the grain-fields so joyous; nor are the autumnal seasons so fruitful in their leafy products. The layers of marble are dug out in less quantity from the disembowelled and wearied mountains; the diminished quantities of gold and silver suggest the early exhaustion of the metals, and the impoverished veins are straitened and decreased day by day; the husbandman is failing in the fields, the sailor at sea, the soldier in the camp, innocence in the market, justice in the tribunal, concord in friendships, skillfulness in the arts, discipline in morals. Think you that the substantial character of a thing that is growing old remains so robust as that wherewith it might previously flourish in its youth while still new and vigorous? Whatever is tending downwards to decay, with its end nearly approaching, must of necessity be weakened. Thus, the sun at his setting darts his rays with a less bright and fiery splendor; thus, in her declining course, the moon wanes with exhausted horns; and the tree, which before had been green and fertile, as its branches dry up, becomes by and by misshapen in a barren old age; and the fountain which once gushed forth liberally from its overflowing veins, as old age causes it to fail, scarcely trickles with a sparing moisture. This is the sentence passed on the world, this is God's law; that everything that has had a beginning should perish, and things that have grown should become old, and that strong things should become weak, and great things become small, and that, when they have become weakened and diminished, they should come to an end.

4. You impute it to the Christians that everything is decaying as the world grows old. What if old men should charge it on the Christians that they grow less strong in their old age; that they no longer, as formerly, have the same facilities, in the hearing of their ears, in the swiftness of their feet, in the keenness of their eyes, in the vigor of their strength, in the freshness of their organic powers, in the fullness of their limbs, and that although once the life of men endured beyond the age of eight and nine hundred years, it can now scarcely attain to its hundredth year? We see grey hairs in boys—the hair fails before it begins to grow; and life does not cease in old age, but it begins with old age. Thus, even at its very commencement, birth hastens to its close;[6] thus, whatever is now born degenerates with the old age of the world itself; so that no one ought to wonder that everything begins to fail in the world, when the whole world itself is already in process of failing, and in its end.

5. Moreover, that wars continue frequently to prevail, that death and famine accumulate anxiety, that health is shattered by raging diseases, that the human race is wasted by the desolation of pestilence, know that this was foretold; that evils should be multiplied in the last times, and that misfortunes should be varied; and that as the day of judgment is now drawing near, the censure of an indignant God should be more and more aroused for the scourging of the human race. For these things happen not, as your false complaining and ignorant inexperience of the truth asserts and repeats, because your gods are not worshipped by us, but because God is not worshipped by you. For since He is Lord and Ruler of the world, and all things are carried on by His will and direction, nor can anything be done save what He Himself has done or allowed to be done, certainly when those things occur which show the anger of an offended God, they happen not on account of us by whom God is worshipped, but they are called down by your sins and deservings, by whom God is neither in any way sought nor feared, because your vain superstitions are not forsaken, nor the true religion known in such wise that He who is the one God over all might alone be worshipped and petitioned.

6. In fine, listen to Himself speaking; Himself with a divine voice at once instructing and warning us: "You shall worship the Lord your God, says He, and Him only shall you serve."[7] And again, "You shall have no other gods but me."[8] And again, "Go not after other gods, to serve them; and worship them not, and provoke not me to anger with the works of your hands to destroy you."[9] Moreover, the prophet, filled with the Holy Spirit, attests and denounces the anger of God, saying, "Thus says the Lord Almighty: Because of mine house that is waste, and you run every man to his own house, therefore the heavens shall be stayed from dew, and the earth shall withhold her fruits: and I will bring a sword upon the earth, and upon the grain, and upon the wine, and upon the oil, and upon men, and upon cattle, and upon all the labors of their hands."[10] Moreover, another prophet repeats, and says, "And I will cause it to rain upon one city, and upon another city I will cause it not to rain. One piece shall be rained upon, and the piece whereon I send no rain shall be withered. And two and three cities shall be gathered into one city to drink water, and shall not be satisfied; and you are not converted unto me, says the Lord."[11]

7. Behold, the Lord is angry and wrathful, and threatens, because you turn not unto Him. And you wonder or complain in this your obstinacy and contempt, if the rain comes down with unusual scarcity; and the earth falls into neglect with dusty corruption; if the barren glebe hardly brings forth a few jejune and pallid blades of grass;[12] if the destroying hail weakens the vines; if the overwhelming whirlwind roots out the olive; if drought stanches the fountain; a pestilent breeze corrupts the air; the weakness of disease wastes away man; although all these things come as the consequence of the sins that provoke them, and God is more deeply indignant when such and so great evils avail nothing! For that these things occur either for the discipline of the obstinate or for the punishment of the evil, the same God declares in the Holy Scriptures, saying, "In vain have I smitten your children; they have not received correction." And the prophet devoted and dedicated to God answers to these words in the same strain, and says, "You have stricken them, but they have not grieved; You have scourged them, but they have refused to receive correction."[13] Lo, stripes are inflicted from God, and there is no fear of God. Lo, blows and scourgings from above are not wanting, and there is no trembling, no fear. What if even no such rebuke as that interfered in human affairs? How much greater still would be the audacity in men, if it were secure in the impunity of their crimes![14]

8. You complain that the fountains are now less plentiful to you, and the breezes less salubrious, and the frequent showers and the fertile earth afford you less ready assistance; that the elements no longer subserve your uses and your pleasures as of old. But do you serve God, by whom all things are ordained to your service; do you wait upon Him by whose good pleasure all things wait upon you? From your slave you yourself require service; and though a man, you compel your fellow-man to submit, and to be obedient to you; and although you share the same lot in respect of being born, the same condition in respect of dying; although you have like bodily substance and a common order of souls, and although you come into this world of ours and depart from it after a time with equal rights, and by the same law; yet, unless you are served by him according to your pleasure, unless you are obeyed by him in conformity to your will, you, as an imperious and excessive exactor of his service, flog and scourge him: you afflict and torture him with hunger, with thirst and nakedness, and even frequently with the sword and with imprisonment. And, wretch that you are, do you not acknowledge the Lord your God while you yourself are thus exercising lordship?

9. And therefore with reason in these plagues that occur, there are not wanting God's stripes and scourges; and since they are of no avail in this matter, and do not convert individuals to God by such terror of destructions, there remains after all the eternal dungeon, and the continual fire, and the everlasting punishment; nor shall the groaning of the suppliants be heard there, because here the terror of the angry God was not heard, crying by His prophet, and saying,"Hear the word of the Lord, you children of Israel: for the judgment of the Lord is against the inhabitants of the earth; because there is neither mercy, nor truth, nor knowledge of God upon the earth. But cursing, and lying, and killing, and stealing, and committing adultery, is broken out over the land, they mingle blood with blood. Therefore shall the land mourn, with every one that dwells therein, with the beasts of the field, with things that creep on the earth, and with the fowls of heaven; and the fishes of the sea shall languish, so that no man shall judge, no man shall rebuke."[15] God says He is wrathful and angry, because there is no acknowledgment of God in the earth, and God is neither known nor feared. The sins of lying, of lust, of fraud, of cruelty, of impiety, of anger, God rebukes and finds fault with, and no one is converted to innocency. Lo, those things are happening which were before foretold by the words of God; nor is any one admonished by the belief of things present to take thought for what is to come. Amongst those very misfortunes wherein the soul, closely bound and shut up, can scarcely breathe, there is still found opportunity for men to be evil, and in such great dangers to judge not so much of themselves as of others. You are indignant that God is angry, as if by an evil life you were deserving any good, as if all things of that kind which happen were not infinitely less and of smaller account than your sins.

10. You who judge others, be for once also a judge of yourself; look into the hiding-places of your own conscience; nay, since now there is not even any shame in your sin, and you are wicked, as if it were rather the very wickedness itself that pleased you, do you, who are seen clearly and nakedly by all other men,[16] yourself also look upon yourself. For either you are swollen with pride, or greedy with avarice, or cruel with anger, or prodigal with gambling, or flushed with intemperance, or envious with jealousy, or unchaste with lust, or violent with cruelty; and do you wonder that God's anger increases in punishing the human race, when the sin that is punished is daily increasing? You complain that the enemy rises up, as if, though an enemy were wanting, there could be peace for you even among the very togas of peace.[17] You complain that the enemy rises up, as if, even although external arms and dangers from barbarians were repressed, the weapons of domestic assault from the calumnies and wrongs of powerful citizens, would not be more ferocious and more harshly wielded within. You complain of barrenness and famine, as if drought made a greater famine than rapacity, as if the fierceness of want did not increase more terribly from grasping at the increase of the year's produce, and the accumulation of their price. You complain that the heaven is shut up from showers, although in the same way the barns are shut up on earth. You complain that now less is produced, as if what had already been produced were given to the indigent. You reproach plague and disease, while by plague itself and disease the crimes of individuals are either detected or increased, while mercy is not manifested to the weak, and avarice and rapine are waiting open-mouthed for the dead. The same men are timid in the duties of affection, but rash in quest of implores gains; shunning the deaths of the dying, and craving the spoils of the dead, so that it may appear as if the wretched are probably forsaken in their sickness for this cause, that they may not, by being cured, escape: for he who enters so eagerly upon the estate of the dying, probably desired the sick man to perish.

11. So great a terror of destruction cannot give the teaching of innocency; and in the midst of a people dying with constant havoc, nobody considers that he himself is mortal. Everywhere there is scattering, there is seizure, there is taking possession; no dissimulation about spoiling, and no delay. As if it were all lawful, as if it were all becoming, as if he who does not rob were suffering loss and wasting his own property, thus every one hastens to the rapine. Among thieves there is at any rate some modesty in their crimes. They love pathless ravines and deserted solitudes; and they do wrong in such a way, that still the crime of the wrong-doers is veiled by darkness and night. Avarice, however, rages openly, and, safe by its very boldness, exposes the weapons of its headlong craving in the light of the market-place. Thence cheats, thence poisoners, thence assassins in the midst of the city, are as eager for wickedness as they are wicked with impunity. The crime is committed by the guilty, and the guiltless who can avenge it is not found. There is no fear from accuser or judge: the wicked obtain impunity, while modest men are silent; accomplices are afraid, and those who are to judge are for sale. And therefore by the mouth of the prophet the truth of the matter is put forth with the divine spirit and instinct: it is shown in a certain and obvious way that God can prevent adverse things, but that the evil deserts of sinners prevent His bringing aid. "Is the Lord's hand," says he, "not strong to save you; or has He made heavy His ear, that He cannot hear you? But your sins separate between you and God; and because of your sins He has hid His face from you, that He may not have mercy."[18] Therefore let your sins and offenses be reckoned up; let the wounds of your conscience be considered; and let each one cease complaining about God, or about us, if he should perceive that himself deserves what he suffers.

12. Look what that very matter is of which is chiefly our discourse—that you molest us, although innocent; that, in contempt of God, you attack and oppress

God's servants. It is little, in your account, that your life is stained with a variety of gross vices, with the iniquity of deadly crimes, with the summary of all bloody rapines; that true religion is overturned by false superstitions; that God is neither sought at all, nor feared at all; but over and above this, you weary God's servants, and those who are dedicated to His majesty and His name, with unjust persecutions. It is not enough that you yourself do not worship God, but, over and above, you persecute those who do worship, with a sacrilegious hostility. You neither worship God, nor do you at all permit Him to be worshipped; and while others who venerate not only those foolish idols and images made by man's hands, but even portents and monsters besides, are pleasing to you, it is only the worshipper of God who is displeasing to you. The ashes of victims and the piles of cattle everywhere smoke in your temples, and God's altars are either nowhere or are hidden. Crocodiles, and apes, and stones, and serpents are worshipped by you; and God alone in the earth is not worshipped. or if worshipped, not with impunity. You deprive the innocent, the just, the dear to God, of their home; you spoil them of their estate, you load them with chains, you shut them up in prison, you punish them with the sword, with the wild beasts, with the flames. Nor, indeed, are you content with a brief endurance of our sufferings, and with a simple and swift exhaustion of pains. You set on foot tedious tortures, by tearing our bodies; you multiply numerous punishments, by lacerating our vitals; nor can your brutality and fierceness be content with ordinary tortures; your ingenious cruelty devises new sufferings.

13. What is this insatiable madness for blood-shedding, what this interminable lust of cruelty? Rather make your election of one of two alternatives. To be a Christian is either a crime, or it is not. If it be a crime, why do you not put the man that confesses it to death? If it be not a crime, why do you persecute an innocent man? For I ought to be put to the torture if I denied it. If in fear of your punishment I should conceal, by a deceitful falsehood, what I had previously been, and the fact that had not worshipped your gods, then I might deserve to be tormented, then I ought to be compelled to confession of my crime by the power of suffering, as in other examinations the guilty, who deny that they are guilty of the crime of which they are accused, are tortured in order that the confession of the reality of the crime, which the tell-tale voice refuses to make, may be wrung out by the bodily suffering. But now, when of my own free will I confess, and cry out, and with words frequent and repeated to the same effect bear witness that I am a Christian, why do you apply tortures to one who avows it, and who destroys your gods, not in hidden and secret places, but openly, and publicly, and in the very market-place, in the hearing of your magistrates and governors; so that, although it was a slight thing which you blamed in me before, that which you ought rather to hate and punish has increased, that by declaring myself a Christian in a frequented place, and with the people standing around, I am confounding both you and your gods by an open and public announcement?[19]

14. Why do you turn your attention to the weakness of our body? Why do you strive with the feebleness of this earthly flesh? Contend rather with the strength of the mind, break down the power of the soul, destroy our faith, conquer if you can by discussion, overcome by reason; or, if your gods have any deity and power, let them themselves rise to their own vindication, let them defend themselves by their own majesty. But what can they advantage their worshippers, if they cannot avenge themselves on those who worship them not? For if he who avenges is of more account than he who is avenged, then you are greater than your gods. And if you are greater than those whom you worship, you ought not to worship them, but rather to be worshipped and feared by them as their lord. Your championship defends them when injured, just as your protection guards them when shut up from perishing. You should be ashamed to worship those whom you yourself defend; you should be ashamed to hope for protection from those whom you yourself protect.

15. Oh, would you but hear and see them when they are adjured by us, and tortured with spiritual scourges, and are ejected from the possessed bodies with tortures of words, when howling and groaning at the voice of man and the power of God, feeling the stripes and blows, they confess the judgment to come![20] Come and acknowledge that what we say is true; and since you say that you thus worship gods, believe even those whom you worship. Or if you will even believe yourself, he—i.e., the demon—who has now possessed your breast, who has now darkened your mind with the night of ignorance, shall speak concerning yourself in your hearing. You will see that we are entreated by those whom you entreat, that we are feared by those whom you fear, whom you adore. You will see that under our hands they stand bound, and tremble as captives, whom you took up to and venerate as lords: assuredly even thus you might be confounded in those errors of yours, when you see and hear your gods, at once upon our interrogation betraying what they are, and even in your presence unable to conceal those deceits and trickeries of theirs.

16. What, then, is that sluggishness of mind; yea, what blind and stupid madness of fools, to be unwilling to come out of darkness into light, and to be unwilling, when bound in the toils of eternal death, to receive the hope of immortality, and not to fear God when He threatens and says, "He that sacrifices unto any gods, but unto the Lord only, shall be rooted out?"[21] And again: "They worshipped them whom their fingers made; and the mean man has bowed down, and the great man has humbled himself, and I will not forgive them."[22] Why do you humble and bend yourself to false gods? Why do you bow your body captive before foolish images and creations of earth? God made you upright; and while other animals are downlooking, and are depressed in posture bending towards the earth, yours is a lofty attitude; and your countenance is raised upwards to heaven, and to God. Look there, lift your eyes thitherward, seek God in the highest, that you may be free from things below; lift your heart to a dependence on high and heavenly things. Why do you prostrate yourself into the ruin of death with the serpent whom you worship? Why do you fall into the destruction of the devil, by his means and in his company? Keep the lofty estate in which you were born. Continue such as you were made by God. To the posture of your countenance and of your body, conform your soul. That you may be able to know God, first know yourself. Forsake the idols which human error has invented. Be turned to God, whom if you implore He will aid you. Believe in Christ, whom the Father has sent to quicken and restore us. Cease to hurt the servants of God and of Christ with your persecutions, since when they are injured the divine vengeance defends them.

17. For this reason it is that none of us, when he is apprehended, makes resistance, nor avenges himself against your unrighteous violence, although our people are numerous and plentiful. Our certainty of a vengeance to follow makes us patient. The innocent give place to the guilty; the harmless acquiesce in punishments and tortures, sure and confident that whatsoever we suffer will not remain unavenged, and that in proportion to the greatness of the injustice of our persecution so will be the justice and the severity of the vengeance exacted for those persecutions. Nor does the wickedness of the impious ever rise up against the name we bear, without immediate vengeance from above attending it. To say nothing of the memories of ancient times, and not to recur with wordy commemoration to frequently repeated vengeance on behalf of God's worshippers, the instance of a recent matter[23] is sufficient to prove that our defense, so speedily, and in its speed so powerfully, followed of late in the ruins of things, in the destruction of wealth, in the waste of soldiers, and the diminution of forts. Nor let any one think that this occurred by chance, or think that it was fortuitous, since long ago Scripture has laid down, and said, "Vengeance is mine; I will repay, says the Lord."[24] And again the Holy Spirit forewarns, and says, "Say not, I will avenge myself of mine enemy, but wait on the Lord, that He may be your help."[25] Whence it is plain and manifest, that not by our means, but for our sakes, all those things are happening which come down from the anger of God.

18. Nor let anybody think that Christians are not avenged by those things that are happening, for the reason that they also themselves seem to be affected by their visitation. A man feels the punishment of worldly adversity, when all his joy and glory are in the world. He grieves and groans if it is ill with him in this life, with whom it cannot be well after this life, all the fruit of whose life is received here, all whose consolation is ended here, whose fading and brief life here reckons some sweetness and pleasure, but when it has departed hence, there remains for him only punishment added to sorrow. But they have no suffering from the assault of present evils who have confidence in future good things. In fact, we are never prostrated by adversity, nor are we broken down, nor do we grieve or murmur in any external misfortune or weakness of body: living by the Spirit rather than by the flesh, we overcome bodily weakness by mental strength. By those very things which torment and weary us, we know and trust that we are proved and strengthened.

19. Do you think that we suffer adversity equally with yourselves, when you see that the same adverse things are not borne equally by us and by you? Among you there is always a clamorous and complaining impatience; with us there is a strong and religious patience, always quiet and always grateful to God. Nor does it claim for itself anything joyous or prosperous in this world, but, meek and gentle and stable against all the gusts of this tossing world, it waits for the time of the divine promise; for as long as this body endures, it must needs have a common lot with others, and its bodily condition must be common. Nor is it given to any of the human race to be separated one from another, except by withdrawal from this present life. In the meantime, we are all, good and evil, contained in one household. Whatever happens within the house, we suffer with equal fate, until, when the end of the temporal life shall be attained, we shall be distributed among the homes either of eternal death or immortality. Thus, therefore, we are not on the same level, and equal with you, because, placed in this present world and in this flesh, we incur equally with you the annoyances of the world and of the flesh; for since in the sense of pain is all punishment, it is manifest that he is not a sharer of your punishment who, you see, does not suffer pain equally with yourselves.[26]

20. There flourishes with us the strength of hope and the firmness of faith. Among these very ruins of a decaying world our soul is lifted up, and our courage unshaken: our patience is never anything but joyous; and the mind is always secure of its God, even as the Holy Spirit speaks through the prophet, and exhorts us, strengthening with a heavenly word the firmness of our hope and faith. "The fig tree," says He, "shall not bear fruit, and there shall be no blossom in the vines. The labor of the olive shall fail, and the fields shall yield no meat. The flock shall be cut off from the fold, and there shall be no herd in the stalls. But I will rejoice in the Lord, and I will joy in the God of my salvation."[27] He says that the man of God and the worshipper of God, depending on the truth of his hope and the steadfastness of his faith, is not moved by the attacks of this world and this life. Although the vine should fail, and the olive deceive, and the field parched with grass dying with drought should wither, what is this to Christians? What to God's servants whom paradise is inviting, whom all the grace and all the abundance of the kingdom of heaven is waiting for? They always exult in the Lord, and rejoice and are glad in their God; and the evils and adversities of the world they bravely suffer, because they are looking forward to gifts and prosperities to come: for we who have put off our earthly birth, and are now created and regenerated by the Spirit, and no longer live to the world but to God, shall not receive God's gifts and promises until we arrive at the presence of God. And yet we always ask for the repulse of enemies, and for obtaining showers, and either for the removal or the moderating of adversity; and we pour forth our prayers, and, propitiating and appeasing God, we entreat constantly and urgently, day and night, for your peace and salvation.[28]

21. Let no one, however, flatter himself, because there is for the present to us and to the profane, to God's worshippers and to God's opponents, by reason of the equality of the flesh and body, a common condition of worldly troubles, in such a way as to think from this, that all those things which happen are not drawn down by you; since by the announcement of God Himself, and by prophetic testimony, it has previously been foretold that upon the unjust should come the wrath of God, and that persecutions which humanly would hurt us should not be wanting; but, moreover, that vengeance, which should defend with heavenly defense those who were hurt, should attend them.

22. And how great, too, are those things which in the meantime are happening in that respect on our behalf! Something is given for an example, that the anger of an avenging God may be known. But the day of judgment is still future which the Holy Scripture denounces, saying, "Howl, for the day of the Lord is at hand, and destruction from God shall come; for, lo, the day of the Lord comes, cruel with wrath and anger, to lay the earth desolate, and to destroy the sinners out of it."[29] And again: "Behold, the day of the Lord comes, burning as an oven; and all the aliens and all that do wickedly shall be as stubble, and the day that comes shall burn them up, says the Lord."[30] The Lord prophesies that the aliens shall be burnt up and consumed; that is, aliens from the divine race, and the profane, those who are not spiritually new-born, nor made children of God. For that those only can escape who have been new-born and signed with the sign of Christ, God says in another place, when, sending forth His angels to the destruction of the world and the death of the human race, He threatens more terribly in the last time, saying, "Go and smite, and let not your eye spare. Have no pity upon old or young, and slay the virgins and the little ones and the women, that they may be utterly destroyed. But touch not any man upon whom is written the mark."[31] Moreover, what this mark is, and in what part of the body it is placed, God sets forth in another place, saying, "Go through the midst of Jerusalem, and set a mark upon the foreheads of the men that sigh and that cry for all the abominations that be done in the midst thereof."[32] And that the sign pertains to the passion and blood of Christ, and that whoever is found in this sign is kept safe and unharmed, is also proved by God's testimony, saying, "And the blood shall be to you for a token upon the houses in which you shall be; and I will see the blood, and will protect you, and the plague of diminution shall not be upon you when I smite the land of Egypt."[33] What previously preceded by a figure in the slain lamb is fulfilled in Christ, the truth which followed afterwards. As, then, when Egypt was smitten, the Jewish people could not escape except by the blood and the sign of the lamb; so also, when the world shall begin to be desolated and smitten, whoever is found in the blood and the sign of Christ alone shall escape.

23. Look, therefore, while there is time, to the true and eternal salvation; and since now the end of the world is at hand, turn your minds to God, in the fear of God; nor let that powerless and vain dominion in the world over the just and meek delight you, since in the field, even among the cultivated and fruitful grain, the tares and the darnel have dominion. Nor say that ill fortunes happen because your gods are not worshipped by us; but know that this is the judgment of God's anger, that He who is not acknowledged on account of His benefits may at least be acknowledged through His judgments. Seek the Lord even late; for long ago, God, forewarning by His prophet, exhorts and says, "Seek the Lord, and your soul shall live."[34] Know God even late; for Christ at His coming admonishes and teaches this, saying, "This is life eternal, that they might know You, the only true God, and Jesus Christ, whom You have sent."[35] Believe Him who deceives not at all. Believe Him who foretold that all these things should come to pass. Believe Him who will give to all that believe the reward of eternal life. Believe Him who will call down on them that believe not, eternal punishments in the fires of Gehenna.

24. What will then be the glory of faith? What the punishment of faithlessness? When the day of judgment shall come, what joy of believers, what sorrow of unbelievers; that they should have been unwilling to believe here, and now that they should be unable to return that they might believe! An ever-burning Gehenna will burn up the condemned, and a punishment devouring with living flames; nor will there be any source whence at any time they may have either respite or end to their torments. Souls with their bodies will be reserved in infinite tortures for suffering. Thus the man will be for ever seen by us who here gazed upon us for a season; and the short joy of those cruel eyes in the persecutions that they made for us will be compensated by a perpetual spectacle,[36] according to the truth of Holy Scripture, which says, "Their worm shall not die, and their fire shall not be quenched; and they shall be for a vision to all flesh."[37] And again: "Then shall the righteous men stand in great constancy before the face of those who have afflicted them, and have taken away their labors. When they see it, they shall be troubled with horrible fear, and shall be amazed at the suddenness of their unexpected salvation; and they, repenting and groaning for anguish of spirit, shall say within themselves, 'These are they whom we had some time in derision, and a proverb of reproach; we fools counted their life madness, and their end to be without honor. How are they numbered among the children of God, and their lot is among the saints! Therefore have we erred from the way of truth, and the light of righteousness has not shined upon us, and the sun rose not on us. We wearied ourselves in the way of wickedness and destruction; we have gone through deserts where there lay no way; but we have not known the way of the Lord. What has pride profited us, or what good has the boasting of riches done us? All those things are passed away like a shadow.'"[38] The pain of punishment will then be without the fruit of penitence; weeping will be useless, and prayer ineffectual. Too late they will believe in eternal punishment who would not believe in eternal life.

25. Provide, therefore, while you may, for your safety and your life. We offer you the wholesome help of our mind and advice. And because we may not hate, and we please God more by rendering no return for wrong, we exhort you while you have the power, while there yet remains to you something of life, to make satisfaction to God, and to emerge from the abyss of darkling superstition into the bright light of true religion. We do not envy your comforts, nor do we conceal the divine benefits. We repay kindness for your hatred; and for the torments and penalties which are inflicted on us, we point out to you the ways of salvation. Believe and live, and do ye who persecute us in time rejoice with us for eternity. When you have once departed there, there is no longer any place for repentance, and no possibility of making satisfaction. Here life is either lost or saved; here eternal safety is provided for by the worship of God and the fruits of faith. Nor let any one be restrained either by his sins or by his years from coming to obtain salvation. To him who still remains in this world no repentance is too late. The approach to God's mercy is open, and the access is easy to those who seek and apprehend the truth. Do you entreat for your sins, although it be in the very end of life, and at the setting of the sun of time; and implore God, who is the one and true God, in confession and faith of acknowledgment of Him, and pardon is granted to the man who confesses, and saving mercy is given from the divine goodness to the believer, and a passage is opened to immortality even in death itself. This grace Christ bestows; this gift of His mercy He confers upon us, by overcoming death in the trophy of the cross, by redeeming the believer with the price of His blood, by reconciling man to God the Father, by quickening our mortal nature with a heavenly regeneration. If it be possible, let us all follow Him; let us be registered in His sacrament and sign. He opens to us the way of life; He brings us back to paradise; He leads us on to the kingdom of heaven. Made by Him the children of God, with Him we shall ever live; with Him we shall always rejoice, restored by His own blood. We Christians shall be glorious together with Christ, blessed of God the Father, always rejoicing with perpetual pleasures in the sight of God, and ever giving thanks to God. For none can be other than always glad and grateful, who, having been once subject to death, has been made secure in the possession of immortality.

NOTES

1. Demetrianus was the Pronconsul (governor) of Africa sometime between 251 and 258, during the reigns of Gallus and Valerian. Cyprian's haughty tone and severe rebukes suggest this was almost certainly written after the complete end of Decius' persecution (251) but prior to the outbreak of the persecution of Valerian (253). Chapter 12, however, suggests that a persecution could have been going on at the time of the letter's publication, as Demetrianus is castigated as a persecutor. A more probable explanation is that Demetrianus had presided over persecutions in the past, though at the time of the letter's composition the persecution had ended. Cyprian would then be rebuking him for sins committed prior, not sins he was currently committing.
2. Prov. 23:9.
3. Prov. 26:4.
4. Matt. 7:6.
5. Cyprian was writing during the middle of the era known in Roman history as the "Crisis of the Third Century," a period lasting from the assassination of Emperor Alexander Severus in 235 to the ascension of Diocletian in 284. During this period, Rome almost collapsed due to the combined pressures of invasion, civil war, plague, and economic depression. This fifty year period saw forty-nine men lay claim to the title of emperor and the secession of Britain, Gaul and large parts of the east.
6. A paraphrase of Wisdom 5:13 in the Septuagint: "Even so we in like manner, as soon as we were born, began to draw to our end, and had no sign of virtue to shew; but were consumed in our own wickedness." The Vulgate translation reads: "So we also being born, forthwith ceased to be: and have been able to shew no mark of virtue: but are consumed in our wickedness."
7. Deut. 6:13.
8. Ex. 29:3.
9. Jer. 25:6.
10. Hag. 1:9.

11. Amos 4:7.
12. Glebe: A Roman legal term, denoting any farm, estate, or parcel of land.
13. Jer. 5:3.
14. The judgments of God are actually manifestations of His mercy.
15. Hos. 4:1-4.
16. Perhaps a reference to Demetrianus' frequenting of the public baths.
17. Because the toga was not worn by soldiers it was regarded as a sign of peace.
18. Isa. 59:1-2.
19. This suggests an atmosphere in which the edicts of persecution are still in force although in practice the authorities have allowed them to lapse, perhaps in the interim between the Decian and Valerian persecutions (251-253). St. Cyprian thus accuses Demetrianus of not being consistent in his application of the law; presumably, the Proconsul is only prosecuting cases against Christians when there is prospect of plunder (see the reference to spoiling of Christian estates in the previous chapter).
20. St. Cyprian, like all of the Fathers, believes that the pagan gods are actually demons pretending to be divinities.
21. Ex. 22:20.
22. Isa. 2:8.
23. A possible reference to the Battle of Abrittus in August of 251, in which the persecuting Emperor Decius was killed and a large part of the Roman army destroyed by the Goths under King Cniva. Decius' successor to the throne, Trebonianus Gallus, secured a humiliating peace treaty with the Goths that allowed them to retire unmolested from Roman territory, retain a large amount of Roman plunder and captives, and promised the Goths an annual tribute or subsidy to deter them from attacking Roman lands.
24. Rom. 12:19.
25. Prov. 20:22.
26. In other words, the essence of simple punishment is not in the physical evil itself, but the pain one endures as a result of the evil. Thus, if a Christian endures the same evils as a pagan (floods, famines, etc.) but does not allow his heart to be disturbed by them, then he cannot be said to be subject to their punishment, even though he undergoes the same trials. The pagans, who face these trials with "a clamorous and complaining impatience" do suffer their punishments, however.
27. Hab. 3:17.
28. Cyprian here is attempting to contradict the notion, common among the pagans, that Christians were unfaithful to Rome and were actually praying for the destruction of the empire. Cyprian says that, on the contrary, the Christians pray for the peace, security and salvation of the empire despite the relentless persecutions against them.
29. Isa. 43:6-9.
30. Mal. 4:1.
31. Ezk. 9:5.
32. Ezk. 9:4.
33. Ex. 12:13.
34. Amos 5:6.
35. John 17:3.
36. This is not too different from St. Thomas Aquinas' teaching that the saints in heaven will see and rejoice in the suffering of the damned, not as taking delight in punishment *qua* punishment, but in that, seeing things through God, they see in the punishment of the damned the ordering of divine justice, in which they do rejoice. See *STh*, Supplementum, Q. 94, Art. 1-2.
37. Isa. 66:24.
38. Wis. 5:1-9.

ON THE VANITY OF IDOLS[1]

1. That those are no gods whom the common people worship, is known from this. They were formerly kings, who on account of their royal memory subsequently began to be adored by their people even in death.[2] Thence temples were founded to them; thence images were sculptured to retain the countenances of the deceased by the likeness; and men sacrificed victims, and celebrated festal days, by way of giving them honor. Thence to posterity those rites became sacred which at first had been adopted as a consolation. And now let us see whether this truth is confirmed in individual instances.

2. Melicertes and Leucothea are precipitated into the sea, and subsequently become sea-divinities. The Castors die by turns, that they may live. Aesculapius is struck by lightning, that he may rise into a god. Hercules, that he may put off the man, is burnt up in the fires of Oeta. Apollo fed the flocks of Admetus; Neptune founded walls for Laomedon, and received—unfortunate builder—no wages for his work. The cave of Jupiter is to be seen in Crete, and his sepulchre is shown; and it is manifest that Saturn was driven away by him, and that from him Latium received its name, as being his lurking-place. He was the first that taught to print letters; he was the first that taught to stamp money in Italy, and thence the treasury is called the treasury of Saturn. And he also was the cultivator of the rustic life, whence he is painted as an old man carrying a sickle.[3] Janus had received him to hospitality when he was driven away, from whose name the Janiculum is so called, and the month of January is appointed. He himself is portrayed with two faces, because, placed in the middle, he seems to look equally towards the commencing and the closing year. The Mauri,[4] indeed, manifestly worship kings, and do not conceal their name by any disguise.

3. From this the religion of the gods is variously changed among individual nations and provinces, inasmuch as no one god is worshipped by all, but by each one the worship of its own ancestors is kept peculiar. Proving that this is so, Alexander the Great writes in the remarkable volume addressed to his mother,[5] that through fear of his power the doctrine of the gods being men, which was kept secret, had been disclosed to him by a priest, that it was the memory of ancestors and kings that was really kept up, and that from this the rites of worship and sacrifice have grown up. But if gods were born at any time, why are they not born in these days also?—unless, indeed, Jupiter possibly has grown too old, or the faculty of bearing has failed Juno.

4. But why do you think that the gods can avail on behalf of the Romans, when you see that they can do nothing for their own worshipers in opposition to the Roman arms? For we know that the gods of the Romans are indigenous. Romulus was made a god by the perjury of Proculus,[6] and Picus, and Tiberinus, and Pilumnus, and Consus, whom as a god of treachery Romulus would have to be worshipped, just as if he had been a god of counsels, when his perfidy resulted in the rape of the Sabines. Tatius also both invented and worshipped the goddess Cloacina; Hostilius, Fear and Paleness. By and by, I know not by whom, Fever was dedicated, and Acca and Flora the harlots. These are the Roman gods. But Mars is a Thracian, and Jupiter a Cretan, and Juno either Argive or Samian or Carthaginian, and Diana of Taurus, and the mother of the gods of Ida; and there are Egyptian monsters, not deities, who assuredly, if they had had any power, would have preserved their own and their people's kingdoms. Certainly there are also among the Romans the conquered Penates whom the fugitive Aeneas introduced there. There is also Venus the bald—far more dishonored by the fact of her baldness in Rome than by her having been wounded in Homer.

5. Kingdoms do not rise to supremacy through merit, but are varied by chance. Empire was formerly held by both Assyrians and Medes and Persians; and we know, too, that both Greeks and Egyptians have had dominion. Thus, in the varying vicissitudes of power, the period of empire has also come to the Romans as to the others. But if you recur to its origin, you must needs blush. A people is collected together from profligates and criminals, and by founding an asylum, impunity for crimes makes the number great; and that their king himself may have a superiority in crime, Romulus becomes a fratricide; and in order to promote marriage, he makes a beginning of that affair of concord by discords. They steal, they do violence, they deceive in order to increase the population of the state; their marriage consists of the broken covenants of hospitality and cruel wars with their fathers-in-law. The consulship, moreover, is the highest degree in Roman honors, yet we see that the consulship began even as did the kingdom. Brutus puts his sons to death, that the commendation of his dignity may increase by the approval of his wickedness. The Roman kingdom, therefore, did not grow from the sanctities of religion, nor from auspices and auguries, but it keeps its appointed time within a definite limit. Moreover, Regulus observed the auspices, yet was taken prisoner; and Mancinus observed their religious obligation, yet was sent under the yoke. Paulus had chickens that fed, and yet he was slain at Cannae. Caius Caesar despised the auguries and auspices that were opposed to his sending ships before the winter to Africa; yet so much the more easily he both sailed and conquered.[7]

6. Of all these, however, the principle is the same, which misleads and deceives, and with tricks which darken the truth, leads away a credulous and foolish rabble. They are impure and wandering spirits, who, after having been steeped in earthly vices, have departed from their celestial vigor by the contagion of earth, and do not cease, when ruined themselves, to seek the ruin of others; and when degraded themselves, to infuse into others the error of their own degradation. These demons the poets also acknowledge, and Socrates declared that he was instructed and ruled at the will of a demon;[8] and thence the Magi have a power either for mischief or for mockery, of whom, however, the chief Hostanes both says that the form of the true God cannot be seen, and declares that true angels stand round about His throne.[9] Wherein Plato also on the same principle concurs, and, maintaining one God, calls the rest angels or demons. Moreover, Hermes Trismegistus speaks of one God, and confesses that He is incomprehensible, and beyond our estimation.[10]

7. These spirits, therefore, are lurking under the statues and consecrated images: these inspire the breasts of their prophets with their afflatus, animate the fibres of the entrails, direct the flights of birds, rule the lots, give efficiency to oracles, are always mixing up falsehood with truth, for they are both deceived and they deceive; they disturb their life, they disquiet their slumbers; their spirits creeping also into their bodies, secretly terrify their minds, distort their limbs, break their health, excite diseases to force them to worship of themselves, so that when glutted with the steam of the altars and the piles of cattle, they may unloose what they had bound, and so appear to have effected a cure.[11] The only remedy from them is when their own mischief ceases; nor have they any other desire than to call men away from God, and to turn them from the understanding of the true religion, to superstition with respect to themselves; and since they themselves are under punishment, [they wish] to seek for themselves companions in punishment whom they may by their misguidance make sharers in their crime. These, however, when adjured by us through the true God, at once yield and confess, and are constrained to go out from the bodies possessed. You may see them at our voice, and by the operation of the hidden majesty, smitten with stripes, burnt with fire, stretched out with the increase of a growing punishment, howling, groaning, entreating, confessing whence they came and when depart, even in the hearing of those very persons who worship them, and either springing forth at once or vanishing gradually, even as the faith of the sufferer comes in aid, or the grace of the healer effects. Hence they urge the common people to detest our name, so that men begin to hate us before they know us, lest they should either imitate us if known, or not be able to condemn us.

8. Therefore the one Lord of all is God. For that sublimity cannot possibly have any peer, since it alone possesses all power. Moreover, let us borrow an illustration for the divine government from the earth. When ever did an alliance in royalty either begin with good faith or end without bloodshed? Thus the brotherhood of the Thebans was broken, and discord endured even in death in their disunited ashes. And one kingdom could not contain the Roman twins, although the shelter of one womb had held them. Pompey and Caesar were kinsmen, and yet they did not maintain the bond of their relationship in their envious power. Neither should you marvel at this in respect of man, since herein all nature consents. The bees have one king, and in the flocks there is one leader, and in the herds one ruler. Much rather is the Ruler of the world one; who commands all things, whatsoever they are, with His word, disposes them by His wisdom, and accomplishes them by His power.

9. He cannot be seen—He is too bright for vision; nor comprehended—He is too pure for our discernment; nor estimated—He is too great for our perception; and therefore we are only worthily estimating Him when we say that He is inconceivable. But what temple can God have, whose temple is the whole world? And while man dwells far and wide, shall I shut up the power of such great majesty within one small building? He must be dedicated in our mind; in our breast He must be consecrated. Neither must you ask the name of God. God is His name.[12] Among those there is need of names where a multitude is to he distinguished by the appropriate characteristics of appellations. To God who alone is, belongs the whole name of God; therefore He is one, and He in His entirety is everywhere diffused. For even the common people in many things naturally confess God, when their mind and soul are admonished of their author and origin. We frequently hear it said, "O God," and "God sees," and "I commend to God," and "God give you," and "as God will," and "if God should grant;" and this is the very height of sinfulness, to refuse to acknowledge Him whom you cannot but know.[13]

10. But that Christ is, and in what way salvation came to us through Him, after this manner is the plan, after this manner is the means. First of all, favor with God was given to the Jews. Thus they of old were righteous; thus their ancestors were obedient to their religious engagements. Thence with them both the loftiness of their rule flourished, and the greatness of their race advanced. But subsequently becoming neglectful of discipline, proud, and puffed up with confidence in their fathers, they despised the divine precepts, and lost the favor conferred upon them. But how profane became their life, what offense to their violated religion was contracted, even they themselves bear witness, since, although they are silent with their voice, they confess it by their end. Scattered and straggling, they wander about; outcasts from their own soil and climate, they are thrown upon the hospitality of strangers.[14]

11. Moreover, God had previously foretold that it would happen, that as the ages passed on, and the end of the world was near at hand, God would gather to Himself from every nation, and people, and place, worshippers much better in obedience and stronger in faith, who would draw from the divine gift that mercy which the Jews had received and lost by despising their religious ordinances. Therefore of this mercy and grace the Word and Son of God is sent as the dispenser and master, who by all the prophets of old was announced as the enlightener and teacher of the human race. He is the power of God, He is the reason, He is His wisdom and glory; He enters into a virgin; being the holy Spirit,[15] He is endued with flesh; God is mingled with man. This is our God, this is Christ, who, as the mediator of the two, puts on man that He may lead them to the Father. What man is, Christ was willing to be, that man also may be what Christ is.

12. And the Jews knew that Christ was to come, for He was always being announced to them by the warnings of prophets. But His advent being signified to them as twofold—the one which should discharge the office and example of a man, the other which should avow Him as God—they did not understand the first advent which preceded, as being hidden in His passion, but believe in the one only which will be manifest in power. But that the people of the Jews could not understand this, was the desert of their sins. They were so punished by their blindness of wisdom and intelligence, that they who were unworthy of life, had life before their eyes, and saw it not.

13. Therefore when Christ Jesus, in accordance with what had been previously foretold by the prophets, drove out from men the demons by His word, and by the command of His voice nerved up the paralytics, cleansed the leprous, enlightened the blind, gave power of movement to the lame, raised the dead again, compelled the elements to obey Him as servants, the winds to serve Him, the seas to obey Him, the lower regions to yield to Him; the Jews, who had believed Him man only from the humility of His flesh and body, regarded Him as a sorcerer for the authority of His power. Their masters and leaders—that is, those whom He subdued both by learning and wisdom—inflamed with wrath and stimulated with indignation, finally seized Him and delivered Him to Pontius Pilate, who was then the procurator of Syria[16] on behalf of the Romans, demanding with violent and obstinate urgency His crucifixion and death.

14. That they would do this He Himself also had foretold; and the testimony of all the prophets had in like manner preceded Him, that it behooved Him to suffer, not that He might feel death, but that He might conquer death, and that, when He should have suffered, He should return again into heaven, to show the power of the divine majesty. Therefore the course of events fulfilled the promise. For when crucified, the office of the executioner being forestalled, He Himself of His own will yielded up His spirit, and on the third day freely rose again from the dead. He appeared to His disciples like as He had been. He gave Himself to the recognition of those that saw Him, associated together with Him; and being evident by the substance of His bodily existence, He delayed for forty days, that they might be instructed by Him in the precepts of life, and might learn what they were to teach. Then in a cloud spread around Him He was lifted up into heaven, that as a conqueror He might bring to the Father man whom He loved, whom He put on, whom He shielded from death; soon to come from heaven for the punishment of the devil and to the judgment of the human race, with the force of an avenger and with the power of a judge; while the disciples, scattered over the world, at the bidding of their Master and God gave forth His precepts for salvation, guided men from their wandering in darkness to the way of light, and gave eyes to the blind and ignorant for the acknowledgment of the truth.

15. And that the proof might not be the less substantial, and the confession of Christ might not be a matter of pleasure, they are tried by tortures, by crucifixions, by many kinds of punishments. Pain, which is the test of truth, is brought to bear, that Christ the Son of God, who is trusted in as given to men for their life, might not only be announced by the heralding of the voice, but by the testimony of suffering. Therefore we accompany Him, we follow Him, we have Him as the Guide of our way, the Source of light, the Author of salvation, promising as well the Father as heaven to those who seek and believe. What Christ is, we Christians shall be, if we imitate Christ.

NOTES

1. In this treatise Cyprian attempts to show the foolishness of paganism by exposing the weakness of the Roman gods in their inability to save their worshippers from peril and their submission before Christian exorcists. St. Augustine, who as bishop of nearby Hippo Regius must have been familiar with this essay, lays out a very similar line of argumentation in *City of God* Book I.

2. This concept of the pagan gods originally being kings was developed by the pagan philosopher Euhemerus of Macedon, who around 300 BC set forward his idea in the book *Sacred History*. This idea, which subsequently became known as *Euhermism*, views the pagan gods as kings or warriors from the distant past around whom mythological elements were allowed to accumulate due to the influence of the poets. Cicero mentions Euhemerism in *De Natura Deorum* 3:53, and the theory is also put forward by the sacred author of the Book of Wisdom 14:12-21, where a Euhemerist explanation is given to explain the origin of idols.

St. Clement of Alexandria wrote, "The native countries of your gods, and their arts and lives, and besides especially their sepulchres, demonstrate them to have been men" (*Exhortation to the Heathen*, 2).

3. According to the Roman's own tradition, Saturn had once been a king in Italy; his reign was known as the Golden Age. See Macrobius *Saturnalia* I,9; Virgil *Aeneid* VII, 49.

4. The Berber Moors of the Numidia.

5. This letter is believed to be apocryphal.

6. According to Livy and Plutarch, it was this Proculus who invented the story of Romulus ascending to heaven to dispel the suspicions of the people that the patricians had in fact murdered him. See Plutarch, *Life of Numa Pompilius* 2:3 and Livy, *History of Rome*, Book I, 1:16.

7. Regulus: Roman general tortured and killed in 250 BC by the Carthaginians during the First Punic War; Mancinus: Roman general who was humiliatingly defeated by the Spanish Numantines in 136 BC; Paulus: Roman consul slain at Cannae fighting Hannibal in 216 BC; Caius Caesar: Julius Caesar, referring to his successful expedition to Egypt in 48 BC in pursuit of his rival Pompeius Magnus.

8. Plato, *Apology* 31c-d, 40a

9. Hostanes, sometimes called Osthanes, was a soothsayer who accompanied King Xerxes of Perisa on his invasion of Greece in 480 BC.

10. Hermes Trismegistus: A fictional character in esoteric Greek philosophy identified with the Greek god Hermes and the Egyptian god Thoth. Several "Hermetic Writings" spuriously attributed to Hermes Trismegistus circulated around the ancient world. The Christians believed him to be a historical person and made him a contemporary of Moses. Many Christian writers, including Lactantius, Augustine, Giordano Bruno, Marsilio Ficino, Campanella and Giovanni Pico della Mirandola considered Hermes Trismegistus to be a wise pagan prophet who foresaw the coming of Christianity.

11. Note that Cyprian does not deny supernatural power to these beings. Like the rest of the Fathers, Cyprian readily acknowledges the pagan gods have power but insists that it is diabolical in origin and only used to bind people in superstition and wickedness.

12. St. Cyprian would not approve of the practice, so popular among modern scholars and song writers, of referring to God casually as "Yahweh." In the following sentences, he goes on to explain that names imply multiplicity, something that cannot be attributed to God.

13. Cyprian means that these are common figures of speech even among the pagans.

14. In other words, the Jews who once testified to God's power by their exaltation even now testify to it by their degradation. St. Augustine makes a similar argument in *City of God*, Book XVIII, Chapter 46.

15. This is a very awkward phrase; some suggest "with the co-operation of the Holy Spirit" is a better rendering.

16. Cyprian is in error here. Pilate, of course, was governor not of Syria but of Judaea.

ON MORTALITY[1]

1. Although in very many of you, dearly beloved brethren, there is a steadfast mind and a firm faith, and a devoted spirit that is not disturbed at the frequency of this present mortality, but, like a strong and stable rock, rather shatters the turbulent onsets of the world and the raging waves of time, while it is not itself shattered, and is not overcome but tried by these temptations; yet because I observe that among the people some, either through weakness of mind, or through decay of faith, or through the sweetness of this worldly life, or through the softness of their sex, or what is of still greater account, through error from the truth, are standing less steadily, and are not exerting the divine and unvanquished vigor of their heart, the matter may not be disguised nor kept in silence, but as far as my feeble powers suffice with my full strength, and with a discourse gathered from the Lord's lessons, the slothfulness of a luxurious disposition must be restrained, and he who has begun to be already a man of God and of Christ, must be found worthy of God and of Christ.

2. For he who wars for God,[2] dearest brethren, ought to acknowledge himself as one who, placed in the heavenly camp, already hopes for divine things, so that we may have no trembling at the storms and whirlwinds of the world, and no disturbance, since the Lord had foretold that these would come.[3] With the exhortation of His fore-seeing word, instructing, and teaching, and preparing, and strengthening the people of His Church for all endurance of things to come, He predicted and said that wars, and famines, and earthquakes, and pestilences would arise in each place; and lest an unexpected and new dread of mischiefs should shake us, He previously warned us that adversity would increase more and more in the last times. Behold, the very things occur which were spoken; and since those occur which were foretold before, whatever things were promised will also follow; as the Lord Himself promises, saying, "But when you see all these things come to pass, know that the kingdom of God is at hand."[4] The kingdom of God, beloved brethren, is beginning to be at hand; the reward of life, and the rejoicing of eternal salvation, and the perpetual gladness and possession lately lost of paradise, are now coming, with the passing away of the world; already heavenly things are taking the place of earthly, and great things of small, and eternal things of things that fade away. What room is there here for anxiety and solicitude? Who, in the midst of these things, is trembling and sad, except he who is without hope and faith? For it is for him to fear death who is not willing to go to Christ. It is for him to be unwilling to go to Christ who does not believe that he is about to reign with Christ.

3. For it is written that the just lives by faith.[5] If you are just, and live by faith, if you truly believe in Christ, why, since you are about to be with Christ, and are secure of the Lord's promise, do you not embrace the assurance that you are called to Christ, and rejoice that you are freed from the devil? Certainly Simeon, that just man, who was truly just, who kept God's commands with a full faith, when it had been pledged him from heaven that he should not die before he had seen the Christ, and Christ had come an infant into the temple with His mother, acknowledged in spirit that Christ was now born, concerning whom it had before been foretold to him; and when he had seen Him, he knew that he should soon die. Therefore, rejoicing concerning his now approaching death, and secure of his immediate summons, he received the child into his arms, and blessing the Lord, he exclaimed, and said, "Now let Your servant depart in peace, according to Your word; for my eyes have seen Your salvation;"[6] assuredly proving and bearing witness that the servants of God then had peace, then free, then tranquil repose, when, withdrawn from these whirlwinds of the world, we attain the harbor of our home and eternal security, when having accomplished this death we come to immortality. For that is our peace, that our faithful tranquillity, that our steadfast, and abiding, and perpetual security.

4. But for the rest, what else in the world than a battle against the devil is daily carried on, than a struggle against his darts and weapons in constant conflicts? Our warfare is with avarice, with immodesty, with anger, with ambition; our diligent and toilsome wrestle with carnal vices, with enticements of the world. The mind of man besieged, and in every quarter invested with the onsets of the devil, scarcely in each point meets the attack, scarcely resists it. If avarice is prostrated, lust springs up. If lust is overcome, ambition takes its place. If ambition is despised, anger exasperates, pride puffs up, wine-bibbing entices, envy breaks concord, jealousy cuts friendship; you are constrained to curse, which the divine law forbids; you are compelled to swear, which is not lawful.

5. So many persecutions the soul suffers daily, with so many risks is the heart wearied, and yet it delights to abide here long among the devil's weapons, although it should rather be our craving and wish to hasten to Christ by the aid of a quicker death; as He Himself instructs us, and says, "Verily, verily, I say unto you, That you shall weep and lament, but the world shall rejoice; and you shall be sorrowful, but your sorrow shall be turned into joy."[7] Who would not desire to be without sadness? Who would not hasten to attain to joy? But when our sadness shall be turned into joy, the Lord Himself again declares, when He says, "I will see you again, and your heart shall rejoice; and your joy no man shall take from you."[8] Since, therefore, to see Christ is to rejoice, and we cannot have joy unless when we shall see Christ, what blindness of mind or what folly is it to love the world's afflictions, and punishments, and tears, and not rather to hasten to the joy which can never be taken away!

6. But, beloved brethren, this is so, because faith is lacking, because no one believes that the things which God promises are true, although He is true, whose word to believers is eternal and unchangeable. If a grave and praiseworthy man should promise you anything, you would assuredly have faith in the promiser, and would not think that you should be cheated and deceived by him whom you knew to be steadfast in his words and his deeds. Now God is speaking with you; and do you faithlessly waver in your unbelieving mind? God promises to you, on your departure from this world, immortality and eternity; and do you doubt? This is not to know God at all; this is to offend Christ, the Teacher of believers, with the sin of incredulity; this is for one established in the Church not to have faith in the house of faith.

7. How great is the advantage of going out of the world, Christ Himself, the Teacher of our salvation and of our good works, shows to us, who, when His disciples were saddened that He said that He was soon to depart, spoke to them, and said, "If you loved me, you would surely rejoice because I go to the Father;"[9] teaching thereby, and manifesting that when the dear ones whom we love depart from the world, we should rather rejoice than grieve. Remembering which truth, the blessed Apostle Paul in his epistle lays it down, saying, "To me to live is Christ, and to die is gain;"[10] counting it the greatest gain no longer to be held by the snares of this world, no longer to be liable to the sins and vices of the flesh, but taken away from smarting troubles, and freed from the envenomed fangs of the devil, to go at the call of Christ to the joy of eternal salvation.

8. But nevertheless it disturbs some that the power of this disease attacks our people equally with the heathens, as if the Christian believed for this purpose, that he might have the enjoyment of the world and this life free from the contact of ills; and not as one who undergoes all adverse things here and is reserved for future joy. It disturbs some that this mortality is common to us with others; and yet what is there in this world which is not common to us with others, so long as this flesh of ours still remains, according to the law of our first birth, common to us with them? So long as we are here in the world, we are associated with the human race in fleshly equality, but are separated in spirit. Therefore until this corruptible shall put on incorruption, and this mortal receive immortality, and the Spirit lead us to God the Father, whatsoever are the disadvantages of the flesh are common to us with the human race. Thus, when the earth is barren with an unproductive harvest, famine makes no distinction; thus, when with the invasion of an enemy any city is taken, captivity at once desolates all; and when the serene clouds withhold the rain, the drought is alike to all; and when the jagged rocks rend the ship, the shipwreck is common without exception to all that sail in her; and the disease of the eyes, and the attack of fevers, and the feebleness of all the limbs is common to us with others, so long as this common flesh of ours is borne by us in the world.

9. Moreover, if the Christian know and keep fast under what condition and what law he has believed, he will be aware that he must suffer more than others in the world, since he must struggle more with the attacks of the devil. Holy Scripture teaches and forewarns, saying, "My son, when you come to the service of God, stand in righteousness and fear, and prepare your soul for temptation."[11] And again: "In pain endure, and in your humility have patience; for gold and silver is tried in the fire, but acceptable men in the furnace of humiliation."[12]

10. Thus Job, after the loss of his wealth, after the death of his children, grievously afflicted, moreover, with sores and worms, was not overcome, but proved; since in his very struggles and anguish, showing forth the patience of a religious mind, he says, "Naked came I out of my mother's womb, naked also I shall go under the earth: the Lord gave, the Lord has taken away; as it seemed fit to the Lord, so it has been done. Blessed be the name of the Lord."[13] And when his wife also urged him, in his impatience at the acuteness of his pain, to speak something against God with a complaining and envious voice, he answered and said, "You speak as one of the foolish women. If we have received good from the hand of the Lord, why shall we not suffer evil? In all these things which befell him, Job sinned not with his lips in the sight of the Lord."[14] Therefore the Lord God gives him a testimony, saying, "Have you considered my servant Job? For there is none like him in all the earth, a man without complaint, a true worshipper of God."[15] And Tobias, after his excellent works, after the many and glorious illustrations of his merciful spirit, having suffered the loss of his sight, fearing and blessing God in his adversity, by his very bodily affliction increased in praise; and even him also his wife tried to pervert, saying, "Where are your righteousnesses? Behold what you suffer."[16] But he, steadfast and firm in respect of the fear of God, and armed by the faith of his religion to all endurance of suffering, yielded not to the temptation of his weak wife in his trouble, but rather deserved better from God by his greater patience; and afterwards Raphael the angel praises him, saying,"It is honorable to show forth and to confess the works of God. For when you prayed, and Sara your daughter-in-law, I did offer the remembrance of your prayer in the presence of the glory of God. And when you buried the dead in singleness of heart, and because you did not delay to rise up and leave your dinner, and went and buried the dead, I was sent to make proof of you. And God again has sent me to heal you and Sara your daughter-in-law. For I am Raphael, one of the seven holy angels, who are present, and go in and out before the glory of God."[17]

11. Righteous men have ever possessed this endurance. The apostles maintained this discipline from the law of the Lord, not to murmur in adversity, but to accept bravely and patiently whatever things happen in the world; since the people of the Jews in this matter always offended, that they constantly murmured against God, as the Lord God bears witness in the Book of Numbers, saying, "Let their murmuring cease from me, and they shall not die."[18] We must not murmur in adversity, beloved brethren, but we must bear with patience and courage whatever happens, since it is written, "The sacrifice to God is a broken spirit; a contrite and humbled heart God does not despise"[19]; since also in Deuteronomy the Holy Spirit warns by Moses and says, "The Lord your God will vex you, and will bring hunger upon you; and it shall be known in your heart if you have well kept His commandments or no."[20] And again: "The Lord your God proves you, that He may know whether you love the Lord your God with all your heart, and with all your soul."[21]

12. Thus Abraham pleased God, who, that he might please God, did not shrink even from losing his son, or from doing an act of parricide. You, who cannot endure to lose your son by the law and lot of mortality, what would you do if you were bidden to slay your son? The fear and faith of God ought to make you prepared for everything, although it should be the loss of private estate, although the constant and cruel harassment of your limbs by agonizing disorders, although the deadly and mournful wrench from wife, from children, from departing dear ones; let not these things be offenses to you, but battles: nor let them weaken nor break the Christian's faith, but rather show forth his strength in the struggle, since all the injury inflicted by present troubles is to be despised in the assurance of future blessings. Unless the battle has preceded, there cannot be a victory: when there shall have been, in the onset of battle, the victory, then also the crown is given to the victors. For the helmsman is recognized in the tempest; in the warfare the soldier is proved. It is a wanton display when there is no danger. Struggle in adversity is the trial of the truth. The tree which is deeply founded in its root is not moved by the onset of winds, and the ship which is compacted of solid timbers is beaten by the waves and is not shattered; and when the threshing-floor brings out the grain, the strong and robust grains despise the winds, while the empty chaff is carried away by the blast that falls upon it.

13. Thus, moreover, the Apostle Paul, after shipwrecks, after scourgings, after many and grievous tortures of the flesh and body, says that he is not grieved, but benefited by his adversity, in order that while he is sorely afflicted he might more truly be proved. "There was given to me," he says, "a thorn in the flesh, the messenger of Satan to buffet me, that I should not be lifted up: for which thing I besought the Lord thrice, that it might depart from me; and He said unto me, 'My grace is sufficient for you, for strength is made perfect in weakness.'"[22] When, therefore, weakness and inefficiency and any destruction seize us, then our strength is made perfect; then our faith, if when tried it shall stand fast, is crowned; as it is written, "The furnace tries the vessels of the potter, and the trial of tribulation just men."[23] This, in short, is the difference between us and others who know not God, that in misfortune they complain and murmur, while adversity does not call us away from the truth of virtue and faith, but strengthens us by its suffering.

14. This trial, that now the bowels, relaxed into a constant flux, discharge the bodily strength; that a fire originated in the marrow ferments into wounds of the fauces[24]; that the intestines are shaken with a continual vomiting; that the eyes are on fire with the injected blood; that in some cases the feet or some parts of the limbs are taken off by the contagion of diseased putrefaction; that from the weakness arising by the maiming and loss of the body, either the gait is enfeebled, or the hearing is obstructed, or the sight darkened—is profitable as a proof of faith.[25] What a grandeur of spirit it is to struggle with all the powers of an unshaken mind against so many onsets of devastation and death! What sublimity, to stand erect amid the desolation of the human race, and not to lie prostrate with those who have no hope in God; but rather to rejoice, and to embrace the benefit of the occasion; that in thus bravely showing forth our faith, and by suffering endured, going forward to Christ by the narrow way that Christ trod, we may receive the reward of His life and faith according to His own judgment! Assuredly he may fear to die, who, not being regenerated of water and the Spirit, is delivered over to the fires of Gehenna; he may fear to die who is not enrolled in the cross and passion of Christ; he may fear to die, who from this death shall pass over to a second death; he may fear to die, whom on his departure from this world eternal flame shall torment with never-ending punishments; he may fear to die who has this advantage in a lengthened delay, that in the meanwhile his groanings and his anguish are being postponed.[26]

15. Many of our people die in this mortality, that is, many of our people are liberated from this world. This mortality, as it is a plague to Jews and Gentiles, and enemies of Christ, so it is a departure to salvation to God's servants. The fact that, without any difference made between one and another, the righteous die as well as the unrighteous, is no reason for you to suppose that it is a common death for the good and evil alike. The righteous are called to their place of refreshing, the unrighteous are snatched away to punishment; safety is the more speedily given to the faithful, penalty to the unbelieving. We are thoughtless and ungrateful, beloved brethren, for the divine benefits, and do not acknowledge what is conferred upon us. Lo, virgins depart in peace, safe with their glory, not fearing the threats of the coming Antichrist, and his corruptions and his brothels. Boys escape the peril of their unstable age, and in happiness attain the reward of continence and innocence. Now the delicate matron does not fear the tortures; for she has escaped by a rapid death the fear of persecution, and the hands and the torments of the executioner. By the dread of the mortality and of the time the lukewarm are inflamed, the slack are nerved up, the slothful are stimulated, the deserters are compelled to return, the heathens are constrained to believe, the ancient congregation of the faithful is called to rest, the new and abundant army is gathered to the battle with a braver vigor, to fight without fear of death when the battle shall come, because it comes to the warfare in the time of the mortality.

16. And further, beloved brethren, what is it, what a great thing is it, how pertinent, how necessary, that pestilence and plague which seems horrible and deadly, searches out the righteousness of each one, and examines the minds of the human race, to see whether they who are in health tend the sick; whether relations affectionately love their kindred; whether masters pity their languishing servants; whether physicians do not forsake the beseeching patients; whether the fierce suppress their violence; whether the rapacious can quench the ever insatiable ardor of their raging avarice even by the fear of death; whether the haughty bend their neck; whether the wicked soften their boldness; whether, when their dear ones perish, the rich, even then bestow anything, and give, when they are to die without heirs. Even although this mortality conferred nothing else, it has done this benefit to Christians and to God's servants that we begin gladly to desire martyrdom as we learn not to fear death. These are trainings for us, not deaths: they give the mind the glory of fortitude; by contempt of death they prepare for the crown.

17. But perchance some one may object, and say, "It is this, then, that saddens me in the present mortality, that I, who had been prepared for confession, and had devoted myself to the endurance of suffering with my whole heart and with abundant courage, am deprived of martyrdom, in that I am anticipated by death." In the first place, martyrdom is not in your power, but in the condescension of

God; neither can you say that you have lost what you do not know whether you would deserve to receive. Then, besides, God the searcher of the reins and heart, and the investigator and knower of secret things, sees you, and praises and approves you; and He who sees that your virtue was ready in you, will give you a reward for your virtue. Had Cain, when he offered his gift to God, already slain his brother? And yet God, foreseeing the fratricide conceived in his mind, anticipated its condemnation. As in that case the evil thought and mischievous intention were foreseen by a foreseeing God, so also in God's servants, among whom confession is purposed and martyrdom conceived in the mind, the intention dedicated to good is crowned by God the judge. It is one thing for the spirit to be wanting for martyrdom, and another for martyrdom to have been wanting for the spirit. Such as the Lord finds you when He calls you, such also He judges you; since He Himself bears witness, and says, "And all the churches shall know that I am the searcher of the reins and heart."[27] For God does not ask for our blood, but for our faith. For neither Abraham, nor Isaac, nor Jacob were slain; and yet, being honored by the deserts of faith and righteousness, they deserved to be first among the patriarchs, to whose feast is collected every one that is found faithful, and righteous, and praiseworthy.[28]

18. We ought to remember that we should do not our own will, but God's, in accordance with what our Lord has bidden us daily to pray. How preposterous and absurd it is, that while we ask that the will of God should be done, yet when God calls and summons us from this world, we should not at once obey the command of His will! We struggle and resist, and after the manner of froward servants we are dragged to the presence of the Lord with sadness and grief, departing hence under the bondage of necessity, not with the obedience of free will; and we wish to be honored with heavenly rewards by Him to whom we come unwillingly. Why, then, do we pray and ask that the kingdom of heaven may come, if the captivity of earth delights us? Why with frequently repeated prayers do we entreat and beg that the day of His kingdom may hasten, if our greater desires and stronger wishes are to obey the devil here, rather than to reign with Christ?

19. Besides, that the indications of the divine providence may be more evidently manifest, proving that the Lord, prescient of the future, takes counsel for the true salvation of His people, when one of our colleagues and fellow priests, wearied out with infirmity, and anxious about the present approach of death, prayed for a respite to himself; there stood by him as he prayed, and when he was now at the point of death, a youth, venerable in honor and majesty, lofty in stature and shining in aspect, and on whom, as he stood by him, the human glance could scarcely look with fleshly eyes, except that he who was about to depart from the world could already behold such a one. And he, not without a certain indignation of mind and voice, rebuked him, and said, "You fear to suffer, you do not wish to depart; what shall I do to you?" It was the word of one rebuking and warning, one who, when men are anxious about persecution, and indifferent concerning their summons, consents not to their present desire, but consults for the future. Our dying brother and colleague heard what he was to say to others. For he who heard when he was dying, heard for the very purpose that he might tell it; he heard not for himself, but for us. For what could he, who was already on the eve of departure, learn for himself? Yea, doubtless, he learned it for us who remain, in order that, when we find the priest who sought for delay rebuked, we might acknowledge what is beneficial for all.

20. To myself also, the very least and last, how often has it been revealed, how frequently and manifestly has it been commanded by the condescension of God, that I should diligently bear witness and publicly declare that our brethren who are freed from this world by the Lord's summons are not to be lamented, since we know that they are not lost, but sent before; that, departing from us, they precede us as travellers, as navigators are accustomed to do; that they should be desired, but not bewailed; that the black garments should not be taken upon us here, when they have already taken upon them white raiment there; that occasion should not be given to the Gentiles for them deservedly and rightly to reprehend us, that we mourn for those, who, we say, are alive with God, as if they were extinct and lost; and that we do not approve wills the testimony of the heart and breast the faith which we express with speech and word. We are prevaricators of our hope and faith: what we say appears to be simulated, feigned, counterfeit. There is no advantage in setting forth virtue by our words, and destroying the truth by our deeds.

21. Finally, the Apostle Paul reproaches, and rebukes, and blames any who are in sorrow at the departure of their friends. "I would not," says he, "have you ignorant, brethren, concerning them which are asleep, that you sorrow not, even as others which have no hope. For if we believe that Jesus died and rose again, even so them which are asleep in Jesus will God bring with Him."[29] He says that those have sorrow in the departure of their friends who have no hope. But we who live in hope, and believe in God, and trust that Christ suffered for us and rose again, abiding in Christ, and through Him and in Him rising again, why either are we ourselves unwilling to depart hence from this life, or do we bewail and grieve for our friends when they depart as if they were lost, when Christ Himself, our Lord and God, encourages us and says, "I am the resurrection and the life: he that believes in me, though he die, yet shall live; and whosoever lives and believes in me shall not die eternally?"[30] If we believe in Christ, let us have faith in His words and promises; and since we shall not die eternally, let us come with a glad security unto Christ, with whom we are both to conquer and to reign forever.

22. That in the meantime we die, we are passing over to immortality by death; nor can eternal life follow, unless it should befall us to depart from this life. That is not an ending, but a transit, and, this journey of time being traversed, a passage to eternity. Who would not hasten to better things? Who would not crave to be changed and renewed into the likeness of Christ, and to arrive more quickly to the dignity of heavenly glory, since Paul the apostle announces and says, "For our conversation is in heaven, from whence also we look for the Lord Jesus Christ; who shall change the body of our humiliation, and conform it to the body of His glory?"[31] Christ the Lord also promises that we shall be such, when, that we may be with Him, and that we may live with Him in eternal mansions, and may rejoice in heavenly kingdoms, He prays the Father for us, saying, "Father, I will that they also whom You have given me be with me where I am, and may see the glory which You have given me before the world was made."[32] He who is to attain to the throne of Christ, to the glory of the heavenly kingdoms, ought not to mourn nor lament, but rather, in accordance with the Lord's promise, in accordance with his faith in the truth, to rejoice in this his departure and translation.

23. Thus, moreover, we find that Enoch also was translated, who pleased God, as in Genesis the Holy Scripture bears witness, and says, "And Enoch pleased God; and afterwards he was not found, because God translated him."[33] To have been pleasing in the sight of God was thus to have merited to be translated from this contagion of the world. And moreover, also, the Holy Spirit teaches by Solomon, that they who please God are more early taken hence, and are more quickly set free, lest while they are delaying longer in this world they should be polluted with the contagions of the world. "He was taken away," says he, "lest wickedness should change his understanding. For his soul was pleasing to God; wherefore hasted He to take him away from the midst of wickedness."[34] So also in the Psalms, the soul that is devoted to its God in spiritual faith hastens to the Lord, saying, "How amiable are your dwellings, O God of hosts! My soul longs, and hastes unto the courts of God."[35]

24. It is for him to wish to remain long in the world whom the world delights, whom this life, flattering and deceiving, invites by the enticements of earthly pleasure. Again, since the world hates the Christian, why do you love that which hates you? And why do you not rather follow Christ, who both redeemed you and loves you? John in his epistle cries, exhorting that we should not follow carnal desires and love the world. "Love not the world, says he, neither the things which are in the world. If any man love the world, the love of the Father is not in him. For all that is in the world is the lust of the flesh, and the lust of the eyes, and the pride of life, which is not of the Father, but of the lust of the world. And the world shall pass away, and the lust thereof; but he who does the will of God abides for ever, even as God abides for ever."[36] Rather, beloved brethren, with a sound mind, with a firm faith, with a robust virtue, let us be prepared for the whole will of God: laying aside the fear of death, let us think on the immortality which follows. By this let us show ourselves to be what we believe, that we do not grieve over the departure of those dear to us, and that when the day of our summons shall arrive, we come without delay and without resistance to the Lord when He Himself calls us.

25. And this, as it ought always to be done by God's servants, much more ought to be done now—now that the world is collapsing and is oppressed with the tempests of mischievous ills; in order that we who see that terrible things have begun, and know that still more terrible things are imminent, may regard it as the greatest advantage to depart from it as quickly as possible. If in your dwelling the walls were shaking with age, the roofs above you were trembling, and the house, now worn out and wearied, were threatening an immediate destruction to its structure crumbling with age, would you not with all speed depart? If, when you were on a voyage, an angry and raging tempest, by the waves violently aroused, foretold the coming shipwreck, would you not quickly seek the harbor? Lo, the world is changing and passing away, and witnesses to its ruin not now by its age, but by the end of things. And do you not give God thanks, do you not congratulate yourself, that by an earlier departure you are taken away, and delivered from the shipwrecks and disasters that are imminent?

26. We should consider, dearly beloved brethren—we should now and always reflect that we have renounced the world, and are in the meantime living here as guests and strangers. Let us greet the day which assigns each of us to his own home, which snatches us hence, and sets us free from the snares of the world, and restores us to paradise and the kingdom. Who that has been placed in foreign lands would not hasten to return to his own country? Who that is hastening to return to his friends would not eagerly desire a prosperous gale, that he might the sooner embrace those dear to him? We regard paradise as our country—we already begin to consider the patriarchs as our parents: why do we not hasten and run, that we may behold our country, that we may greet our parents? There a great number of our dear ones is awaiting us, and a dense crowd of parents, brothers, children, is longing for us, already assured of their own safety, and still solicitous for our salvation.[37] To attain to their presence and their embrace, what a gladness both for them and for us in common! What a pleasure is there in the heavenly kingdom, without fear of death; and how lofty and perpetual a happiness with eternity of living! There the glorious company of the apostles—there the host of the rejoicing prophets—there the innumerable multitude of martyrs, crowned for the victory of their struggle and passion—there the triumphant virgins, who subdued the lust of the flesh and of the body by the strength of their continency—there are merciful men rewarded, who by feeding and helping the poor have done the works of righteousness—who, keeping the Lord's precepts, have transferred their earthly patrimonies to the heavenly treasuries. To these, beloved brethren, let us hasten with an eager desire; let us crave quickly to be with them, and quickly to come to Christ. May God behold this our eager desire; may the Lord Christ look upon this purpose of our mind and faith, He who will give the larger rewards of His glory to those whose desires in respect of Himself were greater!

NOTES

1. Cyprian wrote this treatise to console the faithful at the outset of a terrible plague which ravaged the Roman Empire from 251 and went on intermittently to at least 270. Cyprian's biographer Pontius the Deacon mentions this plague in his narrative of Cyprian's life: "Afterwards there broke out a dreadful plague, and excessive destruction of a hateful disease invaded every house in succession of the trembling populace, carrying off day by day with abrupt attack numberless people, every one from his own house. All were shuddering, fleeing, shunning the contagion, impiously exposing their own friends, as if with the exclusion of the person who was sure to die of the plague, one could exclude death itself also. There lay about the meanwhile, over the whole city, no longer bodies, but the carcases of many, and, by the contemplation of a lot which in their turn would be theirs, demanded the pity of the passers-by for themselves. No one regarded anything besides his cruel gains. No one trembled at the remembrance of a similar event. No one did to another what he himself wished to experience" (*Life and Passion of Cyprian*, 9).
2. "And from the days of John the Baptist until now, the kingdom of heaven suffereth violence, and the violent bear it away" (Matt. 11:12).
3. Matt. 24:7.
4. Luke 21:31.
5. Hab. 2:4; Heb. 10:38.
6. Luke 2:29.
7. John 16:20.
8. John 16:22.
9. John 16:28.
10. Phil. 1:21.
11. Sir. 2:1-2, referred to here as "Holy Scripture."
12. Sir. 2:5.
13. Job 1:21.

14. Job 1:8.
15. Job 2:10.
16. Tob. 2:14.
17. Tob. 12:11-15.
18. Num. 17:10.
19. Ps. 51:17.
20. Deut. 8:2.
21. Deut. 13:3.
22. 2 Cor. 12:7-9.
23. Sir. 27:5.
24. An anatomical term (also known as the oropharyngeal isthmus), the fauces are a part of the oropharynx directly behind the mouth cavity, bounded superiorly by the soft palate, laterally by the palatoglossal arches, and inferiorly by the tongue.
25. This passage is an amazing medical description of the plague then ravaging the empire in Cyprian's day. From this and like descriptions, historians and medical experts believe that the plague Cyprian records was probably small-pox.
26. Note Cyprian's attitude towards suffering: He does not in any way suggest that Christians are immune from the effects of illness or physical pain, nor does he encourage them to seek supernatural healing. Rather, following St. Peter's words, who said, "now for a little while you may have to suffer through various trials, so that the genuineness of your faith, more precious than gold that is perishable even though tested by fire, may prove to be for praise, glory, and honor at the revelation of Jesus Christ" (1 Pet. 1:6-7). Cyprian sees physical suffering as a means of purifying one's faith in God and detaching one's soul from love of the world.
27. Rev. 2:23.
28. A reference to Matt. 8:11.
29. 1 Thess. 4:13-14.
30. John 11:25.
31. Phil. 3:21.
32. John 17:24.
33. Gen. 5:24.
34. Wis. 4:11.
35. Ps. 84:1.
36. 1 John 2:15.
37. St. Cyprian says here that the departed in Christ are "still solicitous for our salvation," implying that the saints in heaven are very aware of what is going on upon earth and interested in the welfare of God's people.

ON WORKS AND ALMS

1. Many and great, beloved brethren, are the divine benefits wherewith the large and abundant mercy of God the Father and Christ both has labored and is always laboring for our salvation: that the Father sent the Son to preserve us and give us life, in order that He might restore us; and that the Son was willing to be sent and to become the Son of man, that He might make us sons of God; humbled Himself, that He might raise up the people who before were prostrate; was wounded that He might heal our wounds; served, that He might draw out to liberty those who were in bondage; underwent death, that He might set forth immortality to mortals. These are many and great boons of divine compassion. But, moreover, what is that providence, and how great the clemency, that by a plan of salvation it is provided for us, that more abundant care should be taken for preserving man after he is already redeemed! For when the Lord at His advent had cured those wounds which Adam had borne, and had healed the old poisons of the serpent, He gave a law to the sound man and bade him sin no more, lest a worse thing should befall the sinner. We had been limited and shut up into a narrow space by the commandment of innocence. Nor would the infirmity and weakness of human frailty have any resource, unless the divine mercy, coming once more in aid, should open some way of securing salvation by pointing out works of justice and mercy, so that by almsgiving we may wash away whatever foulness we subsequently contract.[1]

2. The Holy Spirit speaks in the sacred Scriptures, and says, "By almsgiving and faith sins are purged."[2] Not assuredly those sins which had been previously contracted, for those are purged by the blood and sanctification of Christ. Moreover, He says again, "As water extinguishes fire, so almsgiving quenches sin."[3] Here also it is shown and proved, that as in the laver of saving water the fire of Gehenna is extinguished, so by almsgiving and works of righteousness the flame of sins is subdued. And because in baptism remission of sins is granted once for all, constant and ceaseless labor, following the likeness of baptism, once again bestows the mercy of God.[4] The Lord teaches this also in the Gospel. For when the disciples were pointed out, as eating and not first washing their hands, He replied and said, "He that made that which is within, made also that which is without. But give alms, and behold all things are clean unto you;"[5] teaching hereby and showing, that not the hands are to be washed, but the heart, and that the foulness from inside is to be done away rather than that from outside; but that he who shall have cleansed what is within has cleansed also that which is without; and that if the mind is cleansed, a man has begun to be clean also in skin and body. Further, admonishing, and showing whence we may be clean and purged, He added that alms must be given. He who is pitiful teaches and warns us that pity must be shown; and because He seeks to save those whom at a great cost He has redeemed, He teaches that those who, after the grace of baptism, have become foul, may once more be cleansed.

3. Let us then acknowledge, beloved brethren, the wholesome gift of the divine mercy; and let us, who cannot be without some wound of conscience, heal our wounds by the spiritual remedies for the cleansing and purging of our sins. Nor let any one so flatter himself with the notion of a pure and immaculate heart, as, in dependence on his own innocence, to think that the medicine needs not to be applied to his wounds; since it is written, "Who shall boast that he has a clean heart, or who shall boast that he is pure from sins?"[6] And again, in his epistle, John lays it down, and says, "If we say that we have no sin, we deceive ourselves, and the truth is not in us."[7] But if no one can be without sin, and whoever should say that he is without fault is either proud or foolish; how needful, how kind is the divine mercy, which, knowing that there are still found some wounds in those that have been healed, even after their healing, has given wholesome remedies for the curing and healing of their wounds anew!

4. Finally, beloved brethren, the divine admonition in the Scriptures, as well old as new, has never failed, has never been silent in urging God's people always and everywhere to works of mercy; and in the strain and exhortation of the Holy Spirit, every one who is instructed into the hope of the heavenly kingdom is commanded to give alms. God commands and prescribes to Isaiah: "Cry, says He, with strength, and spare not. Lift up your voice as a trumpet, and declare to my people their transgressions, and to the house of Jacob their sins."[8] And when He had commanded their sins to be charged upon them, and with the full force of His indignation had set forth their iniquities, and had said, that not even though they should use supplications, and prayers, and fastings, should they be able to make atonement for their sins; nor, if they were clothed in sackcloth and ashes, be able to soften God's anger, yet in the last part showing that God can be appeased by almsgiving alone, he added, saying, "Break your bread to the hungry, and bring the poor that are without a home into your house. If you see the naked, clothe him; and despise not the household of your own seed. Then shall your light break forth in season, and your garments shall arise speedily; and righteousness shall go before you, and the glory of God shall surround you. Then shall you cry, and God shall hear you; while yet you are speaking, He shall say, Here I am."[9]

5. The remedies for propitiating God are given in the words of God Himself;

the divine instructions have taught what sinners ought to do, that by works of righteousness God is satisfied, that with the deserts of mercy sins are cleansed. And in Solomon we read, "Shut up alms in the heart of the poor, and these shall intercede for you from all evil."[10] And again: "Whoever stops his ears that he may not hear the weak, he also shall call upon God, and there will be none to hear him."[11] For he shall not be able to deserve the mercy of the Lord, who himself shall not have been merciful; nor shall he obtain anything from the divine pity in his prayers, who shall not have been humane towards the poor man's prayer. And this also the Holy Spirit declares in the Psalms, and proves, saying, "Blessed is he that considers of the poor and needy; the Lord will deliver him in the evil day."[12] Remembering which precepts, Daniel, when king Nebuchadnezzar was in anxiety, being frightened by an adverse dream, gave him, for the turning away of evils, a remedy to obtain the divine help, saying, "Wherefore, O king, let my counsel be acceptable to you; and redeem your sins by almsgivings, and your unrighteousness by mercies to the poor, and God will be patient to your sins."[13] And as the king did not obey him, he underwent the misfortunes and mischiefs which he had seen, and which he might have escaped and avoided had he redeemed his sins by almsgiving. Raphael the angel also witnesses the like, and exhorts that alms should be freely and liberally bestowed, saying, "Prayer is good, with fasting and alms; because alms does deliver from death, and it purges away sins."[14] He shows that our prayers and fastings are of less avail, unless they are aided by almsgiving; that entreaties alone are of little force to obtain what they seek, unless they be made sufficient by the addition of deeds and good works. The angel reveals, and manifests, and certifies that our petitions become efficacious by almsgiving, that life is redeemed from dangers by almsgiving, that souls are delivered from death by almsgiving.

6. Neither, beloved brethren, are we so bringing forward these things, as that we should not prove what Raphael the angel said, by the testimony of the truth. In the Acts of the Apostles the faith of the fact is established; and that souls are delivered by almsgiving not only from the second, but from the first death, is discovered by the evidence of a matter accomplished and completed. When Tabitha, being greatly given to good works and to bestowing alms, fell sick and died, Peter was summoned to her lifeless body; and when he, with apostolic humanity, had come in haste, there stood around him widows weeping and entreating, showing the cloaks, and coats, and all the garments which they had previously received, and praying for the deceased not by their words, but by her own deeds. Peter felt that what was asked in such a way might be obtained, and that Christ's aid would not be wanting to the petitioners, since He Himself was clothed in the clothing of the widows. When, therefore, falling on his knees, he had prayed, and—fit advocate for the widows and poor—had brought to the Lord the prayers entrusted to him, turning to the body, which was now lying washed on the bier, he said, "Tabitha, in the name of Jesus Christ, arise!"[15] Nor did He fail to bring aid to Peter, who had said in the Gospel, that whatever should be asked in His name should be given.[16] Therefore death is suspended, and the spirit is restored, and, to the marvel and astonishment of all, the revived body is quickened into this worldly light once more; so effectual were the merits of mercy, so much did righteous works avail! She who had conferred upon suffering widows the help needful to live, deserved to be recalled to life by the widows' petition.

7. Therefore in the Gospel, the Lord, the Teacher of our life and Master of eternal salvation, quickening the assembly of believers, and providing for them for ever when quickened, among His divine commands and precepts of heaven, commands and prescribes nothing more frequently than that we should devote ourselves to almsgiving, and not depend on earthly possessions, but rather lay up heavenly treasures. "Sell," says He, "your goods, and give alms."[17] And again: "Lay not up for yourselves treasures upon the earth, where moth and rust do corrupt, and where thieves break through and steal. But lay up for yourselves treasures in heaven, where neither moth nor rust does corrupt, and where thieves do not break through nor steal. For where your treasure is, there will your heart be also."[18] And when He wished to set forth a man perfect and complete by the observation of the law, He said, "If you will be perfect, go and sell that you have, and give to the poor, and you shall have treasure in heaven; and come and follow me."[19] Moreover, in another place He says that a merchant of the heavenly grace, and a gainer of eternal salvation, ought to purchase the precious pearl—that is, eternal life—at the price of the blood of Christ, from the amount of his patrimony, parting with all his wealth for it. He says: "The kingdom of heaven is like a merchantman seeking goodly pearls. And when he found a precious pearl, he went away and sold all that he had, and bought it."[20]

8. In fine, He calls those the children of Abraham whom He sees to be laborious in aiding and nourishing the poor. For when Zacchaeus said, "Behold, the half of my goods I give to the poor; and if I have done any wrong to any man, I restore fourfold," Jesus answered and said, "That salvation has this day come to this house, for that he also is a son of Abraham."[21] For if Abraham believed in God, and it was counted unto him for righteousness, certainly he who gives alms according to God's precept believes in God, and he who has the truth of faith maintains the fear of God; moreover, he who maintains the fear of God considers God in showing mercy to the poor. For he labors thus because he believes—because he knows that what is foretold by God's word is true, and that the Holy Scripture cannot lie—that unfruitful trees, that is, unproductive men, are cut off and cast into the fire, but that the merciful are called into the kingdom. He also, in another place, calls laborious and fruitful men faithful; but He denies faith to unfruitful and barren ones, saying, "If you have not been faithful in the unrighteous mammon, who will commit to you that which is true? And if you have not been faithful in that which is another man's, who shall give you that which is your own?"[22]

9. If you dread and fear, lest, if you begin to act thus abundantly, your patrimony being exhausted with your liberal dealing, you may perchance be reduced to poverty; be of good courage in this respect, be free from care: that cannot be exhausted whence the service of Christ is supplied, whence the heavenly work is celebrated. Neither do I vouch for this on my own authority; but I promise it on the faith of the Holy Scriptures, and on the authority of the divine promise. The Holy Spirit speaks by Solomon, and says, "He that gives unto the poor shall never lack, but he that turns away his eye shall be in great poverty;"[23] showing that the merciful and those who do good works cannot want, but rather that the sparing and barren hereafter come to want. Moreover, the blessed Apostle Paul, full of the grace of the Lord's inspiration, says: "He that ministers seed to the sower, shall both minister bread for your food, and shall multiply your seed sown, and shall increase the growth of the fruits of your righteousness, that in all things you may be enriched."[24] And again: "The administration of this service shall not only supply the wants of the saints, but shall be abundant also by many thanksgivings unto God;"[25] because, while thanks are directed to God for our almsgivings and labors, by the prayer of the poor, the wealth of the doer is increased by the retribution of God. And the Lord in the Gospel, already considering the hearts of men of this kind, and with prescient voice denouncing faithless and unbelieving men, bears witness, and says: "Take no thought," saying, "What shall we eat? Or, What shall we drink? Or, Wherewithal shall we be clothed? For these things the Gentiles seek. And your Father knows that you have need of all these things. Seek first the kingdom of God, and His righteousness; and all these things shall be added unto you."[26] He says that all these things shall be added and given to them who seek the kingdom and righteousness of God. For the Lord says, that when the day of judgment shall come, those who have labored in His Church are admitted to receive the kingdom.[27]

10. You are afraid lest perchance your estate should fail, if you begin to act liberally from it; and you do not know, miserable man that you are, that while you are fearing lest your family property should fail you, life itself, and salvation, are failing; and while you are anxious lest any of your wealth should be diminished, you do not see that you yourself are being diminished, in that you are a lover of mammon more than of your own soul; and while you fear, lest for the sake of yourself, you should lose your patrimony, you yourself are perishing for the sake of your patrimony. And therefore the apostle well exclaims, and says: "We brought nothing into this world, neither indeed can we carry anything out. Therefore, having food and clothing, let us therewith be content. For they who will be rich fall into temptation and a snare, and into many and hurtful desires, which drown a man in perdition and in destruction. For covetousness is a root of all evils, which some desiring, have made shipwreck from the faith, and pierced themselves through with many sorrows."[28]

11. Are you afraid that your patrimony perchance may fall short, if you should begin to do liberally from it? Yet when has it ever happened that resources could fail the righteous man, since it is written, "The Lord will not slay with famine the righteous soul?"[29] Elijah in the desert is fed by the ministry of ravens; and a meal from heaven is made ready for Daniel in the den, when shut up by the king's command for a prey to the lions; and you are afraid that food should be wanting to you, laboring and deserving well of the Lord, although He Himself in the Gospel bears witness, for the rebuke of those whose mind is doubtful and faith small, and says: "Behold the fowls of heaven, that they sow not, nor reap, nor gather into barns; and your heavenly Father feeds them: are you not of more value than they?"[30] God feeds the fowls, and daily food is afforded to the sparrows; and to creatures which have no sense of things divine there is no want of drink or food. Do you think that to a Christian—do you think that to a servant of the Lord—do you think that to one given up to good works—do you think that to one that is dear to his Lord, anything will be wanting?

12. Unless you imagine that he who feeds Christ is not himself fed by Christ, or that earthly things will be wanting to those to whom heavenly and divine things are given, whence this unbelieving thought, whence this impious and sacrilegious consideration? What does a faithless heart do in the home of faith? Why is he who does not altogether trust in Christ named and called a Christian? The name of Pharisee is more fitting for you. For when in the Gospel the Lord was discoursing concerning almsgiving, and faithfully and wholesomely warned us to make to ourselves friends of our earthly lucre by provident good works, who might afterwards receive us into eternal dwellings, the Scripture added after this, and said, "But the Pharisees heard all these things, who were very covetous, and they derided Him."[31] Some suchlike we see now in the Church, whose closed ears and darkened hearts admit no light from spiritual and saving warnings, of whom we need not wonder that they condemn the servant in his discourses, when we see the Lord Himself despised by such.

13. Wherefore do you applaud yourself in those vain and silly conceits, as if you were withheld from good works by fear and solicitude for the future? Why do you lay out before you certain shadows and omens of a vain excuse? Yea, confess what is the truth; and since you cannot deceive those who know, utter forth the secret and hidden things of your mind. The gloom of barrenness has besieged your mind; and while the light of truth has departed thence, the deep and profound darkness of avarice has blinded your carnal heart. You are the captive and slave of your money; you are bound with the chains and bonds of covetousness; and you whom Christ had once loosed, are once more in chains. You keep your money, which, when kept, does not keep you. You heap up a patrimony which burdens you with its weight; and you do not remember what God answered to the rich man, who boasted with a foolish exultation of the abundance of his exuberant harvest: "You fool," said He, "this night your soul is required of you; then whose shall those things be which you have provided?"[32] Why do you watch in loneliness over your riches? Why for your punishment do you heap up the burden of your patrimony, that, in proportion as you are rich in this world, you may become poor to God? Divide your returns with the Lord your God; share your gains with Christ; make Christ a partner with you in your earthly possessions, that He also may make you a fellow-heir with Him in His heavenly kingdom.

14. You are mistaken, and are deceived, whosoever you are, that think yourself rich in this world. Listen to the voice of your Lord in the Apocalypse, rebuking men of your stamp with righteous reproaches: 'You say," says He, "I am rich, and increased with goods, and have need of nothing; and know not that you are wretched, and miserable, and poor, and blind, and naked. I counsel you to buy of me gold tried in the fire, that you may be rich; and white raiment, that you may be clothed, and that the shame of your nakedness may not appear in you; and anoint your eyes with eye-salve, that you may see."[33] You therefore, who are rich and wealthy, buy for yourself of Christ gold tried by fire; that you may be pure gold, with your filth burnt out as if by fire, if you are purged by almsgiving and righteous works. Buy for yourself white raiment, that you who had been naked according to Adam, and were before frightful and unseemly, may be clothed with the white garment of Christ. And you who are a wealthy and rich matron in Christ's Church, anoint your eyes, not with the collyrium of the devil,[34] but with Christ's eye-salve, that you may be able to attain to see God, by deserving well of God, both by good works and character.

15. But you who are such as this, cannot labor in the Church. For your eyes, overcast with the gloom of blackness, and shadowed in night, do not see the needy and poor. You are wealthy and rich, and do you think that you celebrate the Lord's Supper, not at all considering the offering, who come to the Lord's Supper without a sacrifice, and yet take part of the sacrifice which the poor man has offered? Consider in the Gospel the widow that remembered the heavenly precepts, doing good even amidst the difficulties and straits of poverty, casting two mites, which were all that she had, into the treasury; whom when the Lord observed and saw, regarding her work not for its abundance, but for its intention, and considering not how much, but from how much, she had given, He answered and said, "Verily I say unto you, that that widow has cast in more than they all into the offerings of God. For all these have, of that which they had in abundance, cast in unto the offerings of God; but she of her penury has cast in all the living that she had."[35] Greatly blessed and glorious woman, who even before the day of judgment hast merited to be praised by the voice of the Judge! Let the rich be ashamed of their barrenness and unbelief. The widow, the widow needy in means, is found rich in works. And although everything that is given is conferred upon widows and orphans, she gives, whom it behooved to receive, that we may know thence what punishment, awaits the barren rich man, when by this very instance even the poor ought to labor in good works. And in order that we may understand that their labors are given to God, and that whoever performs them deserves well of the Lord, Christ calls this the offerings of God, and intimates that the widow has cast in two farthings into the offerings of God, that it may be more abundantly evident that he who has pity on the poor lends to God.[36]

16. But neither let the consideration, dearest brethren, restrain and recall the Christian from good and righteous works, that any one should fancy that he could be excused for the benefit of his children; since in spiritual expenditure we ought to think of Christ, who has declared that He receives them; and not prefer our fellow-servants, but the Lord, to our children, since He Himself instructs and warns us, saying, "He that loves father or mother more than me is not worthy of me, and he that loves son or daughter more than me is not worthy of me."[37] Also in Deuteronomy, for the strengthening of faith and the love of God, similar things are written: "Who say," he says, "unto their father or mother, 'I have not known you;' neither did they acknowledge their children, these have observed Your words, and kept Your covenant."[38] For if we love God with our whole heart, we ought not to prefer either our parents or children to God. And this also John lays down in his epistle, that the love of God is not in them whom we see unwilling to labor for the poor. "Whoso," says he, "has this world's goods, and sees his brother have need, and shuts up his bowels from him, how dwells the love of God in him?"[39] For if by almsgiving to the poor we are lending to God—and when it is given to the least it is given to Christ—there is no ground for any one preferring earthly things to heavenly, nor for considering human things before divine.

17. Thus that widow in the third book of Kings,[40] when in the drought and famine, having consumed everything, she had made of the little meal and oil which was left, a cake upon the ashes, and, having used this, was about to die with her children, Elijah came and asked that something should first be given him to eat, and then of what remained that she and her children should eat. Nor did she hesitate to obey; nor did the mother prefer her children to Elijah in her hunger and poverty. Yea, there is done in God's sight a thing that pleases God: promptly and liberally is presented what is asked for. Neither is it a portion out of abundance, but the whole out of a little, that is given, and another is fed before her hungry children; nor in penury and want is food thought of before mercy; so that while in a saving work the life according to the flesh is contemned, the soul according to the spirit is preserved. Therefore Elijah, being the type of Christ, and showing that according to His mercy He returns to each their reward, answered and said: "Thus says the Lord: The vessel of meal shall not fail, and the cruse of oil shall not be diminished, until the day that the Lord gives rain upon the earth."[41] According to her faith in the divine promise, those things which she gave were multiplied and heaped up to the widow; and her righteous works and deserts of mercy taking augmentations and increase, the vessels of meal and oil were filled. Nor did the mother take away from her children what she gave to Elijah, but rather she conferred upon her children what she did kindly and piously. And she did not as yet know Christ; she had not yet heard His precepts; she did not, as redeemed by His cross and passion, repay meat and drink for His blood. So that from this it may appear how much he sins in the Church, who, preferring himself and his children to Christ, preserves his wealth, and does not share an abundant estate with the poverty of the needy.

18. Moreover, also, (you say) there are many children at home; and the multitude of your children prevents you from giving yourself freely to good works. And yet on this very account you ought to labor the more, for the reason that you are the father of many pledges. There are the more for whom you must beseech the Lord. The sins of many have to be redeemed, the consciences of many to be cleansed, the souls of many to be liberated. As in this worldly life, in the nourishment and bringing up of children, the larger the number the greater also is the expense; so also in the spiritual and heavenly life, the larger the number of children you have, the greater ought to be the outlay of your labors. Thus also Job offered numerous sacrifices on behalf of his children; and as large as was the number of the pledges in his home, so large also was the number of victims given to God.[42]

And since there cannot daily fail to be sins committed in the sight of God, there wanted not daily sacrifices wherewith the sins might be cleansed away. The Holy Scripture proves this, saying: "Job, a true and righteous man, had seven sons and three daughters, and cleansed them, offering for them victims to God according to the number of them, and for their sins one calf."[43] If, then, you truly love your children, if you show to them the full and paternal sweetness of love, you ought to be the more charitable, that by your righteous works you may commend your children to God.

19. Neither should you think that he is father to your children who is both changeable and infirm, but you should obtain Him who is the eternal and unchanging Father of spiritual children. Assign to Him your wealth which you are saving up for your heirs. Let Him be the guardian for your children; let Him be their trustee; let Him be their protector, by His divine majesty, against all worldly injuries. The state neither takes away the property entrusted to God, nor does the exchequer intrude on it, nor does any forensic calumny overthrow it. That inheritance is placed in security which is kept under the guardianship of God. This is to provide for one's dear pledges for the coming time; this is with paternal affection to take care for one's future heirs, according to the faith of the Holy Scripture, which says: "I have been young, and now am old; yet have I not seen the righteous forsaken, nor his seed wanting bread. All the day long he is merciful, and lends; and his seed is blessed."[44] And again: "He who walks without reproach in his integrity shall leave blessed children after him."[45] Therefore you are an unfair and traitorous father, unless you faithfully consult for your children, unless you look forward to preserve them in religion and true piety. You who are careful rather for their earthly than for their heavenly estate, rather to commend your children to the devil than to Christ, are sinning twice, and allowing a double and twofold crime, both in not providing for your children the aid of God their Father, and in teaching your children to love their property more than Christ.

20. Be rather such a father to your children as was Tobias. Give useful and saving precepts to your pledges, such as he gave to his son; command your children what he also commanded his son, saying: "And now, my son, I command you, serve God in truth, and do before Him that which pleases Him; and command your sons, that they exercise righteousness and alms, and be mindful of God, and bless His name always."[46] And again: "All the days of your life, most dear son, have God in your mind, and be not willing to transgress His commandments. Do righteousness all the days of your life, and be not willing to walk in the way of iniquity; because if you deal truly, there will be respect of your works. Give alms of your substance, and turn not away your face from any poor man. So shall it be, that neither shall the face of God be turned away from you. As you have, my son, so do. If your substance is abundant, give alms of it the more. If you have little, communicate of that little. And fear not when you do alms; for you lay up a good reward for yourself against the day of necessity, because that alms do deliver from death, and suffers not to come into Gehenna. Alms is a good gift to all that give it, in the sight of the most high God."[47]

21. What sort of gift is it, beloved brethren, whose setting forth is celebrated in the sight of God? If, in a gift of the Gentiles, it seems a great and glorious thing to have proconsuls or emperors present, and the preparation and display is the greater among the givers, in order that they may please the higher classes; how much more illustrious and greater is the glory to have God and Christ as the spectators of the gift! How much more sumptuous the preparation and more liberal the expense to be set forth in that case, when the powers of heaven assemble to the spectacle, when all the angels come together: where it is not a four-horsed chariot[48] or a consulship that is sought for the giver, but life eternal is bestowed; nor is the empty and fleeting favor of the rabble grasped at, but the perpetual reward of the kingdom of heaven is received!

22. And that the indolent and the barren, and those, who by their covetousness for money do nothing in respect of the fruit of their salvation, may be the more ashamed, and that the blush of dishonor and disgrace may the more strike upon their sordid conscience, let each one place before his eyes the devil with his servants, that is, with the people of perdition and death, springing forth into the midst, and provoking the people of Christ with the trial of comparison—Christ Himself being present, and judging—in these words: "I, for those whom you see with me, neither received buffets, nor bore scourgings, nor endured the cross, nor shed my blood, nor redeemed my family at the price of my suffering and blood; but neither do I promise them a celestial kingdom, nor do I recall them to paradise, having again restored to them immortality. But they prepare for me gifts how precious! How large! With how excessive and tedious a labor procured! And that, with the most sumptuous devices either pledging or selling their means in the procuring of the gift! And, unless a competent manifestation followed, they are cast out with scoffings and hissings, and by the popular fury sometimes they are almost stoned!" Show, O Christ, such givers as these of Yours—those rich men, those men affluent with abounding wealth—whether in the Church wherein You preside and behold, they set forth a gift of that kind—having pledged or scattered their riches, yea, having transferred them, by the change of their possessions for the better, into heavenly treasures! In those spectacles of mine, perishing and earthly as they are, no one is fed, no one is clothed, no one is sustained by the comfort either of any meat or drink. All things, between the madness of the exhibitor and the mistake of the spectator, are perishing in a prodigal and foolish vanity of deceiving pleasures. There, in Your poor, You are clothed and fed; You promise eternal life to those who labor for You; and scarcely are Your people made equal to mine that perish, although they are honored by You with divine wages and heavenly rewards.

23. What do we reply to these things, dearest brethren? With what reason do we defend the minds of rich men, overwhelmed with a profane barrenness and a kind of night of gloom? With what excuse do we acquit them, seeing that we are less than the devil's servants, so as not even moderately to repay Christ for the price of His passion and blood? He has given us precepts; what His servants ought to do He has instructed us; promising a reward to those that are charitable, and threatening punishment to the unfruitful. He has set forth His sentence. He has before announced what He shall judge. What can be the excuse for the laggard? What the defense for the unfruitful? But when the servant does not do what is commanded, the Lord will do what He threatens, seeing that He says: "When the Son of man shall come in His glory, and all the angels with Him, then shall He sit in the throne of His glory: and before Him shall be gathered all nations; and He shall separate them one from another, as a shepherd divides his sheep from the goats: and He shall set the sheep on His right hand, but the goats on the left. Then shall the King say unto them that shall be on His right hand, Come, you blessed of my Father, receive the kingdom that is prepared for you from the foundation of the world. For I was an hungered, and you gave me to eat: I was thirsty, and you gave me to drink: I was a stranger, and you took me in: naked, and you clothed me: I was sick, and you visited me: I was in prison, and you came to me. Then shall the righteous answer Him, saying, Lord, when saw we You an hungered, and fed You? Thirsty, land gave You drink? When saw we You a stranger, and took You in? Naked, and clothed You? Or when saw we You sick, and in prison, and came unto You? Then shall the King answer and say unto them, Verily I say unto you, Insomuch as you did it to one of the least of these my brethren, you did it unto me. Then shall He say also unto those that shall be at His left hand, Depart from me, you cursed, into everlasting fire, which my Father has prepared for the devil and his angels. For I was an hungered, and you gave me not to eat: I was thirsty, and you gave me not to drink: I was a stranger, and you took me not in: naked, and you clothed me not: sick, and in prison, and you visited me not. Then shall they also answer Him, saying, Lord, when saw we You an hungered, or thirsty, or a stranger, or naked, or sick, or in prison, and ministered not unto You? And He shall answer them, Verily I say unto you, In so far as you did it not to one of the least of these, you did it not unto me. And these shall go away into everlasting burning: but the righteous into life eternal."[49] What more could Christ declare unto us? How more could He stimulate the works of our righteousness and mercy, than by saying that whatever is given to the needy and poor is given to Himself, and by saying that He is aggrieved unless the needy and poor be supplied? So that he who in the Church is not moved by consideration for his brother, may yet be moved by contemplation of Christ; and he who does not think of his fellow-servant in suffering and in poverty, may yet think of his Lord, who abides in that very man whom he is despising.

24. And therefore, dearest brethren, whose fear is inclined towards God, and who having already despised and trampled under foot the world, have lifted up your mind to things heavenly and divine, let us with full faith, with devoted mind, with continual labor, give our obedience, to deserve well of the Lord. Let us give to Christ earthly garments, that we may receive heavenly raiment; let us give food and drink of this world, that we may come with Abraham, and Isaac, and Jacob to the heavenly banquet. That we may not reap little, let us sow abundantly.[50] Let us, while there is time, take thought for our security and eternal salvation, according to the admonition of the Apostle Paul, who says: "Therefore, while we have time, let us labor in what is good unto all men, but especially to them that are of the household of faith."[51] But let us not be weary in well-doing, for in its season we shall reap.

25. Let us consider, beloved brethren, what the congregation of believers did in the time of the apostles, when at the first beginnings the mind flourished with greater virtues, when the faith of believers burned with a warmth of faith as yet new. Then they sold houses and farms, and gladly and liberally presented to the apostles the proceeds to be dispensed to the poor; selling and alienating their earthly estate, they transferred their lands there where they might receive the fruits of an eternal possession, and there prepared homes where they might begin an eternal habitation. Such, then, was the abundance in labors, as was the agreement in love, as we read in the Acts of the Apostles: "And the multitude of them that believed acted with one heart and one soul; neither was there any distinction among them, nor did they esteem anything their own of the goods which belonged to them, but they had all things common."[52] This is truly to become sons of God by spiritual birth; this is to imitate by the heavenly law the equity of God the Father. For whatever is of God is common in our use; nor is any one excluded from His benefits and His gifts, so as to prevent the whole human race from enjoying equally the divine goodness and liberality. Thus the day equally enlightens, the sun gives radiance, the rain moistens, the wind blows, and the sleep is one to those that sleep, and the splendor of the stars and of the moon is common. In which example of equality, he who, as a possessor in the earth, shares his returns and his fruits with the fraternity, while he is common and just in his gratuitous bounties, is an imitator of God the Father.

26. What, dearest brethren, will be that glory of those who labor charitably—how great and high the joy when the Lord begins to number His people, and, distributing to our merits and good works the promised rewards, to give heavenly things for earthly, eternal things for temporal, great things for small; to present us to the Father, to whom He has restored us by His sanctification; to bestow upon us immortality and eternity, to which He has renewed us by the quickening of His blood; to bring us anew to paradise, to open the kingdom of heaven, in the faith and truth of His promise! Let these things abide firmly in our perceptions, let them be understood with full faith, let them be loved with our whole heart, let them be purchased by the magnanimity of our increasing labors. An illustrious and divine thing, dearest brethren, is the saving labor of charity; a great comfort of believers, a wholesome guard of our security, a protection of hope, a safeguard of faith, a remedy for sin, a thing placed in the power of the doer, a thing both great and easy, a crown of peace without the risk of persecution; the true and greatest gift of God, needful for the weak, glorious for the strong, assisted by which the Christian accomplishes spiritual grace, deserves well of Christ the Judge, accounts God his debtor. For this palm of works of salvation let us gladly and readily strive; let us all, in the struggle of righteousness, run with God and Christ looking on; and let us who have already begun to be greater than this life and the world, slacken our course by no desire of this life and of this world. If the day shall find us, whether it be the day of reward or of persecution, furnished, if swift, if running in this contest of charity, the Lord will never fail of giving a reward for our merits: in peace He will give to us who conquer, a white crown for our labors; in persecution, He will accompany it with a purple one for our passion.[53]

NOTES

1. "Water quenches a flaming fire, and alms atone for sins" (Sir. 3:29).
2. A rendering of Prov. 16:6: "By mercy and truth iniquity is redeemed; and by the fear of the Lord men depart from evil."
3. Sir. 3:29-30.
4. Christ's death did not make it superfluous to do good works; the grace merited by His death makes meritorious good works truly possible.
5. Luke 11:41.
6. Prov. 20:9.
7. 1 John 1:8.
8. Isa. 58:1.
9. Isa. 58:1-9.
10. Sir. 22:12.
11. Prov. 21:13.

12. Ps. 41:2.
13. Dan. 4:27.
14. Tob. 12:8-9.
15. Acts 9:40.
16. John 14:13; 16:23.
17. Luke 12:33.
18. Matt. 6:19-21.
19. Matt. 19:21.
20. Matt. 13:45-46.
21. Luke 19:8-9.
22. Luke 16:11-12.
23. Prov. 28:27.
24. 2 Cor. 2:9-10.
25. 2 Cor. 9:12.
26. Matt. 6:31-33.
27. Luke 18:29.
28. 1 Tim. 6:7-10.
29. Prov. 10:3.
30. Matt. 5:26.
31. Luke 16:14.
32. Luke 12:20.
33. Rev. 3:17-18.
34. See Cyprian's *On the Dress of Virgins* 7, 14 for the alleged demonic origin of make-up and adornments.
35. Luke 21:3-4.
36. Prov. 19:17.
37. Matt. 10:37.
38. Deut. 33:9. Cyprian takes this verse out of context. It speaks of the Levites, who when Moses came down from Mount Sinai, aided him in destroying the worshipers of the golden calf without regard to family or kinship. The verse does retain a moral lesson on the necessity of believers to put the furtherance of Christ and His kingdom above familial considerations, however.
39. 1 John 3:17.
40. 1 Kings 17. Cyprian is referring to 1 and 2 Samuel as 1 and 2 Kings, so "third Kings" is our 1 Kings.
41. 1 Kings 17:14.
42. Job 1:4-5.
43. Job 1:1-2.
44. Ps. 27:35.
45. Prov. 20:7.
46. Tob. 14:10-11.
47. Tob. 4:5-11.
48. The *quadriga*, the ancient Roman four-horsed chariot, chiefly used as the triumphal car of victorious generals or emperors.
49. Matt. 25:31-46.
50. 2 Cor. 9:6.
51. Gal. 6:10.
52. Acts 4:32.
53. See Letter 8 and Letter 20 for references to the color purple and martyrdom.

ON THE ADVANTAGE OF PATIENCE[1]

1. As I am about to speak, beloved brethren, of patience, and to declare its advantages and benefits, from what point should I rather begin than this, that I see that even at this time, for your audience of me, patience is needful, as you cannot even discharge this duty of hearing and learning without patience? For wholesome discourse and reasoning are then effectually learned, if what is said be patiently heard. Nor do I find, beloved brethren, among the rest of the ways of heavenly discipline wherein the path of our hope and faith is directed to the attainment of the divine rewards, anything of more advantage, either as more useful for life or more helpful to glory, than that we who are laboring in the precepts of the Lord with the obedience of fear and devotion, should especially, with our whole watchfulness, be careful of patience.

2. Philosophers also profess that they pursue this virtue; but in their case the patience is as false as their wisdom also is. For whence can he be either wise or patient, who has neither known the wisdom nor the patience of God? Since He Himself warns us, and says of those who seem to themselves to be wise in this world, "I will destroy the wisdom of the wise, and I will reprove the understanding of the prudent."[2] Moreover, the blessed Apostle Paul, filled with the Holy Spirit, and sent forth for the calling and training of the heathen, bears witness and instructs us, saying, "See that no man despoil you through philosophy and vain deceit, after the tradition of men, after the elements of the world, and not after Christ," because "in Him dwells all the fullness of divinity."[3] And in another place he says: "Let no man deceive himself; if any man among you thinks himself to be wise, let him become a fool to this world, that he may become wise. For the wisdom of this world is foolishness with God. For it is written, 'I will rebuke the wise in their own craftiness.' And again: 'The Lord knows the thoughts of the wise, that they are foolish.'"[4] Wherefore if the wisdom among them be not true, the patience also cannot be true. For if he is wise who is lowly and meek—but we do not see that philosophers are either lowly or meek, but greatly pleasing themselves, and, for the very reason that they please themselves, displeasing God—it is evident that the patience is not real among them where there is the insolent audacity of an affected liberty, and the immodest boastfulness of an exposed and half-naked bosom.[5]

3. But for us, beloved brethren, who are philosophers, not in words, but in deeds, and do not put forward our wisdom in our garb, but in truth—who are better acquainted with the consciousness, than with the boast, of virtues—who do not speak great things, but live them—let us, as servants and worshippers of God, show, in our spiritual obedience, the patience which we learn from heavenly teachings. For we have this virtue in common with God. From Him patience begins; from Him its glory and its dignity take their rise. The origin and greatness of patience proceed from God as its author. Man ought to love the thing which is dear to God; the good which the Divine Majesty loves, it commends. If God is our Lord and Father, let us imitate the patience of our Lord as well as our Father; because it behooves servants to be obedient, no less than it becomes sons not to be degenerate.

4. But what and how great is the patience in God, that, most patiently enduring the profane temples and the images of earth, and the sacrilegious rites instituted by men, in contempt of His majesty and honor, He makes the day to begin and the light of the sun to arise alike upon the good and the evil; and while He waters the earth with showers, no one is excluded from His benefits, but upon the righteous equally with the unrighteous He bestows His undiscriminating rains. We see that with undistinguishing equality of patience, at God's behest, the seasons minister to the guilty and the guiltless, the religious and the impious—those who give thanks and the unthankful; that the elements wait on them; the winds blow, the fountains flow, the abundance of the harvests increases, the fruits of the vineyards ripen, the trees are loaded with apples, the groves put on their leaves, the meadows their verdure; and while God is provoked with frequent, yea, with continual offenses, He softens His indignation, and in patience waits for the day of retribution, once for all determined;[6] and although He has revenge in His power, He prefers to keep patience for a long while, bearing, that is to say, mercifully, and putting off, so that, if it might be possible, the long protracted mischief may at some time be changed, and man, involved in the contagion of errors and crimes, may even though late be converted to God, as He Himself warns and says, "I do not will the death of him that dies, so much as that he may return and live."[7] And again, "Return unto me, says the Lord." And again: "Return to the Lord your God; for He is merciful, and gracious, and patient, and of great pity, and who inclines His judgment towards the evils inflicted."[8] Which, moreover, the blessed apostle referring to, and recalling the sinner to repentance, sets forward, and says: "Or do you despise the riches of His goodness, and forbearance, and long-suffering, not knowing that the patience and goodness of God leads you to repentance? But after your hardness and impenitent heart you store up unto yourself wrath in the day of wrath and of revelation of the righteous judgment of God, who shall render to every one according to his works."[9] He says that God's judgment is just, because it is tardy, because it is long and greatly deferred, so that by the long patience of God man may be benefited for life eternal. Punishment is then executed on the impious and the sinner, when repentance for the sin can no longer avail.

5. And that we may more fully understand, beloved brethren, that patience is a thing of God, and that whoever is gentle, and patient, and meek, is an imitator of God the Father; when the Lord in His Gospel was giving precepts for salvation, and, bringing forth divine warnings, was instructing His disciples to perfection, He laid it down, and said, "You have heard that it is said, You shall love your neighbor, and have your enemy in hatred. But I say unto you, Love your enemies, and pray for them which persecute you; that you may be the children of your Father which is in heaven, who makes His sun to rise on the good and on the evil, and rains upon the just and on the unjust. For if you love them which love you, what reward shall you have? Do not even the publicans the same? And if you shall salute your brethren only, what do you do more (than others)? Do not even the heathens the same thing? Be therefore perfect, even as your Father in heaven is perfect."[10] He said that the children of God would thus become perfect. He showed that they were thus completed, and taught that they were restored by a heavenly birth, if the patience of God our Father dwell in us—if the divine likeness, which Adam had lost by sin, be manifested and shine in our actions. What a glory is it to become like to God! What and how great a felicity, to possess among our virtues, that which may be placed on the level of divine praises!

6. Nor, beloved brethren, did Jesus Christ, our God and Lord, teach this in words only; but He fulfilled it also in deeds. And because He had said that He had come down for this purpose, that He might do the will of His Father;[11] among the other marvels of His virtues, whereby He showed forth the marks of a divine majesty, He also maintained the patience of His Father in the constancy of His endurance. Finally, all His actions, even from His very advent, are characterized by patience as their associate; in that, first of all, coming down from that heavenly sublimity to earthly things, the Son of God did not scorn to put on the flesh of man, and although He Himself was not a sinner, to bear the sins of others. His immortality being in the meantime laid aside, He suffers Himself to become mortal, so that the guiltless may be put to death for the salvation of the guilty. The Lord is baptized by the servant; and He who is about to bestow remission of sins, does not Himself disdain to wash His body in the laver of regeneration. For forty days He fasts, by whom others are feasted. He is hungry, and suffers famine, that they who had been in hunger of the word and of grace may be satisfied with heavenly bread. He wrestles with the devil tempting Him; and, content only to have overcome the enemy, He strives no farther than by words. He ruled over His disciples not as servants in the power of a master; but, kind and gentle, He loved them with a brotherly love. He deigned even to wash the apostles' feet, that since the Lord is such among His servants, He might teach, by His example, what a fellow-servant ought to be among his peers and equals. Nor is it to be wondered at, that among the obedient He showed Himself such, since He could bear Judas even to the last with a long patience—could take meat with His enemy—could know the household foe, and not openly point him out, nor refuse the kiss of the traitor. Moreover, in bearing with the Jews, how great equanimity and how great patience, in turning the unbelieving to the faith by persuasion, in soothing the unthankful by concession, in answering gently to the contradictors, in bearing the proud with clemency, in yielding with humility to the persecutors, in wishing to gather together the slayers of the prophets, and those who were always rebellious against God, even to the very hour of His cross and passion!

7. And moreover, in His very passion and cross, before they had reached the cruelty of death and the effusion of blood, what infamies of reproach were patiently heard, what mockings of contumely were suffered, so that He received the spittings of insulters, who with His spittle had a little before made eyes for a blind man; and He in whose name the devil and his angels is now scourged by His servants, Himself suffered scourgings! He was crowned with thorns, who crowns martyrs with eternal flowers. He was smitten on the face with palms, who gives the true palms to those who overcome. He was despoiled of His earthly garment, who clothes others in the vesture of immortality. He was fed with gall, who gave heavenly food. He was given to drink of vinegar, who appointed the cup of salvation. That guiltless, that just One—nay, He who is innocence itself and justice itself—is counted among transgressors, and truth is oppressed with false witnesses. He who shall judge is judged; and the Word of God is led silently to the slaughter. And when at the cross, of the Lord the stars are confounded, the elements are disturbed, the earth quakes, night shuts out the day, the sun, that he may not be compelled to look on the crime of the Jews, withdraws both his rays and his eyes, He speaks not, nor is moved, nor declares His majesty even in His very passion itself. Even to the end, all things are borne perseveringly and constantly, in order that in Christ a full and perfect patience may be consummated.

8. And after all these things, He still receives His murderers, if they will be converted and come to Him; and with a saving patience, He who is benignant to preserve, closes His Church to none. Those adversaries, those blasphemers, those who were always enemies to His name, if they repent of their sin, if they acknowledge the crime committed, He receives, not only to the pardon of their sin, but to the reward of the heavenly kingdom. What can be said more patient, what more merciful? Even he is made alive by Christ's blood who has shed Christ's blood. Such and so great is the patience of Christ; and had it not been such and so great, the Church would never have possessed Paul as an apostle.

9. But if we also, beloved brethren, are in Christ; if we put Him on, if He is the way of our salvation, who follow Christ in the footsteps of salvation, let us walk by the example of Christ, as the Apostle John instructs us, saying, "He who says he abides in Christ, ought himself also to walk even as He walked."[12] Peter also, upon whom by the Lord's condescension the Church was founded, lays it down in his epistle, and says, "Christ suffered for us, leaving you an example, that you should follow His steps, who did no sin, neither was deceit found in His mouth; who, when He was reviled, reviled not again; when He suffered, threatened not, but gave Himself up to him that judged Him unjustly."[13]

10. Finally, we find that both patriarchs and prophets, and all the righteous men who in their preceding likeness wore the figure of Christ, in the praise of their virtues were watchful over nothing more than that they should preserve patience with a strong and steadfast equanimity. Thus Abel, who first initiated and consecrated the origin of martyrdom, and the passion of the righteous man, makes no resistance nor struggles against his fratricidal brother, but with lowliness and meekness he is patiently slain.[14] Thus Abraham, believing God, and first of all instituting the root and foundation of faith, when tried in respect of his son, does not hesitate nor delay, but obeys the commands of God with all the patience of devotion. And Isaac, prefigured as the likeness of the Lord's victim, when he is presented by his father for immolation, is found patient. And Jacob, driven forth by his brother from his country, departs with patience; and afterwards with greater patience, he suppliantly brings him back to concord with peaceful gifts, when he is even more impious and persecuting. Joseph, sold by his brethren and sent away, not only with patience pardons them, but even bountifully and mercifully bestows gratuitous supplies of grain on them when they come to him. Moses is frequently contemned by an ungrateful and faithless people, and almost stoned; and yet with gentleness and patience he entreats the Lord for those people. But in David, from whom, according to the flesh, the nativity of Christ springs, how great and marvellous and Christian is the patience, that he often had it in his power to be able to kill King Saul, who was persecuting him and desiring to slay him; and yet, chose rather to save him when placed in his hand, and delivered up to him, not repaying his enemy in turn, but rather, on the contrary, even avenging him when slain! In fine, so many prophets were slain, so many martyrs were honored with glorious deaths, who all have attained to the heavenly crowns by the praise of patience. For the crown of sorrows and sufferings cannot be received unless patience in sorrow and suffering precede it.

11. But that it may be more manifestly and fully known how useful and necessary patience is, beloved brethren; let the judgment of God be pondered, which even in the beginning of the world and of the human race, Adam, forgetful of the commandment, and a transgressor of the given law, received. Then we shall know how patient in this life we ought to be who are born in such a state, that we labor here with afflictions and contests. "Because," says He, "you have hearkened to the voice of your wife, and hast eaten of the tree of which alone I had charged you that you should not eat, cursed shall be, the ground in all your works: in sorrow and in groaning shall you eat of it all the days of your life. Thorns and thistles shall it give forth to you, and you shall eat the food of the field. In the sweat of your face shall you eat your bread, till you return into the ground from which you were taken: for dust you are, and to dust shall you go."[15] We are all tied and bound with the chain of this sentence, until, death being expunged, we depart from this life. In sorrow and groaning we must of necessity be all the days of our life: it is necessary that we eat our bread with sweat and labor.

12. Whence every one of us, when he is born and received in the inn of this world,[16] takes his beginning from tears; and, although still unconscious and ignorant of all things, he knows nothing else in that very earliest birth except to weep. By a natural foresight, the untrained soul laments the anxieties and labors of the mortal life, and even in the beginning bears witness by its wails and groans to the storms of the world which it is entering.[17] For the sweat of the brow and labor is the condition of life so long as it lasts. Nor can there be supplied any consolations to those that sweat and toil other than patience; which consolations, while in this world they are fit and necessary for all men, are especially so for us who are more shaken by the siege of the devil, who, daily standing in the battlefield, are wearied with the wrestlings of an inveterate and skillful enemy; for us who, besides the various and continual battles of temptations, must also in the contest of persecutions forsake our patrimonies, undergo imprisonment, bear chains, spend our lives, endure the sword, the wild beasts, fires, crucifixions—in fine, all kinds of torments and penalties, to be endured in the faith and courage of patience; as the Lord Himself instructs us, and says, "These things have I spoken unto you, that in me you might have peace. But in the world you shall have tribulation; yet be confident, for I have overcome the world."[18] And if we who have renounced the devil and the world suffer the tribulations and mischiefs of the devil and the world with more frequency and violence, how much more ought we to keep patience, wherewith as our helper and ally, we may bear all mischievous things!

13. It is the wholesome precept of our Lord and Master: "He that endures," says He, "unto the end, the same shall be saved;"[19] and again, "If you continue," says He, "in my word, you shall be truly my disciples; and you shall know the truth, and the truth shall make you free."[20] We must endure and persevere, beloved brethren, in order that, being admitted to the hope of truth and liberty, we may attain to the truth and liberty itself; for that very fact that we are Christians is the substance of faith and hope. But that hope and faith may attain to their result, there is need of patience. For we are not following after present glory, but future, according to what Paul the apostle also warns us, and says, "We are saved by hope; but hope that is seen is not hope: for what a man sees, why does he hope for? But if we hope for that which we see not, then do we by patience wait for it."[21] Therefore, waiting and patience are needful, that we may fulfil that which we have begun to be, and may receive that which we believe and hope for, according to God's own showing. Moreover, in another place, the same apostle instructs the righteous and the doers of good works, and them who lay up for themselves treasures in heaven with the increase of the divine usury, that they also should be patient; and teaches them, saying, "Therefore, while we have time, let us labor in that which is good unto all men, but especially to them who are of the household of faith. But let us not faint in well-doing, for in its season we shall reap."[22] He admonishes that no man should impatiently faint in his labor, that none should be either called off or overcome by temptations and desist in the midst of the praise and in the way of glory; and the things that are past perish, while those which have begun cease to be perfect; as it is written, "The righteousness of the righteous shall not deliver him in whatever day he shall transgress;"[23] and again, "Hold that which you have, that another take not your crown."[24] Which word exhorts us to persevere with patience and courage, so that he who strives towards the crown with the praise now near at hand, may be crowned by the continuance of patience.

14. But patience, beloved brethren, not only, keeps watch over what is good, but it also repels what is evil. In harmony with the Holy Spirit, and associated with what is heavenly and divine, it struggles with the defense of its strength against the deeds of the flesh and the body, wherewith the soul is assaulted and taken. Let us look briefly into a few things out of many, that from a few the rest also may be understood. Adultery, fraud, manslaughter, are mortal crimes.[25] Let patience be strong and steadfast in the heart; and neither is the sanctified body and temple of God polluted by adultery, nor is the innocence dedicated to righteousness stained with the contagion of fraud; nor, after the Eucharist carried in it, is the hand spotted with the sword and blood.

15. Charity is the bond of brotherhood, the foundation of peace, the holdfast and security of unity, which is greater than both hope and faith, which excels both good works and martyrdoms, which will abide with us always, eternal with God in the kingdom of heaven. Take from it patience; and deprived of it, it does not endure. Take from it the substance of bearing and of enduring, and it continues with no roots nor strength. The apostle, finally, when he would speak of charity, joined to it endurance and patience. "Charity," he says, "is large-souled; charity is kind; charity envies not, is not puffed up, is not provoked, thinks not evil; loves all things, believes all things, hopes all things, bears all things."[26] Thence he shows that it can tenaciously persevere, because it knows how to endure all things. And in another place: "Forbearing one another," he says, "in love, using every effort to keep the unity of the spirit in the bond of peace."[27] He proved that neither unity nor peace could be kept unless brethren should cherish one another with mutual toleration, and should keep the bond of concord by the intervention of patience.

16. What beyond—that you should not swear nor curse; that you should not seek again your goods when taken from you; that, when you receive a buffet, you should give your other cheek to the smiter; that you should forgive a brother who sins against you, not only seven times, but seventy times seven times, but, moreover, all his sins altogether; that you should love your enemies; that you should offer prayer for your adversaries and persecutors? Can you accomplish these things unless you maintain the steadfastness of patience and endurance? And this we see done in the case of Stephen, who, when he was slain by the Jews with violence and stoning, did not ask for vengeance for himself, but for pardon for his murderers, saying, "Lord, lay not this sin to their charge."[28] It behooved the first martyr of Christ thus to be, who, fore-running the martyrs that should follow him in a glorious death, was not only the preacher of the Lord's passion, but also the imitator of His most patient gentleness. What shall I say of anger, of discord, of strife, which things ought not to be found in a Christian? Let there be patience in the breast, and these things cannot have place there; or should they try to enter, they are quickly excluded and depart, that a peaceful abode may continue in the heart, where it delights the God of peace to dwell. Finally, the apostle warns us, and teaches, saying: "Grieve not the Holy Spirit of God, in whom you are sealed unto the day of redemption. Let all bitterness, and anger, and wrath, and clamor, and blasphemy, be put away from you."[29] For if the Christian have departed from rage and carnal contention as if from the hurricanes of the sea, and have already begun to be tranquil and meek in the harbor of Christ, he ought to admit neither anger nor discord within his breast, since he must neither return evil for evil, nor bear hatred.

17. And moreover, also, for the varied ills of the flesh, and the frequent and severe torments of the body, wherewith the human race is daily wearied and harassed, patience is necessary. For since in that first transgression of the commandment strength of body departed with immortality, and weakness came on with death and strength cannot be received unless when immortality also has been received—it behooves us, in this bodily frailty and weakness, always to struggle and to fight. And this struggle and encounter cannot be sustained but by the strength of patience. But as we are to be examined and searched out, diverse sufferings are introduced; and a manifold kind of temptations is inflicted by the losses of property, by the heats of fevers, by the torments of wounds, by the loss of those dear to us. Nor does anything distinguish between the unrighteous and the righteous more, than that in affliction the unrighteous man impatiently complains and blasphemes, while the righteous is proved by his patience, as it is written: "In pain endure, and in your low estate have patience; for gold and silver are tried in the fire."[30]

18. Thus Job was searched out and proved, and was raised up to the very highest pinnacle of praise by the virtue of patience. What darts of the devil were sent forth against him! What tortures were put in use! The loss of his estate is inflicted, the privation of a numerous offspring is ordained for him. The master, rich in estate, and the father, richer in children, is on a sudden neither master nor father! The wasting of wounds is added; and, moreover, an eating pest of worms consumes his festering and wasting limbs. And that nothing at all should remain that Job did not experience in his trials, the devil arms his wife also, making use of that old device of his wickedness, as if he could deceive and mislead all by women, even as he did in the beginning of the world. And yet Job is not broken down by his severe and repeated conflicts, nor the blessing of God withheld from being declared in the midst of those difficulties and trials of his, by the victory of patience. Tobias also, who, after the sublime works of his justice and mercy, was tried with the loss of his eyes, in proportion as he patiently endured his blindness, in that proportion deserved greatly of God by the praise of patience.[31]

19. And, beloved brethren, that the benefit of patience may still more shine forth, let us consider, on the contrary, what mischief impatience may cause. For as patience is the benefit of Christ, so, on the other hand, impatience is the mischief of the devil; and as one in whom Christ dwells and abides is found patient, so he appears always impatient whose mind the wickedness of the devil possesses. Briefly let us look at the very beginnings. The devil suffered with impatience that man was made in the image of God. Hence he was the first to perish and to ruin others.[32] Adam, contrary to the heavenly command with respect to the deadly food, by impatience fell into death; nor did he keep the grace received from God under the guardianship of patience. And in order that Cain should put his brother to death, he was impatient of his sacrifice and gift; and in that Esau descended from the rights of the first-born to those of the younger, he lost his priority by impatience for the pottage. Why was the Jewish people faithless and ungrateful in respect of the divine benefits? Was it not the crime of impatience, that they first departed from God? Not being able to bear the delays of Moses conferring with God, they dared to ask for profane gods, that they might call the head of an ox and an earthen image leaders of their march; nor did they ever desist from their impatience, until, impatient always of docility and of divine admonition, they put to death their prophets and all the righteous men, and plunged even into the crime of the crucifixion and bloodshedding of the Lord. Moreover, impatience makes heretics in the Church, and, after the likeness of the Jews, drives them in opposition to the peace and charity of Christ as rebels, to hostile and raging hatred. And, not at length to enumerate single cases, absolutely everything which patience, by its works, builds up to glory, impatience casts down into ruin.

20. Wherefore, beloved brethren, having diligently pondered both the benefits of patience and the evils of impatience, let us hold fast with full watchfulness the patience whereby we abide in Christ, that with Christ we may attain to God; which patience, copious and manifold, is not restrained by narrow limits, nor confined by strait boundaries. The virtue of patience is widely manifest, and its fertility and liberality proceed indeed from a source of one name, but are diffused by overflowing streams through many ways of glory; nor can anything in our actions avail for the perfection of praise, unless from this it receives the substance of its perfection. It is patience which both commends and keeps us to God. It is patience, too, which assuages anger, which bridles the tongue, governs the mind, guards peace, rules discipline, breaks the force of lust, represses the violence of pride, extinguishes the fire of enmity, checks the power of the rich, soothes the want of the poor, protects a blessed integrity in virgins, a careful purity in widows, in those who are united and married a single affection. It makes men humble in prosperity, brave in adversity, gentle towards wrongs and contempts. It teaches us quickly to pardon those who wrong us; and if you yourself do wrong, to entreat long and earnestly. It resists temptations, suffers persecutions, perfects passions and martyrdoms. It is patience which firmly fortifies the foundations of our faith. It is this which lifts up on high the increase of our hope. It is this which directs our doing, that we may hold fast the way of Christ while we walk by His patience. It is this that makes us to persevere as sons of God, while we imitate our Father's patience.

21. But since I know, beloved brethren, that very many are eager, either on account of the burden or the pain of smarting wrongs, to be quickly avenged of those who act harshly and rage against them, we must not withhold the fact in the furthest particular, that placed as we are in the midst of these storms of a jarring world, and, moreover, the persecutions both of Jews or Gentiles, and heretics, we may patiently wait for the day of [God's] vengeance, and not hurry to revenge our suffering with a querulous haste, since it is written, "Wait upon me, says the Lord, in the day of my rising up for a testimony; for my judgment is to the congregations of the nations, that I may take hold on the kings, and pour out upon them my fury."[33] The Lord commands us to wait, and to bear with brave patience the day of future vengeance; and He also speaks in the Apocalypse, saying, "Seal not the sayings of the prophecy of this book: for now the time is at hand for them that persevere in injuring to injure, and for him that is filthy to be filthy still; but for him that is righteous to do things still more righteous, and likewise for him that is holy to do things still more holy. Behold, I come quickly; and my reward is with me, to render to every man according to his deeds."[34] Whence also the martyrs, crying out and hastening with grief breaking forth to their revenge, are bidden still to wait, and to give patience for the times to be fulfilled and the martyrs to be completed. "And when He had opened," says he, "the fifth seal, I saw under the altar of God the souls of them that were slain for the word of God, and for their testimony; and they cried with a loud voice, saying, 'How long, O Lord, holy and true, do You not judge and avenge our blood on them that dwell on the earth?' And there were given to them each white robes; and it was said unto them that they should rest yet for a little season, until the number of their fellow-servants and brethren is fulfilled, who afterwards shall be slain after their example."[35]

22. But when shall come the divine vengeance for the righteous blood, the Holy Spirit declares by Malachi the prophet, saying, "Behold, the day of the Lord comes, burning as an oven; and all the aliens and all the wicked shall be stubble; and the day that comes shall burn them up, says the Lord."[36] And this we read also in the Psalms, where the approach of God the Judge is announced as worthy to be reverenced for the majesty of His judgment: "God shall come manifest, our God, and I shall not keep silence; a fire shall burn before Him, and round about Him a great tempest. He shall call the heaven above, and the earth beneath, that He may separate His people. Gather His saints together unto Him, who establish

His covenant in sacrifices; and the heavens shall declare His righteousness, for God is the Judge."[37] And Isaiah foretells the same things, saying: "For, behold, the Lord shall come like a fire, and His chariot as a storm, to render vengeance in anger; for in the fire of the Lord they shall be judged, and with His sword shall they be wounded."[38] And again: "The Lord God of hosts shall go forth, and shall crumble the war to pieces; He shall stir up the battle, and shall cry out against His enemies with strength, I have held my peace; shall I always hold my peace?"[39]

23. But who is this that says that he has held his peace before, and will not hold his peace for ever? Surely it is He who was led as a sheep to the slaughter; and as a lamb before its shearer is without voice, so He opened not His mouth. Surely it is He who did not cry, nor was His voice heard in the streets. Surely He who was not rebellious, neither contradicted, when He offered His back to stripes, and His cheeks to the palms of the hands; neither turned away His face from the foulness of spitting. Surely it is He who, when He was accused by the priests and elders, answered nothing, and, to the wonder of Pilate, kept a most patient silence. This is He who, although He was silent in His passion, yet by and by will not be silent in His vengeance. This is our God, that is, not the God of all, but of the faithful and believing; and He, when He shall come manifest in His second advent, will not be silent. For although He came first shrouded in humility, yet He shall come manifest in power.

24. Let us wait for Him, beloved brethren, our Judge and Avenger, who shall equally avenge with Himself the congregation of His Church, and the number of all the righteous from the beginning of the world. Let him who hurries, and is too impatient for his revenge, consider that even He Himself is not yet avenged who is the Avenger. God the Father ordained His Son to be adored; and the Apostle Paul, mindful of the divine command, lays it down, and says: "God has exalted Him, and given Him a name which is above every name, that in the name of Jesus every knee should bow, of things heavenly, and things earthly, and things beneath."[40] And in the Apocalypse the angel withstands John, who wishes to worship him, and says: "Do it not; for I am your fellow-servant, and of your brethren. Worship Jesus the Lord."[41] How great is the Lord Jesus, and how great is His patience, that He who is adored in heaven is not yet avenged on earth! Let us, beloved brethren, consider His patience in our persecutions and sufferings; let us give an obedience full of expectation to His advent; and let us not hasten, servants as we are, to be defended before our Lord with irreligious and immodest eagerness. Let us rather press onward and labor, and, watching with our whole heart, and steadfast to all endurance, let us keep the Lord's precepts; so that when that day of anger and vengeance shall come, we may not be punished with the impious and sinners, but may be honored with the righteous and those that fear God.

NOTES

1. This treatise, written around 256, draws heavily on Tertullian's treatise *Of Patience*.
2. Isa. 29:14.
3. Col. 2:8,10.
4. 1 Cor. 3:18-20.
5. A reference to the Cynic philosophers, who went about bare foot and half-naked, shocking Greco-Roman society by sleeping in tubs by the crossroads and making love in public, making a cult out of shamelessness and immodesty.
6. Unlike some modern theologians who prefer to try to harmonize the positive aspects of all religions by appealing to the "religious sense" in man, St. Cyprian teaches that the very existence of pagan religious rites is a "continual offense" to God that is only tolerated because of His longsuffering in holding off the Day of Judgmemt, not because of any intrinsic good in any non-Christian religion.
7. A paraphrase of Ezk. 18:23: "Is it my will that a sinner should die, saith the Lord God, and not that he should be converted from his ways, and live?"
8. Zech. 1:3, Joel 2:13.
9. Rom. 2:4-6.
10. Matt. 5:43-48.
11. John 6:38.
12. 1 John 2:6.
13. 1 Pet. 2:21.
14. Scripture does not say that Abel did not resist Cain's attack, but it has been tradition to portray it so, since the death of Abel is a type of the death of Christ, who was led to the cross "dumb as a lamb before his shearer" (Isa. 53:7).
15. Gen. 3:17-19.
16. Perhaps a reference to the inn mentioned in the parable of the Good Samaritan in Luke 10: 25-37. According to a common interpretation of the Fathers, the inn is usually seen as the Church. Origen says, "The man who was going down is Adam. Jerusalem is paradise, and Jericho is the world. The robbers are hostile powers. The priest is the Law, the Levite is the prophets, and the Samaritan is Christ. The wounds are disobedience, the beast is the Lord's body, the [inn], which accepts all who wish to enter, is the Church. ... The manager of the [inn] is the head of the Church, to whom its care has been entrusted. And the fact that the Samaritan promises he will return represents the Savior's second coming (Homily 34.4). It is thus unusual that Cyprian should use the word "inn" with reference to the world; he does so probably because the inn, like the world, is only a temporary stop-over on a longer journey, calling to mind our status as *viators*, way-farers, in this life.
17. St. Augustine expresses similar thoughts on infancy in *Confessions*, Book I:6-8.
18. John 16:33.
19. Matt. 10:22.
20. John 8:31-32.
21. Rom. 8:24-25.
22. Gal. 6:10.
23. Ezk. 33:12.
24. Rev. 3:11.
25. Mortal sins.
26. 1 Cor. 3:4-7.
27. Eph. 4:2-3.

28. Acts 7:60.
29. Eph. 4:30-31.
30. Sir. 2:4-5. Note that Cyprian uses the formula "It is written," denoting that what follows is regarded as Sacred Scripture.
31. Job 1-2:10; Tob. 2:10.
32. Like many other Fathers, Cyprian here speculates on the cause of the devil's fall from grace. Whereas Cyprian attributes it to envy at the glory bestowed upon man by being made in God's image (which explains why the devil was so desirous to see the ruin of our first parents), other Fathers and later theologians would see the Incarnation as the reason for Satan's fall; the devil, full of pride, foresaw that God would humble Himself to take on human flesh and was revolted by the idea. Both interpretations center the source of the devil's fall on a contempt for mankind.
33. Zeph. 3:8.
34. Rev. 22:10-12.
35. Rev. 6:9-11.
36. Mal. 4:1.
37. Ps. 50:3-6.
38. Is. 66:15-16.
39. Is. 42:13-14.
40. Phil. 2:9-10.
41. Rev. 19:10.

ON JEALOUSY AND ENVY

1. To be jealous of what you see to be good, and to be envious of those who are better than yourself, seems, beloved brethren, in the eyes of some people to be a slight and petty wrong; and, being thought trifling and of small account, it is not feared; not being feared, it is condoned; being condoned, it is not easily shunned: and it thus becomes a dark and hidden mischief, which, as it is not perceived so as to be guarded against by the prudent, secretly distresses incautious minds. But, moreover, the Lord bade us be prudent, and charged us to watch with careful solicitude, lest the adversary, who is always on the watch and always lying in wait, should creep stealthily into our breast, and blow up a flame from the sparks, magnifying small things into the greatest; and so, while soothing the unguarded and careless with a milder air and a softer breeze, should stir up storms and whirlwinds, and bring about the destruction of faith and the shipwreck of salvation and of life. Therefore, beloved brethren, we must be on our guard, and strive with all our powers to repel, with solicitous and full watch-fullness, the enemy, raging and aiming his darts against every part of our body in which we can be stricken and wounded, in accordance with what the Apostle Peter, in his epistle, forewarns and teaches, saying, "Be sober, and watch; because your adversary the devil, as a roaring lion, goes about seeking any one to devour."[1]

2. He goes about every one of us; and even as an enemy besieging those who are shut up (in a city), he examines the walls, and tries whether there is any part of the walls less firm and less trustworthy, by entrance through which he may penetrate to the inside. He presents to the eyes seductive forms and easy pleasures, that he may destroy chastity by the sight. He tempts the ears with harmonious music, that by the hearing of sweet sounds he may relax and enervate Christian vigor. He provokes the tongue by reproaches; he instigates the hand by exasperating wrongs to the wrecklessness of murder; to make the cheat, he presents dishonest gains; to take captive the soul by money, he heaps together mischievous hoards; he promises earthly honors, that he may deprive of heavenly ones; he makes a show of false things, that he may steal away the true; and when he cannot hiddenly deceive, he threatens plainly and openly, holding forth the fear of turbulent persecution to vanquish God's servants—always restless, and always hostile, crafty in peace, and fierce in persecution.

3. Wherefore, beloved brethren, against all the devil's deceiving snares or open threatenings, the mind ought to stand arrayed and armed, ever as ready to repel as the foe is ever ready to attack. And since those darts of his which creep on us in concealment are more frequent, and his more hidden and secret hurling of them is the more severely and frequently effectual to our wounding, in proportion as it is the less perceived, let us also be watchful to understand and repel these, among which is the evil of jealousy and envy. And if any one closely look into this, he will find that nothing should be more guarded against by the Christian, nothing more carefully watched, than being taken captive by envy and malice, that none, entangled in the blind snares of a deceitful enemy, in that the brother is turned by envy to hatred of his brother, should himself be unwittingly destroyed by his own sword. That we may be able more fully to collect and more plainly to perceive this, let us recur to its fount and origin. Let us consider whence arises jealousy, and when and how it begins. For so mischievous an evil will be more easily shunned by us, if both the source and the magnitude of that same evil be known.

4. From this source, even at the very beginnings of the world, the devil was the first who both perished (himself) and destroyed (others). He who was sustained in angelic majesty, he who was accepted and beloved of God, when he beheld man made in the image of God, broke forth into jealousy with malevolent envy—not hurling down another by the instinct of his jealousy before he himself was first hurled down by jealousy, captive before he takes captive, ruined before he ruins others. While, at the instigation of jealousy, he robs man of the grace of immortality conferred, he himself has lost that which he had previously been. How great an evil is that, beloved brethren, whereby an angel fell, whereby that lofty and illustrious grandeur could be defrauded and overthrown, whereby he who deceived was himself deceived! Thenceforth envy rages on the earth, in that he who is about to perish by jealousy obeys the author of his ruin, imitating the devil in his jealousy; as it is written, "But through envy of the devil death entered into the world. Therefore they who are on his side imitate him."[2]

5. Hence, in fine, began the primal hatreds of the new brotherhood, hence the abominable fratricides, in that the unrighteous Cain is jealous of the righteous Abel, in that the wicked persecutes the good with envy and jealousy. So far prevailed the rage of envy to the consummation of that deed of wickedness, that neither the love of his brother, nor the immensity of the crime, nor the fear of God, nor the penalty of the sin, was considered. He was unrighteously stricken who had been the first to show righteousness; he endured hatred who had not known how to hate; he was impiously slain, who, dying, did not resist. And that Esau was hostile to his brother Jacob, arose from jealousy also. For because the latter had received his father's blessing, the former was inflamed to a persecuting hatred by the brands of jealousy. And that Joseph was sold by his brethren, the reason of their selling him proceeded from envy. When in simplicity, and as a brother to brethren, he set forth to them the prosperity which had been shown to him in visions, their malevolent disposition broke forth into envy. Moreover, that Saul the king hated David, so as to seek by often repeated persecutions to kill him—innocent, merciful, gentle, patient in meekness—what else was the provocation save the spur of jealousy? Because, when Goliath was slain, and by the aid and condescension of God so great an enemy was routed, the wondering people burst forth with the suffrage of acclamation into praises of David, Saul through jealousy conceived the rage of enmity and persecution. And, not to go to the length of numbering each one, let us observe the destruction of a people that perished once for all. Did not the Jews perish for this reason, that they chose rather to envy Christ than to believe Him? Disparaging those great works which He did, they were deceived by blinding jealousy, and could not open the eyes of their heart to the knowledge of divine things.

6. Considering which things, beloved brethren, let us with vigilance and courage fortify our hearts dedicated to God against such a destructiveness of evil. Let the death of others avail for our safety; let the punishment of the unwise confer health upon the prudent. Moreover, there is no ground for any one to suppose that evil of that kind is confined in one form, or restrained within brief limits in a narrow boundary. The mischief of jealousy, manifold and fruitful, extends widely. It is the root of all evils, the fountain of disasters, the nursery of crimes, the material of transgressions. Thence arises hatred, thence proceeds animosity. Jealousy inflames avarice, in that one cannot be content with what is his own, while he sees another more wealthy. Jealousy stirs up ambition, when one sees another more exalted in honors. When jealousy darkens our perceptions, and reduces the secret agencies of the mind under its command, the fear of God is despised, the teaching of Christ is neglected, the day of judgment is not anticipated. Pride inflates, cruelty embitters, faithlessness prevaricates, impatience agitates, discord rages, anger grows hot; nor can he who has become the subject of a foreign authority any longer restrain or govern himself. By this the bond of the Lord's peace is broken; by this is violated brotherly charity; by this truth is adulterated, unity is divided; men plunge into heresies and schisms when priests are disparaged, when bishops are envied, when a man complains that he himself was not rather ordained, or disdains to suffer that another should be put over him. Hence the man who is haughty through jealousy, and perverse through envy, kicks, hence he revolts, in anger and malice the opponent, not of the man, but of the honor.

7. But what a gnawing worm of the soul is it, what a plague-spot of our thoughts, what a rust of the heart, to be jealous of another, either in respect of his virtue or of his happiness; that is, to hate in him either his own deservings or the divine benefits—to turn the advantages of others into one's own mischief—to be tormented by the prosperity of illustrious men—to make other people's glory one's own penalty, and, as it were, to apply a sort of executioner to one's own breast, to bring the tormentors to one's own thoughts and feelings, that they may tear us with intestinal pangs, and may smite the secret recesses of the heart with the hoof of malevolence. To such, no food is joyous, no drink can be cheerful. They are ever sighing, and groaning, and grieving; and since envy is never put off by the envious, the possessed heart is rent without intermission day and night. Other ills have their limit; and whatever wrong is done, is bounded by the completion of the crime. In the adulterer the offense ceases when the violation is perpetrated; in the case of the robber, the crime is at rest when the homicide is committed; and the possession of the booty puts an end to the rapacity of the thief; and the completed deception places a limit to the wrong of the cheat. Jealousy has no limit; it is an evil continually enduring, and a sin without end. In proportion as he who is envied has the advantage of a greater success, in that proportion the envious man burns with the fires of jealousy to an increased heat.

8. Hence the threatening countenance, the lowering aspect, pallor in the face, trembling on the lips, gnashing of the teeth, mad words, unbridled revilings, a hand prompt for the violence of slaughter; even if for the time deprived of a sword, yet armed with the hatred of an infuriate mind. And accordingly the Holy Spirit says in the Psalms: "Be not jealous against him who walks prosperously in his way."[3] And again: "The wicked shall observe the righteous, and shall gnash upon him with his teeth. But God shall laugh at him; for He sees that his day is coming."[4] The blessed Apostle Paul designates and points out these when he says, "The poison of asps is under their lips, and their mouth is full of cursing and bitterness. Their feet are swift to shed blood, destruction and misery are in their ways, who have not known the way of peace; neither is the fear of God before their eyes."[5]

9. The mischief is much more trifling, and the danger less, when the limbs are wounded with a sword. The cure is easy where the wound is manifest; and when the medicament is applied, the sore that is seen is quickly brought to health. The wounds of jealousy are hidden and secret; nor do they admit the remedy of a healing cure, since they have shut themselves in blind suffering within the lurking-places of the conscience. Whoever you are that are envious and malignant, observe how crafty, mischievous, and hateful you are to those whom you hate. Yet you are the enemy of no one's well-being more than your own. Whoever he is whom you persecute with jealousy, he can evade and escape you. You cannot escape yourself. Wherever you may be, your adversary is with you; your enemy is always in your own breast; your mischief is shut up within; you are tied and bound with the links of chains from which you cannot extricate yourself; you are captive under the tyranny of jealousy; nor will any consolations help you. It is a persistent evil to persecute a man who belongs to the grace of God. It is a calamity without remedy to hate the happy.

10. And therefore, beloved brethren, the Lord, taking thought for this risk, that none should fall into the snare of death through jealousy of his brother, when His disciples asked Him which among them should be the greatest, said, "Whosoever shall be least among you all, the same shall be great."[6] He cut off all envy by His reply. He plucked out and tore away every cause and matter of gnawing envy. A disciple of Christ must not be jealous, must not be envious. With us there can be no contest for exaltation; from humility we grow to the highest attainments; we have learned in what way we may be pleasing. And finally, the Apostle Paul, instructing and warning, that we who, illuminated by the light of Christ, have escaped from the darkness of the conversation of night, should walk in the deeds and works of light, writes and says, "The night has passed over, and the day is approaching: let us therefore cast away the works of darkness, and let us put upon us the armor of light. Let us walk honestly, as in the day; not in rioting and drunkenness, not in lusts and wantonness, not in strifes and jealousy."[7] If the darkness has departed from your breast, if the night is scattered therefrom, if the gloom is chased away, if the brightness of day has illuminated your senses, if you have begun to be a man of light, do those things which are Christ's, because Christ is the Light and the Day.

11. Why do you rush into the darkness of jealousy? Why do you enfold yourself in the cloud of malice? Why do you quench all the light of peace and charity in the blindness of envy? Why do you return to the devil, whom you had renounced? Why do you stand like Cain? For that he who is jealous of his brother, and has him in hatred, is bound by the guilt of homicide, the Apostle John declares in his epistle, saying, "Whosoever hates his brother is a murderer; and you know that no murderer has life abiding in him."[8] And again: "He that says he is in the light, and hates his brother, is in darkness even until now, and walks in darkness, and knows not whither he goes, because that darkness has blinded his eyes."[9] "Whosoever hates," says he, "his brother, walks in darkness, and knows not whither he goes."[10] For he goes unconsciously to Gehenna, in ignorance and blindness; he is hurrying into punishment, departing, that is, from the light of Christ, who warns and says, "I am the light of the world. He that follows me shall not walk in darkness, but shall have the light of life."[11] But he follows Christ who stands in His precepts, who walks in the way of His teaching, who follows His footsteps and His ways, who imitates that which Christ both did and taught; in accordance with what Peter also exhorts and warns, saying, "Christ suffered for us, leaving you an example that you should follow His steps."[12]

12. We ought to remember by what name Christ calls His people, by what title He names His flock. He calls them sheep, that their Christian innocence may be like that of sheep; He calls them lambs, that their simplicity of mind may imitate the simple nature of lambs. Why does the wolf lurk under the garb of sheep? Why does he who falsely asserts himself to be a Christian, dishonor the flock of Christ? To put on the name of Christ, and not to go in the way of Christ, what else is it but a mockery of the divine name, but a desertion of the way of salvation; since He Himself teaches and says that he shall come unto life who keeps His commandments, and that he is wise who hears and does His words; that he, moreover, is called the greatest doctor in the kingdom of heaven who thus does and teaches; that, then, will be of advantage to the preacher what has been well and usefully preached, if what is uttered by his mouth is fulfilled by deeds following? But what did the Lord more frequently instill into His disciples, what did He more charge to be guarded and observed among His saving counsels and heavenly precepts, than that with the same love wherewith He Himself loved the disciples, we also should love one another? And in what manner does he keep either the peace or the love of the Lord, who, when jealousy intrudes, can neither be peaceable nor loving?

13. Thus also the Apostle Paul, when he was urging the merits of peace and charity, and when he was strongly asserting and teaching that neither faith nor alms, nor even the passion itself of the confessor and the martyr, would avail him, unless he kept the requirements of charity entire and inviolate, added, and said: "Charity, is magnanimous, charity is kind, charity envies not;"[13] teaching, doubtless, and showing that whoever is magnanimous, and kind, and averse from jealousy and rancor, such a one can maintain charity. Moreover, in another place, when he was advising that the man who has already become filled with the Holy Spirit, and a son of God by heavenly birth, should observe nothing but spiritual and divine things, he lays it down, and says: "And I indeed, brethren, could not speak unto you as unto spiritual, but as unto carnal, even as unto babes in Christ. I have fed you with milk, not with meat: for you were not able hitherto; moreover, neither now are you able. For you are yet carnal: for whereas there are still among you jealousy, and contention, and strifes, are you not carnal, and walk as men?"[14]

14. Vices and carnal sins must be trampled down, beloved brethren, and the corrupting plague of the earthly body[15] must be trodden under foot with spiritual vigor, lest, while we are turned back again to the conversation of the old man, we be entangled in deadly snares, even as the apostle, with foresight and wholesomeness, forewarned us of this very thing, and said: "Therefore, brethren, let us not live after the flesh; for if you live after the flesh, you shall begin to die; but if you, through the Spirit, mortify the deeds of the flesh, you shall live. For as many as are led by the Spirit of God they are the sons of God."[16] If we are the sons of God, if we are already beginning to be His temples, if, having received the Holy Spirit, we are living holily and spiritually, if we have raised our eyes from earth to heaven, if we have lifted our hearts, filled with God and Christ, to things above and divine, let us do nothing but what is worthy of God and Christ, even as the apostle arouses and exhorts us, saying: "If you be risen with Christ, seek those things which are above, where Christ is sitting at the right hand of God; occupy your minds with things that are above, not with things which are upon the earth. For you are dead, and your life is hid with Christ in God. But when Christ, who is your life, shall appear, then shall you also appear with Him in glory."[17] Let us, then, who in baptism have both died and been buried in respect of the carnal sins of the old man, who have risen again with Christ in the heavenly regeneration, both think upon and do the things which are Christ's[18], even as the same apostle again teaches and counsels, saying: "The first man is of the dust of the earth; the second man is from heaven. Such as he is from the earth, such also are they who are from the earth and such as He the heavenly is, such also are they who are heavenly. As we have borne the image of him who is of the earth, let us also bear the image of Him who is from heaven."[19] But we cannot bear the heavenly image, unless in that condition wherein we have already begun to be, we show forth the likeness of Christ.

15. For this is to change what you had been, and to begin to be what you were not, that the divine birth might shine forth in you, that the godly discipline might respond to God, the Father, that in the honor and praise of living, God may be glorified in man; as He Himself exhorts, and warns, and promises to those who glorify Him a reward in their turn, saying, "Them that glorify me I will glorify, and he who despises me shall be despised."[20] For which glorification the Lord, forming and preparing us, and the Son of God instilling the likeness of God the Father, says in His Gospel: "You have heard that it has been said, 'You shall love your neighbor, and hate your enemy.' But I say unto you, Love your enemies, and pray for them which persecute you; that you may be the children of your Father which is in heaven, who makes His sun to rise on the good and on the evil, and sends rain upon the just and on the unjust."[21] If it is a source of joy and glory to men to have children like to themselves—and it is more agreeable to have begotten an offspring then when the remaining progeny responds to the parent with like lineaments— how much greater is the gladness in God the Father, when any one is so spiritually born that in his acts and praises the divine eminence of race is announced! What a palm of righteousness is it, what a crown to be such a one as that the Lord should not say of you, "I have begotten and brought up children, but they have despised me!"[22] Let Christ rather applaud you, and invite you to the reward, saying, "Come, you blessed of my Father, receive the kingdom which is prepared for you from the beginning of the world."[23]

16. The mind must be strengthened, beloved brethren, by these meditations. By exercises of this kind it must be confirmed against all the darts of the devil. Let there be the divine reading in the hands, the Lord's thoughts in the mind; let constant prayer never cease at all; let saving labor persevere. Let us be always busied in spiritual actions, that so often as the enemy approaches, however often he may try to come near, he may find the breast closed and armed against him. For a Christian man's crown is not only that which is received in the time of persecution: peace also has its crowns, wherewith the victors, from a varied and manifold engagement, are crowned, when their adversary is prostrated and subdued. To have overcome lust is the palm of continency. To have resisted against anger, against injury, is the crown of patience. It is a triumph over avarice to despise money. It is the praise of faith, by trust in the future, to suffer the adversity of the world. And he who is not haughty in prosperity, obtains glory for his humility; and he who is disposed to the mercifulness of cherishing the poor, obtains the retribution of a heavenly treasure; and he who knows not to be jealous, and who with one heart and in meekness loves his brethren, is honored with the recompense of love and peace. In this course of virtues we daily run; to these palms and crowns of justice we attain without intermission of time.

17. To these rewards that you also may come who had been possessed with jealousy and rancor, cast away all that malice wherewith you were before held fast, and be reformed to the way of eternal life in the footsteps of salvation. Tear out from your breast thorns and thistles, that the Lord's seed may enrich you with a fertile produce, that the divine and spiritual cornfield may abound to the plentifulness of a fruitful harvest. Cast out the poison of gall, cast out the virus of discords. Let the mind which the malice of the serpent had infected be purged; let all bitterness which had settled within be softened by the sweetness of Christ. If you take both meat and drink from the sacrament of the cross, let the wood which at Marah availed in a figure for sweetening the taste, avail to you in in reality for soothing your softened breast;[24] and you shall not strive for a medicine for your increasing health. Be cured by that whereby you had been wounded. Love those whom you previously had hated; favor those whom you envied with unjust disparagements. Imitate good men, if you are able to follow them; but it you are not able to follow them, at least rejoice with them, and congratulate those who are better than you. Make yourself a sharer with them in united love; make yourself their associate in the alliance of charity and the bond of brotherhood. Your debts shall be remitted to you when you yourself shall have forgiven. Your sacrifices shall be received when you shall come in peace to God. Your thoughts and deeds shall be directed from above, when you consider those things which are divine and righteous, as it is written: "Let the heart of a man consider righteous things, that his steps may be directed by the Lord."[25]

18. And you have many things to consider. Think of paradise, whither Cain does not enter, who by jealousy slew his brother. Think of the heavenly kingdom, to which the Lord does not admit any but those who are of one heart and mind. Consider that those alone can be called sons of God who are peacemakers, who in heavenly birth and by the divine law are made one, and respond to the likeness of God the Father and of Christ. Consider that we are standing under the eyes of God, that we are pursuing the course of our conversation and our life, with God Himself looking on and judging, that we may then at length be able to attain to the result of beholding Him, if we now delight Him who sees us, by our actions, if we show ourselves worthy of His favor and indulgence; if we, who are always to please Him in His kingdom, previously please Him in the world.

NOTES

1. 1 Pet. 5:8.
2. Wis. 2:24.
3. Ps. 37:7.
4. Ps. 37:12-13.
5. Rom. 3:13-18.
6. Luke 9:48.
7. Rom. 13:12-13. This is the same Scripture verse that St. Augustine would read in the garden under the fig tree that led to his conversion in September, 386.
8. 1 John 3:15.
9. 1 John 2:9-11.
10. 1 John 2:11.
11. John 8:12.
12. 1 Pet. 2:21.
13. 1 Cor. 13:4.
14. 1 Cor. 3:1-3.
15. In warning of the "corrupting plague of the earthly body," Cyprian is not condemning the physical body in the Gnostic sense; that is, he is not contrasting flesh with spirit, but the works of the carnal man with the spiritual man—the worldly man with the believer who has become a "son of God by the heavenly birth" of baptism, as St. Paul writes in 1 Cor. 15:47-49.

16. Rom. 8:12-14.
17. Col. 3:1-4.
18. A valuable testimony to patristic belief in the literal washing away of sins accomplished through baptism.
19. 1 Cor. 15:47-49.
20. 1 Sam. 2:30.
21. Matt. 5:43-45.
22. Isa. 1:2.
23. Matt. 25:34.
24. A reference to the episode of the Exodus related in Ex. 15:22-27.
25. Source uncertain; the editors of the Ante-Nicene Fathers believe it to be a Septuagint reference to Proverbs 15:1; this editor thinks Proverbs 21:2 is more likely.

EXHORTATION TO MARTYRDOM, TO FORTUNATUS[1]

Preface

1. You have desired, beloved Fortunatus that, since the burden of persecutions and afflictions is lying heavy upon us, and in the ending and completion of the world the hateful time of Antichrist is already beginning to draw near, I would collect from the sacred Scriptures some exhortations for preparing and strengthening the minds of the brethren, whereby I might animate the soldiers of Christ for the heavenly and spiritual contest. I have been constrained to obey your so needful wish, so that as much as my limited powers, instructed by the aid of divine inspiration, are sufficient, some arms, as it were, and defenses might be brought forth from the Lord's precepts for the brethren who are about to fight. For it is little to arouse God's people by the trumpet call of our voice, unless we confirm the faith of believers, and their valor dedicated and devoted to God, by the divine readings.

2. But what more fitly or more fully agrees with my own care and solicitude, than to prepare the people divinely entrusted to me, and an army established in the heavenly camp, by assiduous exhortations against the darts and weapons of the devil? For he cannot be a soldier fitted for the war who has not first been exercised in the field; nor will he who seeks to gain the crown of contest be rewarded on the racecourse, unless he first considers the use and skillfulness of his powers. It is an ancient adversary and an old enemy with whom we wage our battle: six thousand years are now nearly completed since the devil first attacked man.[2] All kinds of temptation, and arts, and snares for his overthrow, he has learned by the very practice of long years. If he finds Christ's soldier unprepared, if unskilled, if not careful and watching with his whole heart; he circumvents him if ignorant, he deceives him if incautious, he cheats him if inexperienced. But if a man, keeping the Lord's precepts, and bravely adhering to Christ, stands against him, he must needs be conquered, because Christ, whom that man confesses, is un-conquered.

3. And that I might not extend my discourse, beloved brother, to too great a length, and fatigue my hearer or reader by the abundance of a too diffuse style, I have made a compendium; so that the titles being placed first, which every one ought both to know and to have in mind, I might subjoin sections of the Lord's word, and establish what I had proposed by the authority of the divine teaching, in such wise as that I might not appear to have sent you my own treatise so much, as to have suggested material for others to discourse on; a proceeding which will

171

be of advantage to individuals with increased benefit. For if I were to give a man a garment finished and ready, it would be my garment that another was making use of, and probably the thing made for another would be found little fitting for his figure of stature and body. But now I have sent you the very wool and the purple from the Lamb, by whom we were redeemed and quickened; which, when you have received, you will make into a coat for yourself according to your own will, and the rather that you will rejoice in it as your own private and special garment. And you will exhibit to others also what we have sent, that they themselves may be able to finish it according to their will; so that that old nakedness being covered, they may all bear the garments of Christ robed in the sanctification of heavenly grace.[3]

4. Moreover also, beloved brethren, I have considered it a useful and wholesome plan in an exhortation so needful as that which may make martyrs, to cut off all delays and tardiness in our words, and to put away the windings of human discourse, and set down only those things which God speaks, wherewith Christ exhorts His servants to martyrdom. Those divine precepts themselves must be supplied, as it were, for arms for the combatants. Let them be the incitements of the warlike trumpet; let them he the clarion-blast for the warriors. Let the ears be roused by them; let the minds be prepared by them; let the powers both of soul and body be strengthened to all endurance of suffering. Let us only who, by the Lord's permission, have given the first baptism to believers, also prepare each one for the second; urging and teaching that this is a baptism greater in grace, more lofty in power, more precious in honor—a baptism wherein angels baptize—a baptism in which God and His Christ exult—a baptism after which no one sins any more—a baptism which completes the increase of our faith—a baptism which, as we withdraw from the world, immediately associates us with God. In the baptism of water is received the remission of sins, in the baptism of blood the crown of virtues. This thing is to be embraced and desired, and to be asked for in all the entreaties of our petitions, that we who are God's servants should be also His friends.[4]

1. That idols are not gods, and that the elements are not to be worshipped in the place of gods.

In the cxiiith Psalm it is shown that "the idols of the heathen are silver and gold, the work of men's hands. They have a mouth, and speak not; eyes have they, and see not. They have ears, and hear not; neither is there any breath in their mouth. Let those that make them be made like them."[5] Also in the Wisdom of Solomon: "They counted all the idols of the nations to be gods, which neither have the use of eyes to see, nor noses to draw breath, nor ears to hear, nor fingers on their hands to handle; and as for their feet, they are slow to go. For man made them, and he that borrowed his own spirit fashioned them; but no man can make a god like himself. For, since he is mortal, he works a dead thing with wicked hands; for he himself is better than the things which he worships, since he indeed lived once, but they never."[6] In Exodus also: "You shall not make to you an idol, nor the likeness of anything."[7] Moreover, in Solomon, concerning the elements: "Neither by considering the works did they acknowledge who was the workmaster; but deemed either fire, or wind, or the swift air, or the circle of the stars, or the violent water, or the sun, or the moon, to be gods. On account of whose beauty, if they thought this, let them know how much more beautiful is the Lord than they. Or if they admired their powers and operations, let them understand by them, that He that made these mighty things is mightier than they."[8]

2. That God alone must be worshipped

As it is written, "You shall worship the Lord your God, and Him only shall you serve."[9] Also in Exodus: "You shall have none other gods beside me."[10] Also in Deuteronomy: "See, see that I am He, and that there is no God beside me. I will kill, and will make alive; I will smite, and I will heal; and there is none who can deliver out of mine hands."[11] In the Apocalypse, moreover: "And I saw another angel fly in the midst of heaven, having the everlasting Gospel to preach over the earth, and over all nations, and tribes, and tongues, and peoples, saying with a loud voice, 'Fear God rather, and give glory to Him: for the hour of His judgment has come; and worship Him that made heaven and earth, and the sea, and all that therein is.'"[12] So also the Lord, in His Gospel, makes mention of the first and second commandment, saying, "Hear, O Israel, The Lord your God is one God;"[13] and, "You shall love your Lord with all your heart, and with all your soul, and with all your strength. This is the first; and the second is like it, You shall love your neighbor as yourself. On these two commandments hang all the law and the prophets."[14] And once more: "And this is life eternal, that they may know You, the only and true God, and Jesus Christ, whom You have sent."[15]

3. What is God's threatening against those who sacrifice to idols?

In Exodus: "He that sacrifices unto any gods but the Lord only, shall be rooted out."[16] Also in Deuteronomy: "They sacrificed unto demons, and not to God."[17] In Isaiah also: "They worshipped those which their fingers have made; and the mean man was bowed down, and the great man was humbled: and I will not forgive them."[18] And again: "To them have you poured out drink-offerings, and to them you have offered sacrifices. For these, therefore, shall I not be angry, says the Lord?"[19] In Jeremiah also: "Walk not after other gods, to serve them;

and worship them not, and provoke me not in the works of your hands, to destroy you."[20] In the Apocalypse too: "If any man worship the beast and his image, and receive his mark in his forehead or in his hand, he shall also drink of the wine of the wrath of God, which is mixed in the cup of His wrath, and shall be punished with fire and brimstone before the eyes of the holy angels, and before the eyes of the Lamb: and the smoke of their torments shall ascend for ever and ever: and they shall have no rest day or night, whosoever worship the beast and his image."[21]

4. That God does not easily pardon idolaters

Moses in Exodus prays for the people, and does not obtain his prayer, saying: "'I pray, O Lord, this people has sinned a great sin. They have made them gods of gold. And now, if You forgive them their sin, forgive it; but if not, blot me out of the book which You have written.' And the Lord said unto Moses, 'If any one has sinned against me, him will I blot out of my book.'"[22] Moreover, when Jeremiah besought for the people, the Lord speaks to him, saying: "And pray not for this people, and entreat not for them in prayer and supplication; because I will not hear in the time wherein they shall call upon me in the time of their affliction."[23] Ezekiel also denounces this same anger of God upon those who sin against God, and says: "And the word of the Lord came unto me, saying, 'Son of man, whatsoever land sins against me, by committing an offense, I will stretch forth mine hand upon it, and will crush the support of the bread thereof; and I wills send into it famine, and I will take away from it man and beast. And though these three men were in the midst of it, Noah, Daniel, and Job, they shall not deliver sons nor daughters; they themselves only shall be delivered.'"[24] Likewise in the first book of Kings: "If a man sin by offending against another, they shall beseech the Lord for him; but if a man sin against God, who shall entreat for him?"[25]

5. That God is so angry against idolatry, that He has even enjoined those to be slain who persuade others to sacrifice and serve idols

In Deuteronomy: "But if your brother, or your son, or your daughter, or your wife which is in your bosom, or your friend which is the fellow of your own soul, should ask you secretly, saying, 'Let us go and serve other gods, the gods of the nations,' you shall not consent unto him, and you shall not hearken unto him, neither shall your eye spare him, neither shall you conceal him, declaring you shall declare concerning him. Your hand shall be upon him first of all to put him to death, and afterwards the hand of all the people; and they shall stone him, and he shall die, because he has sought to turn you away from the Lord your God."[26] And again the Lord speaks, and says, that neither must a city be spared, even though the whole city should consent to idolatry: "Or if you shall hear in one of the cities which the Lord your God shall give you, to dwell there, saying, 'Let us go and serve other gods, which you have not known,' slaying you shall kill all who are in the city with the slaughter of the sword, and burn the city with fire, and it shall be without habitation for ever. Moreover, it shall no more be rebuilt, that the Lord may be turned from the indignation of His anger. And He will show you mercy, and He will pity you, and will multiply you, if you will hear the voice of the Lord your God, and will observe His precepts."[27] Remembering which precept and its force, Mattathias slew him who had approached the altar to sacrifice.[28] But if before the coming of Christ these precepts concerning the worship of God and the despising of idols were observed, how much more should they be regarded since Christ's advent; since He, when He came, not only exhorted us with words, but with deeds also, but after all wrongs and contumelies, suffered also, and was crucified, that He might teach us to suffer and to die by His example, that there might be no excuse for a man not to suffer for Him, since He suffered for us; and that since He suffered for the sins of others, much rather ought each to suffer for his own sins.[29] And therefore in the Gospel He threatens, and says: "Whosoever shall confess me before men, him will I also confess before my Father which is in heaven; but whosoever shall deny me before men, him will I also deny before my Father which is in heaven."[30] The Apostle Paul also says: "For if we die with Him, we shall also live with Him; if we suffer, we shall also reign with Him; if we deny Him, He also will deny us."[31] John too: "Whosoever denies the Son, the same has not the Father; he that acknowledges the Son, has both the Son and the Father."[32] Whence the Lord exhorts and strengthens us to contempt of death, saying: "Fear not them which kill the body, but are not able to kill the soul; but rather fear Him which is able to kill soul and body in Gehenna."[33] And again: "He that loves his life shall lose it; and he who hates his life in this world, shall keep it unto life eternal."[34]

6. That, being redeemed and quickened by the blood of Christ, we ought to prefer nothing to Christ

In the Gospel the Lord speaks, and says: "He that loves father or mother more than me, is not worthy of me; and he that loves son or daughter more than me, is not worthy of me; and he that takes not his cross and follows me, is not worthy of me."[35] So also it is written in Deuteronomy: "They who say to their father and their mother, 'I have not known you,' and have not acknowledged their own children, these have kept Your precepts, and have observed Your covenant."[36] Moreover, the Apostle Paul says: "Who shall separate us from the love of Christ? Shall tribulation, or distress, or persecution, or hunger, or nakedness, or peril, or sword? As it is written, 'Because for Your sake we are killed all the day long, we are counted as sheep for the slaughter.' Nay, in all these things we overcome on account of Him who has loved us."[37] And again: "You are not your own, for you are bought with a great price. Glorify and bear God in your body."[38] And again: "Christ died for all, that both they which live may not henceforth live unto themselves, but unto Him which died for them, and rose again."[39]

7. That those who are snatched from the jaws of the devil, and delivered from the snares of this world ought not again to return to the world, lest they should lose the advantage of their withdrawal therefrom

In Exodus the Jewish people, prefigured as a shadow and image of us, when, with God for their guardian and avenger, they had escaped the most severe slavery of Pharaoh and of Egypt—that is, of the devil and the world—faithless and ungrateful in respect of God, murmur against Moses, looking back to the discomforts of the desert and of their labor; and, not understanding the divine benefits of liberty and salvation, they seek to return to the slavery of Egypt—that is, of the world whence they had been drawn forth—when they ought rather to have trusted and believed on God, since He who delivers His people from the devil and the world, protects them also when delivered. "'Wherefore have you thus done with us," say they, "in casting us forth out of Egypt? It is better for us to serve the Egyptians than to die in this wilderness.' And Moses said unto the people, 'Trust, and stand fast, and see the salvation which is from the Lord, which He shall do to you today. The Lord Himself shall fight for you, and you shall hold your peace.'"[40] The Lord, admonishing us of this in His Gospel, and teaching that we should not return again to the devil and to the world, which we have renounced, and whence we have escaped, says: "No man looking back, and putting his hand to the plough, is fit for the kingdom of God."[41] And again: "And let him that is in the field not return back. Remember Lot's wife." And lest any one should be retarded by any covetousness of wealth or attraction of his own people from following Christ, He adds, and says: "He that forsakes not all that he has, cannot be my disciple."[42]

8. That we must press on and persevere in faith and virtue, and in completion of heavenly and spiritual grace, that we may attain to the palm and the crown

In the book of Chronicles: "The Lord is with you so long as you also are with Him; but if you forsake Him, He will forsake you."[43] In Ezekiel also: "The righteousness of the righteous shall not deliver him in what day soever he may transgress."[44] Moreover, in the Gospel the Lord speaks, and says: "He that shall endure to the end, the same shall be saved."[45] And again: "If you shall abide in my word, you shall be my disciples indeed; and you shall know the truth, and the truth shall make you free."[46] Moreover, forewarning us that we ought always to be ready, and to stand firmly equipped and armed, He adds, and says: "Let your loins be girded about, and your lamps burning, and you yourselves like men that wait for their lord when he shall return from the wedding, that when he comes and knocks they may open unto him. Blessed are those servants whom their lord, when he comes, shall find watching."[47] Also the blessed Apostle Paul, that our faith may advance and grow, and attain to the highest point, exhorts us, saying: "Do you not know, that they which run in a race run all indeed, yet one receives the prize? So run, that you may obtain. And they, indeed, that they may receive a corruptible crown; but you an incorruptible."[48] And again: "No man that wars for God binds himself to anxieties of this world, that he may be able to please Him to whom he has approved himself. Moreover, also, if a man should contend, he will not be crowned unless he have fought lawfully."[49] And again: "Now I beseech you, brethren, by the mercy of God, that you constitute your bodies a living sacrifice, holy, acceptable unto God; and be not conformed to this world, but be transformed in the renewing of your spirit, that you may prove what is the will of God, good, and acceptable, and perfect."[50] And again: "We are children of God: but if children, then heirs; heirs indeed of God, but joint-heirs with Christ, if we suffer together, that we may also be glorified together."[51] And in the Apocalypse the same exhortation of divine preaching speaks, saying, "Hold fast that which you have, lest another take your crown;"[52] which example of perseverance and persistence is pointed out in Exodus, when Moses, for the overthrow of Amalek, who bore the type of the devil, raised up his open hands in the sign and sacrament of the cross, and could not conquer his adversary unless when he had steadfastly persevered in the sign with hands continually lifted up. "And it came to pass," says he, "when Moses raised up his hands, Israel prevailed; but when he let down his hands, Amalek grew mighty. And they took a stone and placed it under him, and he sate thereon. And Aaron and Hur held up his hands on the one side and on the other side, and Moses' hands were made steady even to the going down of the sun. And Joshua routed Amalek and all his people. And the Lord said unto Moses, 'Write this, and let it be a memorial in a book, and tell it in the ears of Jesus; because in destroying I will destroy the remembrance of Amalek from under heaven.'"[53]

9. That afflictions and persecutions arise for the sake of our being proved

In Deuteronomy, "The Lord your God proves you, that He may know if you love the Lord. your God with all your heart, and with all your soul, and with all your strength."[54] And again, Solomon: "The furnace proves the potter's vessel, and righteous men the trial of tribulation."[55] Paul also testifies similar things, and speaks, saying: "We glory in the hope of the glory of God. And not only so, but we glory in tribulations also; knowing that tribulation works patience, and patience experience, and experience hope; and hope makes not ashamed, because the love of God is shed abroad in our hearts by the Holy Spirit who is given unto us."[56] And Peter, in his epistle, lays it down, and says: "Beloved, be not surprised at the fiery heat which falls upon you, which happens for your trial; and fail not, as if some new thing were happening unto you. But as often as you communicate with the sufferings of Christ, rejoice in all things, that also in the revelation made of His glory you may rejoice with gladness. If you be reproached in the name of Christ, happy are you; because the name of the majesty and power of the Lord rests upon you; which indeed according to them is blasphemed, but according to us is honored."[57]

10. That injuries and penalties of persecutions are not to be feared by us, because greater is the Lord to protect than the devil to assault

John, in his epistle, proves this, saying: "Greater is He who is in you than he that is in the world."[58] Also in the cxviith Psalm: "I will not fear what man can do unto me; the Lord is my helper."[59] And again: "These in chariots, and those in horses; but we will glory in the name of the Lord our God. They themselves are bound, and they have fallen; but we have risen up, and stand upright."[60] And even more strongly the Holy Spirit, teaching and showing that the army of the devil is not to be feared, and that, if the foe should declare war against us, our hope consists rather in that war itself; and that by that conflict the righteous attain to the reward of the divine abode and eternal salvation—lays down in the twenty-sixth Psalm, and says: "Though an host should be arrayed against me, my heart shall not fear; though war should rise up against me, in that will I put my hope. One hope have I sought of the Lord, this will I require; that I may dwell in the house of the Lord all the days of my life."[61] Also in Exodus, the Holy Scripture declares that we are rather multiplied and increased by afflictions, saying: "And the more they afflicted them, so much the more they became greater, and grew stronger."[62] And in the Apocalypse, divine protection is promised to our sufferings. "Fear nothing of these things," it says, "which you shall suffer."[63] Nor does any one else promise to us security and protection, than He who also speaks by Isaiah the prophet, saying: "Fear not; for I have redeemed you, and called you by your name: you are mine. And if you pass through the water, I am with you, and the rivers shall not overflow you. And if you pass through the fire, you shall not be burned, and the flame shall not burn you; for I, the Lord your God, the Holy One of Israel, am He who makes you safe."[64] Who also promises in the Gospel that divine help shall not be wanting to God's servants in persecutions, saying: "But when they shall deliver you up, take no thought how or what you shall speak. For it shall be given you in that hour what you shall speak. For it is not you who speak, but the Spirit of your Father who speaks in you."[65] And again: "Settle it in your hearts not to meditate before how to answer. For I will give you a mouth and wisdom, which your adversaries shall not be able to resist."[66] As in Exodus God speaks to Moses when he delayed and trembled to go to the people, saying: "Who has given a mouth to man? And who has made the stammerer? And who the deaf man? And who the seeing, and the blind man? Have not I, the Lord God? And now go, and I will open your mouth, and will instruct you what you shall say."[67] Nor is it difficult for God to open the mouth of a man devoted to Himself, and to inspire constancy and confidence in speech to His confessor; since in the book of Numbers He made even a she-ass to speak against the prophet Balaam. Wherefore in persecutions let no one think what danger the devil is bringing in, but let him indeed consider what help God affords; nor let human mischief overpower the mind, but let divine protection strengthen the faith; since every one, according to the Lord's promises and the deservings of his faith, receives so much from God's help as he thinks that he receives. Nor is there anything which the Almighty is not able to grant, unless the failing faith of the receiver be deficient and give way.[68]

11. That it was before predicted that the world would hold us in abhorrence, and that it would stir up persecutions against us, and that no new thing is happening to the Christians, since from the beginning of the world the good have suffered, and the righteous have been oppressed and slain by the unrighteous

The Lord in the Gospel forewarns and foretells, saying: "If the world hates you, know that it first hated me. If you were of the world, the world would love what is its own: but because you are not of the world, and I have chosen you out of the world, therefore the world hates you. Remember the word that I spoke unto you, The servant is not greater than his master. If they have persecuted me, they will persecute you also."[69] And again: "The hour will come, that every one that kills you will think that he does God service; but they will do this because they have not known the Father nor me. But these things have I told you, that when the hour shall come you may remember them, because I told you."[70] And again: "Verily, verily, I say unto you, That you shall weep and lament, but the world shall rejoice; you shall be sorrowful, but your sorrow shall be turned into joy."[71] And again: "These things have I spoken unto you, that in me you may have peace; but in the world you shall have tribulation: but be of good confidence, for I have overcome the world."[72] And when He was interrogated by His disciples concerning the sign of His coming, and of the consummation of the world, He answered and said: "Take care lest any deceive you: for many shall come in my name, saying, 'I am Christ;' and shall deceive many. And you shall begin to hear of wars, and rumors of wars; see that you be not troubled: for these things must needs come to pass, but the end is not yet. For nation shall rise against nation, and kingdom against kingdom: and there shall be famines, and earthquakes, and pestilences, in every place. But all these things are the beginnings of travailings. Then they shall deliver you up into affliction, and shall kill you: and you shall be hateful to all nations for my name's sake. And then shall many be offended, and shall betray one another, and shall hate one another. And many false prophets shall arise, and shall seduce many; and because wickedness shall abound, the love of many shall wax cold. But he who shall endure to the end, the same shall be saved. And this Gospel of the kingdom shall be preached through all the world, for a testimony to all nations; and then shall come the end. When, therefore, you shall see the abomination of desolation which is spoken of by Daniel the prophet, standing in the holy place (let him who reads understand), then let them which are in Judea flee to the mountains; and let him which is on the house-roof not go down to take anything from the house; and let him who is in the field not return back to carry away his clothes. But woe to them that are pregnant, and to those that are giving suck in those days! But pray that your flight be not in the winter, nor on the Sabbath day: for there shall be great tribulation, such as has not arisen from the beginning of the world until now, neither shall arise. And unless those days should be shortened, no flesh should be saved; but for the elect's sake those days shall be shortened. Then if any one shall say unto you, Lo, here is Christ, or, Lo, there; believe him not. For there shall arise false Christs, and false prophets, and shall show great signs and wonders, to cause error, if it be possible, even to the elect. But take heed: behold, I have foretold you all things. If, therefore, they shall say to you, 'Lo, he is in the desert;' go not forth: 'Lo, he is in the sleeping chambers;' believe it not. For as the flashing of lightning goes forth from the east, and appears even to the west, so also shall the coming of the Son of man be. Wheresoever the carcass shall be, there shall the eagles be gathered together. But immediately after the affliction of those days the sun shall be darkened, and the moon shall not give her light, and the stars shall fall from heaven, and the powers of heaven shall be moved: and then shall appear the sign of the Son of man in heaven: and all the tribes of the earth shall lament, and shall see the Son of man coming in the clouds of heaven with great power and glory. And He shall send His angels with a great trumpet, and they shall gather together His elect from the four winds, from the heights of heaven, even into the farthest bounds thereof."[73]

And these are not new or sudden things which are now happening to Christians; since the good and righteous, and those who are devoted to God in the law of innocence and the fear of true religion, advance always through afflictions, and wrongs, and the severe and manifold penalties of troubles, in the hardship of a narrow path. Thus, at the very beginning of the world, the righteous Abel was the first to be slain by his brother; and Jacob was driven into exile, and Joseph was sold, and king Saul persecuted the merciful David; and king Ahab endeavored to oppress Elijah, who firmly and bravely asserted the majesty of

God. Zacharias the priest was slain between the temple and the altar, that himself might there become a sacrifice where he was accustomed to offer sacrifices to God. So many martyrdoms of the righteous have, in fact, often been celebrated; so many examples of faith and virtue have been set forth to future generations. The three youths, Ananias, Azarias, and Mishael, equal in age, agreeing in love, steadfast in faith, constant in virtue, stronger than the flames and penalties that urged them, proclaim that they only obey God, that they know Him alone, that they worship Him alone, saying: "O king Nebuchadnezzar, there is no need for us to answer you in this matter. For the God whom we serve is able to deliver us out of the furnace of burning fire; and He will deliver us from your hands, O king. And if not, be it known unto you, that we do not serve your gods, and we do not adore the golden image which you have set up."[74] And Daniel, devoted to God, and filled with the Holy Spirit, exclaims and says: "I worship nothing but the Lord my God, who founded the heaven and the earth."[75] Tobias also, although under a royal and tyrannical slavery, yet in feeling and spirit free, maintains his confession to God, and sublimely announces both the divine power and majesty, saying: "In the land of my captivity I confess to Him, and I show forth His power in a sinful nation."[76] What, indeed, do we find in the Maccabees of seven brethren, equals alike in their lot of birth and virtues, filling up the number seven in the sacrament of a perfected completion? Seven brethren were thus associating in martyrdom. As the first seven days in the divine arrangement containing seven thousand of years,[77] as the seven spirits and seven angels which stand and go in and out before the face of God, and the seven-branched lamp in the tabernacle of witness, and the seven golden candlesticks in the Apocalypse, and the seven columns in Solomon upon which Wisdom built her house, so here also the number seven of the brethren, embracing, in the quantity of their number, the seven churches, as likewise in the first book of Kings we read that the barren has borne seven. And in Isaiah seven women lay hold on one man, whose name they ask to be called upon them. And the Apostle Paul, who refers to this lawful and certain number, writes to the seven churches. And in the Apocalypse the Lord directs His divine and heavenly precepts to the seven churches and their angels, which number is now found in this case, in the seven brethren, that a lawful consummation may be completed. With the seven children is manifestly associated also the mother, their origin and root, who subsequently begot seven churches, she herself having been first, and alone founded upon a rock by the voice of the Lord. Nor is it of no account that in their sufferings the mother alone is with her children. For martyrs who witness themselves as the sons of God in suffering are now no more counted as of any father but God, as in the Gospel the Lord teaches, saying, "Call no man your father upon earth; for one is your Father, which is in heaven."[78]

But what utterances of confessions did they herald forth! How illustrious, how great proofs of faith did they afford! The king Antiochus, their enemy—yea, in Antiochus Antichrist was set forth—sought to pollute the mouths of martyrs, glorious and unconquered in the spirit of confession, with the contagion of swine's flesh; and when he had severely beaten them with whips, and could prevail nothing, commanded iron plates to be heated, which being heated and made to glow, he commanded him who had first spoken, and had more provoked the king with the constancy of his virtue and faith, to be brought up and roasted, his tongue having first been pulled out and cut off, which had confessed God; and this happened the more gloriously to the martyr. For the tongue which had confessed the name of God, ought itself first to go to God. Then in the second, sharper pains having been devised, before he tortured the other limbs, he tore off the skin of his head with the hair, doubtless with a purpose in his hatred. For since Christ is the head of the man, and God is the head of Christ, he who tore the head in the martyr was persecuting God and Christ in that head. But he, trusting in his martyrdom, and promising to himself from the retribution of God the reward of resurrection, exclaimed and said, "You indeed impotently destroy us out of this present life; but the King of the world will raise us up, who die for His laws, unto the eternal resurrection of life."[79] The third being challenged, quickly put forth his tongue; for he had learned from his brother to despise the punishment of cutting off the tongue. Moreover, he firmly held forth his hands to be cut off, greatly happy in such a mode of punishment, since it was his lot to imitate, by stretching forth his hands, the form of his Lord's passion. And also the fourth, with like virtue, despising the tortures, and answering, to restrain the king, with a heavenly voice exclaimed, and said, "It is better that those who are given to death by men should wait for hope from God, to be raised up by Him again to eternal life. For to you there shall be no resurrection to life."[80] The fifth, besides treading under foot the torments of the king, and his severe and various tortures, by the strength of faith, animated to prescience also and knowledge of future events by the Spirit of divinity, foretold to the king the wrath of God, and the vengeance that should swiftly follow. "Having power," said he, "among men, though you are corruptible, you do what you will. But think not that our race is forsaken of God. Abide, and see His great power, how He will torment you and your seed."[81] What alleviation was that to the martyr! How substantial a comfort in his sufferings, not to consider his own torments, but to predict the penalties of his tormentor! But in the sixth, not his bravery only, but also his humility, is to be set forth; that the martyr claimed nothing to himself, nor even made an account of the honor of his own confession with proud words, but rather ascribed it to his sins that he was suffering persecution from the king, while he attributed to God that afterwards he should be avenged. He taught that martyrs are modest, that they were confident of vengeance, and boasted nothing in their suffering. "Do not," said he, "needlessly err; for we on our own account suffer these things, as sinning against our God. But think not that you shall be unpunished, who darest to fight against God."[82] Also the admirable mother, who, neither broken down by the weakness of her sex, nor moved by her manifold bereavement, looked upon her dying children with cheerfulness, and did not reckon those things punishments of her darlings, but glories, giving as great a witness to God by the virtue of her eyes, as her children had given by the tortures and suffering of their limbs; when, after the punishment and slaying of six, there remained one of the brethren, to whom the king promised riches, and power, and many things, that his cruelty and ferocity might be soothed by the satisfaction of even one being subdued, and asked that the mother would entreat that her son might be cast down with herself; she entreated, but it was as became a mother of martyrs—as became one who was mindful of the law and of God—as became one who loved her sons not delicately, but bravely. For she entreated, but it was that he would confess God. She entreated that the brother would not be separated from his brothers in the alliance of praise and glory; then only considering herself the mother of seven sons, if it should happen to her to have brought forth seven sons, not to the world, but to God. Therefore arming him, and strengthening him, and so bearing her son by a more blessed birth, she said, "O son, pity me that bare you ten months in the womb, and gave you milk for three years, and nourished you and brought you up to this age; I pray you, O son, look upon the heaven and the earth; and having considered all the things which are in them, understand that out of nothing God made these things and the human race. Therefore, O son, do not fear that executioner; but being made worthy of your brethren, receive death, that in the same mercy I may receive you with your brethren."[83] The mother's praise was great in her exhortation to virtue, but greater in the fear of God and in the truth of faith, that she promised nothing to herself or her son from the honor of the six martyrs, nor believed that the prayer of the brothers would avail for the salvation of one who should deny, but rather persuaded him to become a sharer in their suffering, that in the day of judgment he might be found with his brethren. After this the mother also dies with her children; for neither was anything else becoming, than that she who had borne and made martyrs, should be joined in the fellowship of glory with them, and that she herself should follow those whom she had sent before to God.

And lest any, when the opportunity either of a certificate[84] or of any such matter is offered to him whereby he may deceive, should embrace the wicked part of deceivers, let us not be silent, moreover, about Eleazar, who, when an opportunity was offered him by the ministers of the king, that having received the flesh which it was allowable for him to partake of, he might pretend, for the misguiding of the king, that he ate those things which were forced upon him from the sacrifices and unlawful meats, would not consent to this deception, saying that it was fitting neither for his age nor nobility to feign that, whereby others would be scandalized and led into error; if they should think that Eleazar, being ninety years old, had left and betrayed the law of God, and had gone over to the manner of aliens; and that it was not of so much consequence to gain the short moments of life, and so incur eternal punishment from an offended God. And he having been long tortured, and now at length reduced to extremity, while he was dying in the midst of stripes and tortures, groaned and said, "O Lord, that hast the holy knowledge, it is manifest that although I might be delivered from death, I suffer the severest pains of body, being beaten with scourges; but with my mind, on account of Your fear, I willingly suffer these things."[85] Assuredly his faith was sincere and his virtue sound, and abundantly pure, not to have regarded king Antiochus, but God the Judge, and to have known that it could not avail him for salvation if he should mock and deceive man, when God, who is the judge of our conscience, and who only is to be feared, cannot at all be mocked nor deceived. If, therefore, we also live as dedicated and devoted to God—if we make our way over the ancient and sacred footsteps of the righteous, let us go through the same proofs of sufferings, the same testimonies of passions, considering the glory of our time the greater on this account, that while ancient examples may be numbered, yet that subsequently, when the abundance of virtue and faith was in excess, the Christian martyrs cannot be numbered, as the Apocalypse testifies and says: "After these things I beheld a great multitude, which no man could number, of every nation, and of every tribe, and people, and language, standing in the sight of the throne and of the Lamb; and they were clothed in white robes, and palms were in their hands; and they said with a loud voice, 'Salvation to our God, who sits upon the throne, and unto the Lamb!' And one of the elders answered and said unto me, 'Who are those which are arrayed in white robes, and whence come they?' And I said unto him, 'My lord, you know.' And he said unto me, 'These are they who have come out of great tribulation, and have washed their robes, and made them white in the blood of the Lamb. Therefore are they before the throne of God, and serve Him day and night in His temple.'"[86] But if the assembly of the Christian martyrs is shown and proved to be so great, let no one think it a hard or a difficult thing to become a martyr, when he sees that the crowd of martyrs cannot be numbered.

12. What hope and reward remains for the righteous and for martyrs after the conflicts and sufferings of this present time
The Holy Spirit shows and predicts by Solomon, saying: "And although in the sight of men they suffered torments, yet their hope is full of immortality. And

having been troubled in a few things, they shall be in many happily ordered, because God has tried them, and has found them worthy of Himself. As gold in the furnace, He has tried them; and as whole burnt-offerings of sacrifice, He has received them, and in its season there will be respect of them. They will shine and run about as sparks in a place set with reeds. They shall judge the nations, and have dominion over the peoples; and their Lord shall reign forever."[87] In the same also our vengeance is described, and the repentance of those who persecute and molest us is announced. "Then," says he, "shall the righteous stand in great constancy before such as have afflicted them, and who have taken away their labors; when they see it, they shall be troubled with a horrible fear: and they shall marvel at the suddenness of their unexpected salvation, saying among themselves, repenting and groaning for anguish of spirit, 'These are they whom we had sometime in derision and as a proverb of reproach. We fools counted their life madness, and their end to be without honor. How are they numbered among the children of God, and their lot is among the saints! Therefore have we erred from the way of truth, and the light of righteousness has not shined unto us, and the sun has not risen upon us. We have been wearied in the way of unrighteousness and perdition, and have walked through hard deserts, but have not known the way of the Lord. What has pride profited us, or what has the boasting of riches brought to us? All these things have passed away like a shadow.'"[88] Likewise in the cxvth Psalm is shown the price and the reward of suffering: "Precious," it says, "in the sight of the Lord is the death of His saints."[89] In the cxxvth Psalm also is expressed the sadness of the struggle, and the joy of the retribution: "They who sow, it says, in tears, shall reap in joy. As they walked, they walked and wept, casting their seeds; but as they come again, they shall come in exultation, bearing their sheaves."[90] And again, in the cxviiith Psalm: "Blessed are those that are undefiled in the way, who walk in the law of the Lord. Blessed are they who search His testimonies, and seek Him out with their whole heart."[91] Moreover, the Lord in the Gospel, Himself the avenger of our persecution and the rewarder of our suffering, says: "Blessed are they who suffer persecution for righteousness' sake, for theirs is the kingdom of heaven."[92] And again: "Blessed shall you be when men shall hate you, and shall separate you, and shall expel you, and shall revile your name as evil, for the Son of man's sake. Rejoice on that day, and leap for joy; for, behold, your reward is great in heaven."[93] And once more: "Whosoever shall lose his life for my sake, the same shall save it."[94] Nor do the rewards of the divine promise attend those alone who are reproached and slain; but if the passion itself, be wanting to the faithful, while their faith has remained sound and unconquered, and having forsaken and contemned all his possessions, the Christian has shown that he is following Christ, even be also is honored by Christ among the martyrs, as He Himself promises and says: "There is no man that leaves house, or land, or parents, or brethren, or wife, or children, for the kingdom of God's sake, but shall receive seven times as much in this present time, and in the world to come eternal life."[95] In the Apocalypse also He says the same thing: "And I saw, says he, the souls of them that were slain for the name of Jesus and the word of God. And when he had placed those who were slain in the first place, he added, saying: And whosoever had not worshipped the image of the beast, neither had received his mark upon their forehead or in their hand;" all these he joins together, as seen by him at one time in the same place, and says, "And they lived and reigned with Christ."[96] He says that all live and reign with Christ, not only who have been slain; but even whosoever, standing in firmness of the faith and in the fear of God, have not worshipped the image of the beast, and have not consented to his deadly and sacrilegious edicts.

13. That we receive more as the reward of our suffering than what we endure here in the suffering itself

The blessed Apostle Paul proves; who by the divine condescension, being caught up into the third heaven and into paradise, testifies that he heard unspeakable words, who boasts that he saw Jesus Christ by the faith of sight, who professes that which he both learned and saw with the greater truth of consciousness, and says: "The sufferings of this present time are not worthy to be compared with the coming glory which shall be revealed in us."[97] Who, then, does not with all his powers labor to attain to such a glory that he may become the friend of God, that he may at once rejoice with Christ, that after earthly tortures and punishments he may receive divine rewards? If to soldiers of this world it is glorious to return in triumph to their country when the foe is vanquished, how much more excellent and greater is the glory, when the devil is overcome, to return in triumph to paradise, and to bring back victorious trophies to that place whence Adam was ejected as a sinner, after casting down him who formerly had cast him down; to offer to God the most acceptable gift—an uncorrupted faith, and an unyielding virtue of mind, an illustrious praise of devotion; to accompany Him when He shall come to receive vengeance from His enemies, to stand at His side when He shall sit to judge, to become co-heir of Christ, to be made equal to the angels; with the patriarchs, with the apostles, with the prophets, to rejoice in the possession of the heavenly kingdom! Such thoughts as these, what persecution can conquer, what tortures can overcome? The brave and steadfast mind, founded in religious meditations, endures; and the spirit abides unmoved against all the terrors of the devil and the threats of the world, when it is strengthened by the sure and solid faith of things to come. In persecutions, earth is shut up, but heaven is opened; Antichrist is threatening, but Christ is protecting; death is brought in, but immortality follows; the world is taken away from him that is slain, but paradise is set forth to him restored; the life of time is extinguished, but the life of eternity is realized. What a dignity it is, and what a security, to go gladly from hence, to depart gloriously in the midst of afflictions and tribulations; in a moment to close the eyes with which men and the world are looked upon, and at once to open them to look upon God and Christ! Of such a blessed departure how great is the swiftness! You shall be suddenly taken away from earth, to be placed in the heavenly kingdoms. It behooves us to embrace these things in our mind and consideration, to meditate on these things day and night. If persecution should fall upon such a soldier of God, his virtue, prompt for battle, will not be able to be overcome. Or if his call should come to him before, his faith shall not be without reward, seeing it was prepared for martyrdom; without loss of time, the reward is rendered by the judgment of God. In persecution, the warfare—in peace, the purity of conscience, is crowned.

NOTES

1. It is uncertain who this Fortunatus is. Presumably he is a fellow bishop; a bishop by that name appears in the records of the Seventh Council of Carthage as leading the Church at Tucca.
2. Though it was not universally believed, Cyprian at least held to a literal view of the chronology of Creation as presented in Genesis.
3. This method of stating an article of faith followed by scriptural articles to support the statement will be used again by Cyprian in the much more voluminous *Three Books of Testimonies Against the Jews.*
4. In contrasting the sacramental baptism with the metaphorical baptism into death, Cyprian explains the fundamental principle behind the Church's teaching on the possibility of baptism of blood. In shedding blood for the Faith the believer is most perfectly conformed to Christ His Master, and thus does Cyprian say that martyrdom "is a baptism greater in grace" than sacramental baptism. He who is sacramentally baptized may sin again, but he who dies faithfully as a martyr is freed from sin and obtains immediate admission to the Beatific Vision.
5. Ps. 135:15-18, 115:4-8.
6. Wis. 15:15-17.
7. Ex. 20:4.
8. Wis. 13:1-4.
9. Deut. 6:13, 10:20.
10. Ex. 20:3.
11. Deut. 32:39.
12. Rev. 14:6-7.
13. Mark 12:29-31.
14. Matt. 22:37-40.
15. John 17:3.
16. Ex. 22:20.
17. Deut. 32:17.
18. Isa. 2:8-9.
19. ibid. 57:6.
20. Jer. 7:6.
21. Rev. 14:9-11.
22. Ex. 32:31-33.

23. Jer. 7:16.
24. Ezk. 14:12-14.
25. 1 Sam 2:25.
26. Deut. 13:6-10.
27. Deut. 13:12-18.
28. A reference to the episode in 1 Macc. 2.
29. This passage demonstrates that Cyprian in no way assumes the later Protestant doctrine that the suffering of Christ renders our suffering superfluous. Rather, the suffering of Christ for our sins empowers us to suffer in and with Him and, in grace, to truly merit grace for ourselves and others.
30. Matt. 10:32-33.
31. 2 Tim. 2:11-12.
32. 1 John 2:23.
33. Matt. 10:28.
34. John 12:25.
35. Matt. 10:37-38.
36. Deut. 33:9.
37. Rom. 8:35-37.
38. 1 Cor. 6:20.
39. 2 Cor. 5:15.
40. Ex. 14:11-14.
41. Luke 9:62.
42. ibid. 17:31-32, 14:33.
43. 2 Chr. 15:2.
44. Ezk. 33:12.
45. Matt. 10:22.
46. John 8:31-32.
47. Luke 12:35-37.
48. 1 Cor. 9:24-25.
49. 2 Tim. 2:4-5.
50. Rom. 12:1-2.
51. ibid. 8:16-17.
52. Rev. 3:11.
53. Ex. 7:11-14.
54. Deut. 13:3.
55. Sir. 27:5.
56. Rom. 5:2-5.
57. 1 Pet. 4:12-14.
58. 1 John 4:4.
59. Ps. 118:6.
60. Ps. 20:7-8.
61. Ps. 27:3-4.
62. Ex. 1:12.
63. Rev. 2:10.
64. Isa. 43:1-3.
65. Matt. 10:10-20.
66. Luke 21:14-15.
67. Ex. 6:11-12.
68. Unlike later theological schools (Thomists, Scotists), St. Cyprian seems to see the reception of God's grace as being triggered by the proper faith or disposition of the believer. If taken strictly, this position could be construed as Semipelagian. This should not alarm us too much: The doctrines of grace were not firmly worked

188

out until the 5th and 6th centuries and Cyprian here was not intending to expound a theology of grace; rather, he intended to exhort the faithful to perseverance by reminding them of God's faithfulness.

69. John 15:18-20.
70. ibid. 16:2-4.
71. ibid. 16:20.
72. ibid. 16:33.
73. Matt. 24:4-31.
74. Dan. 3:16-18.
75. Dan. 14:5 (Bel and the Dragon, 5).
76. Tob. 13:6.
77. If Cyprian believes that the time that has elapsed from the Creation of the world to his own day to be about 6,000 years (see note 2 above), and suggests here that the whole course of the world from beginning to end will be comprised of 7,000 years corresponding to the seven days of Creation, then Cyprian leaves 1,000 years for the Church age. This would put him in the camp of the amillennialists, those who asserted that the Millennium and the age of the Church were synonymous. Whether Cyprian took this thousand years to be literal or symbolic is uncertain.
78. Matt. 23:9.
79. 2 Macc. 7:9.
80. ibid. 7:14.
81. ibid. 7:16.
82. ibid. 7:18.
83. ibid. 7:27.
84. Referring to the certificates offered by the Roman magistrates to those who would sacrifice to the pagan gods. Cyprian here recounts the fortitude of Eleazar against those who, while not apostasizing, would bribe Roman magistrates to obtain the certificate of sacrifice.
85. 2 Macc. 6:30.
86. Rev. 7:9-15.
87. Wis. 3:4-8.
88. Wis. 5:1-9.
89. Ps. 116:15.
90. Ps. 126:5-6.
91. Ps. 119:1-2.
92. Matt. 5:10.
93. Luke 6:22-23.
94. ibid. 9:24.
95. ibid. 18:29-30.
96. Rev. 20:4-5.
97. Rom. 8:18.

THREE BOOKS OF TESTIMONIES AGAINST THE JEWS

BOOK I

Cyprian to his son Quirinus, greeting. It was necessary, my beloved son, that I should obey your spiritual desire, which asked with most urgent petition for those divine teachings wherewith the Lord has condescended to teach and instruct us by the Holy Scriptures, that, being led away from the darkness of error, and enlightened by His pure and shining light, we may keep the way of life through the saving sacraments. And indeed, as you have asked, so has this discourse been arranged by me; and this treatise has been ordered in an abridged compendium, so that I should not scatter what was written in too diffuse an abundance, but, as far as my poor memory suggested, might collect all that was necessary in selected and connected heads, under which I may seem, not so much to have treated the subject, as to have afforded material for others to treat it. Moreover, to readers also, brevity of the same kind is of very great advantage, in that a treatise of too great length dissipates the understanding and perception of the reader, while a tenacious memory keeps that which is read in a more exact compendium. But I have comprised in my undertaking two books of equally moderate length:[1] one wherein I have endeavored to show that the Jews, according to what had before been foretold, had departed from God, and had lost God's favor, which had been given them in past time, and had been promised them for the future, while the Christians had succeeded to their place, deserving well of the Lord by faith, and coming out of all nations and from the whole world. The second book likewise contains the sacrament of Christ,[2] that He has come who was announced according to the Scriptures, and has done and perfected all those things whereby He was foretold as being able to be perceived and known. And these things may be of advantage to you meanwhile, as you read, for forming the first lineaments of your faith. More strength will be given you, and the intelligence of the heart will be effected more and more, as you examine more fully the Scriptures, old and new, and read through the complete volumes of the spiritual books. For now we have filled a small measure from the divine fountains, which in the meantime we would send to you. You will be able to drink more plentifully, and to be more abundantly satisfied, if you also will approach to drink together with us at the same springs of the divine fullness. I bid you, beloved son, always heartily farewell.

1. That the Jews have fallen under the heavy wrath of God because they have forsaken the Lord, and have followed idols.

In Exodus the people said to Aaron: "Arise and make us gods which shall go before us: because as for this man Moses, who brought us out of Egypt, we know not what has become of him."[3] In the same place also Moses says to the Lord: "'O Lord, I pray you, this people have sinned! A great sin. They have made to themselves gods of gold and silver. And now, if you will forgive them their sin, forgive; but if not, blot me out of the book which You have written.' And the Lord said unto Moses, 'If any one has sinned against me, him will I blot out of my book.'"[4] Likewise in Deuteronomy: "They sacrificed unto demons, and not unto God."[5] In the book of Judges too: "And the children of Israel did evil in the sight of the Lord God of their fathers, who brought them out of the land of Egypt, and followed the gods of the peoples that were round about them, and offended the Lord, and forsook God, and served Baal." Also in the same place: "And the children of Israel added again to do evil in the sight of the Lord, and served Baal and the gods of the strangers, and forsook the Lord, and served Him not."[6] In Malachi: "Judah is forsaken, and has become an abomination in Israel and in Jerusalem, because Judah has profaned the holiness of the Lord in those things wherein He has loved, and courted strange gods. The Lord will cut off the man who does this, and he shall be made base in the tabernacles of Jacob."[7]

2. Also because they did not believe the prophets, and put them to death

In Jeremiah the Lord says: "I have sent unto you my servants the prophets. Before the daylight I sent them (and you heard me not, and did not listen with your ears), saying, 'Let every one of you be converted from his evil way, and from your most wicked desires; and you shall dwell in that land which I have given you and your fathers for ever and ever.'" And again: "Go not after other gods, to serve them, and do not worship them; and provoke me not to anger in the works of your hands to scatter you abroad; and you have not hearkened unto me."[8] Also in the third book of the Kings, Elijah says unto the Lord: "In being jealous I have been jealous for the Lord God Almighty; because the children of Israel have forsaken You, have demolished Your altars, and have slain Your prophets with the sword; and I have remained solitary, and they seek my life, to take it away from me."[9] In Ezra also: "They have fallen away from You, and have cast Your law behind their backs, and have killed Your prophets which testified against them that they should return to You."[10]

3. That it was previously foretold that they would neither know the Lord, nor understand, nor receive Him

In Isaiah: "Hear, O heaven, and give ear, O earth: for the Lord has spoken; I have begotten and brought up children, but they have rejected me. The ox knows his owner, and the ass his master's crib: but Israel has not known me, and my people has not perceived me. Ah sinful nation, a people filled with sins, a wicked seed, corrupting children: you have forsaken the Lord, and have sent that Holy One of Israel into anger."[11] In the same also the Lord says: "Go and tell this people, You shall hear with the ear, and shall not understand; and seeing, you shall see, and shall not perceive. For the heart of this people has grown gross, and they hardly hear with their ears, and they have shut up their eyes, lest haply they should see with their eyes, and hear with their ears, and understand with their heart, and should return, and I should heal them."[12] Also in Jeremiah the Lord says: "They have forsaken me, the fountain of living water, and have dug for themselves worn-out cisterns, which could not hold water." Moreover, in the same: "Behold, the word of the Lord has become unto them a reproach, and they do not wish for it."[13] Again in the same the Lord says: "The kite knows his time, the turtle, and the swallow; the sparrows of the field keep the time of their coming in; but my people does not know the judgment of the Lord. How do you say, 'We are wise, and the law of the Lord is with us?' The false measurement has been made vain; the scribes are confounded the wise men have trembled, and been taken, because they have rejected the word of the Lord."[14] In Solomon also: "Evil men seek me, and shall not find me; for they held wisdom in hatred and did not receive the word of the Lord."[15] Also in the twenty-seventh Psalm: "Render to them their deserving, because they have not perceived in the works of the Lord."[16] Also in the eighty-first Psalm: "They have not known, neither have they understood; they shall walk on in darkness."[17] In the Gospel, too, according to John: "He came unto His own, and His own received Him not. As many as received Him, to them gave He power to become the sons of God who believe in His name."[18]

4. That the Jews would not understand the Holy Scriptures, but that they would be intelligible in the last times, after that Christ had come

In Isaiah: "And all these words shall be unto you as the words of a book that is sealed, which, if you shall give to a man that knows letters to read, he shall say, 'I cannot read, for it is sealed.' But in that day the deaf shall hear the words of the book, and they who are in darkness and in a cloud; the eyes of the blind shall see."[19] Also in Jeremiah: "In the last of the days you shall know those things."[20] In Daniel, moreover: "Secure the words, and seal the book until the time of consummation, until many learn, and knowledge is fulfilled, because when there shall be a dispersion they shall know all these things."[21] Likewise in the first Epistle of Paul to the Corinthians: "Brethren, I would not that you should be ignorant, that all our fathers were under the cloud." Also in the second

Epistle to the Corinthians: "Their minds are blinded even unto this day, by this same veil which is taken away in Christ, while this same veil remains in the reading of the Old Testament, which is not unveiled, because it is made void in Christ; and even to this day, if at any time Moses is read, the veil is upon their heart. But by and by, when they shall be turned unto the Lord, the veil shall be taken away."[22] In the Gospel, the Lord after His resurrection says: "'These are the words which I spoke unto you while I was yet with you, that all things must be fulfilled which are written in the law of Moses, and in the prophets, and in the Psalms, concerning me.' Then opened He their understanding, that they might understand the Scriptures; and said unto them, 'That thus it is written, and thus it behooved Christ to suffer, and to rise again from the dead the third day; and that repentance and remission of sins should be preached in His name even among all nations.'"[23]

5. That the Jews could understand nothing of the Scriptures unless they first believed in Christ

In Isaiah: "And if you will not believe, neither will you understand."[24] Also the Lord in the Gospel: "For if you believe not that I am He, you shall die in your sins."[25] Moreover, that righteousness should subsist by faith, and that in it was life, was predicted in Habakkuk: "Now the just shall live by faith of me."[26] Hence Abraham, the father of the nations, believed; in Genesis: "Abraham believed in God, and it was counted unto him for righteousness."[27] In like manner, Paul to the Galatians: "Abraham believed in God, and it was counted unto him for righteousness. You know, therefore, that they which are of faith, the same are children of Abraham. But the Scripture, foreseeing that God justifies the heathens by faith, foretold to Abraham that all nations should be blessed in him. Therefore they who are of faith are blessed with faithful Abraham."[28]

6. That the Jews should lose Jerusalem, and should leave the land which they had received

In Isaiah: "Your country is desolate, your cities are burned with fire: your land, strangers shall devour it in your sight; and the daughter of Zion shall be left deserted, and overthrown by foreign peoples, as a cottage in a vineyard, and as a keeper's lodge in a garden of cucumbers, as a city which is besieged. And unless the Lord of Sabaoth had left us a seed, we should have been as Sodom, and we should have been like Gomorrah."[29] Also in the Gospel the Lord says: "Jerusalem, Jerusalem, that killest the prophets, and stone them that are sent unto you, how often would I have gathered your children as a hen gathers her chickens under her wings, and you would not! Behold, your house shall be left unto you desolate."[30]

7. Also that they should lose the Light of the Lord

In Isaiah: "Come, and let us walk in the light of the Lord. For He has sent away His people, the house of Israel."[31] In His Gospel also, according to John: "That was the true light which lights every man that comes into this world. He was in this world, and the world was made by Him, and the world knew Him not."[32] Moreover, in the same place: "He that believes not is judged already, because he has not believed in the name of the only begotten Son of God. And this is the judgment, that light has come into the world, and men loved darkness rather than light."[33]

8. That the first circumcision of the flesh is made void, and the second circumcision of the spirit is promised instead

In Jeremiah: "Thus says the Lord to the men of Judah, and to them who inhabit Jerusalem, Renew newness among you, and do not sow among thorns: circumcise yourselves to your God, and circumcise the foreskin of your heart; lest my anger go forth like fire, and burn you up, and there be none to extinguish it."[34] Also Moses says: "In the last days God will circumcise your heart, and the heart of your seed, to love the Lord your God."[35] Also in Joshua the son of Nun: "And the Lord said unto Joshua, 'Make you small knives of stone, very sharp, and set about to circumcise the children of Israel for the second time.'"[36] Paul also, to the Colossians: "You are circumcised with the circumcision not made with hands in the putting off of the flesh, but with the circumcision of Christ."[37] Also, because Adam was first made by God uncircumcised, and righteous Abel, and Enoch, who pleased God and was translated; and Noah, who, when the world and men were perishing on account of transgressions, was chosen alone, that in him the human race might be preserved; and Melchizedek, the priest according to whose order Christ was promised. Then, because that sign did not avail women, but all are sealed by the sign of the Lord.[38]

9. That the former law which was given by Moses was to cease

In Isaiah: "Then shall they be manifest who seal the law, that they may not learn; and he shall say, 'I wait upon the Lord, who turns away His face from the house of Jacob, and I shall trust in Him.'"[39] In the Gospel also: "All the prophets and the law prophesied until John."[40]

10. That a new law was to be given

In Micah: "For the law shall go forth out of Zion, and the word of the Lord from Jerusalem. And He shall judge among many peoples, and He shall subdue and uncover strong nations."[41] Also in Isaiah: "For from Zion shall go forth the law, and the word of the Lord from Jerusalem; and He shall judge among the nations."[42] Likewise in the Gospel according to Matthew: "And behold a voice out of the cloud, saying, 'This is my beloved Son, in whom I am well pleased; hear Him.'"[43]

11. That another dispensation and a new covenant was to be given

In Jeremiah: "Behold, the days come, says the Lord, and I will complete for the house of Israel, and for the house of Judah, a new testament, not according to the testament which I ordered with their fathers in that day in which I took hold of their hands to bring them out of the land of Egypt, because they remained not in my testament, and I disregarded them, says the Lord: Because this is the testament which will establish with the house of Israel after those days, says the Lord: I will give them my laws, and into their minds I will write them; and I will be to them for a God, and they shall be to me for a people; and they shall not teach every man his brother, saying, Know the Lord: for all shall know me, from the least even to the greatest of them: for I will be merciful to their iniquities, and will no more be mindful of their sins."[44]

12. That the old baptism should cease, and a new one should begin

In Isaiah: "Therefore remember not the former things, neither reconsider the ancient things. Behold, I make new the things which shall now arise, and you shall know it; and I will make in the desert a way, and rivers in a dry place, to give drink to my chosen race, my people whom I acquired, that they should show forth my praises."[45] In the same also: "If they thirst, He will lead them through the deserts; He will bring forth water from the rock; the rock shall be cloven, and the water shall flow: and my people shall drink."[46] Moreover, in the Gospel according to Matthew, John says: "I indeed baptize you with water unto repentance: but He that comes after me is mightier than I, whose shoes I am not worthy to bear; He shall baptize you with the Holy Ghost, and with fire."[47] Also according to John: "Unless a man be born of water, and of the Spirit, he cannot enter into the kingdom of God. For that which is born of the flesh is flesh, and that which is born of the Spirit is spirit."[48]

13. That the old yoke should be made void, and a new yoke should be given

In the second Psalm: "For what purpose have the heathen raged, and the people imagined vain things? The kings of the earth stood up, and the rulers have gathered together against the Lord, and against His Christ. Let us break their bonds asunder, and cast away their yoke from us."[49] Likewise in the Gospel according to Matthew, the Lord says: "Come unto me, all you that labor and are burdened, and I will cause you to rest. Take my yoke upon you, and learn of me; for I am meek and lowly in heart: and you shall find rest unto your souls. For my yoke is excellent, and my burden is light."[50] In Jeremiah: "In that day I will shatter the yoke from their neck, and will burst their fetters; and they shall not labor for others, but they shall labor for the Lord God; and I will raise up David a king unto them."[51]

14. That the old pastors should cease and new ones begin

In Ezekiel: "Wherefore thus says the Lord, 'Behold, I am above the shepherds; and I will require my sheep from their hands, and I will turn them away from feeding my sheep; and they shall feed them no more, and I will deliver my sheep from their mouth, and I will feed them with judgment.'"[52] In Jeremiah the Lord says: "And I will give you shepherds according to my own heart, and they shall feed you with the food of discipline."[53] In Jeremiah, moreover: "Hear the word of the Lord, you nations, and tell it to the islands which are afar off. Say, He that scatters Israel will gather him, and will keep him as a shepherd his flock: for the Lord has redeemed Jacob, and taken him out from the hand of him that was stronger than he."[54]

15. That Christ should be the house and temple of God, and that the old temple should cease, and the new one should begin

In the second book of Kings: "And the word of the Lord came to Nathan, saying, 'Go and tell my servant David, Thus says the Lord, You shall not build me an house to dwell in; but it shall be, when your days shall be fulfilled, and you shall sleep with your fathers, I will raise up your seed after you, which shall come from your bowels, and I will make ready his kingdom. He shall build me an house in my name, and I will raise up his throne for ever; and I will be to him for a father, and he shall be to me for a son: and his house shall obtain confidence, and his kingdom for evermore in my sight.'"[55] Also in the Gospel the Lord says: "There shall not be left in the temple one stone upon another that shall not be thrown down."[56] And "After three days another shall be raised up without hands."[57]

16. That the ancient sacrifice should be made void, and a new one should be celebrated

In Isaiah: "For what purpose to me is the multitude of your sacrifices? Says the Lord: I am full; I will not have the burnt sacrifices of rams, and fat of lambs, and blood of bulls and goats. For who has required these things from your hands?"[58] Also in the forty-ninth Psalm: "I will not eat the flesh of bulls, nor drink the blood of goats. Offer to God the sacrifice of praise, and pay your vows to the Most High. Call upon me in the day of trouble, and I will deliver you: and you shall glorify me."[59] In the same Psalm, moreover: "The sacrifice of praise shall glorify me: therein is the way in which I will show him the salvation of God."[60] In the fourth Psalm too: "Sacrifice the sacrifice of righteousness, and hope in the Lord."[61] Likewise in Malachi:" I have no pleasure concerning you, says the Lord, and I will not have an accepted offering from your hands. Because from the rising of the sun, even unto the going down of the same, my name is glorified among the Gentiles; and in every place odors of incense are offered to my name, and a pure sacrifice, because great is my name among the nations, says the Lord."[62]

17. That the old priesthood should cease, and a new priest should come, who should be forever

In the cixth Psalm: "Before the morning star I begot you. The Lord has sworn, and He will not repent. You are a priest for ever, after the order of Melchizedek.[63] Also in the first book of Kings, God says to the priest Eli: "And I will raise up to me a faithful priest, who shall do all things which are in my heart: and I will build him a sure house; and he shall pass in the presence of my anointed ones for all days. And it shall be, whosoever shall remain in your house, shall come to worship for an piece of silver, and for one loaf of bread.[64]

18. That another Prophet such as Moses was promised; one who should give a new testament, and who rather ought to be heard

In Deuteronomy God said to Moses: "And the Lord said to me, 'A prophet will I raise up to them from among their brethren, such as you, and I will give my word in His mouth; and He shall speak unto them that which I shall command Him. And whosoever shall not hear whatsoever things that prophet shall speak in my name, I will avenge it."[65] Concerning whom also Christ says in the Gospel according to John: "Search the Scriptures, in which you think you have eternal life. These are they which set forth testimony concerning me; and you will not come to me, that you might have life. Do not think that I accuse you to the Father: there is one that accuses you, even Moses, on whom you hope. For if you had believed Moses, you would also believe me: for he wrote of me. But if you believe not his writings, how shall you believe my words?"[66]

19. That two peoples were foretold, the elder and the younger; that is, the old people of the Jews, and the new one which should consist of us

In Genesis: "And the Lord said unto Rebekah, 'Two nations are in your womb, and two peoples shall be separated from your belly; and the one people shall overcome the other people; and the elder shall serve the younger.'"[67] Also in Hosea: "I will call them my people that are not my people, and her beloved that was not beloved. For it shall be, in that place in which it shall be called not my people, they shall be called the sons of the living God."[68]

198

20. That the Church which before had been barren should have more children from among the Gentiles than what the synagogue had had before

In Isaiah: "Rejoice, you barren, that barest not; and break forth and cry, you that travailest not: because many more are the children of the desolate one than of her who has an husband. For the Lord has said, 'Enlarge the place of your tabernacle, and of your curtains, and fasten them: spare not, make long your measures, and strengthen your stakes: stretch forth yet to your right hand and to your left hand; and your seed shall possess the nations, and shall inhabit the deserted cities. Fear not; because you shall overcome: nor be afraid because you are cursed; for you shall forget your eternal confusion.'"[69] Thus also to Abraham, when his former son was born of a bond-woman, Sarah remained long barren; and late in old age bare her son Isaac, of promise, who was the type of Christ. Thus also Jacob received two wives: the elder Leah, with weak eyes, a type of the synagogue; the younger the beautiful Rachel, a type of the Church, who also remained long barren, and afterwards brought forth Joseph, who also was himself a type of Christ. And in the first of Kings it is said that Elkanah had two wives: Peninnah, with her sons; and Hannah, barren, from whom is born Samuel, not according to the order of generation, but according to the mercy and promise of God, when she had prayed in the temple; and Samuel being born, was a type of Christ. Also in the first book of Kings: "The barren has borne seven and she that had many children has grown weak."[70] But the seven children are the seven churches. Whence also Paul wrote to seven churches;[71] and the Apocalypse sets forth seven churches, that the number seven may be preserved; as the seven days in which God made the world; as the seven angels who stand and go in and out before the face of God, as Raphael the angel says in Tobit;[72] and the sevenfold lamp in the tabernacle of witness; and the seven eyes of God, which keep watch over the world; and the stone with seven eyes, as Zechariah says;[73] and the seven spirits; and the seven candlesticks in the Apocalypse; and the seven pillars upon which Wisdom has built her house in Solomon.

21. That the Gentiles should believe in Christ

In Genesis: "And the Lord God said unto Abraham, 'Go out from your country, and from your kindred, and from your father's house, and go into that land which I shall show you: and I will make of you a great nation, and I will bless you, and I will magnify your name and you shall be blessed: and I will bless him that blesses you, and I will curse him that curses you, and in you shall all the tribes of the earth be blessed."[74] On this same point in Genesis: "And Isaac blessed Jacob. 'Behold, the smell of my son is as the smell of a plentiful field which the Lord has blessed: and God give you of the dew of heaven, and of the fertility of the earth, abundance of grain, and wine, and oil: and peoples shall obey you, and princes shall worship you: and you shall be lord over your brother, and the sons of your father shall worship you; and he that curses you shall be cursed, and he that blesses you shall be blessed.'"[75] On this matter too in Genesis: "But when Joseph saw that his father placed his right hand on the head of Ephraim, it seemed displeasing to him. And Joseph laid hold of his father's hand, to lift it from the head of Ephraim on to the head of Manasseh." Moreover, Joseph said unto his father, "'Not so, my father: this is my first-born; place your right hand upon his head.' But he would not, and said, 'I know it, my son, I know it: and he also shall be a people, and he shall be exalted; but his younger brother shall be greater than he, and his seed shall become a multitude of nations.'"[76] Moreover in Genesis: "Judah, your brethren shall praise you: your hand shall be upon the back of your enemies; the sons of your father shall worship you. Judah is a lion's cub: from the slender twig, my son, you have ascended: you lied down and slept as a lion, and as a lion's cub. Who shall stir him up? There shall not fail a prince from Judah, and a leader from his loins, until those things entrusted to him shall come; and he is the hope of the nations: binding his foal unto the vine, and his ass's colt unto the branch of the vine; he shall wash his garments in wine, and his clothing in the blood of the grape: terrible are his eyes with wine, and his teeth are whiter than milk."[77] Hence in Numbers it is written concerning our people: "Behold, the people shall rise up as a lion-like people."[78] In Deuteronomy: "You Gentiles shall be for the head; but this unbelieving people shall be for the tail."[79] Also in Jeremiah: "Hear the sound of the trumpet. And they said, We will not hear: for this cause the nations shall hear, and they who shall feed their cattle among them."[80] In the seventeenth Psalm: "You shall establish me the head of the nations: a people whom I have not known have served me: at the hearing of the ear they have obeyed me."[81] Concerning this very thing the Lord says in Jeremiah: "Before I formed you in the womb, I knew you; and before you went forth from the womb, I sanctified you, and established you as a prophet among the nations."[82] Also in Isaiah: "Behold, I have manifested him for a witness to the nations, a prince and a commander to the peoples." In the same: "Nations which have not known You shall call upon You; and peoples which were ignorant of You shall flee to You." In the same, moreover: "And in that day there shall be a root of Jesse, which shall rise to rule in all the nations; in Him shall the Gentiles hope: and His rest shall be honor." In the same again: "The land of Zebulon, and the land of Naphtali, by the way of the sea, and you others who inhabit the maritime places, and beyond Jordan of the nations. People that walk in darkness, behold yea great light; you who dwell in the region of the shadow of death, the light shall shine upon you." Also in the same: "Thus says the Lord God to Christ my Lord, whose right hand I hold, that the nations may hear Him; and I will break asunder the strength of kings, I will open before Him gates; and cities shall not be shut." Also in the same: "I come to gather together all nations and tongues; and they shall come, and see my glory. And I will send out over them a standard, and I will send those that are preserved among them to the nations which are afar off, which have not heard my name nor seen my glory; and they shall declare my glory to the nations." Also in the same: "And in all these things they are not converted; therefore He shall lift up a standard to the nations which are afar, and He will draw them from the end of the earth." Also in the same: "Who had not been told of Him shall see, and they who have not heard shall understand." Also in the same: "I have been made manifest to those who seek me not: I have been found of those who asked not after me. I said, 'Lo, here am I, to a nation that has not called upon my name.'"[83] Of this same thing, in the Acts of the Apostles, Paul says: "It was necessary that the word of God should first be shown to you; but since you put it from you, and judged yourselves unworthy of eternal life, lo, we turn to the Gentiles: for thus said the Lord by the Scriptures, 'Behold, I have set You a light among the nations, that You should be for salvation even to the ends of the earth.'"[84]

22. That the Jews would lose while we should receive the bread and the cup of Christ and all His grace, and that the new name of Christians should be blessed in the earth

In Isaiah: "Thus says the Lord, 'Behold, they who serve me shall eat, but you shall be hungry: behold, they who serve me shall drink, but you shall be thirsty: behold, they who serve me shall rejoice, but you shall be confounded; the Lord shall slay you. But to those who serve me a new name shall be named, which shall be blessed in the earth.'"[85] Also in the same place: "Therefore shall He lift up an ensign to the nations which are afar off, and He will draw them from the end of the earth; and, behold, they shall come swiftly with lightness; they shall not hunger nor thirst."[86] Also in the same place: "Behold, therefore, the Ruler, the Lord of Sabaoth, shall take away from Judah and from Jerusalem the healthy man and the strong man, the strength of bread and the strength of water."[87] Likewise in the thirty-third Psalm: "O taste and see how sweet is the Lord. Blessed is the man that hopes in Him. Fear the Lord God, all you His saints: for there is no want to them that fear Him. Rich men have wanted and have hungered; but they who seek the Lord shall never want any good thing."[88] Moreover, in the Gospel according to John, the Lord says: "I am the bread of life: he that comes to me shall not hunger, and he that trusts in me shall never thirst." Likewise He says in that place: "If any one thirst, let him come and drink. He that believes in me, as the Scripture says, out of his belly shall flow rivers of living water." Moreover, He says in the same place: "Unless you eat the flesh of the Son of man, and drink His blood, you shall have no life in you."[89]

23. That the Gentiles rather than the Jews attain to the kingdom of heaven

In the Gospel the Lord says: "Many shall come from the east and from the west, and shall lie down with Abraham, and Isaac, and Jacob, in the kingdom of heaven; but the children of the kingdom shall go out into outer darkness: there shall be weeping and gnashing of teeth."[90]

24. That by this alone the Jews can receive pardon of their sins, if they wash away the blood of Christ slain, in His baptism, and, passing over into His Church, obey His precepts

In Isaiah the Lord says: "Now I will not release your sins. When you stretch forth your hands, I will turn away my face from you; and if you multiply prayers, I will not hear you: for your hands are full of blood. Wash you, make you clean; take away the wickedness from your souls from the sight of my eyes; cease from your wickedness; learn to do good; seek judgment; keep him who suffers wrong; judge for the orphan, and justify the widow. And come, let us reason together, says the Lord: and although your sins be as scarlet, I will whiten them as snow; and although they were as crimson, I will whiten them as wool. And if you be willing and listen to me, you shall eat of the good of the land; but if you be unwilling, and will not hear me, the sword shall consume you; for the mouth of the Lord has spoken these things."[91]

NOTES

1. Cyprian's work against the Jews is divided into two parts (Book I and Book II), while Cyprian's "second book" is actually Book III. This is the traditional division of the work.
2. Cyprian here uses the word *sacramentum* in a more generic way, meaning the "mystery of Christ," as in Col. 1:26-27 and Col. 4:3.
3. Ex. 32:1.
4. Ex. 32:31-33.
5. Deut. 32:17.
6. Judg. 2:11-14, 4:1.
7. Mal. 2:11.
8. Jer. 7:25, 25:6-7.
9. 1 Kings 19:10.
10. Neh. 9:26.
11. Isa. 1:2-4.
12. Isa. 6:9-10.
13. Jer. 2:13, 6:10.
14. Jer. 8:7-9.
15. Prov. 1:28-29.
16. Ps. 28:4.
17. Ps. 82:5.
18. John 1:11-12.
19. Isa. 29:11-18.
20. Jer. 23:20.

21. Dan. 12:4-7.
22. 1 Cor. 10:1, 2 Cor. 3:14-16.
23. Luke 24:44-47.
24. Isa. 7:9.
25. John 8:24.
26. Hab. 2:4.
27. Gen. 15:6.
28. Gal. 3:6-9.
29. Isa. 1:7-9.
30. Matt. 23:37-38.
31. Isa. 2:5-6.
32. John 1:9-10.
33. John 3:18-19.
34. Jer. 4:3-4.
35. Deut. 30:6.
36. Jos. 5:2.
37. Col. 2:11.
38. In other words, righteousness cannot come through circumcision since women cannot be circumcised. Cyprian also cites examples of righteous men who were righteous without cirumcision since they lived before its institution.
39. Isa. 8:16-17.
40. Matt. 11:13.
41. Mic. 4:2-3.
42. Isa. 2:3-4.
43. Matt. 17:5. The implication is that, in commanding men to "hear" Jesus, the Father presents our Lord as a new Lawgiver, just as the Israelites of old were commanded to hear Moses, the old lawgiver. Cyprian might have had Deut. 18:15 in mind: "The Lord thy God will raise up to thee a prophet of thy nation and of thy brethren like unto me: him thou shalt hear."
44. Jer. 31:31-34.
45. Isa. 43:18-21.
46. Isa. 48:21.
47. Matt. 3:11. Note that the baptism "with the Holy Ghost and with fire" mentioned by John is applied by Cyprian to water baptism.
48. John 3:5-6.
49. Ps. 2:1-3.
50. Matt. 11:28-30.
51. Jer. 30:8-9.
52. Ezk. 34:10-16.
53. Jer. 3:15.
54. Jer. 31:10-11.
55. 2 Sam. 7:4,5, 12-16.
56. Matt. 24:2.
57. John 2:19 or Mark 14:58.
58. Isa. 1:11-12.
59. Ps. 50:13-15.
60. Ps. 50:23.
61. Ps. 4:5.
62. Mal. 1:10-11.
63. Ps. 110:3. The word "cixth" is a shorthand way of saying "one hundred and ninth" (C + IX = 109), for Psalm 110 is Psalm 109 according to the old Septuagint-Vulgate numbering.
64. 1 Sam. 2:35, 36.
65. Deut. 18:18-19.

66. John 5:39-40, 45-47.
67. Gen. 25:23. Taken literally, Cyprian misinterprets this passage, which refers not to Jews and Gentiles but to the supremacy of Jacob over Esau. Yet it is valid as an allegorical application. Cyprian implies allegorical intepretations in many of his citations without always explaining them.
68. A combination of Hos. 2:23 and Hos. 1:10.
69. Isa. 54:1-4.
70. 1 Sam. 2:5.
71. Rome, Corinth, Galatia, Ephesus, Colossae, Phillipi, Thessalonica
72. Tob. 12:12-15.
73. Zech. 3:9.
74. Gen. 11:1-3.
75. Gen. 27:27-29.
76. Gen. 48:17-19.
77. Gen. 49:8-12.
78. Num. 23:14.
79. Deut. 28:44.
80. Jer. 6:18.
81. Ps. 18:43, 44.
82. Jer. 1:5.
83. The preceding series of quotes from Isaiah: 55:4, 5; 11:10; 9:1-2; 14:1; 55:18,19; 5:25, 26; 52: 15; 65:1.
84. Acts 13:46-47.
85. Isa. 65:13-15.
86. Isa. 5:26, 27.
87. Isa. 3:1, 2.
88. Ps. 34:8-10.
89. The three preceding quotes from the Gospel of John are taken from 6:35, 7:37-38, 6:53.
90. Matt. 8:11-12.
91. Isa. 1:15-20.

BOOK II

1. That Christ is the First-born, and that He is the Wisdom of God, by whom all things were made

In Solomon in the Proverbs: "The Lord established me in the beginning of His ways, into His works: before the world He rounded me. In the beginning, before He made the earth, and before He appointed the abysses, before the fountains of waters gushed forth, before the mountains were settled, before all the hills, the Lord begot me. He made the countries, and the uninhabitable places, and the uninhabitable bounds under heaven. When He prepared the heaven, I was present with Him; and when He set apart His seat. When He made the strong clouds above the winds, and when He placed the strengthened fountains under heaven, when He made the mighty foundations of the earth, I was by His side, ordering them: I was He in whom He delighted: moreover, I daily rejoiced before His face in all time, when He rejoiced in the perfected earth."[1] Also in the same in Ecclesiasticus: "I went forth out of the mouth of the Most High, first-born before every creature: I made the unwearying light to rise in the heavens, and I covered the whole earth with a cloud: I dwelt in the high places, and my throne in the pillar of the cloud: I compassed the circle of heaven, and I penetrated into the depth of the abyss, and I walked on the waves of the sea, and I stood in all the earth; and in every people and in every nation I had the pre-eminence, and by my own strength I have trodden the hearts of all the excellent and the humble: in me is all hope of life and virtue: pass over to me, all you who desire me."[2] Also in the eighty-eighth Psalm: "And I will establish Him as my first-born, the highest among the kings of the earth. I will keep my mercy for Him for ever, and my faithful covenant for Him; and I will establish his seed for ever and ever. If his children forsake my law, and walk not in my judgments; if they profane my judgments, and do not observe my precepts, I will visit their wickednesses with a rod, and their sins with scourges; but my mercy will I not scatter away from them."[3] Also in the Gospel according to John, the Lord says: "And this is life eternal, that they should know You, the only and true God, and Jesus Christ, whom You have sent. I have glorified You on the earth: I have finished the work which You gave me to do. And now, glorify me with Yourself, with the glory which I had with You before the world was made."[4] Also Paul to the Colossians: "Who is the image of the invisible God, and the first-born of every creature." Also in the same place: "The first-born from the dead, that He might in all things

205

become the holder of the pre-eminence."[5] In the Apocalypse too: "I am Alpha and Omega, the beginning and the end. I will give unto Him that is thirsting from the fountain of the water of life freely."[6] That He also is both the wisdom and the power of God, Paul proves in his first Epistle to the Corinthians: "Because the Jews require a sign, and the Greeks seek after wisdom: but we preach Christ crucified, to the Jews indeed a stumbling-block, and to the Gentiles foolishness; but to them that are called, both Jews and Greeks, Christ the power of God and the wisdom of God."[7]

2. That Christ is the Wisdom of God; and concerning the sacrament of His incarnation and of His passion, and cup and altar; and of the apostles who were sent, and preached

In Solomon in the Proverbs: "Wisdom has built herself an house, and she has placed under it seven pillars; she has slain her victims; she has mingled her wine in the goblet, and has made ready her table, and has sent her servants, calling with a loud announcement to the cup, saying, 'Let him who is foolish turn to me:' and to them that want understanding she has said, 'Come, eat of my loaves, and drink the wine which I have mingled for you. Forsake foolishness, and seek wisdom, and correct knowledge by understanding.'"[8]

3. That the same Christ is the Word of God

In the forty-fourth Psalm: "My heart has breathed out a good Word. I tell my works to the King."[9] Also in the thirty-second Psalm: "By the Word of God were the heavens made fast; and all their strength by the breath of His mouth."[10] Also in Isaiah: "A word completing and shortening in righteousness, because a shortened word will God make in the whole earth."[11] Also in the cvith Psalm: "He sent His Word, and healed them."[12] Moreover, in the Gospel according to John: "In the beginning was the Word, and the Word was with God, and God was the Word. The same was in the beginning with God. All things were made by Him, and without Him was nothing made that was made. In Him was life; and the life was the light of men. And the light shines in darkness; and the darkness comprehended it not."[13] Also in the Apocalypse: "And I saw the heaven opened, and lo, a white horse; and he who sate upon him was called Faithful and True, judging rightly and justly; and He made war. And He was covered with a garment sprinkled with blood; and His name is called the Word of God."[14]

4. That Christ is the Hand and Arm of God

In Isaiah: "Is God's Hand not strong to save? Or has He made His ear heavy, that He cannot hear? But your sins separate between you and God; and on account of your sins He turns His face away from you, that He may not pity.

For your hands are defiled with blood, and your fingers with sins. Moreover, your lips have spoken wickedness, and your tongue meditates unrighteousness. No one speaks truth, nor is there true judgment: they trust in vanity, and speak emptiness, who conceive sorrow, and bring forth wickedness." Also in the same place: "Lord, who has believed our report? And to whom is the Arm of God revealed?" Also in the same: "Thus says the Lord, Heaven is my throne, and the earth is the support of my feet. What house will you build unto me? Or what is the place for my rest? For all these things has mine hand made." Also in the same: "O Lord God, Your Arm is high, and they knew it not; but when they know it, they shall be confounded." Also in the same: "The Lord has revealed His Arm, that holy Arm, in the sight of all nations; all nations, even the ends of the earth, shall see salvation from God." Also in the same place: "Behold, I have made you as the wheels of a thrashing chariot, new and turned back upon themselves; and you shall thrash the mountains, and shall beat the hills small, and shall make them as chaff, and shall winnow them; and the wind shall seize them, and the whirlwind shall scatter them: but you shall rejoice in the saints of Israel; and the poor and needy shall exult. For they shall seek water, and there shall be none. For their tongue shall be dry for thirst. I the Lord God, I the God of Israel, will hear them, and will not forsake them; but I will open rivers in the mountains, and fountains in the midst of the fields. I will make the wildernesses watery groves, and a thirsty land into watercourses. I will establish in the land of drought the cedar-tree and the box-tree, and the myrtle and the cypress, and the elm and the poplar, that they may see and acknowledge, and know and believe together, that the Hand of the Lord has done these things, and the Holy One of Israel has shown them."[15]

5. That Christ is at once Angel and God

In Genesis, to Abraham: "And the Angel of the Lord called him from heaven, and said unto him, 'Abraham, Abraham!' And he said, 'Here am I.' And He said, 'Lay not your hand upon the lad, nor do anything unto him. For now I know that you fear your God, and hast not spared your son, your beloved son, for my sake.'" Also in the same place, to Jacob: "And the Angel of the Lord spoke unto me in dreams, 'I am God, whom you saw in the place of God where you anointed me a pillar of stone, and vowed to me a vow.'"[16] Also in Exodus: "But God went before them by day indeed in a pillar of cloud, to show them the way; and by night in a pillar of fire." And afterwards, in the same place: "And the Angel of God moved forward, which went before the army of the children of Israel." Also in the same place: "Lo, I send my Angel before your face, to keep you in the way, that He may lead you into the land which I have prepared for you. Observe Him, and obey Him, and be not disobedient to Him, and He will not be wanting to you. For my Name is in Him."[17] Whence He Himself says in the Gospel: ""I came in the name of my Father, and you received me not. When another shall come in his own name, him you will receive."[18] And again in the cxviith Psalm: "Blessed is He who comes in the name of the Lord."[19] Also in Malachi: "My covenant of life and peace was with Levi; and I gave him fear, that he should fear me, that he should go from the face of my name. The law of truth was in his mouth, and unrighteousness was not found in his lips. In the peace of the tongue correcting, he walked with us, and turned many away from unrighteousness. Because the lips of the priests shall keep knowledge, and they shall seek the law at His mouth; for He is the Angel of the Almighty."[20]

6. That Christ is God

In Genesis: "And God said unto Jacob, 'Arise, and go up to the place of Bethel, and dwell there; and make there an altar to that God who appeared unto you when thou fleddest from the face of your brother Esau.'"[21] Also in Isaiah: "Thus says the Lord, the God of Sabaoth, Egypt is wearied; and the merchandise of the Ethiopians, and the tall men of the Sabeans, shall pass over unto you, and shall be your servants; and shall walk after you bound with chains; and shall worship you, and shall pray to you, because God is in you, and there is no other God beside you. For you are God, and we knew it not, O God of Israel, our Savior. They shall all be confounded and fear who oppose you, and shall fall into confusion."[22] Likewise in the same: "The voice of one crying in the wilderness, 'Prepare the way of the Lord, make straight the paths of our God. Every channel shall be filled up, and every mountain and hill shall be made low, and all crooked places shall be made straight, and rough places plain; and the glory of the Lord shall be seen, and all flesh shall see the salvation of God, because the Lord has spoken it.'"[23] Moreover, in Jeremiah: "This is our God, and no other shall be esteemed beside Him, who has found all the way of knowledge, and has given it to Jacob His son, and to Israel His beloved. After this He was seen upon earth, and He conversed with men."[24] Also in Zechariah God says: "And they shall cross over through the narrow sea, and they shall smite the waves in the sea, and they shall dry up all the depths of the rivers; and all the haughtiness of the Assyrians shall be confounded, and the sceptre of Egypt shall be taken away. And I will strengthen them in the Lord their God, and in His name shall they glory, says the Lord."[25] Moreover, in Hosea the Lord says: "I will not do according to the anger of mine indignation, I will not allow Ephraim to be destroyed: for I am God, and there is not a holy man in you: and I will not enter into the city; I will go after God."[26] Also in the forty-fourth Psalm: "Your throne, O God, is for ever and ever: the sceptre of righteousness is the sceptre of Your kingdom. You have loved righteousness, and hated iniquity: wherefore God, Your God, has anointed

You with the oil of gladness above Your fellows."[27] So, too, in the forty-fifth Psalm: "Be still, and know that I am God. I will be exalted among the nations, and I will be exalted in the earth."[28] Also in the eighty-first Psalm: "They have not known, neither have they understood: they will walk on in darkness."[29] Also in the sixty-seventh Psalm: "Sing unto God, sing praises unto His name: make a way for Him who goes up into the west: God is His name."[30] Also in the Gospel according to John: "In the beginning was the Word, and the Word was with God, and God was the Word." Also in the same: "The Lord said to Thomas, 'Reach hither your finger, and behold my hands: and be not faithless, but believing.' Thomas answered and said unto Him, 'My Lord and my God.' Jesus says unto him, 'Because you have seen me, you have believed: blessed are they who have not seen, and yet have believed.'"[31] Also Paul to the Romans: "I could wish that I myself were accursed from Christ for my brethren and my kindred according to the flesh: who are Israelites: whose are the adoption, and the glory, and the covenant, and the appointment of the law, and the service [of God], and the promises; whose are the fathers, of whom, according to the flesh, Christ came, who is God over all, blessed for evermore."[32] Also in the Apocalypse: "I am Alpha and Omega, the beginning and the end. I will give to him that is thirsty, of the fountain of living water freely. He that overcomes shall possess these things, and their inheritance; and I will be his God, and he shall be my son."[33] Also in the eighty-first Psalm: "God stood in the congregation of gods, and judging gods in the midst." And again in the same place: "I have said, you are gods; and you are all the children of the Highest: but you shall die like men."[34] But if they who have been righteous, and have obeyed the divine precepts, may be called gods, how much more is Christ, the Son of God, God! Thus He Himself says in the Gospel according to John: "Is it not written in the law, that I said, You are gods? If He called them gods to whom the word of God was given, and the Scripture cannot be relaxed, say to Him whom the Father has sanctified and sent into the world, that you blaspheme because I said, 'I am the Son of God?' But if I do not the works of my Father, believe me not; but if I do, and you will not believe me, believe the works, and know that the Father is in me, and I in Him."[35] Also in the Gospel according to Matthew: "And you shall call His name Emmanuel, which is, being interpreted, God with us."[36]

7. That Christ our God should come, the Enlightener and Savior of the human race

In Isaiah: "Be comforted, you weakened hands; and you weak knees, be strengthened. You who are of a timorous heart, fear not. Our God will recompense judgment, He Himself will come, and will save us. Then shall be opened the eyes of the blind, and the ears of the deaf shall hear. Then the lame man shall leap as a stag, and the tongue of the dumb shall be intelligible; because in the wilderness the water is broken forth, and the stream in the thirsty land." Also in that place: "Not an elder nor an angel, but the Lord Himself shall deliver them; because He shall love them, and shall spare them, and He Himself shall redeem them." Also in the same place: "I the Lord God have called You in righteousness, that I may hold Your hand, and I will comfort You; and I have given You for a covenant of my people, for a light of the nations; to open the eyes of the blind, to bring forth them that are bound from chains, and those who sit in darkness from the prison-house. I am the Lord God, that is my name. I will not give any glory to another, nor my powers to graven images."[37] Also in the twenty-fourth Psalm: "Show me Your ways, Lord, and teach me Your paths, and lead me unto Your truth, and teach me; for You are the God of my salvation."[38] Whence, in the Gospel according to John, the Lord says: "I am the light of the world. He that will follow me shall not walk in darkness, but shall have the light of life."[39] Moreover, in that according to Matthew, the angel Gabriel says to Joseph: "Joseph, you son of David, fear not to take unto you Mary your wife. For that which shall be born to her is of the Holy Ghost. And she shall bring forth a son, and you shall call His name Jesus; for He shall save His people from their sins."[40] Also in that according to Luke: "And Zacharias was filled with the Holy Ghost, and prophesied, saying, 'Blessed be the Lord God of Israel, who has foreseen redemption for His people, and has raised up an horn of salvation for us in the house of His servant David.'" Also in the same place: "The angel said to the shepherds: 'Fear not; for, behold, I bring you tidings that unto you is born this day in the city of David a Savior, which is Christ Jesus.'"[41]

8. That although from the beginning He had been the Son of God, yet He had to be begotten again according to the flesh

In the second Psalm: "The Lord said unto me, 'You are my Son; this day have I begotten You. Ask of me, and I will give You the nations for Your inheritance, and the bounds of the earth for Your possession.'"[42] Also in the Gospel according to Luke: "And it came to pass, when Elizabeth heard the salutation of Mary, the babe leaped in her womb; and she was filled with the Holy Ghost, and she cried out with a loud voice, and said, 'Blessed are you among women, and blessed is the fruit of your womb. And whence does this happen to me, that the mother of my Lord should come to me?'"[43] Also Paul to the Galatians: "But when the fullness of the time had come, God sent His Son, born of a woman."[44] Also in the Epistle of John: "Every spirit which confesses that Jesus Christ has come in the flesh is of God. But whosoever denies that He has come in the flesh is not of God, but is of the spirit of Antichrist."[45]

9. That this should be the sign of His nativity, that He should be born of a virgin—man and God—a son of man and a Son of God

In Isaiah: "And the Lord went on to speak to Ahaz, saying, 'Ask you a sign from the Lord your God, in the height above and in the depth below.' And Ahaz said, 'I will not ask, and I will not tempt the Lord my God.' And He said, 'Hear, therefore, O house of David: it is no trifling contest unto you with men, since God supplies the struggle. On this account God Himself will give you a sign. Behold, a virgin shall conceive, and shall bear a son, and you shall call His name Emmanuel. Butter and honey shall He eat; before that He knows to prefer the evil, He shall exchange the good.'"[46] This seed God had foretold would proceed from the woman that should trample on the head of the devil. In Genesis: "Then God said unto the serpent, 'Because you have done this, cursed are you from every kind of the beasts of the earth. Upon your breast and your belly shall you crawl, and earth shall be your food all the days of your life. And I will place enmity between you and the woman and her seed. He shall regard your head, and you shall watch his heel.'"[47]

10. That Christ is both man and God, compounded of both natures, that He might be a Mediator between us and the Father

In Jeremiah: "And He is man, and who shall know Him?"[48] Also in Numbers: "A star shall arise out of Jacob, and a man shall rise up from Israel." Also in the same place: "A man shall go forth out of his seed, and shall rule over many nations; and His kingdom shall be exalted as Gog, and His kingdom shall be increased; and God brought Him forth out of Egypt. His glory is as of the unicorn, and He shall eat the nations of His enemies, and shall take out the marrow of their fatnesses, and will pierce His enemy with His arrows. He couched and lay down as a lion, and as a lion's cub. Who shall raise Him up? Blessed are they who bless You, and cursed are they who curse You."[49] Also in Isaiah: "The Spirit of the Lord is upon me; on account whereof He has anointed me: He has sent me to tell good tidings to the poor; to heal the bruised in heart, to preach deliverance to the captives, and sight to the blind, to proclaim the acceptable year of the Lord, and the day of retribution."[50] Whence, in the Gospel according to Luke, Gabriel says to Mary: "And the angel, answering, said to her, 'The Holy Ghost shall come upon you, and the power of the Highest shall overshadow you. Wherefore that holy thing which is born of you shall be called the Son of God.'"[51] Also in the first Epistle of Paul to the Corinthians: "The first man is of the mud of the earth; the second man is from heaven. As was he from the soil, such are they also that are of the earth; and as is the heavenly, such also are the heavenly. As we have borne the image of him who is of the earth, let us also bear the image of Him who is from heaven."[52]

211

11. That Christ was to be born of the seed of David, according to the flesh

In the second of Kings: "And the word of the Lord came to Nathan, saying, 'Go and tell my servant David, Thus says the Lord, You shall not build me an house to dwell in; but it shall come to pass, when your days shall be fulfilled, and you shall sleep with your fathers, I will raise up your seed after you who shall come from your loins, and I will establish His kingdom. He shall build me a house in my name, and I will set up His throne for ever; and I will be to Him a Father, and He shall be to me a Son; and His house shall obtain confidence, and His kingdom for ever in my sight.'"[53] Also in Isaiah: "And a rod shall go forth of the root of Jesse, and a flower shall go up from his root; and the Spirit of the Lord shall rest upon Him, the spirit of wisdom and of understanding, the spirit of counsel and might, the spirit of knowledge and piety; and the spirit of the fear of the Lord shall fill Him."[54] Also in the cxxxist Psalm: "God has sworn the truth unto David himself, and He has not repudiated it; of the fruit of your belly will I set upon my throne."[55] Also in the Gospel according to Luke: "And the angel said unto her, 'Fear not, Mary. For you have found favor before God. Behold, you shall conceive, and shall bring forth a son, and shall call His name Jesus. The same shall be great, and He shall be called the Son of the Highest; and the Lord God shall give Him the throne of His father David, and He shall reign over the house of Jacob for ever, and of His kingdom there shall be no end.'"[56] Also in the Apocalypse: "And I saw in the right hand of God, who sate on the throne, a book written within, and on the back sealed with seven seals; and I saw a strong angel proclaiming with a loud voice, 'Who is worthy to receive the book, and to open its seals?' Nor was there any one either in heaven or upon the earth, or under the earth, who was able to open the book, nor even to look into it. And I wept much because nobody was found worthy to open the book, nor to look into it. And one of the elders said unto me, 'Weep not; behold, the Lion of the tribe of Judah, the Root of David, has prevailed to open the book, and to loose its seven seals.'"[57]

12. That Christ should be born in Bethlehem

In Micah: "And you, Bethlehem, house of Ephrata, are not little, that you should be appointed among the thousands of Judah. Out of you shall He come forth to me, that He may be a prince in Israel, and His goings forth from the beginning from the days of old."[58] Also in the Gospel: "And when Jesus was born in Bethlehem of Judah, in the days of Herod the king, behold, Magi came from the east to Jerusalem, saying, Where is He that is born King of the Jews? For we have seen His star in the east, and we have come with gifts to worship Him."[59]

13. That Christ was to come in low estate in His first advent

In Isaiah: "Lord, who has believed our report, and to whom is the Arm of the Lord revealed? We have declared in His presence as children, as a root in a thirsty ground. There is no form nor glory in Him; and we saw Him, and He had no form nor beauty; but His form was without honor, and lacking beyond other men. He was a man set in a plague, and knowing how to bear weakness; because His face was turned away, He was dishonored, and was not accounted of. He bears our sins, and grieves for us; and we thought that He was in grief, and in wounding, and in affliction; but He was wounded for our transgressions, and He was weakened for our sins. The discipline of our peace was upon Him, and with His bruise we are healed. We all like sheep have gone astray; than has gone out of his way. And God has delivered Him for our sins; and He, because He was afflicted, opened not His mouth." Also in the same: "I am not rebellious, nor do I contradict. I gave my back to the stripes, and my cheeks to the palms of the hands. Moreover, I did not turn away my face from the foulness of spitting, and God was my helper." Also in the same: "He shall not cry, nor will any one hear His voice in the streets. He shall not break a bruised reed, and a smoking flax He shall not extinguish; but He shall bring forth judgment in truth. He shall shine forth, and shall not be shaken, until He set judgment in the earth, and in His name shall the nations trust."[60] Also in the twenty-first Psalm: "But I am a worm, and no man; the accursed of man, and the casting away of the people. All they who saw me despised me, and spoke within their lips, and moved their head. 'He hoped in the Lord, let Him deliver him; let Him save him, since he will have Him.'" Also in that place: "My strength is dried up like a potsherd, and my tongue is glued to my jaws."[61] Also in Zechariah: "And the Lord showed me Jesus, that great priest, standing before the face of the Angel of the Lord, and the devil was standing at his right hand to oppose him. And Jesus was clothed in filthy garments, and he stood before the face of the Angel Himself; and He answered and said to them who were standing before His face, saying, 'Take away his filthy garments from him.' And he said to him, 'Behold, I have taken away your iniquities. And put upon him a priestly garment, and set a fair mitre upon his head.'"[62] Also Paul to the Philippians: "Who, being established in the form of God, thought it not robbery that He was equal with God, but emptied Himself, taking the form of a servant, and was made in the likeness of men; and being found in fashion as a man, He humbled Himself, becoming obedient even unto death, even the death of the cross. Wherefore also God exalted Him, and gave Him a name which is above every name, that in the name of Jesus every knee should bow, of things in heaven, of things in earth, and of infernal things, and every tongue should confess that Jesus Christ is Lord in the glory of God the Father."[63]

14. That He is the righteous One whom the Jews should put to death

In the Wisdom of Solomon: "Let us lay hold of the righteous, because He is disagreeable to us, and is contrary to our works, and reproaches us with our transgressions of the law. He professes that He has the knowledge of God, and calls Himself the Son of God; He has become to us an exposure of our thoughts; He is grievous unto us even to look upon, because His life is unlike to others, and His ways are changed. We are esteemed by Him as frivolous, and He restrains Himself from our ways, as if from uncleanness; and He extols the last end of the righteous, and boasts that He has God for His Father. Let us see, then, if His words are true, and let us try what will come to Him. Let us interrogate Him with reproach and torture, that we may know His reverence and prove His patience. Let us condemn Him with a most shameful death. These things they considered, and erred. For their maliciousness has blinded them, and they knew not the sacraments of God."[64] Also in Isaiah: "See how the righteous perishes, and no man understands; and righteous men are taken away, and no man regards. For the righteous man is taken away from the face of unrighteousness, and his burial shall be in peace."[65] Concerning this very thing it was before foretold in Exodus: "You shall not slay the innocent and the righteous."[66] Also in the Gospel: "Judas, led by penitence, said to the priests and elders, I have sinned, in that I have betrayed the innocent blood."[67]

15. That Christ is called a sheep and a lamb who was to be slain, and concerning the sacrament [mystery] of the passion

In Isaiah: "He was led as a sheep to the slaughter, and as a lamb before his shearer is dumb, so He opened not His mouth. In His humiliation His judgment was taken away: who shall relate His nativity? Because His life shall be taken away from the earth. By the transgressions of my people He was led to death; and I will give the wicked for His burial, and the rich themselves for His death; because He did no wickedness, nor deceits with His mouth. Wherefore He shall gain many, and shall divide the spoils of the strong; because His soul was delivered up to death, and He was counted among transgressors. And He bare the sins of many, and was delivered for their offenses."[68] Also in Jeremiah: "Lord, give me knowledge, and I shall know it: then I saw their meditations. I was led like a lamb without malice to the slaughter; against me they devised a device, saying, Come, let us cast the tree into His bread, and let us erase His life from the earth, and His name shall no more be a remembrance."[69] Also in Exodus God said to Moses: "Let them take to themselves each man a sheep, through the houses of the tribes, a sheep without blemish, perfect, male, of a year old it shall be to you. You shall take it from the lambs and from the goats, and all the congregation of the synagogue of the children of Israel shall kill it in the evening; and they shall take of its blood, and shall place it upon the two posts, and upon the threshold in the houses, in the very houses in which they shall eat it. And they shall eat the flesh on the same night, roasted with fire; and they shall eat unleavened bread with bitter herbs. You shall not eat of them raw nor dressed in water, but roasted with fire; the head with the feet and the inward parts. You shall leave nothing of them to the morning; and you shall not break a bone of it. But what of it shall be left to the morning shall be burnt with fire. But thus you shall eat it; your loins girt, and your sandals on your feet, and your staff in your hands; and you shall eat it in haste: for it is the Lord's passover."[70] Also in the Apocalypse: "And I saw in the midst of the throne, and of the four living creatures, and in the midst of the elders, a Lamb standing as if slain, having seven horns and seven eyes, which are the seven spirits of God sent forth throughout all the earth. And He came and took the book from the right hand of God, who sate on the throne. And when He had taken the book, the four living creatures and the four and twenty elders cast themselves before the Lamb, having every one of them harps and golden cups full of odors of supplications, which are the prayers of the saints; and they sang a new song, saying, 'Worthy are You, O Lord, to take the book, and to open its seals: for You were slain, and hast redeemed us with Your blood from every tribe, and people, and nation; and You have made us a kingdom unto our God, and hast made us priests, and they shall reign upon the earth.'"[71] Also in the Gospel: "On the next day John saw Jesus coming to him, and says, 'Behold the Lamb of God, and behold Him that takes away the sins of the world!'"[72]

16. That Christ also is called a Stone

In Isaiah: "Thus says the Lord, Behold, I place on the foundations of Zion a precious stone, elect, chief, a corner stone, honorable; and he who trusts in Him shall not be confounded."[73] Also in the cxviith Psalm: "The stone which the builders rejected, the same has become the head of the corner. This is done by the Lord, and it is wonderful in our eyes. This is the day, which the Lord has made; let us rejoice and be glad in it. O Lord, save therefore, O Lord, direct therefore. Blessed is He who comes in the name of the Lord."[74] Also in Zechariah: "Behold, I bring forth my servant. The Orient is his name, because the stone which I have placed before the face of Jesus; upon that one stone are seven eyes."[75] Also in Deuteronomy: "And you shall write upon the stone all this law, very plainly."[76] Also in Joshua the son of Nun: "And be took a great stone, and placed it there before the Lord; and Joshua said unto the people, 'Behold, this stone shall be to you for a testimony, because it has heard all the things which were spoken by the Lord, which He has spoken to you today; and it shall be for a testimony to you in the last of the days, when you shall have departed from your God.'"[77] Also in the Acts of the Apostles, Peter: "You princes of the people, and elders of Israel, hearken: 'Behold, we are this day interrogated by you about the good deed done to the impotent man, by means of which he is made whole. Be it known unto you all, and to all the people of Israel, that in the name of Jesus Christ of Nazareth, whom you have crucified, whom God has raised up from the dead, by Him he stands whole in your presence, but by none other. This is the stone which was despised by you builders, which has become the head of the corner. For there is no other name given to men under heaven in which we must be saved."[78] This is the stone in Genesis, which Jacob places at his head, because the head of the man is Christ; and as he slept he saw a ladder reaching to heaven, on which the Lord was placed, and angels were ascending and descending.[79] And this stone he designating Christ consecrated and anointed with the sacrament of unction.[80] This is the stone in Exodus upon which Moses sat on the top of a hill when Joshua the son of Nun fought against Amalek; and by the sacrament of the stone, and the steadfastness of his sitting, Amalek was overcome by Joshua, that is, the devil was overcome by Christ. This is the great stone in the first book of Kings, upon which was placed the ark of the covenant when the oxen brought it back in the cart, sent back and returned by the strangers. Also, this is the stone in the first book of Kings, with which David smote the forehead of Goliath and slew him; signifying that the devil and his servants are thereby thrown down—that part of the head, namely, being conquered which they have not had sealed. And by this seal we also are always safe and live. This is the stone which, when Israel had conquered the aliens, Samuel set up and called its name Ebenezer; that is, the stone that helps.

17. That afterwards this Stone should become a mountain, and should fill the whole earth

In Daniel: "And behold a very great image; and the aspect of this image was fearful, and it stood erect before you; whose head was of fine gold, its breast and arms were silver, its belly and thighs were of brass, and its feet were partly indeed of iron, and partly of clay, until that a stone was cut out of the mountain, without the hands of those that should cut it, and struck the image upon the feet of iron and clay, and broke them into small fragments. And the iron, and the clay, and the brass, and the silver, and the gold, was made altogether; and they became small as chaff, or dust in the threshing-floor in summer; and the wind blew them away, so that nothing remained of them. And the stone which struck the image became a great mountain, and filled the whole earth."[81]

18. That in the last times the same mountain should be manifested, and upon it the Gentiles should come, and on it all the righteous should go up

In Isaiah: "In the last times the mountain of the Lord shall be revealed, and the house of God upon the tops of the mountains; and it shall be exalted above the hills, and all nations shall come upon it, and many shall walk and say, Come, and let us go up into the mountain of the Lord, and into the house of the God of Jacob; and He will tell us His way, and we will walk in it. For from Sion shall proceed the law, and the word of the Lord from Jerusalem; and He shall judge among the nations, and shall rebuke much people; and they shall beat their swords into ploughshares, and their spears into pruning-hooks, and they shall no more learn to fight."[82] Also in the twenty-third Psalm: "Who shall ascend into the hill of the Lord, or who shall stand in His holy place? He that is innocent in his hands, and of a clean heart; who has not received his life in vanity, and has not sworn craftily to his neighbor. He shall receive the blessing from the Lord, and mercy from the God that saves him. This is the generation of those who seek Him, that seek the face of the God of Jacob."[83]

19. That Christ is the Bridegroom, having the Church as His bride, from which spiritual children were to be born

In Joel: "Blow with the trumpet in Zion; sanctify a fast, and call a healing; assemble the people, sanctify the Church, gather the elders, collect the little ones that suck the breast; let the Bridegroom go forth of His chamber, and the bride out of her closet."[84] Also in Jeremiah: "And I will take away from the cities of Judah, and from the streets of Jerusalem, the voice of the joyous, and the voice of the glad; the voice of the bridegroom, and the voice of the bride."[85] Also in the eighteenth Psalm: "And he is as a bridegroom going forth from his chamber; he exulted as a giant to run his course. From the height of heaven is his going forth, and his circuit even to the end of it; and there is nothing which is hid from his heat."[86] Also in the Apocalypse: "Come, I will show you the new bride, the Lamb's wife. And he took me in the Spirit to a great mountain, and he showed me the holy city Jerusalem descending out of heaven from God, having the glory of God."[87] Also in the Gospel according to John: "You are my witnesses, that I said to them who were sent from Jerusalem to me, that I am not the Christ, but that I am sent before Him. For he who has the bride is the bridegroom; but the friend of the bridegroom is he who stands and hears him with joy, and rejoices because of the voice of the bridegroom."[88] The mystery of this matter was shown in Joshua the son of Nun, when he was bidden to put his shoes from off him, doubtless because he himself was not the bridegroom. For it was in the law, that whoever should refuse marriage should put off his shoe, but that he should be shod who was to be the bridegroom: "And it happened, when Joshua was in Jericho, he looked around with his eyes, and saw a man standing before his face, and holding a javelin in his hand, and said, 'Are you for us or for our enemies?' And he said, 'I am the leader of the host of the Lord; now draw near.' And Joshua fell on his face to the earth, and said to him, 'Lord, what do You command unto Your servant.' And the leader of the Lord's host said, 'Loose your shoe from your feet, for the place whereon you stand is holy ground.'"[89] Also, in Exodus, Moses is bidden to put off his shoe, because he, too, was not the bridegroom: "And there appeared unto him the angel of the Lord in a flame of fire out of a bush; and he saw that the bush burned with fire, but the bush was not consumed. And Moses said, 'I will pass over and see this great sight, why the bush is not consumed.' But when He saw that he drew near to see, the Lord God called him from the bush, saying, 'Moses, Moses.' And he said, 'What is it?' And He said, 'Draw not near hither, unless you have loosed your shoe from off your feet; for the place on which you stand is holy ground.' And He said unto him, 'I am the God of your father, the God of Abraham, and the God of Isaac, and the God of Jacob.'"[90] This was also made plain in the Gospel according to John: "And John answered them, 'I indeed baptize with water, but there stands One in the midst of you whom you know not: He it is of whom I said, 'The man that comes after me is made before me, the latchet of whose shoe I am not worthy to unloose.'"[91] Also according to Luke: "Let your loins be girt, and your lamps burning, and you like to men that wait for their master when he shall come from the wedding, that when he comes and knocks, they may open unto him. Blessed are those servants whom their Lord, when He comes, shall find watching."[92] Also in the Apocalypse: "The Lord God omnipotent reigns: let us be glad and rejoice, and let us give to Him the honor of glory; for the marriage of the Lamb has come, and His wife has made herself ready."[93]

20. That the Jews would fasten Christ to the cross

In Isaiah: "I have spread out my hands all day to a people disobedient and contradicting me, who walk in ways that are not good, but after their own sins."[94] Also in Jeremiah: "Come, let us cast the tree into His bread, and let us blot out His life from the earth.[95] Also in Deuteronomy: "And Your life shall be hanging (in doubt) before Your eyes; and You shall fear day and night, and shall not trust to Your life."[96] Also in the twenty-first Psalm: "They tore my hands and my feet; they numbered all my bones. And they gazed upon me, and saw me, and divided my garments among them, and upon my vesture they cast a lot. But You, O Lord, remove not Your help far from me; attend unto my help. Deliver my soul from the sword, and my only one from the paw of the dog. Save me from the mouth of the lion, and my lowliness from the horns of the unicorns. I will declare Your name unto my brethren; in the midst of the Church I will praise You."[97] Also in the cxviiith Psalm: "Pierce my flesh with nails through fear of You." Also in the cxlth Psalm: "The lifting up of my hands is an evening sacrifice."[98] Of which sacrifice Zephaniah said: "Fear from the presence of the Lord God, since His day is near, because the Lord has prepared His sacrifice, He has sanctified His elect."[99] Also in Zechariah: "And they shall look upon me, whom they have pierced."[100] Also in the eighty-seventh Psalm: "I have called unto You, O Lord, the whole day; I have stretched out my hands unto You."[101] Also in Numbers: "Not as a man is God suspended, nor as the son of man does He suffer threats."[102] Whence in the Gospel the Lord says: "As Moses lifted up the serpent in the wilderness, even so must the Son of man be lifted up, that whosoever believes in the Son may have life eternal."[103]

21. That in the passion and the sign of the cross is all virtue and power

In Habakkuk: "His virtue covered the heavens, and the earth is full of His praise, and His splendor shall be as the light; there shall be horns in His hands. And there the virtue of His glory was established, and He founded His strong love. Before His face shall go the Word, and shall go forth unto the plains according to His steps."[104] In Isaiah also: "Behold, unto us a child is born, and to us a Son is given, upon whose shoulders shall be government; and His name shall be called the Messenger of a mighty thought."[105] By this sign of the cross also Amalek was conquered by Joshua through Moses. In Exodus Moses said to Joshua: "Choose you out men, and go forth, and order yourselves with Amalek until the morrow. Behold, I will stand on the top of the hill, and the rod of God in mine hand. And it came to pass, when Moses lifted up his hands, Israel prevailed; but when Moses had let down his hands, Amalek grew strong. But the hands of Moses were heavy; and they took a stone, and placed it under him, and he sat upon it and Aaron and Hur held up his hands, on the one side and on the other side; and the hands of Moses were made steady even to the setting of the sun. And Joshua routed Amalek and all his people. And the Lord said unto Moses, Write this, that it may be a memorial in a book, and tell it unto the ears of Joshua, that I may utterly destroy the memory of Amalek from under heaven."[106]

22. That in this sign of the Cross is salvation for all people who are marked on their foreheads[107]

In Ezekiel the Lord says: "Pass through the midst of Jerusalem, and you shall mark the sign I upon the men's foreheads, who groan and grieve for the iniquities which are done in the midst of them." Also in the same place: "Go and smite, and do not spare your eyes. Have no pity on the old man, and the youth, and the virgin, and slay little children and women, that they may be utterly destroyed. But you shall not touch any one upon whom the sign is written, and begin with my holy places themselves."[108] Also in Exodus God says to Moses: "And there shall be blood for a sign to you upon the houses wherein you shall be; and I will look on the blood, and will protect you. And there shall not be in you the plague of wasting when I shall smite the land of Egypt."[109] Also in the Apocalypse:

"And I saw a Lamb standing on Mount Sion, and with Him a hundred and forty and four thousand; and they had His name and the name of His Father written on their foreheads."[110] Also in the same place: "I am Alpha and Omega, the first and the last, the beginning and the end. Blessed are they that do His commandments, that they may have power over the tree of life."[111]

23. That at mid-day in His passion there should be darkness

In Amos: "And it shall come to pass in that day, says the Lord, the sun shall set at noonday, and the day of light shall be darkened; and I will turn your feast-days into grief, and all your songs into lamentation."[112] Also in Jeremiah: "She is frightened that has borne children, and her soul has grown weary. Her sun has gone down while as yet it was mid-day; she has been confounded and accursed: I will give the rest of them to the sword in the sight of their enemies."[113] Also in the Gospel: "Now from the sixth hour there was darkness over all the earth even to the ninth hour."[114]

24. That He was not to be overcome of death, nor should remain in Hades

In the twenty-ninth Psalm: "O Lord, You have brought back my soul from hell."[115] Also in the fifteenth Psalm: "You will not leave my soul in hell, neither will You suffer Your Holy One to see corruption."[116] Also in the third Psalm: "I laid me down and slept, and rose up again, because the Lord helped me."[117] Also according to John: "No man takes away my life from me; but I lay it down of myself. I have the power of laying it down, and I have the power of taking it again. For this commandment I have received from my Father."[118]

25. That He should rise again from the dead on the third day

In Hosea: "After two days He will revive us; we shall rise again on the third day."[119] Also in Exodus: "And the Lord said unto Moses, 'Go down and testify to the people, and sanctify them today and tomorrow; and let them wash their garments, and let them be prepared against the day after tomorrow. For on the third day the Lord will come down on Mount Sinai.'"[120] Also in the Gospel: "A wicked and adulterous generation seeks after a sign; and there shall no sign be given unto it but the sign of the prophet Jonah: for as Jonah was in the whale's belly three days and three nights, so shall the Son of man be three days and three nights in the heart of the earth."[121]

26. That after He had risen again He should receive from His Father all power, and His power should be everlasting

In Daniel: "I saw in a vision by night, and behold as it were the Son of Man, coming in the clouds of heaven, came even to the Ancient of Days, and stood in His sight. And they who stood beside Him brought Him before Him: and to Him was given a royal power, and all the kings of the earth by their generation, and all glory obeying Him: and His power is eternal, which shall not be taken away, and His kingdom shall not be destroyed."[122] Also in Isaiah: "Now will I arise, says the Lord; now will I be glorified, now will I be exalted, now you shall see, now you shall understand, now you shall be confounded. Vain will be the strength of your spirit: the fire shall consume you."[123] Also in the cixth Psalm: "The Lord said unto my Lord, 'Sit on my right hand, until I make Your enemies the footstool of Your feet. God will send the rod of Your power out of Sion, and You shall rule in the midst of Your enemies.'"[124] Also in the Apocalypse: "And I turned and looked to see the voice which spoke with me. And I saw seven golden candlesticks, and in the midst of the candlesticks one like the Son of Man, clothed with a long garment, and He was girt about the paps with a golden girdle. And His head and His hairs were white as wool or snow, and His eyes as a flame of fire, and His feet like to fine brass from a furnace of fire, and His voice like the sound of many waters. And He had in His right hand seven stars: and out of His mouth went a sharp two-edged sword; and His face shone as the sun in his might. And when I saw Him, I fell at His feet as dead. And He laid His right hand upon me, and said, 'Fear not; I am the first and the last, and He that lives and was dead; and, lo, I am living for evermore and I have the keys of death and of hell.'"[125] Likewise in the Gospel, the Lord after His resurrection says to His disciples: "All power is given unto me in heaven and in earth. Go therefore and teach all nations, baptizing them in the name of the Father, and of the Son, and of the Holy Ghost, teaching them to observe all things whatsoever I have commanded you."[126]

27. That it is impossible to attain to God the Father, except by His Son Jesus Christ

In the Gospel: "I am the way, and the truth, and the life: no one comes to the Father but by me." Also in the same place: "I am the door: by me if any man shall enter in, he shall be saved." Also in the same place: "Many prophets and righteous men have desired to see the things which you see, and have not seen them; and to hear those things which you hear, and have not heard them." Also in the same place: "He that believes in the Son has eternal life: he that is not obedient in word to the Son has not life; but the wrath of God shall abide upon him."[127] Also Paul to the Ephesians: "And when He had come, He preached peace to you, to those which are afar off, and peace to those which are near, because through Him we both have access in one Spirit unto the Father."[128] Also to the Romans: "For all have sinned, and fail of the glory of God; but they are justified by His gift and grace, through the redemption which is in Christ Jesus."[129] Also in the Epistle of Peter the apostle: "Christ has died once for our sins, the just for the unjust, that He might present us to God." Also in the same place: "For in this also was it preached to them that are dead, that they might be raised again."[130] Also in the Epistle of John: "Whosoever denies the Son, the same also has not the Father. He that confesses the Son, has both the Son and the Father."[131]

28. That Jesus Christ shall come as a Judge

In Malachi: "Behold, the day of the Lord comes, burning as an oven; and all the aliens and all the wicked shall be as stubble; and the day that comes shall burn them up, says the Lord."[132] Also in the forty-ninth Psalm: "God the Lord of gods has spoken, and called the earth. From the rising of the sun even to the going down thereof, out of Sion is the beauty of His glory. God shall come manifestly, our God, and shall not keep silence. A fire shall burn before Him, and round about Him shall be a great storm. He has called the heaven above, and the earth, that He may separate His people. Gather together His saints unto Him, those who arrange His covenant with sacrifices. And the heavens shall announce His righteousness, for God is the judge."[133] Also in Isaiah: "The Lord God of strength shall go forth, and shall break war in pieces: He shall stir up contest, and shall cry over His enemies with strength. I have been silent; shall I always be silent?"[134] Also in the sixty-seventh Psalm: "Let God arise, and let His enemies be scattered: and let those who hate Him flee from His face. As smoke vanishes, let them vanish: as wax melts from the face of fire, thus let the sinners perish from the face of God. And let the righteous be glad and rejoice in the sight of God: and let them be glad with joyfulness. Sing unto God, sing praises unto His name: make a way to Him who goes up into the west. God is His name. They shall be put to confusion from the face of Him who is the Father of the orphans, and the Judge of the widows. God is in His holy place: God, who makes men to dwell with one mind in an house, bringing forth them that are bound with might, and equally those who provoke unto anger, who dwell in the sepulchres: God, when You went forth in the sight of Your people, in passing into the desert."[135] Also in the eighty-first Psalm: "Arise, O God; judge the earth: for You will exterminate among all nations."[136] Also in the Gospel according to Matthew: "What have we to do with You, You Son of David? Why have you come here to punish us before the time?"[137] Likewise according to John: "The Father judges nothing, but has given all judgment to the Son, that all may honor the Son as they honor the Father. He that honors not the Son, honors not the Father who has sent Him."[138] So too in the second Epistle of Paul to the Corinthians: "We must all appear before the judgment-seat of Christ, that every one may bear the things proper to his body, according to those things which he has done, whether they be good or evil."[139]

29. *That He will reign as a King for ever*

In Zechariah: "Tell the daughter of Zion, Behold, your King comes unto you: just, and having salvation; meek, sitting upon an ass that has not been tamed."[140] Also in Isaiah: "Who will declare to you that eternal place? He that walks in righteousness, and holds back his hands from gifts; stopping his ears. that he may not hear the judgment of blood; and closing his eyes, that he may not see unrighteousness: this man shall dwell in the lofty cavern of the strong rock; bread shall be given him, and his water shall be sure. You shall see the King with glory."[141] Likewise in Malachi: "I am a great King, says the Lord, and my name is illustrious among the nations."[142] Also in the second Psalm: "But I am established as a King by Him upon His holy hill of Zion, announcing His empire."[143] Also in the twenty-first Psalm: "All the ends of the world shall be reminded, and shall turn to the Lord: and all the countries of the nations shall worship in Your sight. For the kingdom is the Lord's: and He shall rule over all nations."[144] Also in the twenty-third Psalm: "Lift up your gates, you princes; and be lifted up, you everlasting doors; and the King of glory shall come in. Who is this King of glory? The Lord strong and mighty, the Lord strong in battle. Lift up your gates, O you princes; and be lifted up, you everlasting doors; and the King of glory shall come in. Who is this King of glory? The Lord of hosts, He is the King of glory."[145] Also in the forty-fourth Psalm: "My heart has breathed forth a good discourse: I tell my works to the king: my tongue is the pen of a writer intelligently writing. You are lovely in beauty above the children of men: grace is shed forth on Your lips, because God has blessed You for ever. Be girt with Your sword on Your thigh, O most mighty. To Your honor and to Your beauty both attend, and direct Yourself, and reign, because of truth, and meekness, and righteousness."[146] Also in the fifth Psalm: "My King, and my God, because unto You will I pray. O Lord, in the morning You shall hear my voice; in the morning I will stand before You, and will contemplate You."[147] Also in the ninety-sixth Psalm: "The Lord has reigned; let the earth rejoice; let the many isles be glad."[148] Moreover, in the forty-fourth Psalm: "The queen stood at your right hand in a golden garment; she is clothed in many colors. Hear, O daughter, and see, and incline your ear, and forget your people and your father's house; for the King has desired your beauty, for He is your Lord God."[149] Also in the seventy-third Psalm: "But God is our King before the world; He has wrought salvation in the midst of the earth."[150] Also in the Gospel according to Matthew: "And when Jesus was born in Bethlehem of Judah in the days of Herod the king, behold, Magi from the east came to Jerusalem, saying, 'Where is He who is born King of the Jews? For we have seen His star in the east, and have come to worship Him.'"[151] Also, according to John, "Jesus said: 'My kingdom is not of this world. If my kingdom were of this world, my servants would be in trouble, that I should not be delivered to the Jews; but now is my kingdom not from hence.' Pilate said, 'Are you a king, then?' Jesus answered, 'You say that I am a king. For this cause I was born, and for this cause I have come into the world, that I might bear testimony to the truth. Every one that is of the truth hears my voice.'"[152]

30. That He Himself is both Judge and King

In the seventy-first Psalm: "O God, give Your judgment to the king, and Your righteousness to the king's son, to judge Your people in righteousness."[153] Also in the Apocalypse: "And I saw the heavens opened, and behold a white horse; and He who sate upon him was called Faithful and True; and He judges justice and righteousness, and makes war. And His eyes were, as it were, a flame of fire, and upon His head were many crowns; and He bare a name written that was known to none other than Himself:' and He was clothed with a garment sprinkled with blood, and His name is called the Word of God. And the armies which are in heaven followed Him on white horses, clothed in linen white and clean. And out of His mouth went forth a sword with two edges, that with it He should smite the nations, which He shall shepherd with a rod of iron; and He shall tread the winepress of the wrath of God Almighty. Also He has on His garment and on His thigh the name written, 'King of kings, and Lord of lords.'"[154] Likewise in the Gospel: "When the Son of man shall come in His glory, and all the angels with Him, then He shall sit in the throne of His glory; and all nations shall be gathered together before Him, and He shall separate them one from another, even as a shepherd separates the sheep from the goats; and He shall place the sheep at His right hand, but the goats at His left hand. Then shall the King say unto them who shall be at His right hand, 'Come, you blessed of my Father, receive the kingdom which is prepared for you from the beginning of the world: for I was hungry, and you gave me to eat: I was thirsty, and you gave me to drink: I was a stranger, and you received me: naked, and you clothed me: sick, and you visited me: I was in prison, and you came unto me.' Then shall the righteous answer, and say unto Him, 'Lord, when saw we You hungry, and fed You? Thirsty, and gave You to drink? And when saw we You a stranger, and received You? Naked, and clothed You? And when saw we You sick, and in prison, and came unto You?' And the King, answering, shall say unto them, 'Verily I say unto you, in as far as you have done it to the least of these my brethren, you have done it unto me.' Then shall He say unto them who shall be on His left hand, 'Depart from me, you cursed, into everlasting fire, which my Father has prepared for the devil and his angels: for I have been hungry, and you gave me not to eat: I have been thirsty, and you gave me not to drink: I was a stranger, and you received me not: naked, and you clothed me not: sick, and in prison, and you visited me not.' Then shall they also answer and say, 'Lord, when saw we You hungry, or thirsty, or a stranger, or naked, or sick, or in prison, and have not ministered unto You?' And He shall answer unto them, 'Verily I say unto you, inasmuch as you have not done it to one of the least of these, you have not done it unto me.' And these shall go away into everlasting burning, but the righteous into life eternal."[155]

NOTES

1. Prov. 8:22-31. This verse would be pivotal in the later Arian controversy in addressing the question of whether or not the Word of God had an eternal preexistence.
2. Sir. 24:3-7.
3. Ps. 89:29-33.
4. John 17:3-5.
5. Col. 1:15, 18.
6. Rev. 21:6.
7. 1 Cor. 1:22-24.
8. Prov. 9:1-6.
9. Ps. 45:1, LXX.
10. Ps. 33:6.
11. Isa. 10:23.
12. Ps. 107:20.
13. John 1:1-5.
14. Rev. 19:11-13.
15. Isa. 59:1-4, 53:1, 66:1-2, 26:11, 52:10, 41:15-20.
16. Gen. 22:11-12, 31:13.
17. Ex. 13:21, 14:19, 23:20-21.
18. John 5:43. In this and the following two citations, Cyprian is attempting to draw a connection between the Angel of the Lord from Exodus, in whom God puts His "name," and Christ as Messiah coming in the name of the Lord. The argument depends upon accepting Cyprian's use of the word "name."
19. Ps. 118:26.
20. Mal. 2:5-7.
21. Gen. 35:1.
22. Isa. 45:14-16.
23. Isa. 40:3-5.
24. Bar. 3:35-37.
25. Zech. 10:11-12.
26. Hos. 11:9-10 from the Septuagint. The Vulgate, and subsequent later translations, says *post Dominum ambulabunt* ("they shall walk after the Lord").
27. Ps. 45:6-7.
28. Ps. 45:10.
29. Ps. 82:5.
30. Ps. 68:4.
31. John 1:1, 20:27-29.
32. Rom. 9:3-5.
33. Rev. 21:6-7.
34. Ps. 82:1, 6-7.
35. John 10:34-38.
36. Matt. 1:23.
37. Isa. 35:3-6, 63:9, 62:6-8.
38. Ps. 25:4-5.
39. John 8:12.

40. Matt. 1:20-21.
41. Luke 1:67-69, 2:10-11.
42. Ps. 2:7-8.
43. Luke 1:41-43.
44. Gal. 4:4.
45. 1 John 4:2-3.
46. Isa. 7:10-15.
47. Gen. 3:14-15. A Septuagint translation. The Vulgate uses the word "crush" instead of "watch," which is the more common translation. In this case, the Vulgate is closer to the original Hebrew, שׁוּף (shuph), which means "to bruise, crush, or strike out at."
48. Jer. 17:9. Cyprian applies this verse to God when in fact, taken in context, it refers to the human heart. From the Septuagint: "The heart is deep beyond all things, and it is the man, and who can know him?"
49. Num. 24:17, 24:7-9.
50. Isa. 61:1-2.
51. Luke 1:35.
52. 1 Cor. 15:47-49.
53. 2 Sam. 7:5, 12-16.
54. Isa. 11:1-3.
55. Ps. 132:11.
56. Luke 1:30-33.
57. Rev. 5:1-5.
58. Mic. 5:2.
59. Matt. 2:1-2.
60. Isa. 53:1-7, 50:5-7, 42:2-4.
61. Ps. 22:6-8, 15.
62. Zech. 3:1,3,5. Jesus is the Greek Septuangint translation of Joshua, which most modern readers will be more familiar with in the context of this passage.
63. Phil. 2:6-11.
64. Wis. 2:12-22.
65. Isa. 57:1-2.
66. Ex. 23:7.
67. Matt. 27:3-4.
68. Isa. 53:7-9, 12.
69. Jer. 11:18-19.
70. Ex. 22:3-12.
71. Rev. 5:6-10.
72. John 1:29.
73. Isa. 28:16.
74. Ps. 118:21-26.
75. Zech. 3:8-19.
76. Deut. 27:8.
77. Jos. 24:26, 27. Cyprian here envisions Jesus Christ as the Stone that bears witness against Israel for the infidelity.
78. Acts 4:1-12.
79. Gen. 49:24.
80. Because the stone was anointed by Jacob, that makes it a *christ* (anointed one), and therefore has special reference to the Lord Jesus.
81. Dan. 2:31-35.
82. Isa. 2:2-4.
83. Ps. 24:3-6.
84. Joel 2:15-16.

85. Jer. 16:9.
86. Ps. 19:5-6. In context, this refers to the sun, which Cyprian and many Fathers see as an image of Christ, the "Sun of Righteousness" (Mal. 4:2).
87. Rev. 21:9-11.
88. John 3:28-29.
89. Jos. 5:13-15.
90. Ex. 3:2-6.
91. John 1:26-27.
92. Luke 12:35-37.
93. Rev. 19:6-7.
94. Isa. 65:2.
95. Jer. 21:19.
96. Deut. 28:66. A very bizarre application of this verse, since in its literal context it is referring to the punishment of disobedient Israelites. It is odd that Cyprian would choose this to apply to the Messiah.
97. Ps. 22:16-22. The word "Church" here is taken from the Septuagint *ekklesia* (assembly); in Hebrew is it *qahal*.
98. Ps. 119:120 (LXX), 141:2.
99. Zeph. 1:7.
100. Zech. 12:10.
101. Ps. 88:9.
102. Num. 23:9.
103. John 3:14-15.
104. Hab. 3:3-5.
105. Isa. 9:6 (LXX).
106. Ex. 7:9-14.
107. A reference to the *sphragis*, the Sign of the Cross traced in consecrated oil on the forehead of the newly baptized. For example, see St. John Chrysostom, *Homilies in 1 Corinthians*, Homily XII:14. The reference here, then, means the Sign of the Cross signifies salvation for all the baptized.
108. Ezk. 9:4-6.
109. Ex. 12:13.
110. Rev. 14:1.
111. Rev. 22:13-14.
112. Amos 8:9-10.
113. Jer. 15:9.
114. Matt. 27:45. The ancient historian S. Julius Africanus mentions that this darkness was referenced in the work of an earlier historian, the Greek Phlegon of Trelles: "Phlegon records that during the reign of Tiberius Caesar there was a complete solar eclipse at full moon from the sixth to the ninth hour." Eusebius also quotes Phlegon: "a great eclipse of the sun occurred at the sixth hour that excelled every other before it, turning the day into such darkness of night that the stars could be seen in heaven, and the earth moved in Bithynia, toppling many buildings in the city of Nicaea." (See: George Syncellus, *Chronography*, 391 and Eusebius, *Chronicle*, Book II, 202nd Olympiad)
115. Ps. 30:3.
116. Ps. 16:10.
117. Ps. 3:5.
118. John 10:18.
119. Hos. 6:2.
120. Ex. 19:10-11.
121. Matt. 12:39-40.
122. Dan. 7:13-14.

123. Isa. 33:10-11.
124. Ps. 110:1-2.
125. Rev. 1:12-18.
126. Matt. 28:18-20.
127. John 14:6, 10:9; Matt. 13:17; John 3:36.
128. Eph. 2:17-18.
129. Rom. 3:23-24.
130. 1 Pet. 3:18, 1 Pet. 4:6.
131. 1 John 2:23.
132. Mal. 4:1.
133. Ps. 50:1-6.
134. Isa. 13:13-14.
135. Ps. 68:1-7.
136. Ps. 82:8.
137. Matt. 8:29.
138. John 5:22-23.
139. 2 Cor. 5:10.
140. Zech. 9:9.
141. Isa. 33:13-17.
142. Mal. 1:14.
143. Ps. 2:6.
144. Ps. 22:27-28.
145. Ps. 24:7-10.
146. Ps. 45:1-4.
147. Ps. 5:2-3.
148. Ps. 97:1.
149. Ps. 45:9-11.
150. Ps. 74:12.
151. Matt. 2:1-2.
152. John 18:36-37.
153. Ps. 72:1-2.
154. Rev. 19:11-16.
155. Matt. 25:31-46.

THREE BOOKS OF TESTIMONIES AGAINST THE JEWS

BOOK III

Cyprian to his son Quirinus, greeting. Of your faith and devotion which you manifest to the Lord God, beloved son, you asked me to gather out for your instruction from the Holy Scriptures some heads bearing upon the religious teaching of our school; seeking for a succinct course of sacred reading, so that your mind, surrendered to God, might not be wearied with long or numerous volumes of books, but, instructed with a summary of heavenly precepts, might have a wholesome and large compendium for nourishing its memory. And because I owe you a plentiful and loving obedience, I have done what you wished. I have labored for once, that you might not always labor. Therefore, as much as my small ability could embrace, I have collected certain precepts of the Lord, and divine teachings, which may be easy and useful to the readers, in that a few things digested into a short space are both quickly read through, and are frequently repeated. I bid you, beloved son, ever heartily farewell.[2]

1. Of the benefit of good works and mercy

In Isaiah: "'Cry aloud," says He, "and spare not; lift up your voice like a trumpet; tell my people their sins, and the house of Jacob their wickednesses. They seek me from day to day, and desire to know my ways, as a people which did righteousness, and did not forsake the judgment of God. They ask of me now a righteous judgment, and desire to approach to God, saying, What! Because we have fasted, and You have not seen: we have humiliated our souls, and You have not known. For in the days of fasting are found your own wills; for either you torment those who are subjected to you, or you fast for strifes and judgments, or you strike your neighbors with fists. For what do you fast unto me, that today your voice should be heard in clamor? This fast I have not chosen, save that a man should humble his soul. And if you shall bend your neck like a ring, and spread under you sackcloth and ashes, neither thus shall it be called an acceptable fast. Not such a fast have I chosen, says the Lord; but loose every knot of unrighteousness, let go the chokings of impotent engagements. Send away the harassed into rest, and scatter every unrighteous contract. Break your bread to the hungry, and bring the houseless poor into your dwelling. If you see the naked, clothe him; and despise not them of your own seed in your house. Then shall your seasonable light break forth, and your garments shall quickly arise; and righteousness shall go before you: and the glory of God shall surround you.

Then you shall cry out, and God shall hear you; while you are yet speaking, He shall say, Here I am."[3] Concerning this same thing in Job: "I have preserved the needy from the hand of the mighty; and I have helped the orphan, to whom there was no helper. The mouth of the widow blessed me, since I was the eye of the blind; I was also the foot of the lame, and the father of the weak."[4] Of this same matter in Tobit: "And I said to Tobias, 'My son, go and bring whatever poor man you shall find out of our brethren, who still has God in mind with his whole heart. Bring him hither, and he shall eat my dinner together with me. Behold, I attend you, my son, until you come.'" Also in the same place: "All the days of your life, my son, keep God in mind, and transgress not His precepts. Do justice all the days of your life, and do not walk in the way of unrighteousness; because if you act truly, there will be respect of your works. Give alms of your substance, and turn not your face from any poor man. So shall it come to pass that the face of God shall not be turned away from you. Even as you have, my son, so do: if you have abundant substance, give the more alms therefrom; if you have little, communicate even of that little. And do not fear when you give alms: you lay up for yourself a good reward against the day of need; because alms delivers from death, and does not suffer to go into darkness. Alms is a good office for all who do it in the sight of the most high God."[5] On this same subject in Solomon in Proverbs: "He that has pity on the poor lends unto the Lord." Also in the same place: "He that gives to the poor shall never want; but he who turns away his eye shall be in much penury." Also in the same place: "Sins are purged away by almsgiving and faith." Again, in the same place: "If your enemy hunger, feed him; and if he thirst, give him to drink: for by doing this you shall scatter live coals upon his head." Again, in the same place: "As water extinguishes fire, so almsgiving extinguishes sin." In the same in Proverbs: "Say not, 'Go away, and return, tomorrow I will give;' when you can do good immediately. For you know not what may happen on the coming day." Also in the same place: "He who stops his ears that he may not hear the weak, shall himself call upon God, and there shall be none to hear him." Also in the same place: "He who has his conversation without reproach in righteousness, leaves blessed children."[6] In the same in Ecclesiasticus: "My son, if you have, do good by yourself, and present worthy offerings to God; remember that death delays not." Also in the same place: "Shut up alms in the heart of the poor, and this will entreat for you from all evil."[7] Concerning this thing in the thirty-sixth Psalm, that mercy is beneficial also to one's posterity: "I have been young, and I have also grown old; and I have not seen the righteous forsaken, nor his seed begging their bread. The whole day he is merciful, and lends; and his seed is in blessing."[8] Of this same thing in the fortieth Psalm: "Blessed is he who considers over the poor and needy: in the evil day God will deliver him."[9] Also in the cxith Psalm: "He has distributed, he has given to the poor; his righteousness shall remain from generation to generation."[10] Of this same thing in Hosea: "I desire mercy rather than sacrifice, and the knowledge of God more than whole burnt-offerings."[11] Of this same thing also in the Gospel according to Matthew: "Blessed are they who hunger and thirst after righteousness: for they shall be satisfied." Also in the same place: "Blessed are the merciful: for they shall obtain mercy." Also in the same place: "Lay up for yourselves treasures in heaven, where neither moth nor rust does corrupt, and where thieves do not dig through and steal: for where your treasure is, there will your heart be also." Also in the same place: "The kingdom of heaven is like a merchant seeking goodly pearls: and when he has found a precious pearl, he went away and sold all that he had, and bought it." That even a small work is of advantage, also in the same place: "And whoever shall give to drink to one of the least of these a cup of cold water in the name of a disciple, verily I say unto you, His reward shall not perish." That alms are to be denied to none, also in the same place: "Give to every one that asks you; and from him who would wish to borrow, be not turned away." Also in the same place: "If you will enter into life, keep the commandments." He says, "Which?" Jesus says unto him, "You shall not kill, You shall not commit adultery, You shall not bear false witness, honor your father and mother: and, You shall love your neighbor as yourself." The young man says unto Him, "All these things have I observed: what lack I yet?" Jesus says unto him, "If you will be perfect, go and sell all that you have, and give to the poor, and you shall have treasure in heaven; and come, follow me." Also in the same place: "When the Son of man shall come in His majesty, and all the angels with Him, then He shall sit on the throne of His glory: and all nations shall be gathered together before Him; and He shall separate them one from another, even as a shepherd separates the sheep from the goats: and He shall place the sheep on the right hand, but the goats on the left hand. Then shall the King say unto them that are on His right hand, 'Come, you blessed of my Father, receive the kingdom prepared for you from the beginning of the world. For I was hungry, and you gave me to eat: I was thirsty, and you gave me to drink: I was a stranger, and you took me in: naked, and you clothed me: I was sick, and you visited me: I was in prison, and you came unto me.' Then shall the righteous answer Him, and say, 'Lord, when saw we You a stranger, and took You in: naked, and clothed You? And when saw we You sick, and in prison, and came to You?' And the King, answering, shall say unto them, 'Verily I say unto you, inasmuch as you did it to one of the least of these my brethren, you did it unto me.' Then shall He say unto them who are on His left hand, 'Depart from me, you cursed, into everlasting fire, which my Father has prepared for the devil and his angels: for I was hungry, and you gave me not to eat: I was thirsty, and you gave me not to drink: I was a stranger, and you took me not in: I was naked, and you clothed me not: sick, and in prison, and you visited me not.' Then shall they also answer, and say, 'Lord, when saw we You hungry, or thirsty, or a stranger, or naked, or sick, or in prison, and did not minister unto You?' And He shall answer them, 'Verily I say unto you, inasmuch as you did it not to one of the least of these, you did it not unto me.' And these shall go away into everlasting burning: but the righteous into life eternal."[12] Concerning this same matter in the Gospel according to Luke: "Sell your possessions, and give alms." Also in the same place: "He who made that which is within, made that which is without also. But give alms, and, behold, all things are pure unto you." Also in the same place: "Behold, the half of my substance I give to the poor; and if I have defrauded any one of anything, I restore him fourfold." And Jesus said unto him: "Salvation has this day been wrought for this house, since he also is a son of Abraham."[13] Of this same thing also in the second Epistle to the Corinthians: "Let your abundance supply their want, that their abundance also may be the supplement of your want, that there may be equality: as it is written, 'He who had much had not excess; and he who had little had no lack.'" Also in the same place: "He who sows sparingly shall reap also sparingly; and he who sows in blessing shall reap also of blessing. But let every one do as he has proposed in his heart: not as if sorrowfully, or of necessity: for God loves a cheerful giver." Also in the same place: "As it is written, 'He has dispersed abroad; he has given to the poor: his righteousness remains for ever.'" Likewise in the same place: "Now he who ministers seed to the sower, shall both supply bread to be eaten, and shall multiply your seed, and shall increase the growth of the fruits of your righteousness: that in all things you may be made rich." Also in the same place: "The administration of this service has not only supplied that which is lacking to the saints, but has abounded by much giving of thanks unto God."[14] Of this same matter in the Epistle of John: "Whoso has this world's substance, and sees his brother desiring, and shuts up his bowels from him, how dwells the love of God in him?"[15] Of this same thing in the Gospel according to Luke: "When you make a dinner or a supper, call not your friends, nor brethren, nor neighbors, nor the rich; lest haply they also invite you again, and a recompense be made you. But when you make a banquet, call the poor, the weak, the blind, and lame: and you shall be blessed; because they have not the means of rewarding you: but you I shall be recompensed in the resurrection of the just."[16]

2. In works and alms, even if by smallness of power less be done, that the will itself is sufficient

In the second Epistle of Paul to the Corinthians: "If there be a ready will, it is acceptable according to what a man has, not according to that which he has not; nor let there be to others a mitigation, but to you a burdening."[17]

3. That charity and brotherly affection are to be religiously and stedfastly practiced

In Malachi: "Has not one God created us? Is there not one Father of us all? Why have you certainly deserted every one his brother?"[18] Of this same thing according to John: "Peace I leave with you, my peace I give unto you." Also in the same place: "This is my commandment, That you love one another, even as I have loved you. Greater love than this has no man, than that one should lay down his life for his friends."[19] Also in the same place: "Blessed are the peacemakers, for they shall be called the sons of God." Also in the same place: "Verily I say unto you, that if two of you shall agree on earth concerning everything, whatever you shall ask it shall be given you from my Father which is in heaven. For wherever two or three are gathered together in my name, I am with them."[20] Of this same thing in the first Epistle to the Corinthians: "And I indeed, brethren, could not speak unto you as to spiritual, but as to carnal, as to babes in Christ. I have given you milk for drink, not meat: for while you were yet little you were not able to bear it, neither now are you able. For you are still carnal: for where there are in you emulation, and strife, and dissensions, are you not carnal, and walk after man?" Likewise in the same place: "And if I should have all faith, so that I can remove mountains, but have not charity, I am nothing. And if I should distribute all my goods for food, and if I should deliver up my body to be burned, but have not charity, I avail nothing. Charity is great-souled; charity is kind; charity envies not; charity deals not falsely; is not puffed up; is not irritated; thinks not evil; rejoices not in injustice, but rejoices in the truth. It loves all things, believes all things, hopes all things, bears all things. Charity shall never fail."[21] Of this same thing to the Galatians: "You shall love your neighbor as yourself. But if you bite and accuse one another, see that you be not consumed one of another."[22] Of this same thing in the Epistle of John: "In this appear the children of God and the children of the devil. Whosoever is not righteous is not of God, and he who loves not his brother. For he who hates his brother is a murderer; and you know that no murderer has eternal life abiding in him." Also in the same place: "If any one shall say that he loves God, and hates his brother, he is a liar: for he who loves not his brother whom he sees, how can he love God whom he sees not?"[23] Of this same thing in the Acts of the Apostles: "But the multitude of them that had believed acted with one soul and mind: nor was there among them any distinction, neither did they esteem as their own anything of the possessions that they had; but all things were common to them."[24] Of this same thing in the Gospel according to Matthew: "If you would offer your gift at the altar, and there rememberest that your brother has ought against you; leave your gift before the altar, and go; first be reconciled to your brother, and then come and offer your gift at the altar."[25] Also in the Epistle of John: "God is love and he that dwells in love dwells in God, and God in him." Also in the same place: "He who says he is in the light, and hates his brother, is a liar, and walks in darkness even until now."[26]

4. That we must boast in nothing, since nothing is our own

In the Gospel according to John: "No one can receive anything, except it were given him from heaven."[27] Also in the first Epistle of Paul to the Corinthians: "For what have you that you have not received? But if you have received it, why do you boast, as if you had not received it?"[28] Also in the first of Kings: "Boast not, neither speak lofty things, and let not great speeches proceed out of your mouth, for the Lord is a God of knowledge." Also in the same place: "The bow of the mighty men has been made weak, and the weak are girt about with strength."[29] Of this same thing in the Maccabees: "It is just to be subjected to God, and that a mortal should not think things equal to God." Also in the same place: "And fear not the words of a man that is a sinner, because his glory shall be filth and worms. Today he shall be lifted up, and tomorrow he shall not be found; because he is turned into his earth, and his thought has perished."[30]

5. That humility and quietness are to be maintained in all things

In Isaiah: "Thus says the Lord God, 'The heaven is my throne, and the earth is the stool of my feet. What seat will you build for me, or what is the place for my rest? For all those things has my hand made, and all those things are mine. And upon whom else will I look, except upon the lowly and quiet man, and him that trembles at my words?'"[31] On this same thing in the Gospel according to Matthew: "Blessed are the meek, for they shall inherit the earth."[32] Of this same thing, too, according to Luke: "He that shall be least among you all, the same shall be great." Also in the same place: "Whosoever exalts himself shall be made low, and whosoever abases himself shall be exalted."[33] Of this same thing to the Romans: "Be not high-minded, but fear; for if God spared not the natural branches, take heed lest He also spare not you."[34] Of this same thing in the thirty-third Psalm: "And He shall save the lowly in spirit."[35] Also to the Romans: "Render to all what is due: tribute to whom tribute is due, custom to whom custom, fear to whom fear, honor to whom honor; owe no man anything, except to love another."[36] Also in the Gospel according to Matthew: "They love the first place of reclining at feasts, and the chief seat in the synagogues, and salutations in the market, and to be called of men Rabbi. But say not Rabbi, for One is your Master."[37] Also in the Gospel according to John: "The servant is not greater than his lord, nor the apostle greater than He that sent himself. If you know these things, blessed shall you be if you shall do them."[38] Also in the eighty-first Psalm: "Do justice to the poor and lowly."[39]

6. That all good and righteous men suffer more, but ought to endure because they are proved

In Solomon: "The furnace proves the vessels of the potter, and the trial of tribulation righteous men."[40] Also in the fiftieth Psalm: "The sacrifice to God is a contrite spirit; a contrite and humbled heart God will not despise." Also in the thirty-third Psalm: "God is nearest to them that are contrite in heart, and He will save the lowly in spirit." Also in the same place: "Many are the afflictions of the righteous, but out of them all the Lord will deliver them."[41] Of this same matter in Job: "Naked came I out of my mother's womb, naked also shall I go under the earth: the Lord gave, and the Lord has taken away: as it has pleased the Lord, so it is done; blessed be the name of the Lord. In all these things which happened to him Job sinned in nothing with his lips in the sight of the Lord."[42] Concerning this same thing in the Gospel according to Matthew: "Blessed are they that mourn, for they shall be comforted."[43] Also according to John: "These things have I spoken unto you, that in me you may have peace. But in the world you shall have affliction; but have confidence, for I have overcome the world."[44] Concerning this same thing in the second Epistle to the Corinthians: "There was given to me a thorn in the flesh, a messenger of Satan to buffet me, that I should not be exalted. For which thing I thrice besought the Lord, that it should depart from me. And He said unto me, 'My grace is sufficient for you; for strength is perfected in weakness.'"[45] Concerning this same thing to the Romans: "We glory in hope of the glory of God. And not only so, but we also glory in afflictions: knowing that affliction works patience; and patience, experience; and experience, hope: and hope does not confound; because the love of God is infused in our hearts by the Holy Spirit, which is given unto us."[46] On this same subject, according to Matthew: "How broad and spacious is the way which leads unto death, and many there are who go in thereby: how straight and narrow is the way that leads to life, and few there are that find it!"[47] Of this same thing in Tobias: "Where are your righteousnesses? Behold what you suffer!"[48] Also in the Wisdom of Solomon: "In the places of the wicked the righteous groan; but at their ruin the righteous will abound."[49]

7. That we must not grieve the Holy Spirit, whom we have received

Paul the apostle to the Ephesians: "Grieve not the Holy Spirit of God, in which you were sealed in the day of redemption. Let all bitterness, and wrath, and indignation, and clamor, and blasphemy, be taken away from you."[50]

8. That anger must be overcome, lest it constrain us to sin

In Solomon in the Proverbs: "Better is a patient man than a strong man; for he who restrains his anger is better than he who takes a city." Also in the same place: "The imprudent man declares his anger on the same day, but the crafty man hides away his dishonor."[51] Of this same thing to the Ephesians: "Be angry, and sin not. Let not the sun set upon your wrath."[52] Also in the Gospel according to Matthew: "You have heard that it was said by the ancients, You shall not kill; and whoever shall kill shall be guilty of the judgment. But I say unto you, That every one who is angry with his brother without cause shall be guilty of the judgment."[53]

9. That brethren ought to support one another

To the Galatians: "Each one having others in consideration, lest you also should be tempted. Bear one another's burdens, and so you shall fulfill the law of Christ."[54]

10. That we must trust in God only, and in Him we must glory

In Jeremiah: "Let not the wise man glory in his wisdom, neither let the strong man glory in his strength, nor let the rich man glory in his riches; but let him that glories glory in this, that he understands and knows that I am the Lord, who do mercy, and judgment, and righteousness upon the earth, because in them is my pleasure, says the Lord."[55] Of the same thing in the fifty-fourth Psalm: "In the Lord have I hoped; I will not fear what man can do unto me." Also in the same place: "To none but God alone is my soul subjected." Also in the cxviith Psalm: "I will not fear what man can do unto me; the Lord is my helper." Also in the same place: "It is good to trust in the Lord rather than to trust in man; it is good to hope in the Lord rather than to hope in princes."[56] Of this same thing in Daniel: "But Shadrach, Meshach, and Abednego answered and said to king Nebuchadnezzar, 'O king, there is no need to answer you concerning this word. For God, whom we serve, is able to deliver us from the furnace of burning fire; and He will deliver us from your hand, O king. And if not, be it known unto you that we serve not your gods, and we adore not the golden image which you have set up.'"[57] Likewise in Jeremiah: "Cursed is the man who has hope in man; and blessed is the man who trusts in the Lord, and his hope shall be in God."[58] Concerning this same thing in Deuteronomy: "You shall worship the Lord your God, and Him only shall you serve."[59] Of this same thing to the Romans: "And they worshipped and served the creature, forsaking the Creator. Wherefore also God gave them up to ignominious passions."[60] Of this thing also in John: "Greater is He who is in you than he who is in this world."[61]

11. That he who has attained to trust, having put off the former man, ought to regard only celestial and spiritual things, and to give no heed to the world which he has already renounced

In Isaiah: "Seek the Lord; and when you have found Him, call upon Him. But when He has come near unto you, let the wicked forsake his ways, and the unrighteous man his thoughts: and let him be turned unto the Lord, and he shall obtain mercy, because He will plentifully pardon your sins."[62] Of this same thing in Solomon: "I have seen all the works which are done under the sun; and, lo, all are vanity."[63] Of this same thing in Exodus: "But thus shall you eat it; your loins girt, and your shoes on your feet, and your staves in your hands: and you shall eat it in haste, for it is the Lord's passover."[64] Of this same thing in the Gospel according to Matthew: "Take no thought, saying, 'What shall we eat? Or, What shall we drink? Or, Wherewith shall we be clothed?' For these things the nations seek after. But your Father knows that you have need of all these things. Seek first the kingdom of God, and His righteousness; and all these things shall be added unto you." Likewise in the same place: "Think not for the morrow, for the morrow shall take thought for itself. Sufficient unto the day is its own evil." Likewise in the same place: "No one looking back, and putting his hands to the plough, is fit for the kingdom of God." Also in the same place: "Behold the fowls of the heaven: for they sow not, nor reap, nor gather into barns; and your heavenly Father feeds them. Are not you of more value than they?"[65] Concerning this same thing, according to Luke: "Let your loins be girded, and your lamps burning; and you like men that wait for their lord, when he comes from the wedding; that, when he comes and knocks, they may open to him. Blessed are those servants, whom their lord, when he comes, shall find watching."[66] Of this same thing in Matthew: "The foxes have holes, and the birds of the heaven have nests; but the Son of man has not where He may lay His head." Also in the same place: "Whoso forsakes not all that he has, cannot be my disciple."[67] Of this same thing in the first to the Corinthians: "You are not your own, for you are bought with a great price. Glorify and bear God in your body." Also in the same place: "The time is limited. It remains, therefore, that both they who have wives be as though they have them not, and they who lament as they that lament not, and they that rejoice as they that rejoice not, and they who buy as they that buy not, and they who possess as they who possess not, and they who use this world as they that use it not; for the fashion of this world passes away." Also in the same place: "The first man is of the clay of the earth, the second man from heaven. As he is of the clay, such also are they who are of the clay; and as is the heavenly, such also are the heavenly. Even as we have borne the image of him who is of the clay, let us bear His image also who is from heaven."[68] Of this same matter to the Philippians: "All seek their own, and not those things which are Christ's; whose end is destruction, whose god is their belly, and their glory is to their confusion, who mind earthly things. For our conversation is in heaven, whence also we expect the Savior, our Lord Jesus Christ, who shall transform the body of our humiliation conformed to the body of His glory."[69] Of this very matter to Galatians: "But be it far from me to boast, except in the cross of our Lord Jesus Christ, by whom the world is crucified unto me, and I unto the world."[70] Concerning this same thing to Timothy: "No man that wars for God binds himself with worldly annoyances, that he may please Him to whom he has approved himself. But and if a man should contend, he will not be crowned unless he fight lawfully."[71] Of this same thing to the Colossians: "If you be dead with Christ from the elements of the world, why still, as if living in the world, do you follow vain things?" Also concerning this same thing: "If you have risen together with Christ, seek those things which are above, where Christ is sitting on the right hand of God. Give heed to the things that are above, not to those things which are on the earth; for you are dead, and your life is hidden with Christ in God. But when Christ your life shall appear, then shall you also appear with Him in glory."[72] Of this same thing to the Ephesians: "Put off the old man of the former conversation, who is corrupted, according to the lusts of deceit. But be renewed in the spirit of your mind, and put on the new man, him who according to God is ordained in righteousness, and holiness, and truth."[73] Of this same thing in the Epistle of Peter: "As strangers and pilgrims, abstain from fleshly lusts, which war against the soul; but having a good conversation among the Gentiles, that while they detract from you as if from evildoers, yet, beholding your good works, they may magnify God."[74] Of this same thing in the Epistle of John: "He who says he abides in Christ, ought himself also to walk even as He walked." Also in the same place: "Love not the world, neither the things that are in the world. If any man loves the world, the love of the Father is not in him. Because everything which is in the world is lust of the flesh, and lust of the eyes, and the ambition of this world, which is not of the Father, but of the lust of this world. And the world shall pass away with its lust. But he that does the will of God abides for ever, even as God abides for ever."[75] Also in the first Epistle of Paul to the Corinthians: "Purge out the old leaven, that you may be a new dough, as you are unleavened. For also Christ our passover is sacrificed. Therefore let us celebrate the feast, not in the old leaven, nor in the leaven of malice and wickedness, but in the unleavened bread of sincerity and truth."[76]

12. *That we must not swear*

In Solomon: "A man that swears much shall be filled with iniquity, and the plague shall not depart from his house; and if he swear vainly, he shall not be justified."[77] Of this same matter, according to Matthew: "Again, you have heard that it was said to them of old, You shall not swear falsely, but shall perform unto the Lord your oaths. I say unto you, Swear not at all: neither by heaven, because it is God's throne; nor by the earth, because it is His footstool; nor by Jerusalem, because it is the city of the great King; neither shall you swear by your head, because you can not make one hair white or black. But let your discourse be, Yea, yea; Nay, nay: for whatever is fuller than these is of evil."[78] Of this same thing in Exodus: "You shall not take the name of the Lord your God in vain."[79]

13. That we must not curse

In Exodus: "You shall not curse nor speak ill of the ruler of your people."[80] Also in the thirty-third Psalm: "Who is the man who desires life, and loves to see good days? Restrain your tongue from evil, and your lips that they speak no guile."[81] Of this same thing in Leviticus: "And the Lord spoke to Moses, saying, 'Bring forth him who has cursed abroad outside the camp; and all who heard him shall place their hands upon his head, and all the assembly of the children of Israel shall stone him.'"[82] Of this same thing in Paul's Epistle to the Ephesians: "Let no evil discourse proceed out of your mouth, but that which is good for the edification of faith, that it may give grace to the hearers."[83] Of this same thing to the Romans: "Blessing, and not cursing."[84] Of this same thing in the Gospel according to Matthew: "He who shall say to his brother, 'You fool!' shall be liable to the Gehenna of fire." Of this same matter, according to the same Matthew: "But I say unto you, that every idle word which men shall speak, they shall give account for it in the day of judgment. For by your words you shall be justified, and by your words you shall be condemned."[85]

14. That we must never murmur, but bless God concerning all things that happen

In Job: "'Say some word against the Lord, and die.' But he, looking upon her, said, 'You speak as one of the foolish women. If we have received good things from the Lord's hand, why shall we not endure evil things?' In all these things which happened unto him, Job sinned not with his lips in the sight of the Lord." Also in the same place: "Have you regarded my servant Job? For there is none like him in the earth: a man without complaint: a true worshipper of God, restraining himself from all evil."[86] Of the same thing in the thirty-third Psalm: "I will bless the Lord at all times: His praise shall ever be in my mouth."[87] Of this same thing in Numbers: "Let their murmuring cease from me, and they shall not die."[88] Of this same thing in the Acts of the Apostles: "But about the middle of the night Paul and Silas prayed and gave thanks to God, and the prisoners heard them."[89] Also in the Epistle of Paul to the Philippians: "But doing all things for love, without murmurings and revilings, that you may be without complaint, and spotless sons of God."[90]

239

15. That men are tried by God for this purpose, that they may be proved

In Genesis: "And God tempted Abraham, and said to him, 'Take your only son whom you love, Isaac, and go into the high land, and offer him there as a burnt-offering on one of the mountains of which I will tell you.'"[91] Of this same thing in Deuteronomy: "The Lord your God proves you, that He may know if you love the Lord your God with all your heart, and with all your soul."[92] Of this same thing in the Wisdom of Solomon: "Although in the sight of men they suffered torments, their hope is full of immortality; and having been in few things distressed, yet in many things they shall be happily ordered, because God tried them, and found them worthy of Himself. As gold in the furnace He proved them, and as a burnt-offering He received them. And in their time there shall be respect of them; they shall judge the nations, and shall rule over the people; and their Lord shall reign for ever."[93] Of this same thing in the Maccabees: "Was not Abraham found faithful in temptation, and it was accounted unto him for righteousness?"[94]

16. Of the benefits of martyrdom

In the Proverbs of Solomon: "The faithful martyr delivers his soul from evils."[95] Also in the same place: "Then shall the righteous stand in great boldness against them who have afflicted them, and who took away their labors. When they see them, they shall be disturbed with a horrible fear; and they shall wonder at the suddenness of their unhoped-for salvation, saying among themselves, repenting and groaning with distress of spirit; These are they whom some time we had in derision, and in the likeness of a proverb; we fools counted their life madness, and their end without honor. How are they reckoned among the children of God, and their lot among the saints! Therefore we have wandered from the way of truth, and the light of righteousness has not shined upon us, and the sun has not risen upon us. We have been wearied in the way of iniquity and of perdition, and we have walked through difficult solitudes; but we have not known the way of the Lord. What has pride profited us? Or what has the boasting of riches brought to us? All these things have passed away as a shadow."[96] Of this same thing in the cxvth Psalm: "Precious in the sight of the Lord is the death of His saints."[97] Also in the cxxvth Psalm: "They who sow in tears shall reap in joy. Walking they walked, and wept as they cast their seeds; but coming they shall come in joy, raising up their laps."[98] Of this same thing in the Gospel according to John: "He who loves his life shall lose it; and he that hates his life in this world shall find it to life eternal." Also in the same place: "But when they shall deliver you up, take no thought what you shall speak; for it is not you who speak, but the Spirit of your Father which speaks in you." Also in the same place: "The hour shall come, that every one that kills you shall think he does service to God, but they shall do this also because they have not known the Father nor me."[99] Of this same matter, according to Matthew: "Blessed are they which shall suffer persecution for righteousness' sake; for theirs is the kingdom of heaven." Also in the same place: "Fear not them which kill the body, but are not able to kill the soul; but rather fear Him which is able to kill the soul and body in Gehenna." Also in the same place: "Whosoever shall confess me before men, him also will I confess before my Father which is in heaven; but he who shall deny me before men, him also will I deny before my Father which is in heaven. And he that shall endure to the end, the same shall be saved."[100] Of this same thing, according to Luke: "Blessed shall you be when men shall hate you, and shall separate you [from their company], and shall drive you out, and shall speak evil of your name, as wicked, for the Son of man's sake. Rejoice in that day, and exult; for, lo, your reward is great in heaven." Also in the same place: "Verily I say unto you, There is no man that leaves house, or parents, or brethren, or wife, or children, for the sake of the kingdom of God, and does not receive seven times as much in this present time, but in the world to come life everlasting."[101] Of this same thing in the Apocalypse: "And when he had opened the fifth seal, I saw under the altar of God the souls of them that were slain on account of the word of God and His testimony. And they cried with a loud voice, saying, 'How long, O Lord, holy and true, do You not judge and avenge our blood on them that dwell on the earth?' And unto every one of them were given white robes; and it was said to them, that they should rest still for a short time, until the number of their fellow-servants, and of their brethren, should be fulfilled, and they who shall afterwards be slain, after their example." Also in the same place: "After these things I saw a great crowd, which no one among them could number, from every nation, and from every tribe, and from every people and tongue, standing before the throne and before the Lamb; and they were clothed with white robes, and palms were in their hands. And they said with a loud voice, 'Salvation to our God, that sits upon the throne, and to the Lamb.' And one of the elders answered and said to me, 'What are these which are clothed with white robes? Who are they, and whence have they come?' And I said unto him, 'My lord, you know.' And he said unto me, 'These are they who have come out of great tribulation, and have washed their robes, and made them white in the blood of the Lamb. Therefore they are before the throne of God, and serve Him day and night in His temple; and He who sits upon the throne shall dwell among them. They shall neither hunger nor thirst ever; and neither shall the sun fall upon them, nor shall they suffer any heat: for the Lamb who is in the midst of the throne shall protect them, and shall lead them to the fountains of the waters of life; and God shall wipe away every tear from their eyes.'" Also in the same place: "He who shall overcome I will give him to eat of the tree of life, which as in the paradise of my

God." Also in the same place: "Be faithful even unto death, and I will give you a crown of life." Also in the same place: "Blessed shall they be who shall watch, and shall keep their garments, lest they walk naked, and they see their shame."[102] Of this same thing, Paul in the second Epistle to Timothy: "I am now offered up, and the time of my assumption is at hand. I have fought a good fight, I have finished my course, I have kept the faith. There now remains for me a crown of righteousness, which the Lord, the righteous Judge, will give me in that day; and not only to me, but to all also who love His appearing."[103] Of this same thing to the Romans: "We are the sons of God: but if sons and heirs of God, we are also joint-heirs with Christ; if we suffer together, that we may also be magnified together."[104] Of this same thing in the cxviiith Psalm: "Blessed are they who are undefiled in the way, and walk in the law of the Lord. Blessed are they who search into His testimonies."[105]

17. That what we suffer in this world is of less account than is the reward which is promised

In the Epistle of Paul to the Romans: "The sufferings of this present time are not worthy of comparison with the glory that is to come after, which shall be revealed in us."[106] Of this same thing in the Maccabees: "O Lord, who hast the holy knowledge, it is manifest that while I might be delivered from death, I am suffering most cruel pains of body, being beaten with whips; yet in spirit I suffer these things willingly, because of the fear of Your own self." Also in the same place: "You indeed, being powerless, destroyest us out of this present life; but the King of the world shall raise us up who have died for His laws into the eternal resurrection of life." Also in the same place: "It is better that, given up to death by men, we should expect hope from God to be raised again by Him. For there shall be no resurrection to life for you." Also in the same place: "Having power among men, although you are corruptible, you do what you will. But think not that our race is forsaken of God. Sustain, and see how His great power will torment, you and your seed." Also in the same place: "Do not err without cause; for we suffer these things on our own accounts, as sinners against our God. But think not that you shall be unpunished, having undertaken to fight against God."[107]

18. That nothing is to be preferred to the love of God and Christ

In Deuteronomy: "You shall love the Lord your God with all your heart, and with all your soul, and with all your might."[108] Also in the Gospel according to Matthew: "He that loves father or mother above me, is not worthy of me; and he that loves son or daughter above me, is not worthy of me; and he that takes not up his cross and follows me, is not my disciple."[109] Also in the Epistle of Paul to the Romans: "Who shall separate us from the love of Christ? Shall tribulation, or distress, or persecution, or famine, or nakedness, or peril, or sword? As it is written, 'Because for your sake we are killed all the day long, we are counted as sheep for the slaughter.' But in all these things we are more than conquerors for His sake who loved us."[110]

19. That we are not to obey our own will, but the will of God

In the Gospel according to John: "I came not down from heaven to do my own will, but the will of Him that sent me."[111] Of this same matter, according to Matthew: "Father, if it be possible, let this cup pass from me; nevertheless, not what I will, but what You will."[112] Also in the daily prayer: "Your will be done, as in heaven, so in earth."[113] Also according to Matthew: "Not every one who says unto me, 'Lord, Lord, shall enter into the kingdom of heaven; but he who does the will of my Father which is in heaven, he shall enter into the kingdom of heaven."[114] Also according to Luke: "But that servant which knows his Lord's will, and obeyed not His will, shall be beaten with many stripes."[115] In the Epistle of John: "But he that does the will of God abides for ever, even as He Himself also abides for ever."[116]

20. That the foundation and strength of hope and faith is fear

In the cxth Psalm: "The fear of the Lord is the beginning of wisdom." Of the same thing in the Wisdom of Solomon: "The beginning of wisdom is to fear God." Also in the Proverbs of the same: "Blessed is the man who reverences all things with fear."[117] Of the same thing in Isaiah: "And upon whom else will I look, except upon him that is lowly and peaceful, and that trembles at my words?"[118] Of this same thing in Genesis: "And the angel of the Lord called him from heaven, and said unto him, 'Abraham, Abraham:' and he said, 'Here am I.' And he said, 'Lay not your hand upon the lad, neither do anything unto him: for now I know that you fear your God, and hast not spared your beloved son for my sake.'"[119] Also in the second Psalm: "Serve the Lord in fear, and rejoice unto Him in trembling."[120] Also in Deuteronomy, the word of God to Moses: "Call the people together to me, and let them hear my words, that they may learn to fear me all the days that they themselves shall live upon the earth."[121] Also in Jeremiah: "Behold, the days come, says the Lord, that I will perfect upon the house of Israel, and in the house of Judah, a new covenant: not according to the covenant that I had ordered with their fathers in the day when I laid hold of their hand to bring them out of the land of Egypt; because they have not abode in my covenant, and I have been unmindful of them, says the Lord; because this is the covenant which I will ordain for the house of Israel. After those days, says the Lord, I will give my law, and will write it in their mind and I will be to them for a God, and they shall be to me for a people. And they shall not teach every man his brother, saying, 'Know the Lord,' because all shall know me, from the least even to the greatest of them: because I will be favorable to their iniquities, and their sins I will not remember any more. If the heaven should be lifted up on high, says the Lord, and if the earth should be made low from beneath, yet I will not cast away the people of Israel, says the Lord, for all the things which they have done. Behold, I will gather them together from every land in which I have scattered them in anger, and in my fury, and in great indignation; and I will grind them down into that place, and I will leave them in fear; and they shall be to me for a people, and I will be to them for a God: and I will give them another way, and another heart, that they may fear me all their days in prosperity with their children: and I will perfect for them an everlasting covenant, which I will not turn away after them; and I will put my fear into their heart, that they may not depart from me: and I will visit upon them to do them good, and to plant them in their land in faith, and with all the heart, and with all the mind."[122] Also in the Apocalypse: "And the four and twenty elders which sit on their thrones in the sight of God fell upon their faces, and worshipped God, saying, 'We give You thanks, O Lord God omnipotent, which art and which wast; because You have taken Your great power, and have reigned. And the nations were angry, and Your wrath has come, and the time in which it should be judged concerning the dead, and the reward should be given to Your servants the prophets, and the saints that fear Your name, small and great; and to disperse those who have corrupted the earth.'" Also in the same place: "And I saw another angel flying through the midst of the heaven, having the everlasting Gospel to preach to those who dwell upon the earth, and to all the nations, and tribes, and tongues, and peoples, saying with a loud voice, 'Fear God, and give Him honor, because the hour of His judgment has come; and adore Him who made the heaven, and the earth, and the sea, and the fountains of waters.'" Also in the same place: "And I saw as it were a sea of glass mingled with fire; and the beasts were feeding with His lambs; and the number of His name a hundred and forty and four, standing upon the sea of glass, having the harps of God; and they sing the song of Moses, the servant of God, and the song of the Lamb, saying, 'Great and marvellous are Your works, O Lord God Almighty; just and true are Your ways, You King of the nations. Who would not fear You, and give honor to Your name? For You only are holy: and because all nations shall come and worship in Your sight, because Your righteousnesses have been made manifest.'"[123] Also in Daniel: "There was a man dwelling in Babylon whose name was Joachim; and he took a wife by name Susanna, the daughter of Helchias, a very beautiful woman, and one that feared the Lord. And her parents were righteous, and taught their daughter according to the law of Moses." Moreover, in Daniel: "And we are lowly this day in all the earth because of our sins, and there is not at this time any prince, or prophet, or leader, or burnt offering, or oblation, or sacrifice, or incense, or place to sacrifice before You, and to find mercy from You. And yet in the soul and spirit of lowliness let us be accepted as the burnt-offerings of rams and bulls, and as it were many thousands of lambs which are fattest. If our offering may be made in Your presence this day, their power shall be consumed, for they shall not be ashamed who put their trust in You. And now we follow with our whole heart, and we fear and seek Your face. Give us not over unto reproach, but do with us according to Your tranquillity, and according to the multitude of Your mercy deliver us." Also in the same place: "And the king exceedingly rejoiced, and commanded Daniel to be taken up out of the den of lions; and the lions had done him no hurt, because he trusted and had believed in his God. And the king commanded, and they brought those men who had accused Daniel; and they cast them in the den of lions, and their wives and their children. And before they had reached the pavement of the den they were seized by the lions, and they broke all their bones in pieces. Then Darius the king wrote, 'To all peoples, tribes, and languages which are in my kingdom, peace be unto you from my face. I decree and ordain that all those who are in my kingdom shall fear and tremble before the most high God whom Daniel serves, because He is the God who lives and abides for ever, and His kingdom shall not pass away, and His dominion goes on for ever; and He alone does signs, and prodigies, and marvellous things in the heaven and the earth, who snatched Daniel from the den of lions.'"[124] Also in Micah: "Wherewith shall I approach the Lord, and lay hold upon Him? In sacrifices, in burnt-offerings, in calves of a year old? Does the Lord favor and receive me with thousands of fat goats? Or shall I give my first-fruits of unrighteousness, the fruit of my belly, the sin of my soul? It is told you, O man, what is good; or what else the Lord does require, save that you should do judgment and justice, and love mercy, and be ready to go with the Lord your God. The voice of the Lord shall be invoked in the city, and He will save those who fear His name." Also in Micah: "Feed Your people with Your rod, the sheep of Your inheritance; and pluck up those who dwell separately in the midst of Carmel. They shall prepare Bashan and Gilead according to the days of the age; and according to the days of their going forth from the land of Egypt I will show them wonderful things. The nations shall see, and be confounded at all their might; and they shall place their hand upon their mouth. Their ears shall be deafened, and they shall lick the dust as do serpents. Dragging the earth, they shall be disturbed, and they shall lick the dust: in their end they shall be afraid towards the Lord their God, and they shall fear because of You. Who is a God as You are, raising up unrighteousness, and passing over impiety?"[125] And in Nahum: "The mountains were moved at Him, and the hills trembled; and the earth was laid bare before His face, and all who dwell therein. From the face of

His anger who shall bear it, and who withstands in the fury of His soul? His rage causes the beginnings to flow, and the rocks were melted by Him. The Lord is good to those who sustain Him in the day of affliction, and knows those who fear Him."[126] Also in Haggai: "And Zerubbabel the son of Salathiel, of the tribe of Judah, and Joshua the son of Josedech, the high priest, and all who remained of the people, obeyed the voice of the Lord their God, because the Lord sent him to them, and the people feared from the face of God."[127] Also in Malachi: "The covenant was with life and peace; and I gave to them the fear to fear me from the face of my name."[128] Also in the thirty-third Psalm: "Fear the Lord, all you His saints: for there is no want to them that fear Him." Also in the eighteenth Psalm: "The fear of the Lord is chaste, abiding for ever."[129]

21. That we must not rashly judge of another

In the Gospel according to Luke: "Judge not, that you be not judged: condemn not, that you be not condemned."[130] Of this same subject to the Romans: "Who are you that judgest another man's servant? To his own master he stands or falls. But he shall stand; for God is able to make him stand." And again: "Wherefore you are without excuse, O every man that judges: for in that in which you judge another, you condemn yourself; for you do the same things which you judge. But you, who judge those who do evil, and do the same, hope that you yourself shall escape the judgment of God."[131] Also in the first Epistle of Paul to the Corinthians: "And let him that thinks he stands take heed lest he fall." And again: "If any man thinks that he knows anything, he knows not yet in what manner he ought to know."[132]

22. That when we have received a wrong, we must remit and forgive it

In the Gospel, in the daily prayer: "Forgive us our debts, even as we forgive our debtors."[133] Also according to Mark: "And when you stand for prayer, forgive, if you have ought against any one; that also your Father who is in heaven may forgive you your sins. But if you do not forgive, neither will your Father which is in heaven forgive you your sins." Also in the same place: "In what measure you mete, in that shall it be measured to you again."[134]

23. That evil is not to be returned for evil

In the Epistle of Paul to the Romans: "Rendering to no man evil for evil." Also in the same place: "Not to be overcome of evil, but overcome evil with good."[135] Of this same thing in the Apocalypse: "And He said unto me, 'Seal not the words of the prophecy of this book; because now the time is at hand. And let those who persist in hurting, hurt: and let him who is filthy, be filthy still: but let the righteous do still more righteousness: and in like manner, let him that is holy do still more holiness. Behold, I come quickly; and my reward is with me, to render to every man according to his deeds.'"[136]

24. That it is impossible to attain to the Father but by His Son Jesus Christ

In the Gospel according to John: "I am the way, the truth, and the life: no man comes unto the Father, but by me." Also in the same place: "I am the door: by me if any man enter in, he shall be saved."[137]

25. That unless a man have been baptized and born again, he cannot attain unto the kingdom of God

In the Gospel according to John: "Unless a man be born again of water and the Spirit, he cannot enter into the kingdom of God. For that which is born of the flesh is flesh; and that which is born of the Spirit is spirit."[138] Also in the same place: "Unless you eat the flesh of the Son of man, and drink His blood, you shall not have life in you."[139]

26. That it is of small account to be baptized and to receive the Eucharist, unless one profit by it both in deeds and works

In the first Epistle of Paul to the Corinthians: "Do you not know, that they which run in a race run indeed all, although one receives the prize? So run, that you may obtain. And those indeed that they may receive a corruptible crown, but we an incorruptible."[140] In the Gospel according to Matthew: "Every tree that brings not forth good fruit shall be cut down, and cast into the fire." Also in the same place: "Many shall say unto me in that day, 'Lord, Lord, have we not prophesied in Your name, and in Your name have cast out devils, and in Your name have done great works?' And then shall I say to them, 'I never knew you; depart from me, you who work iniquity.'" Also in the same place: "Let your light shine before men, that they may see your good works, and glorify your Father which is in heaven."[141] Also Paul to the Philippians: "Shine as lights in the world."[142]

27. That even a baptized person loses the grace that he has attained, unless he keep innocence

In the Gospel according to John: "Lo, you are made whole: sin no more, lest a worse thing happen unto you."[143] Also in the first Epistle of Paul to the Corinthians: "Do you not know that you are the temple of God, and the Spirit of God abides in you? If any one violate the temple of God, him will God destroy."[144] Of this same thing in the Chronicles: "God is with you, while you are with Him: if you forsake Him, He will forsake you."[145]

28. That remission cannot in the Church be granted unto him who has sinned against God (i.e., the Holy Ghost)[146]

In the Gospel according to Matthew: "Whosoever shall say a word against the Son of man, it shall be forgiven him; but whosoever shall speak against the Holy Ghost, it shall not be forgiven him, neither in this world nor in the world to come."[147] Also according to Mark: "All sins shall be forgiven, and blasphemies, to the sons of men; but whoever shall blaspheme against the Holy Ghost, it shall not be forgiven him, but he shall be guilty of eternal sin."[148] Of this same thing in the first book of Kings: "If a man sin by offending against a man, they shall pray the Lord for him; but if a man sin against God, who shall pray for him?"[149]

29. That it was before predicted, concerning the hatred of the Name

In the Gospel according to Luke: "And you shall be hated of all men for my name's sake."[150] Also according to John: "If the world hates you, know that it first hated me. If you were of the world, the world would love what would be its own: but because you are not of the world, and I have chosen you out of the world, therefore the world hates you. Remember the word which I said unto you, 'The servant is not greater than his lord.' If they have persecuted me, they will also persecute you."[151] Also in Baruch: "For the time shall come, and you shall seek me, both you and those who shall be after you, to hear the word of wisdom and of understanding; and you shall not find me. But the nations shall desire to see the wise man, and it shall not happen to them; not because the wisdom of this world shall be wanting, or shall fail to the earth; but neither shall the word of the law be wanting to the world. For wisdom shall be in a few who watch, and are silent and quiet, and who hold converse with one another; because some shall dread them, and shall fear them as evil. But some do not believe the word of the law of the Highest. But some who are amazed in their countenance will not believe; and they also who contradict will believe, and will be contrary to and hindering the spirit of truth. Moreover, others will be wise to the spirit of error, and declaring the edicts, as if of the Highest and the Strong One. Moreover, others are possessors of faith. Others are mighty and strong in the faith of the Highest, and hateful to the stranger."[152]

30. That what any one has vowed to God, he must quickly repay

In Solomon: "According as you have vowed a vow to God, delay not to pay it."[153] Concerning this same thing in Deuteronomy: "But if you have vowed a vow to the Lord your God, you shall not delay to pay it: because the Lord your God inquiring shall seek it of you; and it shall be for a sin. You shall observe those things that shall go forth out of your lips, and shall perform the gift which you have spoken with your mouth."[154] Of this same matter in the forty-ninth

Psalm: "Sacrifice to God the sacrifice of praise, and pay your vows to the Most High. Call upon me in the day of trouble, and I will deliver you, and you shall glorify me."[155] Of this same thing in the Acts of the Apostles: "Why has Satan filled your heart, that you should lie to the Holy Ghost, when your estate was in your own power? You have not lied unto men, but unto God."[156] Also in Jeremiah: "Cursed is he who does the work of God negligently."[157]

31. That he who does not believe is judged already

In the Gospel according to John: "He that believes not is already judged, because he has not believed in the name of the only Son of God. And this is the judgment, that light has come into the world, and men have loved darkness rather than light."[158] Of this also in the first Psalm: "Therefore the ungodly shall not rise up in judgment, nor sinners in the council of the righteous."[159]

32. Of the benefit of virginity and of continency

In Genesis: "Multiplying I will multiply your sorrows and your groanings, and in sorrow shall you bring forth children; and your turning shall be to your husband, and he shall rule over you."[160] Of this same thing in the Gospel according to Matthew: "All men do not receive the word, but they to whom it is given: for there are some eunuchs who were born so from their mother's womb, and there are eunuchs who have been constrained by men, and there are eunuchs who have made themselves eunuchs for the kingdom of heaven's sake. He who can receive it, let him receive it."[161] Also according to Luke: "The children of this world beget, and are begotten. But they who have been considered worthy of that world, and the resurrection from the dead, do not marry, nor are married: for neither shall they begin to die: for they are equal to the angels of God, since they are the children of the resurrection. But, that the dead rise again, Moses intimates when he says in the bush, 'The Lord, the God of Abraham, and the God of Isaac, and the God of Jacob.' He is not the God of the dead, but of the living: for all live unto Him."[162] Also in the first Epistle of Paul to the Corinthians: "It is good for a man not to touch a woman. But, on account of fornication, let every man have his own wife, and every woman have her own husband. Let the husband render what is due to the wife, and similarly the wife to the husband. The wife has not power over her own body, but the husband. And in like manner, the husband has not power over his own body, but the wife. Defraud not one the other, except by agreement for a time, that you may have leisure for prayer; and again return to the same point, lest Satan tempt you on account of your incontinency. This I say by way of allowance, not by way of command. But I wish that all men should be even as I am. But every one has his proper gift from God; one in one way, but another in another way." Also in the same place: "An unmarried man thinks of those things which are the Lord's, in what way he may please God; but he who has contracted marriage thinks of those things that are of this world, in what way he may please his wife. Thus also, both the woman and the unmarried virgin thinks of those things which are the Lord's, that she may be holy both in body and in spirit; but she that has married thinks of those things which are of this world, in what way she may please her husband."[163] Also in Exodus, when the Lord had commanded Moses that he should sanctify the people for the third day, he sanctified them, and added: "Be ready, for three days you shall not approach to women."[164] Also in the first book of Kings: "And the priest answered to David, and said, 'There are no profane loaves in my hand, except one sacred loaf. If the young men have been kept back from women, they shall eat.'"[165] Also in the Apocalypse: "These are they who have not defiled themselves with women, for they have continued virgins; these are they who follow the Lamb wherever He shall go."[166]

33. That the Father judges nothing, but the Son; and that the Father is not glorified by him by whom the Son is not glorified

In the Gospel according to John: "The Father judges nothing, but has given all judgment unto the Son, that all may honor the Son as they honor the Father. He who honors not the Son, honors not the Father who has sent Him."[167] Also in the seventy-first Psalm: "O God, give the king Your judgment, and Your righteousness to the king's son, to judge Your people in righteousness."[168] Also in Genesis: "And the Lord rained upon Sodom and Gomorrah sulphur, and fire from heaven from the Lord."[169]

34. That the believer ought not to live like the Gentile

In Jeremiah: "Thus says the Lord, 'Walk not according to the way of the Gentiles.'"[170] Of this same thing, that one ought to separate himself from the Gentiles, lest he should be a companion of their sin, and become a partaker of their penalty, in the Apocalypse: "And I heard another voice from heaven, saying, 'Go forth from her, my people, lest you be partaker of her crimes, and lest you be stricken with her plagues; because her crimes have reached even to heaven, and the Lord God has remembered her iniquities. Therefore He has returned unto her double, and in the cup which she has mixed double is mingled for her; and in how much she has glorified herself and possessed of delights, in so much is given unto her both torment and grief. For in her heart she says, 'I am a queen, and cannot be a widow, nor shall I see sorrow.' Therefore in one hour her plagues shall come on her, death, grief, and famine; and she shall be burned with fire, because the Lord God is strong who shall judge her. And the kings of the earth shall weep and lament themselves for her, who have committed fornication with her, and have been conversant in her sins.'"[171] Also in Isaiah: "Go forth from the midst of them, you who bear the vessels of the Lord."[172]

35. That God is patient for this end, that we may repent of our sin, and be reformed

In Solomon, in Ecclesiasticus: "Say not, I have sinned, and what sorrow has happened to me? For the Highest is a patient repayer."[173] Also Paul to the Romans: "Or do you despise the riches of His goodness, and forbearance, and patience, not knowing that the goodness of God leads you to repentance? But, according to your hardness and impenitent heart, you store up to yourself wrath in the day of wrath and of revelation of the just judgment of God, who will render to every man according to his deeds."[174]

36. That a woman ought not to be adorned in a worldly fashion

In the Apocalypse: "And there came one of the seven angels having vials, and approached me, saying, 'Come, I will show you the condemnation of the great whore, who sits upon many waters, with whom the kings of the earth have committed fornication.' And I saw a woman who sate upon a beast. And that woman was clothed with a purple and scarlet robe; and she was adorned with gold, and precious stones, and pearls, holding a golden cup in her hand full of curses, and impurity, and fornication of the whole earth."[175] Also to Timothy: "Let your women be such as adorn themselves with shamefacedness and modesty, not with twisted hair, nor with gold, nor with pearls, or precious garments, but as becomes women professing chastity, with a good conversation."[176] Of this same thing in the Epistle of Peter to the people at Pontus: "Let there be in a woman not the outward adorning of ornament, or of gold, or of apparel, but the adorning of the heart."[177] Also in Genesis: "Tamar covered herself with a cloak, and adorned herself; and when Judah beheld her, she appeared to him to be a harlot."[178]

37. That the believer ought not to be punished for other offenses, except for the name he bears

In the Epistle of Peter to them of Pontus: "Nor let any of you suffer as a thief, or a murderer, or as an evil-doer, or as a minder of other people's business, but as a Christian."[179]

38. That the servant of God ought to be innocent, lest he fall into secular punishment

In the Epistle of Paul to the Romans: "Will you not be afraid of the power? Do that which is good, and you shall have praise of it."[180]

39. That there is given to us an example of living in Christ

In the Epistle of Peter to them of Pontus: "For Christ suffered for us, leaving you an example, that you may follow His steps; who did no sin, neither was guile found in His mouth; who, when He was reviled, reviled not again; when He suffered, threatened not, but gave Himself up to him that judges unrighteously."[181] Also Paul to the Philippians: "Who, being appointed in the figure of God, thought it not robbery that He was equal with God; but emptied Himself, taking the form of a servant, He was made in the likeness of man, and was found in fashion as a man. He humbled Himself, becoming obedient even unto death, and the death of the cross. For which cause also God has exalted Him, and has given Him a name, that it may be above every name, that in the name of Jesus every knee should be bowed, of things heavenly, and earthly, and infernal; and that every tongue should confess that the Lord Jesus Christ is in glory of God the Father."[182] Of this same thing in the Gospel according to John: "If I have washed your feet, being your Master and Lord, you also ought to wash the feet of others. For I have given you an example, that as I have done, you also should do to others."[183]

40. That we must not labor noisily nor boastfully

In the Gospel according to Matthew: "Let not your left hand know what your right hand does, that your alms may be in secret; and your Father, which sees in secret, shall render to you." Also in the same place: "When you do an alms, do not sound a trumpet before you, as the hypocrites do in the streets and in the synagogues, that they may be glorified of men. Verily I say unto you, they have fulfilled their reward."[184]

41. That we must not speak foolishly and offensively

In Paul's Epistle to the Ephesians: "Foolish speaking and scurrility, which are not fitting for the occasion, let them not be even named among you."[185]

42. That faith is of advantage altogether, and that we can do as much as we believe

In Genesis: "And Abraham believed God, and it was counted unto him for righteousness."[186] Also in Isaiah: "And if you do not believe, neither shall you understand."[187] Also in the Gospel according to Matthew: "O you of little faith, wherefore did you doubt?" Also in the same place: "If you have faith as a grain of mustard seed, you shall say to this mountain, 'Pass over from here to that place,' and it shall pass over; and nothing shall be impossible unto you."[188] Also according to Mark: "All things whatsoever you pray and ask for, believe that you shall receive them, and they shall be yours." Also in the same place: "All things are possible to him that believes."[189] In Habakkuk: "But the righteous lives by my faith."[190] Also in Daniel: "Ananias, Azarias, and Misael, trusting in God, were delivered from the fiery flame."[191]

43. That he who believes can immediately obtain pardon and peace

In the Acts of the Apostles: "Lo, here is water; what is there which hinders me from being baptized? Then said Philip, 'If you believe with all your heart, you may.'"[192]

44. That believers who differ among themselves ought not to refer to a Gentile judge

In the first Epistle of Paul to the Corinthians: "Dare any of you, having a matter against other, to discuss it among the unrighteous, and not among the saints? Do you not know that the saints shall judge this world?" And again: "Now indeed there is altogether a fault among you, because you have judgments one against another. Why do you not rather suffer injury? Or wherefore are you not rather defrauded? But you do wrong, and defraud, and this your brethren. Do you not know that the unrighteous shall not obtain the kingdom of God?"[193]

45. That hope is of future things, and therefore that our faith concerning those things which are promised ought to be patient

In the Epistle of Paul to the Romans: "We are saved by hope. But hope that is seen is not hope; for what a man sees, why does he hope for? But if we hope for what we see not, we hope for it in patience."[194]

46. That a woman ought to be silent in the church

In the first Epistle of Paul to the Corinthians: "Let women be silent in the church. But if any wish to learn anything, let them ask their husbands at home."[195] Also to Timothy: "Let a woman learn with silence, in all subjection. But I permit not a woman to teach, nor to be set over the man, but to be in silence. For Adam was first formed, then Eve; and Adam was not seduced, but the woman was seduced."[196]

47. That it arises from our fault and our desert that we suffer, and do not perceive God's help in everything

In Hosea: "Hear the word of the Lord, you children of Israel: because judgment is from the Lord against the inhabitants of the earth because there is neither mercy nor truth, nor acknowledgment of God upon the earth; but cursing, and lying, and slaughter, and theft, and adultery is scattered abroad upon the earth: they mingle blood to blood. Therefore the land shall mourn, with all its inhabitants, with the beasts of the field, with the creeping things of the earth, with the birds of heaven; and the fishes of the sea shall fail: so that no man may judge, no man may refute."[197] Of this same thing in Isaiah: "Is not the Lord's hand strong to save, or has He weighed down His ear that He may not hear? But your sins separate between you and God; and on account of your iniquities He turns away His face from you, lest He should pity. For your hands are polluted with blood, and your fingers with sins; and your lips have spoken wickedness, and your tongue devises unrighteousness. No one speaks true things, neither is judgment true. They trust in vanity, and speak emptiness, who conceive sorrow, and bring forth wickedness."[198] Also in Zephaniah: "In failing, let it fail from the face of the earth, says the Lord. Let man fail, and cattle; let the birds of heaven fail, and the fishes of the sea; and I will take away the unrighteous from the face of the earth."[199]

48. That we must not take usury

In the fifteenth Psalm: "He that has not given his money upon usury, and has not received gifts concerning the innocent. He who does these things shall not be moved for ever."[200] Also in Ezekiel: "But the man who will be righteous, shall not oppress a man, and shall return the pledge of the debtor, and shall not commit rapine, and shall give his bread to the hungry, and shall cover the naked, and shall not give his money for usury."[201] Also in Deuteronomy: "You shall not lend to your brother with usury of money, and with usury of victuals."[202]

49. That even our enemies must be loved

In the Gospel according to Luke: "If you love those who love you, what reward do you have? For even sinners love those who love them."[203] Also according to Matthew: "Love your enemies, and pray for those who persecute you, that you may be the children of your Father who is in heaven, who makes His sun to rise upon the good and the evil, and gives rain upon the righteous and the unrighteous."[204]

50. That the sacrament of faith must not be profaned

In Solomon, in the Proverbs: "Say not anything in the ears of a foolish man; lest, when he hears it, he may mock your wise words."[205] Also in the Gospel according to Matthew: "Give not that which is holy to dogs; neither cast your pearls before the swine, lest perchance they trample them down with their feet, and turn again and crush you."[206]

51. That no one should be uplifted in his labor

In Solomon, in Ecclesiasticus: "Extol not yourself in doing your work."[207] Also in the Gospel according to Luke: "Which of you, having a servant ploughing, or a shepherd, says to him when he comes from the field, 'Pass forward and recline?' But he says to him, 'Make ready somewhat that I may sup, and gird yourself, and minister to me, until I eat and drink; and afterwards you shall eat and drink?' Does he thank that servant because he has done what was commanded him? So also you, when you shall have done that which is commanded you, say, 'We are unprofitable servants; we have done what we had to do.'"[208]

52. That the liberty of believing or of not believing is placed in free choice

In Deuteronomy: "Lo, I have set before your face life and death, good and evil. Choose for yourself life, that you may live."[209] Also in Isaiah: "And if you be willing, and hear me, you shall eat the good of the land. But if you be unwilling, and will not hear me, the sword shall consume you. For the mouth of the Lord has spoken these things."[210] Also in the Gospel according to Luke: "The kingdom of God is within you."[211]

53. That he secrets of God cannot be seen through, and therefore that our faith ought to be simple

In the first Epistle of Paul to the Corinthians: "We see now through the glass in an enigma, but then with face to face. Now I know partly; but then I shall know even as also I am known."[212] Also in Solomon, in Wisdom: "And in simplicity of heart seek Him." Also in the same: "He who walks with simplicity, walks trustfully." Also in the same: "Seek not things higher than yourself, and look not into things stronger than yourself." Also in Solomon: "Be not excessively righteous, and do not reason more than is required."[213] Also in Isaiah: "Woe unto them who are convicted in themselves."[214] Also in the Maccabees: "Daniel in his simplicity was delivered from the mouth of the lions."[215] Also in the Epistle of Paul to the Romans: "Oh the depth of the riches of the wisdom and knowledge of God! How incomprehensible are His judgments, and how unsearchable are His ways! For who has known the mind of the Lord? Or who has been His counsellor? Or who has first given to Him, and it shall be recompensed to him again? Because from Him, and through Him, and in Him, are all things: to Him be glory for ever and ever."[216] Also to Timothy: "But foolish and unlearned questions avoid, knowing that they generate strifes. But the servant of God ought not to strive, but to be gentle towards all men."[217]

54. That no one is without filth and without sin[218]

In Job: "For who is pure from filth? Not one; even if his life be of one day on the earth."[219] Also in the fiftieth Psalm: "Behold, I was conceived in iniquities, and in sins has my mother conceived me."[220] Also in the Epistle of John: "If we say that we have no sin, we deceive ourselves, and the truth is not in us."[221]

55. That we must not please men, but God

In the fifty-second Psalm: "They that please men are confounded, because God has made them nothing."[222] Also in the Epistle of Paul to the Galatians: "If I wished to please men, I should not be the servant of Christ."[223]

56. That nothing that is done is hidden from God

In the Wisdom of Solomon: "In every place the eyes of God look upon the good and evil."[224] Also in Jeremiah: "I am a God at hand, and not a God afar off. If a man should be hidden in the secret place, shall I not therefore see him? Do not I fill heaven and earth, says the Lord."[225] Also in the first of Kings: "Man looks on the face, but God on the heart."[226] Also in the Apocalypse: "And all the churches shall know that I am the searcher of the reins and heart; and I will give to every one of you according to his works."[227] Also in the eighteenth Psalm: "Who understands his faults? Cleanse me from my secret sins, O Lord."[228] Also in the second Epistle of Paul to the Corinthians: "We must all be manifested before the tribunal of Christ, that every one may bear again the things which belong to his own body, according to what he has done, whether good or evil."[229]

57. That the believer is amended and reserved

In the cxviith Psalm: "The Lord amending has amended me, and has not delivered me to death."[230] Also in the eighty-eighth Psalm: "I will visit their transgressions with a rod, and their sins with scourges. But my mercy will I not scatter away from them."[231] Also in Malachi: "And He shall sit melting and purifying, as it were, gold and silver; and He shall purify the sons of Levi."[232] Also in the Gospel: "You shall not go out thence until you pay the uttermost farthing."[233]

58. That no one should be made sad by death; since in living is labor and peril, in dying peace and the certainty of resurrection

In Genesis: "Then said the Lord to Adam, 'Because you have hearkened to the voice of your wife, and have eaten of that tree of which alone I commanded you that you should not eat, cursed shall be the ground in all your works; in sadness and groaning shall you eat of it all the days of your life: thorns and thistles shall it cast forth to you; and you shall eat the herb of the field in the sweat of your brow. You shall eat your bread until you return unto the earth from which also you were taken; because earth you are, and to earth you shall go.'"[234] Also in the same place: "And Enoch pleased God, and was not found afterwards: because God translated him."[235] And in Isaiah: "All flesh is grass, and all the glory of it as the flower of grass. The grass withered, and the flower has fallen away; but the word of the Lord abides for ever."[236] In Ezekiel: "They say, 'Our bones have become dry, our hope has perished: we have expired.' Therefore prophesy, and say, 'Thus says the Lord, Behold, I open your monuments, and I will bring you forth from your monuments, and I will bring you into the land of Israel; and I will put my Spirit upon you, and you shall live; and I will place you into your land: and you shall know that I the Lord have spoken, and will do it, says the Lord.'"[237] Also in the Wisdom of Solomon: "He was taken away, lest wickedness should change his understanding; for his soul was pleasing to God."[238] Also in the eighty-third Psalm: "How beloved are your dwellings, You Lord of hosts? My soul desires and hastes to the courts of God."[239] And in the Epistle of Paul to the Thessalonians: "But we would not that you should be ignorant, brethren, concerning those who sleep, that you sorrow not as others which have no hope. For if we believe that Jesus died and rose again, so also them which have fallen asleep in Jesus will God bring with Him."[240] Also in the first Epistle to the Corinthians: "You fool, that which you sow is not quickened except it have first died." And again: "Star differs from star in glory: so also the resurrection. The body is sown in corruption, it rises without corruption; it is sown in ignominy, it rises again in glory; it is sown in weakness, it rises again in power; it is sown an animal body, it rises again a spiritual body." And again: "For this corruptible must put on incorruption, and this mortal put on immortality. But when this corruptible shall have put on incorruption, and this mortal shall have put on immortality, then shall come to pass the word that is written, 'Death is absorbed into striving. Where, O death, is your sting? Where, O death, is your striving?'"[241] Also in the Gospel according to John: "Father, I will that those whom You have given me be with me where I shall be, and may see my glory which You have given me before the foundation of the world."[242] Also according to Luke: "Now let Your servant depart in peace, O Lord, according to the word; for my eyes have seen Your salvation."[243] Also according to John: "If you loved me, you would rejoice because I go to the Father; for the Father is greater than I."[244]

59. Of the idols which the Gentiles think to be gods

In the Wisdom of Solomon: "All the idols of the nations they counted gods, which neither have the use of their eyes for seeing, nor their nostrils to receive breath, nor their ears for hearing, nor the fingers on their hands for handling; but their feet also are slow to walk. For man made them; and he who has borrowed his breath, he fashioned them. But no man will be able to fashion a god like to himself. For since he is mortal, he fashions a dead thing with wicked hands. But he himself is better than they whom he worships, since he indeed lived, but they never." On this same matter: "Neither have they who have regarded the works known who was the artificer, but have thought that either fire, or wind, or the rapid air, or the circle of the stars, or the abundant water, or the sun and moon, were the gods that rule over the world; and if, on account of the beauty of these, they have thought thus, let them know how much more beautiful than these is the Lord; or if they have admired their powers and operations, let them perceive from these very things that He who has established these mighty things is stronger than they."[245] Also in the cxxxivth Psalm: "The idols of the nations are silver and gold, the work of men's hands. They have a mouth, and speak not; they have eyes, and see not; they have ears, and hear not; and neither is there any breath in their mouth. Let them who make them become like them, and all those who trust in them."[246] Also in the ninety-fifth Psalm: "All the gods of the nations are demons, but the Lord made the heavens."[247] Also in Exodus: "You shall not make unto yourselves gods of silver nor of gold." And again: "You shall not make to yourself an idol, nor the likeness of any thing."[248] Also in Jeremiah: "Thus says the Lord, 'Walk not according to the ways of the heathen; for they fear those things in their own persons, because the lawful things of the heathen are vain. Wood cut out from the forest is made. the work of the carpenter, and melted silver and gold are beautifully arranged: they strengthen them with hammers and nails, and they shall not be moved, for they are fixed. The silver is brought from Tharsis, the gold comes from Moab. All things are the works of the artificers; they will clothe it with blue and purple; lifting them, they will carry them, because they will not go forward. Be not afraid of them, because they do no evil, neither is there good in them.' Say thus, 'The gods that have not made the heaven and the earth perish from the earth, and from under this heaven. The heaven has trembled at this, and has shuddered much more vehemently,' says the Lord. 'These evil things have my people done. They have forsaken the fountain of living water, and have dug out for themselves worn-out wells, which could not hold water. Your love has smitten you, and your wickedness shall accuse you. And know and see that it shall be a bitter thing for you that you have forsaken me, says the Lord your God, and you have not hoped in me,' says your Lord. Because of old time you have resented my yoke, and have broken your bonds, and have said, 'I will not serve,' but I will go upon every lofty mountain, and upon every high hill, and upon every shady tree: there I will be confounded with fornication. To the wood and to the stone they have said, 'You are my father;' and to the stone, 'You have begotten me:' and they turned to me their back, and not their face."[249] In Isaiah: "The dragon has fallen or is dissolved; their carved works have become as beasts and cattle. Laboring and hungry, and without strength, you shall bear them bound upon your neck as a heavy burden." And again: "Gathered together, they shall not be able to be saved from war; but they themselves have been led captive with you." And again: "To whom have you likened me? See and understand that you err in your heart, who lavish gold out of the bag, and weigh silver in the balance, bringing it up to the weight. The workmen have made with their hand the things made; and, bowing themselves, they have adored it, and have raised it on their shoulders: and thus they walked. But if they should place them down, they will abide in their place, and will not be moved; and they will not hear those who cry unto them: they will not save them from evils."[250] Also in Jeremiah: "The Lord, who made heaven and earth, in strength has ordered the world, in His wisdom has stretched forth the heaven, and the multitude of the waters in the heaven. He has brought out the clouds from the end of the earth, the lightnings in the clouds; and He has brought forth the winds from His treasures. Every man is made foolish by his knowledge, every artificer is confounded by his graven images; because he has molten a falsehood: there is no breath in them. The works shut up in them are made vain; in the time of their consideration they shall perish."[251] And in the Apocalypse: "And the sixth angel sounded with his trumpet. And I heard one of the four corners of the golden ark, which is in the presence of God, saying to the sixth angel who had the trumpet, 'Loose the four angels which are bound upon the great river Euphrates.' And the four angels were loosed, which were prepared for an hour, and a day, and a month, and a year, to slay the third part of men; and the number of the army of the horsemen was two hundred thousand of thousand: I heard the number of them. And then I saw the horses in the vision, and those that sate upon them, having breastplates of fire, and of hyacinth, and of sulphur: and the heads of the horses as the heads of lions; and out of their mouth went fire, and smoke, and sulphur. By these three plagues the third part of men was slain, by the fire, and the smoke, and the sulphur which went forth from their mouth, and is in their tails: for their tails were like eels; for they had heads, and with them they do mischief. And the rest of the men who were not slain by these plagues, nor repented of the works of the deeds of their hands, that they should not worship demons and idols, that is, images of gold, and of silver, and of brass, and of stone, and of wood, which can neither see nor walk, repented not also of their murders. Also in the same place: And the third angel followed them, saying with a loud voice, 'If any man worship the beast and his image, and has received his mark in his forehead or upon his hand, the same shall drink of the wine of His wrath, and shall be punished with fire and sulphur, under the eyes of the holy angels, and under the eyes of the Lamb; and the smoke of their torments shall ascend up for ever and ever.'"[252]

60. That too great lust of food is not to be desired

In Isaiah: "Let us eat and drink, for tomorrow we shall die. This sin shall not be remitted to you even until you die."[253] Also in Exodus: "And the people sate down to eat and drink, and rose up to play."[254] Paul, in the first to the Corinthians: "Meat commends us not to God; neither if we eat shall we abound, nor if we eat not shall we want." And again: "When you come together to eat, wait one for another. If any is hungry, let him eat at home, that you may not come together for judgment."[255] Also to the Romans: "The kingdom of God is not meat and drink, but righteousness, and peace, and joy in the Holy Ghost."[256] In the Gospel according to John: "I have meat which you know not of. My meat is, that I should do His will who sent me, and should finish His work."[257]

61. That the lust of possessing, and money, are not to be sought after

In Solomon, in Ecclesiasticus: "He that loves silver shall not be satisfied with silver."[258] Also in Proverbs: "He who holds back the grain is cursed among the people; but blessing is on the head of him that communicates it."[259] Also in Isaiah: "Woe unto them who join house to house, and lay field to field, that they may take away something from their neighbor. Will you dwell alone upon the earth?"[260] Also in Zephaniah: "They shall build houses, and shall not dwell in them; and they shall appoint vineyards, and shall not drink the wine of them, because the day of the Lord is near."[261] Also in the Gospel according to Luke: "For what does it profit a man to make a gain of the whole world, but that he should lose himself?" And again: "But the Lord said unto him, 'You fool, this night your soul is required of you. Whose, then, shall those things be which you have provided?'" And again: "Remember that you have received your good things in this life, and likewise Lazarus evil things. But now he is besought, and you grieve."[262] And in the Acts of the Apostles: "But Peter said unto him, 'Silver and gold indeed I have not; but what I have I give unto you: In the name of Jesus Christ of Nazareth, rise up and walk.' And, taking hold of his right hand, he lifted him up."[263] Also in the first to Timothy: "We brought nothing into this world, but neither can we take anything away. Therefore, having maintenance and clothing, let us with these be content. But they who will become rich fall into temptation and a snare, and many and hurtful lusts, which drown man in perdition and destruction. For the root of all evils is covetousness, which some coveting, have made shipwreck from the faith, and have plunged themselves in many sorrows."[264]

62. That marriage is not to be contracted with Gentiles

In Tobias: "Take a wife from the seed of your parents, and take not a strange woman who is not of the tribe of your parents."[265] Also in Genesis, Abraham sends his servant to take from his seed Rebecca, for his son Isaac. Also in Esdras, it was not sufficient for God when the Jews were laid waste, unless they forsook their foreign wives, with the children also whom they had begotten of them. Also in the first Epistle of Paul to the Corinthians: "The woman is bound so long as her husband lives; but if he die, she is freed to marry whom she will, only in the

Lord. But she will be happier if she abide thus." And again: "Do you not know that your bodies are the members of Christ? Shall I take the members of Christ, and make them the members of an harlot? Far be it from me. Or do you not know that he who is joined together with an harlot is one body? For two shall be in one flesh. But he who is joined to the Lord is one spirit."[266] Also in the second to the Corinthians: "Be not joined together with unbelievers. For what participation is there between righteousness and unrighteousness? Or what communication has light with darkness?"[267] Also concerning Solomon in the third book of Kings: "And foreign wives turned away his heart after their gods."[268]

63. That the sin of fornication is grievous

In the first Epistle of Paul to the Corinthians: "Every sin whatsoever a man does is outside the body; but he who commits fornication sins against his own body. You are not your own, for you are bought with a great price. Glorify and bear the Lord in your body."[269]

64. What are those carnal things which beget death, and what are the spiritual things which lead to life

Paul to the Galatians: "The flesh lusts against the Spirit, and the Spirit against the flesh: for these are contrary the one to the other, that you cannot do even those things which you wish. But the deeds of the flesh are manifest, which are: adulteries, fornications, impurities, filthiness, idolatries, sorceries, murders, hatreds, strifes, emulations, animosities, provocations, hatreds, dissensions, heresies, envyings, drunkenness, revellings, and such like: with respect to which I declare, that they who do such things shall not possess the kingdom of God. But the fruit of the Spirit is charity, joy, peace, magnanimity, goodness, faith, gentleness, continency, chastity. For they who are Christ's have crucified their flesh, with its vices and lusts."[270]

65. That all sins are put away in baptism

In the first Epistle of Paul to the Corinthians: "Neither fornicators, nor those who serve idols, nor adulterers, nor effeminate, nor the lusters after mankind, nor thieves, nor cheaters, nor drunkards, nor revilers, nor robbers, shall obtain the kingdom of God. And these things indeed you were: but you are washed, but you are sanctified in the name of our Lord Jesus Christ, and in the Spirit of our God."[271]

66. That the discipline of God is to be observed in Church precepts

In Jeremiah: "And I will give to you shepherds according to my own heart; and they shall feed the sheep, feeding them with discipline."[272] Also in Solomon, in the Proverbs: "My son neglect not the discipline of God, nor fail when rebuked by Him. For whom God loves, He rebukes."[273] Also in the second Psalm: "Keep discipline, lest perchance the Lord should be angry, and you perish from the right way, when His anger shall burn up quickly against you. Blessed are all they who trust in Him."[274] Also in the forty-ninth Psalm: "But to the sinner God says, 'For what do you set forth my judgments, and takest my covenant into your mouth? But you hate discipline, and have cast my words behind you.'"[275] Also in the Wisdom of Solomon: "He who casts away discipline is miserable."[276]

67. That it was foretold that men should despise sound discipline

Paul, in the second to Timothy: "There will be a time when they will not endure sound doctrine; but according to their own lusts will heap to themselves teachers itching in hearing, tickling their ears; and shall turn away their hearing indeed from the truth, but they shall be converted unto fables."[277]

68. That we must depart from him who lives irregularly and contrary to discipline

Paul to the Thessalonians: "But we have commanded you, in the name of Jesus Christ, that you depart from all brethren who walk disorderly, and not according to the tradition which they have received from us."[278] Also in the forty-ninth Psalm: "If you saw a thief, at once you ran with him, and placed your portion with the adulterers."[279]

69. That the kingdom of God is not in the wisdom of the world, nor in eloquence, but in the faith of the cross, and in virtue of conversation[280]

In the first Epistle of Paul to the Corinthians: "Christ sent me to preach, not in wisdom of discourse, lest the cross of Christ should become of no effect. For the word of the cross is foolishness to those who perish; but to those who are saved it is the power of God. For it is written, I will destroy the wisdom of the wise, and I will reprove the prudence of the prudent. Where is the wise? Where is the scribe? Where is the disputer of this world? Hath not God made foolish the wisdom of this world? Since indeed, in the wisdom of God, the world by wisdom knew not God, it pleased God by the foolishness of preaching to save them that believe. Because the Jews desire signs, and the Greeks seek for wisdom: but we preach Christ crucified, to the Jews indeed a stumbling-block, and to the Gentiles foolishness; but to them that are called, Jews and Greeks, Christ the power of God, and the wisdom of God."[281] And again, "Let no man deceive himself. If any man think that he is wise among you, let him become a fool to this world, that he may be wise. For the wisdom of this world is foolishness with God. For it is written, 'You shall rebuke the wise in their own craftiness.'"[282] And again: "The Lord knows the thoughts of the wise, that they are foolish."[283]

70. That we must obey parents

In the Epistle of Paul to the Ephesians: "Children, be obedient to your parents: for this is right. Honor your father and your mother (which is the first command with promise), that it may be well with you, and you may be long-lived on the earth."[284]

71. And that fathers also should not be harsh in respect of their children

Also in the same place: "And, you fathers, drive not your children to wrath: but nourish them in the discipline and rebuke of the Lord."[285]

72. That servants, when they have believed, ought to serve their carnal masters the better

In the Epistle of Paul to the Ephesians: "Servants, obey your fleshly masters with fear and trembling, and in simplicity of your heart. as to Christ; not serving for the eye, as if you were pleasing men; but as servants of God."[286]

73. Moreover, that masters should be the more gentle

Also in the same place: "And, you masters, do the same things to them, forbearing anger: knowing that both your Master and theirs is in heaven; and there is no choice of persons with Him."[287]

74. That all widows that are approved are to be held in honor

In the first Epistle of Paul to Timothy: "Honor widows which are truly widows. But the widow that is wanton, is dead while she lives." And again: "But the younger widows pass by: for when they shall be wanton in Christ, they wish to marry; having judgment, because they have cast off their first faith."[288]

75. That every person ought to have care rather of his own people, and especially of believers

The apostle in his first Epistle to Timothy: "But if any take not care of his own, and especially of those of his own household, he denies the faith, and is worse than an infidel."[289] Of this same thing in Isaiah: "If you shall see the naked, clothe him; and despise not those who are of the household of your own seed."[290] Of which members of the household it is said in the Gospel: "If they have called the master of the house Beelzebub, how much rather them of his household!"[291]

76. That an elder must not be rashly accused

In the first to Timothy: "Against an elder receive not all accusation."[292]

77. That the sinner must be publicly reproved

In the first Epistle of Paul to Timothy: "Rebuke them that sin in the presence of all, that others also may be afraid."[293]

78. That we must not speak with heretics

To Titus: "A man that is an heretic, after one rebuke avoid; knowing that one of such sort is perverted, and sins, and is by his own self condemned."[294] Of this same thing in the Epistle of John: "They went out from among us, but they were not of us; for if they had been of us, they would doubtless have remained with us."[295] Also in the second to Timothy: "Their word does creep as a canker."[296]

79. That innocence asks with confidence, and obtains

In the Epistle of John: "If our heart blame us not, we have confidence towards God; and whatever we ask, we shall receive from Him."[297] Also in the Gospel according to Matthew: "Blessed are they of a pure heart, for they shall see God."[298] Also in the twenty-third Psalm: "Who shall ascend into the hill of the Lord? Or who shall stand in His holy place? The innocent in hands and of a pure heart."[299]

80. That the devil has no power against man unless God have allowed it

In the Gospel according to John: "Jesus said, 'You could have no power against me, unless it were given you from above.'"[300] Also in the third of Kings: "And God stirred up Satan against Solomon himself."[301] Also in Job, first of all God permitted, and then it was allowed to the devil; and in the Gospel, the Lord first permitted, by saying to Judas, "What you do, do quickly."[302] Also in Solomon, in the Proverbs: "The heart of the king is in God's hand."[303]

81. That wages be quickly paid to the hireling

In Leviticus: "The wages of your hireling shall not sleep with you until the morning."[304]

82. That divination must not be used

In Deuteronomy: "Do not use omens nor auguries."[305]

83. That a tuft of hair is not to be worn on the head

In Leviticus: "You shall not make a tuft from the hair of your head."[306]

84. That the beard must not be plucked

"You shall not deface the figure of your beard."[307]

85. That we must rise when a bishop or a presbyter comes

In Leviticus: "You shall rise up before the face of the elder, and shall honor the person of the presbyter."[308]

86. That a schism must not be made, even although he who withdraws should remain in one faith, and in the same tradition

In Ecclesiasticus, in Solomon: "He that cleaves firewood shall be endangered by it if the iron shall fall off."[309] Also in Exodus: "In one house shall it be eaten: you shall not cast forth the flesh abroad out of the house."[310] Also in the cxxxiid Psalm: "Behold how good and how pleasant a thing it is that brethren should dwell in unity!"[311] Also in the Gospel according to Matthew: "He that is not with me is against me; and he that gathers not with me scatters."[312] Also in the first Epistle of Paul to the Corinthians: "But I beseech you, brethren, by the name of our Lord Jesus Christ, that you all say the same thing, and that there be no schisms among you; but that you be all joined together in the same mind and in the same opinion."[313] Also in the sixty-seventh Psalm: "God, who makes men to dwell with one mind in a house."[314]

87. That believers ought to be simple, with prudence

In the Gospel according to Matthew: "Be prudent as serpents, and simple as doves." And again: "You are the salt of the earth. But if the salt have lost his savor, in what shall it be salted? It is good for nothing, but to be cast out abroad, and to be trodden under foot of men."[315]

88. That a brother must not be deceived

In the first Epistle of Paul to the Thessalonians: "That a man do not deceive his brother in a matter, because God is the avenger for all these."[316]

89. That the end of the world comes suddenly

The apostle says: "The day of the Lord shall so come as a thief in the night. When they shall say, 'Peace and security,' then on them shall come sudden destruction."[317] Also in the Acts of the Apostles: "No one can know the times or the seasons which the Father has placed in His own power."[318]

90. That a wife must not depart from her husband; or if she should depart, she must remain unmarried

In the first Epistle of Paul to the Corinthians: "But to them that are married I command, yet not I, but the Lord, that the wife should not be separated from her husband; but if she should depart, that she remain unmarried or be reconciled to her husband: and that the husband should not put away his wife."[319]

91. That every one is tempted so much as he is able to bear

In the first Epistle of Paul to the Corinthians: "No temptation shall take you, except such is human. But God is faithful, who will not suffer you to be tempted above that you are able; but will with the temptation also make a way to escape, that you may be able to bear it."[320]

92. That not everything is to be done which is lawful

Paul, in the first Epistle to the Corinthians: "All things are lawful, but all things are not expedient: all things are lawful, but all things edify not."[321]

93. That it was foretold that heresies would arise

In the first epistle of Paul to the Corinthians: "Heresies must needs be, in order that they which are approved may be made manifest among you."[322]

94. That the Eucharist is to be received with fear and honor

In Leviticus: "But whatever soul shall eat of the flesh of the sacrifice of salvation, which is the Lord's, and his uncleanness is still upon him, that soul shall perish from his people."[323] Also in the first to the Corinthians: "Whosoever shall eat the bread or drink the cup of the Lord unworthily, shall be guilty of the body and blood of the Lord."[324]

95. That we are to live with the good, but to avoid the evil

In Solomon, in the Proverbs: "Bring not the impious man into the habitation of the righteous." Also in the same, in Ecclesiasticus: "Let righteous men be your guests." And again: "The faithful friend is a medicine of life and of immortality." Also in the same place: "Be far from the man who has the power to slay, and you shall not suspect fear." Also in the same place: "Blessed is he who finds a true friend, and who speaks righteousness to the listening ear." Also in the same place: "Hedge your ears with thorns, and hear not a wicked tongue."[325] Also in the seventeenth Psalm: "With the righteous you shall be justified; and with the innocent man you shall be innocent; and with the froward man you shall be froward."[326] Also in the first Epistle of Paul to the Corinthians: "Evil communications corrupt good dispositions."[327]

96. That we must labor not with words, but with deeds

In Solomon, in Ecclesiasticus: "Be not hasty in your tongue, and in your deeds useless and remiss."[328] And Paul, in the first to the Corinthians: "The kingdom of God is not in word, but in power."[329] Also to the Romans: "Not the hearers of the law are righteous before God, but the doers of the law shall be justified."[330] Also in the Gospel according to Matthew: "He who shall do and teach so, shall be called greatest in the kingdom of heaven." Also in the same place: "Every one who hears my words, and does them, I will liken him to a wise man who built his house upon a rock. The rain descended, the floods came, the winds blew, and beat upon that house, and it fell not: for it was founded upon a rock. And every one who hears my words, and does them not, I will liken him to the foolish man, who built his house upon the sand. The rain descended, the floods came, the winds blew, and beat upon that house; and it fell: and its ruin became great."[331]

97. That we must hasten to faith and to attainment

In Solomon, in Ecclesiasticus: "Delay not to be converted to God, and do not put off from day to day; for His anger comes suddenly."[332]

98. That the catechumen ought now no longer to sin

In the Epistle of Paul to the Romans: "Let us do evil until the good things come; whose condemnation is just."[333]

99. That judgment will be according to the times, either of equity before the law, or of law after Moses

Paul to the Romans: "As many as have sinned without law, shall perish without law; and as many as have sinned in the law, shall be judged also by the law."[334]

100. That the grace of God ought to be without price

In the Acts of the Apostles: "Your money be in perdition with yourself, because you have thought that the grace of God is possessed by money."[335] Also in the Gospel: "Freely you have received, freely give." Also in the same place: "You have made my Father's house a house of merchandise; and you have made the house of prayer a den of thieves."[336] Also in Isaiah: "You who thirst, go to the water, and as many as have not money: go, and buy, and drink without money."[337] Also in the Apocalypse: "I am Alpha and Omega, the beginning and the end. I will give to him that thirsts from the fountain of the water of life freely. He who shall overcome shall possess these things, and their inheritance; and I will be his God, and he shall be my son."[338]

101. That the Holy Spirit has frequently appeared in fire

In Exodus: "And the whole of Mount Sinai smoked, because God had come down upon it in fire."[339] Also in the Acts of the Apostles: "And suddenly there was made a sound from heaven, as if a vehement blast were borne along, and it filled the whole of that place in which they were sitting. And there appeared to them cloven tongues as if of fire, which also settled upon each of them; and they were all filled with the Holy Ghost."[340] Also in the sacrifices, whatsoever God accounted accepted, fire descended from heaven, which consumed what was sacrificed. In Exodus: "The angel of the Lord appeared in a flame of fire from the bush."[341]

102. That all good men ought willingly to hear rebuke

In Solomon, in the Proverbs: "He who reproves a wicked man shall be hated by him. Rebuke a wise man, and he will love you."[342]

103. That we must abstain from much speaking

In Solomon: "Out of much speaking you shall not escape sin; but sparing your lips, you shall be wise."[343]

104. That we must not lie

"Lying lips are an abomination to the Lord."[344]

105. That they are frequently to be corrected who do wrong in domestic duty

In Solomon: "He who spares the rod, hates his son." And again: "Do not cease from correcting the child."[345]

106. That when a wrong is received, patience is to be maintained, and vengeance to be left to God

"Say not, 'I will avenge me of mine enemy;' but wait for the Lord, that He may be your help."[346] Also elsewhere: "To me belongs vengeance; I will repay, says the Lord."[347] Also in Zephaniah: "Wait on me, says the Lord, in the day of my rising again to witness; because my judgment is to the congregations of the Gentiles, that I may take kings, and pour out upon them my anger."[348]

107. That we must not use detraction

In Solomon, in the Proverbs: "Love not to detract, lest you be taken away."[349] Also in the forty-ninth Psalm: "You sat, and spoke against your brother; and against the son of your mother you placed a stumbling-block."[350] Also in the Epistle of Paul to the Colossians: "To speak ill of no man, nor to be litigious."[351]

108. That we must not lay snares against our neighbor

In Solomon, in the Proverbs: "He who digs a pit for his neighbor, himself shall fall into it."[352]

109. That the sick are to be visited

In Solomon, in Ecclesiasticus: "Be not slack to visit the sick man; for from these things you shall be strengthened in love."[353] Also in the Gospel: "I was sick, and you visited me; I was in prison, and you came unto me."[354]

110. That tale-bearers are accursed

In Ecclesiasticus, in Solomon: "The talebearer and the double-tongued is accursed; for he will disturb many who have peace."[355]

111. That the sacrifices of the wicked are not acceptable

In the same: "The Highest approves not the gifts of the unrighteous."[356]

112. That those are more severely judged, who in this world have had more power

In Solomon: "The hardest judgment shall be made on those who govern. For to a mean man mercy is granted; but the powerful shall suffer torments mightily."[357] Also in the second Psalm: "And now, you kings, understand; be amended, you who judge the earth."[358]

113. That the widow and orphans ought to be protected

In Solomon: "Be merciful to the orphans as a father, and as a husband to their mother; and you shall be the son of the Highest if you shall obey."[359] Also in Exodus: "You shall not afflict any widow and orphan. But if you afflict them, and they cry out and call unto me, I will hear their cryings, and will be angry in mind against you; and I will destroy you with the sword, and your wives shall be widows, and your children orphans."[360] Also in Isaiah: "Judge for the fatherless, and justify the widow; and come let us reason, says the Lord."[361] Also in Job: "I have preserved the poor man from the hand of the mighty, and I have helped the fatherless who had no helper: the mouth of the widow has blessed me."[362] Also in the sixty-seventh Psalm: "The Father of the orphans, and the Judge of the widows."[363]

114. That one ought to make confession while he is in the flesh

In the fifth Psalm: "But in the grave who will confess unto You?"[364] Also in the twenty-ninth Psalm: "Shall the dust make confession to You?"[365] Also elsewhere that confession is to be made: "I would rather have the repentance of the sinner than his death."[366] Also in Jeremiah: "Thus says the Lord, Shall not he that falls arise? Or shall not he that is turned away be converted?"[367]

115. That flattery is pernicious

In Isaiah: "They who call you blessed, lead you into error, and trouble the paths of your feet."[368]

116. That God is more loved by him who has had many sins forgiven in baptism

In the Gospel according to Luke: "To whom much is forgiven, he loves much; and to whom little is forgiven, the same loves little."[369]

117. That there is a strong conflict to be waged against the devil, and that therefore we ought to stand bravely, that we may be able to conquer

In the Epistle of Paul to the Ephesians: "Our wrestle is not against flesh and blood, but against the powers and princes of this world, and of this darkness; against the spiritual things of wickedness in the heavenly places. Because of this, put on the whole armor of God, that you may be able to resist in the most evil day; that when you have accomplished all, you may stand, having your loins girt in the truth of the Gospel, putting on the breastplate of righteousness, and having your feet shod with the preparation of the Gospel of peace; in all things taking the shield of faith, in which you may extinguish all the fiery darts of the most wicked one; and take the helmet of salvation, and the sword of the Spirit, which is the word of God."[370]

118. Also of Antichrist, that he will come as a man

In Isaiah: "This is the man who arouses the earth, who disturbs kings, who makes the whole earth a desert."[371]

119. That the yoke of the law was heavy, which is cast off by us, and that the Lord's yoke is easy, which is taken up by us

In the second Psalm: "Wherefore have the heathen been in tumult, and the peoples meditated vain things? The kings of the earth have stood up, and their princes have been gathered together against the Lord, and against His Christ. Let us break their bonds asunder, and cast away from us their yoke."[372] Also in the Gospel according to Matthew: "Come unto me, you who labor and are burdened, and I will make you to rest. Take my yoke upon you, and learn of me: for I am meek and lowly of heart, and you shall find rest for your souls. For my yoke is good, and my burden is light."[373] Also in the Acts of the Apostles: "It seemed good to the Holy Ghost, and to us, to impose upon you no other burden than those things which are of necessity, that you should abstain from idolatries, from shedding of blood, and from fornication. And whatsoever you would not to be done unto you, do not to others."[374]

120. That we are to be urgent in prayers

In the Epistle of Paul to the Colossians: "Be instant in prayer, and watch therein."[375] Also in the first Psalm: "But in the law of the Lord is his will, and in His law will he meditate day and night."[376]

NOTES

1. Book III is the "second book" mentioned by Cyprian in his preface to the entire work. It is a catechism of Christian doctrine and ethics, lifted from the words of Scripture.
2. In collecting precepts that are "easy and useful," Cyprian focuses this treatise on practical matters of morality and conduct. Until Augustine, the North African Church ("our school," as Cyprian says) tended to stress practical morality and disciplinary matters over abstract theological speculation.
3. Isa. 58:1-9.
4. Job 29:12-16.
5. Tob. 2:2, 4:5-11.
6. Prov. 19:17, 28:27, 16:6, 25:21, Sir. 3:30, Prov. 3:28, 21:13, 20:7.
7. Sir. 14:11, 29:12. Cyprian is the first Latin father to call this book *Ecclesiasticus*. The Greeks called it *All-Virtuous Wisdom,* from its longer, Hebrew name, *The Book of the All-Virtuous Wisdom of Jesus ben Sirach.*
8. Ps. 37:25-26.
9. Ps. 41:1.
10. Ps. 112:9.
11. Hos. 6:6.
12. Matt. 5:6, 5:7, 6:20-21, 13:45-46, 10:42, 5:42, 19:17-21, 25:31-46.
13. Luke 12:33, 11:40-41, 19:8-9.
14. 2 Cor. 8:14-15, 9:6-7, 9:9, 9:10-11, 9:12.
15. 1 John 3:17.
16. Luke 14:12-14.
17. 2 Cor. 8:12-13.
18. Mal. 2:10.
19. John 14:27, 15:12-13.
20. Matt. 5:9, 18:19-20.
21. 1 Cor. 3:1-3, 13:2-8.
22. Gal. 5:14-15.
23. 1 John 3:10, 15; 4:20.
24. Acts 4:32.
25. Matt. 5:23-24.
26. 1 John 4:16, 2:9.
27. John 3:27.
28. 1 Cor. 4:7.
29. 1 Sam. 2:3-4.
30. 2 Macc. 9:12, 1 Macc. 2:62-63.
31. Isa. 66:1-2.
32. Matt. 5:5.
33. Luke 9:48, 14:11.
34. Rom. 11:20-21.
35. Ps. 34:18.
36. Rom. 13:7-8.
37. Matt. 23:6-8.
38. John 13:16-17.

39. Ps. 82:3.
40. Sir. 27:5. Cyprian, apparently citing this verse from memory, incorrectly attributes it to Solomon.
41. Ps. 51:17; 34:18, 34:19.
42. Job 1:21-22.
43. Matt. 5:4.
44. John 16:33.
45. 2 Cor. 12:7-9.
46. Rom. 5:2-5.
47. Matt. 7:13-14.
48. Tob. 2:14.
49. Prov. 28:28.
50. Eph. 4:30-31.
51. Prov. 16:32, 12:16.
52. Eph. 4:16.
53. Matt. 5:21-22.
54. Gal. 6:1-2.
55. Jer. 9:23-24.
56. Ps. 56:11, 62:1, 118:6, 118:8.
57. Dan. 3:16-18.
58. Jer. 17:5-7.
59. Deut. 6:13.
60. Rom. 1:25-26.
61. 1 John 4:4.
62. Isa. 55:6-7.
63. Eccles. 1:14.
64. Ex. 12:11.
65. Matt. 6:31-33, 34, Luke 9:62, Matt. 6:26.
66. Luke 12:35-37.
67. Matt. 8:20; Luke 14:33.
68. 1 Cor. 6:19-20, 7:29-31, 15:47-49.
69. Phil. 2:21, 3:19-21.
70. Gal. 5:14.
71. 2 Tim. 2:4-5.
72. Col. 2:20, 3:1-4.
73. Eph. 4:22-24.
74. 2 Pet. 2:11-12.
75. 1 John 2:6, 2:15-17.
76. 1 Cor. 5:7-8.
77. Sir. 23:11.
78. Matt. 5:34-37.
79. Ex. 20:7. The citing of this passage by Cyprian here indicates that he views swearing as invoking God's name to witness a rash promise or oath; he does not seem to envisage a universal prohibition against oath-taking as such, as taught by certain Protestant sects. In other words, the problem is not taking the Lord's name to witness something, but taking it "in vain," as the quote from Exodus states.
80. Ex. 22:28.
81. Ps. 34:12-13.
82. Lev. 24:12-14.
83. Eph. 4:29.
84. Rom. 12:14.
85. Matt. 5:22, 12:36-37.

86. Job 2:9-10, 1:8.
87. Ps. 34:1.
88. Num. 17:10.
89. Acts 16:25.
90. Phil. 2:14-15.
91. Gen. 22:1-2.
92. Deut. 13:3.
93. Wis. 3:4-8.
94. 1 Macc. 2:52.
95. Prov. 14:25.
96. Wis. 5:1-9.
97. Ps. 116:5.
98. Ps. 126:5-6.
99. John 12:25, Matt. 10:19-20, John 16:2-3. The fact that Cyprian cites Matthew as being "in the same place" as two passages from John suggests that he is paraphrasing from memory.
100. Matt. 5:10, 10:28, 10:32-33.
101. Luke 6:22-23, 18:29-30.
102. Rev. 6:9-11, 7:9-17, 2:7, 2:10, 16:5.
103. 2 Tim. 4:6-8.
104. Rom. 8:16-17.
105. Ps. 119:1-2.
106. Rom. 8:18.
107. 2 Macc. 6:30, 7:9, 7:14, 7:16-17, 7:18-19. Demonstrating the importance of the tale of the mother and her seven sons from 2 Maccabees 7 in the early Church's doctrine of the Resurrection.
108. Deut. 6:5.
109. Matt. 10:37-38.
110. Rom. 8:35-37.
111. John 6:38.
112. Matt. 26:39.
113. Matt. 6:10. This reference to the Our Father as "the daily prayer" suggests that in Cyprian's time it was already the custom to recite this prayer daily, both within the liturgy and privately, as our Lord indicated.
114. Matt. 7:21.
115. Luke 12:47.
116. 1 John 2:17.
117. Ps. 111:10, Sir. 1:14, Prov. 28:14.
118. Isa. 66:2.
119. Gen. 22:11-12.
120. Ps. 2:11.
121. Deut. 4:10.
122. Jer. 31:31-41.
123. Rev. 11:16-17, 14:16-17, 15:2-4. Cyprian's translation of Rev. 15:2 is very unique. He cites it as " And I saw as it were a sea of glass mingled with fire; and the beasts were feeding with His lambs; and the number of His name a hundred and forty and four, standing upon the sea of glass, having the harps of God." The Latin Vulgate, and most other translations, say: "And I saw as it were a sea of glass mingled with fire: and them that had overcome the beast and his image and the number of his name, standing on the sea of glass, having the harps of God." It is difficult to say where the one hundred and forty four or the "beasts feeding with His lambs" in Cyprian's passage come from, unless he is paraphrasing from memory and confusing 15:2 with 14:1 ("And I looked, and, lo, a Lamb stood on the mount Sion, and with him an hundred forty and four thousand, having his Father's name written in their foreheads").

124. Dan. 13:1-3, 3:37-42, 14-19, 6:24-28.
125. Mic. 6:6-9, 7:14-18.
126. Nah. 1:5-7.
127. Hag. 1:12.
128. Mal. 2:5.
129. Ps. 34:9, 19:9.
130. Luke 6:37.
131. Rom. 13:4, 2:1-3.
132. 1 Cor. 10:12, 8:2.
133. Matt. 6:12. In calling this the "Daily Prayer" Cyprian testifies that in his day the Lord's Prayer was said daily by the Christian community.
134. Actually Matt. 11:25-26. Second quote is Mark 4:24.
135. Rom. 12:17, 22:21.
136. Rev. 22:10-12.
137. John 14:6, 10:9.
138. John 3:5-6. The early Fathers unanimously intepret John 3 as referring to baptism, as Cyprian does here.
139. John 6:53. It is interesting that Cyprian quotes a eucharistic verse in support of his argument about the necessity of baptism. We know that Cyprian certainly interpreted John 6 in a eucharistic sense (for example, *On the Lord's Prayer*, 18), so it seems unlikely that he is here suggesting that eating the flesh of Christ and drinking His blood is synonymous with baptism. It seems that he is rather identifying the eucharist with being born again, as he says "unless a man [is] baptized and born again, he cannot attain unto the kingdom of God," and then goes on to cite John 3 in support of the first point on the necessity of baptism and then John 6 to support his second point, suggesting that we are truly "born again" when we eat the flesh and drink the blood of the Son of God. This is only a theory, and admittedly a stretch, but not as much of a stretch as presuming that eating flesh and blood means baptism. It does have support, however, in the manner Cyprian words the next article, again pairing baptism and eucharist: "That it is of small account to be baptized and to receive the Eucharist, unless one profit by it both in deeds and works."
140. 1 Cor. 9:24-25.
141. Matt. 3:10, 7:22-23, 5:16.
142. Phil. 2:15.
143. John 5:14.
144. 1 Cor. 3:16-17.
145. 2 Chr. 15:2.
146. By qualifying this statement with the phrase "in the Church," Cyprian does not deny that such sins can be forgiven in the absolute sense. Rather, he takes the position that they cannot be *sacramentally* absolved by the Church's ministers. God might still forgive the sinner after sufficient penance, but such a matter was between the sinner and God and the penitent had no confidence of forgiveness during the remainder of his earthly life. Cyprian's comments here on the "unforgivable sin" should be understood in light of the Church's teaching: "'Therefore I tell you, every sin and blasphemy will be forgiven men, but the blasphemy against the Spirit will not be forgiven.' There are no limits to the mercy of God, but anyone who deliberately refuses to accept his mercy by repenting, rejects the forgiveness of his sins and the salvation offered by the Holy Spirit. Such hardness of heart can lead to final impenitence and eternal loss" (CCC 1864).
147. Matt. 12:32.
148. Mark 3:28-29.
149. 1 Sam. 2:25.
150. Luke 21:17.
151. John 15:18-20.

152. This quote that Cyprian attributes to Baruch has never been found in any codice of that book, either in Greek or Latin. Cyprian may have been paraphrasing from memory, skewering the wording of the verse and its authorship as to make it unrecognizable. Its source is unknown.
153. Eccles. 5:4.
154. Deut. 23:21-23.
155. Ps. 50:14-15.
156. Acts 5:3-4.
157. Jer. 48:10.
158. John 3:18-19.
159. Ps. 1:5.
160. Gen. 3:16. In other words, why have children when delivering a baby is such hard work?
161. Matt. 19:11-12.
162. Luke 20:34-38.
163. 1 Cor. 7:1-7, 7:32-34.
164. Ex. 19:15.
165. 1 Sam. 21:4.
166. Rev. 19:4.
167. John 5:22-23.
168. Ps. 72:1-2.
169. Gen. 19:24.
170. Jer. 10:2.
171. Rev. 18:4-9.
172. Isa. 52:11.
173. Sir. 5:4. As in other places, Cyprian attributes the authorship of Sirach to Solomon.
174. Rom. 2:4-6.
175. Rev. 17:1-4.
176. 1 Tim. 2:9-10.
177. 1 Pet. 3:4. Note that Cyprian states the first Epistle of Peter was written to the Church in Pontus. This runs contrary to a larger tradition within the Church that has usually numbered 1 Peter among the "Catholic Epistles;" i.e., circular letters meant for a broad audience, not for any one church community in particular. Cyprian will state this again in Chapter 37 and 39 of the same treatise.
178. Gen. 38:14-15.
179. 1 Pet. 4:15-16.
180. Rom. 13:3.
181. 1 Pet 2:21-23.
182. Phil. 2:6-11.
183. John 13:14-15.
184. Matt. 6:3-4, 6:2.
185. Eph. 5:4.
186. Gen. 15:6.
187. Isa. 7:9.
188. Matt. 14:31, 17:20.
189. Mark 11:24, 9:22.
190. Hab. 2:4.
191. It is clear what story Cyprian is referring to here, but this particular quote does not appear anywhere in the book of Daniel, although verse 3:88 is possibly what Cyprian had in mind: "O Ananias, Azarias, Misael, bless ye the Lord: praise and exalt him above all for ever. For he hath delivered us from hell, and saved us out of the hand of death, and delivered us out of the midst of the burning flame, and saved us out of the midst of the fire."
192. Acts 8:36-37.
193. 1 Cor. 6:1-2, 6:7-9.

194. Rom. 8:24-25.
195. 1 Cor. 14:34-35.
196. 1 Tim. 2:11-14.
197. Hos. 4:1-4.
198. Isa. 59:1-4.
199. Zeph. 1:2-3.
200. Ps. 15:6.
201. Ezk. 18:7-8.
202. Deut. 23:19.
203. Luke 6:32.
204. Matt. 5:44-45.
205. Prov. 23:9.
206. Matt. 7:6.
207. Sir. 10:26.
208. Luke 17:7-10.
209. Deut. 13:9.
210. Isa. 1:19.
211. Luke 17:21.
212. 1 Cor. 13:12.
213. Wis. 1:1, Prov. 10:9, Eccles. 3:21, Sir. 7:17. As we have seen, Cyprian lumps all the writings of Solomon together and also includes Sirach among the writings attributed to Solomon.
214. Isa. 29:15.
215. 1 Macc. 2:60.
216. Rom. 11:33-36.
217. 2 Tim. 2:23-24.
218. It is noteworthy that in attempting to prove the universality of sin, St. Cyprian does not cite Romans 3:9-23, which would later be the prime prooftext for Luther's doctrine of *sola fide*. Though Cyprian and the Fathers certainly admitted the universality of sin, they did not draw the same conclusion as Luther (that there is no place for works) and did not interpret Romans 3 in the way Luther did, and many Protestants do today.
219. Job 14:4-5.
220. Ps. 51:5.
221. 1 John 1:8.
222. Ps. 53:5.
223. Gal. 1:10.
224. Prov. 15:3.
225. Jer. 23:23-24.
226. 1 Sam. 16:7.
227. Rev. 2:23.
228. Ps. 19:12.
229. 2 Cor. 5:10.
230. Ps. 118:18. The Douay-Rheims says: "The Lord chastising hath chastised me: but he hath not delivered me over to death."
231. Ps. 89:32-33.
232. Mal. 3:3.
233. Matt. 5:26.
234. Gen. 3:17-19.
235. Gen. 5:24.
236. Isa. 40:6-7.
237. Ezk. 37:11-14.
238. Wis. 4:11, 14.
239. Ps. 84:1-2.

240. 1 Thess. 4:13-14.
241. 1 Cor. 15:36, 15:41-44, 53-55. This last phrase, "Death is absorbed into striving," is an awkward translation; almost all other translations of this passage say "Death is swallowed up in victory." The Greek word for victory is *nikos* (νικος), a form of *nike*, which is almost always rendered in Latin as *victoria* (Vul: *est absorta est mors in victoria*) and thus in English as "victory." The translation "Death is absorbed into striving" is thus an anomaly.
242. John 17:24.
243. Luke 2:29-30.
244. John 14:28.
245. Wis. 15:15-17, 13:1-4.
246. Ps. 135:16-18.
247. Ps. 96:5.
248. Ex. 20:23, 20:4.
249. Jer. 10: 2–5, 9, 11; 2:12, 13, 19-20, 27.
250. Isa. 46:1-2,5; Jer. 51:15-18 (uncertain); Isa. 46:6-7.
251. Jer. 51:16-19.
252. Rev. 9:13-21.
253. Isa. 22:13-14.
254. Ex. 32:6.
255. 1 Cor. 8:8, 11:33.
256. Rom. 14:17.
257. John 4:32, 34.
258. Sir. 5:10.
259. Prov. 11:26.
260. Isa. 5:8.
261. Zeph. 1:13-14.
262. Luke 9:25, 12:20, 16:25.
263. Acts 3:6.
264. 1 Tim. 6:7-10.
265. Tob. 4:12.
266. 1 Cor. 7:39-40, 6:15-17.
267. 2 Cor. 6:14.
268. 1 Kings 11:4.
269. 1 Cor. 6:18-20.
270. Gal. 5:17-24.
271. 1 Cor. 6:9-11.
272. Jer. 3:15.
273. Prov. 3:11-12.
274. Ps. 2:12.
275. Ps. 50:16.
276. Wis. 3:11.
277. 2 Tim. 4:3-4.
278. 2 Thess. 3:6.
279. Ps. 50:28.
280. Meaning in the power of preaching.
281. 1 Cor. 1:17-24.
282. 1 Cor. 3:18-20.
283. Ps. 93:11.
284. Eph. 6:1-3.
285. Eph. 6:4.
286. Eph. 6:5-6.
287. Eph. 6:9.

288. 1 Tim. 5:3,6; 11-12.
289. 1 Tim. 5:8.
290. Isa. 58:7.
291. Matt. 10:25.
292. 1 Tim. 5:19.
293. 1 Tim. 5:20.
294. Tit. 3:10-11.
295. 1 John 2:19.
296. 2 Tim. 2:17.
297. 1 John 2:21-22.
298. Matt. 5:8.
299. Ps. 24:3-4.
300. John 19:11.
301. 1 Kings 11:23.
302. John 13:27.
303. Prov. 21:1.
304. Lev. 19:13.
305. Deut. 18:10.
306. Lev. 19:27.
307. Ibid.
308. Lev. 19:32.
309. Eccles. 10:9. Actually Ecclesiastes, not Sirach.
310. Ex. 12:4.
311. Ps. 133:1.
312. Matt. 12:30.
313. 1 Cor. 1:10.
314. Ps. 68:6.
315. Matt. 10:16, 5:13.
316. 1 Thess. 4:6.
317. 1 Thess. 5:2-3.
318. Acts 1:7.
319. 1 Cor. 7:10-11.
320. 1 Cor. 10:13.
321. 1 Cor. 10:23.
322. 1 Cor. 11:19.
323. Lev. 7:20.
324. 1 Cor. 11:27.
325. Prov. 24:15, Sir. 9:16; 6:16; 25:9.
326. Ps. 18:25-26.
327. 1 Cor. 15:33.
328. Sir. 4:29.
329. 1 Cor. 4:20.
330. Rom. 2:13.
331. Matt. 5:19; 7:24-27.
332. Sir. 5:7.
333. Rom. 3:8, the entirety of which says, "and why not (as we are slanderously reported, and as some affirm that we say), 'Let us do evil, that good may come?' whose condemnation is just." St. Paul here denies that it is licit for Christians to attain a good end through evil means.
334. Rom. 2:12.
335. Acts 8:20.
336. Matt. 10:8; 21:13.
337. Isa. 55:1.

338. Rev. 21:6-7.
339. Ex. 19:18.
340. Acts 2:2-4.
341. Ex. 3:2.
342. Prov. 9:8.
343. Prov. 9:19.
344. Prov. 12:22.
345. Prov. 13:24, 19:18.
346. Lev. 19:18.
347. Deut. 32:35.
348. Zeph. 3:8.
349. Prov. 20:13 (LXX).
350. Ps. 50:20.
351. A mistaken attribution. This quote is actually from Titus. 3:2.
352. Prov. 26:27.
353. Sir. 7:39.
354. Matt. 25:36.
355. Sir. 28:15.
356. Sir. 34:19.
357. Wis. 6:6.
358. Ps. 2:10.
359. Sir. 4:10.
360. Ex. 22:22-24.
361. Isa. 1:17-18.
362. Job 29:12-13.
363. Ps. 68:5.
364. Ps. 6:5.
365. Ps. 30:9.
366. Ezk. 33:11.
367. Jer. 8:4.
368. Isa. 3:12.
369. Luke 7:47.
370. Eph. 6:12-17.
371. Isa. 14:16.
372. Ps. 2:1-3.
373. Matt. 11:28-30.
374. Acts 15:28-29.
375. Col. 4:2.
376. Ps. 1:2.

PART II:
THE LETTERS OF CYPRIAN

LETTER 1

TO DONATUS[1]

1. Caecilius Cyprian to Donatus sends greeting. You rightly remind me, dearest Donatus, for I not only remember my promise,[2] but I confess that this is the appropriate time for its fulfillment, when the vintage festival invites the mind to unbend in repose, and to enjoy the annual and appointed respite of the declining year. Moreover, the place is in accord with the season, and the pleasant aspect of the gardens harmonizes with the gentle breezes of a mild autumn in soothing and cheering the senses. In such a place as this it is delightful to pass the day in discourse, and, by the (study of the sacred) parables, to train the conscience of the breast to the apprehension of the divine precepts. And that no profane intruder may interrupt our converse, nor any unrestrained clatter of a noisy household disturb it, let us seek this bower. The neighboring thickets ensure us solitude, and the vagrant trailings of the vine branches creeping in pendent mazes among the reeds that support them have made for us a porch of vines and a leafy shelter. Pleasantly here we clothe our thoughts in words; and while we gratify our eyes with the agreeable outlook upon trees and vines, the mind is at once instructed by what we hear, and nourished by what we see, although at the present time your only pleasure and your only interest is in our discourse. Despising the pleasures of sight, your eye is now fixed on me. With your mind as well as your ears you are altogether a listener; and a listener, too, with an eagerness proportioned to your affection.

2. And yet, of what kind or of what amount is anything that my mind is likely to communicate to yours? The poor mediocrity of my shallow understanding produces a very limited harvest, and enriches the soil with no fruitful deposits. Nevertheless, with such powers as I have, I will set about the matter; for the subject itself on which I am about to speak will assist me. In courts of justice, in the public assembly, in political debate, a copious eloquence may be the glory of a voluble ambition; but in speaking of the Lord God, a chaste simplicity of expression strives for the conviction of faith rather with the substance, than with the powers, of eloquence. Therefore accept from me things, not clever but weighty, words, not decked up to charm a popular audience with cultivated rhetoric, but simple and fitted by their unvarnished truthfulness for the proclamation of the divine mercy. Accept what is felt before it is spoken, what has not been accumulated with tardy painstaking during the lapse of years, but has been inhaled in one breath of ripening grace.

3. While I was still lying in darkness and gloomy night, wavering hither and there, tossed about on the foam of this boastful age, and uncertain of my wandering steps, knowing nothing of my real life, and remote from truth and light, I used to regard it as a difficult matter, and especially as difficult in respect of my character at that time, that a man should be capable of being born again—a truth which the divine mercy had announced for my salvation—and that a man quickened to a new life in the laver of saving water should be able to put off what he had previously been;[3] and, although retaining all his bodily structure, should be himself changed in heart and soul. How, said I, is such a conversion possible, that there should be a sudden and rapid divestment of all which, either innate in us has hardened in the corruption of our material nature, or acquired by us has become inveterate by long accustomed use? These things have become deeply and radically ingrained within us. When does he learn thrift who has been used to liberal banquets and sumptuous feasts? And he who has been glittering in gold and purple, and has been celebrated for his costly attire, when does he reduce himself to ordinary and simple clothing? One who has felt the charm of the fasces and of civic honors shrinks from becoming a mere private and inglorious citizen. The man who is attended by crowds of clients, and dignified by the numerous association of an officious train, regards it as a punishment when he is alone. It is inevitable, as it ever has been, that the love of wine should entice, pride inflate, anger inflame, covetousness disquiet, cruelty stimulate, ambition delight, lust hasten to ruin, with allurements that will not let go their hold.

4. These were my frequent thoughts. For as I myself was held in bonds by the innumerable errors of my previous life, from which I did not believe that I could by possibility be delivered, so I was disposed to acquiesce in my clinging vices; and because I despaired of better things, I used to indulge my sins as if they were actually parts of me, and indigenous to me. But after that, by the help of the water of new birth, the stain of former years had been washed away, and a light from above, serene and pure, had been infused into my reconciled heart—after that, by the agency of the Spirit breathed from heaven, a second birth had restored me to a new man—then, in a wondrous manner, doubtful things at once began to assure themselves to me, hidden things to be revealed, dark things to be enlightened, what before had seemed difficult began to suggest a means of accomplishment, what had been thought impossible, to be capable of being achieved; so that I was enabled to acknowledge that what previously, being born of the flesh, had been living in the practice of sins, was of the earth earthly, but had now begun to be of God, and was animated by the Spirit of holiness. You yourself assuredly know and recollect as well as I do what was taken away from us, and what was given to us by that death of evil, and that life of virtue. You yourself know this without my information. Anything like boasting in one's own praise is hateful, although we cannot in reality boast but only be grateful for whatever we do not ascribe to man's virtue but declare to be the gift of God; so that now we sin not is the beginning of the work of faith, whereas that we sinned before was the result of human error. All our power is of God; I say, of God. From Him we have life, from Him we have strength, by power derived and conceived from Him we do, while yet in this world, foreknow the indications of things to come. Only let fear be the keeper of innocence, that the Lord, who of His mercy has flowed into our hearts in the access of celestial grace, may be kept by righteous submissiveness in the hostelry of a grateful mind, that the assurance we have gained may not beget carelessness, and so the old enemy creep upon us again.

5. But if you keep the way of innocence, the way of righteousness, if you walk with a firm and steady step, if, depending on God with your whole strength and with your whole heart, you only be what you have begun to be, liberty and power to do is given you in proportion to the increase of your spiritual grace. For there is not, as is the case with earthly benefits, any measure or stint in the dispensing of the heavenly gift. The Spirit freely flowing forth is restrained by no limits, is checked by no closed barriers within certain bounded spaces; it flows perpetually, it is exuberant in its affluence. Let our heart only be thirsty, and be ready to receive: in the degree in which we bring to it a capacious faith, in that measure we draw from it an overflowing grace. Thence is given power, with modest chastity, with a sound mind, with a simple voice, with unblemished virtue, that is able to quench the virus of poisons for the healing of the sick, to purge out the stains of foolish souls by restored health, to bid peace to those that are at enmity, repose to the violent, gentleness to the unruly—by startling threats to force to avow themselves the impure and vagrant spirits that have betaken themselves into the bodies of men whom they purpose to destroy, to drive them with heavy blows to come out of them, to stretch them out struggling, howling, groaning with increase of constantly renewing pain, to beat them with scourges, to roast them with fire: the matter is carried on there, but is not seen; the strokes inflicted are hidden, but the penalty is manifest. Thus, in respect of what we have already begun to be, the Spirit that we have received possesses its own liberty of action; while in that we have not yet changed our body and members, the carnal view is still darkened by the clouds of this world. How great is this empire of the mind, and what a power it has, not alone that itself is withdrawn from the mischievous associations of the world, as one who is purged and pure can suffer no stain of a hostile irruption, but that it becomes still greater and stronger in its might, so that it can rule over all the imperious host of the attacking adversary with its sway!

6. But in order that the characteristics of the divine may shine more brightly by the development of the truth, I will give you light to apprehend it, the obscurity caused by sin being wiped away. I will draw away the veil from the darkness of this hidden world. For a brief space conceive yourself to be transported to one of the loftiest peaks of some inaccessible mountain, thence gaze on the appearances of things lying below you, and with eyes turned in various directions look upon the eddies of the billowy world, while you yourself are removed from earthly contacts—you will at once begin to feel compassion for the world, and with self-recollection and increasing gratitude to God, you will rejoice with all the greater joy that you have escaped it. Consider the roads blocked up by robbers, the seas beset with pirates, wars scattered all over the earth with the bloody horror of camps. The whole world is wet with mutual blood; and murder, which in the case of an individual is admitted to be a crime, is called a virtue when it is committed wholesale. Impunity is claimed for the wicked deeds, not on the plea that they are guiltless, but because the cruelty is perpetrated on a grand scale.

7. And now, if you turn your eyes and your regards to the cities themselves, you will behold a concourse more fraught with sadness than any solitude. The gladiatorial games are prepared, that blood may gladden the lust of cruel eyes. The body is fed up with stronger food, and the vigorous mass of limbs is enriched with brawn and muscle, that the wretch fattened for punishment may die a harder death. Man is slaughtered that man may be gratified, and the skill that is best able to kill is an exercise and an art. Crime is not only committed, but it is taught. What can be said more inhuman—what more repulsive? Training is undergone to acquire the power to murder, and the achievement of murder is its glory. What state of things, I pray you, can that be, and what can it be like, in which men, whom none have condemned, offer themselves to the wild beasts—men of ripe age, of sufficiently beautiful person, clad in costly garments? Living men, they are adorned for a voluntary death; wretched men, they boast of their own miseries. They fight with beasts, not for their crime, but for their madness. Fathers look on their own sons; a brother is in the arena, and his sister is hard by; and although a grander display of pomp increases the price of the exhibition, yet, oh shame! even the mother will pay the increase in order that she may be present at her own miseries. And in looking upon scenes so frightful and so impious and so deadly, they do not seem to be aware that they are parricides with their eyes.[4]

8. Hence turn your looks to the abominations, not less to be deplored, of another kind of spectacle. In the theaters also you will behold what may well cause you grief and shame. It is the tragic buskin[5] which relates in verse the crimes of ancient days. The old horrors of parricide and incest are unfolded in action calculated to express the image of the truth, so that, as the ages pass by, any crime that was formerly committed may not be forgotten. Each generation is reminded by what it hears, that whatever has once been done may be done again. Crimes never die out by the lapse of ages; wickedness is never abolished by process of time; impiety is never buried in oblivion. Things which have now ceased to be actual deeds of vice become examples. In the mimes, moreover, by the teaching of infamies, the spectator is attracted either to reconsider what he may have done in secret, or to hear what he may do. Adultery is learned while it is seen; and while the mischief having public authority panders to vices, the matron, who perchance had gone to the spectacle a modest woman, returns from it immodest. Still further, what a degradation of morals it is, what a stimulus to abominable deeds, what food for vice, to be polluted by affected gestures, against the covenant and law of one's birth, to gaze in detail upon the endurance of incestuous abominations! Men are emasculated, and all the pride and vigor of their sex is effeminated in the disgrace of their enervated body; and he is most pleasing there who has most completely broken down the man into the woman. He grows into praise by virtue of his crime; and the more he is degraded, the more skillful he is considered to be. Such a one is looked upon—oh shame! And looked upon with pleasure. And what cannot such a creature suggest? He inflames the senses, he flatters the affections, he drives out the more vigorous conscience of a virtuous breast; nor is there wanting authority for the enticing abomination, that the mischief may creep upon people with a less perceptible approach. They picture Venus immodest, Mars adulterous; and that Jupiter of theirs not more supreme in dominion than in vice, inflamed with earthly love in the midst of his own thunders, now growing white in the feathers of a swan, now pouring down in a golden shower, now breaking forth by the help of birds to violate the purity of boys. And now put the question: Can he who looks upon such things be healthy-minded or modest? Men imitate the gods whom they adore, and to such miserable beings their crimes become their religion.[6]

9. Oh, if placed on that lofty watchtower you could gaze into the secret places— if you could open the closed doors of sleeping chambers, and recall their dark recesses to the perception of sight—you would behold things done by immodest persons which no chaste eye could look upon; you would see what even to see is a crime; you would see what people embruted with the madness of vice deny that they have done, and yet hasten to do—men with frenzied lusts rushing upon men, doing things which afford no gratification even to those who do them. I am deceived if the man who is guilty of such things as these does not accuse others of them. The depraved maligns the depraved, and thinks that he himself, though conscious of the guilt, has escaped, as if consciousness were not a sufficient condemnation. The same people who are accusers in public are criminals in private, condemning themselves at the same time as they condemn the culprits; they denounce abroad what they commit at home, willingly doing what, when they have done, they accuse—a daring which assuredly is fitly mated with vice, and an impudence quite in accordance with shameless people. And I beg you not to wonder at the things that persons of this kind speak: the offense of their mouths in words is the least of which they are guilty.

10. But after considering the public roads full of pitfalls, after battles of many kinds scattered abroad over the whole world, after exhibitions either bloody or infamous, after the abominations of lust, whether exposed for sale in brothels or hidden within the domestic walls—abominations, the audacity of which is greater in proportion to the secrecy of the crime—possibly you may think that the Forum at least is free from such things, that it is neither exposed to exasperating wrongs, nor polluted by the association of criminals. Then turn your gaze in that direction: there you will discover things more odious than ever, so that thence you will be more desirous of turning away your eyes, although the laws are carved on twelve tables,[7] and the statutes are publicly prescribed on brazen tablets. Yet wrong is done in the midst of the laws themselves; wickedness is committed in the very face of the statutes; innocence is not preserved even in the place where it is defended. By turns the rancor of disputants rages; and when peace is broken among the togas, the Forum echoes with the madness of strife. There close at hand is the spear and the sword, and the executioner also; there is the claw that tears, the rack that stretches, the fire that burns up—more tortures for one poor human body than it has limbs. And in such cases who is there to help? One's patron? He makes a feint, and deceives. The judge? But he sells his sentence. He who sits to avenge crimes commits them, and the judge becomes the culprit, in order that the accused may perish innocently. Crimes are everywhere common; and everywhere in the multiform character of sin, the pernicious poison acts by means of degraded minds. One man forges a will, another by a capital fraud makes a false deposition; on the one hand, children are cheated of their inheritances, on the other, strangers are endowed with their estates. The opponent makes his charge, the false accuser attacks, the witness defames, on all sides the venal impudence of hired voices sets about the falsification of charges, while in the meantime the guilty do not even perish with the innocent. There is no fear about the laws; no concern for either inquisitor or judge; when the sentence can be bought off for money, it is not cared for. It is a crime now among the guilty to be innocent; whoever does not imitate the wicked is an offense to them. The laws have come to terms with crimes, and whatever is public has begun to be allowed. What can be the modesty, what can be the integrity, that prevails there, when there are none to condemn the wicked, and one only meets with those who ought themselves to be condemned?

11. But that we may not perchance appear as if we were picking out extreme cases, and with the view of disparagement were seeking to attract your attention to those things whereof the sad and revolting view may offend the gaze of a better conscience, I will now direct you to such things as the world in its ignorance accounts good. Among these also you will behold things that will shock you. In respect of what you regard as honors, of what you consider the fasces, what you count affluence in riches, what you think power in the camp, the glory of the purple in the magisterial office, the power of license in the chief command—there is hidden the virus of ensnaring mischief, and an appearance of smiling wickedness, joyous indeed, but the treacherous deception of hidden calamity. Just as some poison, in which the flavor having been medicated with sweetness, craftily mingled in its deadly juices, seems, when taken, to be an ordinary draught, but when it is drunk up, the destruction that you have swallowed assails you. You see, forsooth, that man distinguished by his brilliant dress, glittering, as he thinks, in his purple. Yet with what baseness has he purchased this glitter! What contempts of the proud has he had first to submit to! What haughty thresholds has he, as an early courtier, besieged! How many scornful footsteps of arrogant great men has he had to precede, thronged in the crowd of clients, that by and by a similar procession might attend and precede him with salutations—a train waiting not upon his person, but upon his power! For he has no claim to be regarded for his character, but for his fasces. Of these, finally, you may see the degrading end, when the time-serving sycophant has departed, and the hanger-on, deserting them, has defiled the exposed side of the man who has retired into a private condition. It is then that the mischiefs done to the squandered family-estate smite upon the conscience, then the losses that have exhausted the fortune are known—expenses by which the favor of the populace was bought, and the people's breath asked for with fickle and empty entreaties. Assuredly, it was a vain and foolish boastfulness to have desired to set forth in the gratification of a disappointing spectacle, what the people would not receive, and what would ruin the magistrates.

12. But those, moreover, whom you consider rich, who add forests to forests, and who, excluding the poor from their neighborhood, stretch out their fields far and wide into space without any limits,[8] who possess immense heaps of silver and gold and mighty sums of money, either in built-up heaps or in buried stores—even in the midst of their riches those are torn to pieces by the anxiety of vague thought, lest the robber should spoil, lest the murderer should attack, lest the envy of some wealthier neighbor should become hostile, and harass them with malicious lawsuits. Such a one enjoys no security either in his food or in his sleep. In the midst of the banquet he sighs, although he drinks from a jeweled goblet; and when his luxurious bed has enfolded his body, languid with feasting, in its yielding bosom, he lies wakeful in the midst of the down; nor does he perceive, poor wretch, that these things are merely gilded torments, that he is held in bondage by his gold, and that he is the slave of his luxury and wealth rather than their master. And oh, the odious blindness of perception, and the deep darkness of senseless greed! Although he might disburden himself and get rid of the load, he rather continues to brood over his vexing wealth—he goes on obstinately clinging to his tormenting hoards. From him there is no liberality to dependents, no communication to the poor. And yet such people call that their own money, which they guard with jealous labor, shut up at home as if it were another's, and from which they derive no benefit either for their friends, for their children, or, in fine, for themselves. Their possession amounts to this only, that they can keep others from possessing it; and oh, what a marvelous perversion of names! They call those things goods, which they absolutely put to none but bad uses.

13. Or think you that even those are secure—that those at least are safe with some stable permanence among the chaplets of honor and vast wealth, whom, in the glitter of royal palaces, the safeguard of watchful arms surrounds? They have greater fear than others. A man is constrained to dread no less than he is dreaded. Exaltation exacts its penalties equally from the more powerful, although he may be hedged in with bands of satellites, and may guard his person with the enclosure and protection of a numerous retinue. Even as he does not allow his inferiors to feel security, it is inevitable that he himself should want the sense of security. The power of those whom power makes terrible to others, is, first of all, terrible to themselves. It smiles to rage, it cajoles to deceive, it entices to slay, it lifts up to cast down. With a certain usury of mischief, the greater the height of dignity and honors attained, the greater is the interest of penalty required.

14. Hence, then, the one peaceful and trustworthy tranquility, the one solid and firm and constant security, is this: for a man to withdraw from these eddies of a distracting world, and, anchored on the ground of the harbor of salvation, to lift his eyes from earth to heaven; and having been admitted to the gift of God, and being already very near to his God in mind, he may boast, that whatever in human affairs others esteem lofty and grand, lies altogether beneath his consciousness. He who is actually greater than the world can crave nothing, can desire nothing, from the world. How stable, how free from all shocks is that safeguard; how heavenly the protection in its perennial blessings—to be loosed from the snares of this entangling world, and to be purged from earthly dregs, and fitted for the light of eternal immortality! He will see what crafty mischief of the foe that previously attacked us has been in progress against us. We are constrained to have more love for what we shall be, by being allowed to know and to condemn what we were. Neither for this purpose is it necessary to pay a price either in the way of bribery or of labor; so that man's elevation or dignity or power should be begotten in him with elaborate effort; but it is a gratuitous gift from God, and it is accessible to all. As the sun shines spontaneously, as the day gives light, as the fountain flows, as the shower yields moisture, so does the heavenly Spirit infuse itself into us. When the soul, in its gaze into heaven, has recognized its Author, it rises higher than the sun, and far transcends all this earthly power, and begins to be that which it believes itself to be.

15. Do you, however, whom the celestial warfare has enlisted in the spiritual camp, only observe a discipline uncorrupted and chastened in the virtues of religion. Be constant as well in prayer as in reading; now speak with God, now let God speak with you, let Him instruct you in His precepts, let Him direct you. Whom He has made rich, none shall make poor; for, in fact, there can be no poverty to him whose breast has once been supplied with heavenly food. Ceilings enriched with gold, and houses adorned with mosaics of costly marble, will seem mean to you, now when you know that it is you yourself who are rather to be perfected, you who are rather to be adorned, and that that dwelling in which God has dwelt as in a temple, in which the Holy Spirit has begun to make His abode, is of more importance than all others. Let us embellish this house with the colors of innocence, let us enlighten it with the light of justice: this will never fall into decay with the wear of age, nor shall it be defiled by the tarnishing of the colors of its walls, nor of its gold. Whatever is artificially beautified is perishing; and such things as contain not the reality of possession afford no abiding assurance to their possessors. But this remains in a beauty perpetually vivid, in perfect honor, in permanent splendor. It can neither decay nor be destroyed; it can only be fashioned into greater perfection when the body returns to it.

16. These things, dearest Donatus, briefly for the present. For although what you profitably hear delights your patience, indulgent in its goodness, your well-balanced mind, and your assured faith—and nothing is so pleasant to your ears as what is pleasant to you in God—yet, as we are associated as neighbors, and are likely to talk together frequently, we ought to have some moderation in our conversation; and since this is a holiday rest, and a time of leisure, whatever remains of the day, now that the sun is sloping towards the evening, let us spend it in gladness, nor let even the hour of repast be without heavenly grace. Let the temperate meal resound with psalms; and as your memory is tenacious and your voice musical, undertake this office, as is your wont. You will provide a better entertainment for your dearest friends, if, while we have something spiritual to listen to, the sweetness of religious music charm our ears.

NOTES

1. In this letter Cyprian speaks of his own conversion, the evils attendant upon worldly concerns, and the spiritual blessings that await the righteous. This epistle is commonly accepted as Cyprian's first writing as a Christian.
2. Cyprian had previously promised to write Donatus a letter to converse on divine truths.
3. One of many demonstrations of the Church Fathers' equation of being "born again" with the sacrament of baptism.
4. Reflecting the traditional Catholic teaching that to consent to another's sin or in otherwise to condone it is to be guilty of the sin itself.
5. A *buskin* is a knee- or calf-length boot made of leather or cloth which laces closed, but is open across the toes. It was worn by Athenian tragic actors, hunters and soldiers in Ancient Greek, Etruscan, and Roman societies.
6. "By a like craft, too, did these evil spirits command that theatrical shows, of which I have already spoken, should be instituted and dedicated to them. And in these entertainments the poetical compositions and actions of the drama ascribed such iniquities to the gods, that every one might safely imitate them, whether he believed the gods had actually done such things, or, not believing this, yet perceived that they most eagerly desired to be represented as having done them. And that no one might suppose, that in representing the gods as fighting with one another, the poets had slandered them, and imputed to them unworthy actions, the gods themselves, to complete the deception, confirmed the compositions of the poets by exhibiting their own battles to the eyes of men, not only through actions in the theaters, but in their own persons on the actual field" (St, Augustine, *City of God*, Book II:25). See also *Confessions*, Book III:2-4 on the effects of theatrical spectacles on morality.
7. Reference to the first written Roman legal code, promulgated by the Decemvirs around 451-450 BC.
8. Compare to Isaiah 5:8: "Woe to you that join house to house and lay field to field, even to the end of the place: shall you alone dwell in the midst of the earth?"

LETTER 2

FROM THE ROMAN CLERGY TO THE CARTHAGINIAN CLERGY, CONCERNING THE RETIREMENT OF CYPRIAN

1. We have been informed by Crementius[9] the sub-deacon, who came to us from you, that the blessed father Cyprian has for a certain reason withdrawn;[10] in doing which he acted quite rightly, because he is a person of eminence, and because a conflict is impending, which God has allowed in the world, for the sake of cooperating with His servants in their struggle against the adversary, and was, moreover, willing that this conflict should show to angels and to men that the victor shall be crowned, while the vanquished shall in himself receive the doom which has been made manifest to us. Since, moreover, it devolves upon us who appear to be placed on high;[11] in the place of a shepherd, to keep watch over the flock;[12] if we be found neglectful, it will be said to us, as it was said to our predecessors also, who in such wise negligent had been placed in charge, that we have "not sought for that which was lost, and have not corrected the wanderer, and have not bound up that which was broken, but have eaten their milk, and been clothed with their wool"[13] and then also the Lord Himself, fulfilling what had been written in the law and the prophets, teaches, saying, "I am the good shepherd, who lay down my life for the sheep. But the hireling, whose own the sheep are not, sees the wolf coming, and leaves the sheep, and flees, and the wolf scatters them." To Simon, too, He speaks thus: "Do you love me? He answered, I do love You. He says to him, Feed my sheep."[14] We know that this saying arose out of the very circumstance of his withdrawal, and the rest of the disciples did likewise.

2. We are unwilling, therefore, beloved brethren, that you should be found hirelings, but we desire you to be good shepherds, since you are aware that no slight danger threatens you if you do not exhort our brethren to stand steadfast in the faith, so that the brotherhood be not absolutely rooted out, as being of those who rush headlong into idolatry. Neither is it in words only that we exhort you to this; but you will be able to ascertain from very many who come to you from us, that, God blessing us, we both have done and still do all these things ourselves with all anxiety and worldly risk, having before our eyes rather the fear of God and eternal sufferings than the fear of men and a short-lived discomfort, not forsaking the brethren, but exhorting them to stand firm in the faith, and to be ready to go with the Lord. And we have even recalled those who were ascending to do that to which they were constrained. The Church stands in faith, notwithstanding that some have been driven to fall by very terror, whether that they were persons of eminence, or that they were afraid, when seized, with the fear of man: these, however, we did not abandon, although they were separated from us, but exhorted them, and do exhort them, to repent, if in any way they may receive pardon from Him who is able to grant it; test, haply, if they should be deserted by us, they should become worse.[15]

3. You see, then, brethren, that you also ought to do the like, so that even those who have fallen may amend their minds by your exhortation; and if they should be seized once more, may confess, and may so make amends for their previous sin. And there are other matters which are incumbent on you, which also we have here added, as that if any who may have fallen into this temptation begin to be taken with sickness, and repent of what they have done, and desire communion, it should in any wise be granted them. Or if you have widows or bedridden people who are unable to maintain themselves, or those who are in prisons or are excluded from their own dwellings, these ought in all cases to have some to minister to them. Moreover, catechumens when seized with sickness ought not to be deceived, but help is to be afforded them. And, as matter of the greatest importance, if the bodies of the martyrs and others be not buried, a considerable risk is incurred by those whose duty it is to do this office. By whomsoever of you, then, and on whatever occasion this duty may have been performed, we are sure that he is regarded as a good servant—as one who has been faithful in the least, and will be appointed ruler over ten cities.[16] May God, however, who gives all things to them that hope in Him, grant to us that we may all be found in these works. The brethren who are in bonds greet you, as do the elders, and the whole Church, which itself also with the deepest anxiety keeps watch over all who call on the name of the Lord. And we likewise beg you in your turn to have us in remembrance. Know, moreover, that Bassianus has come to us; and we request of you who have a zeal for God, to send a copy of this letter to whomsoever you are able, as occasions may serve, or make your own opportunities, or send a message, that they may stand firm and steadfast in the faith. We bid you, beloved brethren, ever heartily farewell.

NOTES

9. This Crementius was apparently martyred later in the same year this letter was written; see Letter 3:1 for Cyprian's comments on Crementius's "glorious end."

10. In January of the year 250, the Emperor Decius inaugurated what would come to be known as the Decian Persecution, the first systematic empire-wide persecution of Christians. Under Decius' edicts, bishops were to be put to death and others to be punished and tortured till they recanted. Shortly after the news of these edicts came to Africa, Cyprian fled into hiding, for which he was reproached by his enemies. This letter from the Roman clergy apparently exonerates Cyprian for his prudent retirement from Carthage and gives instructions for the treatment of those Christians who lapsed in their faith during the persecution, though some scholars detect a note of sarcasm here, suggesting that maybe this letter is not meant to exonerate Cyprian but chide him for his flight.

11. "[U]s who appear to be placed on high in place of a shepherd." This wording suggests that this letter was composed senior members of the Roman clergy during the long interregnum between the martyrdom of Pope Fabian on January 20th, 250 and the election of Pope Cornelius on March 6, 251.

12. A reference to John 21:17. Note that this prerogative is claimed exclusively by the See of Rome.

13. Ezk. 34:3-4.

14. John 10:11, 21:17.

15. The issue of how to respond to those scores of Christians who lapsed and apostasized (*lapsi*) during the Decian Persecution would lead to the Novatian schism and cause a major breach between the bishops of Italy and Africa.

16. A reference to Luke 19:17.

LETTER 3

TO THE PRESBYTERS AND DEACONS ABIDING AT ROME[17]

1. Cyprian to the elders and deacons, brethren abiding at Rome, sends, greeting. When the report of the departure of the excellent man, my colleague, was still uncertain among us, my beloved brethren, and I was wavering doubtfully in my opinion on the matter, I received a letter sent to me from you by Crementius the sub-deacon, in which I was most abundantly informed of his glorious end; and I rejoiced greatly that, in harmony with the integrity of his administration, an honorable consummation also attended him. Wherein, moreover, I greatly congratulate you, that you honor his memory with a testimony so public and so illustrious, so that by your means is made known to me, not only what is glorious to you in connection with the memory of your bishop, but what ought to afford to me also an example of faith and virtue. For in proportion as the fall of a bishop is an event which tends ruinously to the fall of his followers, so on the other hand it is a useful and helpful thing when a bishop, by the firmness of his faith, sets himself forth to his brethren as an object of imitation.

2. I have, moreover, read another epistle, in which neither the person who wrote nor the persons to whom it was written were plainly declared; and inasmuch as in the same letter both the writing and the matter, and even the paper itself, gave me the idea that something had been taken away, or had been changed from the original, I have sent you back the epistle as it actually came to hand, that you may examine whether it is the very same which you gave to Crementius the sub-deacon, to carry. For it is a very serious thing if the truth of a clerical letter is corrupted by any falsehood or deceit. In order, then, that we may know this, ascertain whether the writing and subscription are yours, and write me again what is the truth of the matter. I bid you, dearest brethren, ever heartily farewell.[18]

NOTES

17. Written in the year 250 shortly after the outbreak of the Decian Persecution and the flight of Cyprian from Carthage.
18. The letter to which Cyprian is referring has been lost.

LETTER 4

TO THE PRESBYTERS AND DEACONS

1. Cyprian to the presbyters and deacons, his beloved brethren, greeting. Being by the grace of God in safety, dearest brethren, I salute you, rejoicing that I am informed of the prosperity of all things in respect of your safety also; and as the condition of the place does not permit me to be with you now, I beg you, by your faith and your religion, to discharge there both your own office and mine, that there may be nothing wanting either to discipline or diligence. In respect of means, moreover, for meeting the expenses, whether for those who, having confessed their Lord with a glorious voice, have been put in prison, or for those who are laboring in poverty and want, and still stand fast in the Lord, I entreat that nothing be wanting, since the whole of the small sum which was collected there was distributed among the clergy for cases of that kind, that many might have means whence they could assist the necessities and burdens of individuals.

2. I beg also that there may be no lack, on your parts, of wisdom and carefulness to preserve peace. For although from their affection the brethren are eager to approach and to visit those good confessors,[19] on whom by their glorious beginnings the divine consideration has already shed a brightness, yet I think that this eagerness must be cautiously indulged, and not in crowds—not in numbers collected together at once, lest from this very thing ill-will be aroused, and the means of access be denied, and thus, while we insatiably wish for all, we lose all. Take counsel, therefore, and see that this may be more safely managed with moderation, so that the presbyters also, who there offer with the confessors, may one by one take turns with the deacons individually; because, by thus changing the persons and varying the people that come together, suspicion is diminished. For, meek and humble in all things, as befits the servants of God, we ought to accommodate ourselves to the times, and to provide for quietness, and to have regard to the people. I bid you, brethren, beloved and dearly longed-for, always heartily farewell; and have me in remembrance. Greet all the brotherhood. Victor the deacon, and those who are with me, greet you. Farewell!

NOTES

19. During the persecutions, those faithful who had either lapsed or were otherwise under heavy penances were accustomed to visit the confessors in prison to beg for a "letter of peace" (*libellus pacis*) which could be presented to the bishop and stated that he, in consideration of the martyrs' sufferings, might grant the penitents to absolution, thereby releasing them from the punishment they had incurred. Tertullian says, "Which peace some, not having it in the Church, are accustomed to beg from the martyrs in prison; and therefore you should possess and cherish and preserve it in you that so you perchance may be able to grant it to others" (*To the Martyrs*, 1). In this we see the patristic origin of the Catholic doctrine of indulgences. Addressing abuses of the *libelli pacis* will be a prominent theme in many of Cyprian's early letters.

LETTER 5

TO THE PRESBYTERS AND DEACONS

1. Cyprian to the presbyters and deacons, his brethren, greeting. I had wished indeed, beloved brethren, with this my letter to greet the whole of my clergy in health and safety. But since the stormy time which has in a great measure overwhelmed my people, has, moreover, added this enhancement to my sorrows, that it has touched with its desolation even a portion of the clergy, I pray the Lord that, by the divine mercy, I may hereafter greet you at all events as safe, who, as I have learned, stand fast both in faith and virtue. And although some reasons might appear to urge me to the duty of myself hastening to come to you, firstly, for instance, because of my eagerness and desire for you, which is the chief consideration in my prayers, and then, that we might be able to consult together on those matters which are required by the general advantage, in respect of the government of the Church, and having carefully examined them with abundant counsel, might wisely arrange them—yet it seemed to me better, still to preserve my retreat and my quiet for a while, with a view to other advantages connected with the peace and safety of us all—which advantages an account will be given you by our beloved brother Tertullus, who, besides his other care which he zealously bestows on divine labors, was, moreover, the author of this counsel; that I should be cautious and moderate, and not rashly trust myself into the sight of the public; and especially that I should beware of that place where I had been so often inquired for and sought after.

2. Relying, therefore, upon your love and your piety, which I have abundantly known, in this letter I both exhort and command you, that those of you whose presence there is least suspicious and least perilous, should in my stead discharge my duty, in respect of doing those things which are required for the religious administration. In the meantime let the poor be taken care of as much and as well as possible; but especially those who have stood with unshaken faith and have not forsaken Christ's flock, that, by your diligence, means be supplied to them to enable them to bear their poverty, so that what the troubling time has not effected in respect of their faith, may not be accomplished by want in respect of their afflictions. Let a more earnest care, moreover, be bestowed upon the glorious confessors. And although I know that very many of those have been maintained by the vow and by the love of the brethren, yet if there be any who are in want either of clothing or maintenance, let them be supplied, with whatever things are necessary, as I formerly wrote to you, while they were still kept in prison—only let them know from you and be instructed, and learn what, according to the authority of Scripture, the discipline of the Church requires of them, that they ought to be humble and modest and peaceable, that they should maintain the honor of their name, so that those who have achieved glory by what they have testified, may achieve glory also by their characters, and in all things seeking the Lord's approval, may show themselves worthy, in consummation of their praise, to attain a heavenly crown. For there remains more than what is yet seen to be accomplished, since it is written, "Praise not any man before his death;" and again, "Be faithful unto death, and I will give you a crown of life."[20] And the Lord also says, "He that endures to the end, the same shall be saved."[21] Let them imitate the Lord, who at the very time of His passion was not more proud, but more humble. For then He washed His disciples' feet, saying, "If I, your Lord and Master, have washed your feet, you ought also to wash one another's feet. For I have given you an example, that you should do as I have done to you."[22] Let them also follow the example of the Apostle Paul, who, after often-repeated imprisonment, after scourging, after exposures to wild beasts, in everything continued meek and humble; and even after his rapture to the third heaven and paradise, he did not proudly arrogate anything to himself when he said, "Neither did we eat any man's bread for naught, but wrought with labor and travail night and day, that we might not be chargeable to any of you."[23]

3. These several matters, I pray you, suggest to our brethren. And as "he who humbles himself shall be exalted,"[24] now is the time when they should rather fear the ensnaring adversary, who more eagerly attacks the man that is strongest, and becoming more virulent, for the very reason that he is conquered, strives to overcome his conqueror. The Lord grant that I may soon both see them again, and by salutary exhortation may establish their minds to preserve their glory. For I am grieved when I hear that some of them run about wickedly and proudly, and give themselves up to follies or to discords; that members of Christ, and even members that have confessed Christ, are defiled by unlawful concubinage, and cannot be ruled either by deacons or by presbyters, but cause that, by the wicked and evil characters of a few, the honorable glories of many and good confessors are tarnished; whom they ought to fear, lest, being condemned by their testimony and judgment, they be excluded from their fellowship. That, finally, is the illustrious and true confessor, concerning whom afterwards the Church does not blush, but boasts.

4. In respect of that which our fellow presbyters, Donatus and Fortunatus, Novatus and Gordius, wrote to me, I have not been able to reply by myself, since, from the first commencement of my episcopacy, I made up my mind to do nothing on my own private opinion, without your advice and without the consent of the people. But as soon as, by the grace of God, I shall have come to you, then we will discuss in common, as our respective dignity requires, those things which either have been or are to be done. I bid you, brethren beloved and dearly longed-for, ever heartily farewell, and be mindful of me. Greet the brotherhood that is with you earnestly from me, and tell them to remember me. Farewell.

NOTES

20. Sir. 11:28, Rev. 2:10.
21. Matt. 10:22.
22. John 13:14-15.
23. 2 Thess. 3:8.
24. Luke 14:11.

LETTER 6

TO ROGATIANUS THE PRESBYTER, AND THE OTHER CONFESSORS, ad 250

1. Cyprian to the presbyter Rogatianus, and to the other confessors,[25] his brethren, greeting. I had both heretofore, dearly beloved and bravest brethren, sent you a letter, in which I congratulated your faith and virtue with exulting words, and now my voice has no other object, first of all, than with joyous mind, repeatedly and always to announce the glory of your name. For what can I wish greater or better in my prayers than to see the flock of Christ enlightened by the honor of your confession? For although all the brethren ought to rejoice in this, yet, in the common gladness, the share of the bishop is the greatest. For the glory of the Church is the glory of the bishop. In proportion as we grieve over those whom a hostile persecution has cast down, in the same proportion we rejoice over you whom the devil has not been able to overcome.

2. Yet I exhort you by our common faith, by the true and simple love of my heart towards you, that, having overcome the adversary in this first encounter, you should hold fast your glory with a brave and persevering virtue. We are still in the world; we are still placed in the battlefield; we fight daily for our lives. Care must be taken, that after such beginnings as these there should also come an increase, and that what you have begun to be with such a blessed commencement should be consummated in you. It is a slight thing to have been able to attain anything; it is more to be able to keep what you have attained; even as faith itself and saving birth makes alive, not by being received, but by being preserved. Nor is it actually the attainment, but the perfecting, that keeps a man for God. The Lord taught this in His instruction when He said, "Behold, you are made whole; sin no more, lest a worse thing come unto you."[26] Conceive of Him as saying this also to His confessor, "Lo you are made a confessor; sin no more, lest a worse thing come unto you." Solomon also, and Saul, and many others, so long as they walked in the Lord's ways, were able to keep the grace given to them. When the discipline of the Lord was forsaken by them, grace also forsook them.

3. We must persevere in the straight and narrow road of praise and glory; and since peacefulness and humility and the tranquility of a good life is fitting for all Christians, according to the word of the Lord, who looks to none other man than to him that is poor and of a contrite spirit, and that trembles at His word, it the more behooves you confessors, who have been made an example to the rest of the brethren, to observe and fulfill this, as being those whose characters should provoke to imitation the life and conduct of all. For as the Jews were alienated from God, as those on whose account the name of God is blasphemed among the Gentiles,[27] so on the other hand those are dear to God through whose conformity to discipline the name of God is declared with a testimony of praise, as it is written, the Lord Himself forewarning and saying, "Let your light so shine before men that they may see your good works and glorify your Father which is in heaven." And Paul the apostle says, "Shine as lights in the world."[28] And similarly Peter exhorts: "As strangers," says he, "and pilgrims, abstain from fleshly lusts, which war against the soul, having your conversation honest among the Gentiles; that whereas they speak against you as evil-doers, they may by your good works, which they shall behold, glorify the Lord."[29] This, indeed, the greatest part of you, I rejoice to say, are careful for; and, made better by the honor of your confession itself, guard and preserve its glory by tranquil and virtuous lives.

4. But I hear that some infect your number, and destroy the praise of a distinguished name by their corrupt conversation; whom you yourselves, even as being lovers and guardians of your own praise, should rebuke and check and correct. For what a disgrace is suffered by your name, when one spends his days in intoxication and debauchery, another returns to that country whence he was banished, to perish when arrested, not now as being a Christian, but as being a criminal! I hear that some are puffed up and are arrogant, although it is written, "Be not high-minded, but fear: for if God spared not the natural branches, take heed lest He also spare not you."[30] Our Lord was led "as a sheep to the slaughter; and as a lamb before her shearers is dumb, so He opened not His mouth." "I am not rebellious," says He, "neither do I gainsay. I gave my back to the smiters, and my cheeks to the palms of their hands. I hid not my face from the filthiness of spitting."[31] And dares any one now, who lives by and in this very One, lift up himself and be haughty, forgetful, as well of the deeds which He did, as of the commands which He left to us either by Himself or by His apostles? But if the servant is not greater than his Lord. let those who follow the Lord humbly and peacefully and silently tread in His steps, since the lower one is, the more exalted be may become; as says the Lord, "He that is least among you, the same shall be great."[32]

5. What, then, is that—how execrable should it appear to you—which I have learned with extreme anguish and grief of mind, to wit, that there are not wanting those who defile the temples of God, and the members sanctified after confession and made glorious, with a disgraceful and infamous concubinage, associating their beds promiscuously with women's! In which, even if there be no pollution of their conscience, there is a great guilt in this very thing, that by their offense originate examples for the ruin of others. There ought also to be no contentions and emulations among you, since the Lord left to us His peace, and it is written, "You shall love your neighbor as yourself."[33] But if you bite and find fault with one another, take heed that you be not consumed one of another. From abuse and revilings also I entreat you to abstain, for revilers do not attain the kingdom of God; and the tongue which has confessed Christ should be preserved sound and pure with its honor. For he who, according to Christ's precept, speaks things peaceable and good and just, daily confesses Christ. We had renounced the world when we were baptized; but we have now indeed renounced the world when tried and approved by God, we leave all that we have, and have followed the Lord, and stand and live in His faith and fear.

6. Let us confirm one another by mutual exhortations, and let us more and more go forward in the Lord; so that when of His mercy He shall have made that peace which He promises to give, we may return to the Church new and almost changed men, and may be received, whether by our brethren or by the heathen, in all things corrected and renewed for the better; and those who formerly admired our glory in our courage may now admire the discipline in our lives. I bid you, beloved brethren, ever heartily farewell; and be mindful of me.

NOTES

25. See note 54 in *On The Unity of the Church* for the use of the term "confessor" in the early Church.
26. John 5:14.
27. Rom. 2:24.
28. Matt. 5:16, Phil. 2:15.
29. 1 Pet. 2:11-12.
30. Rom. 11:21.
31. Isa. 53:7, 50:6.
32. Luke 9:48.
33. Lev. 19:18.

LETTER 7

TO THE CLERGY, CONCERNING PRAYER TO GOD

1. Cyprian to the presbyters and deacons, his brethren, greeting. Although I know, brethren beloved, that from the fear which we all of us owe to God, you also are instantly urgent in continual petitions and earnest prayers to Him, still I myself remind your religious anxiety, that in order to appease and entreat the Lord, we must lament not only in words, but also with fastings and with tears, and with every kind of urgency. For we must perceive and confess that the so disordered ruin arising from that affliction, which has in a great measure laid waste, and is even still laying waste, our flock, has visited us according to our sins,[34] in that we do not keep the way of the Lord, nor observe the heavenly commandments given to us for our salvation. Our Lord did the will of His Father, and we do not do the will of our Lord; eager about our patrimony and our gain, seeking to satisfy our pride, yielding ourselves wholly to emulation and to strife, careless of simplicity and faith, renouncing the world in words only, and not in deeds, every one of us pleasing himself, and displeasing all others—therefore we are smitten as we deserve, since it is written: "And that servant, which knows his master's will, and has not obeyed his will, shall be beaten with many stripes."[35] But what stripes, what blows, do we not deserve, when even confessors, who ought to be an example of virtuous life to others, do not maintain discipline? Therefore, while an inflated and immodest boastfulness about their own confession excessively elates some, tortures come upon them, and tortures without any cessation of the tormentor, without any end of condemnation, without any comfort of death—tortures which do not easily let them pass to the crown, but wrench them on the rack until they cause them to abandon their faith, unless some one taken away by the divine compassion should depart in the very midst of the torments, gaining glory not by the cessation of his torture, but by the quickness of his death.[36]

2. These things we suffer by our own fault and our own deserving, even as the divine judgment has forewarned us, saying, "If they forsake my law and walk not in my judgments, if they profane my statutes and keep not my commandments, then will I visit their transgressions with the rod, and their iniquities with stripes."[37] It is for this reason that we feel the rods and the stripes, because we neither please God with good deeds nor atone for our sins. Let us of our inmost heart and of our entire mind ask for God's mercy, because He Himself also adds, saying, "Nevertheless my loving-kindness will I not remove from them."[38] Let us ask, and we shall receive; and if there be delay and tardiness in our receiving, since we have grievously offended, let us knock, because to him that knocks also it shall be opened, if only our prayers, our groanings, and our tears, knock at the door; and with these we must be urgent and persevering, even although prayer be offered with one mind.

3. For—which the more induced and constrained me to write this letter to you—you ought to know (since the Lord has condescended to show and to reveal it) that it was said in a vision, "Ask, and you shall obtain." Then, afterwards, that the attending people were bidden to pray for certain persons pointed out to them, but that in their petitions there were dissonant voices, and wills disagreeing, and that this excessively displeased Him who had said, "Ask, and you shall obtain," because the disagreement of the people was out of harmony, and there was not a consent of the brethren one and simple, and a united concord; since it is written, "God who makes men to be of one mind in a house;" and we read in the Acts of the Apostles, "And the multitude of them that believed were of one heart and of one soul."[39] And the Lord has bidden us with His own voice, saying, "This is my command, that you love one another."[40] And again, "I say unto you, that if two of you shall agree on earth as touching anything that you shall ask, it shall be done for you of my Father which is in heaven."[41] But if two of one mind can do so much, what might be effected if the unanimity prevailed among all? But if, according to the peace which our Lord gave us, there were agreement among all brethren, we should before this have obtained from the divine mercy what we seek; nor should we be wavering so long in this peril of our salvation and our faith. Yes, truly, and these evils would not have come upon the brethren, if the brotherhood had been animated with one spirit.[42]

4. For there also was shown that there sat the father of a family, a young man also being seated at his right hand, who, anxious and somewhat sad with a kind of indignation, holding his chin in his right hand, occupied his place with a sorrowful look. But another standing on the left hand, bore a net, which he threatened to throw, in order to catch the people standing round. And when he who saw marveled what this could be, it was told him that the youth who was thus sitting on the right hand was saddened and grieved because his commandments were not observed; but that he on the left was exultant because an opportunity was afforded him of receiving from the father of the family the power of destroying. This was shown long before the tempest of this devastation arose. And we have seen that which had been shown fulfilled; that while we despise the commandments of the Lord, while we do not keep the salutary ordinances of the law that He has given, the enemy was receiving a power of doing mischief, and was overwhelming, by the cast of his net, those who were imperfectly armed and too careless to resist.

5. Let us urgently pray and groan with continual petitions. For know, beloved brethren, that I was not long ago reproached with this also in a vision, that we were sleepy in our prayers, and did not pray with watchfulness; and undoubtedly God, who rebukes whom He loves, when He rebukes, rebukes that He may amend, amends that He may preserve. Let us therefore strike off and break away from the bonds of sleep, and pray with urgency and watchfulness, as the Apostle Paul bids us, saying, "Continue in prayer, and watch in the same."[43] For the

apostles also ceased not to pray day and night; and the Lord also Himself, the teacher of our discipline, and the way of our example, frequently and watchfully prayed, as we read in the Gospel: "He went out into a mountain to pray, and continued all night in prayer to God."[44] And assuredly what He prayed for, He prayed for on our behalf, since He was not a sinner, but bore the sins of others. But He so prayed for us, that in another place we read, "And the Lord said to Peter, 'Behold, Satan has desired to sift you as wheat: but I have prayed for you, that your faith fail not.'"[45] But if for us and for our sins He both labored and watched and prayed, how much more ought we to be instant in prayers; and, first of all, to pray and to entreat the Lord Himself, and then through Him, to make satisfaction to God the Father! We have an advocate and an intercessor for our sins, Jesus Christ the Lord and our God, if only we repent of our sins past, and confess and acknowledge our sins, whereby we now offend the Lord, and for the time to come engage to walk in His ways, and to fear His commandments. The Father corrects and protects us, if we still stand fast in the faith both in afflictions and perplexities, that is to say, cling closely to His Christ; as it is written, "Who shall separate us from the love of Christ? Shall tribulation, or distress, or persecution, or famine or nakedness, or peril, or sword?"[46] None of these things can separate believers, nothing can tear away those who are clinging to His body and blood. Persecution of that kind is an examination and searching out of the heart. God wills us to be sifted and proved, as He has always proved His people; and yet in His trials help has never at any time been wanting to believers.

6. Finally, to the very least of His servants although placed among very many sins, and unworthy of His condescension, yet He has condescended of His goodness towards us to command: "Tell him," said He, "to be safe, because peace is coming; but that, in the meantime, there is a little delay, that some who still remain may be proved." But we are admonished by these divine condescensions both concerning a spare diet and a temperate use of drink; to wit, lest worldly enticement should enervate the breast now elevated with celestial vigor, or lest the mind, weighed down by too abundant feasting, should be less watchful unto prayers and supplication.

7. It was my duty not to conceal these special matters, nor to hide them alone in my own consciousness—matters by which each one of us may be both instructed and guided. And do not you for your part keep this letter concealed among yourselves, but let the brethren have it to read. For it is the part of one who desires that his brother should not be warned and instructed, to intercept those words with which the Lord condescends to admonish and instruct us. Let them know that we are proved by our Lord, and let them never fail of that faith whereby we have once believed in Him, under the conflict of this present affliction. Let each one, acknowledging his own sins, even now put off the conversation of the old man. For no man who looks back as he puts his hand to the plow is fit for the kingdom of God. And, finally, Lot's wife, who, when she was delivered, looked back in defiance of the commandment, lost the benefit of her escape. Let us look not to things which are behind, whither the devil calls us back, but to things which are before, whither Christ calls us. Let us lift up our eyes to heaven, lest the earth with its delights and enticements deceive us. Let each one of us pray God not for himself only, but for all the brethren, even as the Lord has taught us to pray, when He bids to each one, not private prayer, but enjoined them, when they prayed, to pray for all in common prayer and concordant supplication. If the Lord shall behold us humble and peaceable; if He shall see us joined one with another; if He shall see us fearful concerning His anger; if corrected and amended by the present tribulation, He will maintain us safe from the disturbances of the enemy. Discipline has preceded; pardon also shall follow.

8. Let us only, without ceasing to ask, and with full faith that we shall receive, in simplicity and unanimity beseech the Lord, entreating not only with groaning but with tears, as it behooves those to entreat who are situated between the ruins of those who wail, and the remnants of those who fear; between the manifold slaughter of the yielding, and the little firmness of those who still stand. Let us ask that peace may be soon restored; that we may be quickly helped in our concealments and our dangers; that those things may be fulfilled which the Lord deigns to show to his servants—the restoration of the Church, the security of our salvation; after the rains, serenity; after the darkness, light; after the storms and whirlwinds, a peaceful calm; the affectionate aids of paternal love, the accustomed grandeurs of the divine majesty whereby both the blasphemy of persecutors may be restrained, the repentance of the lapsed renewed, and the steadfast faith of the persevering may glory. I bid you, beloved brethren, ever heartily farewell; and have me in remembrance. Salute the brotherhood in my name; and remind them to remember me. Farewell.

NOTES

34. A reference to the persecution of Decius (250-251), then ravaging the North African churches with especial ferocity.
35. Luke 12:47.
36. Cyprian is here condemning the rashness with with some rushed to earn martyrdom, only to succumb to the barbarity of the tortures inflicted and deny their faith.
37. Ps. 89:30-32.
38. Ps. 89:33.
39. Acts 4:32.

40. John 15:12.
41. Matt. 18:19.
42. Cyprian believes that the Church is permitted to be afflicted temporally to the degree that its shepherds waver in their faith; see Letter 7:4.
43. Col. 4:2.
44. Luke 6:12.
45. Luke 22:31-32.
46. Rom. 8:35.

LETTER 8

TO THE MARTYRS AND CONFESSORS

1. Cyprian, to the martyrs and confessors in Christ our Lord and in God the Father, everlasting salvation. I gladly rejoice and am thankful, most brave and blessed brethren, at hearing of your faith and virtue, wherein the Church, our Mother, glories. Lately, indeed, she gloried, when, in consequence of an enduring confession, that punishment was undergone which drove the confessors of Christ into exile; yet the present confession is so much the more illustrious and greater in honor as it is braver in suffering. The combat has increased, and the glory of the combatants has increased also. Nor were you kept back from the struggle by fear of tortures, but by the very tortures themselves you were more and more stimulated to the conflict; bravely and firmly you have returned with ready devotion, to contend in the extremest contest. Of you I find that some are already crowned, while some are even now within reach of the crown of victory; but all whom the danger has shut up in a glorious company are animated to carry on the struggle with an equal and common warmth of virtue, as it behooves the soldiers of Christ in the divine camp: that no allurements may deceive the incorruptible steadfastness of your faith, no threats terrify you, no sufferings or tortures overcome you, because greater is He that is in us, than he that is in the world;[47] nor is the earthly punishment able to do more towards casting down, than is the divine protection towards lifting up. This truth is proved by the glorious struggle of the brethren, who, having become leaders to the rest in overcoming their tortures, afforded an example of virtue and faith, contending in the strife, until the strife yielded, being overcome. With what praises can I commend you, most courageous brethren? With what vocal proclamation can I extol the strength of your heart and the perseverance of your faith? You have borne the sharpest examination by torture, even unto the glorious consummation, and have not yielded to sufferings, but rather the sufferings have given way to you. The end of torments, which the tortures themselves did not give, the crown has given. The examination by torture waxing severer, continued for a long time to this result, not to overthrow the steadfast faith, but to send the men of God more quickly to the Lord. The multitude of those who were present saw with admiration the heavenly contest—the contest of God, the spiritual contest, the battle of Christ—saw that His servants stood with free voice, with unyielding mind, with divine virtue—bare, indeed, of weapons of this world, but believing and armed with the weapons of faith. The tortured stood more brave than the torturers; and the limbs, beaten and torn as they were, overcame the hooks that bent and tore them. The scourge, often repeated with all its rage, could not conquer invincible faith, even although the membrane which enclosed the entrails were broken, and it was no longer the limbs but the wounds of the servants of God that were tortured. Blood was flowing which might quench the blaze of persecution, which might subdue the flames of Gehenna with its glorious gore. Oh, what a spectacle was that to the Lord—how sublime, how great, how acceptable to the eyes of God in the allegiance and devotion of His soldiers! As it is written in the Psalms, when the Holy Spirit at once speaks to us and warns us: "Precious in the sight of the Lord is the death of His saints."[48] Precious is the death which has bought immortality at the cost of its blood, which has received the crown from the consummation of its virtues. How did Christ rejoice therein! How willingly did He both fight and conquer in such servants of His, as the protector of their faith, and giving to believers as much as he who takes believes that he receives! He was present at His own contest; He lifted up, strengthened, animated the champions and assertors of His name. And He who once conquered death on our behalf, always conquers it in us. "When they," says He, "deliver you up, take no thought what you shall speak: for it shall be given you in that hour what you shall speak. For it is not you that speak, but the Spirit of your Father which speaks in you."[49]

2. The present struggle has afforded a proof of this saying. A voice filled with the Holy Spirit broke forth from the martyr's mouth when the most blessed Mappalicus said to the proconsul in the midst of his torments, "You shall see a contest tomorrow." And that which he said with the testimony of virtue and faith, the Lord fulfilled. A heavenly contest was exhibited, and the servant of God was crowned in the struggle of the promised fight. This is the contest which the prophet Isaiah of old predicted, saying, "It shall be no light contest for you with men, since God appoints the struggle."[50] And in order to show what this struggle would be, he added the words, "Behold, a virgin shall conceive and bear a son, and you shall call His name Emmanuel."[51] This is the struggle of our faith in which we engage, in which we conquer, in which we are crowned. This is the struggle which the blessed Apostle Paul has shown to us, in which it behooves us to run and to attain the crown of glory. "Do you not know," says he, "that they which run in a race, run all indeed, but one receives the prize? So run that you may obtain. Now they do it that they may receive a corruptible crown, but we an incorruptible."[52] Moreover, setting forth his own struggle, and declaring that he himself should soon be a sacrifice for the Lord's sake, he says, "I am now ready to be offered, and the time of my assumption is at hand. I have fought a good fight, I have finished my course, I have kept the faith: henceforth there is laid up for me a crown of righteousness, which the Lord, the righteous judge, shall give me at that day; and not to me only, but unto all them also that love His appearing."[53] This fight, therefore, predicted of old by the prophets, begun by the Lord, waged by the apostles, Mappalicus promised again to the proconsul in his own name and that of his colleagues. Nor did the faithful voice deceive in his promise; he exhibited the fight to which he had pledged himself, and he received the reward which he deserved. I not only beseech but exhort the rest of you, that you all should follow that martyr now most blessed, and the other partners of that engagement—soldiers and comrades, steadfast in faith, patient in suffering, victors in tortures—that those who are united at once by the bond of confession, and the entertainment of a dungeon, may also be united in the consummation of their virtue and a celestial crown; that you by your joy may dry the tears of our Mother, the Church, who mourns over the wreck and death of very many; and that you may confirm, by the provocation of your example, the steadfastness of others who stand also. If the battle shall call you out, if the day of your contest shall come engage bravely, fight with constancy, as knowing that you are fighting under the eyes of a present Lord, that you are attaining by the confession of His name to His own glory; who is not such a one as that He only looks on His servants, but He Himself also wrestles in us, Himself is engaged—Himself also in the struggles of our conflict not only crowns, but is crowned. But if before the day of your contest, of the mercy of God, peace shall supervene, let there still remain to you the sound will and the glorious conscience. Nor let any one of you be saddened as if he were inferior to those who before you have suffered tortures, have overcome the world and trodden it under foot, and so have come to the Lord by a glorious road. For the Lord is the searcher out of the reins and the hearts.[54] He looks through secret things, and beholds that which is concealed. In order to merit the crown from Him, His own testimony alone is sufficient, who will judge us. Therefore, beloved brethren, either case is equally lofty and illustrious—the former more secure, to wit, to hasten to the Lord with the consummation of our victory—the latter more joyous; a leave of absence, after glory, being received to flourish in the praises of the Church. O blessed Church of ours, which the honor of the divine condescension illuminates, which in our own times the glorious blood of martyrs renders illustrious! She was white before in the works of the brethren; now she has become purple in the blood of the martyrs. Among her flowers are wanting neither roses nor lilies. Now let each one strive for the largest dignity of either honor. Let them receive crowns, either white, as of labors, or of purple, as of suffering.[55] In the heavenly camp both peace and strife have their own flowers, with which the soldier of Christ may be crowned for glory. I bid you, most brave and beloved brethren, always heartily farewell in the Lord; and have me in remembrance. Farewell.

NOTES

47. 1 John 4:4.
48. Ps. 116:15.
49. Matt. 10:19-20.
50. An extremely awkward paraphrase of Isaiah 7:13: "And he said: Hear ye therefore, O house of David: Is it a small thing for you to be grievous to men, that you are grievous to my God also?"
51. Isa. 7:14.
52. 1 Cor. 9:24-25.
53. 2 Tim. 4:6-8.
54. Rev. 2:23.
55. An early attestation of the association of the color purple with suffering, and hence penance.

LETTER 9

TO THE CLERGY[56]

1. Cyprian to the presbyters and deacons, his brethren, greeting. I have long been patient, beloved brethren, hoping that my forbearing silence would avail to quietness. But since the unreasonable and reckless presumption of some is seeking by its boldness to disturb both the honor of the martyrs, and the modesty of the confessors, and the tranquility of the whole people, it behooves me no longer to keep silence, lest too much reticence should issue in danger both to the people and to ourselves. For what danger ought we not to fear from the Lord's displeasure, when some of the presbyters, remembering neither the Gospel nor their own place, and, moreover, considering neither the Lord's future judgment nor the bishop now placed over them, claim to themselves entire authority—a thing which was never in any wise done under our predecessors—with discredit and contempt of the bishop?

2. And I wish, if it could be so without the sacrifice of our brethren's safety, that they could make good their claim to all things; I could dissemble and bear the discredit of my episcopal authority, as I always have dissembled and borne it. But it is not now the occasion for dissimulating when our brotherhood is deceived by some of you, who, while without the means of restoring salvation they desire to please, become a still greater stumbling-block to the lapsed, for that it is a very great crime which persecution has compelled to be committed, they themselves know who have committed it; since our Lord and Judge has said, "Whosoever shall confess me before men, him will I also confess before my Father which is in heaven; but whosoever shall deny me, him will I also deny."[57] And again He has said, "All sins shall be forgiven unto the sons of men, and blasphemies; but he that shall blaspheme against the Holy Ghost shall not have forgiveness, but is guilty of eternal sin."[58] Also the blessed apostle has said, "You cannot drink the cup of the Lord and the cup of devils; you cannot be partakers of the Lord's table and of the table of devils."[59] He who withholds these words from our brethren deceives them, wretched that they are; so that they who truly repenting might satisfy God, both as the Father and as merciful, with their prayers and works, are seduced more deeply to perish; and they who might raise themselves up fall the more deeply. For although in smaller sins sinners may do penance for a set time, and according to the rules of discipline come to public confession, and by imposition of the hand of the bishop and clergy receive the right of communion: now with their time still unfulfilled, while persecution is still raging, while the peace of the Church itself is not yet restored, they are admitted to communion, and their name is presented; and while the penitence is not yet performed, confession is not yet made, the hands of the bishop and clergy are not yet laid upon them, the eucharist is given to them; although it is written, "Whosoever shall eat the bread and drink the cup of the Lord unworthily, shall be guilty of the body and blood of the Lord."[60]

3. But now they are not guilty who so little observe the law of Scripture; but they will be guilty who are in office and do not suggest these things to brethren, so that, being instructed by those placed above them, they may do all things with the fear of God, and with the observance given and prescribed by Him. Then, moreover, they lay the blessed martyrs open to ill will, and involve the glorious servants of God with the priest of God; so that although they, mindful of my place, have directed letters to me, and have asked that their wishes should then be examined, and peace granted them—when our Mother, the Church herself, should first have received peace for the Lord's mercy, and the divine protection has brought me back to His Church[61]—yet these, disregarding the honor which the blessed martyrs with the confessors maintain for me, despising the Lord's law and that observance, which the same martyrs and confessors bid to be maintained, before the fear of persecution is quenched, before my return, almost even before the departure of the martyrs, communicate with the lapsed, and offer and give them the eucharist: when even if the martyrs, in the heat of their glory, were to consider less carefully the Scriptures, and to desire anything more, they should be admonished by the presbyters' and deacons' suggestions, as was always done in time past.

4. For this reason the divine rebuke does not cease to chastise us night nor day. For besides the visions of the night, by day also, the innocent age of boys is among us filled with the Holy Spirit, seeing in an ecstasy with their eyes, and hearing and speaking those things whereby the Lord condescends to warn and instruct us.[62] And you shall hear all things when the Lord, who bade me withdraw, shall bring me back again to you. In the meanwhile, let those certain ones among you who are rash and incautious and boastful, and who do not regard man, at least fear God, knowing that, if they shall persevere still in the same course, I shall use that power of admonition which the Lord bids me use; so that they may meanwhile be withheld from offering, and have to plead their cause both before me and before the confessors themselves and before the whole people, when, with God's permission, we begin to be gathered together once more into the bosom of the Church, our Mother. Concerning this matter, I have written to the martyrs and confessors, and to the people, letters; both of which I have bidden to be read to you. I wish you, dearly beloved brethren and earnestly longed-for, ever heartily farewell in the Lord; and have me in remembrance. Farewell.

NOTES

56. This letter was written after the conclusion of the Decian persecution and concerns certain priests who had rashly granted reconciliation to the *lapsi* before the persecution had ceased, and without the consent of the bishops.
57. Matt. 10:32-33.
58. Mark 3:28-29.
59. 1 Cor. 10:21.
60. 1. Cor. 11:27.
61. At the writing of this letter (early 250) St. Cyprian was in hiding.
62. Evidence of the charismatic gifts still active in the mid-3rd century.
63. This letter, along with Letter 11, should be read in conjunction with Letter 14.

LETTER 10[63]

TO THE MARTYRS AND CONFESSORS WHO SOUGHT THAT PEACE SHOULD BE GRANTED TO THE LAPSED

1. Cyprian to the martyrs and confessors, his beloved brethren, greeting. The anxiety of my situation and the fear of the Lord constrain me, my brave and beloved brethren, to admonish you in my letters, that those who so devotedly and bravely maintain the faith of the Lord should also maintain the law and discipline of the Lord. For, while it behooves all Christ's soldiers to keep the precepts of their commander, to you it is more especially fitting that you should obey His precepts, inasmuch as you have been made an example to others, both of valour and of the fear of God. And I had indeed believed that the presbyters and deacons who are there present with you would admonish and instruct you more fully concerning the law of the Gospel, as was the case always in times past under my predecessors; so that the deacons passing in and out of the prison controlled the wishes of the martyrs by their counsels, and by the Scripture precepts.[64] But now, with great sorrow of mind, I gather that not only the divine precepts are not suggested to you by them, but that they are even rather restrained, so that those things which are done by you yourselves, both in respect of God with caution, and in respect of God's priest with honor, are relaxed by certain presbyters, who consider neither the fear of God nor the honor of the bishop. Although you sent letters to me in which you ask that your wishes should be examined, and that peace should be granted to certain of the lapsed as soon as with the end of the persecution, we should have begun to meet with our clergy, and to be gathered together once more; those presbyters, contrary to the Gospel law, contrary also to your respectful petition, before penitence was fulfilled, before confession even of the gravest and most heinous sin was made, before hands were placed upon the repentant by the bishops and clergy,[65] dare to offer on their behalf, and to give them the eucharist, that is, to profane the sacred body of the Lord, although it is written, "Whosoever shall eat the bread and drink the cup of the Lord unworthily, shall be guilty of the body and blood of the Lord."[66]

2. And to the lasped indeed pardon may be granted in respect of this thing. For what dead person would not hasten to be made alive? Who would not be eager to attain to his own salvation? But it is the duty of those placed over them to keep the ordinance, and to instruct those that are either hurrying or ignorant, that those who ought to be shepherds of the sheep may not become their butchers. For to concede those things which tend to destruction is to deceive. Nor is the lapsed raised in this manner, but, by offending God, he is more urged on to ruin. Let them learn, therefore, even from you, what they ought to have taught; let them reserve your petitions and wishes for the bishops, and let them wait for ripe and peaceable times to give peace at your requests.[67] The first thing is, that the Mother should first receive peace from the Lord, and then, in accordance with your wishes, that the peace of her children should be considered.

3. And since I hear, most brave and beloved brethren, that you are pressed by the shamelessness of some, and that your modesty suffers violence, I beg you with what entreaties I may, that, as mindful of the Gospel, and considering what and what sort of things in past time your predecessors the martyrs conceded, how careful they were in all respects, you also should anxiously and cautiously weigh the wishes of those who petition you, since, as friends of the Lord, and hereafter to exercise judgment with Him, you must inspect both the conduct and the doings and the deserts of each one. You must consider also the kinds and qualities of their sins, lest, in the event of anything being abruptly and unworthily either promised by you or done by me, our Church should begin to blush, even before the very Gentiles. For we are visited and chastened frequently, and we are admonished, that the commandments of the Lord may be kept without corruption or violation, which I find does not cease to be the case there among you so as to prevent the divine judgment from instructing very many of you also in the discipline of the Church. Now this can all be done, if you will regulate those things that are asked of you with a careful consideration of religion, perceiving and restraining those who, by accepting persons, either make favors in distributing your benefits, or seek to make a profit of an unlawful trade.

4. Concerning this I have written both to the clergy and to the people, both of which letters I have directed to be read to you. But you ought also to bring back and amend that matter according to your diligence, in such a way as to designate those by name to whom you desire that peace should be granted. For I hear that certificates are so given to some as that it is said, 'Let such a one be received to communion along with his friends,' which was never in any case done by the martyrs so that a vague and blind petition should by and by heap reproach upon us. For it opens a wide door to say, 'Such a one with his friends;' and twenty or thirty or more, may be presented to us, who may be asserted to be neighbors and connections, and freedmen and servants, of the man who receives the certificate. And for this reason I beg you that you will designate by name in the certificate those whom you yourselves see, whom you have known, whose penitence you see to be very near to full satisfaction, and so direct to us letters in conformity with faith and discipline. I bid you, very brave and beloved brethren, ever heartily in the Lord farewell; and have me in remembrance. Farewell.

NOTES

64. This passage provides valuable insight into the role of the deacons in the early Church, who "as was always the case in times past," would apparently regulate who could gain access to the imprisoned confessors, who could obtain writs of indulgence (*libelli pacis*) and under what conditions. Cyprian here gently reminds the martyrs that these writs of indulgence should not be given out too liberally and that their distirbution ought to be done in accordance with the dictates of the bishop and under the supervision of the deacons. See Letter 16 for an example of a *libellus pacis.*

65. A glimpse into the ancient method of absolution for post-baptismal sins: the prescription of penance (and its presumed successful completion), confession of sin (usually publicly) to the presbyter or bishop, followed by laying on of hands, which served as an absolution (see also Letter 11:2). This also demonstrates the truth that, in the primitive Church, reconciliation of the Christian sinner with God was considered to be within the authority of the Church. Thus Pope St. Pius X condemns the following proposition in *Lamentabili Sane* (1907): "In the primitive Church there was no concept of the reconciliation of the Christian sinner by the authority of the Church, but the Church by very slow degrees only grew accustomed to this concept. Moreover, even after penance came to be recognized as an institution of the Church, it was not called by the name of sacrament, because it was regarded as an odious sacrament" (46).

66. 1 Cor. 11:27.

67. It is important to note here that Cyprian does not in the least condemn the practice of obtaining

writs of indulgence, only insists that their distribution be handled in an orderly fashion and under the proper ecclesiastical supervision.

LETTER 11

TO THE PEOPLE

1. Cyprian to his brethren among the people who stand fast, greeting. That you bewail and grieve over the downfall of our brethren I know from myself, beloved brethren, who also bewail with you and grieve for each one, and suffer and feel what the blessed apostle said: "Who is weak," said he, "and I am not weak? Who is offended, and I burn not?"[68] And again he has laid it down in his epistle, saying, "Whether one member suffer, all the members suffer with it; or one member rejoice, all the members rejoice with it."[69] I sympathize with you in your suffering and grief, therefore, for our brethren, who, having lapsed and fallen prostrate under the severity of the persecution, have inflicted a like pain on us by their wounds, inasmuch as they tear away part of our bowels with them—to these the divine mercy is able to bring healing. Yet I do not think that there must be any haste, nor that anything must be done incautiously and immaturely, lest, while peace is grasped at, the divine indignation be more seriously incurred. The blessed martyrs have written to me about certain persons, requesting that their wishes may be examined into. When, as soon as peace is given to us all by the Lord, we shall begin to return to the Church, then the wishes of each one shall be looked into in your presence, and with your judgment.[70]

2. Yet I hear that certain of the presbyters, neither mindful of the Gospel nor considering what the martyrs have written to me, nor reserving to the bishop the honor of his priesthood and of his dignity, have already begun to communicate with the lapsed, and to offer on their behalf, and to give them the eucharist, when it was fitting that they should attain to these things in due course. For, as in smaller sins which are not committed against God,[71] penitence may be fulfilled in a set time, and confession may be made with investigation of the life of him who fulfills the penitence, and no one can come to communion unless the hands of the bishop and clergy be first imposed upon him; how much more ought all such matters as these to be observed with caution and moderation, according to the discipline of the Lord, in these gravest and extremest sins! This warning, indeed, our presbyters and deacons ought to have given you, that they might cherish the sheep committed to their care, and by the divine authority might instruct them in the way of obtaining salvation by prayer. I am aware of the peacefulness as well as the fear of our people, who would be watchful in the satisfaction and the deprecation of God's anger, unless some of the presbyters, by way of gratifying them, had deceived them.

3. Even you, therefore, yourselves, guide them each one, and control the minds of the lapsed by counsel and by your own moderation, according to the divine precepts. Let no one pluck the unripe fruit at a time as yet premature. Let no one commit his ship, shattered and broken with the waves, anew to the deep, before he has carefully repaired it. Let none be in haste to accept and to put on a rent tunic, unless he has seen it mended by a skillful workman and has received it arranged by the fuller. Let them bear with patience my advice, I beg. Let them look for my return, that when by God's mercy I come to you, I, with many of my co-bishops, being called together according to the Lord's discipline, and in the presence of the confessors, and with your opinion also, may be able to examine the letters and the wishes of the blessed martyrs.[72] Concerning this matter I have written both to the clergy and to the martyrs and confessors, both of which letters I have directed to be read to you.[73] I bid you, brethren beloved and most longed-for, ever heartily farewell in the Lord; and have me in remembrance. Farewell.

NOTES

68. 2 Cor. 11:29.
69. 1 Cor. 12:26.
70. "[I]n your presence and with your judgment." An indication that confession of sins, such as would have been required by the lapsi for readmission to the Church, would have been made publicly, in the presence of the congregation.
71. Theologically speaking, all sin is ultimately against God (Ps. 51:4, for example). Cyprian does not mean to say that there are certain sins that are not against God, but is referring to sins that have to do specifically with worship of God—in this context, apostasy or sacrificing to pagan idols under fear of death.
72. This would be accomplished at the Synods of Carthage in 251, 252 and 254, where St. Cyprian advocated handling the cases of the *lapsi* on a case by case basis and excommunicated the Novatian bishops, who denied that the Church had the power to reconcile the *lapsi*.
73. Letters 9 and 10.

LETTER 12

TO THE CLERGY, CONCERNING THE LAPSED AND CATECHUMENS

1. Cyprian to the presbyters and deacons, his brethren, greeting. I marvel, beloved brethren, that you have answered nothing to me in reply to my many letters which I have frequently written to you, although as well the advantage as the need of our brotherhood would certainly be best provided for if, receiving information from you, I could accurately investigate and advise upon the management of affairs. Since, however, I see that there is not yet any opportunity of coming to you, and that the summer has already begun[74]—a season that is disturbed with continual and heavy sicknesses—I think that our brethren must be dealt with—that they who have received certificates from the martyrs,[75] and may be assisted by their privilege with God, if they should be seized with any misfortune and peril of sickness, should, without waiting for my presence, before any presbyter who might be present, or if a presbyter should not be found and death begins to be imminent, before even a deacon, be able to make confession of their sin, that, with the imposition of hands upon them for repentance, they should come to the Lord with the peace which the martyrs have desired, by their letters to us, to be granted to them.

2. Cherish also by your presence the rest of the people who are lapsed, and cheer them by your consolation, that they may not fail of the faith and of God's mercy. For those shall not be forsaken by the aid and assistance of the Lord, who meekly, humbly, and with true penitence have persevered in good works; but the divine remedy will be granted to them also. To the hearers also, if there are any overtaken by danger, and placed near to death, let your vigilance not be wanting; let not the mercy of the Lord be denied to those that are imploring the divine favor. I bid you, beloved brethren, ever heartily farewell; and remember me. Greet the whole brotherhood in my name, and remind them and ask them to be mindful of me. Farewell.

NOTES

74. Summer of 250 AD. The persecution of Decius had been in effect for six months at least, though the severity of it was beginning to be relaxed. Therefore the lapsed were beginning to seek reconciliation with the Church, though the persecution had not yet been rescinded and Cyprian had not yet returned from hiding to oversee these affairs himself.
75. The lapsed who, after denying Christ and sacrificing to pagan idols during the persecution, had received writs of indulgence from the confessors to secure their readmission to communion.

LETTER 13
TO THE CLERGY, CONCERNING THOSE
WHO ARE IN HASTE TO RECEIVE PEACE

1. Cyprian to the presbyters and deacons, his brethren, greeting. I have read your letter, beloved brethren, wherein you wrote that your wholesome counsel was not wanting to our brethren, that, laying aside all rash haste, they should manifest a religious patience to God, so that when by His mercy we come together, we may debate upon all kinds of things, according to the discipline of the Church, especially since it is written, "Remember from whence you have fallen, and repent."[76] Now he repents, who, remembering the divine precept, with meekness and patience, and obeying the priests of God, deserves well of the Lord by his obedience and his righteous works.[77]

2. Since, however, you intimate that some are impatient, and eagerly urge their being received to communion, and have desired in this matter that some rule should be given by me to you, I think I have sufficiently written on this subject in the last letter that was sent to you,[78] that they who have received a certificate from the martyrs, and can be assisted by their help with the Lord in respect of their sins, if they begin to be oppressed with any sickness or risk; when they have made confession, and have received the imposition of hands on them by you in acknowledgment of their penitence, should be remitted to the Lord with the peace promised to them by the martyrs. But others who, without having received any certificate from the martyrs, are envious (since this is the cause not of a few, nor of one church, nor of one province, but of the whole world),[79] must wait, in dependence on the protection of the Lord, for the public peace of the Church itself. For this is suitable to the modesty and the discipline, and even the life of all of us, that the chief officers meeting together with the clergy in the presence also of the people who stand fast, to whom themselves, moreover, honor is to be shown for their faith and fear, we may be able to order all things with the religiousness of a common consultation. But how irreligious is it, and mischievous, even to those themselves who are eager, that while such as are exiles, and driven from their country, and spoiled of all their property, have not yet returned to the Church, some of the lapsed should be hasty to anticipate even confessors themselves, and to enter into the Church before them! If they are so over-anxious, they have what they require in their own power, the times themselves offering them freely more than they ask. The struggle is still going forward, and the strife is daily celebrated. If they truly and with constancy repent of what they have done, and the fervor of their faith prevails, he who cannot be delayed may be crowned. I bid you, beloved brethren, ever heartily farewell; and have me in remembrance. Greet all the brotherhood in my name, and tell them to be mindful of me. Farewell.

NOTES

76. Rev. 2:5.
77. An excellent testimony to the fact that the early Church did not believe in justification by faith alone.
78. Letter 12.
79. Here we have St. Cyrpian's valuable testimony that the practice of obtaining *libelli pacis* from the confessors (and the consequent abuses) was not a practice restricted to North Africa but was universal in the early Church.

LETTER 14

TO THE CHURCH AT ROME, IN WHICH CYPRIAN GIVES AN ACCOUNT OF HIS WITHDRAWAL AND OF THE THINGS WHICH HE DID THEREIN[80]

1. Cyprian to his brethren the presbyters and deacons assembled at Rome, greeting. Having ascertained, beloved brethren, that what I have done and am doing has been told to you in a somewhat garbled and untruthful manner, I have thought it necessary to write this letter to you, wherein I might give an account to you of my doings, my discipline, and my diligence; for, as the Lord's commands teach, immediately the first burst of the disturbance arose, and the people with violent clamor repeatedly demanded me. I, taking into consideration not so much my own safety as the public peace of the brethren, withdrew for a while, lest, by my over-bold presence, the tumult which had begun might be still further provoked. Nevertheless, although absent in body, I was not wanting either in spirit, or in act, or in my advice, so as to fail in any benefit that I could afford my brethren by my counsel, according to the Lord's precepts, in anything that my poor abilities enabled me.

2. And what I did, these thirteen letters sent forth at various times declare to you, which I have transmitted to you; in which neither counsel to the clergy, nor exhortation to the confessors, nor rebuke, when it was necessary, to the exiles, nor my appeals and persuasions to the whole brotherhood, that they should entreat the mercy of God, were wanting to the full extent that, according to the law of faith and the fear of God, with the Lord's help, nay poor abilities could endeavor. But afterwards, when tortures came, my words reached both to our tortured brethren and to those who as yet were only imprisoned with a view to torture, to strengthen and console them. Moreover, when I found that those who had polluted their hands and mouths with sacrilegious contact, or had no less infected their consciences with wicked certificates, were everywhere soliciting the martyrs, and were also corrupting the confessors with importunate and excessive entreaties, so that, without any discrimination or examination of the individuals themselves, thousands of certificates were daily given, contrary to the law of the Gospel, I wrote letters in which I recalled by my advice, as much as possible, the martyrs and confessors to the Lord's commands. To the presbyters and deacons also was not wanting the vigor of the priesthood; so that some, too little mindful of discipline, and hasty, with a rash precipitation, who had already begun to communicate with the lapsed, were restrained by my interposition. Among the people, moreover, I have done what I could to quiet their minds, and have instructed them to maintain ecclesiastical discipline.

3. But afterwards, when some of the lapsed, whether of their own accord, or by the suggestion of any other, broke forth with a daring demand, as though they would endeavor by a violent effort to extort the peace that had been promised to them by the martyrs and confessors; concerning this also I wrote twice to the clergy[81], and commanded it to be read to them; that for the mitigation of their violence in any manner for the meantime, if any who had received a certificate from the martyrs were departing from this life, having made confession, and received the imposition of hands on them for repentance, they should be remitted to the Lord with the peace promised them by the martyrs. Nor in this did I give them a law, or rashly constitute myself the author of the direction; but as it seemed fit both that honor should be paid to the martyrs, and that the vehemence of those who were anxious to disturb everything should be restrained; and when, besides, I had read your letter which you lately wrote hither to my clergy by Crementius the sub-deacon, to the effect that assistance should be given to those who might, after their lapse, be seized with sickness, and might penitently desire communion;[82] I judged it well to stand by your judgment, lest our proceedings, which ought to be united and to agree in all things, should in any respect be different.[83] The cases of the rest, even although they might have received certificates from the martyrs, I ordered altogether to be put off, and to be reserved till I should be present, that so, when the Lord has given to us peace, and several bishops shall have begun to assemble into one place, we may be able to arrange and reform everything, having the advantage also of your counsel. I bid you, beloved brethren, ever heartily farewell.

NOTES

80. Cyprian here defends his reasons for fleeing Carthage at the outbreak of the persecution. Some of Cyprian's enemies, possibly Novatianists, had denounced him to Rome as a coward. Here St. Cyprian gives his reply to these charges of cowardice.
81. Letters 12 and 13.
82. Letter 2.
83. Cyprian not only states that the proceedings of the church of Carthage ought to "be united and agree in all things" with the church of Rome, but that Carthage should follow Rome's lead, "to stand by your judgement," lest their proceedings "should in any respect be different." This passage demonstrates implicitly the ideal of the Roman supremacy in the early Church—that the practices and teachings found in Rome ought to be normative and exemplary for the rest of the Church Universal.

LETTER 15[84]

TO MOYSES AND MAXIMUS, AND THE REST OF THE CONFESSORS

1. Cyprian to Moyses and Maximus, the presbyters and the other confessors, his brethren, greeting. Celerinus,[85] a companion both of your faith and virtue, and God's soldier in glorious engagements,[86] has come to me, beloved brethren, and represented all of you, as well as each individual, forcibly to my affection. I beheld in him, when he came, the whole of you; and when he spoke sweetly and often of your love to me, in his words I heard you. I rejoice very greatly when such things are brought to me from you by such men as he. In a certain manner I am also there with you in prison. I think that I who am thus bound to

319

your hearts, enjoy with you the delights of the divine approval. Your individual love associates me with your honor; the Spirit does not allow our love to be separated.[87] Confession shuts you up in prison; affection shuts me up there. And I indeed, remembering you day and night, both when in the sacrifices[88] I offer prayer with many, and when in retirement I pray with private petition, beseech of the Lord a full acknowledgment to your crowns and your praises. But my poor ability is too weak to recompense you; you give more when you remember me in prayer, since, already breathing only celestial things, and meditating only divine things, you ascend to loftier heights, even by the delay of your suffering; and by the long lapse of time, are not wasting, but increasing your glory. A first and single confession makes blessed; you confess as often as, when asked to retire from prison, you prefer the prison with faith and virtue; your praises are as numerous as the days; as the months roll onward, ever your merits increase. He conquers once who suffers at once; but he who continues always battling with punishments, and is not overcome with suffering, is daily crowned.

2. Now, therefore, let magistrates and consuls or proconsuls go by; let them glory in the ensigns of their yearly dignity, and in their twelve fasces. Behold, the heavenly dignity in you is sealed by the brightness of a year's honor, and already, in the continuance of its victorious glory, has passed over the rolling circle of the returning year. The rising sun and the waning moon enlightened the world; but to you, He who made the sun and moon was a greater light in your dungeon, and the brightness of Christ glowing in your hearts and minds, irradiated with that eternal and brilliant light the gloom of the place of punishment, which to others was so horrible and deadly. The winter has passed through the vicissitudes of the months; but you, shut up in prison, were undergoing, instead of the inclemencies of winter, the winter of persecution. To the winter succeeded the mildness of spring, rejoicing with roses and crowned with flowers; but to you were present roses and flowers from the delights of paradise, and celestial garlands wreathed your brows. Behold, the summer is fruitful with the fertility of the harvest, and the threshing-floor is filled with grain; but you who have sown glory, reap the fruit of glory, and, placed in the Lord's threshing-floor, behold the chaff burnt up with unquenchable fire; you yourselves as grains of wheat, winnowed and precious grain, now purged and garnered, regard the dwelling-place of a prison as your granary. Nor is there wanting to the autumn spiritual grace for discharging the duties of the season. The vintage is pressed out of doors, and the grape which shall hereafter flow into the cups is trodden in the presses. You, rich bunches out of the Lord's vineyard, and branches with fruit already ripe, trodden by the tribulation of worldly pressure, fill your wine-press in the torturing prison, and shed your blood instead of wine; brave to bear suffering, you willingly drink the cup of martyrdom. Thus the year rolls on with the Lord's servants—thus is celebrated the vicissitude of the seasons with spiritual deserts, and with celestial rewards.

3. Abundantly blessed are they who, from your number, passing through these footprints of glory, have already departed from the world; and, having finished their journey of virtue and faith, have attained to the embrace and the kiss of the Lord, to the joy of the Lord Himself. But yet your glory is not less, who are still engaged in contest, and, about to follow the glories of your comrades, are long waging the battle, and with an unmoved and unshaken faith standing fast, are daily exhibiting in your virtues a spectacle in the sight of God. The longer is your strife, the loftier will be your crown. The struggle is one, but it is crowded with a manifold multitude of contests; you conquer hunger, and despise thirst, and tread under foot the squalor of the dungeon, and the horror of the very abode of punishment, by the vigor of your courage. Punishment is there subdued; torture is worn out; death is not feared but desired, being overcome by the reward of immortality, so that he who has conquered is crowned with eternity of life. What now must be the mind in you, how elevated, how large the heart, when such and so great things are resolved, when nothing but the precepts of God and the rewards of Christ are considered! The will is then only God's will; and although you are still placed in the flesh, it is the life not of the present world, but of the future, that you now live.

4. It now remains, beloved brethren, that you should be mindful of me; that, among your great and divine considerations, you should also think of me in your mind and spirit; and that I should be in your prayers and supplications, when that voice, which is illustrious by the purification of confession, and praiseworthy for the continual tenor of its honor, penetrates to God's ears, and heaven being open to it, passes from these regions of the world subdued, to the realms above, and obtains from the Lord's goodness even what it asks. For what do you ask from the Lord's mercy which you do not deserve to obtain?—you who have thus observed the Lord's commands, who have maintained the Gospel discipline with the simple vigor of your faith, who, with the glory of your virtue uncorrupted, have stood bravely by the Lord's commands, and by His apostles, and have confirmed the wavering faith of many by the truth of your martyrdom? Truly, Gospel witnesses, and truly, Christ's martyrs, resting upon His roots, founded with strong foundation upon the Rock, you have joined discipline with virtue, you have brought others to the fear of God, you have made your martyrdoms, examples. I bid you, brethren, very brave and beloved, ever heartily farewell, and remember me.

NOTES

84. See also Letter 31. Judging by the metaphor Cyprian uses in section two of this letter, we can probably date it to winter of 250.
85. St. Celerinus of Carthage. Celerinus was imprisoned in Rome and suffered tremendous tortures during the persecution of Decius. He was eventually released and came to Carthage, where Cyprian ordained him a deacon, as recounted in Letter 33. He suffered alongside his two uncles (both named St. Laurentius) and his aunt, St. Clerina, who were all put to death (Feast Day: Feb. 3rd). St. Celerinus' sufferings were so extreme that he was deemed a martyr though still living, much as St. Isaac Jogues would be centuries later.
86. The trials accompanying martyrdom were always seen in terms of combat; see the *Martyrdom of Perpetua and Felicity*, 10 and section 3 of this same letter.
87. A principle behind the communion of the saints: Christians, united in the Spirit, cannot have their love separated by earthly trials, not even death. Christian love continues even after death, because in Christ all are made alive (Luke 20:38, 1 Cor. 15:22).
88. In other words, when he comes together with the Church to offer the sacrifice of the Mass.

LETTER 16

THE CONFESSORS TO CYPRIAN[89]

All the confessors to father Cyprian, greeting. Know that, to all, concerning whom the account of what they have done since the commission of their sin has been, in your estimation, satisfactory, we have granted peace; and we have desired that this rescript should be made known by you to the other bishops also. We bid you to have peace with the holy martyrs. Lucianus wrote this, there being present of the clergy, both an exorcist and a reader.

NOTES

89. A remarkable example of one of the *libelli pacis* of the confessors. See Letters 8, 9, 10 and 17 and *On the Lapsed*, 17-18

LETTER 17

TO THE PRESBYTERS AND DEACONS ABOUT THE FOREGOING AND THE FOLLOWING LETTERS.

Cyprian to the presbyters and deacons, his brethren, greeting. The Lord speaks and says, "Upon whom shall I look, but upon him that is humble and quiet, and that trembles at my words?"[90] Although we ought all to be this, yet especially those ought to be so who must labor, that, after their grave lapse, they may, by true penitence and absolute humility, deserve well of the Lord. Now I have read the letter of the whole body of confessors, which they wish to be made known by me to all my colleagues, and in which they requested that the peace given by themselves should be assured to those concerning whom the account of what they have done since their crime has been, in our estimation, satisfactory; which matter, as it waits for the counsel and judgment of all of us, I do not dare to prejudge, and so to assume a common cause for my own decision. And therefore, in the meantime, let us abide by the letters which I lately wrote to you,[91] of which I have now sent a copy to many of my colleagues, who wrote in reply, that they were pleased with what I had decided, and that there must be no departure therefrom, until, peace being granted to us by the Lord, we shall be able to assemble together into one place, and to examine into the cases of individuals. But that you may know both what my colleague Caldonius wrote to me, and what I replied to him,[92] I have enclosed with my letter a copy of each letter, the whole of which I beg you to read to our brethren, that they may be more and more settled down to patience, and not add another fault to what had hitherto been their former fault, not being willing to obey either me or the Gospel, nor allowing their cases to be examined in accordance with the letters of all the confessors. I bid you, beloved brethren, ever heartily farewell; and have me in remembrance. Salute all the brotherhood. Farewell!

NOTES

90. Isa. 66:2.
91. Letters 8-11. While the confessors plead for a general indulgence (Letter 16), St. Cyprian wishes to wait until the cessation of the persecution and call a general synod to determine the fate of the lapsed. Until then, he wishes their reconciliation to be granted on a case by case basis and pleads that the confessors only grant writs of indulgence to those whose penitence is sincere and under the supervision of the proper ecclesiastical authorities. He here encourages his priests and deacons to abide by his wishes.
92. Letters 18 and 19.

LETTER 18

CALDONIUS TO CYPRIAN

Caldonius to Cyprian and his fellow presbyters abiding at Carthage, greeting. The necessity of the times induces us not hastily to grant peace. But it was well to write to you, that they who, after having sacrificed, were again tried, became exiles.[93] And thus they seem to me to have atoned for their former crime, in that they now let go their possessions and homes, and, repenting, follow Christ. Thus Felix, who assisted in the office of presbyter under Decimus, and was very near to me in bonds (I knew that same Felix very thoroughly), Victoria, his wife, and Lucius, being faithful, were banished, and have left their possessions, which the treasury now has in keeping. Moreover, a woman, Bona by name, who was dragged by her husband to sacrifice, and (with no conscience guilty of the crime, but because those who held her hands, sacrificed) began to cry against them, "I did not do it; you it was who did it!"—was also banished. Since, therefore, all these were asking for peace, saying, "We have recovered the faith which we had lost, we have repented, and have publicly confessed Christ"—although it

323

seems to me that they ought to receive peace—yet I have referred them to your judgment, that I might not appear to presume anything rashly. If, therefore, you should wish me to do anything by the common decision, write to me. Greet our brethren; our brethren greet you. I bid you, beloved brethren, ever heartily farewell.

NOTES

93. Many Roman magistrates, feeling compunction at putting Christians to death for their religion, often preferred to impose upon Christians sentences of exile rather than death.

LETTER 19

CYPRIAN REPLIES TO CALDONIUS

Cyprian to Caldonius, his brother, greeting. We have received your letter, beloved brother, which is abundantly sensible, and full of honesty and faith. Nor do we wonder that, skilled and exercised as you are in the Scriptures of the Lord, you do everything discreetly and wisely. You have judged quite correctly about granting peace to our brethren, which they, by true penitence and by the glory of a confession of the Lord, have restored to themselves, being justified by their words, by which before they had condemned themselves. Since, then, they have washed away all their sin, and their former stain, by the help of the Lord, has been done away by a more powerful virtue, they ought not to lie any longer under the power of the devil, as it were, prostrate; when, being banished and deprived of all their property, they have lifted themselves up and have begun to stand with Christ. And I wish that the others also would repent after their fall, and be transferred into their former condition; and that you may know how we have dealt with these, in their urgent and eager rashness and importunity to extort peace, I have sent a book to you, with letters to the number of five,[94] that I wrote to the clergy and to the people, and to the martyrs also and confessors, which letters have already been sent to many of our colleagues, and have satisfied them; and they replied that they also agree with me in the same opinion according to the Catholic faith; which very thing do you also communicate to as many of our colleagues as you can, that among all these, may be observed one mode of action and one agreement, according to the Lord's precepts. I bid you, beloved brother, ever heartily farewell.

NOTES

94. Letters 9-13.

LETTER 20

CELERINUS TO LUCIAN[95]

1. Celerinus to Lucian, greeting. In writing this letter to you, my lord and brother, I have been rejoicing and sorrowful—rejoicing in that I had heard that you had been tried on behalf of the name of our Lord Jesus Christ our Savior, and had confessed His name in the presence of the magistrates of the world; but sorrowful, in that from the time when I was in your company I have never been able to receive your letters. And now lately a twofold sorrow has fallen upon me; that although you knew that Montanus, our common brother, was coming to me from you out of the dungeon, you did not intimate anything to me concerning your wellbeing, nor about anything that is done in connection with you. This, however, continually happens to the servants of God, especially to those who are appointed for the confession of Christ. For I know that every one looks not now to the things that are of the world, but that he is hoping for a heavenly crown. Moreover, I said that perhaps you had forgotten to write to me. For if from the lowest place I may be called by you yours, or brother, if I should be worthy to hear myself named Celerinus;[96] yet, when I also was in such a purple confession,[96] I remembered my oldest brethren, and I took notice of them in my letters, that their former love was still around me and mine. Yet I beseech, beloved of the Lord, that if, first of all, you are washed in that sacred blood, and have suffered for the name of our Lord Jesus Christ before my letters find you in this world, or should they now reach you, that you would answer them to me. So may He crown you whose name you have confessed. For I believe, that although in this world we do not see each other, yet in the future we shall embrace one another in the presence of Christ. Entreat that I may be worthy, even I, to be crowned along with your company.

2. Know, nevertheless, that I am placed in the midst of a great tribulation; and, as if you were present with me, I remember your former love day and night, God only knows. And therefore I ask that you will grant my desire, and that you will grieve with me at the death of my sister,[97] who in this time of devastation has fallen from Christ; for she has sacrificed and provoked our Lord, as seems manifest to us. And for her deeds, I in this day of paschal rejoicing,[98] weeping day and night, have spent the days in tears, in sackcloth, and ashes, and I am still spending them so to this day, until the aid of our Lord Jesus Christ, and affection manifested through you, or through those my lords who have been crowned, from whom you are about to ask it, shall come to the help of so terrible a shipwreck. For I remember your former love, that you will grieve with all the rest for our sisters whom you also knew well—that is, Numeria and Candida—for whose sin, because they have us as brethren, we ought to keep watch. For I believe that Christ, according to their repentance and the works which they have done towards our banished colleagues who came from you—by whom themselves you will hear of their good works—that Christ, I say, will have mercy upon them, when you, His martyrs, beseech Him.

3. For I have heard that you have received the ministry of the purpled ones. Oh, happy are you, even sleeping on the ground, to obtain your wishes which you have always desired! You have desired to be sent into prison for His name's sake, which now has come to pass; as it is written, "The Lord grant you according to your own heart;"[99] and now made a priest of God over them, and the same their minister has acknowledged it. I ask, therefore my lord, and I entreat by our Lord Jesus Christ, that you will refer the case to the rest of your colleagues, your brethren, my lords, and ask from them, that whichever of you is first crowned, should remit such a great sin to those our sisters, Numeria and Candida. For this latter I have always called Etecusa[100]—God is my witness—because she gave gifts for herself that she might not sacrifice;[101] but she appears only to have ascended to the Tria Fata, and thence to have descended.[102] I know, therefore, that she has not sacrificed. Their cause having been lately heard, the chief rulers commanded them in the meantime to remain as they are, until a bishop should be appointed. But, as far as possible, by your holy prayers and petitions, in which we trust, since you are friends as well as witnesses of Christ, [we pray] that you would be indulgent in all these matters.

4. I entreat, therefore, beloved lord Lucian, be mindful of me, and acquiesce in my petition; so may Christ grant you that sacred crown which he has given you not only in confession but also in holiness, in which you have always walked and have always been an example to the saints as well as a witness, that you will relate to all my lords, your brethren the confessors, all about this matter, that they may receive help from you. For this, my lord and brother, you ought to know, that it is not I alone who ask this on their behalf, but also Statius and Severianus, and all the confessors who have come thence hither from you; to whom these very sisters went down to the harbor and took them up into the city, and they have ministered to sixty-five, and even to this day have tended them in all things, for all are with them. But I ought not to burden that sacred heart of yours any more, since I know that you will labor with a ready will. Macharius, with his sisters Cornelia and Emerita, salute you, rejoicing in your sanguinary confession, as well as in that of all the brethren, and Saturninus, who himself also wrestled with the devil, who also bravely confessed the name of Christ, who moreover, under the torture of the grappling claws, bravely confessed, and who also strongly begs and entreats this. Your brethren Calpurnius and Maria, and all the holy brethren, salute you. For you ought to know this too, that I have written also to my lords your brethren letters, which I request that you will deign to read to them.

NOTES

95. Though not written by or addressed to St. Cyprian, this letter is included in the *epistulae* because it concerns the reconciliation of the lapsed, something Cyprian wrote so extensively about, and is addressed to the confessors of Carthage. Cyprian will also get involved in this discussion afterwards (Letter 23).
96. A popular name for martyrdom int he 3rd century was the "purple confession," regarding to the garments of the martyrs being "purpled" by their blood. See Cyprian's use of this term in the conclusion of Letter 8.
97. Spiritual death, for his sister had apostasized during the persecution.
98. "[T]his day of paschal rejoicing;" this can only refer to Easter Sunday. Since the tone of this letter and the following apparenntly suggests that the persecution of Decius is still going on at this point, we can date the composition of this letter to Easter Sunday, 250 AD, which in that year fell on March 31st.
99. Ps. 20:4
100. Candida's nickname *Etecusa*, "because she gave gifts," is unintelligible etymologically. Some suggest this nickname is derived from *excusatam* (to make an excuse for or plead exemption for). Others suggest that Etecusa is the proper name and it is Numeria that is the nickname, because of its relation to the Latin verb *numeravit*, "she paid." The ambiguity of the passage is due to the poor grammar of Celerinus' writing.
101. This Etecusa had bribed the magistrates to obtain the required certificate of sacrifice without having to go through with the offering. This would have made her one of the *libellatici* (as opposed to the *lapsi*, who had actually sacrificed). Libellatici were usually subject to a two year penance.
102. The Tria Fata were statues of the three Fates or Sibyls supposedly set up by the Roman King Tarquinus Priscus (616-579 BC), making them the oldest statues in Rome. The statues still existed in the time of Augustus and stood near the Rostra Augusti in front of the Curia Iulia. By Cyprian's time the name Tria Fata referred to the whole area of the Roman Forum in front of the Curia Iulia, the location where accused Christians were compelled to sacrifice to the Roman gods. The aforesaid Etecusa went up to steps to the place of sacrifice at Tria Fata, but as she had bribed the magistrates to avoid having to sacrifice, she merely gave the appearance of sacrificing without actually doing so.

LETTER 21

LUCIAN REPLIES TO CELERINUS

1. Lucian to Celerinus, his lord,[103] and (if I shall be worthy to be called so) colleague in Christ, greeting. I have received your letter, most dearly beloved lord and brother, in which you have so laden me with expressions of kindness, that by reason of your so burdening me I was almost overcome with such excessive joy; so that I exulted in reading, by the benefit of your so great humility, the letter, which I also earnestly desired after so long a time to read, in which you deigned to call me to remembrance, saying to me in your writing, if I may be worthy to be called your brother, of a man such as I am who confessed the name of God with trembling before the inferior magistrates. For you, by God's will, when you confessed, not only frightened back the great serpent himself, the pioneer of Antichrist, but have conquered him, by that voice and those divine words, whereby I know how you love the faith, and how zealous you are for Christ's discipline, in which I know and rejoice that you are actively occupied. Now beloved, already to be esteemed among the martyrs, you have wished to overload me with your letter, in which you told us concerning our sisters, on whose behalf I wish that we could by possibility mention them without remembering also so great a crime committed. Assuredly we should not then think of them with so many tears as we do now.

2. You ought to know what has been done concerning us. When the blessed martyr Paulus[104] was still in the body, he called me and said to me: "Lucian, in the presence of Christ I say to you, if any one, after my being called away, shall ask for peace from you, grant it in my name."[105] Moreover, all of us whom the Lord has condescended in such tribulation to call away, by our letters, by mutual agreement, have given peace to all. You see, then, brother, how I have done this in part of what Paulus bade me, as what we in all cases decreed when we were in this tribulation, wherein by the command of the emperor we were ordered to be put to death by hunger and thirst, and were shut up in two cells, that so they might weaken us by hunger and thirst. Moreover, the fire from the effect of our torture was so intolerable that nobody could bear it. But now we have attained the brightness itself. And therefore, beloved brother, greet Numeria and Candida, who [shall have peace] according to the precept of Paulus,[106] and the rest of the martyrs whose names I subjoin: viz., Bassus in the dungeon of the perjured, Mappalicus at the torture, Fortunio in prison, Paulus after torture, Fortunata, Victorinus, Victor, Herennius, Julia, Martial, and Aristo, who by God's will were put to death in the prison by hunger, of whom in a few days you will hear of me as a companion. For now there are eight days, from the day in which I was shut up again, to the day in which I wrote my letter to you. For before these eight days, for five intervening days, I received a morsel of bread and water by measure. And therefore, brother, as here, since the Lord has begun to give peace to the Church itself, according to the precept of Paulus, and our tractate, the case being set forth before the bishop, and confession being made, I ask that not only these may have peace, but also [all] those whom you know to be very near to our heart.

3. All my colleagues greet you. Do you greet the confessors of the Lord who are there with you, whose names you have intimated, among whom also are Saturninus, with his companions, but who also is my colleague, and Maris,

Collecta, and Emerita, Calpurnius and Maria, Sabina, Spesina, and the sisters, Januaria, Dativa, Donata. We greet Saturus with his family, Bassianus and all the clergy, Uranius, Alexius, Quintainus, Colonica, and all whose names I have not written, because I am already weary. Therefore they must pardon me. I bid you heartily farewell, and Alexius, and Getulicus, and the money-changers, and the sisters. My sisters Januaria and Sophia, whom I commend to you, greet you.

NOTES

103. *Lord* was a common title of respect for bishops. We are reminded by St. Ignatius of Antioch that "we ought to regard the bishop as the Lord Himself" (*Ad Eph.*, 6:1).
104. Martyred in Carthage in 250 at the outbreak of the Decian persecution.
105. Some have attempted to attribute to this Paulus the origins of the whole practice of obtaining *libelli pacis* from the martyrs. However, the true origin of the practice goes back much further: Tertullian complains about abuses of *libelli pacis* in *Ad Martryas* 1 and *On Modesty* 22, the former of which was probably written around the year 200. In that passage, Tertullian mentions the seeking of *libelli pacis* from the martyrs as something the faithful "had been used" to doing, suggesting its origin lies even further back.
106. The ease with which Lucian granted indulgence to Numeria and Candida, without scrutinizing their cases individually or consulting the bishop, will lead Cyrpian to complain of this indulgence to the See of Rome. Of this letter Cyprian said, "Lucian wrote a letter in the name of all the confessors, in which well near every bond of faith, and fear of God, and the Lord's command, and the sacredness and sincerity of the Gospel were dissolved" (Letter 23:2).

LETTER 22

TO THE CLERGY ABIDING AT ROME, CONCERNING MANY OF THE CONFESSORS, AND CONCERNING THE FORWARDNESS OF LUCIAN AND THE MODESTY OF CELERINUS THE CONFESSOR

1. Cyprian to the presbyters and deacons abiding at Rome, his brethren, greeting. After the letters that I wrote to you,[107] beloved brethren, in which what I had done was explained, and some slight account was given of my discipline and diligence, there came another matter which, any more than the others, ought not to be concealed from you. For our brother Lucian, who himself also is one of the confessors, earnest indeed in faith, and robust in virtue, but little established in the reading of the Lord's word, has attempted certain things, constituting himself for a time an authority for unskilled people, so that certificates written by his hand were given indiscriminately to many persons in the name of Paulus; whereas Mappalicus the martyr, cautious and modest, mindful of the law and discipline, wrote no letters contrary to the Gospel, but only, moved with domestic affection for his mother, who had fallen, commanded peace to be given to her. Saturninus, moreover, after his torture, still remaining in prison, sent out no letters of this kind. But Lucian, not only while Paulus was still in prison, gave everywhere in his name certificates written with his own hand, but even after his decease persisted in doing the same things under his name, saying that this had been commanded him by Paulus, ignorant that he must obey the Lord rather than his fellow-servant. In the name also of Aurelius, a young man who had undergone the torture, many certificates were given, written by the hand of the same Lucian, because Aurelius did not know how to write himself.

2. In order, in some measure, to put a stop to this practice, I wrote letters to them, which I have sent to you under the enclosure of the former letter, in which I did not fail to ask and persuade them that consideration might be had for the law of the Lord and the Gospel. But after I sent my letters to them, that, as it were, something might be done more moderately and temperately; the same Lucian wrote a letter in the name of all the confessors, in which well near every bond of faith, and fear of God, and the Lord's command, and the sacredness and sincerity of the Gospel were dissolved. For he wrote in the name of all, that they had given peace to all, and that he wished that this decree should be communicated through me to the other bishops, of which letter I transmitted a copy to you. It was added indeed, of whom the account of what they have done since their crime has been satisfactory, a thing this which excites a greater odium against me, because I, when I have begun to hear the cases of each one and to examine into them, seem to deny to many what they now are all boasting that they have received from the martyrs and confessors.[108]

3. Finally, this seditious practice has already begun to appear; for in our province, through some of its cities, an attack has been made by the multitude upon their rulers, and they have compelled that peace to be given to them immediately which they all cried out had been once given to them by the martyrs and confessors.[109] Their rulers, being frightened and subdued, were of little avail to resist them, either by vigor of mind or by strength of faith. With us, moreover, some turbulent spirits, who in time past were with difficulty governed by me, and were delayed till my coming, were inflamed by this letter as if by a firebrand, and began to be more violent, and to extort the peace granted to them.[110] I have sent a copy to you of the letters that I wrote to my clergy about these matters, and, moreover, what Caldonius, my colleague, of his integrity and faithfulness wrote, and what I replied to him. I have sent both to you to read. Copies also of the letter of Celerinus, the good and stout confessor, which he wrote to Lucian the same confessor—also what Lucian replied to him—I have sent to you; that you may know both my labor in respect of everything, and my diligence, and might learn the truth itself, how moderate and cautious is Celerinus the confessor, and how reverent both in his humility and fear for our faith; while Lucian, as I have said, is less skillful concerning the understanding of the Lord's word, and by his facility, is mischievous on account of the dislike that he causes for my reverential dealing. For while the Lord has said that the nations are to be baptized in the name of the Father, and of the Son, and of the Holy Ghost, and their past sins are to be done away in baptism; this man, ignorant of the precept and of the law, commands peace to be granted and sins to be done away in the name of Paulus;[111] and he says that this was commanded him by Paulus, as you will observe in the letter sent by the same Lucian to Celerinus, in which he very little considered that it is not martyrs that make the Gospel, but that martyrs are made by the Gospel; since Paul also, the apostle whom the Lord called a chosen vessel unto Him, laid down in his epistle: "I marvel that you are so soon removed from Him that called you into the grace of Christ, unto another gospel: which is not another; but there be some that trouble you, and would pervert the Gospel of Christ. But though we, or an angel from heaven, preach any other gospel unto you than that which we have preached unto you, let him be accursed. As we said before, so say I now again, If any man preach any other gospel unto you than that you have received, let him be accursed."[112]

4. But your letter, which I received, written to my clergy, came opportunely; as also did those which the blessed confessors, Moyses and Maximus, Nicostratus, and the rest, sent to Saturninus and Aurelius, and the others, in which are contained the full vigor of the Gospel and the robust discipline of the law of the Lord. Your words much assisted me as I labored here, and withstood with the whole strength of faith the onset of ill-will, so that my work was shortened from above, and that before the letters which I last sent you reached you, you declared to me, that according to the Gospel law, your judgment also strongly and unanimously concurred with mine. I bid you, brethren, beloved and longed for, ever heartily farewell.

NOTES

107. Letter 3.
108. In reading this passage, it is important to keep in mind that Cyprian is not denying the practice of obtaining *libelli pacis* outright; he has no problem with the practice itself provided it is done circumspectly, under the authority of the bishop and supervision of the deacons. This letter should be read in conjunction with Letters 9 and 10 to the Carthaginian clergy.
109. Notice the novelty that Cyprian attributes to this practice. This is valuable testimony to the important role that penitence played in reconciliation during the first centuries of the Church.
110. Cyprian's opponents, possibly the same who complained to Rome of his departure at the outbreak of the persecution, have used the contention brought about by the *lapsi* controversy to further oppose Cyprian's governance of the church at Carthage. These opponents were led by Novatian, future anti-pope.
111. Besides being a valuable testimony to patristic belief in the regenerative powers of baptism, this passage also reveals an important distinction Cyprian develops between the forgiveness

of sins per se and the commutation of penance granted through the indulgence of the martyrs. He fears that, through a commutation of penance that is granted too hastily, the faithful will begin to confuse the forgiveness of sins obtained through baptism with the commutation of the penalties due to sin obtained through the indulgence. We see in this controversy the genesis of the distinction between the guilt of sin and the temporal punishment due to sin.

112. Gal. 1:8-9.

LETTER 23

TO THE CLERGY, ON THE LETTERS SENT TO ROME

Cyprian to the presbyters and deacons, his brethren, greeting. That nothing may be unknown to your consciousness, beloved brethren, of what was written to me and what I replied, I have sent you a copy of each letter, and I believe that my rejoinder will not displease you. But I ought to acquaint you in my letter concerning this, that for a very urgent reason I have sent a letter to the clergy who abide in the city. And since it behooved me to write by clergy, while I know that very many of ours are absent, and the few that are there are hardly sufficient for the ministry of the daily duty, it was necessary to appoint some new ones, who might be sent. Know, then, that I have made Saturus a reader, and Optatus, the confessor, a sub-deacon; whom already, by the general advice, we had made next to the clergy, in having entrusted to Saturus on Easter Day, once and again, the reading; and when with the teacher-presbyters we were carefully trying readers— in appointing Optatus from among the readers to be a teacher of the hearers[113]— examining, first of all, whether all things were found fitting in them, which ought to be found in such as were in preparation for the clerical office. Nothing new, therefore, has been done by me in your absence; but what, on the general advice of all of us had been begun, has, upon urgent necessity, been accomplished. I bid you, beloved brethren, ever heartily farewell; and remember me. Farewell.

NOTE

113. "Hearers;" in Latin *audientes*, a special class denoting those who were present in church but not yet baptized, so named because they would be conducted from the church after the readings, psalms and homily. In Carthage, these audientes were placed under the specific care of a catechist or teacher, called the *Audientium Doctor*. It is this office that Saturus has been elevated to by Cyprian.

LETTER 24

TO MOYSES AND MAXIMUS AND THE REST OF THE CONFESSORS AT ROME[114]

1. Cyprian to Moyses and Maximus, the presbyters, and to the other confessors, his very beloved brethren, greeting. I had already known from rumor, most brave and blessed brethren, the glory of your faith and virtue, rejoicing greatly and abundantly congratulating you, that the highest condescension of our Lord Jesus Christ should have prepared you for the crown by confession of His name. For you, who have become chiefs and leaders in the battle of our day, have set forward the standard of the celestial warfare; you have made a beginning of the spiritual contest which God has purposed to be now waged by your valor; you, with unshaken strength and unyielding firmness, have broken the first onset of the rising war. Thence have arisen happy openings of the fight; thence have begun good auspices of victory. It happened that here martyrdoms were consummated by tortures. But he who, preceding in the struggle, has been made an example of virtue to the brethren, is on common ground with the martyrs in honor. Hence you have delivered to us garlands woven by your hand, and have pledged your brethren from the cup of salvation.

2. To these glorious beginnings of confession and the omens of a victorious warfare, has been added the maintenance of discipline, which I observed from the vigor of your letter that you lately sent to your colleagues joined with you to the Lord in confession, with anxious admonition, that the sacred precepts of the Gospel and the commandments of life once delivered to us should be kept with firm and rigid observance. Behold another lofty degree of your glory; behold, with confession, a double title to deserving well of God—to stand with a firm step, and to drive away in this struggle, by the strength of your faith, those who endeavor to make a breach in the Gospel, and bring impious hands to the work of undermining the Lord's precepts—to have before afforded the indications of courage, and now to afford lessons of life. The Lord, when, after His resurrection, He sent forth His apostles, charges them, saying, "All power is given unto me in heaven and in earth. Go therefore, and teach all nations, baptizing them in the name of the Father, and of the Son, and of the Holy Ghost: teaching them to observe all things whatsoever I have commanded you."[115] And the Apostle John, remembering this charge, subsequently lays it down in his epistle: "Hereby," says he, "we do know that we know Him, if we keep His commandments. He that says he knows Him, and keeps not His commandments, is a liar, and the truth is not in him."[116] You prompt the keeping of these precepts; you observe the divine and heavenly commands. This is to be a confessor of the Lord; this is to be a martyr of Christ—to keep the firmness of one's profession inviolate among all evils, and secure. For to wish to become a martyr for the Lord, and to try to overthrow the Lord's precepts; to use against Him the condescension that He has granted you—to become, as it were, a rebel with arms that you have received from Him—this is to wish to confess Christ, and to deny Christ's Gospel. I rejoice, therefore, on your behalf, most brave and faithful brethren; and as much as I congratulate the martyrs there honored for the glory of their strength, so much do I also equally congratulate you for the crown of the Lord's discipline. The Lord has shed forth His condescension in manifold kinds of liberality. He has distributed the praises of good soldiers and their spiritual glories in plentiful variety. We also are sharers in your honor; we count your glory our glory, whose times have been brightened by such a felicity, that it should be the fortune of our day to see the proved servants of God and Christ's soldiers crowned. I bid you, most brave and blessed brethren, ever heartily farewell; and remember me.

NOTES

114. Written during the Decian persecution, 250 AD.
115. Matt. 28:18-20.
116. 1 John 2:3-4.

LETTER 25

MOYSES, MAXIMUS, NICOSTRATUS, AND THE OTHER CONFESSORS ANSWER THE FOREGOING LETTER, AD 250.

1. To Caecilius Cyprian, bishop of the church of the Carthaginians, Moyses and Maximus, presbyters, and Nicostratus and Rufinus, deacons, and the other confessors persevering in the faith of the truth, in God the Father, and in His Son Jesus Christ our Lord, and in the Holy Spirit, greeting. Placed, brother, as we are among various and manifold sorrows, on account of the present desolations of many brethren throughout almost the whole world, this chief consolation has reached us, that we have been lifted up by the receipt of your letter, and have gathered some alleviation for the griefs of our saddened spirit. From which we can already perceive that the grace of divine providence wished to keep us so long shut up in the prison chains, perhaps for no other reason than that, instructed and more vigorously animated by your letter, we might with a more earnest will attain to the destined crown. For your letter has shone upon us as a calm in the midst of a tempest, and as the longed-for tranquillity in the midst of a troubled sea, and as repose in labors, as health in dangers and pains, as in the densest darkness, the bright and glowing light. Thus we drank it up with a thirsty spirit, and received it with a hungry desire; so that we rejoice to find ourselves by it sufficiently fed and strengthened for encounter with the foe.[117] The Lord will reward you for that love of yours, and will restore you the fruit due to this so good work; for he who exhorts is not less worthy of the reward of the crown than he who suffers; not less worthy of praise is he who has taught, than he who has acted also; he is not less to be honored who has warned, than he who has fought; except that sometimes the weight of glory more redounds to him who trains, than to him who has shown himself a teachable learner; for the latter, perchance, would not have had what he has practiced, unless the former had taught him.

2. Therefore, again, we say, brother Cyprian, we have received great joy, great comfort, great refreshment, especially in that you have described, with glorious and deserved praises, the glorious, I will not say, deaths, but immortalities of martyrs. For such departures should have been proclaimed with such words, that the things which were related might be told in such manner as they were done. Thus, from your letter, we saw those glorious triumphs of the martyrs; and with our eyes in some sort have followed them as they went to heaven, and have contemplated them seated among angels, and the powers and dominions of heaven. Moreover, we have in some manner perceived with our ears the Lord giving them the promised testimony in the presence of the Father.[118] It is this, then, which also raises our spirit day by day, and inflames us to the following of the track of such dignity.

3. For what more glorious, or what more blessed, can happen to any man from the divine condescension, than to confess the Lord God, in death itself, before his very executioners? Than among the raging and varied and exquisite tortures of worldly power, even when the body is racked and torn and cut to pieces, to confess Christ the Son of God with a spirit still free, although departing? Than to have mounted to heaven with the world left behind? Than, having forsaken men, to stand among the angels? Than, all worldly impediments being broken through, already to stand free in the sight of God? Than to enjoy the heavenly kingdom without any delay? Than to have become an associate of Christ's passion in Christ's name? Than to have become by the divine condescension the judge of one's own judge? Than to have brought off an unstained conscience from the confession of His name? Than to have refused to obey human and sacrilegious laws against the faith? Than to have borne witness to the truth with a public testimony? Than, by dying, to have subdued death itself, which is dreaded by all? Than, by death itself, to have attained immortality? Than when torn to pieces, and tortured by all the instruments of cruelty, to have overcome the torture by the tortures themselves? Than by strength of mind to have wrestled with all the agonies of a mangled body? Than not to have shuddered at the flow of one's own blood? Than to have begun to love one's punishments, after having faith to bear them? Than to think it an injury to one's life not to have left it?

4. For to this battle our Lord, as with the trumpet of His Gospel, stimulates us when He says, "He that loves father or mother more than me is not worthy of me: and he that loves his own soul more than me is not worthy of me. And he that takes not his cross, and follows after me, is not worthy of me."[119] And again, "Blessed are they which are persecuted for righteousness' sake: for theirs is the kingdom of heaven. Blessed shall you be, when men shall persecute you, and hate you. Rejoice, and be exceeding glad: for so did their fathers persecute the prophets which were before you."[120] And again, "Because you shall stand before kings and powers, and the brother shall deliver up the brother to death, and the father the son, and he that endures to the end shall be saved;" and "To him that overcomes will I give to sit on my throne, even as I also overcame and am set down on the throne of my Father."[121] Moreover the apostle: "Who shall separate us from the love of Christ? Shall tribulation, or distress, or persecution, or famine, or nakedness, or peril, or sword? (As it is written, "For your sake are we killed all the day long; we are accounted as sheep for the slaughter.") Nay, in all these things we are more than conquerors for Him who has loved us."[122]

5. When we read these things, and things of the like kind, brought together in the Gospel, and feel, as it were, torches placed under us, with the Lord's words to inflame our faith, we not only do not dread, but we even provoke the enemies of the truth; and we have already conquered the opponents of God, by the very fact of our not yielding to them, and have subdued their nefarious laws against the truth. And although we have not yet shed our blood, we are prepared to shed it. Let no one think that this delay of our departure is any clemency; for it obstructs us, it makes a hindrance to our glory, it puts off heaven, it withholds the glorious sight of God. For in a contest of this kind, and in the kind of contest when faith is struggling in the encounter, it is not true clemency to put off martyrs by delay. Entreat therefore, beloved Cyprian, that of His mercy the Lord will every day more and more arm and adorn every one of us with greater abundance and readiness, and will confirm and strengthen us by the strength of His power; and, as a good captain, will at length bring forth His soldiers, whom He has hitherto trained and proved in the camp of our prison, to the field of the battle set before them. May He hold forth to us the divine arms, those weapons that know not how to be conquered—the breastplate of righteousness, which is never accustomed to be broken—the shield of faith, which cannot be pierced through—the helmet of salvation, which cannot be shattered—and the sword of the Spirit, which has never been wont to be injured. For to whom should we rather commit these things for him to ask for us, than to our so reverend bishop, as destined victims asking help of the priest?

6. Behold another joy of ours, that, in the duty of your episcopate, although in the meantime you have been, owing to the condition of the times, divided from your brethren, you have frequently confirmed the confessors by your letters; that you have ever afforded necessary supplies from your own just acquisitions; that in all things you have always shown yourself in some sense present; that in no part of your duty have you hung behind as a deserter. But what more strongly stimulated us to a greater joy we cannot be silent upon, but must describe with all the testimony of our voice. For we observe that you have both rebuked with fitting censure, and worthily, those who, unmindful of their sins, had, with hasty and eager desire, extorted peace from the presbyters in your absence, and those who, without respect for the Gospel, had with profane facility granted the holiness of the Lord unto dogs, and pearls to swine; although a great crime, and one which has extended with incredible destructiveness almost over the whole earth, ought only, as you yourself write, to be treated cautiously and with moderation, with the advice of all the bishops, presbyters, deacons, confessors, and even the laymen who abide fast, as in your letters you yourself also testify; so that, while wishing unseasonably to bring repairs to the ruins, we may not appear to be bringing about other and greater destruction, for where is the divine word left, if pardon be so easily granted to sinners?[123] Certainly their spirits are to be cheered and to be nourished up to the season of their maturity, and they are to be instructed from the Holy Scriptures how great and surpassing a sin they have committed. Nor let them be animated by the fact that they are many, but rather let them be checked by the fact that they are not few. An unblushing number has never been accustomed to have weight in extenuation of a crime; but shame, modesty, patience, discipline, humility, and subjection, waiting for the judgment of others upon itself, and bearing the sentence of others upon its own judgment—this it is which proves penitence; this it is which skins over a deep wound; this it is which raises up the ruins of the fallen spirit and restores them, which quells and restrains the burning vapor of their raging sins. For the physician will not give to the sick the food of healthy bodies, lest the unseasonable nourishment, instead of repressing, should stimulate the power of the raging disease—that is to say, lest what might have been sooner diminished by abstinence, should, through impatience, be prolonged by growing indigestion.

7. Hands, therefore, polluted with impious sacrifices must be purified with good works, and wretched mouths defiled with accursed food must be purged with words of true penitence, and the spirit must be renewed and consecrated in the recesses of the faithful heart. Let the frequent groanings of the penitents be heard; let faithful tears be shed from the eyes not once only, but again and again, so that those very eyes which wickedly looked upon idols may wash away, with tears that satisfy God, the unlawful things that they had done. Nothing is necessary for diseases but patience: they who are weary and weak wrestle with their pain; and so at length hope for health, if, by tolerating it, they can overcome their suffering; for unfaithful is the scar which the physician has too quickly produced; and the healing is undone by any little casualty, if the remedies be not used faithfully from their very slowness. The flame is quickly recalled again to a conflagration, unless the material of the whole fire be extinguished even to the extremest spark; so that men of this kind should justly know that even they themselves are more advantaged by the very delay, and that more trusty remedies are applied by the necessary postponement. Besides, where shall it be said that they who confess Christ are shut up in the keeping of a squalid prison, if they who have denied Him are in no peril of their faith?[124] Where, that they are bound in the cincture of chains in God's name, if they who have not kept the confession of God are not deprived of communion? Where, that the imprisoned martyrs lay down their glorious lives, if those who have forsaken the faith do not feel the magnitude of their dangers and their sins? But if they betray too much impatience, and demand communion with intolerable eagerness, they vainly utter with petulant and unbridled tongues those querulous and invidious reproaches which avail nothing against the truth, since they might have retained by their own right what now by a necessity, which they of their own free will have sought, they are compelled to sue for. For the faith which could confess Christ, could also have been kept by Christ in communion. We bid you, blessed and most glorious father, ever heartily farewell in the Lord; and have us in remembrance.

NOTES

117. Confession for Christ is a battle, a confrontation with the devil. See section 5 of the same letter.
118. Luke 12:18.
119. Matt. 10:37-38.
120. Matt. 5:10-12.
121. Mark 13:12; Rev. 3:21.
122. Rom. 8:35.
123. See *On the Lapsed* and Letters 8-13.
124. The premature reconciliation of the lapsed is an affront to the sacrifice martyrs.

LETTER 26

CYPRIAN TO THE LAPSED

1. Our Lord, whose precepts and admonitions we ought to observe, describing the honor of a bishop and the order of His Church, speaks in the Gospel, and says to Peter: "I say unto you, That you are Peter, and upon this rock will I build my Church; and the gates of hell shall not prevail against it. And I will give unto you the keys of the kingdom of heaven: and whatsoever you shall bind on earth shall be bound in heaven: and whatsoever you shall loose on earth shall be loosed in heaven."[125] Thence, through the changes of times and successions, the ordering of bishops and the plan of the Church flow onwards; so that the Church is founded upon the bishops, and every act of the Church is controlled by these same rulers. Since this, then, is founded on the divine law, I marvel that some, with daring temerity, have chosen to write to me as if they wrote in the name of the Church; when the Church is established in the bishop and the clergy, and all who stand fast in the faith. For far be it from the mercy of God and His uncontrolled might to suffer the number of the lapsed to be called the Church;[126] since it is written, "God is not the God of the dead, but of the living."[127] For we indeed desire that all may be made alive; and we pray that, by our supplications and groans, they may be restored to their original state. But if certain lapsed ones claim to be the Church, and if the Church be among them and in them, what is left but for us to ask of these very persons that they would deign to admit us into the Church? Therefore it behooves them to be submissive and quiet and modest, as those who ought to appease God, in remembrance of their sin, and not to write letters in the name of the Church, when they should rather be aware that they are writing to the Church.

2. But some who are of the lapsed have lately written to me, and are humble and meek and trembling and fearing God, and who have always labored in the Church gloriously and liberally, and who have never made a boast of their labor to the Lord, knowing that He has said, "When you shall have done all these things, say, 'We are unprofitable servants: we have done that which was our duty to do.'"[128] Thinking of which things, and although they had received certificates from the martyrs, nevertheless, that their satisfaction might be admitted by the Lord, these persons beseeching have written to me that they acknowledge their sin, and are truly repentant, and do not hurry rashly or importunately to secure peace; but that they are waiting for my presence, saying that even peace itself, if they should receive it when I was present, would be sweeter to them. How greatly I congratulate these, the Lord is my witness, who has condescended to tell what such, and such sort of servants deserve of His kindness. Which letters, as I lately received, and now read that you have written very differently, I beg that you will discriminate between your wishes; and whoever you are who have sent this letter, add your names to the certificate, and transmit the certificate to me with your several names. For I must first know to whom I have to reply; then I will respond to each of the matters that you have written, having regard to the mediocrity of my place and conduct. I bid you, beloved brethren, ever heartily farewell, and live quietly and tranquilly according to the Lord's discipline. Farewell.

NOTES

125. Matt. 16:18-19.

126. The sin of apostasy automatically put one outside the Church. Notice that St. Cyprian does not view spiritual life as possible without being in union with the Church. Those who have sinned by lapsing are called spiritually "dead" and are not regarded as part of the Church. To be cut off from the Church cuts one off from God, and if one loses God's grace through serious, public sin, they are presumed to be out of communion with the Church as well.

127. Matt. 22:32.
128. Luke 17:10.

LETTER 27

TO THE PRESBYTERS AND DEACONS[129]

1. Cyprian to the presbyters and deacons, his brethren, greeting. You have done uprightly and with discipline, beloved brethren, that, by the advice of my colleagues who were present, you have decided not to communicate[130] with Gaius the presbyter of Didda, and his deacon; who, by communicating with the lapsed,[131] and offering their oblations, have been frequently taken in their wicked errors; and who once and again, as you wrote to me, when warned by my colleagues not to do this, have persisted obstinately, in their presumption and audacity, deceiving certain brethren also from among our people, whose benefit we desire with all humility to consult, and whose salvation we take care for, not with affected adulation, but with sincere faith, that they may supplicate the Lord with true penitence and groaning and sorrow, since it is written, "Remember from whence you are fallen, and repent."[132] And again, the divine Scripture says, "Thus says the Lord, 'When you shall be converted and lament, then you shall be saved, and shall know where you have been.'"[133]

2. Yet how can those mourn and repent, whose groanings and tears some of the presbyters obstruct when they rashly think that they may be communicated with, not knowing that it is written, "They who call you happy cause you to err, and destroy the path of your feet?"[134] Naturally, our wholesome and true counsels have no success, while the salutary truth is hindered by mischievous blandishments and flatteries, and the wounded and unhealthy mind of the lapsed suffers what those also who are bodily diseased and sick often suffer; that while they refuse wholesome food and beneficial drink as bitter and distasteful, and crave those things which seem to please them and to be sweet for the present, they are inviting to themselves mischief and death by their recklessness and intemperance. Nor does the true remedy of the skillful physician avail to their safety, while the sweet enticement is deceiving with its charms.

3. Do you, therefore, according to my letters, take counsel about this faithfully and wholesomely, and do not recede from better counsels; and be careful to read these same letters to my colleagues also, if there are any present, or if any should come to you; that, with unanimity and concord, we may maintain a healthful plan for soothing and healing the wounds of the lapsed, intending to deal very fully with all when, by the Lord's mercy, we shall begin to assemble together. In the meantime, if any unrestrained and impetuous person, whether of our presbyters or deacons or of strangers, should dare, before our decree, to communicate with the lapsed, let him be expelled from our communion, and plead the cause of his rashness before all of us when, by the Lord's permission, we shall assemble together again. Moreover, you wished me to reply what I thought concerning Philumenus and Fortunatus, sub-deacons, and Favorinus, an acolyte, who retired in the midst of the time of trial, and have now returned. Of which thing I cannot make myself sole judge, since many of the clergy are still absent, and have not considered, even thus late, that they should return to their place; and this case of each one must be considered separately and fully investigated, not only with my colleagues, but also with the whole of the people themselves. For a matter which hereafter may constitute an example as regards the ministers of the Church must be weighed and adjudged with careful deliberation. In the meanwhile, let them only abstain from the monthly division, not so as to seem to be deprived of the ministry of the Church, but that all matters being in a sound state, they may be reserved till my coming. I bid you, beloved brethren, ever heartily farewell. Greet all the brotherhood, and farewell.

NOTES

129. Written towards the end of the Decian persecution but while many of the clergy were still in hiding, as Cyprian says "many of the clergy are still absent."
130. Communicate in the sense of the receive Holy Communion with.
131. The assumption here is that these are *lapsi* who have not yet confessed and been absolved from their sin but are nevertheless receiving Holy Communion.
132. Rev. 2:5.
133. Isa. 30:15.
134. The Septuagint translation of Isaiah 3:12.

LETTER 28

TO THE PRESBYTERS AND DEACONS
ABIDING AT ROME

Cyprian to the presbyters and deacons abiding at Rome, his brethren, greeting. Both our common love and the reason of the thing demand, beloved brethren, that I should keep back from your knowledge nothing of those matters which are transacted among us, that so we may have a common plan for the advantage of the administration of the Church.[135] For after I wrote to you the letter which I sent by Saturus the reader, and Optatus the sub-deacon, the combined temerity of certain of the lapsed, who refuse to repent and to make satisfaction to God, wrote to me, not asking that peace might be given to them, but claiming it as already given; because they say that Paulus has given peace to all,[136] as you will read in their letter of which I have sent you a copy, as well as what I briefly replied to them in the meantime. But that you may also know what sort of a letter I afterwards wrote to the clergy, I have, moreover, sent you a copy of this.[137] But if, after all, their temerity should not be repressed either by my letters or by yours, and should not yield to wholesome counsels, I shall take such proceedings as the Lord, according to His Gospel, has enjoined to be taken. I bid you, beloved brethren, ever heartily farewell.

NOTES

135. Cyprian sees it as essential to his episcopal mission that his bishopric and the See of Rome be united in their course of action; see also Letter 14:3.
136. See Letter 21 for Paulus.
137. Letter 23.

LETTER 29

THE PRESBYTERS AND DEACONS ABIDING
AT ROME, TO CYPRIAN[138]

1. The presbyters and deacons abiding at Rome, to Father Cyprian, greeting. When, beloved brother, we carefully read your letter which you had sent by Fortunatus the sub-deacon, we were smitten with a double sorrow, and disordered with a twofold grief, that there was not any rest given to you in such necessities of the persecution, and that the unreasonable petulance of the lapsed brethren was declared to be carried even to a dangerous boldness of expression. But although those things which we have spoken of severely afflicted us and our spirit, yet your rigor and the severity that you have used, according to the proper discipline, moderates the so heavy load of our grief, in that you rightly restrain the wickedness of some, and, by your exhortation to repentance, show the legitimate way of salvation. That they should have wished to hurry to such an extreme as this, we are indeed considerably surprised; as that with such urgency, and at so unseasonable and bitter a time, being in so great and excessive a sin, they should not so much ask for, as claim, peace for themselves; nay, should say that they already have it in heaven. If they have it, why do they ask for what they possess? But if, by the very fact that they are asking for it, it is proved that they have it not, wherefore do they not accept the judgment of those from whom they have thought fit to ask for the peace, which they certainly have not got? But if they think that they have from any other source the prerogative of communion, let them try to compare it with the Gospel, that so at length it may abundantly avail them, if it is not out of harmony with the Gospel law.[139] But on what principle can that give Gospel communion which seems to be established contrary to Gospel truth? For since every prerogative contemplates the privilege of association, precisely on the assumption of its not being out of harmony with the will of Him with whom it seeks to be associated; then, because this is alien from His will with whom it seeks to be associated, it must of necessity lose the indulgence[140] and privilege of the association.[141]

2. Let them, then, see what it is they are trying to do in this matter. For if they say that the Gospel has established one decree, but the martyrs have established another; then they, setting the martyrs at variance with the Gospel, will be in danger on both sides. For, on the one hand, the majesty of the Gospel will already appear shattered and cast down, if it can be overcome by the novelty of another decree; and, on the other, the glorious crown of confession will be taken from the heads of the martyrs, if they be not found to have attained it by the observation of that Gospel whence they become martyrs;[142] so that, reasonably, no one should be more careful to determine nothing contrary to the Gospel, than he who strives to receive the name of martyr from the Gospel. We should like, besides, to be informed of this: if martyrs become martyrs for no other reason than that by not sacrificing they may keep the peace of the Church even to the shedding of their own blood, lest, overcome by the suffering of the torture, by losing peace, they might lose salvation; on what principle do they think that the salvation, which if they had sacrificed they thought that they should not have, was to be given to those who are said to have sacrificed;[143] although they ought to maintain that law in others which they themselves appear to have held before their own eyes? In which thing we observe that they have put forward against their own cause the very thing which they thought made for them. For if the martyrs thought that peace was to be granted to them, why did not they themselves grant it? Why did they think that, as they themselves say, they were to be referred to the bishops? For he who orders a thing to be done, can assuredly do that which he orders to be done. But, as we understand, nay, as the case itself speaks and proclaims, the most holy martyrs thought that a proper measure of modesty and of truth must be observed on both sides. For as they were urged by many, in remitting them to the bishop they conceived that they would consult their own modesty so as to be no further disquieted; and in themselves not holding communion with them, they judged that the purity of the Gospel law ought to be maintained unimpaired.[144]

3. But of your charity, brother, never desist from soothing the spirits of the lapsed and affording to the erring the medicine of truth, although the temper of the sick is wont to reject the kind offices of those who would heal them. This wound of the lapsed is as yet fresh, and the sore is still rising into a tumor; and therefore we are certain, that when, in the course of more protracted time, that urgency of theirs shall have worn out, they will love that very delay which refers them to a faithful medicine; if only there be not those who arm them for their own danger, and, instructing them perversely, demand on their behalf, instead of the salutary remedies of delay, the fatal poisons of a premature communion. For we do not believe, that without the instigation of certain persons they would all have dared so petulantly to claim peace for themselves. We know the faith of the Carthaginian church, we know her training, we know her humility; whence also we have marvelled that we should observe certain things somewhat rudely suggested against you by letter, although we have often become aware of your mutual love and charity, in many illustrations of reciprocal affection of one another. It is time, therefore, that they should repent of their fault, that they should prove their grief for their lapse, that they should show modesty, that they should manifest humility, that they should exhibit some shame, that, by their submission, they should appeal to God's clemency for themselves, and by due honor for God's priest should draw forth upon themselves the divine mercy. How vastly better would have been the letters of these men themselves, if the prayers of those who stood fast had been aided by their own humility, since that which is asked for is more easily obtained when he for whom it is asked is worthy, that what is asked should be obtained.

4. In respect, however, of Privatus of Lambesa, you have acted as you usually do, in desiring to inform us of the matter, as being an object of anxiety; for it becomes us all to watch for the body of the whole Church, whose members are scattered through every various province. But the deceitfulness of that crafty man could not be hid from us even before we had your letters; for previously, when from the company of that very wickedness a certain Futurus came, a standard-bearer of Privatus, and was desirous of fraudulently obtaining letters from us, we were neither ignorant who he was, nor did he get the letters which he wanted. We bid you heartily farewell in the Lord.

NOTES

138. This letter is a response to Letter 28.
139. A reference to Matthew 10:33 and its parallel Luke 12:9, which reads, "But he that shall deny me before men, I will also deny him before my Father who is in heaven." This was the "Gospel law" regarding apostasy, which the Roman presbyters here argue trumps any claims to the contrary made by the unreconciled *lapsi*.
140. *Indulgentia*, the terms that would later be applied to the remission of the temporal punishments due to sin that finds its origin in the letters of peace (*libelli pacis*) granted by the martyrs.
141. In other words, all of the promises and blessings promised in the Gospel to the faithful presuppose that they remain in communion with the Church and have not, through apostasy or some other sin, cut themselves off from God's grace and put themselves outside the Church's communion. It is therefore foolish for the lapsed to speak about the promises and prerogatives of the Gospel promised to the faithful if they themselves are no longer counted among the faithful, having lost the "privilege of association."
142. The arrogant presumption of the lapsed is offensive to the sacrifice of the martyrs. St. Cyprian makes a similar argument in Letter 25:7
143. The *libellatici*, those who bribed a magistrate to obtain a certificate of sacrifice (*libellus*)

without actually making a sacrifice.

144. The Roman presbyters are here commending the practice of those prudent confessors who, rather than grant peace liberally to all the lapsed who asked for it, followed the advice of Cyprian and others of like opinion in awaiting the judgment of the bishops in the matter. See Letters 9 and 10.

LETTER 30

THE ROMAN CLERGY TO CYPRIAN

1. To Father Cyprian, the presbyters and deacons abiding at Rome, greeting.[145] Although a mind conscious to itself of uprightness, and relying on the vigor of evangelical discipline, and made a true witness to itself in the heavenly decrees, is accustomed to be satisfied with God for its only judge, and neither to seek the praises nor to dread the charges of any other, yet those are worthy of double praise, who, knowing that they owe their conscience to God alone as the judge, yet desire that their doings should be approved also by their brethren themselves. It is no wonder, brother Cyprian, that you should do this, who, with your usual modesty and inborn industry, have wished that we should be found not so much judges of, as sharers in, your counsels, so that we might find praise with you in your doings while we approve them; and might be able to be fellow-heirs with you in your good counsels, because we entirely accord with them. In the same way we are all thought to have labored in that in which we are all regarded as allied in the same agreement of censure and discipline.[146]

2. For what is there either in peace so suitable, or in a war of persecution so necessary, as to maintain the due severity of the divine rigor? Which he who resists, will of necessity wander in the unsteady course of affairs, and will be tossed here and there by the various and uncertain storms of things; and the helm of counsel being, as it were, wrenched from his hands he will drive the ship of the Church's safety among the rocks; so that it would appear that the Church's safety can be no otherwise secured, than by repelling any who set themselves against it as adverse waves, and by maintaining the ever-guarded rule of discipline itself as if it were the rudder of safety in the tempest. Nor is it now but lately that this counsel has been considered by us, nor have these sudden appliances against the wicked but recently occurred to us; but this is read of among us as the ancient severity, the ancient faith, the ancient discipline, since the apostle would not have published such praise concerning us, when he said that "your faith is spoken of throughout the whole world"[147] unless already from thence that vigor had borrowed the roots of faith from those times; from which praise and glory it is a very great crime to have become degenerate. For it is less disgrace never to have attained to the heraldry of praise, than to have fallen from the height of praise; it is a smaller crime not to have been honored with a good testimony, than

345

to have lost the honor of good testimonies; it is less discredit to have lain without the announcement of virtues, ignoble without praise, than, disinherited of the faith, to have lost our proper praises. For those things which are proclaimed to the glory of any one, unless they are maintained by anxious and careful pains, swell up into the odium of the greatest crime.[148]

3. That we are not saying this dishonestly, our former letters have proved, wherein we have declared our opinion to you with a very plain statement, both against those who had betrayed themselves as unfaithful by the unlawful presentation of wicked certificates, as if they thought that they would escape those ensnaring nets of the devil; whereas, not less than if they had approached to the wicked altars, they were held fast by the very fact that they had testified to him; and against those who had used those certificates when made, although they had not been present when they were made, since they had certainly asserted their presence by ordering that they should be so written. For he is not guiltless of wickedness who has bidden it to be done; nor is he unconcerned in the crime with whose consent it is publicly spoken of, although it was not committed by him. And since the whole mystery of faith is understood to be contained in the confession of the name of Christ, he who seeks for deceitful tricks to excuse himself, has denied Christ; and he who wants to appear to have satisfied either edicts or laws put forth against the Gospel, has obeyed those edicts by the very fact by which he wished to appear to have obeyed them. Moreover, also, we have declared our faith and consent against those, too, who had polluted their hands and their mouths with unlawful sacrifices, whose own minds were before polluted; whence also their very hands and mouths were polluted also. Far be it from the Roman Church to slacken her vigor with so profane a facility, and to loosen the nerves of her severity by overthrowing the majesty of faith;[149] so that, when the wrecks of your ruined brethren are still not only lying, but are falling around, remedies of a too hasty kind, and certainly not likely to avail, should be afforded for communion; and by a false mercy, new wounds should be impressed on the old wounds of their transgression; so that even repentance should be snatched from these wretched beings, to their greater overthrow. For where can the medicine of indulgence profit, if even the physician himself, by intercepting repentance, makes easy way for new dangers, if he only hides the wound, and does not suffer the necessary remedy of time to close the scar? This is not to cure, but, if we wish to speak the truth, to slay.

4. Nevertheless, you have letters agreeing with our letters from the confessors, whom the dignity of their confession has still shut up here in prison, and whom, for the Gospel contest, their faith has once already crowned in a glorious confession; letters wherein they have maintained the severity of the Gospel discipline, and have revoked the unlawful petitions, so that they might not be a disgrace to the Church. Unless they had done this, the ruins of Gospel discipline would not easily be restored, especially since it was to none so fitting to maintain the tenor of evangelical vigor unimpaired, and its dignity, as to those who had given themselves up to be tortured and cut to pieces by raging men on behalf of the Gospel, that they might not deservedly forfeit the honor of martyrdom, if, on the occasion of martyrdom, they had wished to be betrayers of the Gospel. For he who does not guard what he has, in that condition whereon he possesses it, by violating the condition whereon he possesses it, loses what he possessed.

5. In which matter we ought to give you also, and we do give you, abundant thanks, that you have brightened the darkness of their prison by your letters; that you came to them in whatever way you could enter; that you refreshed their minds, robust in their own faith and confession, by your addresses and letters; that, following up their felicities with worthy praises, you have inflamed them to a much more ardent desire of heavenly glory; that you urged them forward; that you animated, by the power of your discourse, those who, as we believe and hope, will be victors by and by; so that although all may seem to come from the faith of those who confess, and from the divine mercy, yet they seem in their martyrdom to have become in some sort debtors to you. But once more, to return to the point whence our discourse appears to have digressed, you shall find subjoined the sort of letters that we also sent to Sicily; although upon us is incumbent a greater necessity of delaying this affair; having, since the departure of Fabian of most noble memory,[150] had no bishop appointed as yet,[151] on account of the difficulties of affairs and times, who can arrange all things of this kind, and who can take account of those who are lapsed, with authority and wisdom. However, what you also have yourself declared in so important a matter, is satisfactory to us, that the peace of the Church must first be maintained; then, that an assembly for counsel being gathered together, with bishops, presbyters, deacons, and confessors, as well as with the laity who stand fast, we should deal with the case of the lapsed. For it seems extremely invidious and burdensome to examine into what seems to have been committed by many, except by the advice of many; or that one should give a sentence when so great a crime is known to have gone forth, and to be diffused among so many; since that cannot be a firm decree which shall not appear to have had the consent of very many. Look upon almost the whole world devastated, and observe that the remains and the ruins of the fallen are lying about on every side, and consider that therefore an extent of counsel is asked for, large in proportion as the crime appears to be widely propagated. Let not the medicine be less than the wound, let not the remedies be fewer than the deaths, that in the same manner as those who fell, fell for this reason that they were too incautious with a blind rashness, so those who strive to set in order this mischief should use every moderation in counsels, lest anything done as it ought not to be, should, as it were, be judged by all of no effect.

6. Thus, with one and the same counsel, with the same prayers and tears, let us, who up to the present time seem to have escaped the destruction of these times of ours, as well as those who appear to have fallen into those calamities of the time, entreat the divine majesty, and ask peace for the Church's name. With mutual prayers, let us by turns cherish, guard, arm one another; let us pray for the lapsed, that they may be raised up; let us pray for those who stand, that they may not be tempted to such a degree as to be destroyed; let us pray that those who are said to have fallen may acknowledge the greatness of their sin, and may perceive that it needs no momentary nor over-hasty cure; let us pray that penitence may follow also the effects of the pardon of the lapsed; that so, when they have understood their own crime, they may be willing to have patience with us for a while, and no longer disturb the fluctuating condition of the Church, lest they may seem themselves to have inflamed an internal persecution for us, and the fact of their unquietness be added to the heap of their sins. For modesty is very greatly fitting for them in whose sins it is an immodest mind that is condemned. Let them indeed knock at the doors, but assuredly let them not break them down; let them present themselves at the threshold of the church, but certainly let them not leap over it; let them watch at the gates of the heavenly camp, but let them be armed with modesty, by which they perceive that they have been deserters; let them resume the trumpet of their prayers, but let them not therewith sound a point of war; let them arm themselves indeed with the weapons of modesty, and let them resume the shield of faith, which they had put off by their denial through the fear of death, but let those that are even now armed believe that they are armed against their foe, the devil, not against the Church, which grieves over their fall. A modest petition will much avail them; a bashful entreaty, a necessary humility, a patience which is not careless. Let them send tears as their ambassadors for their sufferings; let groanings, brought forth from their deepest heart, discharge the office of advocate, and prove their grief and shame for the crime they have committed.

7. Nay, if they shudder at the magnitude of the guilt incurred; if with a truly medicinal hand they deal with the deadly wound of their heart and conscience and the deep recesses of the subtle mischief, let them blush even to ask; except, again, that it is a matter of greater risk and shame not to have besought the aid of peace. But let all this be in the sacrament;[152] in the law of their very entreaty let consideration be had for the time; let it be with downcast entreaty, with subdued petition, since he also who is besought ought to be bent, not provoked; and as the divine clemency ought to be looked to, so also ought the divine censure; and as it is written, "I forgave you all that debt, because you desired me,"[153] so it is written, "Whosoever shall deny me before men, him will I also deny before my Father and before His angels."[154] For God, as He is merciful, so He exacts obedience to His precepts, and indeed carefully exacts it; and as He invites to the banquet, so the man that has not a wedding garment He binds hands and feet, and casts him out beyond the assembly of the saints.[155] He has prepared heaven, but He has also prepared hell. He has prepared places of refreshment, but He has also prepared eternal punishment. He has prepared the light that none can approach unto, but He has also prepared the vast and eternal gloom of perpetual night.

8. Desiring to maintain the moderation of this middle course in these matters, we for a long time, and indeed many of us, and, moreover, with some of the bishops who are near to us and within reach, and some whom, placed afar off, the heat of the persecution had driven out from other provinces, have thought that nothing new was to be done before the appointment of a bishop; but we believe that the care of the lapsed must be moderately dealt with, so that, in the meantime, while the grant of a bishop is withheld from us by God, the cause of such as are able to bear the delays of postponement should be kept in suspense; but of such as impending death does not suffer to bear the delay, having repented and professed a detestation of their deeds with frequency; if with tears, if with groans, if with weeping they have betrayed the signs of a grieving and truly penitent spirit, when there remains, as far as man can tell, no hope of living; to them, finally, such cautious and careful help should be ministered, God Himself knowing what He will do with such, and in what way He will examine the balance of His judgment; while we, however, take anxious care that neither ungodly men should praise our smooth facility, nor truly penitent men accuse our severity as cruel. We bid you, most blessed and glorious father, ever heartily farewell in the Lord; and have us in memory.

NOTES

145. Mention of the Bishop of Rome is absent is these letters, as Pope Fabian had been martyred in January, 250 at the outset of the persecution. The See of Rome would remain vacant for fourteen months until the election of Pope Cornelius in March, 251.

146. An interesting passage: the Roman presbyters seem to suggest that, although they could have approved Cyprian's leadership as "judges," by the affection they bear him and by his modesty they prefer to address him "not so much judges of" his conduct, but rather as "sharers" in his labors. This suggests the existence formal authority of the See of Rome over the church of Carthage which was in practice governed by charity and mutual affection. This paternal authority of Rome over the universal Church is also possibly hinted at in Letter 29:4: "For it

becomes us all [the clergy of the Roman See?] to watch for the body of the whole Church, whose members are scattered through every various province."

147. Rom. 1:8

148. The Roman presbyters suggest that "by careful and anxious pains" they have maintained the "ever-guarded rule of discipline," that "ancient faith" and have not lost their "good testimonies" and "proper praises."

149. The Roman presbyters consider it preposterous that the Roman Church should ever "overthrow the majesty of faith."

150. Pope St. Fabian, martyed January, 250; Feast Day January 20th. The Roman Martyrology for the day says: "At Rome, the birthday of St. Fabian, pope, who suffered martyrdom in the time of Decius, and was buried in the cemetery of Callistus."

151. There was a fourteen month interregnum between the martyrdom of Fabian in January, 250 and the election of Cornelius in March, 251.

152. *In sacramento*, perhaps meaning in a manner keeping with ecclesiastical discipline, or perhaps a reference to the sacrament of penance and the expected dispositions the Roman presbyters have of the penitents who approach the Church for forgiveness.

153. Matt. 18:32.

154. Matt. 10:33.

155. Matt. 22:11-12.

LETTER 31

TO THE CARTHAGINIAN CLERGY,
ABOUT THE LETTERS SENT TO ROME

Cyprian to the presbyters and deacons, his brethren, greeting. That you, my beloved brethren, might know what letters I have sent to the clergy acting at Rome, and what they have replied to me, and, moreover, what Moyses and Maximus, the presbyters, and Rufinus and Nicostratus, the deacons, and the rest of the confessors that with them are kept in prison, replied likewise to my letters, I have sent you copies to read. Do you take care, with as much diligence as you can, that what I have written, and what they have replied, be made known to our brethren. And, moreover, if any bishops from foreign places, my colleagues, or presbyters, or deacons, should be present, or should arrive among you, let them hear all these matters from you; and if they wish to transcribe copies of the letters and to take them to their own people, let them have the opportunity of transcribing them; although I have, moreover, bidden Saturus the reader, our brother, to give liberty of copying them to any individuals who wish it; so that, in ordering, for the present, the condition of the Church in any manner, an agreement, one and faithful, may be observed by all. But about the other matters which were to be dealt with, as I have also written to several of my colleagues, we will more fully consider them in a common council, when, by the Lord's permission, we shall begin to assemble into one place. I bid you, brethren, beloved and longed-for, ever heartily farewell. Salute the brotherhood. Farewell.

LETTER 32

TO THE CLERGY AND PEOPLE, ABOUT THE ORDINATION OF AURELIUS AS A READER.

1. Cyprian to the elders and deacons, and to the whole people, greeting. In ordinations of the clergy, beloved brethren, we usually consult you beforehand, and weigh the character and deserts of individuals, with the general advice. But human testimonies must not be waited for when the divine approval precedes. Aurelius, our brother, an illustrious youth, already approved by the Lord, and dear to God, in years still very young, but, in the praise of virtue and of faith, advanced; inferior in the natural abilities of his age, but superior in the honor he has merited—has contended here in a double conflict, having twice confessed and twice been glorious in the victory of his confession, both when he conquered in the course and was banished, and when at length he fought in a severer conflict, he was triumphant and victorious in the battle of suffering. As often as the adversary wished to call forth the servants of God, so often this prompt and brave soldier both fought and conquered. It had been a slight matter, previously to have engaged under the eyes of a few when he was banished; he deserved also in the forum to engage with a more illustrious virtue so that, after overcoming the magistrates, he might also triumph over the proconsul, and, after exile, might vanquish tortures also. Nor can I discover what I ought to speak most of in him— the glory of his wounds or the modesty of his character; that he is distinguished by the honor of his virtue, or praiseworthy for the admirableness of his modesty. He is both so excellent in dignity and so lowly in humility, that it seems that he is divinely reserved as one who should be an example to the rest for ecclesiastical discipline, of the way in which the servants of God should in confession conquer by their courage, and, after confession, be conspicuous for their character.[156]

2. Such a one, to be estimated not by his years but by his deserts, merited higher degrees of clerical ordination and larger increase. But, in the meantime, I judged it well, that he should begin with the office of reading;[157] because nothing is more suitable for the voice which has confessed the Lord in a glorious utterance, than to sound Him forth in the solemn repetition of the divine lessons; than, after the sublime words which spoke out the witness of Christ, to read the Gospel of Christ whence martyrs are made; to come to the desk after the scaffold; there to have been conspicuous to the multitude of the Gentiles, here to be beheld by the brethren; there to have been heard with the wonder of the surrounding people, here to be heard with the joy of the brotherhood. Know, then, most beloved brethren, that this man has been ordained by me and by my colleagues who were then present. I know that you will both gladly welcome these tidings, and that you desire that as many such as possible may be ordained in our church. And since joy is always hasty, and gladness can bear no delay, he reads on the Lord's day, in the meantime, for me;[158] that is, he has made a beginning of peace, by solemnly entering on his office of a reader. Do you frequently be urgent in supplications, and assist my prayers by yours, that the Lord's mercy favoring us may soon restore both the priest safe to his people, and the martyr for a reader with the priest. I bid you, beloved brethren in God the Father, and in Jesus Christ, ever heartily farewell.

NOTES

156. In Aurelius we see it evident that not all those who confessed Christ were subsequently put to death but suffered according to the whim of their judges, sometimes more, sometimes less than the law demanded. In Aurelius' case, he confessed before local magistrates (and later a proconsul) and suffered exile and torture.

157. The office of *lector* was an eminent position in the early Church, requiring a higher standard of education than most offices. The lectors were ordained by the laying on of hands by the bishop, accompanied by certain prayers, and were responsible for reading all the lessons in the liturgy, including the Epistle and Gospel. The Council of Carthage (398) lays down the following rule for the appointment of lectors by the bishop: "When a reader is ordained let the bishop speak about him to the people, pointing out his faith and life and skill" (Canon 8), which is what we see Cyprian doing here by letter, though a century and a half earlier. The role of reading the Gospel was taken over by the deacons around the 5th century, while the reading of the Epistle later fell to the sub-deacon.

158. He performs the readings for Cyprian in his absence.

LETTER 33

TO THE CLERGY AND PEOPLE, ABOUT THE ORDINATION
OF CELERINUS AS READER[159]

1. Cyprian to the presbyters and deacons, and to the whole people, his brethren in the Lord, greeting. The divine benefits, beloved brethren, should be acknowledged and embraced, wherewith the Lord has condescended to embellish and illustrate His Church in our times by granting a respite to His good confessors and His glorious martyrs, that they who had grandly confessed Christ should afterwards adorn Christ's clergy in ecclesiastical ministries. Exult, therefore, and rejoice with me on receiving my letter, wherein I and my colleagues who were then present mention to you Celerinus, our brother, glorious alike for his courage and his character, as added to our clergy, not by human recommendation, but by divine condescension; who, when he hesitated to yield to the Church, was constrained by her own admonition and exhortation, in a vision by night, not to refuse our persuasions;[160] and she had more power, and constrained him, because it was not right, nor was it becoming, that he should be without ecclesiastical honor, whom the Lord honored with the dignity of heavenly glory.

2. This man was the first in the struggle of our days; he was the leader among Christ's soldiers; he, in the midst of the burning beginnings of the persecution, engaged with the very chief and author of the disturbance, in conquering with invincible firmness the adversary of his own conflict. He made a way for others to conquer; a victor with no small amount of wounds, but triumphant by a miracle, with the long-abiding and permanent penalties of a tedious conflict. For nineteen days, shut up in the close guard of a dungeon, he was racked and in irons; but although his body was laid in chains, his spirit remained free and at liberty. His flesh wasted away by the long endurance of hunger and thirst; but God fed his soul, that lived in faith and virtue, with spiritual nourishments. He lay in punishments, the stronger for his punishments; imprisoned, greater than those that imprisoned him; lying prostrate, but loftier than those who stood; as bound, and firmer than the links which bound him; judged, and more sublime than those who judged him; and although his feet were bound on the rack, yet the serpent was trodden on and ground down and vanquished. In his glorious body shine the bright evidences of his wounds; their manifest traces show forth, and appear on the man's sinews and limbs, worn out with tedious wasting away. Great things are they—marvellous things are they—which the brotherhood may hear of his virtues and of his praises. And should any one appear like Thomas, who has little faith in what he hears, the faith of the eyes is not wanting, so that what one hears he may also see. In the servant of God, the glory of the wounds made the victory; the memory of the scars preserves that glory.

3. Nor is that kind of title to glories in the case of Celerinus, our beloved, an unfamiliar and novel thing. He is advancing in the footsteps of his kindred; he rivals his parents and relations in equal honors of divine condescension. His grandmother, Celerina, was some time since crowned with martyrdom. Moreover, his paternal and maternal uncles, Laurentius and Egnatius, who themselves also were once warring in the camps of the world, but were true and spiritual soldiers of God, casting down the devil by the confession of Christ, merited palms and crowns from the Lord by their illustrious passion. We always offer sacrifices for them,[161] as you remember, as often as we celebrate the passions and days of the martyrs in the annual commemoration. Nor could he, therefore, be degenerate and inferior whom this family dignity and a generous nobility provoked, by domestic examples of virtue and faith. But if in a worldly family it is a matter of heraldry and of praise to be a patrician, of how much greater praise and honor is it to become of noble rank in the celestial heraldry! I cannot tell whom I should call more blessed—whether those ancestors, for a posterity so illustrious, or him, for an origin so glorious. So equally between them does the divine condescension flow, and pass to and fro, that, just as the dignity of their offspring brightens their crown, so the sublimity of his ancestry illuminates his glory.

4. When this man, beloved brethren, came to us with such condescension of the Lord, illustrious by the testimony and wonder of the very man who had persecuted him, what else behooved to be done except that he should be placed on the pulpit, that is, on the tribunal of the Church; that, resting on the loftiness of a higher station, and conspicuous to the whole people for the brightness of his honor, he should read the precepts and Gospel of the Lord, which he so bravely and faithfully follows? Let the voice that has confessed the Lord daily be heard in those things which the Lord spoke. Let it be seen whether there is any further degree to which he can be advanced in the Church. There is nothing in which a confessor can do more good to the brethren than that, while the reading of the Gospel is heard from his lips, every one who hears should imitate the faith of the reader. He should have been associated with Aurelius in reading; with whom, moreover, he was associated in the alliance of divine honor; with whom, in all the insignia of virtue and praise, he had been united. Equal both, and each like to the other, in proportion as they were sublime in glory, in that proportion they were humble in modesty. As they were lifted up by divine condescension, so they were lowly in their own peacefulness and tranquillity, and equally affording examples to every one of virtues and character, and fitted both for conflict and for peace; praiseworthy in the former for strength, in the latter for modesty.

5. In such servants the Lord rejoices; in confessors of this kind He glories—whose way and conversation is so advantageous to the announcement of their glory, that it affords to others a teaching of discipline. For this purpose Christ has willed them to remain long here in the Church; for this purpose He has kept them safe, snatched from the midst of death—a kind of resurrection, so to speak, being wrought on their behalf; so that, while nothing is seen by the brethren loftier in honor, nothing more lowly in humility, the way of life of the brotherhood may accompany these same persons. Know, then, that these for the present are appointed readers, because it was fitting that the candle should be placed in a candlestick, whence it may give light to all, and that their glorious countenance should be established in a higher place, where, beheld by all the surrounding brotherhood, they may give an incitement of glory to the beholders. But know that I have already purposed the honor of the presbytery for them, that so they may be honored with the same presents as the presbyters, and may share the monthly divisions in equalled quantities, to sit with us hereafter in their advanced and strengthened years; although in nothing can he seem to be inferior in the qualities of age who has consummated his age by the dignity of his glory. I bid you, brethren, beloved and earnestly longed-for, ever heartily farewell.

NOTES

159. St. Celerinus, the Roman confessor mentioned in Letter 15 who would go on to be gloriously martyred.
160. Apparently Celerinus was reluctant to be ordained lector until convinced by a heavenly vision.
161. The sacrifice of the Mass was not offered "for" the martyrs in the sense that Masses are offered for the repose of a departed soul; they Masses were offered "for" the martyrs in the sense that they were in honor of the martyrs, as it was never the Church's custom to pray for the souls of the martyrs but rather to invoke their prayers (see *On the Lapsed,* 18; Letter 56).

LETTER 34

TO THE SAME, ABOUT THE ORDINATION
OF NUMIDICUS AS PRESBYTER

Cyprian to the presbyters and deacons, and to the whole people, his brethren, very dear and longed-for, greeting. That which belongs, dearest brethren, both to the common joy and to the greatest glory of our Church ought to be told to you; for you must know that I have been admonished and instructed by divine condescension, that Numidicus[162] the presbyter should be appointed in the number of Carthaginian presbyters, and should sit with us among the clergy—a man illustrious by the brightest light of confession, exalted in the honor both of virtue and of faith; who by his exhortation sent before himself an abundant number of martyrs, slain by stones and by the flames, and who beheld with joy his wife abiding by his side, burned (I should rather say, preserved) together with the rest. He himself, half consumed, overwhelmed with stones, and left for dead—when afterwards his daughter, with the anxious consideration of affection, sought for the corpse of her father—was found half dead, was drawn out and revived, and remained unwillingly from among the companions whom he himself had sent before. But the reason of his remaining behind, as we see, was this: that the Lord might add him to our clergy, and might adorn with glorious priests the number of our presbyters that had been desolated by the lapse of some. And when God permits, he shall be advanced to a larger office in his region, when, by the Lord's protection, we have come into your presence once more. In the meantime, let what is revealed be done, that we receive this gift of God with thanksgiving, hoping from the Lord's mercy more ornaments of the same kind, that so the strength of His Church being renewed, He may make men so meek and lowly to flourish in the honor of our assembly. I bid you, brethren, very dear and longed-for, ever heartily farewell.

NOTES

162. St. Numidicus (Feast Day Aug. 9th); the Roman Martyrology for the day recounts his story: "In Africa, the commemoration of many holy martyrs during the persecution of Valerian.

Being exhorted by St. Numidicus, they obtained the palm of martyrdom by being cast into the fire, but Numidicus, although thrown into the flames with the others and overwhelmed with stones, was nevertheless taken out by his daughter. Found half dead, he was restored and deserved afterwards by his virtue to be made priest of the Church of Carthage by blessed Cyprian." The martyrology places his martyrdom during the persecution of Valerian (258); he may have suffered under Decius, however (250), for Cyprian in this same letter mentions that he is still in hiding, which places the letter and ordination as taking place during the year 250 or early 251 at the latest, unless Cyprian is referring to the time of exile he spent in 257 in Curubis prior to his own martyrdom (see *Life and Passion of Cyprian*, 12).

LETTER 35

TO THE CLERGY, CONCERNING THE CARE
OF THE POOR AND STRANGERS

Cyprian to the presbyters and deacons, his beloved brethren, greeting. In safety, by God's grace, I greet you, beloved brethren, desiring soon to come to you, and to satisfy the wish as well of myself and you, as of all the brethren. It behooves me also, however, to have regard to the common peace, and, in the meantime, although with weariness of spirit, to be absent from you, lest my presence should provoke the jealousy and violence of the heathens, and I should be the cause of breaking the peace, who ought rather to be careful for the quiet of all. When, therefore, you write that matters are arranged, and that I ought to come, or if the Lord should condescend to intimate it to me before, then I will come to you. For where could I be better or more joyful than there where the Lord willed me both to believe and to grow up? I request that you will diligently take care of the widows, and of the sick, and of all the poor. Moreover, you may supply the expenses for strangers, if any should be indigent, from my own portion, which I have left with Rogatianus, our fellow presbyter; which portion, lest it should be all appropriated, I have supplemented by sending to the same by Naricus the acolyte another share, so that the sufferers may be more largely and promptly dealt with. I bid you, beloved brethren, ever heartily farewell; and have me in remembrance. Greet your brotherhood in my name, and tell them to be mindful of me.

LETTER 36

TO THE CLERGY, BIDDING THEM SHOW EVERY KINDNESS
TO THE CONFESSORS IN PRISON

1. Cyprian to the presbyters and deacons, his brethren, greeting. Although I know, dearest brethren, that you have frequently been admonished in my letters to manifest all care for those who with a glorious voice have confessed the Lord, and are confined in prison; yet, again and again, I urge it upon you, that no consideration be wanting to them to whose glory there is nothing wanting. And

I wish that the circumstances of the place and of my station would permit me to present myself at this time with them; promptly and gladly would I fulfil all the duties of love towards our most courageous brethren in my appointed ministry. But I beseech you, let your diligence be the representative of my duty, and do all those things which behoove to be done in respect of those whom the divine condescension has rendered illustrious in such merits of their faith and virtue. Let there be also a more zealous watchfulness and care bestowed upon the bodies of all those who, although they were not tortured in prison, yet depart thence by the glorious exit of death.[163] For neither is their virtue nor their honor too little for them also to be allied with the blessed martyrs. As far as they could, they bore whatever they were prepared and equipped to bear. He who under the eyes of God has offered himself to tortures and to death, has suffered whatever he was willing to suffer; for it was not he that was wanting to the tortures, but the tortures that were wanting to him. "Whosoever shall confess me before men, him will I also confess before my Father which is in heaven,"[164] says the Lord. They have confessed Him. "He that endures to the end, the same shall be saved,"[165] says the Lord. They have endured and have carried the uncorrupted and unstained merits of their virtues through, even unto the end. And, again, it is written, "Be faithful unto death, and I will give you a crown of life."[166] They have persevered in their faithfulness, and steadfastness, and invincibleness, even unto death. When to the willingness and the confession of the name in prison and in chains is added also the conclusion of dying, the glory of the martyr is consummated.

2. Finally, also, take note of their days on which they depart, that we may celebrate their commemoration among the memorials of the martyrs, although Tertullus, our most faithful and devoted brother, who, in addition to the other solicitude and care which he shows to the brethren in all service of labor, is not wanting besides in that respect in any care of their bodies, has written, and does write and intimate to me the days, in which our blessed brethren in prison pass by the gate of a glorious death to their immortality; and there are celebrated here by us oblations and sacrifices for their commemorations, which things, with the Lord's protection, we shall soon celebrate with you. Let your care also (as I have already often written) and your diligence not be wanting to the poor—to such, I mean, as stand fast in the faith and bravely fight with us, and have not left the camp of Christ; to whom, indeed, we should now show a greater love and care, in that they are neither constrained by poverty nor prostrated by the tempest of persecution, but faithfully serve with the Lord, and have given an example of faith to the other poor. I bid you, brethren beloved, and greatly longed-for, ever heartily farewell; and remember me. Greet the brotherhood in my name. Farewell.

163. In other words, those who died in prison from natural causes or from conditions relating to their imprisonment should be counted among the martyrs. This is because, though not tortured or killed, by confessing Christ and suffering imprisonment they show that they have nevertheless offered themselves as martyrs, since torture and death were always possibilities when confessing Christ publicly.
164. Matt. 10:32.
165. Matt. 10:22.
166. Rev. 2:10.

LETTER 37[167]

TO CALDONIUS, HERCULANUS, AND OTHERS, ABOUT THE EXCOMMUNICATION OF FELICISSIMUS

1. Cyprian to Caldonius[168] and Herculanus, his colleagues, also to Rogatianus and Numidicus, his fellow presbyters, greeting. I have been greatly grieved, dearest brethren, at the receipt of your letter, that although I have always proposed to myself and wished to keep all our brotherhood safe, and to preserve the flock unharmed, as charity requires, you tell me now that Felicissimus has been attempting many things with wickedness and craft; so that, besides his old frauds and plundering, of which I had formerly known a good deal, he has now, moreover, tried to divide with the bishop a portion of the people; that is, to separate the sheep from the shepherd, and sons from their parents, and to scatter the members of Christ. And although I sent you as my substitutes to discharge the necessities of our brethren, with funds, and if any, moreover, wished to exercise their crafts, to assist their wishes with such an addition as might be sufficient, and at the same time also to take note of their ages and conditions and deserts—that I also, upon whom falls the charge of knowing all of them thoroughly, might promote any that were worthy and humble and meek to the offices of the ecclesiastical administration—he has interfered, and directed that no one should be relieved, and that those things which I had desired should not be ascertained by careful examination; he has also threatened our brethren, who had first approached to be relieved, with a wicked exercise of power, and with a violent dread that those who desired to obey me should not communicate with him in death.[169]

2. And since, after all these things, neither moved by the honor of my station, nor shaken by your authority and presence, but of his own impulse, disturbing the peace of the brethren he has rushed forth with many more, and asserted himself as a leader of a faction and chief of a sedition with a hasty madness—in which respect, indeed, I congratulate several of the brethren that they have withdrawn from this boldness, and have rather chosen to consent with you, so that they may remain with the Church, their mother, and receive their stipends from the bishop who dispenses them, which, indeed, I know for certain, that others also will peaceably do, and will quickly withdraw from their rash error—in the meantime, since Felicissimus has threatened that they should not communicate with him in death who had obeyed us, that is, who communicated with us, let him receive the sentence which he first of all declared, that he may know that he is excommunicated by us; inasmuch as he adds to his frauds and rapines, which we have known by the clearest truth, the crime also of adultery, which our brethren, grave men, have declared that they have discovered, and have asseverated that they will prove; all which things we shall then judicially examine, when, with the Lord's permission, we shall assemble in one place with many of our colleagues. But Augendus also, who, considering neither his bishop nor his Church, has equally associated himself with him in this conspiracy and faction, if he should further persevere with him, let him bear the sentence which that factious and impetuous man has provoked on himself. Moreover, whoever shall ally himself with his conspiracy and faction, let him know that he shall not communicate in the Church[170] with us, since of his own accord he has preferred to be separated from the Church. Read this letter of mine to our brethren, and also transmit it to Carthage to the clergy, the names being added of those who have joined themselves with Felicissimus. I bid you, beloved brethren, ever heartily farewell; and remember me. Farewell.

NOTES

167. This letter shows us the unfolding of a schism regarding the *lapsi*, such as Cyprian had worried about in previous letters. This Felicissimus had been ordained a deacon by Novatus without the permission of Cyprian, who declared that his prerogatives had been encroached upon. While Cyprian was absent during the Decian persecution, some presbyters on their own authority began to readmit the *lapsi* to the communion (Letters 9 & 10, for example). Before his return Cyprian interfered and sent a commission to investigate. Felicissimus denounced him for encroaching upon his rights as a deacon, and his church became a center for *lapsi* wishing to have their cases decided quickly. When Cyprian returned in 251, a synod met and excommunicated Felicissimus, along with five presbyters who were his adherents. This only increased the renown of Felicissimus and brought him more followers, including several local bishops. This burgeoning schismatic sect elected Fortunatus, one of the five presbyters, as bishop (or rather "anti-bishop") of Carthage. Felicissimus was sent to Rome to press for the removal of Cyprian by Pope Cornelius, but was unsuccessful. The schism seems to have petered out after this. Note also the assumption that the Bishop of Rome has the authority to remove a sitting bishop of another See.

168. Presumably the same Caldonius that had addressed St. Cyprian in Letter 18.

169. This phrase "communicate with him in death" occurs twice in Letter 37 (*In morte non communicarent* and *Non communicaturos in morte*). As this phrase makes very little sense, it has been suspected that this is a mistranslation going back at least to the English translation done in the *Ante-Nicene Fathers* series, Volume V, in the late 19th century. It has been suggested that early on there was a mistranslation regarding the word *morte* ("in death"), some favoring *monte*, ("on the mountain"), since it would be very easy for a copyist to have

mistaken the *n* for an *r*, and that the English translators mistakenly rendered the word as "in death." If this is the case, the real phrase should be "communicate with him on the mountain," which would make much more sense. Since Felicissimus was setting up a schismatic movement, "the mountain" could have been the location of their gatherings, as opposed to the official churches which would have remained under Cyprian's control. This is the most plausible explanation of this mysterious phrase.

170. This phrase, "communicate with us in the Church," seems to lend more weight to the above explanation. Cyprian is contrasting licit communion "in the Church" with schismatic communion "on the mountain."

LETTER 38

THE LETTER OF CALDONIUS, HERCULANUS, AND OTHERS, ON THE EXCOMMUNICATION OF FELICISSIMUS WITH HIS PEOPLE

Caldonius, with Herculanus and Victor, his colleagues, also with Rogatianus and Numidicus, presbyters. We have rejected Felicissimus and Augendus from communion; also Repostus from among the exiles, and Irene of the Blood-stained ones;[171] and Paula the sempstress;[172] which you ought to know from my subscription; also we have rejected Sophronius and Soliassus the vessel maker[173]—himself also one of the exiles.

NOTES

171. Those who had shed their blood during the Decian persecution.
172. Sempstress: An old fashioned word for seamstress.
173. This phrase (Lat: *budinarius*) is ambiguous; it could also mean "mule carrier" or be a proper name.

LETTER 39

TO THE PEOPLE, CONCERNING FIVE SCHISMATIC PRESBYTERS OF THE FACTION OF FELICISSIMUS

1. Cyprian to the whole people, greeting. Although, dearest brethren, Virtius, a most faithful and upright presbyter, and also Rogatianus and Numidicus, presbyters, confessors, and illustrious by the glory of the divine condescension, and also the deacons, good men and devoted to the ecclesiastical administration in all its duties, with the other ministers, afford you the full attention of their presence, and do not cease to confirm individuals by their assiduous exhortations, and, moreover, to govern and reform the minds of the lapsed by their wholesome counsels, yet, as much as I can, I admonish, and as I can, I visit you with my letters. By my letters I say, dearest brethren; for the malignity and treachery of certain of the presbyters has accomplished this, that I should not be allowed to come to you before Easter-day; since mindful of their conspiracy, and retaining that ancient venom against my episcopate, that is, against your suffrage and

God's judgment, they renew their old attack upon me, and once more begin their sacrilegious machinations with their accustomed craft. And, indeed, of God's providence, neither by our wish nor desire, nay, although we were forgiving and silent, they have suffered the punishment which they had deserved; so that, not cast out by us, they of their own accord have cast themselves out. They themselves, before their own conscience, have passed sentence on themselves in accordance with your suffrages and the divine. These conspirators and evil men of their own accord have driven themselves from the Church.[174]

2. Now it has appeared whence came the faction of Felicissimus; on what root and by what strength it stood. These men supplied in former times encouragements and exhortations to certain confessors, not to agree with their bishop, not to maintain the ecclesiastical discipline with faith and quietness according to the Lord's precepts, not to keep the glory of their confession with an uncorrupt and unspotted conversation.[175] And lest it should be too little to have corrupted the minds of certain confessors, and to have wished to arm a portion of our broken fraternity against God's priesthood, they have now turned their attention with their envenomed deceitfulness to the ruin of the lapsed, to turn away from the healing of their wound the sick and the wounded, and those who, by the misfortune of their fall, are less fit and less sturdy to take stronger counsel; and invite them, by the falsehood of a fallacious peace, to a fatal rashness, leaving off prayers and supplications, whereby, with long and continual satisfaction, the Lord is to be appeased.[176]

3. But I pray you, brethren, watch against the snares of the devil, and, taking care for your own salvation, be diligently on your guard against this death-bearing fallacy. This is another persecution and another temptation. Those five presbyters are none other than the five leaders who were lately associated with the magistrates in an edict, that they might overthrow our faith, that they might turn away the feeble hearts of the brethren to their deadly nets by the prevarication of the truth. Now the same scheme, the same overturning, is again brought about by the five presbyters, linked with Felicissimus, to the destruction of salvation, that God should not be besought, and that he who has denied Christ should not appeal for mercy to the same Christ whom he had denied; that after the fault of the crime, repentance also should be taken away;[177] and that the Lord should not be appeased through bishops and priests, but that the Lord's priests being, forsaken, a new tradition of a sacrilegious appointment should arise, contrary to the evangelical discipline. And although it was once arranged as well by us as by the confessors and the city clergy, and moreover by all the bishops appointed either in our province or beyond the sea, that no novelty should be introduced in respect of the case of the lapsed unless we all assembled into one place, and our counsels being compared, should decide upon a moderate sentence, tempered alike with discipline and with mercy—against this our counsel they have rebelled, and all priestly authority and power is destroyed by factious conspiracies.

4. What sufferings do I now endure, dearest brethren, that I myself am not able to come to you at the present juncture, that I myself cannot approach you each one, that I myself cannot exhort you according to the teaching of the Lord and of His Gospel! An exile of, now, two years[178] was not sufficient, and a mournful separation from you, from your countenance, and from your sight—continual grief and lamentation, which, in my loneliness without you, breaks me to pieces with my constant mourning, nor my tears flowing day and night, that there is not even an opportunity for the priest, whom you made with so much love and eagerness, to greet you, nor to be enfolded in your embraces. This greater grief is added to my worn spirit, that in the midst of so much solicitude and necessity I am not able myself to hasten to you, since, by the threats and by the snares of perfidious men, we are anxious that on our coming a greater tumult may not arise there; and so, although the bishop ought to be careful for peace and tranquillity in all things, he himself should seem to have afforded material for sedition, and to have embittered persecution anew. Hence, however, beloved brethren, I not only admonish but counsel you, not rashly to trust to mischievous words, nor to yield an easy consent to deceitful sayings, nor to take darkness for light, night for day, hunger for food, thirst for drink, poison for medicine, death for safety. Let not the age nor the authority deceive you of those who, answering to the ancient wickedness of the two elders; as they attempted to corrupt and violate the chaste Susannah, are thus also attempting, with their adulterous doctrines, to corrupt the chastity of the Church and violate the truth of the Gospel.[179]

5. The Lord cries aloud, saying, "Hearken not unto the words of the false prophets, for the visions of their own hearts deceive them. They speak, but not out of the mouth of the Lord. They say to them that despise the word of the Lord, 'You shall have peace.'"[180] They are now offering peace who have not peace themselves. They are promising to bring back and recall the lapsed into the Church, who themselves have departed from the Church. There is one God, and Christ is one, and there is one Church, and one chair founded upon the rock by the word of the Lord. Another altar cannot be constituted nor a new priesthood be made, except the one altar and the one priesthood. Whosoever gathers elsewhere, scatters. Whatsoever is appointed by human madness, so that the divine disposition is violated, is adulterous, is impious, is sacrilegious. Depart far from the contagion of men of this kind. and flee from their words, avoiding them as a cancer and a plague, as the Lord warns you and says, They are blind leaders of the blind. "But if the blind lead the blind, they shall both fall into the ditch."[181] They intercept your prayers, which you pour forth with us to God day and night, to appease Him with a righteous satisfaction. They intercept your tears with which you wash away the guilt of the sin you have committed; they intercept the peace which you truly and faithfully ask from the mercy of the Lord; and they do not know that it is written, "And that prophet, or that dreamer of dreams, that has spoken to turn you away from the Lord your God, shall be put to death."[182] Let no one, beloved brethren, make you to err from the ways of the Lord; let no one snatch you, Christians, from the Gospel of Christ; let no one take sons of the Church away from the Church; let them perish alone for themselves who have wished to perish; let them remain outside the Church alone who have departed from the Church; let them alone be without bishops who have rebelled against bishops; let them alone undergo the penalties of their conspiracies who formerly, according to your votes, and now according to God's judgment, have deserved to undergo the sentence of their own conspiracy and malignity.

6. The Lord warns us in His Gospel, saying, "You reject the commandment of God, that you may establish your own tradition."[183] Let them who reject the commandment of God and endeavor to keep their own tradition be bravely and firmly rejected by you; let one downfall be sufficient for the lapsed; let no one by his fraud hurl down those who wish to rise; let no one cast down more deeply and depress those who are down, on whose behalf we pray that they may be raised up by God's hand and arm; let no one turn away from all hope of safety those who are half alive and entreating that they may receive their former health; let no one extinguish every light of the way of salvation to those that are wavering in the darkness of their lapse. The apostle instructs us, saying, "If any man teach otherwise, and consent not to the wholesome words of our Lord Jesus Christ and His doctrine, he is lifted up with foolishness: from such withdraw yourself."[184] And again he says, "Let no man deceive you with vain words; for because of these things comes the wrath of God upon the children of disobedience."[185] Be not therefore partakers with them. There is no reason that you should be deceived with vain words, and begin to be partakers of their depravity. Depart from such, I entreat you, and acquiesce in our counsels, who daily pour out for you continual prayers to the Lord, who desire that you should be recalled to the Church by the clemency of the Lord, who pray for the fullest peace from God, first for the mother, and then for her children. Join also your petitions and prayers with our prayers and petitions; mingle your tears with our wailings. Avoid the wolves who separate the sheep from the shepherd; avoid the envenomed tongue of the devil, who from the beginning of the world, always deceitful and lying, lies that he may deceive, cajoles that he may injure, promises good that he may give evil, promises life that he may put to death. Now also his words are evident, and his poisons are plain. He promises peace, in order that peace may not possibly be attained; he promises salvation, that he who has sinned may not come to salvation; he promises a Church, when he so contrives that he who believes him may utterly perish apart from the Church.

7. It is now the occasion, dearly beloved brethren, both for you who stand fast to persevere bravely, and to maintain your glorious stability, which you kept in persecution with a continual firmness; and if any of you by the circumvention of the adversary have fallen, that in this second temptation you should faithfully take counsel for your hope and your peace; and in order that the Lord may pardon you, that you should not depart from the priests of the Lord, since it is written, "And the man that will do presumptuously, and will not hearken unto the priest or unto the judge that shall be in those days, even that man shall die."[186] Of this persecution this is the latest and final temptation, which itself also, by the Lord's protection, shall quickly pass away; so that I shall be again presented to you after Easter-day with my colleagues, who, being present, we shall be able as well to arrange as to complete the matters which require to be done according to your judgment and to the general advice of all of us as it has been decided before. But if anybody, refusing to repent and to make satisfaction to God, shall yield to the party of Felicissimus and his satellites, and shall join himself to the heretical faction, let him know that he cannot afterwards return to the Church and communicate with the bishops and the people of Christ. I bid you, dearest brethren, ever heartily farewell, and that you plead with me in continual prayer that the mercy of God may be entreated.

NOTES

174. See note 67 for Letter 37.
175. Felicissimus and his party were among those presbyters who encouraged confessors to grant *libelli pacis* to the *lapsi* outside of episcopal discretion, contrary to Cyprian's explicit wishes as laid down in Letters 9 and 10.
176. A testimony to the patristic belief that even after the guilt of sin is forgiven, "prayers...supplications" and "continual satisfaction" on the part of penitents were needed before the Lord was "appeased;" that is, before the temporal punishment due to sin was wiped away.
177. The argument here is that the quick and painless reconciliation offered by the adherents of Felicissimus to the lapsed precludes any prolonged period of repentance and contrition. Cyprian worries that a reconciliation granted too easily will lead the lapsed to neglect the customary penance that such a sin would normally have merited, and thus, will continue to lull them into the same state of inconstancy and weakness that led to their apostasy in the first place.
178. Not two years inclusive; the actual duration of Cyprian's exile was only fourteen months, from 250 to 251.
179. A reference to Daniel 13.

180. Jer. 23:16-17.
181. Matt. 15:14.
182. Deut. 13:5.
183. Mark 7:9.
184. 1 Tim. 6:3-5.
185. Eph. 5:6.
186. Deut. 17:12. This citation from Deuteronomy shows that Cyprian, and presumably the fathers in general, see the New Testament priesthood as the continuation of the Old Testament priesthood, albeit in a superior and transfigured way. This is why he quotes a precept regarding the Old Covenant priesthood with direct reference to the priests of the New Covenant.

LETTER 40

TO POPE CORNELIUS, ON HIS REFUSAL TO RECEIVE NOVATIAN'S ORDINATION[187]

1. Cyprian to Cornelius, his brother, greeting. There have come to us, beloved brother, sent by Novatian, Maximus the presbyter, and Augendus the deacon, and a certain Machaeus and Longinus. But, as we discovered, as well from the letters which they brought with them, as from their discourse and declaration, that Novatian had been made bishop; disturbed by the wickedness of an unlawful ordination made in opposition to the Catholic Church, we considered at once that they must be restrained from communion with us; and having, in the meanwhile, refuted and repelled the things which they pertinaciously and obstinately endeavored to assert, I and several of my colleagues, who had come together to me, were awaiting the arrival of our colleagues Caldonius and Fortunatus, whom we had lately sent to you as ambassadors, and to our fellow bishops, who were present at your ordination, in order that, when they came and reported the truth of the matter,[188] the wickedness of the adverse party might be quelled through them, by greater authority and manifest proof. But there came, in addition, Pompeius and Stephanus, our colleagues, who themselves also, by way of instructing us thereon, put forward manifest proofs and testimonies in conformity with their gravity and faithfulness, so that it was not even necessary that those who had come, as sent by Novatian, should be heard any further. And when in our solemn assembly they burst in with invidious abuse and turbulent clamor, demanding that the accusations, which they said that they brought and would prove, should be publicly investigated by us and by the people, we said that it was not consistent with our gravity to suffer the honor of our colleague, who had already been chosen and ordained and approved by the laudable sentence of many, to be called into question any further by the abusive voice of rivals. And because it would be a long business to collect into a letter the matters in which they have been refuted and repressed, and in which they have been manifested as having caused heresy by their unlawful attempts, you shall hear everything most fully from Primitivus our co-presbyter, when he shall come to you.

2. And lest their raging boldness should ever cease, they are striving here also to distract the members of Christ into schismatical parties,[189] and to cut and tear the one body of the Catholic Church, so that, running about from door to door, through the houses of many, or from city to city, through certain districts, they seek for companions in their obstinacy and error to join to themselves in their schism. To whom we have once given this reply, nor shall we cease to command them to lay aside their pernicious dissensions and disputes, and to be aware that it is an impiety to forsake their Mother; and to acknowledge and understand that when a bishop is once made and approved by the testimony and judgment of his colleagues and the people, another can by no means be appointed. Thus, if they consult their own interest peaceably and faithfully, if they confess themselves to be maintainers of the Gospel of Christ, they must return to the Church. I bid you, dearest brother, ever heartily farewell.

NOTES

187. Here we see the unfolding of the Novatian schism. In the controversy over the *lapsi*, Novatian had been a rigorist, teaching that the lapsed could not be reconciled with the Church during their lifetime. The prior schism of Felicissimus had taken the opposite extreme, that of reconciling the lapsed prematurely and without sufficient penance. Despite this, Novatian had supported Felicissimus against Cyprian in order to challenge the latter's authority. Novatian had been one of the Roman priests who governed the See of Rome after the martyrdom of Fabius (January, 250). After the death of Decius and the end of persecution (March, 251), the Church of Rome elected Cornelius as their bishop. Novatian, dissenting from the outcome of the election, hastily summoned several bishops from remote parts of Italy and staged a spurious election that proclaimed him pope. Novatian hastily sent messengers to the various churches of Christendom, hoping thereby to get them to recognize his election. Cyprian here writes to Cornelius of the arrival of Novatian's delegates and how the Carthaginian Church remained steadfast in their support of Cornelius, the true pope.

188. "[T]*he truth of the matter*"—Novatian accused Cornelius of being elected through bribery and extortion; the witnesses of the election Cyprian speaks of debunked these rumors by their testimony.

189. The followers of Novatian tried to set up rival bishops in the churches they visited, attempting to establish a rival hierarchy. Pope Cornelius did the same in churches where the local bishops resisted his authority; it is important to note that the authority of the Bishop of Rome to depose and appoint bishops was unchallenged in Cyprian's time. If the popes did not have this authority, then Novatian, the antipope, would not have tried to mimick it by appointing his own bishops.

LETTER 41

TO CORNELIUS, ABOUT CYPRIAN'S APPROVAL OF HIS ORDINATION, AND CONCERNING FELICISSIMUS

1. Cyprian to Cornelius his brother, greeting. As was fitting for God's servants, and especially for upright and peaceable priests, dearest brother, we recently sent our colleagues Caldonius and Fortunatus, that they might, not only by the persuasion of our letters, but by their presence and the advice of all of you, strive and labor with all their power to bring the members of the divided body into the unity of the Catholic Church,[190] and associate them into the bond of Christian charity. But since the obstinate and inflexible pertinacity of the adverse party has not only rejected the bosom and the embrace of its root and Mother, but even, with a discord spreading and reviving itself worse and worse, has appointed a bishop for itself, and, contrary to the sacrament once delivered of the divine appointment and of Catholic unity, has made an adulterous and opposed head[191] outside the Church; having received your letters as well as those of our colleagues, at the coming also of our colleagues Pompeius and Stephanus, good men and very dear to us, by whom all these things were undoubtedly alleged and proved to us with general gladness, in conformity with the requirements alike of the sanctity and the truth of the divine tradition and ecclesiastical institution, we have directed our letters to you. Moreover, bringing these same things under the notice of our several colleagues throughout the province, we have bidden also that our brethren, with letters from them, be directed to you.

2. This has been done, although our mind and intention had been already plainly declared to the brethren, and to the whole of the people in this place, when, having received letters lately from both parties, we read your letters, and intimated your ordination to the episcopate, in the ears of every one. Moreover, remembering the common honor, and having respect for the sacerdotal gravity and sanctity, we repudiated those things which from the other party had been heaped together with bitter virulence into a document transmitted to us; alike considering and weighing, that in so great and so religious an assembly of brethren, in which God's priests were sitting together, and His altar was set, they ought neither to be read nor to be heard. For those things should not easily be put forward, nor carelessly and rudely published, which may move a scandal by means of a quarrelsome pen in the minds of the hearers, and confuse brethren, who are placed far apart and dwelling across the sea, with uncertain opinions. Let those beware, who, obeying either their own rage or lust, and unmindful of the divine law and holiness, rejoice to throw abroad in the meantime things which they cannot prove; and although they may not be successful in destroying and ruining innocence, are satisfied with scattering stains upon it with lying reports and false rumors. Assuredly, we should exert ourselves, as it is fitting for prelates and priests to do, that such things, when they are written by any, should be repudiated as far as we are concerned. For otherwise, what will become of that which we learn and which we declare to be laid down in Scripture: "Keep your tongue from evil, and your lips from speaking guile"?[192] And elsewhere:

"Your mouth abounded in malice, and your tongue embraced deceit. You sat and spoke against your brother, and slandered your own mother's son."[193] Also whist the apostle says: "Let no corrupt communication proceed from your mouth, but that which is good to the edifying of faith, that it may minister grace unto the hearers."[194] Further, we show what the right course of conduct to pursue is, if, when such things are written by the calumnious temerity of some, we do not allow them to be read among us: and therefore, dearest brother, when such letters came to me against you, even though they were the letters of your co-presbyter sitting with you, as they breathed a tone of religious simplicity, and did not echo with any barkings of curses and revilings, I ordered them to be read to the clergy and the people.

3. But in desiring letters from our colleagues, who were present at your ordination at that place, we did not forget the ancient usage, nor did we seek for any novelty. For it was sufficient for you to announce yourself by letters to have been made bishop, unless there had been a dissenting faction on the other side, who by their slanderous and calumnious fabrications disturbed the minds and perplexed the hearts of our colleagues, as well as of several of the brethren. To set this matter at rest, we judged it necessary to obtain thence the strong and decided authority of our colleagues who wrote to us; and they, declaring the testimony of their letters to be fully deserved by your character, and life, and teaching, have deprived even your rivals, and those who delight either in novelty or evil, of every scruple of doubt or of difference; and, according to our advice weighed in wholesome reason, the minds of the brethren tossing about in this sea have sincerely and decidedly approved your priesthood. For this, my brother, we especially both labor after, and ought to labor after, to be careful to maintain as much as we can the unity delivered by the Lord,[195] and through His apostles to us their successors, and, as far as in us lies, to gather into the Church the dispersed and wandering sheep which the willful faction and heretical temptation of some is separating from their Mother; those only being left outside, who by their obstinacy and madness have persisted, and have been unwilling to return to us; who themselves will have to give an account to the Lord of the dissension and separation made by them, and of the Church that they have forsaken.

4. But, so far as pertains to the cause of certain presbyters here, and of Felicissimus, that you may know what has been done here, our colleagues have sent you letters subscribed by their own hand, that you may learn, when you have heard the parties, from their letters what they have thought and what they have pronounced. But you will do better, brother, if you will also bid copies of the letters which I had sent[196] lately by our colleagues Caldonius and Fortunatus to you, to he read for the common satisfaction, which I had written concerning the same Felicissimus and his presbytery to the clergy there, and also to the people, to be read to the brethren there; declaring your ordination, and the course of the whole transaction, that so as well there as here the brotherhood may be informed of all things by us. Moreover, I have here transmitted also copies of the same by Mettius the sub-deacon, sent by me, and by Nicephorus the acolyte. I bid you, dearest brother, ever heartily farewell.

NOTES

190. Note that Cyprian views the Body of Christ as identical with the Catholic Church, in which physical membership is vital. He knows nothing of the "invisible church" proposed by Luther and the Protestants.
191. By calling the antipope the "opposed Head" of the Church he infers that the true pope is the rightful Head of the Church on earth.
192. Ps. 34:14.
193. Ps. 50:19-20.
194. Eph. 4:29.
195. The physical unity of the Church is considered a gift to it passed on by Christ. This is the Church's *oneness*, one of its four marks, of which the Catechism says, "What are these bonds of unity? Above all, charity "binds everything together in perfect harmony." But the unity of the pilgrim Church is also assured by visible bonds of communion: profession of one faith received from the Apostles; common celebration of divine worship, especially of the sacraments; apostolic succession through the sacrament of Holy Orders, maintaining the fraternal concord of God's family" (CCC 815).
196. Letters 39 and 40.

LETTER 42

TO POPE CORNELIUS, ON HIS HAVING SENT LETTERS TO THE CONFESSORS WHOM NOVATIAN HAD SEDUCED[197]

Cyprian to Cornelius his brother, greeting. I have though it both obligatory on me, and necessary for you, dearest brother, to write a short letter[198] to the confessors who are there with you, and, seduced by the obstinacy and depravity of Novatian and Novatus,[199] have departed from the Church; in which letter I might induce them, for the sake of our mutual affection, to return to their Mother, that is, to the Catholic Church. This letter I have first of all entrusted to you by Mettius the sub-deacon for your perusal, lest any one should pretend that I had written otherwise than according to the contents of my letter. I have, moreover, charged the same Mettius sent by me to you, that he should be guided by your decision; and if you should think that this letter should be given to the confessors, then that he should deliver it. I bid you, dearest brother, ever heartily farewell.

NOTES

197. This letter was sent at the same time as Letters 41 and 43.

198. Letter 43.

199. Novatian was sometimes referred to in other writings as Novatus. It appears that Cyprian at the time had heard both of these names associated with the schism and assumed they were different persons.

LETTER 43

TO THE ROMAN CONFESSORS, THAT THEY SHOULD RETURN TO UNITY

Cyprian to Maximus and Nicostratus, and the other confessors, greeting.[200] As you have frequently gathered from my letters, beloved, what honor I have ever observed in my mode of speaking for your confession, and what love for the associated brotherhood; believe, I entreat you, and acquiesce in these my letters, wherein I both write and with simplicity and fidelity consult for you, and for your doings, and for your praise. For it weighs me down and saddens me, and the intolerable grief of a smitten, almost prostrate, spirit seizes me, when I find that you there, contrary to ecclesiastical order, contrary to evangelical law, contrary to the unity of the Catholic institution, had consented that another bishop should be made. That is what is neither right nor allowable to be done; that another church should be set up; that Christ's members should be torn asunder; that the one mind and body of the Lord's flock should be lacerated by a divided emulation. I entreat that in you, at all events, that unlawful rending of our brotherhood may not continue; but remembering both your confession and the divine tradition, you may return to the Mother whence you have gone forth; whence you came to the glory of confession with the rejoicing of the same Mother. And think not that you are thus maintaining the Gospel of Christ when you separate yourselves from the flock of Christ, and from His peace and concord; since it is more fitting for glorious and good soldiers to sit down within their own camp, and so placed within to manage and provide for those things which are to be dealt with in common. For as our unanimity and concord ought by no means to be divided, and because we cannot forsake the Church and go outside her to come to you, we beg and entreat you with what exhortations we can, rather to return to the Church your Mother, and to our brotherhood. I bid you, dearest brethren, ever heartily farewell.

NOTE

200. These confessors had been carried away in the schism of Novatian.

LETTER 44

TO CORNELIUS, CONCERNING POLYCARP THE ADRUMETINE

1. Cyprian to Cornelius his brother, greeting. I have read your letters, dearest brother, which you sent by Primitivus our co-presbyter, in which I perceived that you were annoyed that, whereas letters from the Adrumetine colony[201] in the name of Polycarp were directed to you, yet after Liberalis and I came to that place, letters began to be directed thence to the presbyters and to the deacons.[202]

2. In respect of which I wish you to know, and certainly to believe, that it was done from no levity or contempt. But when several of our colleagues who had assembled into one place had determined that, while our co-bishops Caldonius and Fortunatus were sent as ambassadors to you, all things should be in the meantime suspended as they were, until the same colleagues of ours, having reduced matters there to peace, or, having discovered their truth. should return to us; the presbyters and deacons abiding in the Adrumetine colony; in the absence of our co-bishop Polycarp, were ignorant of what had been decided in common by us. But when we came before them, and our purpose was understood, they themselves also began to observe what the others did, so that the agreement of the churches abiding there was in no respect broken.

3. Some persons, however, sometimes disturb men's minds and spirits by their words, in that they relate things otherwise than is the truth. For we, who furnish every person who sails hence with a plan that they may sail without any offense, know that we have exhorted them to acknowledge and hold the root and matrix of the Catholic Church. But since our province is wide-spread, and has Numidia and Mauritania attached to it; lest a schism made in the city should confuse the minds of the absent with uncertain opinions, we decided—having obtained by means of the bishops the truth of the matter, and having got a greater authority for the proof of your ordination, and so at length every scruple being got rid of from the breast of every one—that letters should be sent you by all who were placed anywhere in the province; as in fact is done, that so the whole of our colleagues might decidedly approve of and maintain both you and your communion, that is as well to the unity of the Catholic Church as to its charity. That all which has by God's direction come to pass, and that our design has under Providence been forwarded, we rejoice.

4. For thus as well the truth as the dignity of your episcopate has been established in the most open light, and with the most manifest and substantial approval; so that from the replies of our colleagues, who have thence written to us, and from the account and from the testimonies of our co-bishops Pompeius, and Stephanus, and Caldonius, and Fortunatus, both the needful cause and the right order, and moreover the glorious innocence, of your ordination might be known by all. That we, with the rest of our colleagues, may steadily and firmly administer this office, and keep it in the concordant unanimity of the Catholic Church, the divine condescension will accomplish; so that the Lord who condescends to elect and appoint for Himself priests in His Church, may protect them also when elected and appointed by His good-will and help, inspiring them to govern, and supplying both vigor for restraining the contumacy of the wicked, and gentleness for cherishing the penitence of the lapsed. I bid you, dearest brother, ever heartily farewell.

NOTES

201. The city of Hadramentum, modern day Sousse in Tunisia.
202. Since this took place during the period of the Novatian schism, letters being addressed to the Roman clergy and not to the bishop could suggest that the clergy of North Africa did not recognize Cornelius as legitimate pope or otherwise thought the See vacant. Cyprian writes to deny any such intent on the part of his clergy. As Cyprian explains below, the Adrumetine clergy had heard of the schism but did not yet know which claimant Cyprian regarded as legitimate. Therefore, they thought it best to avoid commiting to either Cornelius or Novatian by addressing the letter simply to the Roman clergy.

LETTER 45

POPE CORNELIUS TO CYPRIAN, ON THE RETURN OF THE CONFESSORS TO UNITY[203]

1. Cornelius to Cyprian his brother, greeting. In proportion to the solicitude and anxiety that we sustained in respect of those confessors who had been circumvented and almost deceived and alienated from the Church by the craft and malice of that wily and subtle man,[204] was the joy with which we were affected, and the thanks which we gave to Almighty God and to our Lord Christ, when they, acknowledging their error, and perceiving the poisoned cunning of the malignant man, as if of a serpent, came back, as they with one heart profess, with singleness of will to the Church from which they had gone forth. And first, indeed, our brethren of approved faith, loving peace and desiring unity, announced that the swelling pride of these men was already soothed; yet there was no fitting assurance to induce us easily to believe that they were thoroughly changed. But afterwards, Urbanus and Sidonius the confessors came to our presbyters, affirming that Maximus the confessor and presbyter, equally with themselves, desired to return into the Church;[205] but since many things had preceded this which they had contrived, of which you also have been made aware from our co-bishops and from my letters, so that faith could not hastily be reposed in them, we determined to hear from their own mouth and confession those things which they had sent by the messengers. And when they came, and were required by the presbyters to give an account of what they had done, and were charged with having very lately repeatedly sent letters full of calumnies and reproaches, in their name, through all the churches, and had disturbed nearly all the churches; they affirmed that they had been deceived, and that they had not known what was in those letters; that only through being misled they had also committed schismatical acts, and been the authors of heresy, so that they suffered hands to be imposed on him as if upon a bishop. And when these and other matters had been charged upon them, they entreated that they might be done away and altogether discharged from memory.

2. The whole of this transaction therefore being brought before me, I decided that the presbytery should be brought together; (for there were present five bishops, who were also present today) so that by well-grounded counsel it might be determined with the consent of all what ought to be observed in respect of their persons. And that you may know the feeling of all, and the advice of each one, I decided also to bring to your knowledge our various opinions, which you will read subjoined. When these things were done, Maximus, Urbanus, Sidonius, and several brethren who had joined themselves to them, came to the presbytery, desiring with earnest prayers that what had been done before might fall into oblivion, and no mention might be made of it; and promising that henceforth, as though nothing had been either done or said, all things on both sides being forgiven, they would now exhibit to God a heart clean and pure, following the evangelical word which says, "Blessed are the pure in heart, for they shall see God."[206] What remained was, that the people should be informed of all this proceeding, that they might see those very men established in the Church whom they had long seen and mourned as wanderers and scattered. Their will being known, a great concourse of the brotherhood was assembled. There was one voice from all, giving thanks to God; all were expressing the joy of their heart by tears, embracing them as if they had this day been set free from the penalty of the dungeon. And to quote their very own words—"We," they say, "know that Cornelius is bishop of the most holy Catholic Church elected by Almighty God, and by Christ our Lord. We confess our error; we have suffered imposture; we were deceived by captious perfidy and loquacity. For although we seemed, as it were, to have held a kind of communion with a man who was a schismatic and a heretic, yet our mind was always sincere in the Church. For we are not ignorant that there is one God; that there is one Christ the Lord whom we have confessed, and one Holy Spirit; and that in the Catholic Church there ought to be one bishop. Were we not rightly induced by that confession of theirs, to allow that what they had confessed before the power of the world they might approve when established in the Church? Wherefore we bade Maximus the presbyter to take his own place; the rest we received with great approbation of the people. But we remitted all things to Almighty God, in whose power all things are reserved."[207]

3. These things therefore, brother, written to you in the same hour, at the same moment, we have transmitted; and I have sent away at once Nicephorus the acolyte, hastening to descend to embarkation, that so, no delay being made, you might, as if you had been present among that clergy and in that assembly of people, give thanks to Almighty God and to Christ our Lord. But we believe—nay, we confide in it for certain—that the others also who have been ranged in this error will shortly return into the Church when they see their leaders acting with us. I think, brother, that you ought to send these letters also to the other churches, that all may know that the craft and prevarication of this schismatic and heretic are from day to day being reduced to nothing. Farewell, dearest brother.

NOTES

203. This and the following letters deal with the rejoicing of the Churches of Rome and Carthage at the return of the Roman confessors to the Pope after their brief adherence to the schism of Novatian.
204. Novatian.
205. Notice the tone of Pope Cornelius' words: to follow leaders outside of the institutional, apostolic Church was nothing other than to leave the Church. Hence he sees their abandomnment of Novatian as a "return to the Church."
206. Matt. 5:8.
207. This is a very interesting confession of faith by the Roman confessors. Cornelius is not called simply "Bishop of Rome" but "bishop of the holy Catholic Church," which always implies the Church in its universality. His election is said not only to be valid but by "Almighty God and Christ our Lord." They go on to state that "in the Catholic Church there ought to be one bishop." This could be interpreted as meaning that there should only be one Bishop of Rome presiding over the Church, or it could also mean that there should be but one episcopate in the Church, from which it is unlawful to depart and set up a rival. Either interprtation is favorable from a Catholic viewpoint; if the former, the supremacy of the Bishop of Rome is affirmed, if the latter, the necessity of a visible, apostolic episcopate.

LETTER 46

CYPRIAN'S ANSWER TO CORNELIUS, CONGRATULATING HIM ON THE RETURN OF THE CONFESSORS FROM THE SCHISM OF NOVATIAN

1. Cyprian to Cornelius his brother, greeting. I profess that I both have rendered and do render the greatest thanks without ceasing, dearest brother, to God the Father Almighty, and to His Christ the Lord and our God and Savior, that the

Church is thus divinely protected, and its unity and holiness is not constantly nor altogether corrupted by the obstinacy of perfidy and heretical wickedness. For we have read your letter, and have exultingly received the greatest joy from the fulfilment of our common desire; to wit, that Maximus the presbyter, and Urbanus, the confessors, with Sidonius and Macarius, have re-entered into the Catholic Church, that is, that they have laid aside their error, and given up their schismatical, nay, their heretical madness, and have sought again in the soundness of faith the home of unity and truth; that whence they had gone forth to glory, there they might gloriously return; and that they who had confessed Christ should not afterwards desert the camp of Christ, and that they might not tempt the faith of their charity and unity, who had not been overcome in strength and courage. Behold the safe and unspotted integrity of their praise; behold the uncorrupted and substantial dignity of these confessors, that they have departed from the deserters and fugitives, that they have left the betrayers of the faith, and the impugners of the Catholic Church. With reason did both the people and the brotherhood receive them when they returned, as you write, with the greatest joy; since in the glory of confessors who had maintained their glory, and returned to unity, there is none who does not reckon himself a partner and a sharer.

2. We can estimate the joy of that day from our own feelings. For if, in this place, the whole number of the brethren rejoiced at your letter which you sent concerning their confession, and received this tidings of common rejoicing with the greatest alacrity, what must have been the joy there when the matter itself, and the general gladness, was carried on under the eyes of all? For since the Lord in His Gospel says that there is the highest joy in heaven over one sinner that repents, how much greater is the joy in earth, no less than in heaven, over confessors who return with their glory and with praise to the Church of God, and make a way of returning for others by the faith and approval of their example? For this error had led away certain of our brethren, so that they thought they were following the communion of confessors. When this error was removed, light was infused into the breasts of all, and the Catholic Church has been shown to be one, and to be able neither to be cut nor divided.[208] Nor can any one now be easily deceived by the talkative words of a raging schismatic, since it has been proved that good and glorious soldiers of Christ could not long be detained without the Church by the deceitfulness and perfidy of others. I bid you, dearest brother, ever heartily farewell.

NOTES

208. The unity of the Church of Christ is manifest in communion with the validly consecrated successors of the apostles, the bishops. The mystical oneness of the Church is thus manifest in a very tangible way, so that, as Pope Pius XII said, "[T]here is only one chief Head of this Body, namely Christ, who never ceases Himself to guide the Church invisibly, though at

the same time He rules it visibly, through him who is His representative on earth" (*Mystici Corporis Christi*, 40). There is no such thing as the Calvinist "invisible church;" the spiritual unity of the Church is manifest visibly in communion with the bishops.

LETTER 47

CORNELIUS TO CYPRIAN, CONCERNING THE FACTION OF NOVATIAN WITH HIS PARTY

Cornelius to Cyprian his brother, greeting. That nothing might be wanting to the future punishment of this wretched man, when cast down by the powers of God, (on the expulsion by you of Maximus, and Longinus, and Machaeus) he has risen again; and, as I intimated in my former letter which I sent to you by Augendus the confessor, I think that Nicostratus, and Novatus, and Evaristus, and Primus, and Dionysius, have already come there. Therefore let care be taken that it be made known to all our co-bishops and brethren, that Nicostratus is accused of many crimes, and that not only has he committed frauds and plunders on his secular patroness, whose affairs he managed; but, moreover (which is reserved to him for a perpetual punishment), he has abstracted no small deposits of the Church; that Evaristus has been the author of a schism; and that Zetus has been appointed bishop in his place, and his successor to the people over whom he had previously presided. But he contrived greater and worse things by his malice and insatiable wickedness than those which he was then always practicing among his own people; so that you may know what kind of leaders and protectors that schismatic and heretic constantly had joined to his side. I bid you, dearest brother, ever heartily fare well.

LETTER 48

CYPRIAN'S ANSWER TO CORNELIUS, CONCERNING THE CRIMES OF NOVATUS

1. Cyprian to Cornelius his brother, greeting. You have acted, dearest brother, both with diligence and love, in sending us in haste Nicephorus the acolyte, who both told us the glorious gladness concerning the return of the confessors, and most fully instructed us against the new and mischievous devices of Novatian and Novatus[209] for attacking the Church of Christ. For whereas on the day before, that mischievous faction of heretical wickedness had arrived here, itself already lost and ready to ruin others who should join it, on the day after, Nicephorus arrived with your letter. From which we both learned ourselves, and have begun to teach and to instruct others, that Evaristus from being a bishop has now not remained even a layman;[210] but, banished from the see and from the people, and an exile from the Church of Christ, he roves about far and wide through other provinces, and, himself having made shipwreck of truth and faith, is preparing for some who are like him, as fearful shipwrecks. Moreover, that Nicostratus, having lost the diaconate of sacred administrations,[211] because he had abstracted the Church's money by a sacrilegious fraud, and disowned the deposits of the widows and orphans, did not wish so much to come into Africa as to escape there from the city, from the consciousness of his rapines and his frightful crimes. And now a deserter and a fugitive from the Church, as if to have changed the clime were to change the man, he goes on to boast and announce himself a confessor, although *he* can no longer either be or be called a confessor of Christ who has denied Christ's Church. For when the Apostle Paul says, "For this cause shall a man leave his father and mother, and shall cleave unto his wife; and they two shall be one flesh. This is a great mystery; but I speak concerning Christ and the Church;"[212]—when, I say, the blessed apostle says this, and with his sacred voice testifies to the unity of Christ with the Church, cleaving to one another with indivisible links, how can he be with Christ who is not with the spouse of Christ, and in His Church? Or how does he assume to himself the charge of ruling or governing the Church, who has spoiled and wronged the Church of Christ?

2. For about Novatus there need have been nothing told by you to us, since Novatus ought rather to have been shown by us to you, as always greedy of novelty, raging with the rapacity of an insatiable avarice, inflated with the arrogance and stupidity of swelling pride; always known with bad repute to the bishops there; always condemned by the voice of all the priests as a heretic and a perfidious man; always inquisitive, that he may betray: he flatters for the purpose of deceiving, never faithful that he may love; a torch and fire to blow up the flames of sedition; a whirlwind and tempest to make shipwrecks of the faith; the foe of quiet, the adversary of tranquillity, the enemy of peace. Finally, when Novatus withdrew thence from among you, that is, when the storm and the whirlwind departed, calm arose there in part, and the glorious and good confessors who by his instigation had departed from the Church, after he retired from the city, returned to the Church. This is the same Novatus who first sowed among us the flames of discord and schism; who separated some of the brethren here from the bishop;[213] who, in the persecution itself, was to our people, as it were, another persecution, to overthrow the minds of the brethren. He it is who, without my leave or knowledge, of his own factiousness and ambition appointed his attendant Felicissimus[214] a deacon, and with his own tempest sailing also to Rome to overthrow the Church, endeavored to do similar and equal things there, forcibly separating a part of the people from the clergy, and dividing the concord of the fraternity that was firmly knit together and mutually loving one another. Since Rome from her greatness plainly ought to take precedence over Carthage, he there committed still greater and graver crimes.[215] He who in the one place had made a deacon contrary to the Church, in the other made a bishop. Nor let any one be surprised at this in such men. The wicked are always madly carried away by their own furious passions; and after they have committed crimes, they are agitated by the very consciousness of a depraved mind. Neither can those remain in God's Church, who have not maintained its divine and ecclesiastical discipline, either in the conversation of their life or the peace of their character. Orphans despoiled by him, widows defrauded, moneys moreover of the Church withheld, exact from him those penalties which we behold inflicted in his madness. His father also died of hunger in the street, and afterwards even in death was not buried by him. The womb of his wife was smitten by a blow of his heel; and in the miscarriage that soon followed, the offspring was brought forth, the fruit of a father's murder. And now does he dare to condemn the hands of those who sacrifice, when he himself is more guilty in his feet, by which the son, who was about to be born, was slain?[216]

3. He long ago feared this consciousness of crime. On account of this he regarded it as certain that he would not only be turned out of the presbytery, but restrained from communion; and by the urgency of the brethren, the day of investigation was coming on, on which his cause was to be dealt with before us, if the persecution had not prevented. He, welcoming this, with a sort of desire of escaping and evading condemnation, committed all these crimes, and wrought all this stir; so that he who was to be ejected and excluded from the Church, anticipated the judgment of the priests by a voluntary departure, as if to have anticipated the sentence were to have escaped the punishment.

4. But in respect to the other brethren, over whom we grieve that they were circumvented by him, we labor that they may avoid the mischievous neighborhood of the crafty impostor, that they may escape the deadly nets of his solicitations, that they may once more seek the Church from which he deserved by divine authority to be expelled. Such indeed, with the Lord's help, we trust may return by His mercy, for one cannot perish unless it is plain that he must perish, since the Lord in His Gospel says, "Every planting which my heavenly Father has not planted shall be rooted up."[217] He alone who has not been planted in the precepts and warnings of God the Father, can depart from the Church: he alone can forsake the bishops and abide in his madness with schismatics and heretics. But the mercy of God the Father, and the indulgence of Christ our Lord, and our own patience, will unite the rest with us. I bid you, dearest brother, ever heartily farewell.

NOTES

209. See footnote for Letter 42 on the the apparent confusion over Novatian's name.
210. The Catholic Church teaches that the Sacrament of Holy Orders confers in indelible mark

upon its recipient similar to baptism, meaning that once a man receives this mark it can never be undone ("once a bishop, always a bishop;" see CCC 1558). St. Cyprian does not mean that Evaristus has lost the Sacrament of Holy Orders; rather, he means that by adhering to the schism of Novatian, Evaristus as severed himself from the unity of the Church. Cyprian's point is that even a layman is more united to Christ than Evaristus; though the latter is a bishop, his adherence to the schism puts him further out of unity with Christ than the humblest layman.

211. "Lost the diaconate." See the above note. Nicostratus did not efface the Sacrament of Orders, but lost his ministry within the Church due to his adherence to the schism.

212. Eph. 5:31-32.

213. Novatian was responsible for stirring up opposition to Cyprian both in Carthage and at Rome during the time Cyprian was in hiding during the persecution of Decius.

214. See Letter 37.

215. A plain admission by Cyprian that not all episcopal sees were considered equal in the ancient Church. Rome's preeminence over Carthage is "plainly" known to Cyprian; that is, it is obvious to all Christians.

216. This passage is interesting for two reasons. First, note that the offering of the Eucharist by the priests is called a sacrifice. Second, that the killing of an unborn child in the womb is described as "murder."

217. Matt. 15:13.

LETTER 49

MAXIMUS AND THE OTHER CONFESSORS TO CYPRIAN, ABOUT THEIR RETURN FROM SCHISM

Maximus, Urbanus, Sidonius, and Macharius, to Cyprian their brother, greeting. We are certain, dearest brother, that you also rejoice together with us with equal earnestness, that we having taken advice, and especially, considering the interests and the peace of the Church, having passed by all other matters, and reserved them to God's judgment, have made peace with Cornelius our bishop, as well as with the whole clergy. You ought most certainly to know from these our letters that this was done with the joy of the whole Church, and even with the forward affection of the brethren. We pray, dearest brother, that for many years you may fare well.[218]

NOTES

218. Union with the Church of Christ is manifest by visible unity with the local bishop. The Church is not simply an invisible community of individuals, but a corporate and visible unity of belivers gathered around the bishop, the visible source of unity (see CCC 886).

LETTER 50

FROM CYPRIAN TO THE ROMAN CONFESSORS, CONGRATULATING THEM ON THEIR RETURN FROM SCHISM

1. Cyprian to Maximus the presbyter, also to Urbanus, and Sidonius, and Macharius, his brethren, greeting. When I read your letters, dearest brethren, that you wrote to me about your return, and about the peace of the Church, and the brotherly restoration, I confess that I was as greatly overjoyed as I had before been overjoyed when I learned the glory of your confession, and thankfully received tidings of the heavenly and spiritual renown of your warfare. For this, moreover, is another confession of your faith and praise; to confess that the Church is one,[219] and not to become a sharer in other men's error, or rather wickedness; to seek anew the same camp whence you went forth, whence with the most vigorous strength you leapt forth to wage the battle and to subdue the adversary. For the trophies from the battlefield ought to be brought back there whence the arms for the field had been received, lest the Church of Christ should not retain those same glorious warriors whom Christ had furnished for glory. Now, however, you have kept in the peace of the Lord the fitting tenor of your faith and the law of undivided charity and concord, and have given by your walk an example of love and peace to others; so that the truth of the Church, and the unity of the Gospel mystery which is held by us, are also linked together by your consent and bond; and confessors of Christ do not become the leaders of error, after having stood forth as praiseworthy originators of virtue and honor.

2. Let others consider how much they may congratulate you, or how much each one may glory for himself: I confess that I congratulate you more, and I more boast of you to others, in respect of this your peaceful return and charity. For you ought in simplicity to hear what was in my heart. I grieved vehemently, and I was greatly afflicted, that I could not hold communion with those whom once I had begun to love. After the schismatical and heretical error laid hold of you, on your going forth from prison, it seemed as if your glory had been left in the dungeon. For there the dignity of your name seemed to have stayed behind when the soldiers of Christ did not return from the prison to the Church, although they had gone into the prison with the praise and congratulations of the Church.

3. For although there seem to be tares in the Church, yet neither our faith nor our charity ought to be hindered, so that because we see that there are tares in the Church we ourselves should withdraw from the Church: we ought only to labor that we may be wheat, that when the wheat shall begin to be gathered into the Lord's barns, we may receive fruit for our labor and work. The apostle in his epistle says, "In a great house there are not only vessels of gold and silver, but also of wood and of earth, and some to honor and some to dishonor.[220] Let us strive, dearest brethren, and labor as much as we possibly can, that we may be vessels of gold or silver. But to the Lord alone it is granted to break the vessels of earth, to whom also is given the rod of iron. The servant cannot be greater than his lord, nor may any one claim to himself what the Father has given to the Son alone, so as to think that he can take the fan for winnowing and purging the threshing-floor, or can separate by human judgment all the tares from the wheat. That is a proud obstinacy and a sacrilegious presumption which a depraved madness assumes to itself. And while some are always assuming to themselves more dominion than meek justice demands, they perish from the Church; and while they insolently extol themselves, blinded by their own swelling, they lose the light of truth. For which reason we also, keeping moderation, and considering the Lord's balances, and thinking of the love and mercy of God the Father, have long and carefully pondered with ourselves, and have weighed what was to be done with due moderation.

4. All which matters you can look into thoroughly, if you will read the tracts[221] which I have lately read here, and have, for the sake of our mutual love, transmitted to you also for you to read; wherein there is neither wanting for the lapsed, censure which may rebuke, nor medicine which may heal. Moreover, my feeble ability has expressed as well as it could the unity of the Catholic Church. Which treatise I now more and more trust will be pleasing to you, since you now read it in such a way as both to approve and love it; inasmuch as what we have written in words you fulfil in deeds, when you return to the Church in the unity of charity and peace. I bid you, dearest brethren, and greatly longed-for, ever heartily farewell.

NOTES

219. The Church's oneness is a visible oneness. When Christ willed that His Church be one (John 17:21), the oneness He willed was a visible, corporate unity.
220. 2 Tim. 2:20.
221. *On the Unity of the Church.* Cyprian prepared a special edition of this treatise for the benefit of the Church of Rome. Cyprian edited the treatise in which he praised the Roman See in particular as the visible source of unity in the Church (see *On the Unity of the Church*, 4). This edited "Roman edition" of the treatise circulated alongside the original, meaning different manuscripts did or did not contain the amended passage depending on whether they were copied from the Carthaginian original or the Roman edition.

LETTER 51

TO ANTONIANUS ABOUT CORNELIUS AND NOVATIAN

1. Cyprian to Antonianus his brother, greeting. I received your first letters, dearest brother, firmly maintaining the concord of the priestly college, and adhering to the Catholic Church, in which you intimated that you did not hold communion with Novatian, but followed my advice, and held one common agreement with Cornelius our co-bishop.[222] You wrote, moreover, for me to transmit a copy of those same letters to Cornelius our colleague, so that he might lay aside all anxiety, and know at once that you held communion with him, that is, with the Catholic Church.[223]

2. But subsequently there arrived other letters of yours sent by Quintus our co-presbyter, in which I observed that your mind, influenced by the letters of Novatian, had begun to waver. For although previously you had settled your opinion and consent firmly, you desired in these letters that I should write to you once more what heresy Novatian had introduced, or on what grounds Cornelius holds communion with Trophimus and the sacrificers.[224] In which matters, indeed, if you are anxiously careful, from solicitude for the faith, and are diligently seeking out the truth of a doubtful matter, the hesitating anxiety of a mind undecided in the fear of God, is not to be blamed.

3. Yet, as I see that after the first opinion expressed in your letter, you have been disturbed subsequently by letters of Novatian, I assert this first of all, dearest brother, that grave men, and men who are once established upon the strong rock with solid firmness, are not moved, I say not with a light air, but even with a wind or a tempest, lest their mind, changeable and uncertain, be frequently agitated here and there by various opinions, as by gusts of wind rushing on them, and so be turned from its purpose with some reproach of levity. That the letters of Novatian may not do this with you, nor with any one, I will set before you, as you have desired, my brother, an account of the matter in few words. And first of all indeed, as you also seem troubled about what I too have done, I must clear my own person and cause in your eyes, lest any should think that I have lightly withdrawn from my purpose, and while at first and at the commencement I maintained evangelical vigor, yet subsequently I seem to have turned my mind from discipline and from its former severity of judgment, so as to think that those who have stained their conscience with certificates, or have offered abominable sacrifices, are to have peace made easy to them. Both of which things have been done by me, not without long-balanced and pondered reasons.

4. For when the battle was still going on, and the struggle of a glorious contest was raging in the persecution, the courage of the soldiers had to be excited with every exhortation, and with full urgency, and especially the minds of the lapsed had to be roused with the trumpet call, as it were, of my voice, that they might pursue the way of repentance, not only with prayers and lamentations; but, since an opportunity was given of repeating the struggle and of regaining salvation, that they might be reproved by my voice, and stimulated rather to the ardor of confession and the glory of martyrdom. Finally, when the presbyters and deacons had written to me about some persons, that they were without moderation and were eagerly pressing forward to receive communion; replying to them in my letter which is still in existence,[225] then I added also this: If these are so excessively eager, they have what they require in their own power, the time itself providing for them more than they ask: the battle is still being carried on, and the struggle is daily celebrated: if they truly and substantially repent of what they have done, and the ardor of their faith prevails, he who cannot be delayed may be crowned. But I put off deciding what was to be arranged about the case of the lapsed, so that when quiet and tranquillity should be granted, and the divine indulgence should allow the bishops to assemble into one place, then the advice gathered from the comparison of all opinions being communicated and weighed, we might determine what was necessary to be done. But if any one, before our council, and before the opinion decided upon by the advice of all, should rashly wish to communicate with the lapsed, he himself should be withheld from communion.

5. And this also I wrote very fully to Rome, to the clergy who were then still acting without a bishop, and to the confessors, Maximus the presbyter, and the rest who were then shut up in prison, but are now in the Church, joined with Cornelius. You may know that I wrote this from their reply, for in their letter they wrote thus: "However, what you have yourself also declared in so important a matter is satisfactory to us, that the peace of the Church must first be maintained; then, that an assembly for counsel being gathered together, with bishop, presbyters, deacons, and confessors, as well as with the laity who stand fast, we should deal with the case of the lapsed." It was added also—Novatian then writing, and reciting with his own voice what he had written, and the presbyter Moyses,[226] then still a confessor, but now a martyr, subscribing—that peace ought to be granted to the lapsed who were sick and at the point of departure. Which letter was sent throughout the whole world, and was brought to the knowledge of all the churches and all the brethren.

6. According, however, to what had been before decided, when the persecution was quieted, and opportunity of meeting was afforded, a large number of bishops, whom their faith and the divine protection had preserved in soundness and safety, we met together; and the divine Scriptures being brought forward on both sides, we balanced the decision with wholesome moderation, so that neither should hope of communion and peace be wholly denied to the lapsed, lest they should fail still more through desperation, and, because the Church was closed to them, should, like the world, live as heathens; nor yet, on the other hand, should the censure of the Gospel be relaxed, so that they might rashly rush to communion, but that repentance should be long protracted, and the paternal clemency be sorrowfully besought, and the cases, and the wishes, and the necessities of individuals be examined into, according to what is contained in a little book, which I trust has come to you, in which the several heads of our decisions are collected. And lest perchance the number of bishops in Africa should seem unsatisfactory, we also wrote to Rome, to Cornelius our colleague, concerning this thing, who himself also holding a council with very many bishops, concurred in the same opinion as we had held, with equal gravity and wholesome moderation.

7. Concerning which it has now become necessary to write to you, that you may know that I have done nothing lightly, but, according to what I had before comprised in my letters, had put off everything to the common determination of our council, and indeed communicated with no one of the lapsed as yet, so long as there still was an opening by which the lapsed might receive not only pardon, but also a crown. Yet afterwards, as the agreement of our college, and the advantage of gathering the fraternity together and of healing their wound required, I submitted to the necessity of the times, and thought that the safety of the many must be provided for; and I do not now recede from these things which have once been determined in our council by common agreement, although many things are ventilated by the voices of many, and lies against God's priests uttered from the devil's mouth, and tossed about everywhere, to the rupture of the concord of Catholic unity. But it behooves you, as a good brother and a fellow priest like-minded, not easily to receive what malignants and apostates may say, but carefully to weigh what your colleagues, modest and grave men, may do, from an investigation of our life and teaching.

8. I come now, dearest brother, to the character of Cornelius our colleague, that with us you may more justly know Cornelius, not from the lies of malignants and detractors, but from the judgment of the Lord God, who made him a bishop, and from the testimony of his fellow bishops, the whole number of whom has agreed with an absolute unanimity throughout the whole world. For—a thing which with laudable announcement commends our dearest Cornelius to God and Christ, and to His Church, and also to all his fellow priests—he was not one who on a sudden attained to the episcopate; but, promoted through all the ecclesiastical offices, and having often deserved well of the Lord in divine administrations, he ascended by all the grades of religious service to the lofty summit of the priesthood. Then, moreover, he did not either ask for the episcopate itself, nor did he wish it; nor, as others do when the swelling of their arrogance and pride inflates them, did he seize upon it; but quite otherwise, and meek and such as those are accustomed to be who are chosen of God to this office, having regard to the modesty of his virgin continency, and the humility of his inborn and guarded veneration, he did not, as some do, use force to be made a bishop, but he himself suffered compulsion, so as to be forced to receive the episcopal office. And he was made bishop by very many of our colleagues who were then present in the city of Rome, who sent to us letters concerning his ordination, honorable and laudatory, and remarkable for their testimony in announcement of him. Moreover, Cornelius was made bishop by the judgment of God and of His Christ, by the testimony of almost all the clergy, by the suffrage of the people who were then present, and by the assembly of ancient priests and good men, when no one had been made so before him, when the place of Fabian, that is, when the place of Peter and the degree of the sacerdotal throne was vacant; which being occupied by the will of God, and established by the consent of all of us, whosoever now wishes to become a bishop, must needs be made from without; and he cannot have the ordination of the Church who does not hold the unity of the Church. Whoever he may be, although greatly boasting about himself, and claiming very much for himself, he is profane, he is an alien, he is without. And as after the first there cannot be a second, whosoever is made after one who ought to be alone, is not second to him, but is in fact none at all.

9. Then afterwards, when he had undertaken the episcopate, not obtained by solicitation nor by extortion, but by the will of God who makes priests; what a virtue there was in the very undertaking of his episcopate, what strength of mind, what firmness of faith—a thing that we ought with simple heart both thoroughly to look into and to praise—that he intrepidly sat at Rome in the sacerdotal chair at that time when a tyrant, odious to God's priests, was threatening things that can, and cannot be spoken, inasmuch as he would much more patiently and tolerantly hear that a rival prince was raised up against himself than that a priest of God was established at Rome. Is not this man, dearest brother, to be commended with the highest testimony of virtue and faith? Is not he to be esteemed among the glorious confessors and martyrs, who for so long a time sate awaiting the manglers of his body and the avengers of a ferocious tyrant, who, when Cornelius resisted their deadly edicts, and trampled on their threats and sufferings and tortures by the vigor of his faith, would either rush upon him with the sword, or crucify him, or scorch him with fire, or rend his bowels and his limbs with some unheard-of kind of punishment? Even though the majesty and goodness of the protecting Lord guarded, when made, the priest whom He willed to be made; yet Cornelius, in what pertains to his devotion and fear, suffered whatever he could suffer, and conquered the tyrant first of all by his priestly office, who was afterwards conquered in arms and in war.

10. But in respect to certain discreditable and malignant things that are bandied about concerning him, I would not have you wonder when you know that this is always the work of the devil, to wound God's servants with lies, and to defame a glorious name by false opinions, so that they who are bright in the light of their own conscience may be tarnished by the reports of others. Moreover, you are to know that our colleagues have investigated, and have certainly discovered that he has been blemished with no stain of a certificate, as some intimate; neither has he mingled in sacrilegious communion with the bishops who have sacrificed, but has merely associated with us those whose cause had been heard, and whose innocence was approved.[227]

11. For with respect to Trophimus also, of whom you wished tidings to be written to you, the case is not as the report and the falsehood of malignant people had conveyed it to you. For, as our predecessors often did, our dearest brother, in bringing together the brethren, yielded to necessity; and since a very large part of the people had withdrawn with Trophimus, now when Trophimus returned to the Church, and atoned for, and with the penitence of prayer confessed his former error, and with perfect humility and satisfaction recalled the brotherhood whom he had lately taken away, his prayers were heard; and not only Trophimus, but a very great number of brethren who had been with Trophimus, were admitted into the Church of the Lord, who would not all have returned to the Church unless they had come in Trophimus' company. Therefore the matter being considered there with several colleagues, Trophimus was received, for whom the return of the brethren and salvation restored to many made atonement. Yet Trophimus was admitted in such a manner as only to communicate as a layman, not, according to the information given to you by the letters of the malignants, in such a way as to assume the place of a priest.

12. But, moreover, in respect of what has been told you, that Cornelius communicates everywhere with those who have sacrificed, this intelligence has also arisen from the false reports of the apostates. For neither can they praise us who depart from us, nor ought we to expect to please them, who, while they displease us, and revolt against the Church, violently persist in soliciting brethren away from the Church. Wherefore, dearest brethren, do not with facility either hear or believe whatever is currently rumored against Cornelius and about me.

13. For if any are seized with sicknesses, help is given to them in danger, as it has been decided.[228] Yet after they have been assisted, and peace has been granted to them in their danger, they cannot be suffocated by us, or destroyed, or by our force or hands urged on to the result of death; as if, because peace is granted to the dying, it were necessary that those who have received peace should die; although the token of divine love and paternal lenity appears more in this way, that they, who in peace given to them receive the pledge of life, are moreover here bound to life by the peace they have received. And therefore, if with peace received, a reprieve is given by God, no one ought to complain of the priests for this, when once it has been decided that brethren are to be aided in peril. Neither must you think, dearest brother, as some do, that those who receive certificates are to be put on a par with those who have sacrificed; since even among those who have sacrificed, the condition and the case are frequently different. For we must not place on a level one who has at once leapt forward with good-will to the abominable sacrifice, and one who, after long struggle and resistance, has reached that fatal result under compulsion; one who has betrayed both himself and all his connections, and one who, himself approaching the trial in behalf of all, has protected his wife and his children, and his whole family, by himself undergoing the danger; one who has compelled his inmates or friends to the crime, and one who has spared inmates and servants, and has even received many brethren who were departing to banishment and flight, into his house and hospitality; showing and offering to the Lord many souls living and safe to entreat for a single wounded one.

14. Since, then, there is much difference between those who have sacrificed, what a want of mercy it is, and how bitter is the hardship, to associate those who have received certificates, with those who have sacrificed, when he by whom the certificate has been received may say, I had previously read, and had been made aware by the discourse of the bishop, that we must not sacrifice to idols, that the servant of God ought not to worship images; and therefore, in order that I might not do this which was not lawful, when the opportunity of receiving a certificate was offered, which itself also I should not have received, unless the opportunity had been put before me, I either went or charged some other person going to the magistrate, to say that I am a Christian, that I am not allowed to sacrifice, that I cannot come to the devil's altars, and that I pay a price for this purpose, that I may not do what is not lawful for me to do. Now, however, even he who is stained with having received a certificate—after he has learned from our admonitions that he ought not even to have done this, and that although his hand is pure, and no contact of deadly food has polluted his lips, yet his conscience is nevertheless polluted, weeps when he hears us, and laments, and is now admonished of the thing wherein he has sinned, and having been deceived, not so much by guilt as by error, bears witness that for another time he is instructed and prepared.[229]

15. If we reject the repentance of those who have some confidence in a conscience that may be tolerated; at once with their wife, with their children, whom they had kept safe, they are hurried by the devil's invitation into heresy or schism; and it will be attributed to us in the day of judgment, that we have not cared for the wounded sheep, and that on account of a single wounded one we have lost many sound ones. And whereas the Lord left the ninety and nine that were whole, and sought after the one wandering and weary, and Himself carried it, when found, upon His shoulders, we not only do not seek the lapsed, but even drive them away when they come to us; and while false prophets are not ceasing to lay waste and tear Christ's flock, we give an opportunity to dogs and wolves, so that those whom a hateful persecution has not destroyed, we ruin by our hardness and inhumanity. And what will become, dearest brother, of what the apostle says: "I please all men in all things, not seeking my own profit, but the profit of many, that they may be saved. Be followers of me, as I also am of Christ."[230] And again: "To the weak I became as weak, that I might gain the weak."[231] And again: "Whether one member suffer, all the members suffer with it; or one member rejoice, all the members rejoice with it."[232]

16. The principle of the philosophers and Stoics is different, dearest brother, who say that all sins are equal, and that a grave man ought not easily to be moved.[233] But there is a wide difference between Christians and philosophers. And when the apostle says, "Beware, lest any man spoil you through philosophy and vain deceit,"[234] we are to avoid those things which do not come from God's clemency, but are begotten of the presumption of a too rigid philosophy. Concerning Moses, moreover, we find it said in the Scriptures, "Now the man Moses was very meek;"[235] and the Lord in His Gospel says, "Be merciful, as your Father also had mercy upon you;"[236] and again, "They that be whole need not a physician, but they that are sick."[237] What medical skill can he exercise who says, "I cure the sound only, who have no need of a physician?" We ought to give our assistance, our healing art, to those who are wounded; neither let us think them dead, but rather let us regard them as lying half alive, whom we see to have been wounded in the fatal persecution, and who, if they had been altogether dead, would never from the same men become afterwards both confessors and martyrs.

17. But since in them there is that, which, by subsequent repentance, may be strengthened into faith; and by repentance strength is armed to virtue, which could not be armed if one should fall away through despair; if, hardly and cruelly separated from the Church, he should turn himself to Gentile ways and to worldly works, or, if rejected by the Church, he should pass over to heretics and schismatics; where, although he should afterwards be put to death on account of the name, still, being placed outside the Church, and divided from unity and from charity, he could not in his death be crowned. And therefore it was decided, dearest brother, the case of each individual having been examined into, that the receivers of certificates should in the meantime be admitted, that those who had sacrificed should be assisted at death, because there is no confession in the place of the departed, nor can any one be constrained by us to repentance, if the fruit of repentance be taken away. If the battle should come first, strengthened by us, he will be found ready armed for the battle; but if sickness should press hard upon him before the battle, he departs with the consolation of peace and communion.

18. Moreover, we do not prejudge when the Lord is to be the judge; save that if He shall find the repentance of the sinners full and sound, He will then ratify what shall have been here determined by us.[238] If, however, any one should delude us with the pretence of repentance, God, who is not mocked, and who looks into man's heart, will judge of those things which we have imperfectly looked into, and the Lord will amend the sentence of His servants; while yet, dearest brother, we ought to remember that it is written, "A brother that helps a brother shall be exalted;" and that the apostle also has said, "Let all of you severally have regard to yourselves, lest you also be tempted. Bear one another's burdens, and so fulfil the law of Christ;"[239] also that, rebuking the haughty, and breaking down their arrogance, he says in his epistle, "Let him that thinks he stands, take heed lest he fall;"[240] and in another place he says, "Who are you that judgest another man's servant? To his own master he stands or falls; yea, he shall stand, for God is able to make him stand."[241] John also proves that Jesus Christ the Lord is our Advocate and Intercessor for our sins, saying, "My little children, these things write I unto you, that you sin not. And if any man sin, we have an Advocate with the Father, Jesus Christ the Supporter: and He is the propitiation for our sins."[242] And Paul also, the apostle, in his epistle, has written, "If, while we were yet sinners, Christ died for us; much more, being now justified by His blood, we shall be saved from wrath through Him."[243]

19. Considering His love and mercy, we ought not to be so bitter, nor cruel, nor inhuman in cherishing the brethren, but to mourn with those that mourn, and to weep with them that weep, and to raise them up as much as we can by the help and comfort of our love; neither being too ungentle and pertinacious in repelling their repentance; nor, again, being too lax and easy in rashly yielding communion. Lo! A wounded brother lies stricken by the enemy in the field of battle. There the devil is striving to slay him whom he has wounded; here Christ is exhorting that he whom He has redeemed may not wholly perish. Whether of the two do we assist? On whose side do we stand? Whether do we favor the devil, that he may destroy, and pass by our prostrate lifeless brother, as in the Gospel did the priest and Levite; or rather, as priests of God and Christ, do we imitate what Christ both taught and did, and snatch the wounded man from the jaws of the enemy, that we may preserve him cured for God the judge?

20. And do not think, dearest brother, that either the courage of the brethren will be lessened, or that martyrdoms will fail for this cause, that repentance is relaxed to the lapsed, and that the hope of peace is offered to the penitent. The strength of the truly believing remains unshaken; and with those who fear and love God with their whole heart, their integrity continues steady and strong. For to adulterers even a time of repentance is granted by us, and peace is given. Yet virginity is not therefore deficient in the Church, nor does the glorious design of continence languish through the sins of others.[244] The Church, crowned with so many virgins, flourishes; and chastity and modesty preserve the tenor of their glory. Nor is the vigor of continence broken down because repentance and pardon are facilitated to the adulterer. It is one thing to stand for pardon, another thing to attain to glory: it is one thing, when cast into prison, not to go out thence until one has paid the last penny;[245] another thing at once to receive the wages of faith and courage. It is one thing, tortured by long suffering for sins, to be cleansed and long purged by fire; another to have purged all sins by suffering.[246] It is one thing, in fine, to be in suspense till the sentence of God at the day of judgment; another to be at once crowned by the Lord.

21. And, indeed, among our predecessors, some of the bishops here in our province thought that peace was not to be granted to adulterers, and wholly closed the gate of repentance against adultery. Still they did not withdraw from the assembly of their co-bishops, nor break the unity of the Catholic Church by the persistency of their severity or censure; so that, because by some peace was granted to adulterers, he who did not grant it should be separated from the Church. While the bond of concord remains, and the undivided sacrament of the Catholic Church endures, every bishop disposes and directs his own acts, and will have to give an account of his purposes to the Lord.

22. But I wonder that some are so obstinate as to think that repentance is not to be granted to the lapsed, or to suppose that pardon is to be denied to the penitent, when it is written, "Remember whence you are fallen, and repent, and do the first works,"[247] which certainly is said to him who evidently has fallen, and whom the Lord exhorts to rise up again by his works, because it is written, "Alms do deliver from death,"[248] and not, assuredly, from that death which once the blood of Christ extinguished, and from which the saving grace of baptism and of our Redeemer has delivered us, but from that which subsequently creeps in through sins.[249] Moreover, in another place time is granted for repentance; and the Lord threatens him that does not repent: "I have," says He, "many things against you, because you suffer your wife Jezebel, which calls herself a prophetess, to teach and to seduce my servants to commit fornication, and to eat things sacrificed to idols; and I gave her a space to repent, and she will not repent of her fornication. Behold, I will cast her into a bed, and them that commit adultery with her into great tribulation, except they repent of their deeds;"[250] whom certainly the Lord would not exhort to repentance, if it were not that He promises mercy to them that repent. And in the Gospel He says, "I say unto you, that likewise joy shall be in heaven over one sinner that repents, more than over ninety and nine just persons that need no repentance."[251] For since it is written, "God did not make death, neither has He pleasure in the destruction of the living,"[252] assuredly He who wills that none should perish, desires that sinners should repent, and by repentance should return again to life. Thus also He cries by Joel the prophet, and says, "And now, thus says the Lord your God, Turn even to me with all your heart, and with fasting, and with weeping, and with mourning; and rend your heart, and not your garments, and return unto the Lord your God; for He is gracious and merciful, slow to anger, and of great kindness, and repents Him of the evil appointed."[253] In the Psalms, also, we read as well the rebuke as the clemency of God, threatening at the same time as He spares, punishing that He may correct; and when He has corrected, preserving. "I will visit," He says, "their transgressions with the rod, and their iniquity with stripes. Nevertheless, my loving-kindness will I not utterly take from them."[254]

23. The Lord also in His Gospel, setting forth the love of God the Father, says, "What man is there of you, whom, if his son ask bread, will he give him a stone? Or if he ask a fish, will he give him a serpent? If you then, being evil, know how to give good gifts unto your children, how much I more shall your heavenly Father give good things to them that ask Him?"[255] The Lord is here comparing the father after the flesh, and the eternal and liberal love of God the Father. But if that evil father upon earth, deeply offended by a sinful and evil son, yet if he should see the same son afterwards reformed, and, the sins of his former life being put away, restored to sobriety and morality and to the discipline of innocence by the sorrow of his repentance, both rejoices and gives thanks, and with the eagerness of a father's exultation, embraces the restored one, whom before he had cast out; how much more does that one and true Father, good, merciful, and loving—yea, Himself Goodness and Mercy and Love—rejoice in the repentance of His own sons! Nor threatens punishment to those who are now repenting, or mourning and lamenting, but rather promises pardon and clemency. Whence the Lord in the Gospel calls those that mourn, blessed; because he who mourns calls forth mercy. He who is stubborn and haughty heaps up wrath against himself, and the punishment of the coming judgment. And therefore, dearest brother, we have decided that those who do not repent, nor give evidence of sorrow for their sins with their whole heart, and with manifest profession of their lamentation, are to be absolutely restrained from the hope of communion and peace if they begin to beg for them in the midst of sickness and peril; because it is not repentance for sin, but the warning of urgent death, that drives them to ask; and he is not worthy to receive consolation in death who has not reflected that he was about to die.

24. In reference, however, to the character of Novatian, dearest brother, of whom you desired that intelligence should be written you what heresy he had introduced; know that, in the first place, we ought not even to be inquisitive as to what he teaches, so long as he teaches out of the pale of unity. Whoever he may be, and whatever he may be, he who is not in the Church of Christ is not a Christian. Although he may boast himself, and announce his philosophy or eloquence with lofty words, yet he who has not maintained brotherly love or ecclesiastical unity has lost even what he previously had been. Unless he seems to you to be a bishop, who—when a bishop has been made in the Church by sixteen co-bishops—strives by bribery to be made an adulterous and extraneous bishop by the hands of deserters; and although there is one Church, divided by Christ throughout the whole world into many members, and also one episcopate diffused through a harmonious multitude of many bishops; in spite of God's tradition, in spite of the combined and everywhere compacted unity of the Catholic Church, is endeavoring to make a human church, and is sending his new apostles through very many cities, that he may establish some new foundations of his own appointment. And although there have already been ordained in each city, and through all the provinces, bishops old in years, sound in faith, proved in trial, proscribed in persecution, this one dares to create over these other and false bishops: as if he could either wander over the whole world with the persistence of his new endeavor, or break asunder the structure of the ecclesiastical body, by the propagation of his own discord, not knowing that schismatics are always ferent at the beginning, but that they cannot increase nor add to what they have unlawfully begun, but that they immediately fail together with their evil emulation. But he could not hold the episcopate, even if he had before been made bishop, since he has cut himself off from the body of his fellow bishops, and from the unity of the Church; since the apostle admonishes that we should mutually sustain one another, and not withdraw from the unity which God has appointed, and says, "Bearing with one another in love, endeavoring to keep the unity of the Spirit in the bond of peace."[256] He then who neither maintains the unity of the Spirit nor the bond of peace, and separates himself from the band of the Church, and from the assembly of priests, can neither have the power nor the honor of a bishop, since he has refused to maintain either the unity or the peace of the episcopate.[257]

25. Then, moreover, what a swelling of arrogance it is, what oblivion of humility and gentleness, what a boasting of his own arrogance, that any one should either dare, or think that he is able, to do what the Lord did not even grant to the apostles; that he should think that he can discern the tares from the wheat, or, as if it were granted to him to bear the fan and to purge the threshing-floor, should endeavor to separate the chaff from the wheat; and since the apostle says, "But in a great house there are not only vessels of gold and of silver, but also of wood and of earth,"[258] should think to choose the vessels of gold and of silver, to despise, to cast away, and to condemn the vessels of wood and of clay; while the vessels of wood are not burnt up except in the day of the Lord by the flame of the divine burning, and the vessels of clay are only broken by Him to whom is given the rod of iron.

26. Or if he appoints himself a searcher and judge of the heart and reins, let him in all cases judge equally. And as he knows that it is written, "Behold, you are made whole; sin no more, lest a worse thing happen unto you,"[259] let him separate the fraudulent and adulterers from his side and from his company, since the case of an adulterer is by far both graver and worse than that of one who has taken a certificate, because the latter has sinned by necessity, the former by free will: the latter, thinking that it is sufficient for him that he has not sacrificed, has been deceived by an error; the former, a violator of the matrimonial tie of another, or entering a brothel, into the sink and filthy gulf of the common people, has befouled by detestable impurity a sanctified body and God's temple, as says the apostle: "Every sin that a man does is without the body, but he that commits fornication sins against his own body."[260] And yet to these persons themselves repentance is granted, and the hope of lamenting and atoning is left, according to the saying of the same apostle: "I fear lest, when I come to you, I shall bewail many of those who have sinned already, and have not repented of the uncleanness, and fornication, and lasciviousness which they have committed."[261]

27. Neither let the new heretics flatter themselves in this, that they say that they do not communicate with idolaters; although among them there are both adulterers and fraudulent persons, who are held guilty of the crime of idolatry, according to the saying of the apostle: "For know this with understanding, that no whoremonger, nor unclean person, nor covetous man, whose guilt is that of idolatry, has any inheritance in the kingdom of Christ and of God."[262] And again: "Mortify therefore your members which are upon the earth; putting off fornication, uncleanness, and evil concupiscence, and covetousness, which are the service of idols: for which things' sake comes the wrath of God."[263] For as our bodies are members of Christ, and we are each a temple of God, whosoever violates the temple of God by adultery, violates God; and he who, in committing sins, does the will of the devil, serves demons and idols. For evil deeds do not come from the Holy Spirit, but from the prompting of the adversary, and lusts born of the unclean spirit constrain men to act against God and to obey the devil. Thus it happens that if they say that one is polluted by another's sin, and if they contend, by their own assertion, that the idolatry of the delinquent passes over to one who is not guilty according to their own word; they cannot be excused from the crime of idolatry, since from the apostolic proof it is evident that the adulterers and defrauders with whom they communicate are idolaters. But with us, according to our faith and the given rule of divine preaching, agrees the principle of truth, that every one is himself held fast in his own sin; nor can one become guilty for another, since the Lord forewarns us, saying, "The righteousness of the righteous shall be upon him, and the wickedness of the wicked shall be upon him."[264] And again: "The fathers shall not die for the children, and the children shall not die for the fathers. Every one shall die in his own sin."[265] Reading and observing this, we certainly think that no one is to be restrained from the fruit of satisfaction, and the hope of peace, since we know, according to the faith of the divine Scriptures, God Himself being their author, and exhorting in them, both that sinners are brought back to repentance, and that pardon and mercy are not denied to penitents.

28. And oh, mockery of a deceived fraternity! Oh, vain deception of miserable and senseless mourners! Oh, ineffectual and profitless tradition of heretical institution! To exhort to the repentance of atonement, and to take away the healing from the atonement; to say to our brethren, "Mourn and shed tears, and groan day and night, and labor largely and frequently for the washing away and cleansing of your sin; but, after all these things, you shall die without the pale of the Church. Whatsoever things are necessary to peace, you shall do, but none of that peace which you seek shall you receive!"[266] Who would not perish at once? Who would not fall away, from very desperation? Who would not turn away his mind from all design of lamentation? Do you think that the husbandman could labor if you should say, "Till the field with all the skill of husbandry, diligently persevere in its cultivation; but you shall reap no harvest, you shall press no vintage, you shall receive no fruits of your olive-yard, you shall gather no apples from the trees;" or if, urging upon any one the possession and use of ships, you were to say, "Purchase, my brother, material from excellent woods; inweave your keel with the strongest and chosen oak; labor on the rudder, the ropes, the sails, that the ship may be constructed and fitted; but when you have done this, you shall never behold the result from its doings and its voyages?"

29. This is to shut up and to cut off the way of grief and of repentance; so that while in all Scripture the Lord God sooths those who return to Him and repent, repentance itself is taken away by our hardness and cruelty, which intercepts the fruits of repentance. But if we find that none ought to be restrained from repenting, and that peace may be granted by His priests to those who entreat and beseech the Lord's mercy, inasmuch as He is merciful and loving, the groaning of those who mourn is to be admitted, and the fruit of repentance is not to be denied to those who grieve. And because in the place of the departed there is no confession, neither can confession be made there, they who have repented from their whole heart, and have asked for it, ought to be received within the Church, and to be kept in it for the Lord, who will of a surety judge, when He comes to His Church, those whom He shall find within it. But apostates and deserters, or adversaries and enemies, and those who lay waste the Church of Christ, cannot, even if outside the Church they have been slain for His name, according to the apostle, be admitted to the peace of the Church, since they have neither kept the unity of the spirit nor of the Church.

30. These few things for the present, out of many, dearest brother, I have run over as briefly as I could, that I might thereby both satisfy your desire, and might link you more and more closely to the society of our college and body. But if there should arise to you an opportunity and power of coming to us, we shall be able to confer more fully together, and to consider more fruitfully and more at large the things which make for a salutary agreement. I bid you, dearest brother, ever heartily farewell.

NOTES

222. Since Cyprian just admitted above (Letter 48:2) that the See of Rome takes precedence over Carthage, and since in other places he speaks of the See of Rome as the visible source of the Church's unity (*On the Unity of the Church*, 4), Cyprian's statement here should not be construed in such a manner as to deny the precedence or preeminence of the Roman pontiff. It must be remembered that the Roman pontiff is another bishop, and insofar as Holy Orders are concerned, he is equal in dignity to the other bishops. Even now it is common for the popes to address the bishops in their official pronouncements as "my venerable brother bishops."

223. To hold communion with the Pope is to hold communion with the Catholic Church. "He that holds not this unity of the Church, does he think that he holds the faith? He who deserts the chair of Peter, upon whom the Church is founded, is he confident that he is in the Church?" (*On the Unity of the Church*, 4).

224. The *lapsi*, those Christians who sacrificed to idols during the persecution and had not yet been reconciled to the Church.

225. See Letters 9-13.

226. See Letter 24.

227. Some had accused Pope Cornelius of being one of the *libellatici*, those who had avoided sacrificing to idols during the persecution by bribing the Magistrate to obtain a certificate stating that they had sacrificed. Cyprian strenuously defends Pope Cornelius against this accusation.

228. Cyprian is here arguing that he has not been holding communion with the unreconciled *lapsi*, as he is accused of, but that he will reconcile them if they are in danger of death by virtue

of sickness, which had long been his policy. Cyprian states that it is not his fault if some of the lapsed who are granted reconciliation during their illness go on to survive. If they are reconciled and survive their illness, this should be seen as the mercy of God, against which no person should complain.

229. Those who sacrificed (*lapsi*) are guilty of a greater sin than those who bribed the magistrates (*libellatici*). The former actually pollute themselves by offering sacrifices to idols while the latter only lead men to believe that they have. This is still a sin, but is not so deadly as that of the former.

230. 1 Cor. 10:33.

231. 1 Cor. 9:22.

232. 1 Cor. 12:26.

233. St. Cyprian here bears witness to the perennial belief of the Church that there are indeed different degrees of sin, the most evident being the difference between mortal and venial.

234. Col. 2:8.

235. Num. 12:3.

236. Luke 6:36.

237. Matt. 9:12.

238. In other words, so long as the contrition of a sinner is sincere, God will always honor and "ratify" the absolution granted by the priests of the Church. "Whose sins you shall forgive, they are forgiven them: and whose sins you shall retain, they are retained" (John 20:23).

239. Gal. 6:1-2. This is the corrolary to Cyprian's foregoing point: if repentance is sincere, God will confirm and ratify the absolution granted by the priest; however if repentance is insincere, then God, who judges a man's heart, will hold him accountable, even if the priest granting the absolution is deceived about the quality of the sinner's repentance.

240. 1 Cor. 10:12.

241. Rom. 14:4.

242. 1 John 2:1.

243. Rom. 5:8-9.

244. "Christ, 'holy, innocent, and undefiled,' knew nothing of sin, but came only to expiate the sins of the people. The Church, however, clasping sinners to her bosom, at once holy and always in need of purification, follows constantly the path of penance and renewal." All members of the Church, including her ministers, must acknowledge that they are sinners. In everyone, the weeds of sin will still be mixed with the good wheat of the Gospel until the end of time. Hence the Church gathers sinners already caught up in Christ's salvation but still on the way to holiness" (CCC § 827).

245. Luke 12:49. The Fathers often quote this verse with reference to Purgatory.

246. Note the implicit belief in Purgatory; Cyprian contrasts the virgins and martyrs, who have "purged all sins by suffering" with those who do not do penance and will subsequently have "to be cleansed and long purged by fire."

247. Rev. 2:5.

248. Tob. 4:10.

249. In other words, penitential acts done in grace are not capable of atoning for mortal sin or granting justification, which is solely the work of Christ's death mediated to us through baptism. Penance is done for the purpose of purifying the heart from the effects of sin and countering the tendency to venial sin which exists even in belivers with the the best of intentions.

250. Rev. 2:20-22.

251. Luke 15:7.

252. Wis. 1:13.

253. Joel 2:12-13.

254. Ps. 89:3.

255. Matt. 7:9-11.

256. Eph. 4:2-3. St. Cyprian interprets the unity Paul speaks of as a visible, ecclesial unity.

257. St. Cyprian's theology of the nature of Holy Orders must be viewed in light of his tendency to overemphasize the worthiness of the minister. His statement here apparently suggests a belief that a bishop can "lose" the sacrament of orders, just as he believes heretics cannot validly baptize; both positions stem from an incomplete view of the nature of the sacraments. The Church's teaching is that Holy Orders, validly conferred, confers an indelible mark that can never be effaced, regardless of heresy or schism. An alternate interpretation is that he means that such person lose their canonical office, but not the sacramental character, which would be more in line with subsequent developments in sacramental theology.

258. 2 Tim. 2:20.

259. John 5:14.

260. 1 Cor. 6:18.

261. 2 Cor. 12:21.

262. Eph. 5:5.

263. Col. 3:5-6.

264. Ezk. 18:20.

265. Deut. 24:26.

266. Referring to the rigorist practice of condemning the lapsed to perpetual penance but witholding sacramental absolution.

LETTER 52

TO FORTUNATUS, CONCERNING THOSE
WHO YIELDED TO TORTURES.

1. Cyprian to Fortunatus, Ahymnus, Optatus, Privatianus, Donatulus, and Felix, his brethren, greeting, You have written to me, dearest brethren, that when you were in the city of Capsa for the purpose of ordaining a bishop, Superius, our brother and colleague brought before you, that Ninus, Clementianus, and Florus, our brethren, who had been previously laid hold of in the persecution, and confessing the name of the Lord, had overcome the violence of the magistracy, and the attack of a raging populace, afterwards, when they were tortured before the proconsul with severe sufferings, were vanquished by the acuteness of the torments, and fell, through their lengthened agonies, from the degree of glory to which in the full virtue of faith they were tending, and after this grave lapse, incurred not willingly but of necessity, had not yet ceased their repentance for the space of three years: of whom you thought it right to consult whether it was well to receive them now to communion.

2. And indeed, in respect of my own opinion, I think that the Lord's mercy will not be wanting to those who are known to have stood in the ranks of battle, to have confessed the name, to have overcome the violence of the magistrates and the rush of the raging populace with the persistency of unshaken faith, to have suffered imprisonment, to have long resisted, amidst the threats of the proconsul and the warring of the surrounding people, torments that wrenched and tore them with protracted repetition; so that in the last moment to have been vanquished by the infirmity of the flesh, may be extenuated by the plea of preceding deserts. And it may be sufficient for such to have lost their glory, but that we ought not, moreover, to close the place of pardon to them, and deprive them of their Father's love and of our communion; to whom we think it may be sufficient for entreating the mercy of the Lord, that for three years continually and sorrowfully, as you write, they have lamented with excessive penitential mourning. Assuredly I do not think that peace is incautiously and over-hastily granted to those, who by the bravery of their warfare, have not, we see, been previously wanting to the battle; and who, if the struggle should come on anew, might be able to regain their glory. For when it was decided in the council that penitents in peril of sickness should be assisted, and have peace granted to them, surely those ought to precede in receiving peace whom we see not to have fallen by weakness of mind, but who, having engaged in the conflict, and being wounded, have not been able to sustain the crown of their confession through weakness of the flesh; especially since, in their desire to die, they were not permitted to be slain, but the tortures wrenched their wearied frames long enough, not to conquer their faith, which is unconquerable, but to exhaust the flesh, which is weak.

3. Since, however, you have written for me to give full consideration to this matter with many of my colleagues; and so great a subject claims greater and more careful counsel from the conference of many; and as now almost all, during the first celebrations of Easter, are dwelling at home with their brethren: when they shall have completed the solenmity to be celebrated among their own people, and have begun to come to me, I will consider it more at large with each one, so that a decided opinion, weighed in the council of many priests, on the subject on which you have consulted me, may be established among us, and may be written to you. I bid you, dearest brethren, ever heartily farewell.

LETTER 53
TO CORNELIUS, ON GRANTING PEACE
TO THE LAPSED

1. Cyprian, Liberalis, Caldonius, Nicomedes, Caecilius, Junius, Marrutius, Felix, Successus, Faustinus, Fortunatus, Victor, Saturninus, another Saturninus, Rogatianus, Tertullus, Lucianus, Eutyches, Amplus, Sattius, Secundinus, another Saturninus, Aurelius, Priscus, Herculanus, Victoricus, Quintus, Honoratus, Montanus, Hortensianus, Verianus, Iambus, Donatus, Pompeius, Polycarpus, Demetrius, another Donatus, Privatianus, another Fortunatus, Rogatus and Monulus, to Cornelius their brother, greeting. We had indeed decided some time ago, dearest brother, having mutually taken counsel one with another, that they who, in the fierceness of persecution, had been overthrown by the adversary, and had lapsed, and had polluted themselves with unlawful sacrifices, should undergo a long and full repentance; and if the risk of sickness should be urgent, should receive peace on the very point of death. For it was not right, neither did the love of the Father nor divine mercy allow, that the Church should be closed to those that knock, or the help of the hope of salvation be denied to those who mourn and entreat, so that when they pass from this world, they should be dismissed to their Lord without communion and peace; since He Himself who gave the law, that things which were bound on earth should also be bound in heaven, allowed, moreover, that things might be loosed there which were here first loosed in the Church.[267] But now, when we see that the day of another trouble is again beginning to draw near,[268] and are admonished by frequent and repeated intimations that we should be prepared and armed for the struggle which the enemy announces to us, that we should also prepare the people committed to us by divine condescension, by our exhortations, and gather together from all parts all the soldiers of Christ who desire arms, and are anxious for the battle within the Lord's camp: under the compulsion of this necessity, we have decided that peace is to be given to those who have not withdrawn from the Church of the Lord, but have not ceased from the first day of their lapse to repent, and to lament, and to beseech the Lord; and we have decided that they ought to be armed and equipped for the battle which is at hand.

2. For we must comply with fitting intimations and admonitions, that the sheep may not be deserted in danger by the shepherds, but that the whole flock may be gathered together into one place, and the Lord's army may be arrived for the contest of the heavenly warfare. For the repentance of the mourners was reasonably prolonged for a more protracted time, help only being afforded to the sick in their departure, so long as peace and tranquillity prevailed, which permitted the long postponement of the tears of the mourners, and late assistance in sickness to the dying. But now indeed peace is necessary, not for the sick, but for the strong; nor is communion to be granted by us to the dying, but to the living, that we may not leave those whom we stir up and exhort to the battle unarmed and naked, but may fortify them with the protection of Christ's body and blood. And, as the Eucharist is appointed for this very purpose that it may be a safeguard to the receivers, it is needful that we may arm those whom we wish to be safe against the adversary with the protection of the Lord's abundance. For how do we teach or provoke them to shed their blood in confession of His name if we deny to those who are about to enter on the warfare the blood of Christ? Or how do we make them fit for the cup of martyrdom, if we do not first admit them to drink, in the Church, the cup of the Lord by the right of communion?

3. We should make a difference, dearest brother, between those who either have apostatized, and, having returned to the world which they have renounced, are living heathenish lives, or, having become deserters to the heretics, are daily taking up parricidal arms against the Church; and those who do not depart from the Church's threshold, and, constantly and sorrowfully imploring divine and paternal consolation, profess that they are now prepared for the battle, and ready to stand and fight bravely for the name of their Lord and for their own salvation. In these times we grant peace, not to those who sleep, but to those who watch. We grant peace, not amid indulgences, but amid arms. We grant peace, not for rest, but for the field of battle. If, according to what we hear, and desire, and believe of them, they shall stand bravely, and shall overthrow the adversary with us in the encounter, we shall not repent of having granted peace to men so brave. Yea, it is the great honor and glory of our episcopate to have granted peace to martyrs, so that we, as priests, who daily celebrate the sacrifices of God, may prepare offerings and victims for God.[269] But if—which may the Lord avert from our brethren—any one of the lapsed should deceive, seeking peace by guile, and at the time of the impending struggle receiving peace without any purpose of doing battle, he betrays and deceives himself, hiding one thing in his heart and pronouncing another with his voice. We, so far as it is allowed to us to see and to judge, look upon the face of each one; we are not able to scrutinize the heart and to inspect the mind. Concerning these the Discerner and Searcher of hidden things judges, and He will quickly come and judge of the secrets and hidden things of the heart. But the evil ought not to stand in the way of the good, but rather the evil ought to be assisted by the good. Neither is peace, therefore, to be denied to those who are about to endure martyrdom, because there are some who will refuse it, since for this purpose peace should be granted to all who are about to enter upon the warfare, that through our ignorance he may not be the first one to be passed over, who in the struggle is to be crowned.

4. Nor let any one say, that he who accepts martyrdom is baptized in his own blood, and peace is not necessary to him from the bishop, since he is about to have the peace of his own glory, and about to receive a greater reward from the condescension of the Lord.[270] First of all, he cannot be fitted for martyrdom who is not armed for the contest by the Church; and his spirit is deficient which the Eucharist received does not raise and stimulate. For the Lord says in His Gospel: "But when they deliver you up, take no thought what you shall speak; for it shall be given you in that hour what you shall speak. For it is not you that speak, but the Spirit of your Father which speaks in you."[271] Now, since He says that the Spirit of the Father speaks in those who are delivered up and set in the confession of His name, how can he be found prepared or fit for that confession who has not first, in the reception of peace, received the Spirit of the Father, who, giving strength to His servants, Himself speaks and confesses in us?[272] Then, besides—if, having forsaken everything that he has, a man shall flee, and dwelling in hiding-places and in solitude, shall fall by chance among thieves, or shall die in fever and in weakness, will it not be charged upon us that so good a soldier, who has forsaken all that he has, and contemning his house, and his parents, and his children, has preferred to follow his Lord, dies without peace and without communion? Will not either inactive negligence or cruel hardness be ascribed to us in the day of judgment, that, pastors though we are, we have neither been willing to take care of the sheep trusted and committed to us in peace, nor to arm them in battle? Would not the charge be brought against us by the Lord, which by His prophet He utters and says, "Behold, you consume the milk, and you clothe you with the wool, and you kill them that are fed; but feed not my flock. You have not strengthened the weak; neither have you healed that which was sick, neither have you comforted that which was broken, neither have you brought again that which strayed, neither have you sought that which was lost, and that which was strong you wore out with labor."[273] And "My sheep were scattered, because there were no shepherds: and they became meat to all the beasts of the field; and there was none who sought after them, nor brought them back.[274] Therefore thus says the 'Lord, Behold, I am against the shepherds; and I will require my sheep of their hand, and cause them to cease from feeding my sheep; neither shall they feed them any more: and I will deliver my sheep from their mouth, and I will feed them with judgment.'"

5. Lest, then, the sheep committed to us by the Lord be demanded back from our mouth, wherewith we deny peace, wherewith we oppose to them rather the severity of human cruelty than the benignity of divine and paternal love; we have determined by the suggestion of the Holy Spirit and the admonition of the Lord, conveyed by many and manifest visions[275], because the enemy is foretold and shown to be at hand, to gather within the camp the soldiers of Christ, to examine the cases of each one, and to grant peace to the lapsed, yea, rather to furnish arms to those who are about to fight. And this, we trust, will please you in contemplation of the paternal mercy. But if there be any of our colleagues who, now that the contest is urgent, thinks that peace should not be granted to our brethren and sisters, he shall give an account to the Lord in the day of judgment, either of his grievous rigor or of his inhuman hardness. We, as befitted our faith and charity and solicitude, have laid before you what was in our own mind, namely, that the day of contest has approached, that a violent enemy will soon rise up against us, that a struggle is coming on, not such as it has been, but much more serious and fierce. This is frequently shown to us from above; concerning this we are often admonished by the providence and mercy of the Lord, of whose help and love we who trust in Him may be secure, because He who in peace foretells to His soldiers that the battle will come, will give to them when they are warring victory in the encounter. We bid you, dearest brother, ever heartily farewell.

NOTES

267. Cyprian's citation of Matthew 18:18 in this context demonstrates that the early Church interpreted "binding and loosing" in temrs of dictating the conditions upon which a person could be admitted to fellowship and, if they had fallen, what sort of penance was necessary to restore that fellowship.
268. A reference to the brief but fierce persecution of Trebonianus Gallus of 252-253, in which Pope Cornelius would be killed.
269. Cyprian draws a parallel between the martyrs and the sacrifice of the Mass: just as the priest of God daily offers the sacrifice of the Mass to God, so, through his ministry to the confessors, does he prepare believers for martyrdom ("offerings and victims for God").
270. Cyprian is not here doubting the validity of baptism of blood itself, but rather is questioning its efficacy for those lapsed or heretics who have not yet been reconciled to the Church.
271. Matt. 10:19-20.
272. The implication being that the grace of the Holy Spirit is imparted through the mediation of the sacramental ministry of the Church.
273. Ezk. 34:3-4.
274. Ezk. 34:6-10.
275. Though Cyprian regrettably does not give us any details about these visions, they clearly show the charismatic gifts still operating among the churches in the mid-3rd century.

LETTER 54

TO CORNELIUS, AGAINST THE HERETICS FORTUNATUS AND FELICISSIMUS[276]

1. I have read your letter, dearest brother, which you sent by Saturus our brother the acolyte, abundantly full of fraternal love and ecclesiastical discipline and priestly reproof; in which you signified that Felicissimus, no new enemy of Christ,[277] but long ago excommunicated for his very many and grave crimes, and condemned not only by my judgment, but also by that of very many of my fellow bishops, has been rejected by you there, and that when he came attended by a band and faction of desperate men, he was driven from the Church with the full rigor with which it behooves a bishop to act. From which Church long ago he was driven, with others like himself, by the majesty of God and the severity of Christ our Lord and Judge; that the author of schism and disagreement, the fraudulent user of money entrusted to him, the violator of virgins, the destroyer and corrupter of many marriages, should not, by the dishonor of his presence and his immodest and incestuous contact, violate further the spouse of Christ, hitherto uncorrupt, holy, modest.

2. But yet, when I read your other letter, brother, which you subjoined to your first one, I was considerably surprised at observing that you were in some degree disturbed by the threats and terrors of those who had come, when, according to what you wrote, they had attacked and threatened you with the greatest desperation, that if you would not receive the letters which they had brought, they would read them publicly, and would utter many base and disgraceful things, and such as were worthy of their mouth. But if the matter is thus, dearest brother, that the audacity of the most wicked men is to be dreaded, and that what evil men cannot do rightly and equitably, they may accomplish by daring and desperation, there is an end of the vigor of the episcopacy, and of the sublime and divine power of governing the Church; nor can we continue any longer, or in fact now be Christians, if it has come to this, that we are to be afraid of the threats or the snares of outcasts. For both Gentiles and Jews threaten, and heretics and all those, of whose hearts and minds the devil has taken possession, daily attest their venomous madness with furious voice. We are not, therefore, to yield because they threaten; nor is the adversary and enemy on that account greater than Christ, because he claims for himself and assumes so much in the world. There ought to abide with us, dearest brother, an immovable strength of faith; and against all the irruptions and onsets of the waves that roar against us, a steady and unshaken courage should plant itself as with the fortitude and mass of a resisting rock. Nor does it matter whence comes the terror or the danger to a bishop, who lives subject to terrors and dangers, and is nevertheless made glorious by those very terrors and dangers. For we ought not to consider and regard the mere threats of the Gentiles or of the Jews, when we see that the Lord Himself was deserted by His brethren, and was betrayed by him whom He Himself had chosen among His apostles; that also in the beginning of the world it was none other than a brother who slew righteous Abel, and an angry brother pursued the fleeing Jacob, and the youthful Joseph was sold by the act of his brethren. In the Gospel also we read that it was foretold that our foes should rather be of our own household, and that they who have first been associated in the sacrament of unity shall be they who shall betray one another. It makes no difference who delivers up or who rages, since God permits those to be delivered up whom He appoints to be crowned. For it is no ignominy to us to suffer from our brethren what Christ suffered, nor is it glory to them to do what Judas did. But what insolence it is in them, what swelling and inflated and vain boasting on the part of these threateners, there to threaten me in my absence, when here they have me present in their power! I do not fear their reproaches with which they daily wound themselves and their own life; I do not tremble at their clubs and stones and swords, which they brandish with parricidal words: as far as lies in their power such men are homicides before God. Yet they are not able to slay unless the Lord have allowed them to slay; and although I must die but once, yet they daily slay me by their hatred, their words, and their villainies.

3. But, dearest brother, ecclesiastical discipline is not on that account to be forsaken, nor priestly censure to be relaxed, because we are disturbed with reproaches or are shaken with terrors; since Holy Scripture meets and warns us, saying, "But he who presumes and is haughty, the man who boasts of himself, who has enlarged his soul as hell, shall accomplish nothing."[278] And again: "And fear not the words of a sinful man, for his glory shall be dung and worms. Today he is lifted up, and tomorrow he shall not be found, because he is turned into his earth, and his thought shall perish."[279] And again: "I have seen the wicked exalted, and raised above the cedars of Lebanon: I went by, and, lo, he was not; yea, I sought him, and his place was not found."[280] Exaltation, and puffing up, and arrogant and haughty boastfulness, spring not from the teaching of Christ who teaches humility, but from the spirit of Antichrist, whom the Lord rebukes by His prophet, saying, "For you have said in your heart, 'I will ascend into heaven, I will place my throne above the stars of God: I will sit on a lofty mountain, above the lofty mountains to the north: I will ascend above the clouds; I will be like the Most High.'"[281] And he added, saying, "Yet you shall descend into hell, to the foundations of the earth; and they that see you shall wonder at you."[282] Whence also divine Scripture threatens a like punishment to such in another place, and says, "For the day of the Lord of hosts shall be upon every one that is injurious and proud, and upon every one that is lifted up, and lofty."[283] By his mouth, therefore, and by his words, is every one at once betrayed; and whether he has Christ in his heart, or Antichrist, is discerned in his speaking, according to what the Lord says in His Gospel, "O generation of vipers, how can you, being evil, speak good things? For out of the abundance of the heart the mouth speaks. A good man out of the good treasure brings forth good things; and an evil man out of the evil treasure brings forth evil things."[284] Whence also that rich sinner who implores help from Lazarus, then laid in Abraham's bosom, and established in a place of comfort, while he, writhing in torments, is consumed by the heats of burning flame, suffers most punishment of all parts of his body in his mouth and his tongue, because doubtless in his mouth and his tongue he had most sinned.[285]

4. For since it is written, "Neither shall revilers inherit the kingdom of God," and again the Lord says in His Gospel, "Whosoever shall say to his brother, 'You fool;' and whosoever shall say, "Raca," shall be in danger of the hell fire;"[286] how can they evade the rebuke of the Lord the avenger, who heap up such expressions, not only on their brethren, but also on the priests, to whom is granted such honor of the condescension of God, that whosoever should not obey his priest, and him that judges here for the time, was immediately to be slain? In Deuteronomy the Lord God speaks, saying, "And the man that will do presumptuously, and will not hearken unto the priest or to the judge, whosoever he shall be in those days, that man shall die; and all the people, when they hear, shall fear, and shall do no more wickedly."[287] Moreover, to Samuel when he was despised by the Jews, God says; "They have not rejected you, but they have rejected me." And the Lord also in the Gospel says, "He that hears you, hears me, and Him that sent me; and he that rejects you, rejects me; and he that rejects me, rejects Him that sent me."[288] And when he had cleansed the leprous man, he said, "Go, show yourself to the priest." And when afterwards, in the time of His passion, He had received a buffet from a servant of the priest, and the servant said to Him, "Do you answer the high priest so?" the Lord said nothing reproachfully against the high priest, nor detracted anything from the priest's honor; but rather asserting His own innocence, and showing it, He says, "If I have spoken evil, bear witness of the evil; but if well, why do you smite me?"[289] Also subsequently, in the Acts of the Apostles, the blessed Apostle Paul, when it was said to him, "Do you revile God's priest?"[290]—although they had begun to be sacrilegious, and impious, and bloody, the Lord having already been crucified, and had no longer retained anything of the priestly honor and authority—yet Paul, considering the name itself, however empty, and the shadow, as it were, of the priest, said, "I knew not, brethren, that he was the high priest: for it is written, 'You shall not speak evil of the ruler of your people.'"[291]

5. When, then, such and so great examples, and many others, are precedents whereby the priestly authority and power by the divine condescension is established, what kind of people, think you, are they who, being enemies of the priests, and rebels against the Catholic Church, are frightened neither by the threatening of a forewarning Lord, nor by the vengeance of coming judgment? For neither have heresies arisen, nor have schisms originated, from any other source than from this, that God's priest is not obeyed; nor do they consider that there is one person for the time priest in the Church, and for the time judge in the stead of Christ;[292] whom, if, according to divine teaching, the whole fraternity should obey, no one would stir up anything against the college of priests; no one, after the divine judgment, after the suffrage of the people, after the consent of the co-bishops, would make himself a judge, not now of the bishop, but of God. No one would rend the Church by a division of the unity of Christ. No one, pleasing himself, and swelling with arrogance, would found a new heresy, separate and without, unless any one be of such sacrilegious daring and abandoned mind, as to think that a priest is made without God's judgment, when the Lord says in His Gospel, "Are not two sparrows sold for a farthing? And one of them does not fall to the ground without the will of your Father."[293] When He says that not even the least things are done without God's will, does any one think that the highest and greatest things are done in God's Church either without God's knowledge or permission, and that priests—that is, His stewards—are not ordained by His decree? This is not to have faith, whereby we live; this is not to give honor to God, by whose direction and decision we know and believe that all things are ruled and governed. Undoubtedly there are bishops made, not by the will of God, but they are such as are made outside of the Church—such as are made contrary to the ordinance and tradition of the Gospel, as the Lord Himself in the twelve prophets asserts, saying, "They have set up a king for themselves, and not by me." And again: "Their sacrifices are as the bread of mourning; all that eat thereof shall be polluted." And the Holy Spirit also cries by Isaiah, and says, "Woe unto you, children that are deserters. Thus says the Lord, 'You have taken counsel, but not of me; and you have made a covenant, but not of my Spirit, that you may add sin to sin.'"[294]

6. But—I speak to you as being provoked; I speak as grieving; I speak as constrained—when a bishop is appointed into the place of one deceased, when he is chosen in time of peace by the suffrage of an entire people,[295] when he is protected by the help of God in persecution, faithfully linked with all his colleagues, approved to his people by now four years' experience in his episcopate; observant of discipline in time of peace; in time of disturbance, proscribed with the name of his episcopate applied and attached to him; so often asked for in the circus for the lions; in the amphitheatre, honored with the testimony of the divine condescension; even in these very days on which I have written this letter to you, on account of the sacrifices which, by proclaimed edict, the people were commanded to celebrate, demanded anew in the circus for the lions by the clamor of the populace—when such a one, dearest brother, is seen to be assailed by some desperate and reckless men, and by those who have their place outside the Church, it is manifest who assails him: not assuredly Christ, who either appoints or protects his priests; but he who, as the adversary of Christ and the foe to His Church, for this purpose persecutes with his malice the ruler of the Church, that when the pilot is removed, he may rage more atrociously and more violently with a view to the Church's dispersion.

7. Nor ought it, my dearest brother, to disturb any one who is faithful and mindful of the Gospel, and retains the commands of the apostle who forewarns us; if in the last days certain persons, proud, contumacious, and enemies of God's priests, either depart from the Church or act against the Church, since both the Lord and His apostles have previously foretold that there should be such. Nor let any one wonder that the servant placed over them should be forsaken by some, when His own disciples forsook the Lord Himself, who performed such great and wonderful works, and illustrated the attributes of God the Father by the testimony of His doings. And yet He did not rebuke them when they went away, nor even severely threaten them; but rather, turning to His apostles, He said, "Will you also go away?"[296] manifestly observing the law whereby a man left to his own liberty, and established in his own choice, himself desires for himself either death or salvation. Nevertheless, Peter, upon whom by the same Lord the Church had been built, speaking one for all, and answering with the voice of the Church, says, "Lord, to whom shall we go? You have the words of eternal life;" and "we believe, and are sure that You are the Christ, the Son of the living God"[297]signifying, doubtless, and showing that those who departed from Christ perished by their own fault, yet that the Church which believes on Christ, and holds that which it has once learned, never departs from Him at all, and that those are the Church who remain in the house of God; but that, on the other hand, they are not the plantation planted by God the Father, whom we see not to be established with the stability of wheat, but blown about like chaff by the breath of the enemy scattering them, of whom John also in his epistle says, "They went out from us, but they were not of us; for if they had been of us, no doubt they would have continued with us."[298] Paul also warns us, when evil men perish out of the Church, not to be disturbed, nor to let our faith be lessened by the departure of the faithless. "For what," he says, "if some of them have departed from the faith? Has their unbelief made the faith of God of none effect? God forbid! For God is true, but every man a liar."[299]

8. For our own part, it befits our conscience, dearest brother, to strive that none should perish going out of the Church by our fault; but if any one, of his own accord and by his own sin, should perish, and should be unwilling to repent and to return to the Church, that we who are anxious for their well-being should be blameless in the day of judgment, and that they alone should remain in punishment who refused to be healed by the wholesomeness of our advice. Nor ought the reproaches of the lost to move us in any degree to depart from the right path and from the sure rule, since also the apostle instructs us, saying, "If I should please men, I should not be the servant of Christ."[300] There is a great difference whether one desires to deserve well of men or of God. If we seek to please men, the Lord is offended. But if we strive and labor that we may please God, we ought to contemn human reproaches and abuse.

9. But that I did not immediately write to you, dearest brother, about Fortunatus, that pseudo-bishop, constituted by a few, and those, inveterate heretics, the matter was not such as ought at once and hastily to be brought under your notice, as if it were great or to be feared; especially since you already know well enough the name of Fortunatus, who is one of the five presbyters who some time back deserted from the Church, and were lately excommunicated by the judgment of our fellow bishops, men both numerous and entitled to the greatest respect, who on this matter wrote to you last year. Also you would recognize Felicissimus, the standard-bearer of sedition, who himself also is comprised in those same letters long ago written to you by our co-bishops, and who not only was excommunicated by them here, but moreover was lately driven from the Church by you there. Since I was confident that these things were in your knowledge, and knew for certain that they abode in your memory and discipline, I did not think it necessary that the follies of heretics should be told you quickly and urgently. For indeed it ought not to pertain to the majesty or the dignity of the Catholic Church, to concern itself with what the audacity of heretics and schismatics may attempt among themselves. For Novatian's party is also said to have now made Maximus the presbyter—who was lately sent to us as an ambassador for Novatian, and rejected from communion with us—their false bishop in that place; and yet I had not written to you about this, since all these things are slighted by us; and I had sent to you lately the names of the bishops appointed there, who with wholesome and sound discipline govern the brethren in the Catholic Church. And this certainly, therefore, it was decided by the advice of all of us to write to you, that there might be found a short method of destroying error and of finding out truth, that you and our colleagues might know to whom to write, and reciprocally, from whom it behooved you to receive letters; but if any one, except those whom we have comprised in our letter, should dare to write to you, you would know either that he was polluted by sacrifice, or by receiving a certificate, or that he was one of the heretics, and therefore perverted and profane. Nevertheless, having gained an opportunity, by means of a very great friend and a clerk, I have written to you by Felicianus the acolyte, whom you had sent with Perseus our colleague, among other matters which were to be brought under your notice from their party, about that Fortunatus also. But while our brother Felicianus is either retarded there by the wind or is detained by receiving other letters from us, he has been forestalled by Felicissimus hastening to you. For thus wickedness always hastens, as if by its speed it could prevail against innocence.

10. But I intimated to you, my brother, by Felicianus, that there had come to Carthage, Privatus, an old heretic in the colony of Lambesa[301], many years ago condemned for many and grave crimes by the judgment of ninety bishops, and severely remarked upon in the letters of Fabian and Donatus, also our predecessors, as is not hidden from your knowledge; who, when he said that he wished to plead his cause before us in the council which we held on the Ides of May then past, and was not permitted, made for himself that Fortunatus a pretended bishop, worthy of his college. And there had also come with him a certain Felix, whom he himself had formerly appointed a pseudo-bishop outside the Church, in heresy. But Jovinus also, and Maximus, were present as companions with the proved heretic, condemned for wicked sacrifices and crimes proved against them by the judgment of nine bishops, our colleagues, and again excommunicated also by many of us last year in a council. And with these four was also joined Repostus of Suturnica, who not only fell himself in the persecution, but cast down by sacrilegious persuasion the greatest part of his people. These five, with a few who either had sacrificed, or had evil consciences, concurred in desiring Fortunatus as a false bishop for themselves, that so, their crimes agreeing, the ruler should be such as those who are ruled.

11. Hence also, dearest brother, you may now know the other falsehoods which desperate and abandoned men have there spread about, that although, of the sacrificers, or of the heretics, there were not more than five false bishops who came to Carthage, and appointed Fortunatus as the associate of their madness; yet they, as children of the devil, and full of lies, dared, as you write, to boast that there were present twenty-five bishops; which falsehood they boasted here also before among our brethren, saying that twenty-five bishops would come from Numidia to make a bishop for them. After they were detected and confounded in this their lie (only five who had made shipwreck coming together, and these being excommunicated by us), they sailed to Rome with the reward of their lies, as if the truth could not sail after them, and convict their lying tongues by proof of the certainty. And this, my brother, is real madness, not to think nor to know that lies do not long deceive, that the night only lasts so long as until the day brightens; but that when the day is clear and the sun has arisen, the darkness and gloom give place to light, and the robberies which were going on through the night cease. In fine, if you were to seek the names from them, they would have none which they could even falsely give. For such among them is the penury even of wicked men, that neither of sacrificers nor of heretics can there be collected twenty-five for them; and yet, for the sake of deceiving the ears of the simple and the absent, the number is exaggerated by a lie, as if, even if this number were true, either the Church would be overcome by heretics, or righteousness by the unrighteous.

12. Nor does it behoove me, dearest brother, to do like things to them, and to go through in my discourse those things which they have committed, and still commit, since we have to consider what it becomes God's priests to utter and to write. Nor ought grief to speak among us so much as shame, and I ought not to seem provoked rather to heap together reproaches than crimes and sins.

Therefore I am silent upon the deceits practiced in the Church. I pass over the conspiracies and adulteries, and the various kinds of crimes. That circumstance alone, however, of their wickedness, in which the cause is not mine, nor man's, but God's, I do not think must be withheld; that from the very first day of the persecution, while the recent crimes of the guilty were still hot, and not only the devil's altars, but the very hands and the mouths of the lapsed, were still smoking with the abominable sacrifices, they did not cease to communicate with the lapsed, and to interfere with their repentance. God cries, "He that sacrifices unto any gods, save unto the Lord only, shall be rooted out."[302] And in the Gospel the Lord says, "Whosoever shall deny me, him will I deny." And in another place the divine indignation and anger are not silent, saying, "To them have you poured out a drink-offering, and to them have you offered a meat-offering. Shall I not be angry with these things? says the Lord."[303] And they interfere that God may not be entreated, who Himself declares that He is angry; they interpose that Christ may not be besought with prayers and satisfactions, who professes that him who denies Him He will deny.

13. In the very time of persecution we wrote letters on this matter, but we were not attended to. A full council being held, we decreed, not only with our consent, but also with our threatening, that the brethren should repent, and that none should rashly grant peace to those who did not repent. And those sacrilegious persons rush with impious madness against God's priests, departing from the Church; and raising their parricidal arms against the Church, in order that the malice of the devil may consummate their work, take pains that the divine clemency may not heal the wounded in His Church. They corrupt the repentance of the wretched men by the deceitfulness of their lies, that it may not satisfy an offended God—that he who has either blushed or feared to be a Christian before, may not afterwards seek Christ his Lord, nor he return to the Church who had departed from the Church. Efforts are used that the sins may not be atoned for with just satisfactions and lamentations, that the wounds may not be washed away with tears. True peace is done away by the falsehood of a false peace; the healthful bosom of a mother is closed by the interference of the stepmother, that weeping and groaning may not be heard from the breast and from the lips of the lapsed. And beyond this, the lapsed are compelled with their tongues and lips, in the Capitol wherein before they had sinned, to reproach the priests—to assail with contumelies and with abusive words the confessors and virgins, and those righteous men who are most eminent for the praise of the faith, and most glorious in the Church. By which things, indeed, it is not so much the modesty and the humility and the shame of our people that are smitten, as their own hope and life that are lacerated. For nor is it he who hears, but he who utters the reproach, that is wretched; nor is it he who is smitten by his brother, but he who smites a brother, that is a sinner under the law; and when the guilty do a wrong to the innocent, they suffer the injury who think that they are doing it. Finally, their mind is smitten by these things, and their spirit is dull, and their sense of right is estranged: it is God's wrath that they do not perceive their sins, lest repentance should follow as it is written, "And God gave them the spirit of stupor," that is, that they may not return and be healed, and be made whole after their sins by just prayers and satisfactions.[304] Paul the apostle in his epistle lays it down, and says, "They received not the love of the truth, that they might be saved. And for this cause God shall send them strong delusion, that they should believe a lie: that they all might be judged who believed not the truth, but had pleasure in unrighteousness."[305] The highest degree of happiness is, not to sin; the second, to acknowledge our sins. In the former, innocence flows pure and unstained to preserve us; in the latter, there comes a medicine to heal us. Both of these they have lost by offending God, both because the grace is lost which is received from the sanctification of baptism, and repentance comes not to their help, whereby the sin is healed. Think you, brother, that their wickednesses against God are trifling, their sins small and moderate—since by their means the majesty of an angry God is not besought, since the anger and the fire and the day of the Lord is not feared—since, when Antichrist is at hand the faith of the militant people is disarmed by the taking away of the power of Christ and His fear? Let the laity see to it how they may amend this. A heavier labor is incumbent on the priests in asserting and maintaining the majesty of God, that we seem not to neglect anything in this respect, when God admonishes us, and says, "And now, O you priests, this commandment is for you. If you will not hear, and if you will not lay it to heart, to give glory unto my name, says the Lord, I will even send a curse upon you, and I will curse your blessing."[306] Is honor, then, given to God when the majesty and decree of God are so condemned, that when He declares that He is indignant and angry with those who sacrifice, and when He threatens eternal penalties and perpetual punishments, it is proposed by the sacrilegious, and said, "Let not the wrath of God be considered, let not the judgment of the Lord be feared, let not any knock at the Church of Christ; but repentance being done away with, and no confession of sin being made, the bishops being despised and trodden under foot, let peace be proclaimed by the presbyters in deceitful words; and lest the lapsed should rise up, or those placed without should return to the Church, let communion be offered to those who are not in communion?"

14. To these also it was not sufficient that they had withdrawn from the Gospel, that they had taken away from the lapsed the hope of satisfaction and repentance, that they had taken away those involved in frauds or stained with adulteries, or polluted with the deadly contagion of sacrifices, lest they should entreat God, or make confession of their crimes in the Church,[307] from all feeling and fruit of repentance; that they had set up outside for themselves—outside the Church, and opposed to the Church, a conventicle of their abandoned faction, when there had flowed together a band of creatures with evil consciences, and unwilling to entreat and to satisfy God. After such things as these, moreover, they still dare—a false bishop having been appointed for them by, heretics—to set sail and to bear letters from schismatic and profane persons to the throne of Peter, and to the chief church whence priestly unity takes its source;[308] and not to consider that these were the Romans whose faith was praised in the preaching of the apostle, to whom faithlessness could have no access. But what was the reason of their coming and announcing the making of the pseudo-bishop in opposition to the bishops? For either they are pleased with what they have done, and persist in their wickedness; or, if they are displeased and retreat, they know whither they may return. For, as it has been decreed by all of us—and is equally fair and just—that the case of every one should be heard there where the crime has been committed; and a portion of the flock has been assigned to each individual pastor, which he is to rule and govern, having to give account of his doing to the Lord; it certainly behooves those over whom we are placed not to run about nor to break up the harmonious agreement of the bishops with their crafty and deceitful rashness, but there to plead their cause, where they may be able to have both accusers and witnesses of their crime; unless perchance the authority of the bishops constituted in Africa seems to a few desperate and abandoned men to be too little, who have already judged concerning them, and have lately condemned, by the gravity of their judgment, their conscience bound in many bonds of sins. Already their case has been examined, already sentence concerning them has been pronounced; nor is it fitting for the dignity of priests to be blamed for the levity of a changeable and inconstant mind, when the Lord teaches and says, "Let your communication be, Yea, yea; Nay, nay."[309]

15. If the number of those who judged concerning them last year be reckoned with the presbyters and deacons, then there were more present to the judgment and hearing than are those very same persons who now seem to be associated with Fortunatus. For you ought to know, dearest brother, that after he was made a pseudo-bishop by the heretics, he was at once deserted by almost all. For those to whom in past time delusions were offered, and deceitful words were given, to the effect that they were to return to the Church together; after they saw that a false bishop was made there, learned that they had been fooled and deceived, and are daily returning and knocking at the door of the Church; while we, meanwhile, by whom account is to be given to the Lord, are anxiously weighing and carefully examining who ought to be received and admitted into the Church. For some are either hindered by their crimes to such a degree, or they are so obstinately and firmly opposed by their brethren, that they cannot be received at all except with offense and risk to a great many, For neither must some putridities be so collected and brought together, that the parts which are sound and whole should be injured; nor is that pastor serviceable or wise who so mingles the diseased and affected sheep with his flock as to contaminate the whole flock with the infection of the clinging evil. (Do not pay attention to their number. For one who fears God is better than a thousand impious sons, as the Lord spoke by the prophet, saying, "O son, do not delight in ungodly sons, though they multiply to you, except the fear of the Lord be with them."[310]) Oh, if you could, dearest brother, be with us here when those evil and perverse men return from schism, you would see what labor is mine to persuade patience to our brethren, that they should calm their grief of mind, and consent to receive and heal the wicked. For as they rejoice and are glad when those who are endurable and less guilty return, so, on the other hand, they murmur and are dissatisfied as often as the incorrigible and violent, and those who are contaminated either by adulteries or by sacrifices, and who, in addition to this, are proud besides, so return to the Church, as to corrupt the good dispositions within it. Scarcely do I persuade the people; nay, I extort it from them, that they should suffer such to be admitted. And the grief of the fraternity is made the more just, from the fact that one and another who, notwithstanding the opposition and contradiction of the people, have been received by my facility, have proved worse than they had been before, and have not been able to keep the faith of their repentance, because they had not come with true repentance.

16. But what am I to say of those who have now sailed to you with Felicissimus, guilty of every crime, as ambassadors sent by Fortunatus the pseudo-bishop, bringing to you letters as false as he himself is false, whose letters they bring, as his conscience is full of sins, as his life is execrable, as it is disgraceful; so that, even if they were in the Church, such people ought to be expelled from the Church. In addition, since they have known their own conscience, they do not dare to come to us or to approach to the threshold of the Church, but wander about, without her, through the province, for the sake of circumventing and defrauding the brethren; and now, being sufficiently known to all, and everywhere excluded for their crimes, they sail there also to you. For they cannot have the face to approach to us, or to stand before us, since the crimes which are charged upon them by the brethren are most grievous and grave. If they wish to undergo our judgment, let them come. Finally, if they can find any excuse or defense. let us see what thought they have of making satisfaction, what fruit of repentance they bring forward. The Church is neither closed here to any one, nor is the bishop denied to any.

Our patience, and facility, and humanity are ready for those who come. I entreat all to return into the Church. I beg all our fellow-soldiers to be included within the camp of Christ, and the dwelling-place of God the Father. I remit everything. I shut my eyes to many things, with the desire and the wish to gather together the brotherhood. Even those things which are committed against God I do not investigate with the full judgment of religion. I almost sin myself, in remitting sins more than I ought. I embrace with prompt and full love those who return with repentance, confessing their sin with lowly and unaffected atonement.

17. But if there are some who think that they can return to the Church not with prayers but with threats, or suppose that they can make a way for themselves, not with lamentation and atonements, but with terrors, let them take it for certain that against such the Church of the Lord stands closed; nor does the camp of Christ, unconquered and firm with the Lord's protection, yield to threats. The priest of God holding fast the Gospel and keeping Christ's precepts may be slain; he cannot be conquered. Zacharias, God's priest, suggests and furnishes to us examples of courage and faith, who, when he could not be terrified with threats and stoning, was slain in the temple of God, at the same time crying out and saying, what we also cry out and say against the heretics, "Thus says the Lord, You have forsaken the ways of the Lord, and the Lord will forsake you."[311] For because a few rash and wicked men forsake the heavenly and wholesome ways of the Lord, and not doing holy things are deserted by the Holy Spirit, we also ought not therefore to be unmindful of the divine tradition,[312] so as to think that the crimes of madmen are greater than the judgments of priests; or conceive that human endeavors can do more to attack, than divine protection avails to defend.

18. Is the dignity of the Catholic Church, dearest brother, to be laid aside, is the faithful and uncorrupted majesty of the people placed within it, and the priestly authority and power also, all to be laid aside for this, that those who are set without the Church may say that they wish to judge concerning a prelate in the Church? Heretics concerning a Christian? Wounded men about a whole man? Maimed concerning a sound man? Lapsed concerning one who stands fast? Guilty concerning their judge? Sacrilegious men concerning a priest? What is left but that the Church should yield to the Capitol, and that, while the priests depart and remove the Lord's altar, the images and idols should pass over with their altars into the sacred and venerable assembly of our clergy, and a larger and fuller material for declaiming against us and abusing us be afforded to Novatian; if they who have sacrificed and have publicly denied Christ should begin not only to be entreated and admitted without penance done, but, moreover, in addition, to domineer by the power of their terror?

19. If they desire peace, let them lay aside their arms. If they make atonement, why do they threaten? Or if they threaten, let them know that they are not feared by God's priests. For even Antichrist, when he shall begin to come, shall not enter into the Church because he threatens; neither shall we yield to his arms and violence, because he declares that he will destroy us if we resist. Heretics arm us when they think that we are terrified by their threatenings; nor do they cast us down on our face, but rather they lift us up and inflame us, when they make peace itself worse to the brethren than persecution. And we desire, indeed, that they may not fill up with crime what they speak in madness, that they who sin with perfidious and cruel words may not also sin in deeds. We pray and beseech God, whom they do not cease to provoke and exasperate, that He will soften their hearts, that they may lay aside their madness, and return to soundness of mind; that their breasts, covered over with the darkness of sins, may acknowledge the light of repentance, and that they may rather seek that the prayers and supplications of the priest may be poured out on their behalf, than themselves pour out the blood of the priest. But if they continue in their madness, and cruelly persevere in these their parricidal deceits and threats, no priest of God is so weak, so prostrate, and so abject, so inefficient by the weakness of human infirmity, as not to be aroused against the enemies and impugners of God by strength from above; as not to find his humility and weakness animated by the vigor and strength of the Lord who protects him. It matters nothing to us by whom, or when we are slain, since we shall receive from the Lord the reward of our death and of our blood. Their concision is to be mourned and lamented, whom the devil so blinds, that, without considering the eternal punishments of Gehenna, they endeavor to imitate the coming of Antichrist, who is now approaching.

20. And although I know, dearest brother, from the mutual love which we owe and manifest one towards another, that you always read my letters to the very distinguished clergy who preside with you there, and to your very holy and large congregation, yet now I both warn and ask you to do by my request what at other times you do of your own accord and courtesy; that so, by the reading of this my letter, if any contagion of envenomed speech and of pestilent propagation has crept in there, it may be all purged out of the ears and of the hearts of the brethren, and the sound and sincere affection of the good may be cleansed anew from all the filth of heretical disparagement.

21. But for the rest, let our most beloved brethren firmly decline, and avoid the words and conversations of those whose word creeps onwards like a cancer; as the apostle says, "Evil words corrupt good morals."[313] And again: "A man that is an heretic, after one admonition, reject: knowing that he that is such is subverted, and sins, being condemned of himself."[314] And the Holy Spirit speaks by Solomon, saying, "A perverse man carries perdition in his mouth; and in his lips he hides a fire."[315] Also again, he warns us, and says, "Hedge in your ears with thorns, and hearken not to a wicked tongue." And again: "A wicked doer gives heed to the tongue of the unjust; but a righteous man does not listen to lying lips."[316] And although I know that our brotherhood there, assuredly fortified by your foresight, and besides sufficiently cautious by their own vigilance, cannot be taken nor deceived by the poisons of heretics, and that the teachings and precepts of God prevail with them only in proportion as the fear of God is in them; yet, even although needlessly, either my solicitude or my love persuaded me to write these things to you, that no commerce should be entered into with such; that no banquets nor conferences be entertained with the wicked; but that we should be as much separated from them, as they are deserters from the Church; because it is written, "If he shall neglect to hear the Church, let him be unto you as a heathen man and a publican."[317] And the blessed apostle not only warns, but also commands us to withdraw from such. "We command you," he says, "in the name of Jesus Christ our Lord, that you withdraw yourselves from every brother that walks disorderly, and not after the tradition which he received of us."[318] There can be no fellowship between faith and faithlessness. He who is not with Christ, who is an adversary of Christ, who is hostile to His unity and peace, cannot be associated with us. If they come with prayers and atonements, let them be heard; if they heap together curses and threats, let them be rejected. I bid you, dearest brother, ever heartily farewell.

NOTES

276. As the Novatian schism continues to unfold, the heretics Fortunatus and Felicissimus have written to Pope Cornelius making various accusations against Cyprian. Cyprian here answers his accusers and encourages the pope to be bold against the heretics.
277. See Letters 29, 37 and 38.
278. Hab. 2:5.
279. 1 Macc. 2:62-63.
280. Ps. 37:35-36.
281. Isa. 14:13-14.
282. Isa. 14:15-16.
283. Isa. 2:12.
284. Matt. 12:34-35.
285. Luke 16.
286. 1 Cor. 6:10, Matt. 5:22.
287. Deut. 17:12-13.
288. 1 Sam. 8:7, Luke 10:16.
289. Matt. 8:4, John 18:22, 23.
290. Acts 23:4.
291. Acts 23:5. In these series of quotes, St. Cyprian teaches that the office of the priesthood itself is worthy of honor even if the men who hold the office are not.

292. The bishop, who possesses the fullness of Holy Orders, acts *in persona Christi capitis*, "in the person of Christ the head."
293. Matt. 10:29.
294. Hos. 8:4, 9:4; Isa. 30:1.
295. An important witness to apostolic succession; each bishop is succeeded by another, "appointed into the place [or office] of the one deceased."
296. John 6:67.
297. John 6:68, 69.
298. 1 John 2:19.
299. Rom. 3:3-4.
300. Gal. 1:10.
301. See Letter 29.
302. Ex. 22:20.
303. Matt. 10:53; Isa. 57:6.
304. Rom. 11:8.
305. 2 Thess. 2:10-12.
306. Mal. 2:1-2.
307. A testimony to public nature of the sacrament of penance in the patristic age.
308. The pope, though in the hierarchy of Holy Orders is simply another bishop, nevertheless, by virtue of his succession to the throne of Peter, is the source of unity for the whole episcopate. The Second Vatican Council taught, "The Roman Pontiff, as the successor of Peter, is the perpetual and visible principle and foundation of unity of both the bishops and of the faithful" (*Lumen Gentium* 23).
309. Matt. 5:37.
310. A paraphrase of Sirach 16:1: "Rejoice not in ungodly children, if they be multiplied: neither be delighted in them, if the fear of God be not with them."
311. 2 Chron. 24:20.
312. An interesting phrase, Cyprian here acknowledges that not only the Sacred Scriptures but also the Sacred Tradition are of divine origin. "There exists a close connection and communication between sacred tradition and Sacred Scripture. For both of them, flowing from the same divine wellspring, in a certain way merge into a unity and tend toward the same end" (*Dei Verbum*, 9).
313. 1 Cor. 15:53.
314. Tit. 3:10-11.
315. Prov. 16:27.
316. Sir. 28:28; Prov. 17:4.
317. Matt. 18:17.

LETTER 55

TO THE PEOPLE OF THIBARIS[319]

1. Cyprian to the people abiding at Thibaris, greeting. I had indeed thought, beloved brethren, and prayerfully desired—if the state of things and the condition of the times permitted, in conformity with what you frequently desired—myself to come to you; and being present with you, then to strengthen the brotherhood with such moderate powers of exhortation as I possess. But since I am detained by such urgent affairs, that I have not the power to travel far from this place, and to be long absent from the people over whom by divine mercy I am placed, I have written in the meantime this letter, to be to you in my stead. For as, by the condescension of the Lord instructing me,[320] I am very often instigated and warned, I ought to bring unto your conscience also the anxiety of my warning. For you ought to know and to believe, and hold it for certain, that the day of affliction has begun to hang over our heads, and the end of the world and the time of Antichrist to draw near, so that we must all stand prepared for the battle; nor consider anything but the glory of life eternal, and the crown of the confession of the Lord; and not regard those things which are coming as being such as were those which have passed away. A severer and a fiercer fight is now threatening, for which the soldiers of Christ ought to prepare themselves with uncorrupted faith and robust courage, considering that they drink the cup of Christ's blood daily, for the reason that they themselves also may be able to shed their blood for Christ. For this is to wish to be found with Christ, to imitate that which Christ both taught and did, according to the Apostle John, who said, "He that says he abides in Christ, ought himself also so to walk even as He walked." Moreover, the blessed Apostle Paul exhorts and teaches, saying, "We are God's children; but if children, then heirs of God, and joint-heirs with Christ; if so be that we suffer with Him, that we may also be glorified together."[321]

2. Which things must all now be considered by us, that no one may desire anything from the world that is now dying, but may follow Christ, who both lives for ever, and quickens His servants, who are established in the faith of His name. For there comes the time, beloved brethren, which our Lord long ago foretold and taught us was approaching, saying, "The time comes, that whosoever kills you will think that he does God service. And these things they will do unto you, because they have not known the Father nor me. But these things have I told you, that when the time shall come, you may remember that I told you of them."[322] Nor let any one wonder that we are harassed with constant persecutions, and continually tried with increasing afflictions, when the Lord before predicted that these things would happen in the last times, and has instructed us for the warfare by the teaching and exhortation of His words. Peter also, His apostle, has taught that persecutions occur for the sake of our being proved, and that we also should, by the example of righteous men who have gone before us, be joined to the love of God by death and sufferings. For he wrote in his epistle, and said, "Beloved, think it not strange concerning the fiery trial which is thing happened unto you; but as often as you partake in Christ's sufferings, rejoice in all things, that when His glory shall be revealed, you may be glad also with exceeding joy. If you are reproached in the name of Christ, happy are you; for the name of the majesty and power of the Lord rests on you, which indeed on their part is blasphemed, but on our part is glorified."[323] Now the apostles taught us those things which they themselves also learnt from the Lord's precepts and the heavenly commands, the Lord Himself thus strengthening us, and saying, "There is no man that has left house, or land, or parents, or brethren, or sisters, or wife, or children, for the kingdom of God's sake, who shall not receive sevenfold more in this present time, and in the world to come life everlasting."[324] And again He says, "Blessed are you when men shall hate you, and shall separate you from their company, and shall cast you out, and shall reproach your name as evil for the Son of man's sake. Rejoice in that day, and leap for joy; for, behold your reward is great in heaven."[325]

3. The Lord desired that we should rejoice and leap for joy in persecutions, because, when persecutions occur, then are given the crowns of faith, then the soldiers of God are proved then the heavens are opened to martyrs. For we have not in such a way given our name to warfare that we ought only to think about peace and draw back from and refuse war, when in this very warfare the Lord walked first—the Teacher of humility, and endurance, and suffering—so that what He taught to be done, He first of all did, and what He exhorts to suffer, He Himself first suffered for us. Let it be before your eyes beloved brethren, that He who alone received all judgment from the Father, and who will come to judge, has already declared the decree of His judgment and of His future recognition, foretelling and testifying that He will confess those before His Father who confess Him, and will deny those who deny Him. If we could escape death, we might reasonably fear to die. But since, on the other hand, it is necessary that a mortal man should die, we should embrace the occasion that comes by the divine promise and condescention, and accomplish the ending provided by death with the reward of immortality; nor fear to be slain, since we are sure when we are slain to be crowned.

4. Nor let any one, beloved brethren, when he beholds our people driven away and scattered by the fear of persecution, be disturbed at seeing the brotherhood gathered together, nor the bishops discoursing. All are not able to be there together, who may not kill, but who must be killed. Wherever, in those days, each one of the brethren shall be separated from the flock for a time, by the necessity of the season, in body, not in spirit, let him not be moved at the terror of that flight; nor, if he withdraw and be concealed, let him be alarmed at the solitude of the desert place. He is not alone, whose companion in flight Christ is; he is not alone who, keeping God's temple wheresoever he is, is not without God. And if a robber should fall upon you, a fugitive in the solitude or in the mountains; if a wild beast should attack you; if hunger, or thirst, or cold should distress you, or the tempest and the storm should overwhelm you hastening in a rapid voyage over the seas, Christ everywhere looks upon His soldier fighting;

and for the sake of persecution, for the honor of His name, gives a reward to him when he dies, as He has promised that He will give in the resurrection. Nor is the glory of martyrdom less that he has not perished publicly and before many, since the cause of perishing is to perish for Christ. That Witness who proves martyrs, and crowns them, suffices for a testimony of his martyrdom.

5. Let us, beloved brethren, imitate righteous Abel, who initiated martyrdoms, he first being slain for righteousness' sake. Let us imitate Abraham, the friend of God, who did not delay to offer his son as a victim with his own hands, obeying God with a faith of devotion. Let us imitate the three children Ananias, Azarias, and Misael, who, neither frightened by their youthful age nor broken down by captivity, Judea, being conquered and Jerusalem taken, overcame the king by the power of faith in his own kingdom; who, when bidden to worship the image which Nebuchadnezzar the king had made, stood forth stronger both than the king's threats and the flames, calling out and attesting their faith by these words: "O king Nebuchadnezzar, we are not careful to answer you in this matter. For the God whom we serve is able to deliver us from the burning fiery furnace; and He will deliver us out of your hands, O king. But if not, be it known to you, that we do not serve your gods, nor worship the golden image which you have set up."[326] They believed that they might escape according to their faith, but they added, and if not, that the king might know that they could also die for the God they worshipped. For this is the strength of courage and of faith, to believe and to know that God can deliver from present death, and yet not to fear death nor to give way, that faith may be the more mightily proved. The uncorrupted and unconquered might of the Holy Spirit broke forth by their mouth, so that the words which the Lord in His Gospel spoke are seen to be true: "But when they shall seize you, take no thought what you shall speak; for it shall be given you in that hour what you shall speak. For it is not you that speak, but the Spirit of your Father which speaks in you."[327] He said that what we are able to speak and to answer is given to us in that hour from heaven, and supplied; and that it is not then we who speak, but the Spirit of God our Father, who, as He does not depart nor is separated from those who confess Him, Himself both speaks and is crowned in us. So Daniel, too, when he was required to worship the idol Bel, which the people and the king then worshipped, in asserting the honor of his God, broke forth with full faith and freedom, saying, "I worship nothing but the Lord my God, who created the heaven and the earth."[328]

6. What shall we say of the cruel tortures of the blessed martyrs in the Maccabees, and the multiform sufferings of the seven brethren, and the mother comforting her children in their agonies, and herself dying also with her children?[329] Do not they witness the proofs of great courage and faith, and exhort us by their sufferings to the triumphs of martyrdom? What of the prophets whom the Holy Spirit quickened to the foreknowledge of future events? What of the apostles whom the Lord chose? Since these righteous men were slain for righteousness' sake, have they not taught us also to die? The nativity of Christ witnessed at once the martyrdom of infants, so that they who were two years old and under were slain for His name's sake. An age not yet fitted for the battle appeared fit for the crown. That it might be manifest that they who are slain for Christ's sake are innocent, innocent infancy was put to death for His name's sake. It is shown that none is free from the peril of persecution, when even these accomplished martyrdoms. But how grave is the case of a Christian man, if he, a servant, is unwilling to suffer, when his Master first suffered; and that we should be unwilling to suffer for our own sins, when He who had no sin of His own suffered for us! The Son of God suffered that He might make us sons of God, and the son of man will not suffer that he may continue to be a son of God! If we suffer from the world's hatred, Christ first endured the world's hatred. If we suffer reproaches in this world, if exile, if tortures, the Maker and Lord of the world experienced harder things than these, and He also warns us, saying, "If the world hate you, remember that it hated me before you. If you were of the world, the world would love its own: but because you are not of the world, but I have chosen you out of the world, therefore the world hates you. Remember the word that I said unto you, 'The servant is not greater than his lord.' If they have persecuted me, they will also persecute you."[330] Whatever our Lord and God taught, He also did, that the disciple might not be excused if he learns and does not.

7. Nor let any one of you, beloved brethren, be so terrified by the fear of future persecution, or the coming of the threatening Antichrist, as not to be found armed for all things by the evangelical exhortations and precepts, and by the heavenly warnings. Antichrist is coming, but above him comes Christ also. The enemy goes about and rages, but immediately the Lord follows to avenge our sufferings and our wounds. The adversary is enraged and threatens, but there is One who can deliver us from his hands. He is to be feared whose anger no one can escape, as He Himself forewarns, and says: "Fear not them which kill the body, but are not able to kill the soul; but rather fear Him which is able to destroy both body and soul in hell."[331] And again: "He that loves his life, shall lose it; and he that hates his life in this world, shall keep it unto life eternal."[332] And in the Apocalypse He instructs and forewarns, saying, "If any man worship the beast and his image, and receive his mark in his forehead or in his hand, the same also shall drink of the wine of the wrath of God, mixed in the cup of His indignation, and he shall be tormented with fire and brimstone in the presence of the holy angels, and in the presence of the Lamb; and the smoke of their torments shall ascend up for ever and ever; and they shall have no rest day nor night, who worship the beast and his image."[333]

8. For the secular contest men are trained and prepared, and reckon it a great glory of their honor if it should happen to them to be crowned in the sight of the people, and in the presence of the emperor. Behold a lofty and great contest, glorious also with the reward of a heavenly crown, inasmuch as God looks upon us as we struggle, and, extending His view over those whom He has condescended to make His sons, He enjoys the spectacle of our contest. God looks upon us in the warfare, and fighting in the encounter of faith; His angels look on us, and Christ looks on us. How great is the dignity, and how great the happiness of the glory, to engage in the presence of God, and to be crowned, with Christ for a judge! Let us be armed, beloved brethren, with our whole strength, and let us be prepared for the struggle with an uncorrupted mind, with a sound faith, with a devoted courage. Let the camp of God go forth to the battle-field which is appointed to us. Let the sound ones be armed, lest he that is sound should lose the advantage of having lately stood; let the lapsed also be armed, that even the lapsed may regain what he has lost: let honor provoke the whole; let sorrow provoke the lapsed to the battle. The Apostle Paul teaches us to be armed and prepared, saying, "We wrestle not against flesh and blood, but against powers, and the princes of this world and of this darkness, against spirits of wickedness in high places. Wherefore put on the whole armor, that you may be able to withstand in the most evil day, that when you have done all you may stand; having your loins girt about with truth, and having put on the breastplate of righteousness; and your feet shod with the preparation of the Gospel of peace; taking the shield of faith, wherewith you shall be able to quench all the fiery darts of the wicked one; and the helmet of salvation, and the sword of the Spirit, which is the word of God."[334]

9. Let us take these arms, let us fortify ourselves with these spiritual and heavenly safeguards, that in the most evil day we may be able to withstand, and to resist the threats of the devil: let us put on the breastplate of righteousness, that our breast may be fortified and safe against the darts of the enemy: let our feet be shod with evangelical teaching, and armed, so that when the serpent shall begin to be trodden and crushed by us, he may not be able to bite and trip us up: let us bravely bear the shield of faith, by the protection of which, whatever the enemy darts at us may be extinguished: let us take also for protection of our head the helmet of salvation, that our ears may be guarded from hearing the deadly edicts; that our eyes may be fortified, that they may not see the odious images; that our brow may be fortified, so as to keep safe the sign of God;[335] that our mouth may be fortified, that the conquering tongue may confess Christ its Lord: let us also arm the right hand with the sword of the Spirit, that it may bravely reject the deadly sacrifices; that, mindful of the Eucharist, the hand which has received the Lord's body may embrace the Lord Himself, hereafter to receive from the Lord the reward of heavenly crowns.

10. Oh, what and how great will that day be at its coming, beloved brethren, when the Lord shall begin to count up His people, and to recognize the deservings of each one by the inspection of His divine knowledge, to send the guilty to Gehenna, and to set on fire our persecutors with the perpetual burning of a penal fire, but to pay to us the reward of our faith and devotion! What will be the glory and how great the joy to be admitted to see God, to be honored to receive with Christ, your Lord God, the joy of eternal salvation and light—to greet Abraham, and Isaac, and Jacob, and all the patriarchs, and prophets, and apostles, and martyrs—to rejoice with the righteous and the friends of God in the kingdom of heaven, with the pleasure of immortality given to us—to receive there what neither eye has seen, nor ear heard, neither has entered into the heart of man! For the apostle announces that we shall receive greater things than anything that we here either do or suffer, saying, "The sufferings of this present time are not worthy to be compared with the glory to come hereafter which shall be revealed in us."[336] When that revelation shall come, when that glory of God shall shine upon us, we shall be as happy and joyful, honored with the condescension of God, as they will remain guilty and wretched, who, either as deserters from God or rebels against Him, have done the will of the devil, so that it is necessary for them to be tormented with the devil himself in unquenchable fire.

11. Let these things, beloved brethren, take hold of our hearts; let this be the preparation of our arms, this our daily and nightly meditation, to have before our eyes and ever to revolve in our thoughts and feelings the punishments of the wicked and the rewards and the deservings of the righteous: what the Lord threatens by way of punishment against those that deny Him; what, on the other hand, He promises by way of glory to those that confess Him. If, while we think and meditate on these things, there should come to us a day of persecution, the soldier of Christ instructed in His precepts and warnings is not fearful for the battle, but is prepared for the crown. I bid you, dearest brethren, ever heartily farewell.

NOTES

318. 2 Thess. 3:6.
319. This letter was probably written in 252 or early 253 at the outset of the shortlived persecution

of Trebonianus Gallus.

320. Cyprian previously indicated that he had been warned of the approaching persecution through visions granted to Him by the Lord; see Letter 53:5.

321. 1 John 2:6; Rom. 8:17.

322. John 16:2-4.

323. 1 Pet. 12-14.

324. Luke 18:29.

325. Matt. 5:11-12.

326. Dan. 3:16-18.

327. Matt. 10:19-20.

328. Dan. 14:5. This is from one of the Deuterocanonical portions of Daniel, found only in Catholic bibles.

329. An allusion to the tale of the seven brothers in 2 Macc. 7.

330. John 15:18-20.

331. Matt. 10:28.

332. John 12:25.

333. Rev. 14:9-11.

334. Eph. 6:12-17.

335. A reference to the *sphragis*, the "sealing" of the believer in the Holy Spirit conferred at Confirmation, imparted by the tracing of the sign of the cross on ther forehead in blessed oil. Fr. John Hardon, S.J., says of the *sphragis*: "The term originally used by the Fathers of the Church to identify the sacramental character conferred at baptism, confirmation, and orders. Literally it means a seal or identifying sign and describes the indelible and unloseable assimilation to Christ possessed by one who has the character. One is permanently and unalterably changed, so that nothing one ever does or becomes later on can eradicate this unique relationship to Christ" (*Modern Catholic Dictionary,* Fr. John Hardon, S.J.).

336. Rom. 8:18.

LETTER 56

TO CORNELIUS IN EXILE[337]

1. Cyprian to Cornelius his brother, greeting. We have been made acquainted, dearest brother, with the glorious testimonies of your faith and courage, and have received with such exultation the honor of your confession, that we count ourselves also sharers and companions in your merits and praises. For as we have one Church, a mind united, and a concord undivided, what priest does not congratulate himself on the praises of his fellow-priest as if on his own; or what brotherhood would not rejoice in the joy of its brethren? It cannot be sufficiently declared how great was the exultation and how great the joy here, when we had heard of your success and bravery, that you had stood forth as a leader of confession to the brethren there; and, moreover, that the confession of the leader had increased by the consent of the brethren; so that, while you precede them to glory, you have made many your companions in glory, and have persuaded the people to become a confessor by being first prepared to confess on behalf of all; so that we are at a loss what we ought first of all to commend in you, whether your prompt and decided faith, or the inseparable love of the brethren. Among you the courage of the bishop going before has been publicly proved, and the unitedness of the brotherhood following has been shown. As with you there is one mind and one voice, the whole Roman Church has confessed.

2. The faith, dearest brethren, which the blessed apostle commended in you has shone brightly.[338] He even then in the spirit foresaw this praise of courage and firmness of strength; and, attesting your merits by the commendation of your future doings, in praising the parents he provokes the children. While you are thus unanimous, while you are thus brave, you have given great examples both of unanimity and of bravery to the rest of the brethren. You have taught them deeply to fear God, firmly to cling to Christ; that the people should be associated with the priests in peril; that the brethren should not be separated from brethren in persecution that a concord, once established, can by no means be overcome; that whatsoever is at the same time sought for by all, the God of peace will grant to the peaceful. The adversary had leapt forth to disturb the camp of Christ with violent terror; but, with the same impetuosity with which he had come, he was beaten back and conquered; and as much fear and terror as he had brought, so much bravery and strength he also found. He had thought that he could again overthrow the servants of God, and agitate them in his accustomed manner, as if they were novices and inexperienced—as if little prepared and little cautious. He attacked one first, as a wolf had tried to separate the sheep from the flock, as a hawk to separate the dove from the flying troop; for he who has not sufficient strength against all, seeks to gain advantage from the solitude of individuals. But when beaten back as well by the faith as by the vigor of the combined army, he perceived that the soldiers of Christ are now watching, and stand sober and armed for the battle; that they cannot be conquered, but that they can die; and that by this very fact they are invincible, that they do not fear death; that they do not in turn assail their assailants, since it is not lawful for the innocent even to kill the guilty; but that they readily deliver up both their lives and their blood; that since such malice and cruelty rages in the world, they may the more quickly withdraw from the evil and cruel. What a glorious spectacle was that under the eyes of God! What a joy of His Church in the sight of Christ, that not single soldiers, but the whole camp, at once went forth to the battle which the enemy had tried to begin! For it is plain that all would have come if they could have heard, since whoever heard ran hastily and came. How many lapsed were there restored by a glorious confession! They bravely stood, and by the very suffering of repentance were made braver for the battle, that it might appear that lately they had been taken at unawares, and had trembled at the fear of a new and unaccustomed thing, but that they had afterwards returned to themselves; that true faith and their strength, gathered from the fear of God, had constantly and firmly strengthened them to all endurance; and that now they do not stand for pardon of their crime, but for the crown of their suffering.

3. What does Novatian say to these things, dearest brother? Does he yet lay aside his error? Or, indeed, as is the custom of foolish men, is he more driven to fury by our very benefits and prosperity; and in proportion as the glory of love and faith grows here more and more, does the madness of dissension and envy break out anew there? Does the wretched man not cure his own wound, but wound both himself and his friends still more severely, clamoring with his tongue to the ruin of the brethren, and hurling darts of poisonous eloquence, more severe in accordance with the wickedness of a secular philosophy than peaceable with the gentleness of the Lord's wisdom—a deserter of the Church, a foe to mercy, a destroyer of repentance a teacher of arrogance, a corrupter of truth, a murderer of love? Does he now acknowledge who is the priest of God; which is the Church and the house of Christ; who are God's servants, whom the devil molests; who the Christians, whom Antichrist attacks? For neither does he seek those whom he has already subdued, nor does he take the trouble to overthrow those whom he has already made his own. The foe and enemy of the Church despises and passes by those whom he has alienated from the Church, and led without as captives and conquered; he goes on to harass those in whom he sees Christ dwell.[339]

4. Even although any one of such should have been seized, there is no reason for his flattering himself, as if in the confession of the name; since it is manifest that, if people of this sort should be put to death outside the Church, it is no crown of faith, but is rather a punishment of treachery. Nor will those dwell in the house of God among those that are of one mind, whom we see to have withdrawn by the madness of discord from the peaceful and divine household.

5. We earnestly exhort as much as we can, dearest brother, for the sake of the mutual love by which we are joined one to another, that since we are instructed by the providence of the Lord, who warns us, and are admonished by the wholesome counsels of divine mercy, that the day of our contest and struggle is already approaching, we should not cease to be instant with all the people in fastings, in watchings, in prayers. Let us be urgent, with constant groanings and frequent prayers. For these are our heavenly arms, which make us to stand fast and bravely to persevere. These are the spiritual defenses and divine weapons which defend us. Let us remember one another in concord and unanimity. Let us on both sides always pray for one another. Let us relieve burdens and afflictions by mutual love, that if any one of us, by the swiftness of divine condescension, shall go hence the first, our love may continue in the presence of the Lord, and our prayers for our brethren and sisters not cease in the presence of the Father's mercy. I bid you, dearest brother, ever heartly farewell.

NOTES

337. This letter must have been written between June, 252, when the persecution of Gallus began and Pope Cornelius was exiled to Centumcellae, Italy, and June, 253, when Cornelius died in exile.

338. Cyprian is not the only Father to appropriate St. Paul's words in Romans 1:8, alluded to here, to the Roman Church itself. Thus, Paul's words in praise of the Roman Church, "your faith is being proclaimed throughout the whole world," are appropriated to the Roman Church of all generations.

339. One sign of the true Church, according to Cyprian, is that it is always the subject of the most vicious attacks of the evil one. One of the marks of the true Church, according to St. Robert Bellarmine, is the opposition that the Church arouses among those who attack her on the very grounds that Christ was opposed by His enemies. See also Cyprian's Letter 57:3.

LETTER 57

TO LUCIUS THE BISHOP OF ROME[340]

1. Cyprian, with his colleagues, to Lucius his brother, greeting. We had lately also congratulated you indeed, dearest brother, when the divine condescension, by a double honor, appointed you in the administration of God's Church, as well a confessor as a priest.[341] But now also we no less congratulate you and your companions, and the whole fraternity, that the benignant and liberal protection of the Lord has brought you back again to His own with the same glory, and with praises to you; that so the shepherd might be restored to feed his flock, and the pilot to manage the ship, and the ruler to govern the people; and that it might appear that your banishment was so divinely arranged, not that the bishop banished and driven away should be wanting to the Church, but that he should return to the Church greater than he had left it.

2. For the dignity of martyrdom was not the less in the case of the three youths, because, their death being frustrated, they came forth safe from the fiery furnace; nor did Daniel stand forth uncompleted in the praise he deserved, because, when he had been sent to the lions for a prey, he was protected by the Lord, and lived to glory. Among confessors of Christ, martyrdoms deferred do not diminish the merits of confession, but show forth the greatness of divine protection. We see represented in you what the brave and illustrious youths announced before the king, that they indeed were prepared to be burnt in the flames, that they might not serve his gods, nor worship the image which he had made; but that the God whom they worshipped, and whom we also worship, was able even to rescue them from the fiery furnace, and to deliver them from the hands of the king, and from imminent sufferings. This we now find carried out in the faith of your confession, and in the Lord's protection over you; so that while you were prepared and ready to undergo all punishment, yet the Lord withdrew you from punishment, and preserved you for the Church. In your return the dignity of his confession has not been abridged in the bishop, but the priestly authority has rather increased; so that a priest is assisting at the altar of God, who exhorts the people to take up the arms of confession, and to submit to martyrdom, that Antichrist is near, prepares the soldiers for the battle, not only by the urgency of his speech and his words, but by the example of his faith and courage.

3. We understand, dearest brother, and we perceive with the whole light of our heart, the salutary and holy plans of the divine majesty, whence the sudden persecution lately arose there—whence the secular power suddenly broke forth against the Church of Christ and the bishop Cornelius, the blessed martyr, and all of you; so that, for the confusion and beating down of heretics, the Lord might show which was the Church—which is its one bishop chosen by divine appointment—which presbyters are associated with the bishop in priestly honor—which is the united and true people of Christ, linked together in the love of the Lord's flock—who they were whom the enemy would harass; whom, on the other hand, the devil would spare as being his own. For Christ's adversary does not persecute and attack any except Christ's camp and soldiers; heretics, once prostrated and made his own, he despises and passes by. He seeks to cast down those whom he sees to stand.

4. And I wish, dearest brother, that the power were now given us to be with you there on your return, that we ourselves, who love you with mutual love, might, being present with the rest, also receive the very joyous fruit of your coming. What exultation among all the brethren there; what running together and embracing of each one as they arrive! Scarcely can you be satisfied with the kisses of those who cling to you; scarcely can the very faces and eyes of the people be satiated with seeing. At the joy of your coming the brotherhood there has begun to recognize what and how great a joy will follow when Christ shall come. For because His advent will quickly approach, a kind of representation has now gone before in you; that just as John, His forerunner and preparer of His way, came and preached that Christ had come, so, now that a bishop returns as a confessor of the Lord, and His priest, it appears that the Lord also is now returning. But I and my colleagues, and all the brotherhood, send this letter to you in the stead of us, dearest brother; and setting forth to you by our letter our joy, we express the faithful inclination of our love here also in our sacrifices and our prayers, not ceasing to give thanks to God the Father, and to Christ His Son our Lord; and as well to pray as to entreat, that He who is perfect, and makes perfect, will keep and perfect in you the glorious crown of your confession, who perchance has called you back for this purpose, that your glory should not be hidden, if the martyrdom of your confession should be consummated away from home. For the victim which affords an example to the brotherhood both of courage and of faith, ought to be offered up when the brethren are present. We bid you, dearest brother, ever heartily farewell.

NOTES

340. Pope Lucius (253-254) was elevated to the papacy following the death of Cornelius in June, 253. He was banished upon assuming the Chair of Peter but was shortly recalled, which occasioned this letter from Cyprian. Lucius would die soon after, on March 5th, 254. He is listed in the Roman Martyrology, though it does not state that he suffered martyrdom, only that "for his faith in Christ he suffered exile and acted as an outstanding confessor of the faith, with moderation and prudence, in the difficult times that were his." Because the facts surrounding his martyrdom are uncertain, his feast was moved in the Roman Martyrology to the day of his death and omitted from the General Calendar in 1969.

341. Notice that Cyprian refers to Lucius as administering not the "Church of Rome," but "God's Church," implying that he who administers the Church of Rome in fact administers God's Church. See also Letter 44:3, where Cyprian refers to the local Church at Rome as the "root and matrix" of the Church universal, and Letter 65:2, where Pope Cornelius is said to be ordained not "in the Church of Rome" but "in the Catholic Church."

LETTER 58[342]

ON THE BAPTISM OF INFANTS

1. Cyprian, and others his colleagues who were present in council, in number sixty-six, to Fidus their brother, greeting. We have read your letter, dearest brother, in which you intimated concerning Victor, formerly a presbyter, that our colleague Therapius, rashly at a too early season, and with over-eager haste, granted peace to him before he had fully repented, and had satisfied the Lord God, against whom he had sinned; which thing rather disturbed us, that it was a departure from the authority of our decree, that peace should be granted to him before the legitimate and full time of satisfaction, and without the request and consciousness of the people—no sickness rendering it urgent, and no necessity compelling it. But the judgment being long weighed among us, it was considered sufficient to rebuke Therapius our colleague for having done this rashly, and to have instructed him that he should not do the like with any other. Yet we did not think that the peace once granted in any wise by a priest of God was to be taken away, and for this reason have allowed Victor to avail himself of the communion granted to him.

2. But in respect of the case of the infants, which you say ought not to be baptized within the second or third day after their birth, and that the law of ancient circumcision should be regarded, so that you think that one who is just born should not be baptized and sanctified within the eighth day, we all thought very differently in our council. For in this course which you thought was to be taken, no one agreed; but we all rather judge that the mercy and grace of God is not to be refused to any one born of man. For as the Lord says in His Gospel, "The Son of man is not come to destroy men's lives, but to save them."[343] As far as we can we must strive that, if possible, no soul be lost. For what is wanting to him who has once been formed in the womb by the hand of God? To us, indeed, and to our eyes, according to the worldly course of days, they who are born appear to receive an increase. But whatever things are made by God, are completed by the majesty and work of God their Maker.

3. Moreover, belief in divine Scripture declares to us, that among all, whether infants or those who are older, there is the same equality of the divine gift. Elisha, beseeching God, so laid himself upon the infant son of the widow, who was lying dead, that his head was applied to his head, and his face to his face, and the limbs of Elisha were spread over and joined to each of the limbs of the child, and his feet to his feet. If this thing be considered with respect to the inequality of our birth and our body, an infant could not be made equal with a person grown up and mature, nor could its little limbs fit and be equal to the larger limbs of a man. But in that is expressed the divine and spiritual equality, that all men are like and equal, since they have once been made by God; and our age may have a difference in the increase of our bodies, according to the world, but not according to God; unless that very grace also which is given to the baptized is given either less or more, according to the age of the receivers, whereas the Holy Spirit is not given with measure, but by the love and mercy of the Father alike to all. For God, as He is no respecter of persons, is no respecter of age; since He shows Himself Father to all with well-weighed equality for the attainment of heavenly grace.

4. For, with respect to what you say, that the aspect of an infant in the first days after its birth is not pure, so that any one of us would still shudder at kissing it, we do not think that this ought to be alleged as any impediment to heavenly grace. For it is written, "To the pure all things are pure."[344] Nor ought any of us to shudder at that which God has condescended to make. For although the infant is still fresh from its birth, yet it is not such that any one should shudder at kissing it in giving grace and in making peace; since in the kiss of an infant every one of us ought for his very religion's sake, to consider the still recent hands of God themselves, which in some sort we are kissing, in the man lately formed and freshly born, when we are embracing that which God has made. For in respect of the observance of the eighth day in the Jewish circumcision of the flesh, a sacrament was given beforehand in shadow and in usage; but when Christ came, it was fulfilled in truth. For because the eighth day, that is, the first day after the Sabbath, was to be that on which the Lord should rise again, and should quicken us, and give us circumcision of the spirit, the eighth day, that is, the first day after the Sabbath, and the Lord's day, went before in the figure; which figure ceased when by and by the truth came, and spiritual circumcision was given to us.

5. For which reason we think that no one is to be hindered from obtaining grace by that law which was already ordained, and that spiritual circumcision ought not to be hindered by carnal circumcision, but that absolutely every man is to be admitted to the grace of Christ, since Peter also in the Acts of the Apostles speaks, and says, "The Lord has said to me that I should call no man common or unclean."[345] But if anything could hinder men from obtaining grace, their more heinous sins might rather hinder those who are mature and grown up and older. But again, if even to the greatest sinners, and to those who had sinned much against God, when they subsequently believed, remission of sins is granted— and nobody is hindered from baptism and from grace—how much rather ought we to shrink from hindering an infant, who, being lately born, has not sinned, except in that, being born after the flesh according to Adam, he has contracted the contagion of the ancient death at its earliest birth, who approaches the more easily on this very account to the reception of the forgiveness of sins—that to him are remitted, not his own sins, but the sins of another?

6. And therefore, dearest brother, this was our opinion in council, that by us no one ought to he hindered from baptism and from the grace of God, who is merciful and kind and loving to all. Which, since it is to he observed and maintained in respect of all, we think is to be even more observed in respect of infants and newly-born persons, who on this very account deserve more from our help and from the divine mercy, that immediately, on the very beginning of their birth, lamenting and weeping, they do nothing else but entreat. We bid you, dearest brother, ever heartily farewell.

NOTES

342. While Cyprian's letter is not about infant baptism per se, but rather how soon after birth infants should be baptized, his argument presumes a general acceptance of the principle of infant baptism, which is aptly summed up in his statement that "the mercy and grace of God is not to be refused of to any one born of man...whether infants or those who are older, there is the same quality of divine gift" (58:2,3). The practice of infant baptism was universally acknowledged in the early Church. See also CCC 1250.
343. Luke 4:56
344. Tit. 1:15
345. Acts 10:28

LETTER 59

TO THE BISHOPS OF NUMIDIA, ON THE REDEMPTION OF THEIR BRETHREN FROM SLAVERY AMONG THE BARBARIANS[346]

1. Cyprian to Januarius, Maximus, Proculus, Victor, Modianus, Nemesianus, Nampulus, and Honoratus, his brethren, greeting. With excessive grief of mind, and not without tears, dearest, brethren, I have read your letter which you wrote to me from the solicitude of your love, concerning the captivity of our brethren and sisters. For who would not grieve at misfortunes of that kind, or who would not consider his brother's grief his own, since the Apostle Paul speaks, saying, "Whether one member suffer, all the members suffer with it; or one member rejoice, all the members rejoice with it;" and in another place he says, "Who is weak, and I am not weak?"[347] Wherefore now also the captivity of our brethren must be reckoned as our captivity, and the grief of those who are endangered is to be esteemed as our grief, since indeed there is one body of our union; and not love only, but also religion, ought to instigate and strengthen us to redeem the members of the brethren.

2. For inasmuch as the Apostle Paul says again, "Do you not know that you are the temple of God, and that the Spirit of God dwells in you?"[348]—even although love urged us less to bring help to the brethren, yet in this place we must have considered that it was the temples of God which were taken captive, and that we ought not by long inactivity and neglect of their suffering to allow the temples of God to be long captive, but to strive with what powers we can, and to act quickly by our obedience, to deserve well of Christ our Judge and Lord and God. For as the Apostle Paul says, "As many of you as have been baptized into Christ have put on Christ,"[349] Christ is to be contemplated in our captive brethren, and He is to be redeemed from the peril of captivity who redeemed us from the peril of death; so that He who took us out of the jaws of the devil, who abides and dwells in us, may now Himself be rescued and redeemed from the hands of barbarians by a sum of money—who redeemed us by His cross and blood—who suffers these things to happen for this reason, that our faith may be tried, whether each one of us will do for another what he would wish to be done for himself, if he himself were held captive among barbarians. For who that is mindful of humanity, and reminded of mutual love, if he be a father, will not now consider that his sons are there; if he be a husband, will not think that his wife is there kept captive, with as much grief as shame for the marriage tie? But how great is the general grief among all of us, and suffering concerning the peril of virgins who are kept there, on whose behalf we must bewail not only the loss of liberty, but of modesty; and must lament the bonds of barbarians less than the violence of seducers and abominable places, lest the members dedicated to Christ, and devoted for ever in honor of continence by modest virtue, should be sullied by the lust and contagion of the insulter.

3. Our brotherhood, considering all these things according to your letter, and sorrowfully examining, have all promptly and willingly and liberally gathered together supplies of money for the brethren, being always indeed, according to the strength of their faith, prone to the work of God, but now even more stimulated to salutary works by the consideration of so great a suffering. For since the Lord in His Gospel says, "I was sick, and you visited me,"[350] with how much greater reward for our work will He say now, "I was captive, and you redeemed me!" And since again He says, "I was in prison, and you came unto me,"[351] how much more will it be when He begins to say, "I was in the dungeon of captivity, and I lay shut up and bound among barbarians, and from that prison of slavery you delivered me, being about to receive a reward from the Lord when the day of judgment shall come!" Finally, we give you the warmest thanks that you have wished us to be sharers in your anxiety, and in so great and necessary a work—that you have offered us fruitful fields in which we might cast the seeds of our hope, with the expectation of a harvest of the most abundant fruits which will proceed from this heavenly and saving operation. We have then sent you a sum of one hundred thousand sesterces, which have been collected here in the Church over which[352] by the Lord's mercy we preside, by the contributions of the clergy and people established with us, which you will there dispense with what diligence you may.

4. And we wish, indeed, that nothing of such a kind may happen again, and that our brethren, protected by the majesty of the Lord, may be preserved safe from perils of this kind. If, however, for the searching out of the love of our mind, and for the testing of the faith of our heart, any such thing should happen, do not delay to tell us of it in your letters, counting it for certain that our church and the whole fraternity here beseech by their prayers that these things may not happen again; but if they happen, that they will willingly and liberally render help. But that you may have in mind in your prayers our brethren and sisters who have labored so promptly and liberally for this needful work, that they may always labor; and that in return for their good work you may present them in your sacrifices and prayers, I have subjoined the names of each one; and moreover also I have added the names of my colleagues and fellow priests, who themselves also, as they were present, contributed some little according to their power, in their own names and the name of their people. And besides our own amount, I have intimated and sent their small sums, all of whom, in conformity with the claims of faith and charity, you ought to remember in your supplications and prayers. We bid you, dearest brethren, ever heartily farewell, and remember us.

NOTES

346. Probably native Numidian Berbers.
347. 1 Cor. 12:26, 2 Cor. 11:29
348. 1 Cor. 3:16
349. Gal. 3:27
350. Matt. 25:36
351. Ibid.
352. One hundred thousand sesterces approximates to around $125,000 American (c. 2012). The fact that Cyprian was able to raise this much so quickly for the redemption of captives indicates that the Church of Carthage was large and affluent enough to easily furnish such a sum.

LETTER 60

AN ACTOR IS THREATENED WITH EXCOMMUNICATION

1. Cyprian to Euchratius his brother, greeting. From our mutual love and your reverence for me you have thought that I should be consulted, dearest brother, as to my opinion concerning a certain actor, who, being settled among you, still persists in the discredit of the same art of his; and as a master and teacher, not for the instruction, but for the destruction of boys, that which he has unfortunately learned he also imparts to others: you ask whether such a one ought to communicate with us.[353] This, I think, neither befits the divine majesty nor the discipline of the Gospel, that the modesty and credit of the Church should be polluted by so disgraceful and infamous a contagion. For since, in the law, men are forbidden to put on a woman's garment, and those that offend in this manner are judged accursed, how much greater is the crime, not only to take women's garments, but also to express base and effeminate and luxurious gestures, by the teaching of an immodest art?

2. Nor let any one excuse himself that he himself has given up the theater, while he is still teaching the art to others. For he cannot appear to have given it up who substitutes others in his place, and who, instead of himself alone, supplies many in his stead; against God's appointment, instructing and teaching in what way a man may be broken down into a woman, and his sex changed by art, and how the devil who pollutes the divine image may be gratified by the sins of a corrupted and enervated body. But if such a one alleges poverty and the necessity of small means, his necessity also can be assisted among the rest who are maintained by the support of the Church; if he be content, that is, with very frugal but innocent food. And let him not think that he is redeemed by an allowance to cease from sinning, since this is an advantage not to us, but to himself. What more he may wish he must seek thence, from such gain as takes men away from the banquet of Abraham, and Isaac, and Jacob, and leads them down, sadly and perniciously fattened in this world, to the eternal torments of hunger and thirst; and therefore, as far as you can, recall him from this depravity and disgrace to the way of innocence, and to the hope of eternal life, that he may be content with the maintenance of the Church, sparing indeed, but wholesome. But if the Church with you is not sufficient for this, to afford support for those in need, he may transfer himself to us, and here receive what may be necessary to him for food and clothing, and not teach deadly things to others without the Church, but himself learn wholesome things in the Church. I bid you, dearest brother, ever heartily farewell.

NOTES

353. In ancient Rome, acting was a disreputable profession, and acting troupes were often practitioners of transvetitism, pedophilia, pederasty, homosexuality and all manner of promiscuity.

LETTER 61

TO POMPONIUS, CONCERNING SOME VIRGINS

1. Cyprian, Caecilius, Victor, Sedatus, Tertullus, with the presbyters who were present with them, to Pomponius their brother, greeting. We have read, dearest brother, your letter which you sent by Paconius our brother, asking and desiring us to write again to you, and say what we thought of those virgins who, after having once determined to continue in their condition, and firmly to maintain their continency, have afterwards been found to have remained in the same bed side by side with men; of whom you say that one is a deacon; and yet that the same virgins who have confessed that they have slept with men declare that they are chaste. Concerning which matters, since you have desired our advice, know that we do not depart from the traditions of the Gospel and of the apostles, but with constancy and firmness take counsel for our brethren and sisters, and maintain the discipline of the Church by all the ways of usefulness and safety, since the Lord speaks, saying, "And I will give you pastors according to mine heart, and they shall feed you with discipline."[354] And again it is written; "Whoever despises discipline is miserable;"[355] and in the Psalms also the Holy Spirit admonishes and instructs us, saying, "Keep discipline, lest haply the Lord be angry, and you perish from the right way, when His anger shall quickly burn against you."[356]

2. In the first place, therefore, dearest brother, both by overseers and people nothing is to be more eagerly sought after, than that we who fear God should keep the divine precepts with every observation of discipline, and should not suffer our brethren to stray, and to live according to their own fancy and lust; but that we should faithfully consult for the life of each one, and not suffer virgins to dwell with men—I do not say to sleep together, but to live together—since both their weak sex and their age, still critical, ought to be bridled in all things and ruled by us, lest an occasion should be given to the devil who ensnares us, and desires to rage over us, to hurt them, since the apostle also says, "Do not give place to the devil."[357] The ship is watchfully to be delivered from perilous places, that it may not be broken among the rocks and cliffs; the baggage must swiftly be taken out of the fire, before it is burnt up by the flames reaching it. No one who is near to danger is long safe, nor will the servant of God be able to escape the devil if he has entangled himself in the devil's nets. We must interfere at once with such as these, that they may be separated while yet they can be separated in innocence; because by and by they will not be able to be separated by our interference, after they have become joined together by a very guilty conscience. Moreover, what a number of serious mischiefs we see to have arisen hence; and what a multitude of virgins we behold corrupted by unlawful and dangerous conjunctions of this kind, to our great grief of mind! But if they have faithfully dedicated themselves to Christ, let them persevere in modesty and chastity, without incurring any evil report, and so in courage and steadiness await the reward of virginity. But if they are unwilling or unable to persevere, it is better that they should marry, than that by their crimes they should fall into the fire. Certainly let them not cause a scandal to the brethren or sisters, since it is written, "If meat cause my brother to offend, I will eat no flesh while the world stands, lest I make my brother to offend."[358]

3. Nor let any one think that she can be defended by this excuse, that she may be examined and proved whether she be a virgin; since both the hands and the eyes of the midwives are often deceived; and if she be found to be a virgin in that particular in which a woman may be so, yet she may have sinned in some other part of her body, which may be corrupted and yet cannot be examined. Assuredly the mere lying together, the mere embracing, the very talking together, and the act of kissing, and the disgraceful and foul slumber of two persons lying together, how much of dishonor and crime does it confess! If a husband come upon his wife, and see her lying with another man, is he not angry and raging, and by the passion of his rage does he not perhaps take his sword into his hand? And what shall Christ and our Lord and Judge think, when He sees His virgin, dedicated to Him, and destined for His holiness, lying with another? How indignant and angry is He, and what penalties does He threaten against such unchaste connections! Whose spiritual sword and the coming day of judgment, that every one of the brethren may be able to escape, we ought with all our counsel to provide and to strive. And since it behooves all by all means to keep discipline, much more is it right that overseers and deacons should be careful for this, that they may afford an example and instruction to others concerning their conversation and character. For how can they direct the integrity and continence of others, if the corruptions and teachings of sin begin to proceed from themselves?

4. And therefore you have acted advisedly and with vigor, dearest brother, in excommunicating the deacon who has often abode with a virgin; and, moreover, the others who had been used to sleep with virgins. But if they have repented of this their unlawful lying together, and have mutually withdrawn from one another, let the virgins meantime be carefully inspected by midwives; and if they should be found virgins, let them be received to communion, and admitted to the Church; yet with this threatening, that if subsequently they should return to the same men, or if they should dwell together with the same men in one house or under the same roof, they should be ejected with a severer censure, nor should such be afterwards easily received into the Church. But if any one of them be found to be corrupted, let her abundantly repent, because she who has been guilty of this crime is an adulteress, not against a husband, but against Christ; and therefore, a due time being appointed, let her afterwards, when confession has been made, return to the Church. But if they obstinately persevere, and do not mutually separate themselves, let them know that, with this their immodest obstinacy, they can never be admitted by us into the Church, lest they should begin to set an example to others to go to ruin by their crimes. Nor let them think that the way of life or of salvation is still open to them, if they have refused to obey the bishops and priests, since in Deuteronomy the Lord God says, "And the man that will do presumptuously, and will not hearken unto the priest or judge, whosoever be shall be in those days, that man shall die, and all the people shall hear and fear, and do no more presumptuously."[359] God commanded those who did not obey His priests to be slain, and those who did not hearken to His judges who were appointed for the time. And then indeed they were slain with the sword, when the circumcision of the flesh was yet in force; but now that circumcision has begun to be of the spirit among God's faithful servants, the proud and contumacious are slain with the sword of the Spirit, in that they are cast out of the Church. For they cannot live out of it, since the house of God is one, and there can be no salvation to any except in the Church. But the divine Scripture testifies that the undisciplined perish, because they do not listen to, nor obey wholesome precepts; for it says, "An undisciplined man loves not him that corrects him. But they who hate reproof shall be consumed with disgrace."[360]

5. Therefore, dearest brother, endeavor that the undisciplined should not be consumed and perish, that as much as you can, by your salutary counsels, you should rule the brotherhood, and take counsel of each one with a view to his salvation. Strait and narrow is the way through which we enter into life, but excellent and great is the reward when we enter into glory. Let those who have once made themselves eunuchs for the kingdom of heaven please God in all things, and not offend God's priests nor the Lord's Church by the scandal of their wickedness. And if, for the present, certain of our brethren seem to be made sorry by us, let us nevertheless remain in our wholesome persuasion, knowing that an apostle also has said, "Am I therefore become your enemy because I tell you the truth?"[361] But if they shall obey us, we have gained our brethren, and have formed them as well to salvation as to dignity by our address. But if some of the perverse persons refuse to obey, let us follow the same apostle, who says, "If I please men, I should not be the servant of Christ."[362] If we cannot please some, so as to make them please Christ, let us assuredly, as far as we can, please Christ our Lord and God, by observing His precepts. I bid you, brother beloved and much longed-for, heartily farewell in the Lord.

NOTES

354. Jer. 3:15.
355. Wis. 3:11.
356. Ps. 2:12.
357. Eph. 4:27.
358. 1 Cor. 8:13.
359. Deut. 17:12-13.
360. Prov. 15:12, 10.
361. Gal. 4:16.
362. Gal. 1:10.

LETTER 62

TO CAECILIUS ON THE SACRAMENT OF THE LORD'S CUP

1. Cyprian to Caecilius[363] his brother, greeting. Although I know, dearest brother, that very many of the bishops who are set over the churches of the Lord by divine condescension, throughout the whole world, maintain the plan of evangelical truth, and of the tradition of the Lord, and do not by human and novel institution depart from that which Christ our Master both prescribed and did; yet since some, either by ignorance or simplicity in sanctifying the cup of the Lord, and in ministering to the people, do not do that which Jesus Christ, our Lord and God, the founder and teacher of this sacrifice, did and taught, I have thought it as well a religious as a necessary thing to write to you this letter, that, if any one is still kept in this error, he may behold the light of truth, and return to the root and origin of the tradition of the Lord. Nor must you think, dearest brother, that I am writing my own thoughts or man's; or that I am boldly assuming this to myself of my own voluntary will, since I always hold my mediocrity with lowly and modest moderation. But when anything is prescribed by the inspiration and command of God, it is necessary that a faithful servant should obey the Lord, acquitted by all of assuming anything arrogantly to himself, seeing that he is constrained to fear offending the Lord unless he does what he is commanded.

2. Know then that I have been admonished that, in offering the cup, the tradition of the Lord must be observed, and that nothing must be done by us but what the Lord first did on our behalf, as that the cup which is offered in remembrance of Him should be offered mingled with wine. For when Christ says, "I am the true vine,"[364] the blood of Christ is assuredly not water, but wine; neither can His blood by which we are redeemed and quickened appear to be in the cup, when in the cup there is no wine whereby the blood of Christ is shown forth, which is declared by the sacrament and testimony of all the Scriptures.[365]

3. For we find in Genesis also, in respect of the sacrament in Noah, this same thing was to them a precursor and figure of the Lord's passion; that he drank wine; that he was drunken; that he was made naked in his household; that he was lying down with his thighs naked and exposed; that the nakedness of the father was observed by his second son, and was told abroad, but was covered by two, the eldest and the youngest; and other matters which it is not necessary to follow out, since this is enough for us to embrace alone, that Noah, setting forth a type of the future truth, did not drink water, but wine, and thus expressed the figure of the passion of the Lord.

4. Also in the priest Melchizedek we see prefigured the sacrament of the sacrifice of the Lord, according to what divine Scripture testifies, and says, "And Melchizedek, king of Salem, brought forth bread and wine."[366] Now he was a priest of the most high God, and blessed Abraham. And that Melchizedek bore a type of Christ, the Holy Spirit declares in the Psalms, saying from the person of the Father to the Son: "Before the morning star I begot You; You are a priest for ever, after the order of Melchizedek;"[367] which order is assuredly this coming from that sacrifice and thence descending; that Melchizedek was a priest of the most high God; that he offered wine and bread; that he blessed Abraham. For who is more a priest of the most high God than our Lord Jesus Christ, who offered a sacrifice to God the Father, and offered that very same thing which Melchizedek had offered, that is, bread and wine, to wit, His body and blood? And with respect to Abraham, that blessing going before belonged to our people. For if Abraham believed in God, and it was accounted unto him for righteousness, assuredly whosoever believes in God and lives in faith is found righteous, and already is blessed in faithful Abraham, and is set forth as justified; as the blessed Apostle Paul proves, when he says, "Abraham believed God, and it was accounted to him for righteousness."[368] You know, then, that they which are of faith, these are the children of Abraham. But the Scripture, foreseeing that God would justify the Gentiles through faith, pronounced before to Abraham that all nations should be blessed in him; "therefore they who are of faith are blessed with faithful Abraham."[369] Whence in the Gospel we find that children of Abraham are raised from stones, that is, are gathered from the Gentiles.[370] And when the Lord praised Zacchaeus, He answered and said, "This day is salvation come to this house, forasmuch as he also is a son of Abraham."[371] In Genesis, therefore, that the benediction, in respect of Abraham by Melchizedek the priest, might be duly celebrated, the figure of Christ's sacrifice precedes, namely, as ordained in bread and wine; which thing the Lord, completing and fulfilling, offered bread and the cup mixed with wine, and so He who is the fullness of truth fulfilled the truth of the image prefigured.[372]

5. Moreover the Holy Spirit by Solomon shows before the type of the Lord's sacrifice, making mention of the immolated victim, and of the bread and wine, and, moreover, of the altar and of the apostles, and says, "Wisdom has built her house, she has underlaid her seven pillars; she has killed her victims; she has mingled her wine in the chalice; she has also furnished her table: and she has sent forth her servants, calling together with a lofty announcement to her cup, saying, 'Whoever is simple, let him turn to me;' and to those that want understanding she has said, 'Come, eat of my bread, and drink of the wine which I have mingled for you.'"[373] He declares the wine mingled, that is, he foretells with prophetic voice the cup of the Lord mingled with water and wine, that it may appear that that was done in our Lord's passion which had been before predicted.

6. In the blessing of Judah also this same thing is signified, where there also is expressed a figure of Christ, that He should have praise and worship from his brethren; that He should press down the back of His enemies yielding and fleeing, with the hands with which He bore the cross and conquered death; and that He Himself is the Lion of the tribe of Judah, and should couch sleeping in His passion, and should rise up, and should Himself be the hope of the Gentiles. To which things divine Scripture adds, and says, "He shall wash His garment in wine, and His clothing in the blood of the grape."[374] But when the blood of the grape is mentioned, what else is set forth than the wine of the cup of the blood of the Lord?

7. In Isaiah also the Holy Spirit testifies this same thing concerning the Lord's passion, saying, "Wherefore are Your garments red, and Your apparel as from the treading of the wine-press full and well trodden?"[375] Can water make garments red? Or is it water in the wine-press which is trodden by the feet, or pressed out by the press? Assuredly, therefore, mention is made of wine, that the Lord's blood may be understood, and that which was afterwards manifested in the cup of the Lord might be foretold by the prophets who announced it. The treading also, and pressure of the wine-press, is repeatedly dwelt on; because just as the drinking of wine cannot be attained to unless the bunch of grapes be first trodden and pressed, so neither could we drink the blood of Christ unless Christ had first been trampled upon and pressed, and had first drunk the cup of which He should also give believers to drink.

8. But as often as water is named alone in the Holy Scriptures, baptism is referred to, as we see intimated in Isaiah: "Remember not," says he, "the former things, and consider not the things of old. Behold, I will do a new thing, which shall now spring forth; and you shall know it. I will even make a way in the wilderness, and rivers in the dry place, to give drink to my elected people, my people whom I have purchased, that they might show forth my praise."[376] There God foretold by the prophet, that among the nations, in places which previously had been dry, rivers should afterwards flow plenteously, and should provide water for the elected people of God, that is, for those who were made sons of God by the generation of baptism. Moreover, it is again predicted and foretold before, that the Jews, "if they should thirst and seek after Christ, should drink with us, that is, should attain the grace of baptism. If they shall thirst," he says, "He shall lead them through the deserts, shall bring forth water for them out of the rock; the rock shall be cloven, and the water shall flow, and my people shall drink;"[377] which is fulfilled in the Gospel, when Christ, who is the Rock, is cloven by a stroke of the spear in His passion; who also, admonishing what was before announced by the prophet, cries and says, "If any man thirst, let him come and drink. He that believes in me, as the Scripture says, out of his belly shall flow rivers of living water."[378] And that it might be more evident that the Lord is speaking there, not of the cup, but of baptism, the Scripture adds, saying, "But this spoke He of the Spirit, which they that believe in Him should receive."[379] For by baptism the Holy Spirit is received; and thus by those who are baptized, and have attained to the Holy Spirit, is attained the drinking of the Lord's cup. And let it disturb no one, that when the divine Scripture speaks of baptism, it says that we thirst and drink, since the Lord also in the Gospel says, "Blessed are they which do hunger and thirst after righteousness;"[380] because what is received with a greedy and thirsting desire is drunk more fully and plentifully. As also, in another place, the

Lord speaks to the Samaritan woman, saying, "Whosoever drinks of this water shall thirst again; but whosoever drinks of the water that I shall give him, shall not thirst for ever."[381] By which is also signified the very baptism of saving water, which indeed is once received, and is not again repeated. But the cup of the Lord is always both thirsted for and drunk in the Church.[382]

9. Nor is there need of very many arguments, dearest brother, to prove that baptism is always indicated by the appellation of water, and that thus we ought to understand it, since the Lord, when He came, manifested the truth of baptism and the cup in commanding that that faithful water, the water of life eternal, should be given to believers in baptism, but, teaching by the example of His own authority, that the cup should be mingled with a union of wine and water.[383] For, taking the cup on the eve of His passion, He blessed it, and gave it to His disciples, saying, "Drink all of this; for this is my blood of the New Testament, which shall be shed for many, for the remission of sins. I say unto you, I will not drink henceforth of this fruit of the vine, until that day in which I shall drink new wine with you in the kingdom of my Father."[384] In which portion we find that the cup which the Lord offered was mixed, and that that was wine which He called His blood. Whence it appears that the blood of Christ is not offered if there be no wine in the cup, nor the Lord's sacrifice celebrated with a legitimate consecration unless our oblation and sacrifice respond to His passion. But how shall we drink the new wine of the fruit of the vine with Christ in the kingdom of His Father, if in the sacrifice of God the Father and of Christ we do not offer wine, nor mix the cup of the Lord by the Lord's own tradition?

10. Moreover, the blessed Apostle Paul, chosen and sent by the Lord, and appointed a preacher of the Gospel truth, lays down these very things in his epistle, saying, "The Lord Jesus, the same night in which He was betrayed, took bread; and when He had given thanks, He broke it, and said, 'This is my body, which shall be given for you: do this in remembrance of me.' After the same manner also He took the cup, when he had supped, saying, 'This cup is the new testament in my blood: this do, as oft as you drink it, in remembrance of me.' For as often as you eat this bread and drink this cup, you shall show forth the Lord's death until He comes."[385] But if it is both enjoined by the Lord, and the same thing is confirmed and delivered by His apostle, that as often as we drink, we do in remembrance of the Lord the same thing which the Lord also did, we find that what was commanded is not observed by us, unless we also do what the Lord did; and that mixing the Lord's cup in like manner we do not depart from the divine teaching; but that we must not at all depart from the evangelical precepts, and that disciples ought also to observe and to do the same things which the

Master both taught and did. The blessed apostle in another place more earnestly and strongly teaches, saying, "I wonder that you are so soon removed from Him that called you into grace, unto another gospel, which is not another; but there are some that trouble you, and would pervert the Gospel of Christ. But though we, or an angel from heaven, preach any otherwise than that which we have preached to you, let him be anathema. As we said before, so say I now again, If any man preach any other gospel unto you than that you have received, let him be anathema."[386]

11. Since, then, neither the apostle himself nor an angel from heaven can preach or teach any otherwise than Christ has once taught and His apostles have announced, I wonder very much whence has originated this practice, that, contrary to evangelical and discipline, water is offered in some places in the Lord's cup, which water by itself cannot express the blood of Christ. The Holy Spirit also is not silent in the Psalms on the sacrament of this thing, when He makes mention of the Lord's cup, and says, "Your inebriating cup, how excellent it is!"[387] Now the cup which inebriates is assuredly mingled with wine, for water cannot inebriate anybody. And the cup of the Lord in such wise inebriates, as Noah also was intoxicated drinking wine, in Genesis. But because the intoxication of the Lord's cup and blood is not such as is the intoxication of the world's wine, since the Holy Spirit said in the Psalm, "Your inebriating cup," He added, "how excellent it is," because doubtless the Lord's cup so inebriates them that drink, that it makes them sober; that it restores their minds to spiritual wisdom; that each one recovers from that flavor of the world to the understanding of God; and in the same way, that by that common wine the mind is dissolved, and the soul relaxed, and all sadness is laid aside, so, when the blood of the Lord and the cup of salvation have been drunk, the memory of the old man is laid aside, and there arises an oblivion of the former worldly conversation, and the sorrowful and sad breast which before was oppressed by tormenting sins is eased by the joy of the divine mercy; because that only is able to rejoice him who drinks in the Church which, when it is drunk, retains the Lord's truth.

12. But how perverse and how contrary it is, that although the Lord at the marriage made wine of water, we should make water of wine, when even the sacrament of that thing ought to admonish and instruct us rather to offer wine in the sacrifices of the Lord. For because among the Jews there was a want of spiritual grace, wine also was wanting. For the vineyard of the Lord of hosts was the house of Israel; but Christ, when teaching and showing that the people of the Gentiles should succeed them, and that by the merit of faith we should subsequently attain to the place which the Jews had lost, of water made wine;

that is, He showed that at the marriage of Christ and the Church, as the Jews failed, the people of the nations should rather flow together and assemble: for the divine Scripture in the Apocalypse declares that the waters signify the people, saying, "The waters which you saw, upon which the whore sits, are peoples and multitudes, and nations of the Gentiles, and tongues,"[388] which we evidently see to be contained also in the sacrament of the cup.

13. For because Christ bore us all, in that He also bore our sins, we see that in the water is understood the people, but in the wine is showed the blood of Christ. But when the water is mingled in the cup with wine, the people is made one with Christ, and the assembly of believers is associated and conjoined with Him on whom it believes; which association and conjunction of water and wine is so mingled in the Lord's cup, that that mixture cannot any more be separated.[389] Whence, moreover, nothing can separate the Church—that is, the people established in the Church, faithfully and firmly persevering in that which they have believed—from Christ, in such a way as to prevent their undivided love from always abiding and adhering. Thus, therefore, in consecrating the cup of the Lord, water alone cannot be offered, even as wine alone cannot be offered. For if any one offer wine only, the blood of Christ is dissociated from us; but if the water be alone, the people are dissociated from Christ; but when both are mingled, and are joined with one another by a close union, there is completed a spiritual and heavenly sacrament. Thus the cup of the Lord is not indeed water alone, nor wine alone, unless each be mingled with the other; just as, on the other hand, the body of the Lord cannot be flour alone or water alone, unless both should be united and joined together and compacted in the mass of one bread; in which very sacrament our people are shown to be made one, so that in like manner as many grains, collected, and ground, and mixed together into one mass, make one bread; so in Christ, who is the heavenly bread, we may know that there is one body, with which our number is joined and united.

14. There is then no reason, dearest brother, for any one to think that the custom of certain persons is to be followed, who have thought in you past that water alone should be offered in the cup of the Lord. For we must inquire whom they themselves have followed. For if in the sacrifice which Christ offered none is to be followed but Christ, assuredly it behooves us to obey and do that which Christ did, and what He commanded to be done, since He Himself says in the Gospel, "If you do whatsoever I command you, henceforth I call you not servants, but friends."[390] And that Christ alone ought to be heard, the Father also testifies from heaven, saying, "This is my well-beloved Son, in whom I am well pleased; hear Him."[391] Wherefore, if Christ alone must be heard, we ought not to give heed to what another before us may have I thought was to be done, but what Christ, who is before all, first did. Neither is it becoming to follow the practice of man, but the truth of God; since God speaks by Isaiah the prophet, and says, "In vain do they worship me, teaching the commandments and doctrines of men."[392] And again the Lord in the Gospel repeats this same saying, and says, "You reject the commandment of God, that you may keep your own tradition."[393] Moreover, in another place He establishes it, saying, "Whosoever shall break one of these least commandments, and shall teach men so, he shall be called the least in the kingdom of heaven."[394] But if we may not break even the least of the Lord's commandments, how much rather is it forbidden to infringe such important ones, so great, so pertaining to the very sacrament of our Lord's passion and our own redemption, or to change it by human tradition into anything else than what was divinely appointed![395] For if Jesus Christ, our Lord and God, is Himself the chief priest of God the Father, and has first offered Himself a sacrifice to the Father, and has commanded this to be done in commemoration of Himself, certainly that priest truly discharges the office of Christ, who imitates that which Christ did;[396] and he then offers a true and full sacrifice in the Church to God the Father, when he proceeds to offer it according to what he sees Christ Himself to have offered.

15. But the discipline of all religion and truth is overturned, unless what is spiritually prescribed be faithfully observed; unless indeed any one should fear in the morning sacrifices, lest by the taste of wine he should be redolent of the blood of Christ. Therefore thus the brotherhood is beginning even to be kept back from the passion of Christ in persecutions, by learning in the offerings to be disturbed concerning His blood and His blood-shedding. Moreover, however, the Lord says in the Gospel, "Whosoever shall be ashamed of me, of him shall the Son of man be ashamed."[397] And the apostle also speaks, saying, "If I pleased men, I should not be the servant of Christ."[398] But how can we shed our blood for Christ, who blush to drink the blood of Christ?

16. Does any one perchance flatter himself with this notion, that although in the morning, water alone is seen to be offered, yet when we come to supper we offer the mingled cup? But when we sup, we cannot call the people together to our banquet, so as to celebrate the truth of the sacrament in the presence of all the brotherhood. But still it was not in the morning, but after supper, that the Lord offered the mingled cup. Ought we then to celebrate the Lord's cup after supper, that so by continual repetition of the Lord's supper we may offer the mingled cup? It behooved Christ to offer about the evening of the day, that the very hour of sacrifice might show the setting and the evening of the world; as it is written in Exodus, "And all the people of the synagogue of the children of Israel shall kill it in the evening."[399] And again in the Psalms, "Let the lifting up of my hands be an evening sacrifice."[400] But we celebrate the resurrection of the Lord in the morning.

17. And because we make mention of His passion in all sacrifices (for the Lord's passion is the sacrifice which we offer), we ought to do nothing else than what He did. For Scripture says, "For as often as you eat this bread and drink this cup, you do show forth the Lord's death till He come."[401] As often, therefore, as we offer the cup in commemoration of the Lord and of His passion, let us do what it is known the Lord did. And let this conclusion be reached, dearest brother: if from among our predecessors any have either by ignorance or simplicity not observed and kept this which the Lord by His example and teaching has instructed us to do, he may, by the mercy of the Lord, have pardon granted to his simplicity. But we cannot be pardoned who are now admonished and instructed by the Lord to offer the cup of the Lord mingled with wine according to what the Lord offered, and to direct letters to our colleagues also about this, so that the evangelical law and the Lord's tradition may be everywhere kept, and there be no departure from what Christ both taught and did.[402]

18. To neglect these things any further, and to persevere in the former error, what is it else than to fall under the Lord's rebuke, who in the psalm reproves, and says, "What have you to do to declare my statutes, or that you should take my covenant into your mouth, seeing you hate instruction and castest my words behind you? When you saw a thief, you consented with him, and hast been partaker with adulterers."[403] For to declare the righteousness and the covenant of the Lord, and not to do the same that the Lord did, what else is it than to cast away His words and to despise the Lord's instruction, to commit not earthly, but spiritual thefts and adulteries? While any one is stealing from evangelical truth the words and doings of our Lord, he is corrupting and adulterating the divine precepts, as it is written in Jeremiah. He says, "What is the chaff to the wheat? Therefore, behold, I am against the prophets, says the Lord, who steal my words every one from his neighbor, and cause my people to err by their lies and by their lightness." Also in the same prophet, in another place, He says, "She committed adultery with stones and trees, and yet for all this she turned not unto me."[404] That this theft and adultery may not fall unto us also, we ought to be anxiously careful, and fearfully and religiously to watch. For if we are priests of God and of Christ, I do not know any one whom we ought rather to follow than God and Christ, since He Himself emphatically says in the Gospel, "I am the light of the world; he that follows me shall not walk in darkness, but shall have the light of life."[405] Lest therefore we should walk in darkness, we ought to follow Christ, and to observe his precepts, because He Himself told His apostles in another place, as He sent them forth, "All power is given unto me in heaven and earth. Go, therefore, and teach all nations, baptizing them in the name of the Father, and of the Son, and of the Holy Ghost: teaching them to observe all things whatsoever I have commanded you."[406] Wherefore, if we wish to walk in the light of Christ, let us not depart from His precepts and admonitions, giving thanks that, while He instructs for the future what we ought to do, He pardons for the past wherein we in our simplicity have erred. And because already His second coming draws near to us, His benign and liberal condescension is more and more illuminating our hearts with the light of truth.

19. Therefore it befits our religion, and our fear, and the place itself, and the office of our priesthood, dearest brother, in mixing and offering the cup of the Lord, to keep the truth of the Lord's tradition, and, on the warning of the Lord, to correct that which seems with some to have been erroneous; so that when He shall begin to come in His brightness and heavenly majesty, He may find that we keep what He admonished us; that we observe what He taught; that we do what He did. I bid you, dearest brother, ever heartily farewell.

NOTES

363. Probably the same Caecilius mentioned in Pontius' *Life and Passion of Cyprian* (4), the elderly presbyter, "who had converted him from his worldly errors to the acknowledgment of the true divinity" (*Life and Passion of Cyprian*, 4).

364. John 15:1.

365. Apparently, there was a practice in some places of offering the Eucharist with water alone instead of grape wine, which Cyprian unhesitating condemns as against apostolic tradition ("contrary to evangelical discipline, water is offered in some places in the Lord's cup" (Letter 62:11). Notice the nascent sacramental theology in Cyprian's words: in order for the blood "appear to be in the cup," not only the intention and words of the minister are needed, but also the proper material, in this case, wine. He says later in the same letter, "Whence it appears that the blood of Christ is not offered if there be no wine in the cup, nor the Lord's sacrifice celebrated with a legitimate consecration unless our oblation and sacrifice respond to His passion" (9). The necessity of wine is settled by apostolic usage going back to our Lord's institution of the Eucharist: "In offering the cup, the tradition of the Lord must be observed, and that nothing must be done by us but what the Lord first did on our behalf." We see here the beginnings of a sacramental theology of form and matter.

366. Gen. 14:8.

367. Ps. 110:4.

368. Rom. 4:3.

369. Gal. 3:6-9.

370. Matt. 3:9. A testimony to the patristic belief that the Church is the true Israel; note that this is not the same as saying that the Church replaced Israel—rather the Church is, and has always been, Israel, for true Israel is those who hold the faith of Abraham.

371. Luke 19:9.

372. The identification of the sacrifice of Melchizedek with the Eucharist is, of course, found in the

current Canon of the Mass: "Look with favor on these offerings and accept them as once you accepted the gifts of your servant Abel, the sacrifice of Abraham, our Father in faith, and the bread and wine offered by your priest Melchizedek. Almighty God, we pray that your angel may take this sacrifice to your altar in heaven. Then, as we receive from this altar the sacred body and blood of your Son, let us be filled with every grace and blessing."

373. Prov. 9:1-9.

374. Gen. 49:11.

375. Isa. 63:2.

376. Isa. 43:18-21.

377. Isa. 48:21.

378. John 7:38.

379. John 7:39.

380. Matt. 5:6.

381. John 4:13-14.

382. Notice that Cyprian, a Latin African Father, makes free and easy use of the allegorical sense of Scripture and presumes that his readers understand it as well. This should be sufficient in itself to refute those who assert that the allegorical tradition was restricted to the Alexandrian school. Allegorcial approaches to Scripture were common among all the Fathers. See also Bl. John Henry Newman, *An Essay on the Development of Christian Doctrine*, Chap. VII, Sect. I§4.

383. Cyprian's argument here is complex but powerful. He begins by presuming that there are certain typological truths in the Old Testament—Old Testament signs or passages that signify New Testament realities. He then goes on to say that, whenever water is mentioned in the Old or New Testaments, it always signifies baptism, not Eucharist. That the Church has never understood these passages to refer to the cup of the Lord is evident since, even though they refer to drinking, they are types not of the Eucharist but of baptism.

384. Matt. 26:28-29.

385. 1 Cor. 11:23-26.

386. Gal. 1:6-9.

387. The Vulgate translation of Psalm 23:5, (22:5 in the Vulgate), unfamiliar to most English speakers who are accustomed to this phrase being rendered simply, "My cup overflows." The Latin says, *pones coram me mensam ex adverso hostium meorum inpinguasti oleo caput meum calix meus inebrians* ("Thou hast prepared a table before me against them that afflict me. Thou hast anointed my head with oil; and my chalice which inebreateth me, how goodly is it!")

388. Rev. 17:15.

389. An interesting interpretation of this liturgical action, since it has become common to see the mingling of the water and the wine as signifying the mingling of human nature with the Word in the Hypostatic Union: "By the mystery of this water and wine may we come to share in the divinity of Christ who humbled himself to share in our humanity" (Prayer from the Preparation of the Gifts, Roman Missal).

390. John 15:14-15.

391. Matt. 17:5.

392. Isa. 29:13.

393. Mark 7:13.

394. Matt. 5:19.

395. Clearly St. Cyprian believes that how one celebrates the sacraments of the Lord is of tremendous importance, as contrary to those modern liturgists who claim that in liturgical celebrations the form is not as important as the intention of the ministers.

396. The doctrine that the consecrated priest acts *In persona Christi capitis*. "Only to the apostles, and thenceforth to those on whom their successors have imposed hands, is granted the power of the priesthood, in virtue of which they represent the person of Jesus Christ before their

people, acting at the same time as representatives of their people before God....The priest is the same, Jesus Christ, whose sacred Person His minister represents. Now the minister, by reason of the sacerdotal consecration which he has received, is made like to the High Priest and possesses the power of performing actions in virtue of Christ's very person" (Pope Pius XII, *Mediator Dei*, 40, 69).

397. Luke 9:26.

398. Gal. 1:10.

399. Ex. 12:6.

400. Ps. 141:2.

401. 1 Cor. 11:26.

402. Not only the sacraments simply, but in this case their form and matter are part of apostolic tradition. Some sacraments, such as baptism and Eucharist, were instituted by Christ *in specie*, meaning in their specific matter and form; others, such as Holy Orders and Confirmation, are instituted *in genere*, meaning only in a general way, the specifics being left to the discretion of the Church. The Council of Trent taught that "the Church may, according to circumstances, times and places, determine or change whatever she may judge most expedient for those receiving them or for the veneration of the sacraments; and this power has always been hers" (Council of Trent, Session XXI, cap. ii). This applies more to some sacraments than to others; Cyprian rightly believes that, in the case of the Eucharist, which has been instituted *in specie*, the question of omitting the wine falls outside the pale of this authority.

403. Ps. 50:16-18.

404. Jer. 23:28, 3:9.

405. John 8:12.

406. Matt. 28:18-20.

LETTER 63

TO EPICTETUS OF ASSURAE, CONCERNING FORTUNATIANUS, FORMERLY BISHOP OF ASSURAE

1. Cyprian to Epictetus his brother, and to the people established at Assurae, greeting. I was gravely and grievously disturbed, dearest brethren, at learning that Fortunatianus, formerly bishop among you, after the sad lapse of his fall, was now wishing to act as if he were sound, and beginning to claim for himself the episcopate. Which thing distressed me; in the first place, on his own account, who, wretched man that he is, being either wholly blinded in the darkness of the devil, or deceived by the sacrilegious persuasion of certain persons; when he ought to be making atonement, and to give himself to the work of entreating the Lord night and day, by tears, and supplications, and prayers, dares still to claim to himself the priesthood which he has betrayed, as if it were right, from the altars of the devil, to approach to the altar of God. Or as if he would not provoke a greater wrath and indignation of the Lord against himself in the day of judgment, who, not being able to be a guide to the brethren in faith and virtue, stands forth as a teacher in perfidy, in boldness, and in temerity; and he who has not taught the brethren to stand bravely in the battle, teaches those who are conquered and prostrate not even to ask for pardon; although the Lord says, "To them have you poured a drink-offering, and to them have you offered a meat-offering. Shall I not be angry for these things, says the Lord?"[407] And in another place, "He that sacrifices to any god, save unto the Lord only, shall be destroyed."[408] Moreover, the Lord again speaks, and says, "They have worshipped those whom their own fingers have made: and the mean man bows down, and the great man humbles himself: and I will not forgive them."[409] In the Apocalypse also, we read the anger of the Lord threatening, and saying, "If any man worship the beast and his image, and receive his mark in his forehead or in his hand, the same shall drink of the wine of the wrath of God mixed in the cup of His anger; and he shall be tormented with fire and brimstone in the presence of the holy angels, and in the presence of the Lamb: and the smoke of their torments shall ascend up for ever and ever; neither shall they have rest day nor night, who worship the beast and his image."[410]

2. Since, therefore, the Lord threatens these torments, these punishments in the day of judgment, to those who obey the devil and sacrifice to idols, how does he think that he can act as a priest of God who has obeyed and served the priests of the devil; or how does he think that his hand can be transferred to the sacrifice of God and the prayer of the Lord which has been captive to sacrilege and to crime, when in the sacred Scriptures God forbids the priests to approach to sacrifice even if they have been in lighter guilt; and says in Leviticus: "The man in whom there shall be any blemish or stain shall not approach to offer gifts to God"?[411] Also in Exodus: "And let the priests which come near to the Lord God sanctify themselves, lest perchance the Lord forsake them."[412] And again: "And when they come near to minister at the altar of the Holy One, they shall not bring sin upon them, lest they die."[413] Those, therefore, who have brought grievous sins upon themselves, that is, who, by sacrificing to idols, have offered sacrilegious sacrifices, cannot claim to themselves the priesthood of God,[414] nor make any prayer for their brethren in His sight; since it is written in the Gospel, "God hears not a sinner; but if any man be a worshipper of God, and does His will, him He hears."[415] Nevertheless the profound gloom of the falling darkness has so blinded the hearts of some, that they receive no light from the wholesome precepts, but, once turned away from the direct path of the true way, they are hurried headlong and suddenly by the night and error of their sins.

3. Nor is it wonderful if now those reject our counsels, or the Lord's precepts, who have denied the Lord. They desire gifts, and offerings, and gain, for which formerly they watched insatiably. They still long also for suppers and banquets, whose debauch they belched forth in the indigestion lately left to the day, most manifestly proving now that they did not before serve religion, but rather their belly and gain, with profane cupidity. Whence also we perceive and believe that this rebuke has come from God's searching out, that they might not continue to stand at the altar; and any further, as unchaste persons, to have to do with modesty; as perfidious, to have to do with faith; as profane, with religion; as earthly, with things divine; as sacrilegious, with things sacred. That such persons may not return again to the profanation of the altar, and to the contagion of the brethren, we must keep watch with all our powers, and strive with all our strength, that, as far as in us lies, we may keep them back from this audacity of their wickedness, that they attempt not any longer to act in the character of priest; who, cast down to the lowest pit of death, have gone headlong with the weight of a greater destruction beyond the lapses of the laity.

4. But if, among these insane persons, their incurable madness shall continue, and, with the withdrawal of the Holy Spirit, the blindness which has begun shall remain in its deep night, our counsel will be to separate individual brethren from their deceitfulness; and, lest any one should run into the toils of their error, to separate them from their contagion. Since neither can the oblation be consecrated where the Holy Spirit is not;[416] nor can the Lord avail to any one by the prayers and supplications of one who himself has done despite to the Lord. But if Fortunatianus, either by the blindness induced by the devil forgetful of his crime, or become a minister and servant of the devil for deceiving the brotherhood, shall persevere in this his madness, do you, as far as in you lies, strive, and in this darkness of the rage of the devil, recall the minds of the brethren from error, that they may not easily consent to the madness of another; that they may not make themselves partakers in the crimes of abandoned men; but being sound, let them maintain the constant tenor of their salvation, and of the integrity preserved and guarded by them.

5. Let the lapsed, however, who acknowledge the greatness of their sin, not depart from entreating the Lord, nor forsake the Catholic Church, which has been appointed one and alone by the Lord; but, continuing in their atonements and entreating the Lord's mercy, let them knock at the door of the Church, that they may be received there where once they were, and may return to Christ from whom they have departed, and not listen to those who deceive them with a fallacious and deadly seduction; since it is written, "Let no man deceive you with vain words, for because of these things comes the wrath of God upon the children of disobedience; be not therefore partakers with them."[417] Therefore let no one associate himself with the contumacious, and those who do not fear God, and those who entirely withdraw from the Church. But if any one should be impatient of entreating the Lord who is offended, and should be unwilling to obey us, but should follow desperate and abandoned men, he must take the blame to himself when the day of judgment shall come. For how shall he be able in that day to entreat the Lord, who has both before this denied Christ, and now also the Church of Christ, and not obeying bishops sound and wholesome and living, has made himself an associate and a partaker with the dying? I bid you, dearest brethren and longed-for, ever heartily farewell.

NOTES

407. Isa. 57:6.

408. Ex. 22:20.

409. Isa. 2:8-9.

410. Rev. 14:9-11.

411. Lev. 21:7.

412. Ex. 19:22.

413. Ex. 28:43.

414. It is uncertain whether Cyprian means that the apostate priest actually loses his priesthood or simply loses the his office, which is a different matter. Given the Catholic teaching that the imposition of Holy Orders leaves an indelible mark that can never be effaced, Cyprian may have meant this in the more orthodox sense, referring not of the priesthood itself. He admits in Letter 67:5 that not even the collegial episcopate can "rescind ordination rightly perfected." But then again, given Cyprian's quasi-Donatist belief that the administration of the sacraments was bound up with the worthiness of the minister, maybe not. See Cyprian's comments at the Seventh Council of Carthage.

415. John 9:31.

416. The commission of a mortal sin, such as apostasy, means the loss of the Holy Spirit's presence and of sanctifying grace. According to Cyprian, this means also a loss in the priest's ability to confect the sacraments. Therefore, any priest in mortal sin would be unable to exercise his sacerdotal ministry. In this, Cyprian errs. St. Augustine would later clarify the true Catholic teaching: that the true minister of every sacrament is Christ, and that the power to confect the sacraments comes from God, not from the priest.

417. Eph. 5:6-7.

LETTER 64

TO ROGATIANUS, CONCERNING A DEACON
WHO CONTENDED AGAINST THE BISHOP

1. Cyprian to his brother Rogatianus, greeting. I and my colleagues who were present with me were deeply and grievously distressed, dearest brother, on reading your letter in which you complained of your deacon, that, forgetful of your priestly station, and unmindful of his own office and ministry, he had provoked you by his insults and injuries. And you indeed have acted worthily, and with your accustomed humility towards us, in rather complaining of him to us; although you have power, according to the vigor of the episcopate and the authority of your See, whereby you might be justified on him at once, assured that all we your colleagues would regard it as a matter of satisfaction, whatever you should do by your priestly power in respect of an insolent deacon, as you have in respect of men of this kind divine commands. Inasmuch as the Lord God says in Deuteronomy, "And the man that will do presumptuously, and will not hearken unto the priest or the judge, whoever he shall be in those days, that man shall die; and all the people, when they hear, shall fear, and shall no more do impiously."[418] And that we may know that this voice of God came forth with His true and highest majesty to honor and avenge His priests; when three of the ministers—Korah, Dathan, and Abiram—dared to deal proudly, and to exalt their neck against Aaron the priest, and to equal themselves with the priest set over them; they were swallowed up and devoured by the opening of the earth, and so immediately suffered the penalty of their sacrilegious audacity. Nor they alone, but also two hundred and fifty others, who were their companions in boldness, were consumed by a fire breaking forth from the Lord, that it might be proved that God's priests are avenged by Him who makes priests. In the book of Kings also, when Samuel the priest was despised by the Jewish people on account of his age, as you are now, the Lord in wrath exclaimed, and said, "They have not rejected you, but they have rejected me."[419] And that He might avenge this, He set over them Saul as a king, who afflicted them with grievous injuries, and trod on the people, and pressed down their pride with all insults and penalties, that the despised priest might be avenged by divine vengeance on a proud people.

2. Moreover also Solomon, established in the Holy Spirit, testifies and teaches what is the priestly authority and power, saying, "Fear the Lord with all your soul, and reverence His priests;"[420] and again, "Honor God with all your soul, and honor His priests."[421] Mindful of which precepts, the blessed Apostle Paul, according to what we read in the Acts of the Apostles, when it was said to him, "Do you revile thus God's high priest?" answered and said, "I knew not, brethren, that he was the high priest; for it is written, 'You shall not speak evil of the ruler of your people.'"[422] Moreover, our Lord Jesus Christ Himself, our King, and Judge, and God, even to the very day, of His passion observed the honor to priests and high priests, although they observed neither the fear of God nor the acknowledgment of Christ. For when He had cleansed the leper, He said to him, "Go, show yourself to the priest, and offer the gift."[423] With that humility which taught us also to be humble, He still called him a priest whom He knew to be sacrilegious; also under the very sting of His passion, when He had received a blow, and it was said to Him, "Do you answer the high priest so?" He said nothing reproachfully against the person of the high priest, but rather maintained His own innocence saying, "If I have spoken evil, bear witness of the evil; but if well, why do you smite me?"[424] All which things were therefore done by Him humbly and patiently, that we might have an example of humility and patience;

for He taught that true priests were lawfully and fully to be honored, in showing Himself such as He was in respect of false priests.

3. But deacons ought to remember that the Lord chose apostles, that is, bishops and overseers; while apostles appointed for themselves deacons after the ascent of the Lord into heaven, as ministers of their episcopacy and of the Church. But if we may dare anything against God who makes bishops, deacons may also dare against us by whom they are made; and therefore it behooves the deacon of whom you write to repent of his audacity, and to acknowledge the honor of the priest, and to satisfy the bishop set over him with full humility. For these things are the beginnings of heretics, and the origins and endeavors of evil-minded schismatics—to please themselves, and with swelling haughtiness to despise him who is set over them. Thus they depart from the Church—thus a profane altar is set up outside—thus they rebel against the peace of Christ, and the appointment and the unity of God. But if, further, he shall harass and provoke you with his insults, you must exercise against him the power of your dignity, by either deposing him or excommunicating him. For if the Apostle Paul, writing to Timothy, said, "Let no man despise your youth,"[425] how much rather must it he said by your colleagues to you, "Let no man despise your age?" And since you have written, that one has associated himself with that same deacon of yours, and is a partaker of his pride and boldness, you may either restrain or excommunicate him also, and any others that may appear of a like disposition, and act against God's priest. Unless, as we exhort and advise, they should rather perceive that they have sinned and make satisfaction, and suffer us to keep our own purpose; for we rather ask and desire to overcome the reproaches and injuries of individuals by clemency and patience, than to punish them by our priestly power. I bid you, dearest brother, ever heartily farewell.

NOTES

418. Deut. 17:12-13.
419. 1 Sam. 8:7.
420. Sir. 7:29.
421. Sir. 7:31.
422. Acts 23:4-5.
423. Mark 1:44.
424. John 18:23.
425. 1 Tim. 4:12.

LETTER 65

TO THE CLERGY AND PEOPLE ABIDING AT FURNI, ABOUT VICTOR[426]

1. Cyprian to the presbyters, and deacons, and people abiding at Furni,[427] greeting. I and my colleagues who were present with me were greatly disturbed, dearest brethren, as were also our fellow presbyters who sate with us, when we were made aware that Geminius Victor, our brother, when departing this life, had named Geminius Faustinus the presbyter executor to his will, although long since it was decreed, in a council of the bishops, that no one should appoint any of the clergy and the ministers of God executor or guardian by his will, since every one honored by the divine priesthood, and ordained in the clerical service, ought to serve only the altar and sacrifices, and to have leisure for prayers and supplications. For it is written: "No man that wars for God entangles himself with the affairs of this life, that he may please Him to whom he has pledged himself."[428] As this is said of all men, how much rather ought those not to be bound by worldly anxieties and involvements, who, being busied with divine and spiritual things, are not able to withdraw from the Church, and to have leisure for earthly and secular doings! The form of which ordination and engagement the Levites formerly observed under the law, so that when the eleven tribes divided the land and shared the possessions, the Levitical tribe, which was left free for the temple and the altar, and for the divine ministries, received nothing from that portion of the division; but while others cultivated the soil, that portion only cultivated the favor of God, and received the tithes from the eleven tribes, for their food and maintenance, from the fruits which grew. All which was done by divine authority and arrangement, so that they who waited on divine services might in no respect be called away, nor be compelled to consider or to transact secular business. Which plan and rule is now maintained in respect of the clergy, that they who are promoted by clerical ordination in the Church of the Lord may be called off in no respect from the divine administration, nor be tied down by worldly anxieties and matters; but in the honor of the brethren who contribute, receiving as it were tenths of the fruits, they may not withdraw from the altars and sacrifices, but may serve day and night in heavenly and spiritual things.

2. The bishops our predecessors religiously considering this, and wholesomely providing for it, decided that no brother departing should name a cleric for executor or guardian; and if any one should do this, no offering should be made for him, nor any sacrifice be celebrated for his repose.[429] For he does not deserve to be named at the altar of God in the prayer of the priests, who has wished to call away the priests and ministers from the altar. And therefore, since Victor, contrary to the rule lately made in council by the priests, has dared to appoint

Geminius Faustinus, a presbyter, his executor, it is not allowed that any offering be made by you for his repose, nor any prayer be made in the church in his name, that so the decree of the priests, religiously and needfully made, may be kept by us; and, at the same time, an example be given to the rest of the brethren, that no one should call away to secular anxieties the priests and ministers of God who are occupied with the service of His altar and Church. For care will probably be taken in time to come that this happen not with respect to the person of clerics any more, if what has now been done has been punished. I bid you, dearest brethren, ever heartily farewell.

NOTES

425. Some date this letter from before the Decian persecution, perhaps as early as 249, though this is uncertain.
426. Now El-Msaadin in Tunisia.
427. 2 Tim. 2:4
428. An explicit testimony to the offering of Masses for the dead in the time of Cyprian.

LETTER 66

TO POPE STEPHEN, CONCERNING MARCIAN OF ARLES, WHO HAD JOINED THE NOVATIANS

1. Cyprian to his brother Stephen, greeting. Faustinus our colleague, abiding at Lyons, has once and again written to me, dearest brother, informing me of those things which also I certainly know to have been told to you, as well by him as by others our fellow bishops established in the same province, that Marcian, who abides at Aries, has associated himself with Novatian, and has departed from the unity of the Catholic Church, and from the agreement of our body and priesthood, holding that most extreme depravity of heretical presumption, that the comforts and aids of divine love and paternal tenderness are closed to the servants of God who repent, and mourn, and knock at the gate of the Church with tears, and groans, and grief; and that those who are wounded are not admitted for the soothing of their wounds, but that, forsaken without hope of peace and communion, they must be thrown to become the prey of wolves and the booty of the devil; which matter, dearest brother, it is our business to advise for and to aid in, since we who consider the divine clemency, and hold the balance in governing the Church, do thus exhibit the rebuke of vigor to sinners in such a way as that, nevertheless, we do not refuse the medicine of divine goodness and mercy in raising the lapsed and healing the wounded.

2. Wherefore it behooves you to write a very copious letter to our fellow bishops appointed in Gaul, not to suffer any longer that Marcian, froward and haughty, and hostile to the divine mercy and to the salvation of the brotherhood, should insult our assembly, because he does not yet seem to be excommunicated by us; in that he now for a long time boasts and announces that, adhering to Novatian, and following his frowardness, he has separated himself from our communion; although Novatian himself, whom he follows, has formerly been excommunicated, and judged an enemy to the Church; and when he sent ambassadors to us into Africa, asking to be received into our communion, he received back word from a council of several priests who were here present, that he himself had excluded himself, and could not by any of us be received into communion, as he had attempted to erect a profane altar, and to set up an adulterous throne, and to offer sacrilegious sacrifices opposed to the true priest; while the Bishop Cornelius was ordained in the Catholic Church by the judgment of God, and by the suffrages of the clergy and people.[430] Therefore, if he were willing to return to a right mind, and to come to himself, he should repent and return to the Church as a suppliant. How vain it is, dearest brother, when Novatian has lately been repulsed and rejected, and excommunicated by God's priests throughout the whole world, for us still to suffer his flatterers now to jest with us, and to judge of the majesty and dignity of the Church!

3. Let letters be directed by you into the province and to the people abiding at Arles, by which, Marcian being excommunicated, another may be substituted in his place, and Christ's flock, which even to this day is contemned as scattered and wounded by him, may be gathered together. Let it suffice that many of our brethren have departed in these late years in those parts without peace; and certainly let the rest who remain be helped, who groan both day and night, and beseeching the divine and fatherly mercy, entreat the comfort of our succor. For, for that reason, dearest brother, the body of priests is abundantly large, joined together by the bond of mutual concord, and the link of unity; so that if any one of our college should try to originate heresy, and to lacerate and lay waste Christ's flock, others may help, and as it were, as useful and merciful shepherds, gather together the Lord's sheep into the flock. For what if any harbor in the sea shall begin to be mischievous and dangerous to ships, by the breach of its defenses; do not the navigators direct their ships to other neighboring ports where there is a safe and practicable entrance, and a secure station? Or if, on the road, any inn should begin to be beset and occupied by robbers, so that whoever should enter would be caught by the attack of those who lie in wait there; do not the travellers, as soon as this its character is discovered, seek other houses of entertainment on the road, which shall be safer, where the lodging is trustworthy, and the inns safe for the travellers? And this ought now to be the case with us, dearest brother, that we should receive to us with ready and kindly humanity our brethren, who, tossed on the rocks of Marcian, are seeking the secure harbors of the Church; and that we afford such a place of entertainment for the travellers as is that in the Gospel, in which those who are wounded and maimed by robbers may be received and cherished, and protected by the host.

4. For what is a greater or a more worthy care of overseers, than to provide by diligent solicitude and wholesome medicine for cherishing and preserving the sheep? Since the Lord speaks, and says, "The diseased you have not strengthened, neither have you healed that which was sick, neither have you bound up that which was broken, neither have you brought again that which was driven away, neither have you sought that which was lost. And my sheep were scattered because there is no shepherd; and they became meat to all the beasts of the field, and none did search or seek after them. Therefore thus says the Lord, Behold, I am against the shepherds, and I will require my flock at their hands, and cause them to cease from feeding the flock; neither shall they feed them any more: for I will deliver them from their mouth, and I will feed them with judgment."[431] Since therefore the Lord thus threatens such shepherds by whom the Lord's sheep are neglected and perish, what else ought we to do, dearest brother, than to exhibit full diligence in gathering together and restoring the sheep of Christ, and to apply the medicine of paternal affection to cure the wounds of the lapsed, since the Lord also in the Gospel warns, and says, "They that be whole need not a physician, but they that are sick?"[432] For although we are many shepherds, yet we feed one flock, and ought to collect and cherish all the sheep which Christ by His blood and passion sought for; nor ought we to suffer our suppliant and mourning brethren to be cruelly despised and trodden down by the haughty presumption of some, since it is written, "But the man that is proud and boastful shall bring nothing at all to perfection, who has enlarged his soul as hell."[433] And the Lord, in His Gospel, blames and condemns men of that kind, saying, "You are they which justify yourselves before men, but God knows your hearts: for that which is highly esteemed among men is abomination in the sight of God."[434] He says that those are execrable and detestable who please themselves, who, swelling and inflated, arrogantly assume anything to themselves. Since then Marcian has begun to be of these, and, allying himself with Novatian, has stood forth as the opponent of mercy and love, let him not pronounce sentence, but receive it; and let him not so act as if he himself were to judge of the college of priests, since he himself is judged by all the priests.

5. For the glorious honor of our predecessors, the blessed martyrs Cornelius and Lucius, must be maintained, whose memory as we hold in honor, much more ought you, dearest brother, to honor and cherish with your weight and authority, since you have become their vicar and successor. For they, full of the Spirit of God, and established in a glorious martyrdom, judged that peace should be granted to the lapsed, and that when penitence was undergone, the reward of peace and communion was not to be denied; and this they attested by their letters, and we all everywhere and entirely have judged the same thing. For there could not be among us a diverse feeling in whom there was one spirit; and therefore it is manifest that he does not hold the truth of the Holy Spirit with the rest, whom we observe to think differently. Intimate plainly to us who has been substituted at Arles in the place of Marcian, that we may know to whom to direct our brethren, and to whom we ought to write. I bid you, dearest brother, ever heartily farewell.[435]

NOTES

430. Note that Cornelius is said not to be ordained in the Church of Rome, but in the Catholic Church. See Letter 57:1 for similar language about Pope Lucius: "appointed...in the administration of God's Church."
431. Ezk. 34:1-10.
432. Matt. 9:12.
433. Heb. 2:5.
434. Luke 16:15.
435. Though Cyprian acknowledges that Marcian has already been condemned by the episcopal college ("judged by all the priests"), he implores Pope Stephen to invoke his authority and act so that the matter may be more plainly settled and peace restored to the Church of Arles. We see here a primitive testimony to the role of the Bishop of Rome as the final arbiter of all disputes within the episcopal college, a tribunal of ultimate appeal.

LETTER 67

TO THE CLERGY AND PEOPLE OF SPAIN, CONCERNING BASILIDES AND MARTIAL[436]

1. Cyprian, Caecilius, Primus, Polycarp, Nicomedes, Lucilianus, Successus, Sedatus, Fortunatus, Januarius, Secundinus, Pomponius, Honoratus, Victor, Aurelius, Sattius, Petrus, another Januarius, Saturninus, another Aurelius, Venantius, Quietus, Rogatianus, Tenax, Felix, Faustinus, Quintus, another Saturninus, Lucius, Vincentius, Libosus, Geminius, Marcellus, Iambus, Adelphius, Victoricus, and Paulus, to Felix the presbyter, and to the peoples abiding at Legio and Asturica, also to Laelius the deacon, and the people abiding at Emerita, brethren in the Lord, greeting. When we had come together, dearly beloved brethren, we read your letters, which according to the integrity of your faith and your fear of God you wrote to us by Felix and Sabinus our fellow bishops, signifying that Basilides and Martial, being stained with the certificates of idolatry,[437] and bound with the consciousness of wicked crimes, ought not to hold the episcopate and administer the priesthood of God; and you desired an answer to be written to you again concerning these things, and your solicitude, no less just than needful, to be relieved either by the comfort or by the help of our judgment. Nevertheless to this your desire not so much our counsels as the divine precepts reply, in which it is long since bidden by the voice of Heaven and prescribed by the law of God, who and what sort of persons ought to serve the altar and to celebrate the divine sacrifices. For in Exodus God speaks to Moses, and warns him, saying, "Let the priests which come near to the Lord God sanctify themselves, lest the Lord forsake them." And again: "And when they come near to the altar of the Holy One to minister they shall not bring sin upon them, lest they die."[438] Also in Leviticus the Lord commands and says, "Whosoever has any spot or blemish upon him, shall not approach to offer gifts to God."[439]

2. Since these things are announced and are made plain to us, it is necessary that our obedience should wait upon the divine precepts; nor in matters of this kind can human indulgence accept any man's person, or yield anything to any one, when the divine prescription has interfered, and establishes a law. For we ought not to be forgetful what the Lord spoke to the Jews by Isaiah the prophet, rebuking, and indignant that they had despised the divine precepts and followed human doctrines. "This people," he says, "honors me with their lips, but their heart is widely removed from me; but in vain do they worship me, teaching the doctrines and commandments of men."[440] This also the Lord repeats in the Gospel, and says, "You reject the commandment of God, that you may establish your own tradition."[441] Having which things before our eyes, and solicitously and religiously considering them, we ought in the ordinations of priests to choose none but unstained and upright ministers, who, holily and worthily offering sacrifices to God, may be heard in the prayers which they make for the safety of the Lord's people, since it is written, "God hears not a sinner; but if any man be a worshipper of God, and does His will, him He hears."[442] On which account it is fitting, that with full diligence and sincere investigation those should be chosen for God's priesthood whom it is manifest God will hear.

3. Nor let the people flatter themselves that they can be free from the contagion of sin, while communicating with a priest who is a sinner, and yielding their consent to the unjust and unlawful episcopacy of their overseer, when the divine reproof by Hosea the prophet threatens, and says, "Their sacrifices shall be as the bread of mourning; all that eat thereof shall be polluted,"[443] teaching manifestly and showing that all are absolutely bound to the sin who have been contaminated by the sacrifice of a profane and unrighteous priest. Which, moreover, we find to be manifested also in Numbers, when Korah, and Dathan, and Abiram claimed for themselves the power of sacrificing in opposition to Aaron the priest. There also the Lord commanded by Moses that the people should be separated from them, lest, being associated with the wicked, themselves also should be bound closely in the same wickedness. "Separate yourselves," said He, "from the tents of these wicked and hardened men, and touch not those things which belong to them, lest you perish together in their sins."[444] On which account a people obedient to the Lord's precepts, and fearing God, ought to separate themselves from a sinful prelate, and not to associate themselves with the sacrifices of a sacrilegious priest, especially since they themselves have the power either of choosing worthy priests, or of rejecting unworthy ones.

4. Which very thing, too, we observe to come from divine authority, that the priest should be chosen in the presence of the people under the eyes of all, and should be approved worthy and suitable by public judgment and testimony; as in the book of Numbers the Lord commanded Moses, saying, "Take Aaron your brother, and Eleazar his son, and place them in the mount, in the presence of all the assembly, and strip Aaron of his garments, and put them upon Eleazar his son; and let Aaron die there, and be added to his people."[445] God commands a priest to be appointed in the presence of all the assembly; that is, He instructs and shows that the ordination of priests ought not to be solemnized except with the knowledge of the people standing near, that in the presence of the people either the crimes of the wicked may be disclosed, or the merits of the good may be declared, and the ordination, which shall have been examined by the suffrage and judgment of all, may be just and legitimate. And this is subsequently observed, according to divine instruction, in the Acts of the Apostles, when Peter speaks to the people of ordaining an apostle in the place of Judas. "Peter," it says, "stood up in the midst of the disciples, and the multitude were in one place."[446] Neither do we observe that this was regarded by the apostles only in the ordinations of bishops and priests, but also in those of deacons, of which matter itself also it is written in their Acts: "And they twelve called together," it says, "the whole congregation of the disciples, and said to them,"[447] which was done so diligently and carefully, with the calling together of the whole of the people, surely for this reason, that no unworthy person might creep into the ministry of the altar, or to the office of a priest. For that unworthy persons are sometimes ordained, not according to the will of God, but according to human presumption, and that those things which do not come of a legitimate and righteous ordination are displeasing to God, God Himself manifests by Hosea the prophet, saying, "They have set up for themselves a king, but not by me."[448]

5. For which reason you must diligently observe and keep the practice delivered from divine tradition and apostolic observance, which is also maintained among us, and almost throughout all the provinces; that for the proper celebration of ordinations all the neighboring bishops of the same province should assemble with that people for which a prelate is ordained. And the bishop should be chosen in the presence of the people, who have most fully known the life of each one, and have looked into the doings of each one as respects his habitual conduct.[449] And this also, we see, was done by you in the ordination of our colleague Sabinus; so that, by the suffrage of the whole brotherhood, and by the sentence of the bishops who had assembled in their presence, and who had written letters to you concerning him, the episcopate was conferred upon him, and hands were imposed on him in the place of Basilides. Neither can it rescind an ordination rightly perfected, that Basilides, after the detection of his crimes, and the baring of his conscience even by his own confession, went to Rome and deceived Stephen our colleague, placed at a distance, and ignorant of what had been done, and of the truth, to canvass that he might be replaced unjustly in the episcopate from which he had been righteously deposed.[450] The result of this is, that the sins of Basilides are not so much abolished as enhanced, inasmuch as to his former sins he has also added the crime of deceit and circumvention. For he is not so much to be blamed who has been through heedlessness surprised by fraud, as he is to be execrated who has fraudulently taken him by surprise. But if Basilides could deceive men, he cannot deceive God, since it is written, "God is not mocked."[451] But neither can deceit advantage Martialis, in such a way as that he who also is involved in great crimes should hold his bishopric, since the apostle also warns, and says, "A bishop must be blameless, as the steward of God."[452]

6. Wherefore, since as you have written, dearly beloved brethren, and as Felix and Sabinus our colleagues affirm, and as another Felix of Caesar Augusta, a maintainer of the faith and a defender of the truth, signifies in his letter, Basilides and Martialis have been contaminated by the abominable certificate of idolatry; and Basilides, moreover, besides the stain of the certificate, when he was prostrate in sickness, blasphemed against God, and confessed that he blasphemed; and because of the wound to his own conscience, voluntarily laying down his episcopate, turned himself to repentance, entreating God, and considering himself sufficiently happy if it might be permitted him to communicate even as a layman:[453] Martialis also, besides the long frequenting of the disgraceful and filthy banquets of the Gentiles in their college, and placing his sons in the same college, after the manner of foreign nations, among profane sepulchres, and burying them together with strangers, has also affirmed, by acts which are publicly taken before a ducenarian procurator,[454] that he had yielded himself to idolatry, and had denied Christ; and as there are many other and grave crimes in which Basilides and Martialis are held to be implicated; such persons attempt to claim for themselves the episcopate in vain; since it is evident that men of that kind may neither rule over the Church of Christ, nor ought to offer sacrifices to God, especially since Cornelius also, our colleague, a peaceable and righteous priest, and moreover honored by the condescension of the Lord with martyrdom, has long ago decreed with us, and with all the bishops appointed throughout the whole world, that men of, this sort might indeed be admitted to repentance, but were prohibited from the ordination of the clergy, and from the priestly honor.[455]

7. Nor let it disturb you, dearest brethren, if with some, in these last times, either an uncertain faith is wavering, or a fear of God without religion is vacillating, or a peaceable concord does not continue. These things have been foretold as about to happen in the end of the world; and it was predicted by the voice of the Lord, and by the testimony of the apostles, that now that the world is failing, and the Antichrist is drawing near, everything good shall fail, but evil and adverse things shall prosper.

8. Yet although, in these last times, evangelic rigor has not so failed in the Church of God, nor the strength of Christian virtue or faith so languished, that there is not left a portion of the priests which in no respect gives way under these ruins of things and wrecks of faith; but, bold and steadfast, they maintain the honor of the divine majesty and the priestly dignity, with full observance of fear. We remember and keep in view that, although others succumbed and yielded, Mattathias boldly vindicated God's law;[456] that Elijah, when the Jews gave way and departed from the divine religion, stood and nobly contended; that Daniel, deterred neither by the loneliness of a foreign country nor by the harassment of continual persecution, frequently and gloriously suffered martyrdoms; also that the three youths, subdued neither by their tender years nor by threats, stood up faithfully against the Babylonian fires, and conquered the victor king even in their very captivity itself. Let the number either of prevaricators or of traitors see to it, who have now begun to rise in the Church against the Church, and to corrupt as well the faith as the truth. Among very many there still remains a sincere mind and a substantial religion, and a spirit devoted to nothing but the Lord and its God. Nor does the perfidy of others press down the Christian faith into ruin, but rather stimulates and exalts it to glory, according to what the blessed Apostle Paul exhorts, and says: "For what if some of these have fallen from their faith: has their unbelief made the faith of God of none effect? God forbid. For God is true, but every man a liar."[457] But if every man is a liar, and God only true, what else ought we, the servants, and especially the priests, of God, to do, than forsake human errors and lies, and continue in the truth of God, keeping the Lord's precepts?

9. Wherefore, although there have been found: some among our colleagues, dearest brethren, who think that the godly discipline may be neglected, and who rashly hold communion with Basilides and Martialis, such a thing as this ought not to trouble our faith, since the Holy Spirit threatens such in the Psalms, saying, "But you hate instruction, and cast my words behind you: when you saw a thief, you consented unto him, and hast been partaker with adulterers."[458] He shows that they become sharers and partakers of other men's sins who are associated with the delinquents. And besides, Paul the apostle writes, and says the same thing: "Whisperers, backbiters, haters of God, injurious, proud, boasters of themselves, inventors of evil things, who, although they knew the judgment of God, did not understand that they which commit such things are worthy of death, not only they which commit those things, but they also which consent unto those who do these things."[459] Since they, says he, who do such things are worthy of death, he makes manifest and proves that not only they are worthy of death, and come into punishment who do evil things, but also those who consent unto those who do such things—who, while they are mingled in unlawful communion with the evil and sinners, and the unrepenting, are polluted by the contact of the guilty, and, being joined in the fault, are thus not separated in its penalty. For which reason we not only approve, but applaud, dearly beloved brethren, the religious solicitude of your integrity and faith, and exhort you as much as we can by our letters, not to mingle in sacrilegious communion with profane and polluted priests, but maintain the sound and sincere constancy of your faith with religious fear. I bid you, dearest brethren, ever heartily farewell.

NOTES

436. In this letter Cyprian argues that bishops who wavered in their faith during the persecution and obtained certificates of sacrifice should lose their episcopal office, and he commends the bishops of Spain for refusing to have communion with two such bishops. It is uncertain whether Cyprian here suggests that such bishops actually lose their ordination; he is clear that they lose their ministerial office. In some places he seems to suggest that a rightly performed ordination can never be undone (67:5) but in others seems to suggest that bishops guilty of serious sins actually lose their ordination and become laymen (67:6). To the degree that he means the latter, we can see these statements as quasi-Donatist, as they tend towards the position that a minister's personal unworthiness invalidates his sacramental ministry, a position he would later defend at the Seventh Council of Carthage.
437. Most likely these bishops are *libellatici*, those who had procured certificates of sacrifice by bribery or other means without actually participating in pagan sacrifices. This is indicated by Cyprian's explicit mention of certificates.
438. Ex. 19:22, 28:43.
439. Lev. 21:17.
440. Isa. 29:13.
441. Mark 7:13.
442. John 9:31.
443. Hos. 9:4.

444. Num. 16:26.

445. Num. 20:25-26.

446. Acts 1:15.

447. Acts 4:2.

448. Hos. 8:4.

449. Though the presence of multiple bishops at an episcopal ordination was common in patristic times, it has not been understood to itself be necessary for a valid ordination. Canon 1014 and the Catechism § 1559 make reference to the practice of having a bishop consecrated by three bishops. However, the Catechism says that this practice was only to evidence the "collegial nature" of the episcopate (CCC 1559)—it is a symbolic recalling of the unity of the College of Apostles. The commentary in the official CIC says that this was instituted "for organizational reasons" (p. 635). While canon 1014 mandates three bishops present, the Catechism and the CIC commentary make clear that this does not pertain to validity.

450. Again, we see the See of Rome being used as a court of final appeal. See the note for Letter 67:5. Basilides was ejected from his see in Spain; therefore he goes to Rome in order that "he might be replaced" in his see. Such an appeal would be fruitless if the pope did not actually have the power to depose or reinstate individual bishops.

451. Gal. 6:7.

452. Tit. 1:7.

453. See footnote 95 on Letter 63:2.

454. A high ranking imperial official in charge of important ministries, many of them related to finances or tax collection. The adjective *ducenarian* indicates that this official was paid a salary of 200,000 sesterces per year. Apparently in Cyprian's time one of their duties was to try the cases of accused Christians.

455. Cyprian here cites Pope Cornelius in order to establish his argument. The discipline maintained by the Bishop of Rome was seen as normative in the Church.

456. 1 Maccabees 2.

457. Rom. 3:3-4.

458. Ps. 50:17-18.

459. Rom. 1:30-32.

LETTER 68

TO FLORENTIUS PUPIANUS, IN WHICH CYPRIAN DEFENDS HIMSELF AGAINST SLANDER

1. Cyprian, who is also called Thascius, to Florentius, who is also Pupianus, his brother, greeting. I had believed, brother, that you were now at length turned to repentance for having either rashly heard or believed in time past things so wicked, so disgraceful, so execrable even among Gentiles, concerning me. But even now in your letter I perceive that you are still the same as you were before—that you believe the same things concerning me, and that you persist in what you did believe, and, lest by chance the dignity of your eminence and your martyrdom should be stained by communion with me, that you are inquiring carefully into my character; and after God the Judge who makes priests, that you wish to judge—I will not say of me, for what am I?—but of the judgment of God and of Christ. This is not to believe in God—this is to stand forth as a rebel against Christ and His Gospel; so that although He says, "Are not two sparrows sold for a farthing? And neither of them falls to the ground without the will of my Father,"[460] and His majesty and truth prove that even things of little consequence are not done without the consciousness and permission of God, you think that God's priests are ordained in the Church without His knowledge. For to believe that they who are ordained are unworthy and unchaste, what else is it than to believe that his priests are not appointed in the Church by God, nor through God?[461]

2. Think you that my testimony of myself is better than that of God? When the Lord Himself teaches, and says that testimony is not true, if any one himself appears as a witness concerning himself, for the reason that every one would assuredly favor himself. Nor would any one put forward mischievous and adverse things against himself, but there may be a simple confidence of truth if, in what was announced of us, another is the announcer and witness. "If," He says, "I bear witness of myself, my testimony is not true; but there is another who bears witness of me."[462] But if the Lord Himself, who will by and by judge all things, was unwilling to be believed on His own testimony, but preferred to be approved by the judgment and testimony of God the Father, how much more does it behoove His servants to observe this, who are not only approved by, but even glory in the judgment and testimony of God! But with you the fabrication of hostile and malignant men has prevailed against the divine decree, and against our conscience resting upon the strength of its faith, as if among lapsed and profane persons placed outside the Church, from whose breasts the Holy Spirit has departed, there could be anything else than a depraved mind and a deceitful tongue, and venomous hatred, and sacrilegious lies, which whosoever believes, must of necessity be found with them when the day of judgment shall come.

3. But with respect to what you have said, that priests should be lowly, because both the Lord and His apostles were lowly; both all the brethren and Gentiles also well know and love my humility; and you also knew and loved it while you were still in the Church, and were in communion with me. But which of us is far from humility: I, who daily serve the brethren, and kindly receive with good-will and gladness every one that comes to the Church; or you, who appoint yourself bishop of a bishop, and judge of a judge, given for the time by God? Although the Lord God says in Deuteronomy, "And the man that will do presumptuously, and will not hearken unto the priests or unto the judge who shall be in those days, even that man shall die; and all the people, when they hear, shall fear, and do no more presumptuously."[463] And again He speaks to Samuel, and says, "They have not despised you, but they have despised me."[464] And moreover the Lord, in the Gospel, when it was said to Him, "Do you answer the high priest so?" guarding the priestly dignity, and teaching that it ought to be maintained, would say nothing against the high priest, but only clearing His own innocence, answered, saying, "If I have spoken evil, bear witness of the evil; but if well, why do you smite me?"[465] The blessed apostle also, when it was said to him, "Do you revile God's high priest?" spoke nothing reproachfully against the priest, when he might have lifted up himself boldly against those who had crucified the Lord, and who had already sacrificed God and Christ, and the temple and the priesthood; but even although in false and degraded priests, considering still the mere empty shadow of the priestly name, he said, "I knew not, brethren, that he was the high priest; for it is written, 'You shall not speak evil of the ruler of your people.'"[466]

4. Unless perchance I was a priest to you before the persecution, when you held communion with me, and ceased to be a priest after the persecution! For the persecution, when it came, lifted you to the highest sublimity of martyrdom. But it depressed me with the burden of proscription, since it was publicly declared, "If any one holds or possesses any of the property of Caecilius Cyprian, bishop of the Christians;" so that even they who did not believe in God appointing a bishop, could still believe in the devil proscribing a bishop. Nor do I boast of these things, but with grief I bring them forward, since you constitute yourself a judge of God and of Christ, who says to the apostles, and thereby to all chief rulers, who by vicarious ordination succeed to the apostles:[467] "He that hears you, hears me; and he that hears me, hears Him that sent me; and he that despises you, despises me, and Him that sent me."[468]

5. For from this have arisen, and still arise, schisms and heresies, in that the bishop who is one and rules over the Church is contemned by the haughty presumption of some persons; and the man who is honored by God's condescension, is judged unworthy by men. For what swelling of pride is this, what arrogance of soul, what inflation of mind, to call prelates and priests to one's own recognition, and unless I may be declared clear in your sight and absolved by your judgment, behold now for six years the brotherhood has neither had a bishop, nor the people a prelate, nor the flock a pastor, nor the Church a governor, nor Christ a representative, nor God a priest![469] Pupianus must come to the rescue, and give judgment, and declare the decision of God and Christ accepted, that so great a number of the faithful who have been summoned away, under my rule, may not appear to have departed without hope of salvation and of peace; that the new crowd of believers may not be considered to have failed of attaining any grace of baptism and the Holy Spirit by my ministry; that the peace conferred upon so many lapsed and penitent persons, and the communion vouchsafed by my examination, may not be abrogated by the authority of your judgment. Condescend for once, and deign to pronounce concerning us, and to establish our episcopate by the authority of your recognition, that God and His Christ may thank you, in that by your means a representative and ruler has been restored as well to their altar as to their people!

6. Bees have a king, and cattle a leader, and they keep faith to him. Robbers obey their chief with an obedience full of humility. How much more simple and better than you are the brute cattle and dumb animals, and robbers, although bloody, and raging among swords and weapons! The chief among them is acknowledged and feared, whom no divine judgment has appointed, but on whom an abandoned faction and a guilty band have agreed.

7. You say, indeed, that the scruple into which you have fallen ought to be taken from your mind.[470] You have fallen into it, but it was by your irreligious credulity. You have fallen into it, but it was by your own sacrilegious disposition and will in easily hearkening to unchaste, to impious, to unspeakable things against your brother, against a priest, and in willingly believing them in defending other men's falsehoods, as if they were your own and your private property; and in not remembering that it is written, "Hedge your ears with thorns, and hearken not to a wicked tongue;"[471] and again: "A wicked doer gives heed to the tongue of the unjust; but a righteous man regards not lying lips."[472] Wherefore have not the martyrs fallen into this scruple, full of the Holy Ghost, and already by their passion near to the presence of God and of His Christ; martyrs who, from their dungeon, directed letters to Cyprian the bishop, acknowledging the priest of God, and bearing witness to him? Wherefore have not so many bishops, my colleagues, fallen into this scruple, who either, when they departed from the midst of us, were proscribed, or being taken were cast into prison and were in chains; or who, sent away into exile, have gone by an illustrious road to the Lord; or who in some places, condemned to death, have received heavenly crowns from the glorification of the Lord? Wherefore have not they fallen into this scruple, from among that people of ours which is with us, and is by God's condescension committed to us—so many confessors who have been put to the question and tortured, and glorious by the memory of illustrious wounds and scars; so many chaste virgins, so many praiseworthy widows; finally, all the churches throughout the whole world who are associated with us in the bond of unity? Unless all these, who are in communion with me, as you have written, are polluted with the pollution of my lips, and have lost the hope of eternal life by the contagion of my communion. Pupianus alone, sound, inviolate, holy, modest, who would not associate himself with us, shall dwell alone in paradise and in the kingdom of heaven.

8. You have written also, that on my account the Church has now a portion of herself in a state of dispersion, although the whole people of the Church are collected, and united, and joined to itself in an undivided concord: they alone have remained without, who even, if they had been within, would have had to be cast out. Nor does the Lord, the protector of His people, and their guardian, suffer the wheat to be snatched from His floor; but the chaff alone can be separated from the Church, since also the apostle says, "For what if some of them have departed from the faith? Shall their unbelief make the faith of God of none effect? God forbid; for God is true, but every man a liar."[473] And the Lord also in the Gospel, when disciples forsook Him as He spoke, turning to the twelve, said, "Will you also go away?" Then Peter answered Him, "Lord, to whom shall we go? You have the word of eternal life; and we believe, and are sure, that You are the Son of the Living God."[474] Peter speaks there, on whom the Church was to be built, teaching and showing in the name of the Church, that although a rebellious and arrogant multitude of those who will not hear and obey may depart, yet the Church does not depart from Christ; and they are the Church who are a people united to the priest, and the flock which adheres to its pastor. Whence you ought to know that the bishop is in the Church, and the Church in the bishop; and if any one be not with the bishop, that he is not in the Church, and that those flatter themselves in vain who creep in, not having peace with God's priests, and think that they communicate secretly with some; while the Church, which is Catholic and one, is not cut nor divided, but is indeed connected and bound together by the cement of priests who cohere with one another.

9. Wherefore, brother, if you consider God's majesty who ordains priests, if you will for once have respect to Christ, who by His decree and word, and by His presence, both rules prelates themselves, and rules the Church by prelates; if you will trust, in respect of the innocence of bishops, not human hatred, but the divine judgment; if you will begin even a late repentance for your temerity, and pride, and insolence; if you will most abundantly make satisfaction to God and His Christ whom I serve, and to whom with pure and unstained lips I ceaselessly offer sacrifices, not only in peace, but in persecution; we may have some ground for communion with you, even although there still remain among us respect and fear for the divine censure; so that first I should consult my Lord whether He would permit peace to be granted to you, and you to be received to the communion of His Church by His own showing and admonition.

10. For I remember what has already been manifested to me, nay, what has been prescribed by the authority of our Lord and God to an obedient and fearing servant; and among other things which He condescended to show and to reveal,

He also added this: "Whoever therefore does not believe Christ, who makes the priest, shall hereafter begin to believe Him who avenges the priest."[475] Although I know that to some men dreams seem ridiculous and visions foolish, yet assuredly it is to such as would rather believe in opposition to the priest, than believe the priest. But it is no wonder, since his brethren said of Joseph, "Behold, this dreamer comes; come now therefore, let us slay him."[476] And afterwards the dreamer attained to what he had dreamed; and his slayers and sellers were put to confusion, so that they, who at first did not believe the words, afterwards believed the deeds. But of those things that you have done, either in persecution or in peace, it is foolish for me to pretend to judge you, since you rather appoint yourself a judge over us. These things, of the pure conscience of my mind, and of my confidence in my Lord and my God, I have written at length. You have my letter, and I yours. In the day of judgment, before the tribunal of Christ, both will be read.

NOTES

460. Matt. 10:29.
461. It is amusing to see St. Cyprian here change his argument from the preceding letter. Previously, he had admitted that unworthy priests may sometimes be ordained outside of the will of God (67:4). When he himself is accused of perhaps being among the unworthy, he responds that no priest is ordained apart from God's will.
462. John 5:31-32.
463. Deut. 17:12-13.
464. 1 Sam. 8:7.
465. John 18:23.
466. Acts 23:4-5.
467. A very clear proof of the doctrine of Apostolic Succession—that the authority of the Apostles was handed on in the episcopate through what Cyprian calls "vicarious ordination."
468. Luke 10:16.
469. This statement dates this letter to the year 256, only two years before Cyprian's death.
470. Pupianus had apparently hearkened to some gossip concerning Cyprian, probably from the same group of detractors who had been Cyprian's opponents throughout his entire episcopacy.
471. Sir. 28:24.
472. Prov. 17:4.
473. Rom. 3:3-4.
474. John 6:67-69.
475. This saying of our Lord comes from a vision granted to Cyprian in the form of a dream, as he narrates.
476. Gen. 37:19.

LETTER 69

TO JANUARIUS AND THE NUMIDIAN BISHOPS
ON THE BAPTISM OF HERETICS[477]

1. Cyprian, Liberalis, Caldonius, Junius, Primus, Caecilius, Polycarp, Nicomedes, Felix, Marrutius, Successus, Lucianus, Honoratus, Fortunatus, Victor, Donatus, Lucius, Herculanus, Pomponius, Demetrius, Quintus, Saturninus, Januarius, Marcus, another Saturninus, another Donatus, Rogatianus, Sedatus, Tertullus, Hortensianus, still another Saturninus, Sattius, to their brethren Januarius, Saturninus, Maximus, Victor, another Victor, Cassius, Proculus, Modianus, Cittinus, Gargilius, Eutycianus, another Gargilius, another Saturninus, Nemesianus, Nampulus, Antonianus, Rogatianus, Honoratus, greeting. When we were together in council, dearest brethren, we read your letter which you wrote to us concerning those who seem to be baptized by heretics and schismatics, asking whether, when they come to the Catholic Church, which is one, they ought to be baptized. On which matter, although you yourselves hold thereupon the truth and certainty of the Catholic rule, yet since you have thought that of our mutual love we ought to be consulted, we put forward our opinion, not as a new one, but we join with you in equal agreement, in an opinion long since decreed by our predecessors, and observed by us—judging, namely, and holding it for certain that no one can be baptized abroad outside the Church, since there is one baptism appointed in the holy Church.[478] And it is written in the words of the Lord, "They have forsaken me, the fountain of living waters, and hewed them out broken cisterns, which can hold no water."[479] And again, sacred Scripture warns, and says, "Keep you from the strange water, and drink not from a fountain of strange water."[480] It is required, then, that the water should first be cleansed and sanctified by the priest, that it may wash away by its baptism the sins of the man who is baptized; because the Lord says by Ezekiel the prophet: "Then will I sprinkle clean water upon you, and you shall be cleansed from all your filthiness; and from all your idols will I cleanse you: a new heart also will I give you, and a new spirit will I put within you."[481] But how can he cleanse and sanctify the water who is himself unclean, and in whom the Holy Spirit is not? Since the Lord says in the book of Numbers, "And whatsoever the unclean person touches shall be unclean."[482] Or how can he who baptizes give to another remission of sins who himself, being outside the Church, cannot put away his own sins?[483]

2. But, moreover, the very interrogation which is put in baptism is a witness of the truth. For when we say, "Do you believe in eternal life and remission of sins through the holy Church?" we mean that remission of sins is not granted except in the Church, and that among heretics, where there is no Church, sins cannot be put away. Therefore they who assert that heretics can baptize, must either change the interrogation or maintain the truth; unless indeed they attribute a church also to those who, they contend, have baptism. It is also necessary that he should be anointed who is baptized; so that, having received the chrism, that is, the anointing, he may be anointed of God, and have in him the grace of Christ.[484] Further, it is the Eucharist whence the baptized are anointed with the oil sanctified on the altar. But he cannot sanctify the creature of oil, who has neither an altar nor a church; whence also there can be no spiritual anointing among heretics, since it is manifest that the oil cannot be sanctified nor the Eucharist celebrated at all among them. But we ought to know and remember that it is written, "Let not the oil of a sinner anoint my head,"[485] which the Holy Spirit before forewarned in the Psalms, lest any one going out of the way and wandering from the path of truth should be anointed by heretics and adversaries of Christ. Besides, what prayer can a priest who is impious and a sinner offer for a baptized person? Since it is written, "God hears not a sinner; but if any man be a worshipper of God, and does His will, him He hears."[486] Who, moreover, can give what he himself has not?[487] Or how can he discharge spiritual functions who himself has lost the Holy Spirit? And therefore he must be baptized and renewed who comes untrained to the Church, that he may be sanctified within by those who are holy, since it is written, "Be holy, for I am holy, says the Lord."[488] So that he who has been seduced into error, and baptized outside of the Church, should lay aside even this very thing in the true and ecclesiastical baptism, viz., that he a man coming to God, while he seeks for a priest, fell by the deceit of error upon a profane one.

3. But it is to approve the baptism of heretics and schismatics, to admit that they have truly baptized. For therein a part cannot be void, and part be valid. If one could baptize, he could also give the Holy Spirit.[489] But if he cannot give the Holy Spirit, because he that is appointed without is not endowed with the Holy Spirit, he cannot baptize those who come; since both baptism is one and the Holy Spirit is one, and the Church founded by Christ the Lord upon Peter, by a source and principle of unity, is one also.[490] Hence it results, that since with them all things are futile and false, nothing of that which they have done ought to be approved by us. For what can be ratified and established by God which is done by them whom the Lord calls His enemies and adversaries? Setting forth in His Gospel, "He that is not with me is against me; and he that gathers not with me, scatters."[491] And the blessed Apostle John also, keeping the commandments and precepts of the Lord, has laid it down in his epistle, and said, "You have heard that antichrist shall come: even now there are many antichrists; whereby we know that it is the last time. They went out from us, but they were not of us; for if they had been of us, no doubt they would have continued with us."[492] Whence we also ought to gather and consider whether they who are the Lord's adversaries, and are called antichrists, can give the grace of Christ. Wherefore we who are with the Lord, and maintain the unity of the Lord, and according to His condescension administer His priesthood in the Church, ought to repudiate and reject and regard as profane whatever His adversaries and the antichrists do; and to those who, coming out of error and wickedness, acknowledge the true faith of the one Church, we should give the truth both of unity and faith, by means of all the sacraments of divine grace.[493] We bid you, dearest brethren, ever heartily farewell.

NOTES

477. Here we see the beginning of that famous contention between St. Cyprian and Pope St. Stephen over the legitimacy of baptism performed by heretics. This dispute will dominate the remainder of Cyprian's episcopate.

478. It is interesting that here St. Cyprian asserts rebaptism is "an opinion long since decreed by our predecessors," since at the Seventh Council of Carthage the African bishops will all admit that the Roman practice of not rebaptizing was in fact the long existing custom. Presumably at this stage in the controversy Cyprian was not yet aware of anything to the contrary in other churches.

479. Jer. 2:13.

480. The Septuagint translation of Proverbs 9:18: "But he knows that mighty men die by her, and he falls in with a snare of hell. But hasten away, delay not in the place, neither fix thine eye upon her: for thus shalt thou go through strange water; but do thou abstain from strange water, and drink not of a strange fountain, that thou mayest live long, and years of life may be added to thee." The Vulgate text simply reads, "And he did not know that giants are there, and that her guests are in the depths of hell."

481. Ezk. 36:25-26.

482. Num. 19:22.

483. Cyprian is here attributing the power of the sacraments too much to the minister and is negating the operation of God's grace working through the minister, whose unworthiness does not invalidate God's goodness.

484. A reference to the Sacrament of Confirmation.

485. Ps. 141:5 (LXX).

486. John 9:31.

487. This is the crux if Cyprian's entire argument in favor of rebaptism of heretics. Yet, as mentioned above and exemplified by this formula, Cyprian views the sacramental power of God as primarily originating with the minister.

488. Lev. 19:2.

489. In other words, he could administer Confirmation.

490. The Church is here said to be founded by Christ upon Peter, and this is the Church's "source and principal of unity."

491. Luke 11:23.

492. 1 John 2:18-19.

493. Because of the imperfect development of sacramental theology during Cyprian's day, he did not understand that different sacraments may have different ministers. It is the Church's teaching authority (ultimately meaning the See of Rome in union with the Pope) that

determines under what conditions sacraments are lawfully and validly administered. Thus, regarding Cyprian's argument above that a heretic cannot administer Confirmation and so also cannot administer baptism, it can be pointed out that the minister of Confirmation is different from the minister of baptism. Only a bishop or a priest lawfully delegated by a bishop may confirm; but in the case of baptism, though the proper minister is still a priest, the Church recognizes that anyone, even a non-believer, may administer a valid baptism in the case of an emergency.

LETTER 70

TO QUINTUS, ON THE BAPTISM OF HERETICS

1. Cyprian to Quintus his brother, greeting. Lucian, our co-presbyter, has reported to me, dearest brother, that you have wished me to declare to you what I think concerning those who seem to have been baptized by heretics and schismatics; of which matter, that you may know what several of us fellow bishops, with the brother presbyters who were present, lately determined in council, I have sent you a copy of the same epistle.[494] For I know not by what presumption some of our colleagues are led to think that they who have been dipped by heretics ought not to be baptized when they come to us, for the reason that they say that there is one baptism which indeed is therefore one, because the Church is one, and there cannot be any baptism out of the Church. For since there cannot be two baptisms, if heretics truly baptize, they themselves have this baptism.[495] And he who of his own authority grants this advantage to them yields and consents to them, that the enemy and adversary of Christ should seem to have the power of washing, and purifying, and sanctifying a man. But we say that those who come thence are not re-baptized among us, but are baptized. For indeed they do not receive anything there, where there is nothing; but they come to us, that here they may receive where there is both grace and all truth, because both grace and truth are one. But again some of our colleagues would rather give honor to heretics than agree with us; and while by the assertion of one baptism they are unwilling to baptize those that come, they thus either themselves make two baptisms in saying that there is a baptism among heretics; or certainly, which is a matter of more importance, they strive to set before and prefer the sordid and profane washing of heretics to the true and only and legitimate baptism of the Catholic Church, not considering that it is written, "He who is baptized by one dead, what avails his washing?"[496] Now it is manifest that they who are not in the Church of Christ are reckoned among the dead; and another cannot be made alive by him who himself is not alive, since there is one Church which, having attained the grace of eternal life, both lives for ever and quickens the people of God.

2. And they say that in this matter they follow ancient custom; although among the ancients these were as yet the first beginnings of heresy and schisms, so that those were involved in them who departed from the Church, having first been baptized therein; and these, therefore, when they returned to the Church and repented, it was not necessary to baptize. Which also we observe in the present day, that it is sufficient to lay hands for repentance upon those who are known to have been baptized in the Church, and have gone over from us to the heretics, if, subsequently acknowledging their sin and putting away their error, they return to the truth and to their parent; so that, because it had been a sheep, the Shepherd may receive into His fold the estranged and vagrant sheep. But if he who comes from the heretics has not previously been baptized in the Church, but comes as a stranger and entirely profane, he must be baptized, that he may become a sheep, because in the holy Church is the one water which makes sheep. And therefore, because there can be nothing common to falsehood and truth, to darkness and light, to death and immortality, to Antichrist and Christ, we ought by all means to maintain the unity of the Catholic Church, and not to give way to the enemies of faith and truth in any respect.

3. Neither must we prescribe this from custom, but overcome opposite custom by reason. For neither did Peter, whom first the Lord chose, and upon whom He built His Church, when Paul disputed with him afterwards about circumcision, claim anything to himself insolently, nor arrogantly assume anything, so as to say that he held the primacy, and that he ought rather to be obeyed by novices and those lately come.[497] Nor did he despise Paul because he had previously been a persecutor of the Church, but admitted the counsel of truth, and easily yielded to the lawful reason which Paul asserted, furnishing thus an illustration to us both of concord and of patience, that we should not obstinately love our own opinions, but should rather adopt as our own those which at any time are usefully and wholesomely suggested by our brethren and colleagues, if they be true and lawful. Paul, moreover, looking forward to this, and consulting faithfully for concord and peace, has laid down in his epistle this rule: "Moreover, let the prophets speak two or three, and let the rest judge. But if anything be revealed to another that sits by, let the first hold his peace."[498] In which place he has taught and shown that many things are revealed to individuals for the better, and that each one ought not obstinately to contend for that which he had once imbibed and held; but if anything has appeared better and more useful, he should gladly embrace it. For we are not overcome when better things are presented to us, but we are instructed, especially in those matters which pertain to the unity of the Church and the truth of our hope and faith; so that we, priests of God and prelates of His Church, by His condescension, should know that remission of sins cannot be given save in the Church, nor can the adversaries of Christ claim to themselves anything belonging to His grace.[499]

4. Which thing, indeed, Agrippinus also, a man of worthy memory, with his other fellow bishops, who at that time governed the Lord's Church in the province of Africa and Numidia, decreed, and by the well-weighed examination of the common council established: whose opinion, as being both religious and lawful and salutary, and in harmony with the Catholic faith and Church, we also have followed. And that you may know what kind of letters we have written on this subject, I have transmitted for our mutual love a copy of them, as well for your own information as for that of our fellow bishops who are in those parts. I bid you, dearest brother, ever heartily farewell.

NOTES

494. A reference to the Seventh Council of Carthage. By this time, Cyprian was known across the Church as the defender of the rigorist position on the question of heretic baptism.

495. See the footnotes on the Seventh Council of Carthage for a more detailed exposition of Cyprian's sacramental theology *vis-a-vis* that of St. Augustine and where the former errs.

496. This is a sloppy paraphrase of Sirach 31:25 in the Septuagint: "He that washeth himself after the touching of a dead body, if he touch it again, what availeth his washing?" In the Vulgate, this is Sirach 34:30: "He that washeth himself after touching the dead, if he toucheth him again, what doth his washing avail?" Cyprian's interpretation is supported by neither translation.

497. St. Cyprian is certainly not denying the Roman primacy, which he asserts in many other places (Letters 39:5, 44:3, 54:14, 68:8, 69:3, and especially *On the Unity of the Church*, 4, where he plainly says, "The other Apostles were indeed what Peter was, but the primacy is given to Peter, and the Church and the chair is shown to be one"). The statement needs to be taken in context of the whole argument. Cyprian's larger argument is that, although it is custom to not baptize heretics who have a Trinitarian baptism, it may be prudent, for the sake of concord and patience, not to insist on custom and to let the opinions of others prevail. Thus, he uses the example of Peter and Paul's meeting in Galatians 2:11-21. The argument is that, while Peter could have insisted on his primacy and on obedience, he chose not to, voluntarily humbling himself to listen to the rebuke of St. Paul. He could have argued his point from authority, but instead chose to not cling "obstinately" to his own opinions and listened to the advice of Paul. Cyprian thus draws a connection between Peter, the first pope, and Stephen, and insinuates that the latter should follow the precedent set by the former in the controversy. The primacy itself is not denied; rather, it is the perceived heavy-handedness Pope Stephen in disregarding the opinions of the African bishops that Cyprian finds so appalling.

498. 1 Cor. 14:29.

499. This is the essence of St. Cyprian's argument against a custom he disagrees with.

LETTER 71

TO POPE STEPHEN, CONCERNING A COUNCIL

1. Cyprian and others, to Stephen their brother, greeting. We have thought it necessary for the arranging of certain matters, dearest brother, and for their investigation by the examination of a common council, to gather together and to hold a council, at which many priests were assembled at once; at which, moreover, many things were brought forward and transacted. But the subject in regard to which we had chiefly to write to you, and to confer with your gravity and wisdom, is one that more especially pertains both to the priestly authority and to the unity, as well as the dignity, of the Catholic Church, arising as these do from the ordination of the divine appointment; to wit, that those who have been dipped abroad outside the Church, and have been stained among heretics and schismatics with the taint of profane water, when they come to us and to the Church which is one, ought to be baptized, for the reason that it is a small matter to lay hands on them that they may receive the Holy Ghost, unless they receive also the baptism of the Church. For then finally can they be fully sanctified, and be the sons of God, if they be born of each sacrament; since it is written, "Unless a man be born again of water, and of the Spirit, he cannot enter into the kingdom of God."[500] For we find also, in the Acts of the Apostles, that this is maintained by the apostles, and kept in the truth of the saving faith, so that when, in the house of Cornelius the centurion, the Holy Ghost had descended upon the Gentiles who were there, fervent in the warmth of their faith, and believing in the Lord with their whole heart; and when, filled with the Spirit, they blessed God in various tongues, still none the less the blessed Apostle Peter, mindful of the divine precept and the Gospel, commanded that those same men should be baptized who had already been filled with the Holy Spirit, that nothing might seem to be neglected to the observance by the apostolic instruction in all things of the law of the divine precept and Gospel.[501] But that that is not baptism which the heretics use; and that none of those who oppose Christ can profit by the grace of Christ; has lately been set forth with care in the letter which was written on that subject to Quintus, our colleague, established in Mauritania; as also in a letter which our colleagues previously wrote to our fellow bishops presiding in Numidia, of both which letters I have subjoined copies.[502]

2. We add, however, and connect with what we have said, dearest brother, with common consent and authority, that if, again, any presbyters or deacons, who either have been before ordained in the Catholic Church, and have subsequently stood forth as traitors and rebels against the Church, or who have been promoted among the heretics by a profane ordination by the hands of false bishops and antichrists contrary to the appointment of Christ, and have attempted to offer; in opposition to the one and divine altar, false and sacrilegious sacrifices without, that these also be received when they return, on this condition, that they communicate as laymen, and hold it to be enough that they should be received to peace, after having stood forth as enemies of peace; and that they ought not, on returning, to retain those arms of ordination and honor with which they rebelled against us. For it behooves priests and ministers, who wait upon the altar and sacrifices, to be sound and stainless; since the Lord God speaks in Leviticus, and says, "No man that has a stain or a blemish shall come near to offer gifts to the Lord."[503] Moreover, in Exodus, He prescribes this same thing, and says, "And let the priests which come near to the Lord God sanctify themselves, lest the Lord forsake them."[504] And again: "And when they come near to minister at the altar of the holy place, they shall not bear iniquity upon them, lest they die."[505] But what can be greater iniquity, or what stain can be more odious, than to have stood in opposition to Christ; than to have scattered His Church, which He purchased and founded with His blood; than, unmindful of evangelical peace and love, to have fought with the madness of hostile discord against the unanimous and accordant people of God? Such as these, although they themselves return to the Church, still cannot restore and recall with them those who, seduced by them, and forestalled by death without, have perished outside the Church without communion and peace; whose souls in the day of judgment shall be required at the hands of those who have stood forth as the authors and leaders of their ruin. And therefore to such, when they return, it is sufficient that pardon should be granted; since perfidy ought certainly not to receive promotion in the household of faith. For what do we reserve for the good and innocent, and those who do not depart from the Church, if we honor those who have departed from us, and stood in opposition to the Church?

3. We have brought these things, dearest brother, to your knowledge, for the sake of our mutual honor and sincere affection; believing that, according to the truth of your religion and faith, those things which are no less religious than true will be approved by you. But we know that some will not lay aside what they have once imbibed, and do not easily change their purpose; but, keeping fast the bond of peace and concord among their colleagues, retain certain things peculiar to themselves, which have once been adopted among them. In which behalf we neither do violence to, nor impose a law upon, any one, since each prelate has in the administration of the Church the exercise of his will free, as he shall give an account of his conduct to the Lord. We bid you, dearest brother, ever heartily farewell.

NOTES

500. John 3:5.
501. Acts 10.
502. Letters 70 and 69, respectively.
503. Lev. 21:21.
504. Ex. 19:22.
505. Ex. 28:43.

LETTER 72

TO JUBAIANUS, CONCERNING THE BAPTISM OF HERETICS

1. Cyprian to Jubaianus his brother, greeting. You have written to me, dearest brother, wishing that the impression of my mind should be signified to you, as to what I think concerning the baptism of heretics; who, placed without, and established outside the Church, arrogate to themselves a matter neither within their right nor their power. This baptism we cannot consider as valid or legitimate, since it is manifestly unlawful among them;[506] and since we have already expressed in our letters what we thought on this matter, I have, as a compendious method, sent you a copy of the same letters, what we decided in council when very many of us were present, and what, moreover, I subsequently wrote back to Quintus, our colleague, when he asked about the same thing. And now also, when we had met together, bishops as well of the province of Africa as of Numidia, to the number of seventy-one, we established this same matter once more by our judgment, deciding that there is one baptism which is appointed in the Catholic Church; and that by this those are not re-baptized, but baptized by us, who at any time come from the adulterous and unhallowed water to be washed and sanctified by the truth of the saving water.

2. Nor does what you have described in your letters disturb us, dearest brother, that the Novatians re-baptize those whom they entice from us, since it does not in any wise matter to us what the enemies of the Church do, so long as we ourselves hold a regard for our power, and the steadfastness of reason and truth. For Novatian, after the manner of apes—which, although they are not men, yet imitate human doings—wishes to claim to himself the authority and truth of the Catholic Church, while he himself is not in the Church; nay, moreover, has stood forth hitherto as a rebel and enemy against the Church. For, knowing that there is one baptism, he arrogates to himself this one, so that he may say that the Church is with him, and make us heretics. But we who hold the head and root of the one Church know, and trust for certain, that nothing is lawful there outside the Church, and that the baptism which is one is among us, where he himself also was formerly baptized, when he maintained both the wisdom and truth of the divine unity. But if Novatian thinks that those who have been baptized in the Church are to be re-baptized outside—without the Church—he ought to begin by himself, that he might first be re-baptized with an extraneous and heretical baptism, since he thinks that after the Church, yea, and contrary to the Church, people are to be baptized without. But what sort of a thing is this, that, because Novatian dares to do this thing, we are to think that we must not do it! What

479

then? Because Novatian also usurps the honor of the priestly throne, ought we therefore to renounce our throne?[507] Or because Novatian endeavors wrongfully to set up an altar and to offer sacrifices, does it behoove us to cease from our altar and sacrifices, lest we should appear to be celebrating the same or like things with him? Utterly vain and foolish is it, that because Novatian arrogates to himself outside the Church the image of the truth, we should forsake the truth of the Church.

3. But among us it is no new or sudden thing for us to judge that those are to be baptized who come to the Church from among the heretics, since it is now many years and a long time ago, that, under Agrippinus—a man of worthy memory—very many bishops assembling together have decided this;[508] and thenceforward until the present day, so many thousands of heretics in our provinces have been converted to the Church, and have neither despised nor delayed, nay, they have both reasonably and gladly embraced, the opportunity to attain the grace of the life-giving laver and of saving baptism. For it is not difficult for a teacher to insinuate true and lawful things into his mind, who, having condemned heretical pravity, and discovered the truth of the Church, comes for this purpose, that he may learn, and learns for the purpose that he may live. We ought not to increase the stolidity of heretics by the patronage of our consent, when they gladly and readily obey the truth.

4. Certainly, since I found in the letter the copy of which you transmitted to me, that it was written, "That it should not be asked who baptized, since he who is baptized might receive remission of sins according to what he believed," I thought that this topic was not to be passed by, especially since I observed in the same epistle that mention was also made of Marcion, saying that even those that came from him did not need to be baptized, because they seemed to have been already baptized in the name of Jesus Christ. Therefore we ought to consider their faith who believe without, whether in respect of the same faith they can obtain any grace. For if we and heretics have one faith, we may also have one grace. If the Patripassians, Anthropians, Valentinians, Apelletians, Ophites,[509] Marcionites, and other pests, and swords, and poisons of heretics for subverting the truth, confess the same Father, the same Son, the same Holy Ghost, the same Church with us, they may also have one baptism if they have also one faith.

5. And lest it should be wearisome to go through all the heresies, and to enumerate either the follies or the madness of each of them, because it is no pleasure to speak of that which one either dreads or is ashamed to know, let us examine in the meantime about Marcion alone, the mention of whom has been made in the letter transmitted by you to us, whether the ground of his baptism can be made good. For the Lord after His resurrection, sending His disciples, instructed and taught them in what manner they ought to baptize, saying, "All power is given unto me in heaven and in earth. Go, therefore, and teach all nations, baptizing them in the name of the Father, and of the Son, and of the Holy Ghost."[510] He suggests the Trinity, in whose sacrament the nations were to be baptized. Does Marcion then maintain the Trinity? Does he then assert the same Father, the Creator, as we do? Does he know the same Son, Christ born of the Virgin Mary, who as the Word was made flesh, who bare our sins, who conquered death by dying, who by Himself first of all originated the resurrection of the flesh, and showed to His disciples that He had risen in the same flesh? Widely different is the faith with Marcion, and, moreover, with the other heretics nay, with them there is nothing but perfidy, and blasphemy, and contention, which is hostile to holiness and truth. How then can one who is baptized among them seem to have obtained remission of sins, and the grace of the divine mercy, by his faith, when he has not the truth of the faith itself? For if, as some suppose, one could receive anything abroad out of the Church according to his faith, certainly he has received what he believed; but if he believes what is false, he could not receive what is true; but rather he has received things adulterous and profane, according to what he believed.

6. This matter of profane and adulterous baptism Jeremiah the prophet plainly rebukes, saying, "Why do they who afflict me prevail? My wound is hard; whence shall I be healed? While it has indeed become unto me as deceitful water which has no faithfulness."[511] The Holy Spirit makes mention by the prophet of deceitful water which has no faithfulness. What is this deceitful and faithless water? Certainly that which falsely assumes the resemblance of baptism, and frustrates the grace of faith by a shadowy pretence. But if, according to a perverted faith, one could be baptized without, and obtain remission of sins, according to the same faith he could also attain the Holy Spirit; and there is no need that hands should be laid on him when he comes, that he might obtain the Holy Ghost, and be sealed. Either he could obtain both privileges without by his faith, or he who has been without has received neither.[512]

7. But it is manifest where and by whom remission of sins can be given; to wit, that which is given in baptism. For first of all the Lord gave that power to Peter, upon whom He built the Church, and whence He appointed and showed the source of unity—the power, namely, that whatsoever he loosed on earth should be loosed in heaven. And after the resurrection, also, He speaks to the apostles, saying, "As the Father has sent me, even so I send you. And when He had said this, He breathed on them, and says, unto them, 'Receive the Holy Ghost: whosesoever sins you remit, they are remitted unto them; and whosesoever sins you retain, they are retained.'"[513] Whence we perceive that only they who are set over the Church and established in the Gospel law, and in the ordinance of the Lord, are allowed to baptize and to give remission of sins; but that without, nothing can either be bound or loosed, where there is none who can either bind or loose anything.

8. Nor do we propose this, dearest brother, without the authority of divine Scripture, when we say that all things are arranged by divine direction by a certain law and by special ordinance, and that none can usurp to himself, in opposition to the bishops and priests, anything which is not of his own right and power. For Korah, Dathan, and Abiram endeavored to usurp, in opposition to Moses and Aaron the priest, the power of sacrificing; and they did not do without punishment what they unlawfully dared. The sons of Aaron also, who placed strange fire upon the altar, were at once consumed in the sight of an angry Lord; which punishment remains to those who introduce strange water by a false baptism, that the divine vengeance may avenge and chastise when heretics do that in opposition to the Church, which the Church alone is allowed to do.

9. But in respect of the assertion of some concerning those who had been baptized in Samaria, that when the Apostles Peter and John came, only hands were imposed on them, that they might receive the Holy Ghost, yet that they were not re-baptized; we see that that place does not, dearest brother, touch the present case. For they who had believed in Samaria had believed with a true faith; and within, in the Church which is one, and to which alone it is granted to bestow the grace of baptism and to remit sins, had been baptized by Philip the deacon, whom the same apostles had sent. And therefore, because they had obtained a legitimate and ecclesiastical baptism, there was no need that they should be baptized any more, but only that which was needed was performed by Peter and John; viz., that prayer being made for them, and hands being imposed, the Holy Spirit should be invoked and poured out upon them, which now too is done among us, so that they who are baptized in the Church are brought to the prelates of the Church, and by our prayers and by the imposition of hands obtain the Holy Spirit, and are perfected with the Lord's seal.[514]

10. There is no ground, therefore, dearest brother, for thinking that we should give way to heretics so far as to contemplate the betrayal to them of that baptism, which is only granted to the one and only Church. It is a good soldier's duty to defend the camp of his general against rebels and enemies. It is the duty of an

illustrious leader to keep the standards entrusted to him. It is written, "The Lord your God is a jealous God."[515] We who have received the Spirit of God ought to have a jealousy for the divine faith; with such a jealousy as that wherewith Phineas both pleased God and justly allayed His wrath when He was angry, and the people were perishing. Why do we receive as allowed an adulterous and alien church, a foe to the divine unity, when we know only one Christ and His one Church? The Church, setting forth the likeness of paradise, includes within her walls fruit-bearing trees, whereof that which does not bring forth good fruit is cut off and is cast into the fire. These trees she waters with four rivers, that is, with the four Gospels, wherewith, by a celestial inundation, she bestows the grace of saving baptism. Can any one water from the Church's fountains who is not within the Church? Can one impart those wholesome and saving draughts of paradise to any one if he is perverted, and of himself condemned, and banished outside the fountains of paradise, and has dried up and failed with the dryness of an eternal thirst?

11. The Lord cries aloud, that whosoever thirsts should come and drink of the rivers of living water that flowed out of His bosom.[516] Whither is he to come who thirsts? Shall he come to the heretics, where there is no fountain and river of living water at all; or to the Church which is one, and is founded upon one who has received the keys of it by the Lord's voice? It is she who holds and possesses alone all the power of her spouse and Lord. In her we preside; for her honor and unity we fight; her grace, as well as her glory, we defend with faithful devotedness. We by the divine permission water the thirsting people of God; we guard the boundaries of the living fountains. If, therefore, we hold the right of our possession, if we acknowledge the sacrament of unity, wherefore are we esteemed prevaricators against truth? Wherefore are we judged betrayers of unity? The faithful, and saving, and holy water of the Church cannot be corrupted and adulterated, as the Church herself also is uncorrupted, and chaste, and modest. If heretics are devoted to the Church and established in the Church, they may use both her baptism and her other saving benefits. But if they are not in the Church, nay more, if they act against the Church, how can they baptize with the Church's baptism?

12. For it is no small and insignificant matter, which is conceded to heretics, when their baptism is recognized by us; since thence springs the whole origin of faith and the saving access to the hope of life eternal, and the divine condescension for purifying and quickening the servants of God. For if any one could be baptized among heretics, certainly he could also obtain remission of sins. If he attained remission of sins, he was also sanctified. If he was sanctified, he also was made the temple of God. I ask, of what God? If of the Creator; he could not be, because he has not believed in Him. If of Christ; he could not become His temple, since he denies that Christ is God. If of the Holy Spirit; since the three are one, how can the Holy Spirit be at peace with him who is the enemy either of the Son or of the Father?

13. Hence it is in vain that some who are overcome by reason oppose to us custom, as if custom were greater than truth; or as if that were not to be sought after in spiritual matters which has been revealed as the better by the Holy Spirit. For one who errs by simplicity may be pardoned, as the blessed Apostle Paul says of himself, "I who at first was a blasphemer, and a persecutor, and injurious; yet obtained mercy, because I did it ignorantly."[517] But after inspiration and revelation made to him, he who intelligently and knowingly perseveres in that course in which he had erred, sins without pardon for his ignorance. For he resists with a certain presumption and obstinacy, when he is overcome by reason. Nor let any one say, "We follow that which we have received from the apostles," when the apostles only delivered one Church, and one baptism, which is not ordained except in the same Church. And we cannot find that any one, when he had been baptized by heretics, was received by the apostles in the same baptism, and communicated in such a way as that the apostles should appear to have approved the baptism of heretics.[518]

14. For as to what some say, as if it tended to favor heretics, that the Apostle Paul declared, "Only every way, whether in pretence or in truth, let Christ be preached,"[519] we find that this also can avail nothing to their benefit who support and applaud heretics. For Paul, in his epistle, was not speaking of heretics, nor of their baptism, so that anything can be shown to have been alleged which pertained to this matter. He was speaking of brethren, whether as walking disorderly and against the discipline of the Church, or as keeping the truth of the Gospel with the fear of God. And he said that certain of them spoke the word of God with constancy and courage, but some acted in envy and dissension; that some maintained towards him a benevolent love, but that some indulged a malevolent spirit of dissension; but yet that he bore all patiently, so long only as, whether in truth or in pretence, the name of Christ which Paul preached might come to the knowledge of many; and the sowing of the word, which as yet had been new and irregular, might increase through the preaching of the speakers. Besides, it is one thing for those who are within the Church to speak concerning the name of Christ; it is another for those who are without, and act in opposition to the Church, to baptize in the name of Christ. Wherefore, let not those who favor heretics put forward what Paul spoke concerning brethren, but let them show if he thought anything was to be conceded to the heretic, or if he approved of their faith or baptism, or if he appointed that perfidious and blasphemous men could receive remission of their sins outside the Church.

15. But if we consider what the apostles thought about heretics, we shall find that they, in all their epistles, execrated and detested the sacrilegious wickedness of heretics. For when they say that their word creeps as a canker,[520] how is such a word as that able to give remission of sins, which creeps like a canker to the ears of the hearers? And when they say that there can be no fellowship between righteousness and un-righteousness, no communion between light and darkness,[521] how can either darkness illuminate, or unrighteousness justify? And when they say that they are not of God, but are of the spirit of antichrist,[522] how can they transact spiritual and divine matters, who are the enemies of God, and whose hearts the spirit of antichrist has possessed? Wherefore, if, laying aside the errors of human dispute, we return with a sincere and religious faith to the evangelical authority and to the tradition, we shall perceive that they may do nothing towards conferring the ecclesiastical and saving grace, who, scattering and attacking the Church of Christ, are called adversaries by Christ Himself, but by His apostles, antichrists.

16. Again, there is no ground for any one, for the circumvention of Christian truth, opposing to us the name of Christ, and saying, "All who are baptized everywhere, and in any manner, in the name of Jesus Christ, have obtained the grace of baptism"—when Christ Himself speaks, and says, "Not every one that says unto me, Lord, Lord, shall enter into the kingdom of heaven."[523] And again, He forewarns and instructs, that no one should be easily deceived by false prophets and false Christs in His name. "Many," He says, "shall come in my name, saying, 'I am Christ,' and shall deceive many." And afterwards He added: "But take heed; behold, I have foretold you all things."[524] Whence it appears that all things are not at once to be received and assumed which are boasted of in the name of Christ, but only those things which are done in the truth of Christ.

17. For whereas in the Gospels, and in the epistles of the apostles, the name of Christ is alleged for the remission of sins; it is not in such a way as that the Son alone, without the Father, or against the Father, can be of advantage to anybody; but that it might be shown to the Jews, who boasted as to their having the Father, that the Father would profit them nothing, unless they believed on the Son whom He had sent. For they who know God the Father the Creator, ought also to know Christ the Son, lest they should flatter and applaud themselves about the Father alone, without the acknowledgment of His Son, who also said, "No man comes to the Father but by me."[525] But He, the same, sets forth, that it is the knowledge of the two which saves, when He says, "And this is life eternal, that they might know You, the only true God, and Jesus Christ, whom you have sent."[526] Since, therefore, from the preaching and testimony of Christ Himself, the Father who sent must be first known, then afterwards Christ, who was sent, and there cannot be a hope of salvation except by knowing the two together; how, when God the Father is not known, nay, is even blasphemed, can they who among the heretics are said to be baptized in the name of Christ, be judged to have obtained the remission of sins? For the case of the Jews under the apostles was one, but the condition of the Gentiles is another. The former, because they had already gained the most ancient baptism of the law and Moses, were to be baptized also in the name of Jesus Christ, in conformity with what Peter tells them in the Acts of the Apostles, saying, "Repent, and be baptized every one of you in the name of the Lord Jesus Christ, for the remission of sins, and you shall receive the gift of the Holy Ghost. For this promise is unto you, and to your children, and to all that are afar off, even as many as the Lord our God shall call."[527] Peter makes mention of Jesus Christ, not as though the Father should be omitted, but that the Son also might be joined to the Father.

18. Finally, when, after the resurrection, the apostles are sent by the Lord to the heathens, they are bidden to baptize the Gentiles in the name of the Father, and of the Son, and of the Holy Ghost. How, then, do some say, that a Gentile baptized without, outside the Church, yea, and in opposition to the Church, so that it be only in the name of Jesus Christ, everywhere, and in whatever manner, can obtain remission of sin, when Christ Himself commands the heathen to be baptized in the full and united Trinity?[528] Unless while one who denies Christ is denied by Christ, he who denies His Father whom Christ Himself confessed is not denied; and he who blasphemes against Him whom Christ called His Lord and His God, is rewarded by Christ, and obtains remission of sins, and the sanctification of baptism! But by what power can he who denies God the Creator, the Father of Christ, obtain, in baptism, the remission of sins, since Christ received that very power by which we are baptized and sanctified, from the same Father, whom He called greater than Himself, by whom He desired to be glorified, whose will He fulfilled even unto the obedience of drinking the cup, and of undergoing death? What else is it then, than to become a partaker with blaspheming heretics, to wish to maintain and assert, that one who blasphemes and gravely sins against the Father and the Lord and God of Christ, can receive remission of sins in the name of Christ? What, moreover, is that, and of what kind is it, that he who denies the Son of God has not the Father, and he who denies the Father should be thought to have the Son, although the Son Himself testifies, and says, "No man can come unto me except it were given unto him of my Father?"[529] So that it is evident, that no remission of sins can be received in baptism from the Son, which it is not plain that the Father has granted. Especially, since He further repeats, and says, "Every plant which my heavenly Father has not planted shall be rooted up."[530]

19. But if Christ's disciples are unwilling to learn from Christ what veneration and honor is due to the name of the Father, still let them learn from earthly and secular examples, and know that Christ has declared, not without the strongest rebuke, "The children of this world are wiser in their generation than the children of light."[531] In this world of ours, if any one have offered an insult to the father of any; if in injury and frowardness he have wounded his reputation and his honor by a malevolent tongue, the son is indignant, and wrathful, and with what means he can, strives to avenge his injured father's wrong? Think you that Christ grants impunity to the impious and profane, and the blasphemers of His Father, and that He puts away their sins in baptism, who it is evident, when baptized, still heap up evil words on the person of the Father, and sin with the unceasing wickedness of a blaspheming tongue? Can a Christian, can a servant of God, either conceive this in his mind, or believe it in faith, or put it forward in discourse? And what will become of the precepts of the divine law, which say, "Honor your father and your mother?"[532] If the name of father, which in man is commanded to be honored, is violated with impunity in God, what will become of what Christ Himself lays down in the Gospel, and says, "He that curses father or mother, let him die the death;"[533] if He who bids that those who curse their parents after the flesh should be punished and slain, Himself quickens those who revile their heavenly and spiritual Father, and are hostile to the Church, their Mother? An execrable and detestable thing is actually asserted by some, that He who threatens the man who blasphemes against the Holy Spirit, that he shall be guilty of eternal sin, Himself condescends to sanctify those who blaspheme against God the Father with saving baptism. And now, those who think that they must communicate with such as come to the Church without baptism, do not consider that they are becoming partakers with other men's, yea, with eternal sins, when they admit without baptism those who cannot, except in baptism, put off the sins of their blasphemies.

20. Besides, how vain and perverse a thing it is, that when the heretics themselves, having repudiated and forsaken either the error or the wickedness in which they had previously been, acknowledge the truth of the Church, we should mutilate the rights and sacrament of that same truth, and say to those who come to us and repent, that they had obtained remission of sins when they confess that they have sinned, and are for that reason come to seek the pardon of the Church! Wherefore, dearest brother, we ought both firmly to maintain the faith and truth of the Catholic Church, and to teach, and by all the evangelical and precepts to set forth, the plan of the divine dispensation and unity.

21. Can the power of baptism be greater or of more avail than confession, than suffering, when one confesses Christ before men and is baptized in his own blood? And yet even this baptism does not benefit a heretic, although he has confessed Christ, and been put to death outside the Church, unless the patrons and advocates of heretics declare that the heretics who are slain in a false confession of Christ are martyrs, and assign to them the glory and the crown of martyrdom contrary to the testimony of the apostle, who says that it will profit them nothing although they were burnt and slain.[534] But if not even the baptism of a public confession and blood can profit a heretic to salvation, because there is no salvation out of the Church,[535] how much less shall it be of advantage to him, if in a hiding-place and a cave of robbers, stained with the contagion of adulterous water, he has not only not put off his old sins, but rather heaped up still newer and greater ones! Wherefore baptism cannot be common to us and to heretics, to whom neither God the Father, nor Christ the Son, nor the Holy Ghost, nor the faith, nor the Church itself, is common. And therefore it behooves those to be baptized who come from heresy to the Church, that so they who are prepared, in the lawful, and true, and only baptism of the holy Church, by divine regeneration, for the kingdom of God, may be born of both sacraments, because it is written, "Unless a man be born of water and of the Spirit, he cannot enter into the kingdom of God."[536]

22. On which place some, as if by human reasoning they were able to make void the truth of the Gospel declaration, object to us the case of catechumens; asking if any one of these, before he is baptized in the Church, should be apprehended and slain on confession of the name, whether he would lose the hope of salvation and the reward of confession, because he had not previously been born again of water? Let men of this kind, who are aiders and favorers of heretics, know therefore, first, that those catechumens hold the sound faith and truth of the Church, and advance from the divine camp to do battle with the devil, with a full and sincere acknowledgment of God the Father, and of Christ, and of the Holy Ghost; then, that they certainly are not deprived of the sacrament of baptism who are baptized with the most glorious and greatest baptism of blood, concerning which the Lord also said, that He had another baptism to be baptized with. But the same Lord declares in the Gospel, that those who are baptized in their own blood, and sanctified by suffering, are perfected, and obtain the grace of the divine promise, when He speaks to the thief believing and confessing in His very passion, and promises that he should be with Himself in paradise. Wherefore we who are set over the faith and truth ought not to deceive and mislead those who come to the faith and truth, and repent, and beg that their sins should be remitted to them; but to instruct them when corrected by us, and reformed for the kingdom of heaven by celestial discipline.[537]

23. But some one says, "What, then, shall become of those who in past times, coming from heresy to the Church, were received without baptism?" The Lord is able by His mercy to give indulgence, and not to separate from the gifts of His Church those who by simplicity were admitted into the Church, and in the Church have fallen asleep. Nevertheless it does not follow that, because there was error at one time, there must always be error; since it is more fitting for wise and God-fearing men, gladly and without delay to obey the truth when laid open and perceived, than pertinaciously and obstinately to struggle against brethren and fellow priests on behalf of heretics.[538]

24. Nor let any one think that, because baptism is proposed to them, heretics will be kept back from coming to the Church, as if offended at the name of a second baptism; nay, but on this very account they are rather driven to the necessity of coming by the testimony of truth shown and proved to them. For if they shall see that it is determined and decreed by our judgment and sentence, that the baptism wherewith they are there baptized is considered just and legitimate, they will think that they are justly and legitimately in possession of the Church also, and the other gifts of the Church; nor will there be any reason for their coming to us, when, as they have baptism, they seem also to have the rest. But further, when they know that there is no baptism without, and that no remission of sins can be given outside the Church, they more eagerly and readily hasten to us, and implore the gifts and benefits of the Church our Mother, assured that they can in no wise attain to the true promise of divine grace unless they first come to the truth of the Church. Nor will heretics refuse to be baptized among us with the lawful and true baptism of the Church, when they shall have learned from us that they also were baptized by Paul, who already had been baptized with the baptism of John, as we read in the Acts of the Apostles.

25. And now by certain of us the baptism of heretics is asserted to occupy the [same] ground, and, as if by a certain dislike of re-baptizing, it is counted unlawful to baptize after God's enemies. And this, although we find that they were baptized whom John had baptized: John, esteemed the greatest among the prophets; John, filled with divine grace even in his mother's womb; who was sustained with the spirit and power of Elijah; who was not an adversary of the Lord, but His precursor and announcer; who not only foretold our Lord in words, but even showed Him to the eyes; who baptized Christ Himself by whom others are baptized. But if on that account a heretic could obtain the right of baptism, because he first baptized, then baptism will not belong to the person that has it, but to the person that seizes it. And since baptism and the Church can by no means be separated from one another, and divided, he who has first been able to lay hold on baptism has equally also laid hold on the Church[539]; and you begin to appear to him as a heretic, when you being anticipated, have begun to be last, and by yielding and giving way have relinquished the right which you had received. But how dangerous it is in divine matters, that any one should depart from his right and power, Holy Scripture declares when, in Genesis, Esau thence lost his birthright, nor was able afterwards to regain that which he had once given up.

26. These things, dearest brother, I have briefly written to you, according to my abilities, prescribing to none, and prejudging none, so as to prevent any one of the bishops doing what he thinks well, and having the free exercise of his judgment. We, as far as in us lies, do not contend on behalf of heretics with our colleagues and fellow bishops, with whom we maintain a divine concord and the peace of the Lord; especially since the apostle says, "If any man, however, is thought to be contentious, we have no such custom, neither the Church of God."[540] Charity of spirit, the honor of our college, the bond of faith, and priestly concord, are maintained by us with patience and gentleness. For this reason, moreover, we have with the best of our poor abilities, with the permission and inspiration of the Lord, written a treatise on the Benefit of Patience, which for the sake of our mutual love we have transmitted to you. I bid you, dearest brother, ever heartily farewell.

NOTES

506. Cyprian here confuses *sacramental validity* with *sacramental liciety*. A sacrament may of course be valid while being illicit (illegal), as in the case of baptism by heretics.
507. References to *cathedra*, the episcopal chair from which bishops preached.
508. A reference to the synod convened in Carthage during the episcopacy of Agrippinus around 220, which dealt with proper reception of heretics and schismatics into the Church. Cyprian infers here that Agrippinus' discipline included re-baptism.
509. An obscure gnostic sect that venerated the serpent.
510. Matt. 28:18.
511. Jer. 15:18, Septuagint version.
512. Apart from the immediate context, notice that St. Cyprian assumes that faith alone is not sufficient to receive the graces which only come through the sacraments.
513. John 20:21-23.
514. A testimony to the practice of Confirmation in the early Church.
515. Deut. 4:24.

516. John 7:37-38.

517. 1 Tim. 1:13.

518. It is interesting that in this, and in other arguments against "custom" (see the statement of Libosus of Vaga in the Seventh Council of Carthage), it becomes evident that it had been the Tradition of the Church to not rebaptize heretics. This exposes the position of Cyprian as novel and against apostolic custom. He does not argue that it is not customary to rebaptize heretics; he rather argues that the custom is wrong, though in doing so he acknowledges that such a custom exists and that he is arguing from outside the Tradition.

519. Phil. 1:18.

520. 2 Tim. 2:17.

521. 2 Cor. 6:14.

522. 1 John 4:3.

523. Matt. 7:21.

524. Matt. 24:5, 25.

525. John 14:6.

526. John 17:3.

527. Acts 2:38-39.

528. Cyprian seems to be asserting that the baptism of the heretics made use of improper form (baptism "in the name of Jesus Christ" rather than in the name of the Trinity). If this is the case, it brings another question into the debate: baptism done in the proper form but with an improper minister (say, a heretic) can be valid though illicit, but baptism done with the incorrect form, regardless of who performs it, would be invalid as well as illicit. Cyprian does not distinguish between the question of validity and the question if liciety, which makes his argument somewhat muddled.

529. John 6:65.

530. Matt. 15:13.

531. Luke 16:8.

532. Ex. 20:12.

533. Matt. 15:4.

534. 1 Cor. 13:3.

535. The origin of the famous saying, *Salus extra ecclesiam non est.*

536. John 3:5.

537. An important affirmation of the traditional Catholic teaching on the baptism of blood.

538. Cyprian again finds himself having to argue awkwardly against the Church's tradition. See note 91 above.

539. One of the fruits of baptism is incorporation into the Church: "From the baptismal fonts is born the one People of God of the New Covenant, which transcends all the natural or human limits of nations, cultures, races, and sexes: 'For by one Spirit we were all baptized into one body'" (CCC 1267).

540. 1 Cor. 11:16.

LETTER 73

TO POMPEY, AGAINST THE EPISTLE OF STEPHEN ABOUT THE BAPTISM OF HERETICS[541]

1. Cyprian to his brother Pompeius, greeting. Although I have fully comprised what is to be said concerning the baptism of heretics in the letters of which I sent you copies, dearest brother, yet, since you have desired that what Stephen our brother replied to my letters should be brought to your knowledge, I have sent you a copy of his reply; on the reading of which, you will more and more observe his error in endeavoring to maintain the cause of heretics against Christians, and against the Church of God. For among other matters, which were either haughtily assumed, or were not pertaining to the matter, or contradictory to his own view, which he unskilfully and without foresight wrote, he moreover added this saying: "If any one, therefore, come to you from any heresy whatever, let nothing be innovated (or done) which has not been handed down, to wit, that hands be imposed on him for repentance; since the heretics themselves, in their own proper character, do not baptize such as come to them from one another, but only admit them to communion."[542]

2. He forbade one coming from any heresy to be baptized in the Church; that is, he judged the baptism of all heretics to be just and lawful. And although special heresies have special baptisms and different sins, he, holding communion with the baptism of all, gathered up the sins of all, heaped together into his own bosom. And he charged that nothing should be innovated except what had been handed down; as if he were an innovator, who, holding the unity, claims for the one Church one baptism; and not manifestly he who, forgetful of unity, adopts the lies and the contagions of a profane washing. "Let nothing be innovated," says he, "nothing maintained, except what has been handed down." Whence is that tradition? Whether does it descend from the authority of the Lord and of the Gospel, or does it come from the commands and the epistles of the apostles? For that those things which are written must be done, God witnesses and admonishes, saying to Joshua the son of Nun: "The book of this law shall not depart out of your mouth; but you shall meditate in it day and night, that you may observe to do according to all that is written therein."[543] Also the Lord, sending His apostles, commands that the nations should be baptized, and taught to observe all things which He commanded. If, therefore, it is either prescribed in the Gospel, or contained in the epistles or Acts of the Apostles, that those who come from any heresy should not be baptized, but only hands laid upon them to repentance, let this divine and holy tradition be observed. But if everywhere heretics are called nothing else than adversaries and antichrists, if they are pronounced to be people to be avoided, and to be perverted and condemned of their own selves, wherefore is it that they should not be thought worthy of being condemned by us, since it is evident from the apostolic testimony that they are of their own selves condemned? So that no one ought to defame the apostles as if they had approved of the baptisms of heretics, or had communicated with them without the Church's baptism, when they, the apostles, wrote such things of the heretics. And this, too, while as yet the more terrible plagues of heresy had not broken forth; while Marcion of Pontus had not yet emerged from Pontus, whose master Cerdon[544] came to Rome—while Hyginus was still bishop, who was the ninth bishop in that city—whom Marcion followed, and with greater impudence adding other enhancements to his crime, and more daringly set himself to blaspheme against God the Father, the Creator, and armed with sacrilegious arms the heretical madness that rebelled against the Church with greater wickedness and determination.

3. But if it is evident that subsequently heresies became more numerous and worse; and if, in time past, it was never at all prescribed nor written that only hands should be laid upon a heretic for repentance, and that so he might be communicated with; and if there is only one baptism, which is with us, and is within, and is granted of the divine condescension to the Church alone, what obstinacy is that, or what presumption, to prefer human tradition to divine ordinance, and not to observe that God is indignant and angry as often as human tradition relaxes and passes by the divine precepts, as He cries out, and says by Isaiah the prophet, "This people honors me with their lips, but their heart is far from me. But in vain do they worship me, teaching the doctrines and commandments of men."[545] Also the Lord in the Gospel, similarly rebuking and reproving, utters and says, "You reject the commandment of God, that you may keep your own tradition."[546] Mindful of which precept, the blessed Apostle Paul himself also warns and instructs, saying, "If any man teach otherwise, and consent not to the wholesome words of our Lord Jesus Christ, and to His doctrine, he is proud, knowing nothing: from such withdraw yourself."[547]

4. Certainly an excellent and lawful tradition is set before us by the teaching of our brother Stephen, which may afford us a suitable authority! For in the same place of his epistle he has added and continued: "Since those who are specially heretics do not baptize those who come to them from one another, but only receive them to communion." To this point of evil has the Church of God and spouse of Christ been developed, that she follows the examples of heretics; that for the purpose of celebrating the celestial sacraments, light should borrow her discipline from darkness, and Christians should do that which antichrists do. But what is that blindness of soul, what is that degradation of faith, to refuse to recognize the unity which comes from God the Father, and from the tradition of Jesus Christ the Lord and our God! For if the Church is not with heretics, therefore, because it is one, and cannot be divided; and if thus the Holy Spirit is not there, because He is one, and cannot be among profane persons, and those who are without; certainly also baptism, which consists in the same unity, cannot be among heretics, because it can neither be separated from the Church nor from the Holy Spirit.

5. Or if they attribute the effect of baptism to the majesty of the name, so that they who are baptized anywhere and anyhow, in the name of Jesus Christ, are judged to be renewed and sanctified; wherefore, in the name of the same Christ, are not hands laid upon the baptized persons among them, for the reception of the Holy Spirit? Why does not the same majesty of the same name avail in the imposition of hands, which, they contend, availed in the sanctification of baptism?[551] For if any one born out of the Church can become God's temple, why cannot the Holy Spirit also be poured out upon the temple? For he who has been sanctified, his sins being put away in baptism, and has been spiritually reformed into a new man, has become fitted for receiving the Holy Spirit; since the apostle says, "As many of you as have been baptized into Christ have put on Christ."[552] He who, having been baptized among the heretics, is able to put on Christ, may much more receive the Holy Spirit whom Christ sent. Otherwise He who is sent will be greater than Him who sends; so that one baptized without may begin indeed to put on Christ, but not to be able to receive the Holy Spirit, as if Christ could either be put on without the Spirit, or the Spirit be separated from Christ. Moreover, it is silly to say, that although the second birth is spiritual, by which we are born in Christ through the laver of regeneration, one may be born spiritually among the heretics, where they say that the Spirit is not. For water alone is not able to cleanse away sins, and to sanctify a man, unless he have also the Holy Spirit. Wherefore it is necessary that they should grant the Holy Spirit to be there, where they say that baptism is; or else there is no baptism where the Holy Spirit is not, because there cannot be baptism without the Spirit.[553]

6. But what a thing it is, to assert and contend that they who are not born in the Church can be the sons of God! For the blessed apostle sets forth and proves that baptism is that wherein the old man dies and the new man is born, saying, "He saved us by the washing of regeneration."[548] But if regeneration is in the washing, that is, in baptism, how can heresy, which is not the spouse of Christ, generate sons to God by Christ? For it is the Church alone which, conjoined and united with Christ, spiritually bears sons; as the same apostle again says, "Christ loved the Church, and gave Himself for it, that He might sanctify it, cleansing it with the washing of water."[549] If, then, she is the beloved and spouse who alone is sanctified by Christ, and alone is cleansed by His washing, it is manifest that heresy, which is not the spouse of Christ, nor can be cleansed nor sanctified by His washing, cannot bear sons to God.

7. But further, one is not born by the imposition of hands when he receives the Holy Spirit, but in baptism, that so, being already born, he may receive the Holy Spirit, even as it happened in the first man Adam. For first God formed him, and then breathed into his nostrils the breath of life. For the Spirit cannot be received, unless he who receives first have an existence. But as the birth of Christians is in baptism, while the generation and sanctification of baptism are with the spouse of Christ alone, who is able spiritually to conceive and to bear sons to God, where and of whom and to whom is he born, who is not a son of the Church, so as that he should have God as his Father, before he has had the Church for his Mother? But as no heresy at all, and equally no schism, being without, can have the sanctification of saving baptism, why has the bitter obstinacy of our brother Stephen broken forth to such an extent, as to contend that sons are born to God from the baptism of Marcion; moreover, of Valentinus and Apelles, and of others who blaspheme against God the Father; and to say that remission of sins is granted in the name of Jesus Christ where blasphemy is uttered against the Father and against Christ the Lord God?

8. In which place, dearest brother, we must consider, for the sake of the faith and the religion of the sacerdotal office which we discharge, whether the account can be satisfactory in the day of judgment for a priest of God, who maintains, and approves, and acquiesces in the baptism of blasphemers, when the Lord threatens, and says, "And now, O you priests, this commandment is for you: if you will not hear, and if you will not lay it to heart to give glory unto my name, says the Lord Almighty, I will even send a curse upon you, and I will curse your blessings."[550] Does he give glory to God, who communicates with the baptism of Marcion? Does he give glory to God, who judges that remission of sins is granted among those who blaspheme against God? Does he give glory to God, who affirms that sons are born to God without, of an adulterer and a harlot? Does he give glory to God, who does not hold the unity and truth that arise from the divine law, but maintains heresies against the Church? Does he give glory to God, who, a friend of heretics and an enemy to Christians,[554] thinks that the priests of God, who support the truth of Christ and the unity of the Church, are to be excommunicated? If glory is thus given to God, if the fear and the discipline of God is thus preserved by His worshippers and His priests, let us cast away our arms; let us give ourselves up to captivity; let us deliver to the devil the ordination of the Gospel, the appointment of Christ, the majesty of God; let the sacraments of the divine warfare be loosed; let the standards of the heavenly camp be betrayed; and let the Church succumb and yield to heretics, light to darkness, faith to perfidy, hope to despair, reason to error, immortality to death, love to hatred, truth to falsehood, Christ to Antichrist! Deservedly thus do heresies and schisms arise day by day, more frequently and more fruitfully grow up, and with serpents' locks shoot forth and cast out against the Church of God with greater force the poison of their venom; while, by the advocacy of some, both authority and support are afforded them; while their baptism is defended, while faith, while truth, is betrayed; while that which is done without against the Church is defended within in the very Church itself.

9. But if there be among us, most beloved brother, the fear of God, if the maintenance of the faith prevail, if we keep the precepts of Christ, if we guard the incorrupt and inviolate sanctity of His spouse, if the words of the Lord abide in our thoughts and hearts, when he says, "Do you think, when the Son of man comes, shall He find faith on the earth"[555] then, because we are God's faithful soldiers, who war for the faith and sincere religion of God, let us keep the camp entrusted to us by God with faithful valor. Nor ought custom, which had crept in among some, to prevent the truth from prevailing and conquering; for custom without truth is the antiquity of error. On which account, let us forsake the error and follow the truth, knowing that in Esdras also the truth conquers, as it is written: "Truth endures and grows strong to eternity, and lives and prevails for ever and ever. With her there is no accepting of persons or distinctions; but what is just she does: nor in her judgments is there unrighteousness, but the strength, and the kingdom, and the majesty, and the power of all ages. Blessed be the Lord God of truth!"[556] This truth Christ showed to us in His Gospel, and said, "I am the truth."[557] Wherefore, if we are in Christ, and have Christ in us, if we abide in the truth, and the truth abides in us, let us keep fast those things which are true.

10. But it happens, by a love of presumption and of obstinacy, that one would rather maintain his own evil and false position, than agree in the right and true which belongs to another. Looking forward to which, the blessed Apostle Paul writes to Timothy, and warns him that a bishop must not be litigious, nor contentious, but gentle and teachable. Now he is teachable who is meek and gentle to the patience of learning. For it behooves a bishop not only to teach, but also to learn; because he also teaches better who daily increases and advances by learning better; which very thing, moreover, the same Apostle Paul teaches, when he admonishes, that if anything better be revealed to one sitting by, the first should hold his peace.[558] But there is a brief way for religious and simple minds, both to put away error, and to find and to elicit truth. For if we return to the head and source of divine tradition, human error ceases; and having seen the reason of the heavenly sacraments, whatever lay hid in obscurity under the gloom and cloud of darkness, is opened into the light of the truth. If a channel supplying water, which formerly flowed plentifully and freely, suddenly fail, do we not go to the fountain, that there the reason of the failure may be ascertained, whether from the drying up of the springs the water has failed at the fountainhead, or whether, flowing thence free and full, it has failed in the midst of its course; that so, if it has been caused by the fault of an interrupted or leaky channel, that the constant stream does not flow uninterruptedly and continuously, then the channel being repaired and strengthened, the water collected may be supplied for the use and drink of the city, with the same fertility and plenty with which it issues from the spring? And this it behooves the priests of God to do now, if they would keep the divine precepts, that if in any respect the truth have wavered and vacillated, we should return to our original and Lord, and to the evangelical and tradition; and thence may arise the ground of our action, whence has taken rise both our order and our origin.

11. For it has been delivered to us, that there is one God, and one Christ, and one hope, and one faith, and one Church, and one baptism ordained only in the one Church, from which unity whosoever will depart must needs be found with heretics; and while he upholds them against the Church, he impugns the sacrament of the divine tradition. The sacrament of which unity we see expressed also in the Canticles, in the person of Christ, who says, "A garden enclosed is my sister, my spouse, a fountain sealed, a well of living water, a garden with the fruit of apples."[559] But if His Church is a garden enclosed, and a fountain sealed, how can he who is not in the Church enter into the same garden, or drink from its fountain? Moreover, Peter himself, showing and vindicating the unity, has commanded and warned us that we cannot be saved, except by the one only baptism of one Church. "In the ark," says he, "of Noah, few, that is, eight souls, were saved by water, as also baptism shall in like manner save you."[560] In how short and spiritual a summary has he set forth the sacrament of unity! For as, in that baptism of the world in which its ancient iniquity was purged away, he who was not in the ark of Noah could not be saved by water, so neither can he appear to be saved by baptism who has not been baptized in the Church which is established in the unity of the Lord according to the sacrament of the one ark.

12. Therefore, dearest brother, having explored and seen the truth; it is observed and held by us, that all who are converted from any heresy whatever to the Church must be baptized by the only and lawful baptism of the Church, with the exception of those who had previously been baptized in the Church, and so had passed over to the heretics. For it behooves these, when they return, having repented, to be received by the imposition of hands only, and to be restored by the shepherd to the sheep-fold whence they had strayed. I bid you, dearest brother, ever heartily farewell.

NOTES

541. In his book against the Donatists, St. Augustine mentions this letter, saying: "Cyprian writes also to Pompcius about this selfsame matter, and clearly shows in that letter that Stephen, who, as we learn, was then bishop of the Roman Church, not only did not agree with him

upon the points before us, but even wrote and taught the opposite views. But Stephen certainly did not "communicate with heretics," merely because he did not dare to impugn the baptism of Christ, which he knew remained perfect in the midst of their perversity. For if none have baptism who entertain false views about God, it has been proved sufficiently, in my opinion, that this may happen even within the Church. The apostles, indeed, gave no injunctions on the point; but the custom, which is opposed to Cyprian, may be supposed to have had its origin in apostolic tradition, just as there are many things which are observed by the whole Church, and therefore are fairly held to have been enjoined by the apostles, which yet are not mentioned in their writings" (*On Baptism, Against the Donatists*, Book V, Chapter 23:31).

542. Pope Stephen here maintains the traditional custom, and hence argues from authority and tradition, while Cyprian argues against the Roman custom.

543. Jos. 1:8.

544. "But one Cerdon himself also, taking occasion in like manner from these heretics and Simon, affirms that the God preached by Moses and the prophets was not Father of Jesus Christ. For he contends that this Father had been known, whereas that the Father of Christ was unknown, and that the former was just, but the latter good. And Marcion corroborated the tenet of this heretic in the work which he attempted to write, and which he styled *Antitheses*. And he was in the habit, in this book, of uttering whatever slanders suggested themselves to his mind against the Creator of the universe. In a similar manner likewise (acted) Lucian, the disciple of this heretic" (St. Hippolytus, *Refutation of All Heresies*, Book VII, Chap. 25).

545. Isa. 29:13. This is a fascinating passage, for St. Cyprian here admits that Pope Stephen does hold to the tradition, but denies that the tradition is correct, pitting Scripture against Tradition in a regrettable moment of proto-Protestantism.

546. Mark 7:13

547. 1 Tim. 6:3-5. Cyprian is here being disingenuous, arguing as though the rigorist position on the question were clearly set forth in Scripture, whereas the truth of the matter is as Augustine says, the Apostles gave no injunctions on the question either for or against baptism of heretics.

548. The answer to this question, as later developments in sacramental theology attest, is that the sacraments of baptism and confirmation have different requirements for valid administration. Though the proper minister of baptism is a local ordinary or a local pastor, any person may administer a valid baptism, though the Church envisions this happening only in emergencies (see 1917 C.I.C 738§ 1, 741 and 1983 C.I.C. 861§1-2). This is not the case with confirmation, which can only be administered by a bishop or a lawfully delegated priest (1983 C.I.C 882, 883§ 1-3).

549. Gal. 3:27.

550. In Cyprian's day the sacrament of confirmation was administered immediately after baptism. So united were these two sacraments that Cyprian sees a baptism without confirmation as incomplete. This is not true, strictly speaking, although it is the case that confirmation is seen to be a "completion" and "deepening" of baptismal grace (CCC 1285, 1303).

551. Tit. 3:5.

552. Eph. 5:25-26.

553. Mal. 2:1-2.

554. Here Cyprian indulges in some regrettable character defamation; Stephen, though in disagreement with Cyprian, could hardly be called "a friend of heretics and an enemy of Christians."

555. Luke 18:8.

556. 1 Esdras 4:38-40 in the Septuagint.

557. John 14:6.

558. 1 Cor. 14:30.

559. Song of Solomon 4:12-13.

560. 1 Pet. 3:20-21.

LETTER 74

BISHOP FIRMILIAN OF CAESAREA IN CAPPADOCIA, TO CYPRIAN, AGAINST THE LETTER OF STEPHEN[561]

1. to Cyprian, his brother in the Lord, greeting. We have received by Rogatian, our beloved deacon, the letter sent by you which you wrote to us, well-beloved brother; and we gave the greatest thanks to the Lord, because it has happened that we who are separated from one another in body are thus united in spirit, as if we were not only occupying one country, but inhabiting together one and the self-same house. Which also it is becoming for us to say, because, indeed, the spiritual house of God is one. For it shall come to pass in the last days, says the prophet, that the mountain of the Lord shall be manifest, and the house of God above the tops of the mountains.[562] Those that come together into this house are united with gladness, according to what is asked from the Lord in the psalm, to dwell in the house of the Lord all the days of one's life.[563] Whence in another place also it is made manifest, that among the saints there is great and desirous love for assembling together. "Behold," he says, "how good and how pleasant a thing it is for brethren to dwell together in unity!"[564]

2. For unity and peace and concord afford the greatest pleasure not only to men who believe and know the truth, but also to heavenly angels themselves, to whom the divine word says it is a joy when one sinner repents and returns to the bond of unity. But assuredly this would not be said of the angels, who have their conversation in heaven, unless they themselves also were united to us, who rejoice at our unity; even as, on the other hand, they are assuredly saddened when they see the diverse minds and the divided wills of some, as if not only they do not together invoke one and the same God, but as if, separated and divided from one another, they can neither have a common conversation nor discourse. Except that we may in this matter give thanks to Stephen, that it has now happened through his unkindness that we receive the proof of your faith and wisdom. But although we have received the favor of this benefit on account of Stephen, certainly Stephen has not done anything deserving of kindness and thanks. For neither can Judas be thought worthy by his perfidy and treachery wherewith he wickedly dealt concerning the Savior, as though he had been the cause of such great advantages, that through him the world and the people of the Gentiles were delivered by the Lord's passion.

3. But let these things which were done by Stephen be passed by for the present, lest, while we remember his audacity and pride, we bring a more lasting sadness on ourselves from the things that he has wickedly done.[565] And knowing, concerning you, that you have settled this matter, concerning which there is now a question, according to the rule of truth and the wisdom of Christ; we have exulted with great joy, and have given God thanks that we have found in brethren placed at such a distance such a unanimity of faith and truth with us.[566] For the grace of God is mighty to associate and join together in the bond of charity and unity even those things which seem to be divided by a considerable space of earth, according to the way in which of old also the divine power associated in the bond of unanimity Ezekiel and Daniel, though later in their age, and separated from them by a long space of time, to Job and Noah, who were among the first; so that although they were separated by long periods, yet by divine inspiration they felt the same truths. And this also we now observe in you, that you who are separated from us by the most extensive regions, approve yourselves to be, nevertheless, joined with us in mind and spirit. All which arises from the divine unity. For even as the Lord who dwells in us is one and the same, He everywhere joins and couples His own people in the bond of unity, whence their sound has gone out into the whole earth, who are sent by the Lord swiftly running in the spirit of unity; as, on the other hand, it is of no advantage that some are very near and joined together bodily, if in spirit and mind they differ, since souls cannot at all be united which divide themselves from God's unity. For, lo, it says, they that are far from You shall perish. But such shall undergo the judgment of God according to their desert, as depart from His words who prays to the Father for unity, and says, "Father, grant that, as You and I are one, so they also may be one in us."[567]

4. But we receive those things which you have written as if they were our own; nor do we read them cursorily, but by frequent repetition have committed them to memory. Nor does it hinder saving usefulness, either to repeat the same things for the confirmation of the truth, or, moreover, to add some things for the sake of accumulating proof. But if anything has been added by us, it is not added as if there had been too little said by you; but since the divine discourse surpasses human nature, and the soul cannot conceive or grasp the whole and perfect word, therefore also the number of prophets is so great, that the divine wisdom in its multiplicity may be distributed through many. Whence also he who first speaks in prophecy is bidden to be silent if a revelation be made to a second.[568] For which reason it happens of necessity among us, that year by year we, the elders and prelates, assemble together to arrange those matters which are committed to our care, so that if any things are more serious they may be directed by the common counsel. Moreover, we do this that some remedy may be sought for by repentance for lapsed brethren, and for those wounded by the devil after the saving laver, not as though they obtained remission of sins from us, but that by our means they may be converted to the understanding of their sins, and may be compelled to give fuller satisfaction to the Lord.

5. But since that messenger sent by you was in haste to return to you, and the winter season was pressing, we replied what we could to your letter. And indeed, as respects what Stephen has said, as though the apostles forbade those who come from heresy to be baptized, and delivered this also to be observed by their successors, you have replied most abundantly, that no one is so foolish as to believe that the apostles delivered this, when it is even well known that these heresies themselves, execrable and detestable as they are, arose subsequently; when even Marcion the disciple of Cerdo is found to have introduced his sacrilegious tradition against God long after the apostles, and after long lapse of time from them. Apelles, also consenting to his blasphemy, added many other new and more important matters hostile to faith and truth. But also the time of Valentinus and Basilides is manifest, that they too, after the apostles, and after a long period, rebelled against the Church of God with their wicked lies. It is plain that the other heretics, also, afterwards introduced their evil sects and perverse inventions, even as every one was led by error; all of whom, it is evident, were self-condemned, and have declared against themselves an inevitable sentence before the day of judgment; and he who confirms the baptism of these, what else does he do but adjudge himself with them, and condemn himself, making himself a partaker with such?

6. But that they who are at Rome do not observe those things in all cases which are handed down from the beginning, and vainly pretend the authority of the apostles; any one may know also from the fact, that concerning the celebration of Easter, and concerning many other sacraments of divine matters, he may see that there are some diversities among them, and that all things are not observed among them alike, which are observed at Jerusalem, just as in very many other provinces also many things are varied because of the difference of the places and names. And yet on this account there is no departure at all from the peace and unity of the Catholic Church, such as Stephen has now dared to make; breaking the peace against you, which his predecessors have always kept with you in mutual love and honor, even herein defaming Peter and Paul the blessed apostles, as if the very men delivered this who in their epistles execrated heretics, and warned us to avoid them. Whence it appears that this tradition is of men which maintains heretics, and asserts that they have baptism, which belongs to the Church alone.[569]

7. But, moreover, you have well answered that part where Stephen said in his letter that heretics themselves also are of one mind in respect of baptism; and that they do not baptize such as come to them from one another, but only communicate with them; as if we also ought to do this. In which place, although you have already proved that it is sufficiently ridiculous for any one to follow those that are in error, yet we add this moreover, over and above, that it is not wonderful for heretics to act thus, who, although in some lesser matters they differ, yet in that which is greatest they hold one and the same agreement to blaspheme the Creator, figuring for themselves certain dreams and phantasms of an unknown God. Assuredly it is but natural that these should agree in having a baptism which is unreal, in the same way as they agree in repudiating the truth of the divinity. Of whom, since it is tedious to reply to their several statements, either wicked or foolish, it is sufficient shortly to say in sum, that they who do not hold the true Lord the Father cannot hold the truth either of the Son or of the Holy Spirit; according to which also they who are called Cataphrygians,[570] and endeavor to claim to themselves new prophecies, can have neither the Father, nor the Son, nor the Holy Spirit, of whom, if we ask what Christ they announce, they will reply that they preach Him who sent the Spirit that speaks by Montanus and Prisca. And in these, when we observe that there has been not the spirit of truth, but of error, we know that they who maintain their false prophesying against the faith of Christ cannot have Christ. Moreover, all other heretics, if they have separated themselves from the Church of God, can have nothing of power or of grace, since all power and grace are established in the Church where the elders preside, who possess the power both of baptizing, and of imposition of hands, and of ordaining.[571] For as a heretic may not lawfully ordain nor lay on hands, so neither may he baptize, nor do any thing holily or spiritually, since he is an alien from spiritual and deifying sanctity. All which we some time back confirmed in Iconium, which is a place in Phrygia, when we were assembled together with those who had gathered from Galatia and Cilicia, and other neighboring countries, as to be held and firmly vindicated against heretics, when there was some doubt in certain minds concerning that matter.

8. And as Stephen and those who agree with him contend that putting away of sins and second birth may result from the baptism of heretics, among whom they themselves confess that the Holy Spirit is not; let them consider and understand that spiritual birth cannot be without the Spirit; in conformity with which also the blessed Apostle Paul baptized anew with a spiritual baptism those who had already been baptized by John before the Holy Spirit had been sent by the Lord, and so laid hands on them that they might receive the Holy Spirit. But what kind of a thing is it, that when we see that Paul, after John's baptism, baptized his disciples again, we are hesitating to baptize those who come to the Church from heresy after their unhallowed and profane dipping. Unless, perchance, Paul was inferior to the bishops of these times, so that these indeed can by imposition of hands alone give the Holy Spirit to those heretics who come (to the Church), while Paul was not fitted to give the Holy Spirit by imposition of hands to those who had been baptized by John, unless he had first baptized them also with the baptism of the Church.[572]

9. That, moreover, is absurd, that they do not think it is to be inquired who was the person that baptized, for the reason that he who has been baptized may have obtained grace by the invocation of the Trinity, of the names of the Father, and of the Son, and of the Holy Spirit. Then this will be the wisdom which Paul writes is in those who are perfected. But who in the Church is perfect and wise who can either defend or believe this, that this bare invocation of names is sufficient to the remission of sins and the sanctification of baptism; since these things are only then of advantage, when both he who baptizes has the Holy Spirit, and the baptism itself also is not ordained without the Spirit? But, say they, he who in any manner whatever is baptized without, may obtain the grace of baptism by his disposition and faith, which doubtless is ridiculous in itself, as if either a wicked disposition could attract to itself from heaven the sanctification of the righteous, or a false faith the truth of believers.[573] But that not all who call on the name of Christ are heard, and that their invocation cannot obtain any grace, the Lord Himself manifests, saying, "Many shall come in my name, saying, 'I am Christ,' and shall deceive many."[574] Because there is no difference between a false prophet and a heretic. For as the former deceives in the name of God or Christ, so the latter deceives in the sacrament of baptism. Both strive by falsehood to deceive men's wills.

10. But I wish to relate to you some facts concerning a circumstance which occurred among us, pertaining to this very matter. About two-and-twenty years ago, in the times after the Emperor Alexander,[575] there happened in these parts many struggles and difficulties, either in general to all men, or privately to Christians. Moreover, there were many and frequent earthquakes, so that many places were overthrown throughout Cappadocia and Pontus; even certain cities, dragged into the abyss, were swallowed up by the opening of the gaping earth. So that from this also a severe persecution arose against us of the Christian name; and this after the long peace of the previous age arose suddenly, and with its unusual evils was made more terrible for the disturbance of our people. Serenianus was then governor in our province, a bitter and terrible persecutor. But the faithful being set in this state of disturbance, and fleeing here and there for fear of the persecution, and leaving their country and passing over into other regions—for there was an opportunity of passing over, for the reason that that persecution was not over the whole world, but was local—there arose among us on a sudden a certain woman, who in a state of ecstasy announced herself as a prophetess, and acted as if filled with the Holy Spirit. And she was so moved by the impetus of the principal demons, that for a long time she made anxious and deceived the brotherhood, accomplishing certain wonderful and portentous things, and promised that she would cause the earth to be shaken. Not that the power of the demon was so great that he could prevail to shake the earth, or to disturb the elements; but that sometimes a wicked spirit, prescient, and perceiving that there will be an earthquake, pretends that he will do what he sees will happen. By these lies and boastings he had so subdued the minds of individuals, that they obeyed him and followed wherever he commanded and led. He would also make that woman walk in the keen winter with bare feet over frozen snow, and not to be troubled or hurt in any degree by that walking. Moreover, she would say that she was hurrying to Judea and to Jerusalem, feigning as if she had come thence. Here also she deceived one of the presbyters, a countryman, and another, a deacon, so that they had intercourse with that same woman, which was shortly afterwards detected. For on a sudden there appeared unto her one of the exorcists, a man approved and always of good conversation in respect of religious discipline, who, stimulated by the exhortation also of very many brethren who were themselves strong and praiseworthy in the faith, raised himself up against that wicked spirit to overcome it; which moreover, by its subtle fallacy, had predicted this a little while before, that a certain adverse and unbelieving tempter would come. Yet that exorcist, inspired by God's grace, bravely resisted, and showed that that which was before thought holy, was indeed a most wicked spirit. But that woman, who previously by wiles and deceitfulness of the demon was attempting many things for the deceiving of the faithful, among other things by which she had deceived many, also had frequently dared this; to pretend that with an invocation not to be contemned she sanctified bread and celebrated the Eucharist, and to offer sacrifice to the Lord, not without the sacrament of the accustomed utterance; and also to baptize many, making use of the usual and lawful words of interrogation, that nothing might seem to be different from the ecclesiastical rule.

11. What, then, shall we say about the baptism of this woman, by which a most wicked demon baptized through means of a woman? Do Stephen and they who agree with him approve of this also especially when neither the symbol of the Trinity nor the legitimate and ecclesiastical interrogatory were wanting to her? Can it be believed that either remission of sins was given, or the regeneration of the saving laver duly completed, when all things, although after the image of truth, yet were done by a demon? Unless, perchance, they who defend the baptism of heretics contend that the demon also conferred the grace of baptism in the name of the Father, and of the Son, and of the Holy Spirit. Among them, no doubt, there is the same error—it is the very deceitfulness of devils, since among them the Holy Spirit is not at all.

12. Moreover, what is the meaning of that which Stephen would assert, that the presence and holiness of Christ is with those who are baptized among heretics? For if the apostle does not speak falsely when he says, "As many of you as are baptized into Christ, have put on Christ,"[576] certainly he who has been baptized among them into Christ, has put on Christ. But if he has put on Christ, he might also receive the Holy Spirit, who was sent by Christ, and hands are vainly laid upon him who comes to us for the reception of the Spirit; unless, perhaps, he has not put on the Spirit from Christ, so that Christ indeed may be with heretics, but the Holy Spirit not be with them.

13. But let us briefly run through the other matters also, which were spoken of by you abundantly and most fully, especially as Rogatianus, our well-beloved deacon, is hurrying to you. For it follows that they must be asked by us, when they defend heretics, whether their baptism is carnal or spiritual. For if it is carnal, they differ in no respect from the baptism of the Jews, which they use in such a manner that in it, as if in a common and vulgar laver, only external filth is washed away. But if it is spiritual, how can baptism be spiritual among those among whom there is no Holy Spirit? And thus the water wherewith they are washed is to them only a carnal washing, not a sacrament of baptism.[577]

14. But if the baptism of heretics can have the regeneration of the second birth, those who are baptized among them must be counted not heretics, but children of God. For the second birth, which occurs in baptism, begets sons of God.[578] But if the spouse of Christ is one, which is the Catholic Church, it is she herself who alone bears sons of God. For there are not many spouses of Christ, since the apostle says, "I have espoused you, that I may present you as a chaste virgin to Christ;"[579] and, "Hearken, O daughter, and consider, and incline your ear; forget also your own people, for the King has greatly desired your beauty;"[580] and, "Come with me, my spouse, from Lebanon; you shall come, and shall pass over from the source of your faith;"[581] and, "I have come into my garden, my sister, my spouse."[582] We see that one person is everywhere set forward, because also the spouse is one. But the synagogue of heretics is not one with us, because the spouse is not an adulteress and a harlot. Whence also she cannot bear children of God; unless, as appears to Stephen, heresy indeed brings them forth and exposes them, while the Church takes them up when exposed, and nourishes those for her own whom she has not born, although she cannot be the mother of strange children. And therefore Christ our Lord, setting forth that His spouse is one, and declaring the sacrament of His unity, says, "He that is not with me is against me, and he that gathers not with me scatters."[583] For if Christ is with us, but the heretics are not with us, certainly the heretics are in opposition to Christ; and if we gather with Christ, but the heretics do not gather with us, doubtless they scatter.

15. But neither must we pass over what has been necessarily remarked by you, that the Church, according to the Song of Songs, is a garden enclosed, and a fountain sealed, a paradise with the fruit of apples.[584] They who have never entered into this garden, and have not seen the paradise planted by God the Creator, how shall they be able to afford to another the bring water of the saving laver from the fountain which is enclosed within, and sealed with a divine seal? And as the ark of Noah was nothing else than the sacrament of the Church of Christ, which then, when all without were perishing, kept those only safe who were within the ark, we are manifestly instructed to look to the unity of the Church.[585] Even as also the Apostle Peter laid down, saying, "Thus also shall baptism in like manner make you safe,"[586] showing that as they who were not in the ark with Noah not only were not purged and saved by water, but at once perished in that deluge; so now also, whoever are not in the Church with Christ will perish outside, unless they are converted by penitence to the only and saving laver of the Church.

16. But what is the greatness of his error, and what the depth of his blindness, who says that remission of sins can be granted in the synagogues of heretics, and does not abide on the foundation of the one Church which was once based by Christ upon the rock, may be perceived from this, that Christ said to Peter alone, "Whatsoever you shall bind on earth shall be bound in heaven, and whatsoever you shall loose on earth shall be loosed in heaven."[587] And again, in the Gospel, when Christ breathed on the apostles alone, saying, "Receive the Holy Spirit: whose soever sins you remit they are remitted unto them, and whose soever sins you retain they are retained."[588] Therefore the power of remitting sins was given to the apostles, and to the churches which they, sent by Christ, established, and to the bishops who succeeded to them by vicarious ordination.[589] But the enemies of the one Catholic Church in which we are, and the adversaries of us who have succeeded the apostles, asserting for themselves, in opposition to us, unlawful priesthoods, and setting up profane altars, what else are they than Korah, Dathan, and Abiram, profane with a like wickedness, and about to suffer the same punishments which they did, as well as those who agree with them, just as their partners and abettors perished with a like death to theirs?

17. And in this respect I am justly indignant at this so open and manifest folly of Stephen, that he who so boasts of the place of his episcopate, and contends that he holds the succession from Peter, on whom the foundations of the Church were laid, should introduce many other rocks and establish new buildings of many churches;[590] maintaining that there is baptism in them by his authority. For they who are baptized, doubtless, fill up the number of the Church. But he who approves their baptism maintains, of those baptized, that the Church is also with them. Nor does he understand that the truth of the Christian Rock is overshadowed, and in some measure abolished, by him when he thus betrays and deserts unity.[591] The apostle acknowledges that the Jews, although blinded by ignorance, and bound by the grossest wickedness, have yet a zeal for God. Stephen, who announces that he holds by succession the throne of Peter, is stirred with no zeal against heretics, when he concedes to them, not a moderate, but the very greatest power of grace: so far as to say and assert that, by the sacrament of baptism, the filth of the old man is washed away by them, that they pardon the former mortal sins, that they make sons of God by heavenly regeneration, and renew to eternal life by the sanctification of the divine laver. He who concedes and gives up to heretics in this way the great and heavenly gifts of the Church, what else does he do but communicate with them for whom he maintains and claims so much grace?[592] And now he hesitates in vain to consent to them, and to be a partaker with them in other matters also, to meet together with them, and equally with them to mingle their prayers, and appoint a common altar and sacrifice.[593]

18. But, says he, the name of Christ is of great advantage to faith and the sanctification of baptism; so that whosoever is anywhere so-ever baptized in the name of Christ, immediately obtains the grace of Christ: although this position may be briefly met and answered, that if baptism without in the name of Christ availed for the cleansing of man; in the name of the same Christ, the imposition of hands might avail also for the reception of the Holy Spirit; and the other things also which are done among heretics will begin to seem just and lawful when they are done in the name of Christ; as you have maintained in your letter that the name of Christ could be of no avail except in the Church alone, to which alone Christ has conceded the power of heavenly grace.[594]

19. But with respect to the refutation of custom which they seem to oppose to the truth, who is so foolish as to prefer custom to truth, or when he sees the light, not to forsake the darkness?—unless most ancient custom in any respect avail the Jews, upon the advent of Christ, that is, the Truth, in remaining in their old usage, and forsaking the new way of truth. And this indeed you Africans are able to say against Stephen, that when you knew the truth you forsook the error of custom. But we join custom to truth, and to the Romans' custom we oppose custom, but the custom of truth; holding from the beginning that which was delivered by Christ and the apostles.[595] Nor do we remember that this at any time began

507

among us, since it has always been observed here, that we knew none but one Church of God, and accounted no baptism holy except that of the holy Church.[596] Certainly, since some doubted about the baptism of those who, although they receive the new prophets,[597] yet appear to recognize the same Father and Son with us; very many of us meeting together in Iconium very carefully examined the matter, and we decided that every baptism was altogether to be rejected which is arranged for without the Church.

20. But to what they allege and say on behalf of the heretics, that the apostle said, "Whether in pretence or in truth, Christ is preached,"[598] it is idle for us to reply; when it is manifest that the apostle, in his epistle wherein he said this, made mention neither of heretics nor of baptism of heretics, but spoke of brethren only, whether as perfidiously speaking in agreement with himself, or as persevering in sincere faith; nor is it needful to discuss this in a long argument, but it is sufficient to read the epistle itself, and to gather from the apostle himself what the apostle said.

21. What then, say they, will become of those who, coming from the heretics, have been received without the baptism of the Church? If they have departed this life, they are reckoned in the number of those who have been catechumens indeed among us, but have died before they were baptized—no trifling advantage of truth and faith, to which they had attained by forsaking error, although, being prevented by death, they had not gained the consummation of grace. But they who still abide in life should be baptized with the baptism of the Church, that they may obtain remission of sins, lest by the presumption of others they remain in their old error, and die without the completion of grace. But what a crime is theirs on the one hand who receive, or on the other, theirs who are received, that their foulness not being washed away by the laver of the Church, nor their sins put away, communion being rashly seized, they touch the body and blood of the Lord, although it is written, "Whosoever shall eat the bread or drink the cup of the Lord unworthily, shall be guilty of the body and blood of the Lord!"[599]

22. We have judged, that those also whom they, who had formerly been bishops in the Catholic Church, and afterwards had assumed to themselves the power of clerical ordination, had baptized, are to be regarded as not baptized. And this is observed among us, that whosoever dipped by them come to us are baptized among us as strangers and having obtained nothing, with the only and true baptism of the Catholic Church, and obtain the regeneration of the laver of life. And yet there is a great difference between him who unwillingly and constrained by the necessity of persecution has given way, and him who with a profane will boldly rebels against the Church, or with impious voice blasphemes against the Father and God of Christ and the Creator of the whole world. And Stephen is not ashamed to assert and to say that remission of sins can be granted by those who are themselves set fast in all kinds of sins, as if in the house of death there could be the laver of salvation.

23. What, then, is to be made of what is written, "Abstain from strange water, and drink not from a strange fountain,"[600] if, leaving the sealed fountain of the Church, you take up strange water for your own, and pollute the Church with unhallowed fountains? For when you communicate with the baptism of heretics, what else do you do than drink from their slough and mud; and while you yourself are purged with the Church's sanctification, you become befouled with the contact of the filth of others? And do you not fear the judgment of God when you are giving testimony to heretics in opposition to the Church, although it is written, "A false witness shall not be unpunished?"[601] But indeed you are worse than all heretics. For when many, as soon as their error is known, come over to you from them that they may receive the true light of the Church, you assist the errors of those who come, and, obscuring the light of ecclesiastical truth, you heap up the darkness of the heretical night; and although they confess that they are in sins, and have no grace, and therefore come to the Church, you take away from them remission of sins, which is given in baptism, by saying that they are already baptized and have obtained the grace of the Church outside the Church, and you do not perceive that their souls will be required at your hands when the day of judgment shall come, for having denied to the thirsting the drink of the Church, and having been the occasion of death to those that were desirious of living. And, after all this, you are indignant!

24. Consider with what want of judgment you dare to blame those who strive for the truth against falsehood. For who ought more justly to be indignant against the other?—whether he who supports God's enemies, or he who, in opposition to him who supports God's enemies, unites with us on behalf of the truth of the Church?—except that it is plain that the ignorant are also excited and angry, because by the want of counsel and discourse they are easily turned to wrath; so that of none more than of you does divine Scripture say, "A wrathful man stirs up strifes, and a furious man heaps up sins."[602] For what strifes and dissensions have you stirred up throughout the churches of the whole world! Moreover, how great sin have you heaped up for yourself, when you cut yourself off from so many flocks! For it is yourself that you have cut off. Do not deceive yourself, since he is really the schismatic who has made himself an apostate from the communion of ecclesiastical unity. For while you think that all may be excommunicated by you, you have excommunicated yourself alone from all; and not even the precepts of an apostle have been able to mould you to the rule of truth and peace, although he warned, and said, "I therefore, the prisoner of the Lord, beseech you that you walk worthy of the vocation wherewith you are called, with all lowliness and meekness, with long-suffering, forbearing one another in love; endeavoring to keep the unity of the Spirit in the bond of peace. There is one body and one Spirit, even as you are called in one hope of your calling; one Lord, one faith, one baptism; one God and Father of all, who is above all, and through all, and in us all."[603]

25. How carefully has Stephen fulfilled these salutary commands and warnings of the apostle, keeping in the first place lowliness of mind and meekness! For what is more lowly or meek than to have disagreed with so many bishops throughout the whole world, breaking peace with each one of them in various kinds of discord: at one time with the eastern churches, as we are sure you know; at another time with you who are in the south, from whom he received bishops as messengers sufficiently patiently and meekly not to receive them even to the speech of an ordinary conference; and even more, so mindful of love and charity as to command the entire fraternity, that no one should receive them into his house, so that not only peace and communion, but also a shelter and entertainment, were denied to them when they came! This is to have kept the unity of the Spirit in the bond of peace, to cut himself off from the unity of love, and to make himself a stranger in all respects from his brethren, and to rebel against the sacrament and the faith with the madness of contumacious discord! With such a man can there be one Spirit and one body, in whom perchance there is not even one mind, so slippery, and shifting, and uncertain is it?

26. But as far as he is concerned, let us leave him; let us rather deal with that concerning which there is the greatest question. They who contend that persons baptized among the heretics ought to be received as if they had obtained the grace of lawful baptism, say that baptism is one and the same to them and to us, and differs in no respect. But what says the Apostle Paul? "One Lord, one faith, one baptism, one God."[604] If the baptism of heretics be one and the same with ours, without doubt their faith also is one; but if our faith is one, assuredly also we have one Lord: if there is one Lord, it follows that we say that He is one. But if this unity which cannot be separated and divided at all, is itself also among heretics, why do we contend any more? Why do we call them heretics and not Christians? Moreover, since we and heretics have not one God, nor one Lord, nor one Church, nor one faith, nor even one Spirit, nor one body, it is manifest that neither can baptism be common to us with heretics, since between us there is nothing at all in common. And yet Stephen is not ashamed to afford patronage to such in opposition to the Church, and for the sake of maintaining heretics to divide the brotherhood and in addition, to call Cyprian a false Christ and a false apostle, and a deceitful worker. And he, conscious that all these characters are in himself, has been in advance of you, by falsely objecting to another those things which he himself ought deservedly to hear. We all bid you, for all our sakes, with all the bishops who are in Africa, and all the clergy, and all the brotherhood, farewell; that, constantly of one mind, and thinking the same thing, we may find you united with us even though afar off.[605]

NOTES

561. Written in 256 by Firmilian, Bishop of Caesarea Mazaca in Asia Minor, now Kayseri, in central Turkey. Firmilian held the episcopate of Caeasarea for forty years and was a personal acquaintance and disciple of Origen. St. Gregory of Nyssa tells us that Firmilian was a Cappdocian. For his vocal opposition to the teaching of Pope Stephen he was excommunicated, but he appears to have been reconciled by Stephen's successors. Unlike St. Cyprian, Firmilian would survive the coming persecution of Valerian and go on to take part in the proceedings against the heretic Paul of Samosata, eventually dying naturally in 268.

562. Isa. 2:2.

563. Ps. 23:6.

564. Ps. 133:1.

565. The "things done by Stephen" refer to the pope's acceptance of baptisms performed by heretics and the writing of letters to the various churches advocating this practice.

566. Firmilian of Cappadocia here acknowledges that the rigorist position held by Cyprian was by no means universal.

567. John 17:21.

568. A fascinating glimpse into the charismatic life of the early Church. Prophecy was alive and well in the Church in the days of St. Cyprian.

569. This is a blatant attack upon the primacy of the Roman Church by Firmilian. Yet, the fact that Firmilian is able to make this attack suggests that Rome was at that time making the counter-claim: to preserve, intact, the tradition of the apostles and the authority of Peter. Firmilian here makes the mistake of confounding disciplines, those "many things that are varied because of the difference of the places and names," and those substantial matters of faith that must be believed by all everywhere, as St. Vincent of Lerins would say.

570. Montanist heretics from Phrygia.

571. Like Cyprian, Firmilian sees the powers of administering the sacraments as too intimately united with the worthiness of the minister. He also mistakenly assumes that the proper minister of each of the three sacraments mentioned is the same, where in fact the sacrament of baptism, unlike confirmation or holy orders, can be administered in case of emergency by any individual seeking to do what the Church does, even a heretic. This is based in the absolute necessity of the grace of baptism for salvation and God's will to save all men. These developments in sacramental theology were worked out during the Donatist controversy and would not be formalized until the early Middle Ages.

572. The difference here is that the baptism of the heretics was, in many cases, a Trinitarian baptism whereas the baptism of John the Baptist was simply a symbolic washing to signify repentance and preparation for the Messiah.

573. Neither Firmilian, Cyprian nor Pope Stephen agree that a sacrament becomes valid by faith alone, as Firmilian here points out. The sacraments confer grace objectively (*ex opere*

operato) although one's disposition will make reception of the sacraments more effacacious (*ex opera operantis*). Thus, whatever we want to say about Cyprian's dispute with the pope, he certainly does not adopt a Protestant position on what makes the sacraments effectual.

574. Mark 13:6.

575. Alexander Severus (222-235), last emperor of the Severan dynasty.

576. Gal. 3:27.

577. Firmilian seems to disregard the fact that the *form* of baptism used by the Jews was entirely different than that used by Christians. Those using proper Trinitarian form and intending to validly baptize may do so, despite that fact that baptism by other than a properly ordained minister (except in instances of a grave emergency) is illicit and sinful.

578. Note how all parties concerned in this controversy assume an objective regeneration that occurs in baptism, *contra* many modern forms of Protestantism. See also Letter 74:15.

579. 2 Cor. 11:2.

580. Ps. 45:10.

581. Song of Solomon 4:8.

582. Song of Solomon 5:1.

583. Luke 11:23.

584. Song of Solomon, 4:12-13.

585. The ark of Noah as a type of the Church was a very prominent image in patristic ecclesiology.

586. 1 Pet. 3:21.

587. Matt. 16:19. Even the opponents of Pope Stephen acknowledged that the Church was built upon the rock and that this rock was Peter. Firmilian does not deny that Stephen is the successor to the Petrine ministry, but accuses him of leading the Church in a manner unworthy of the ministry he received. See 74:17.

588. John 20:22-23.

589. An excellent testimony to the belief of the early Christians that the forgiveness of God was mediated through the ministry of the episcopate, and that the power of forgiveness or retention of sins granted in John 20:22-23 was understood in a strict, literal sense.

590. Another reference to Peter as the foundation stone of the Church.

591. The truth of the unity of the Church is vouchsafed and signified through the ministry of Peter, the Rock upon whom the Church is built. The argument is that Pope Stephen, in allowing the legitimacy of baptism outside the visible confines of the Church, actually uses his Petrine authority to undermine the unity of the Church as established in and through Peter. This unity cannot ultimately be undone, which is why Firmilian hesitates here and says the unity brought about by the Christian Rock is "in *some* measure abolished;" in other words, Firmilian accuses Stephen of being a hypocrite by using his authority to undermine the unity of the Church, the very unity which his authority was meant to preserve. Notice how Firmilian's argument only makes sense if we assume that Peter is the Rock and the visible source of the Church's unity.

592. Again, Firmilian and the enemies of the pope exaggerate; to admit that baptism may be valid outside the visible confines of the Church is not the same as communicating with them.

593. Firmilian is assuming that the validity of baptism outside of the visible Church implies that there would arise a real and perfect unity between Christians and heretics, something neither he, nor Cyprian, nor Pope Stephen would admit. The pope understood this, which is why, though admitting a more universal application of baptism, refused, as Firmilian noted, "to be a partaker with them in other matters also, to meet together with them, and equally with them to mingle their prayers, and appoint a common altar and sacrifice." This is because Pope Stephen's teaching implied no real communion with heretics, the focus of the argument being on the efficacy of the sacrament, not on those administering it.

594. See Letter 74:7, footnote 31.

595. The question here is not of custom versus Scripture, but of custom versus custom. Which

custom is truly universal, "that which was delivered by Christ to the apostles," the Roman or the African?

596. It is interesting to note that those opponents of Catholicism who would adopt Firmilian's arguments against papal authority would end up having to affirm that there is no salvation outside of the institutional Catholic Church, which is actually the hinge of Firmilian's argument.

597. Those who recognize the "new prophets" are probably the Montanists.

598. Php. 1:18.

599. 1 Cor. 11:27. An affirmation of both the regenerative nature of baptism and of the Real Presence of our Lord in the Eucharist.

600. A Septuagint translation of Prov. 9:18. This verse appears in the Vulgate as Prov. 9:17 and reads, "Stolen waters are sweeter, and hidden bread is more pleasant."

601. Prov. 19:5.

602. Prov. 29:22.

603. Eph. 4:1-6. Firmilian here does nothing less than accuse the pope of promoting schism and rending the Body of Christ.

604. Eph. 4:5-6.

605. For a more thorough treatment of the points raised by Firmilian in this last section, see the footnotes for the Seventh Coucil of Carthage.

LETTER 75

TO MAGNUS, ON BAPTIZING THE NOVATIANS, AND GRACE AVAILABLE TO THE SICK

1. Cyprian to Magnus his son, greeting. With your usual religious diligence, you have consulted my poor intelligence, dearest son, as to whether, among other heretics, they also who come from Novatian ought, after his profane washing, to be baptized, and sanctified in the Catholic Church, with the lawful, and true, and only baptism of the Church. Respecting which matter, as much as the capacity of my faith and the sanctity and truth of the divine Scriptures suggest, I answer, that no heretics and schismatics at all have any power or right. For which reason Novatian neither ought to be nor can be expected, inasmuch as he also is without the Church and acting in opposition to the peace and love of Christ, from being counted among adversaries and antichrists. For our Lord Jesus Christ, when He testified in His Gospel that those who were not with Him were His adversaries, did not point out any species of heresy, but showed that all whatsoever who were not with Him, and who, not gathering with Him, were scattering His flock, were His adversaries; saying, "He that is not with me is against me, and he that gathers not with me scatters."[606] Moreover, the blessed Apostle John himself distinguished no heresy or schism, neither did he set down any as specially separated; but he called all who had gone out from the Church, and who acted in opposition to the Church, antichrists, saying, "You have heard that Antichrist comes, and even now have come many antichrists; wherefore we know that this is the last time. They went out from us, but they were not of us; for if they had been of us, they would have continued with us."[607] Whence it appears, that all are adversaries of the Lord and antichrists, who are known to have departed from charity and from the unity of the Catholic Church.[611] In addition, moreover, the Lord establishes it in His Gospel, and says, "But if he neglect to hear the Church, let him be unto you as a heathen man and a publican."[612] Now if they who despise the Church are counted heathens and publicans, much more certainly is it necessary that rebels and enemies, who forge false altars, and lawless priesthoods,[613] and sacrilegious sacrifices, and corrupter names, should be counted among heathens and publicans; since they who sin less, and are only despisers of the Church, are by the Lord's sentence judged to be heathens and publicans.

2. But that the Church is one, the Holy Spirit declares in the Song of Songs, saying, in the person of Christ, "My dove, my undefiled, is one; she is the only one of her mother, she is the choice one of her that bare her."[608] Concerning which also He says again, "A garden enclosed is my sister, my spouse; a spring sealed up, a well of living water."[609] But if the spouse of Christ, which is the Church, is a garden enclosed; a thing that is closed up cannot lie open to strangers and profane persons. And if it is a fountain sealed, he who, being placed without has no access to the spring, can neither drink thence nor be sealed. And the well also of living water, if it is one and the same within, he who is placed without cannot be quickened and sanctified from that water of which it is only granted to those who are within to make any use, or to drink. Peter also, showing this, set forth that the Church is one, and that only they who are in the Church can be baptized; and said, "In the ark of Noah, few, that is, eight souls, were saved by water; the like figure where-unto even baptism shall save you;"[610] proving and attesting that the one ark of Noah was a type of the one Church. If, then, in that baptism of the world thus expiated and purified, he who was not in the ark of Noah could be saved by water, he who is not in the Church to which alone baptism is granted, can also now be quickened by baptism. Moreover, too, the Apostle Paul, more openly and clearly still manifesting this same thing, writes to the Ephesians, and says, "Christ loved the Church, and gave Himself for it, that He might sanctify and cleanse it with the washing of water."[614] But if the Church is one which is loved by Christ, and is alone cleansed by His washing, how can he who is not in the Church be either loved by Christ, or washed and cleansed by His washing?

3. Wherefore, since the Church alone has the living water, and the power of baptizing and cleansing man, he who says that any one can be baptized and sanctified by Novatian must first show and teach that Novatian is in the Church or presides over the Church. For the Church is one, and as she is one, cannot be both within and without. For if she is with Novatian, she was not with Cornelius. But if she was with Cornelius, who succeeded the bishop Fabian by lawful ordination, and whom, beside the honor of the priesthood, the Lord glorified also with martyrdom, Novatian is not in the Church; nor can he be reckoned as a bishop, who, succeeding to no one, and despising the evangelical and apostolic tradition, sprang from himself. For he who has not been ordained in the Church can neither have nor hold to the Church in any way.

4. For the faith of the sacred Scripture sets forth that the Church is not without, nor can be separated nor divided against itself, but maintains the unity of an inseparable and undivided house; since it is written of the sacrament of the passover, and of the lamb, which Lamb designated Christ: "In one house shall it be eaten: you shall not carry forth the flesh abroad out of the house."[618] Which also we see expressed concerning Rahab, who herself also bore a type of the Church, who received the command which said, "You shall bring your father, and your mother, and your brethren, and all your father's household unto you into your house; and whosoever shall go out of the doors of your house into the street, his blood shall be upon him."[619] In which mystery is declared, that they who will live, and escape from the destruction of the world, must be gathered together into one house alone, that is, into the Church; but whosoever of those thus collected together shall go out abroad, that is, if any one, although he may have obtained grace in the Church, shall depart and go out of the Church, that his blood shall be upon him; that is, that he himself must charge it upon himself that he perishes; which the Apostle Paul explains, teaching and enjoining that a heretic must be avoided, as perverse, and a sinner, and as condemned of himself. For that man will be guilty of his own ruin, who, not being cast out by the bishop, but of his own accord deserting from the Church is by heretical presumption condemned of himself.

5. And therefore the Lord, suggesting to us a unity that comes from divine authority, lays it down, saying, "I and my Father are one."[620] To which unity reducing His Church, He says again, "And there shall be one flock, and one shepherd."[615] But if the flock is one, how can he be numbered among the flock who is not in the number of the flock? Or how can he be esteemed a pastor, who—while the true shepherd remains and presides over the Church of God by successive ordination—succeeding to no one, and beginning from himself, becomes a stranger and a profane person, an enemy of the Lord's peace and of the divine unity, not dwelling in the house of God, that is, in the Church of God, in which none dwell except they are of one heart and one mind, since the Holy Spirit speaks in the Psalms, and says, "It is God who makes men to dwell of one mind in a house."[616]

6. Besides even the Lord's sacrifices themselves declare that Christian unanimity is linked together with itself by a firm and inseparable charity, for when the

Lord calls bread, which is combined by the union of many grains, His body, He indicates our people whom He bore as being united; and when He calls the wine, which is pressed from many grapes and clusters and collected together, His blood, He also signifies our flock linked together by the mingling of a united multitude.[617] If Novatian is united to this bread of the Lord, if he also is mingled with this cup of Christ, he may also seem to be able to have the grace of the one baptism of the Church, if it be manifest that he holds the unity of the Church. In fine, how inseparable is the sacrament of unity, and how hopeless are they, and what excessive ruin they earn for themselves from the indignation of God, who make a schism, and, forsaking their bishop, appoint another false bishop for themselves without—Holy Scripture declares in the books of Kings, where ten tribes were divided from the tribe of Judah and Benjamin, and, forsaking their king, appointed for themselves another one without. It says, "And the Lord was very angry with all the seed of Israel, and removed them away, and delivered them into the hand of spoilers, until He had cast them out of His sight; for Israel was scattered from the house of David, and they made themselves a king, Jeroboam the son of Nebat."[621] It says that the Lord was very angry, and gave them up to perdition, because they were scattered from unity, and had made another king for themselves. And so great was the indignation of the Lord against those who had made the schism, that even when the man of God was sent to Jeroboam, to charge upon him his sins, and predict the future vengeance, he was forbidden to eat bread or to drink water with them. And when he did not observe this, and took meat against the command of God, he was immediately smitten by the majesty of the divine judgment, so that returning thence he was slain on the way by the jaws of a lion which attacked him. And dares any one to say that the saving water of baptism and heavenly grace can be in common with schismatics, with whom neither earthly food nor worldly drink ought to be in common? Moreover, the Lord satisfies us in His Gospel, and shows forth a still greater light of intelligence, that the same persons who had then divided themselves from the tribe of Judah and Benjamin, and forsaking Jerusalem had seceded to Samaria, should be reckoned among profane persons and Gentiles. For when first He sent His disciples on the ministry of salvation, He bade them, saying, "Go not into the way of the Gentiles, and into any city of the Samaritans enter not."[622] Sending first to the Jews, He commands the Gentiles as yet to be passed over; but by adding that even the city of the Samaritans was to be omitted, where there were schismatics, He shows that schismatics were to be put on the same level as Gentiles.[623]

7. But if any one objects, by way of saying that Novatian holds the same law which the Catholic Church holds, baptizes with the same symbol with which we baptize, knows the same God and Father, the same Christ the Son, the same Holy Spirit, and that for this reason he may claim the power of baptizing, namely, that he seems not to differ from us in the baptismal interrogatory; let any one that thinks that this may be objected, know first of all, that there is not one law of the Creed, nor the same interrogatory common to us and to schismatics. For when they say, "Do you believe the remission of sins and life eternal through the holy Church?" they lie in their interrogatory, since they have not the Church. Then, besides, with their own voice they themselves confess that remission of sins cannot be given except by the holy Church; and not having this, they show that sins cannot be remitted among them.

8. But that they are said to have the same God the Father as we, to know the same Christ the Son, the same Holy Spirit, can be of no avail to such as these. For even Korah, Dathan, and Abiram knew the same God as did the priest Aaron and Moses.[624] Living under the same law and religion, they invoke the one and true God, who was to be invoked and worshipped; yet, because they transgressed the ministry of their office in opposition to Aaron the priest, who had received the legitimate priesthood by the condescension of God and the ordination of the Lord, and claimed to themselves the power of sacrificing, divinely stricken, they immediately suffered punishment for their unlawful endeavors; and sacrifices offered irreligiously and lawlessly, contrary to the right of divine appointment, could not be accepted, nor profit them. Even those very censers in which incense had been lawlessly offered, lest they should any more be used by the priests, but that they might rather exhibit a memorial of the divine vengeance and indignation for the correction of their successors, being by the command of the Lord melted and purged by fire, were beaten out into flexible plates, and fastened to the altars, according to what the Holy Scripture says, to be, it says, a memorial to the children of Israel, that no stranger which is not of the seed of Aaron come near to offer incense before the Lord, that he be not as Korah. And yet those men had not made a schism, nor had gone out abroad, and in opposition to God's priests rebelled shamelessly and with hostility; but this these men are now doing who divide the Church, and, as rebels against the peace and unity of Christ, attempt to establish a throne for themselves, and to assume the primacy, and to claim the right of baptizing and of offering. How can they complete what they do, or obtain anything by lawless endeavors from God, seeing that they are endeavoring against God what is not lawful to them? Wherefore they who patronize Novatian or other schismatics of that kind, contend in vain that any one can be baptized and sanctified with a saving baptism among them, when it is plain that he who baptizes has not the power of baptizing.

9. And, moreover, that it may be better understood what is the divine judgment against audacity of the like kind, we find that in such wickedness, not only the leaders and originators, but also the partakers, are destined to punishment, unless they have separated themselves from the communion of the wicked; as the Lord by Moses commands, and says, "Separate yourselves from the tents of these most hardened men, and touch nothing of theirs, lest you be consumed in their sins."[625] And what the Lord had threatened by Moses He fulfilled, that whosoever had not separated himself from Korah and Dathan, and Abiram, immediately suffered punishment for his impious communion. By which example is shown and proved, that all will be liable to guilt as well as its punishment, who with irreligious boldness mingle themselves with schismatics in opposition to prelates and priests; even as also by the prophet Hosea the Holy Spirit witnesses, and says, "Their sacrifices shall be unto them as the bread of mourning; all that thereof shall be polluted;"[626] teaching, doubtless, and showing that all are absolutely joined with the leaders in punishment, who have been contaminated by their crime.

10. What, then, can be their deservings in the sight of God, on whom punishment are divinely denounced? Or how can such persons justify and sanctify the baptized, who, being enemies of the priests, strive to usurp things foreign and lawless, and by no right conceded to them? And yet we do not wonder that, in accordance with their wickedness, they do contend for them. For it is necessary that each one of them should maintain what they do; nor when vanquished will they easily yield, although they know that what they do is not lawful. That is to be wondered at, yea, rather to be indignant and aggrieved at, that Christians should support antichrists; and that prevaricators of the faith, and betrayers of the Church, should stand within in the Church itself. And these, although otherwise obstinate and unteachable, yet still at least confess this that all, whether heretics or schismatics, are without the Holy Spirit, and therefore can indeed baptize, but cannot confer the Holy Spirit; and at this very point they are held fast by us, inasmuch as we show that those who have not the Holy Spirit are not able to baptize at all.[627]

11. For since in baptism every one has his own sins remitted, the Lord proves and declares in His Gospel that sins can only be put away by those who have the Holy Spirit. For after His resurrection, sending forth His disciples, He speaks to them, and says, "As the Father has sent me, even so send I you. And when He had said this, He breathed on them, and said to them, 'Receive the Holy Spirit. Whose soever sins you remit, they shall be remitted unto them; and whose soever sins you retain, they shall be retained.'"[628] In which place He shows, that he alone can baptize and give remission of sins who has the Holy Spirit. Moreover, John, who was to baptize Christ our Lord Himself, previously received the Holy Spirit while he was yet in his mother's womb, that it might be certain and manifest that none can baptize save those who have the Holy Spirit. Therefore those who patronize heretics or schismatics must answer us whether they have or have not the Holy Spirit. If they have, why are hands imposed on those who are baptized among them when they come to us, that they may receive the Holy Spirit, since He must surely have been received there, where if He was He could be given? But if heretics and schismatics baptized without have not the Holy Spirit, and therefore hands are imposed on them among us, that here may be received what there neither is nor can be given; it is plain, also, that remission of sins cannot be given by those who, it is certain, have not the Holy Spirit. And therefore, in order that, according to the divine arrangement and the evangelical truth, they may be able to obtain remission of sins, and to be sanctified, and to become temples of God, they must all absolutely be baptized with the baptism of the Church who come from adversaries and antichrists to the Church of Christ.

12. You have asked also, dearest son, what I thought of those who obtain God's grace in sickness and weakness, whether they are to be accounted legitimate Christians, for that they are not to be washed, but sprinkled, with the saving water.[629] In this point, my diffidence and modesty prejudges none, so as to prevent any from feeling what he thinks right, and from doing what he feels to be right. As far as my poor understanding conceives it, I think that the divine benefits can in no respect be mutilated and weakened; nor can anything less occur in that case, where, with full and entire faith both of the giver and receiver, is accepted what is drawn from the divine gifts. For in the sacrament of salvation the contagion of sins is not in such wise washed away, as the filth of the skin and of the body is washed away in the carnal and ordinary washing, as that there should be need of saltpetre and other appliances also, and a bath and a basin wherewith this vile body must be washed and purified. Otherwise is the breast of the believer washed; otherwise is the mind of man purified by the merit of faith. In the sacraments of salvation, when necessity compels, and God bestows His mercy, the divine methods confer the whole benefit on believers; nor ought it to trouble any one that sick people seem to be sprinkled or affused, when they obtain the Lord's grace, when Holy Scripture speaks by the mouth of the prophet Ezekiel, and says, "Then will I sprinkle clean water upon you, and you shall be clean: from all your filthiness and from all your idols will I cleanse you. And I will give you a new heart, and a new spirit will I put within you."[630] Also in Numbers: "And the man that shall be unclean until the evening shall be purified on the third day, and on the seventh day shall be clean: but if he shall not be purified on the third day, on the seventh day he shall not be clean. And that soul shall be cut off from Israel: because the water of sprinkling has not been sprinkled upon him."[631] And again: "And the Lord spoke unto Moses saying, Take the Levites from among the children of Israel, and cleanse them. And thus shall you do unto them, to cleanse them: you shall sprinkle them with the water of purification."[632] And again: "The water of sprinkling is a purification."[633] Whence it appears that the sprinkling also of water prevails equally with the washing of salvation; and that when this is done in the Church, where the faith both of receiver and giver is sound, all things hold and may be consummated and perfected by the majesty of the Lord and by the truth of faith.

13. But, moreover, in respect of some calling those who have obtained the peace of Christ by the saving water and by legitimate faith, not Christians, but Clinics,[634] I do not find whence they take up this name, unless perhaps, having read more, and of a more recondite kind, they have taken these Clinics from Hippocrates or Soranus. For I, who know of a Clinic in the Gospel, know that to that paralytic and infirm man, who lay on his bed during the long course of his life, his infirmity presented no obstacle to his attainment in the fullest degree of heavenly strength. Nor was he only raised from his bed by the divine indulgence, but he also took up his bed itself with his restored and increased strength. And therefore, as far as it is allowed me by faith to conceive and to think, this is my opinion, that any one should be esteemed a legitimate Christian, who by the law and right of faith shall have obtained the grace of God in the Church. Or if any one think that those have gained nothing by having only been sprinkled with the saving water, but that they are still empty and void, let them not be deceived, so as if they escape the evil of their sickness, and get well, they should seek to be baptized. But if they cannot be baptized who have already been sanctified by ecclesiastical baptism, why are they offended in respect of their faith and the mercy of the Lord? Or have they obtained indeed the divine favor, but in a shorter and more limited measure of the divine gift and of the Holy Spirit, so as indeed to be esteemed Christians, but yet not to be counted equal with others?

14. Nay, verily, the Holy Spirit is not given by measure, but is poured out altogether on the believer. For if the day rises alike to all, and if the sun is diffused with like and equal light over all, how much more does Christ, who is the true sun and the true day, bestow in His Church the light of eternal life with the like equality![635] Of which equality we see the sacrament celebrated in Exodus, when the manna flowed down from heaven, and, prefiguring the things to come, showed forth the nourishment of the heavenly bread and the food of the coming Christ. For there, without distinction either of sex or of age, an omer was collected equally by each one. Whence it appeared that the mercy of Christ, and the heavenly grace that would subsequently follow, was equally divided among all; without difference of sex, without distinction of years, without accepting of persons, upon all the people of God the gift of spiritual grace was shed. Assuredly the same spiritual grace which is equally received in baptism by believers, is subsequently either increased or diminished in our conversation and conduct; as in the Gospel the Lord's seed is equally sown, but, according to the variety of the soil, some is wasted, and some is increased into a large variety of plenty, with an exuberant fruit of either thirty or sixty or a hundred fold. But, once more, when each was called to receive a penny, wherefore should what is distributed equally by God be diminished by human interpretation?

15. But if any one is moved by this, that some of those who are baptized in sickness are still tempted by unclean spirits, let him know that the obstinate wickedness of the devil prevails even up to the saving water, but that in baptism it loses all the poison of his wickedness. An instance of this we see in the king Pharaoh, who, having struggled long, and delayed in his perfidy, could resist and prevail until he came to the water; but when he had come there, he was both conquered and destroyed. And that that sea was a sacrament of baptism, the blessed Apostle Paul declares, saying, "Brethren, I would not have you ignorant how that all our fathers were under the cloud, and all passed through the sea, and were all baptized unto Moses in the cloud and in the sea;" and he added, saying, "Now all these things were our examples."[636] And this also is done in the present day, in that the devil is scourged, and burned, and tortured by exorcists, by the human voice, and by divine power; and although he often says that he is going out, and will leave the men of God, yet in that which he says he deceives, and puts in practice what was before done by Pharaoh with the same obstinate and fraudulent deceit. When, however, they come to the water of salvation and to the sanctification of baptism, we ought to know and to trust that there the devil is beaten down, and the man, dedicated to God, is set free by the divine mercy. For as scorpions and serpents, which prevail on the dry ground, when cast into water, cannot prevail nor retain their venom; so also the wicked spirits, which are called scorpions and serpents, and yet are trodden under foot by us, by the power given by the Lord, cannot remain any longer in the body of a man in whom, baptized and sanctified, the Holy Spirit is beginning to dwell.[637]

16. This, finally, in very fact also we experience, that those who are baptized by urgent necessity in sickness, and obtain grace, are free from the unclean spirit wherewith they were previously moved, and live in the Church in praise and honor, and day by day make more and more advance in the increase of heavenly grace by the growth of their faith. And, on the other hand, some of those who are baptized in health, if subsequently they begin to sin, are shaken by the return of the unclean spirit, so that it is manifest that the devil is driven out in baptism by the faith of the believer, and returns if the faith afterwards shall fail. Unless, indeed, it seems just to some, that they who, outside the Church among adversaries and antichrists, are polluted with profane water, should be judged to be baptized; while they who are baptized in the Church are thought to have attained less of divine mercy and grace; and so great consideration be had for heretics, that they who come from heresy are not interrogated whether they are washed or sprinkled, whether they be clinics or peripatetics; but among us the sound truth of faith is disparaged, and in ecclesiastical baptism its majesty and sanctity suffer derogation.

17. I have replied, dearest son, to your letter, so far as my poor ability prevailed; and I have shown, as far as I could, what I think; prescribing to no one, so as to prevent any prelate from determining what he thinks right, as he shall give an account of his own doings to the Lord, according to what the blessed Apostle Paul in his Epistle to the Romans writes and says: "Every one of us shall give account for himself: let us not therefore judge one another."[638] I bid you, dearest son, ever heartily farewell.

NOTES

606. Matt. 12:30

607. 1 John 2:18-19

608. Cyprian here mentions charity and unity with the Catholic Church as those two things which put one in friendship with God. This is very similar to what would later be taught by the Second Vatican Council: "They are fully incorporated in the society of the Church who, possessing the Spirit of Christ accept her entire system and all the means of salvation given to her, and are united with her as part of her visible bodily structure and through her with Christ, who rules her through the Supreme Pontiff and the bishops...He is not saved, however, who, though part of the body of the Church, does not persevere in charity. He remains indeed in the bosom of the Church, but, as it were, only in a 'bodily' manner and not 'in his heart' (*Lumen Gentium*, 14).

609. Matt. 18:17.

610. Other claims to authority in the Church outside of those standing in the legitimate apostolic succession are "lawless priesthoods."

611. Song of Solomon 6:9.

612. Song of Solomon 4:12. For more images from the Song of Solomon applied to the Church, see Letter 74.

613. 1 Pet. 3:20-21.

614. Eph. 5:25-26. Most Protestants assume the "washing" in this verse refers to reading the Bible; Cyprian very clearly applies it to baptism.

615. Ex. 12:46.

616. Jos. 2:18-19.

617. John 10:30.

618. John 10:16.

619. Ps. 67:7 (Vulgate).

620. Cyprian is here not suggesting that the Eucharist is merely symbolic, especially in light of many of his other statements (*On the Lord's Prayer*, 18; Letter 53:2, 55:1, 62:6). Rather, he is pointing out that the physical nature of the Eucharistic elements (grains of wheat brought together into bread, and grapes pressed into wine) are apt symbols of the unity of the Church. He draws an appropriate symbolic parallel without denying the literal truth of Christ's Real Presence.

621. 2 Kings 17:20-21.

622. Matt. 10:5.

623. If this is the true reason why Christ told His disciples to avoid Samaria, it is unclear why He Himself preaches there in John 4.

624. The story of Korah, Dathan and Abiram is from Numbers 16.

625. Num. 16:26.

626. Hos. 9:4.

627. Again, Cyprian mistakenly presumes that the conditions governing who can administer Confirmation are identical with those governing the administration of baptism.

628. John 20:21-23. Cyprian cites this passage in reference to baptism, though most subsequent theologians, both medieval and modern, see John 20 as applying primarily to the sacrament of penance, not baptism.

629. Due to the nature of their sickness, these Christians were baptized by aspersion (sprinkling) rather than immersion. Cyprian opines that either method is acceptable, and even cites Ezekiel and Numbers in support of aspersion.

630. Ezk. 36:25-26.

631. Num. 19:8, 12, 13.

632. Num. 8:5-7.

633. Num. 19:9.

634. The argument seems to have been that ill persons who received baptism by aspersion were Christians, thought not as fully as those baptized by immersion. Thus, the term "Clinics," describing them as a sort of incomplete Christian.

635. It is interesting that, in light of attempts by anti-Catholics to link Catholicism with the later cult of Sol Invictus ("The Unconquerable Sun"), Cyprian, an ardent defender of orthodoxy and no compromiser with pagans, here uses the image of the sun to refer to Christ. The symbolism of Christ as the sun is a thoroughly Christian one that does not depend upon allusions to the pagan cult of Sol Invictus.

636. 1 Cor. 10:1-2, 6.

637. Cyprian here simply means that baptism washes away all sin and drives out all demons; he does not mean to imply that a Christian cannot fall again under the power of the evil one.

638. Rom. 14:12-13.

LETTER 76

CYPRIAN TO NEMESIANUS AND THE MARTYRS
OF THE MINES

1. Cyprian to Nemesianus, Felix, Lucius, another Felix, Litteus, Polianus, Victor, Jader, and Dativus, his fellow bishops, also to his fellow presbyters and deacons, and the rest of the brethren in the mines, martyrs of God the Father Almighty, and of Jesus Christ our Lord, and of God our preserver, everlasting greeting. Your glory, indeed, would demand, most blessed and beloved brethren, that I myself should come to see and to embrace you, if the limits of the place appointed me did not restrain me, banished as I am for the sake of the confession of the Name.[639] But in what way I can, I bring myself into your presence; and even though it is not permitted me to come to you in body and in movement, yet in love and in spirit I come expressing my mind in my letter, in which mind I joyfully exult in those virtues and praises of yours, counting myself a partaker with you, although not in bodily suffering, yet in community of love. Could I be silent and restrain my voice in stillness, when I am made aware of so many and such glorious things concerning my dearest friends, things with which the divine condescension has honored you, so that part of you have already gone before by the consummation of their martyrdom to receive from their Lord the crown of their deserts? Part still abide in the dungeons of the prison, or in the mines and in chains, exhibiting by the very delays of their punishments, greater examples for the strengthening and arming of the brethren, advancing by the tediousness of their tortures to more ample titles of merit, to receive as many payments in heavenly rewards, as days are now counted in their punishments. I do not marvel, most brave and blessed brethren, that these things have happened to you in consideration of the desert of your religion and your faith; that the Lord should thus have lifted you to the lofty height of glory by the honor of His glorification, seeing that you have always flourished in His Church, guarding the tenor of the faith, keeping firmly the Lord's commands; in simplicity, innocence; in charity, concord; modesty in humility, diligence in administration, watchfulness in helping those that suffer, mercy in cherishing the poor, constancy in defending the truth, judgment in severity of discipline. And that nothing should be wanting to the example of good deeds in you, even now, in the confession of your voice and the suffering of your body, you provoke the minds of your brethren to divine martyrdom, by exhibiting yourselves as leaders of virtue, that while the flock follows its pastors, and imitates what it sees to be done by those set over it, it may be crowned with the like merits of obedience by the Lord.

2. But that, being first severely beaten with clubs, and ill-used, you have begun by sufferings of that kind, the glorious firstlings of your confession, is not a matter to be execrated by us. For a Christian body is not very greatly terrified at clubs, seeing all its hope is in the wood. The servant of Christ acknowledges the sacrament of his salvation: redeemed by wood to life eternal, he is advanced by wood to the crown. But what wonder if, as golden and silver vessels, you have been committed to the mine that is the home of gold and silver, except that now the nature of the mines is changed, and the places which previously had been accustomed to yield gold and silver have begun to receive them? Moreover, they have put fetters on your feet, and have bound your blessed limbs, and the temples of God with disgraceful chains, as if the spirit also could be bound with the body, or your gold could be stained by the contact of iron. To men who are dedicated to God, and attesting their faith with religious courage, such things are ornaments, not chains; nor do they bind the feet of the Christians for infamy, but glorify them for a crown. Oh feet blessedly bound, which are loosed, not by the smith but by the Lord! Oh feet blessedly bound, which are guided to paradise in the way of salvation! Oh feet bound for the present time in the world, that they may be always free with the Lord! Oh feet, lingering for a while among the fetters and cross-bars, but to run quickly to Christ on a glorious road! Let cruelty, either envious or malignant, hold you here in its bonds and chains as long as it will, from this earth and from these sufferings you shall speedily come to the kingdom of heaven. The body is not cherished in the mines with couch and cushions, but it is cherished with the refreshment and solace of Christ. The frame wearied with labors lies prostrate on the ground, but it is no penalty to lie down with Christ. Your limbs unbathed, are foul and disfigured with filth and dirt; but within they are spiritually cleansed, although without the flesh is defiled. There the bread is scarce; but man lives not by bread alone, but by the word of God. Shivering, you want clothing; but he who puts on Christ is both abundantly clothed and adorned. The hair of your half-shorn bead seems repulsive; but since Christ is the head of the man, anything whatever must needs become that head which is illustrious on account of Christ's name. All that deformity, detestable and foul to Gentiles, with what splendor shall it be recompensed! This temporal and brief suffering, how shall it be exchanged for the re ward of a bright and eternal honor, when, according to the word of the blessed apostle, the Lord shall change the body of our humiliation, that it may be fashioned like to the body of His brightness![640]

3. But there cannot be felt any loss of either religion or faith, most beloved brethren, in the fact that now there is given no opportunity there to God's priests for offering and celebrating the divine sacrifices; yea, you celebrate and offer a sacrifice to God equally precious and glorious, and that will greatly profit you for the retribution of heavenly rewards, since the sacred Scripture speaks, saying, "The sacrifice of God is a broken spirit; a contrite and humbled heart God does not despise."[641] You offer this sacrifice to God; you celebrate this sacrifice without intermission day and night, being made victims to God, and exhibiting yourselves as holy and unspotted offerings, as the apostle exhorts and says, "I beseech you therefore, brethren, by the mercies of God, that you present your bodies a living sacrifice, holy, acceptable unto God. And be not conformed to this world; but be you transformed by the renewing of your mind, that you may prove what is that good, and acceptable, and perfect will of God."[642]

4. For this it is which especially pleases God; it is this wherein our works with greater deserts are successful in earning God's good-will; this it is which alone the obedience of our faith and devotion can render to the Lord for His great and saving benefits, as the Holy Spirit declares and witnesses in the Psalms: "What shall I render," says He, "to the Lord for all His benefits towards me? I will take the cup of salvation, and I will call upon the name of the Lord. Precious in the sight of the Lord is the death of His saints."[643] Who would not gladly and readily receive the cup of salvation? Who would not with joy and gladness desire that in which he himself also may render somewhat unto His Lord? Who would not bravely and unfalteringly receive a death precious in the sight of the Lord, to please His eyes, who, looking down from above upon us who are placed in the conflict for His name, approves the willing, assists the struggling, crowns the conquering with the recompense of patience, goodness, and affection, rewarding in us whatever He Himself has bestowed, and honoring what He has accomplished?

5. For that it is His doing that we conquer, and that we attain by the subduing of the adversary to the palm of the greatest contest, the Lord declares and teaches in His Gospel, saying, "But when they deliver you up, take no thought how or what you shall speak; for it shall be given you in that same hour what you shall speak. For it is not you that speak, but the Spirit of your Father which speaks in you."[644] And again: "Settle it therefore in your hearts, not to meditate before what you shall answer; for I will give you a mouth and wisdom, which your adversaries shall not be able to resist."[645] In which, indeed, is both the great confidence of believers, and the gravest fault of the faithless, that they do not trust Him who promises to give His help to those who confess Him, and do not on the other hand fear Him who threatens eternal punishment to those who deny Him.

6. All which things, most brave and faithful soldiers of Christ, you have suggested to your brethren, fulfilling in deeds what you have previously taught in words, hereafter to be greatest in the kingdom of heaven, as the Lord promises and says, "Whosoever shall do and teach so, shall be called the greatest in the kingdom of heaven."[646] Moreover, a manifold portion of the people, following your example, have confessed alike with you, and alike have been crowned, associated with you in the bond of the strongest charity, and separated from their prelates neither by the prison nor by the mines; in the number of whom neither are there wanting virgins in whom the hundred-fold are added to the fruit of sixty-fold,[647] and whom a double glory has advanced to the heavenly crown. In boys also a courage greater than their age has surpassed their years in the praise of their confession, so that every sex and every age should adorn the blessed flock of your martyrdom.

7. What now must be the vigor, beloved brethren, of your victorious consciousness, what the loftiness of your mind, what exultation in feeling, what triumph in your breast, that every one of you stands near to the promised reward of God, are secure from the judgment of God, walk in the mines with a body captive indeed, but with a heart reigning, that you know Christ is present with you, rejoicing in the endurance of His servants, who are ascending by His footsteps and in His paths to the eternal kingdoms! You daily expect with joy the saving day of your departure; and already about to withdraw from the world, you are hastening to the rewards of martyrdom, and to the divine homes, to behold after this darkness of the world the purest light, and to receive a glory greater than all sufferings and conflicts, as the apostle witnesses, and says, "The sufferings of this present time are not worthy to be compared with the glory that shall be revealed in us."[648] And because now your word is more effectual in prayers, and supplication is more quick to obtain what is sought for in afflictions, seek more eagerly, and ask that the divine condescension would consummate the confession of all of us; that from this darkness and these snares of the world God would set us also free with you, sound and glorious; that we who here are united in the bond of charity and peace, and have stood together against the wrongs of heretics and the oppressions of the heathens, may rejoice together in the heavenly kingdom. I bid you, most blessed and most beloved brethren, ever farewell in the Lord, and always and everywhere remember me.

NOTES

639. This sentence indicates that the letter was composed during 257, the year Cyprian spent in exile immediately prior to his execution during the persecution of Valerian (257-259). These last seven letters (76-82) are all very brief and deal with the final months of Cyprian's life leading up to his execution on September 14th, 258.
640. Phil. 3:21.
641. Ps. 51:18.
642. Rom. 12:1-2.
643. Ps. 116:12-13, 15.
644. Mark 13:11.
645. Luke 21:14-15.
646. Matt. 5:19.
647. An allusion to Matt. 13:8.
648. Rom. 8:18.

LETTER 77

THE REPLY OF NEMESIANUS TO CYPRIAN

1. Nemesianus, Dativus, Felix, and Victor, to their brother Cyprian, in the Lord eternal salvation. You speak, dearly beloved Cyprian, in your letters always with deep meaning, as suits the condition of the time, by the assiduous reading of which letters both the wicked are corrected and men of good faith are confirmed. For while you do not cease in your writings to lay bare the hidden mysteries, you thus make us to grow in faith, and men from the world to draw near to belief. For by whatever good things you have introduced in your many books, unconsciously you have described yourself to us. For you are greater than all men in discourse, in speech more eloquent, in counsel wiser, in patience more simple, in works more abundant, in abstinence more holy, in obedience more humble, and in good deeds more innocent. And you yourself know, beloved, that our eager wish was, that we might see you, our teacher and our lover, attain to the crown of a great confession.

2. For, in the proceedings before the proconsul, as a good and true teacher you first have pronounced that which we your disciples, following you, ought to say before the president. And, as a sounding trumpet, you have stirred up God's soldiers, furnished with heavenly arms, to the close encounter; and fighting in the first rank, you have slain the devil with a spiritual sword: you have also ordered the troops of the brethren, on the one hand and on the other, with your words, so that snares were on all sides laid for the enemy, and the severed sinews of the very carcass of the public foe were trodden under foot. Believe us, dearest, that your innocent spirit is not far from the hundred-fold reward,[649] seeing that it has feared neither the first onsets of the world, nor shrunk from going into exile, nor hesitated to leave the city, nor dreaded to dwell in a desert place; and since it furnished many with an example of confession, itself first spoke the martyr-witness. For it provoked others to acts of martyrdom by its own example; and not only began to be a companion of the martyrs already departing from the world, but also linked a heavenly friendship with those who should be so.

3. Therefore they who were condemned with us give you before God the greatest thanks, beloved Cyprian, that in your letter you have refreshed their suffering breasts; have healed their limbs wounded with clubs; have loosened their feet bound with fetters; have smoothed the hair of their half-shorn head; have illuminated the darkness of the dungeon; have brought down the mountains of the mine to a smooth surface; have even placed fragrant flowers to their nostrils, and have shut out the foul odor of the smoke. Moreover, your continued gifts, and those of our beloved Quirinus, which you sent to be distributed by Herennianus the sub-deacon, and Lucian, and Maximus, and Amantius the acolytes, provided a supply of whatever had been wanting for the necessities of their bodies. Let us, then, be in our prayers helpers of one another: and let us ask, as you have bidden us, that we may have God and Christ and the angels as supporters in all our actions. We bid you, lord and brother, ever heartily farewell, and have us in mind.

Greet all who are with you. All ours who are with us love you, and greet you, and desire to see you.

NOTES

649. For the hundred-fold referring to the crown earned by martyrdom, see Cyprian's letter 75:14, 76:6, *On the Dress of Virgins*, 21; also St. Augstine *On Holy Virginity,* 46; St. Jerome Letter XLVIII:2; Origen *Exhortation to Martyrdom*, 14.

LETTER 78
LUCIUS TO CYPRIAN[650]

1. To Cyprian our brother and colleague, Lucius, and all the brethren who are with me in the Lord, greeting. Your letter came to us, dearest brother, while we were exulting and rejoicing in God that He had armed us for the struggle, and had made us by His condescension conquerors in the battle; the letter, namely, which you sent to us by Herennianus the sub-deacon, and Lucian, and Maximus, and Amantius the acolytes, which when we read we received a relaxation in our bonds, a solace in our affliction, and a support in our necessity; and we were aroused and more strenuously animated to bear whatever more of punishment might be awaiting us. For before our suffering we were called forth by you to glory, who first afforded us guidance to confession of the name of Christ. We indeed, who follow the footsteps of your confession, hope for an equal grace with you. For he who is first in the race is first also for the reward; and you who first occupied the course thence have communicated this to us from what you began, showing doubtless the undivided love wherewith you have always loved us, so that we who had one Spirit in the bond of peace might have the grace of your prayers, and one crown of confession.

2. But in your case, dearest brother, to the crown of confession is added the reward of your labors—an abundant measure which you shall receive from the Lord in the day of retribution, who have by your letter presented yourself to us, as you manifested to us that candid and blessed breast of yours which we have ever known, and in accordance with its largeness have uttered praises to God with us, not as much as we deserve to hear, but as much as you are able to utter. For with your words you have both adorned those things which had been less instructed in us, and have strengthened us to the sustaining of those sufferings which we bear, as being certain of the heavenly rewards, and of the crown of martyrdom, and of the kingdom of God, from the prophecy which, being filled with the Holy Spirit, you have pledged to us in your letter.[651] All this will happen, beloved, if you will have us in mind in your prayers, which I trust you do even as we certainly do.

3. And thus, O brother most longed-for, we have received what you sent to us from Quirinus and from yourself, a sacrifice from every clean thing.[652] Even as Noah offered to God, and God was pleased with the sweet savor, and had respect unto his offering, so also may He have respect unto yours, and may He be pleased to return to you the reward of this so good work. But I beg that you will command the letter which we have written to Quirinus to be sent forward. I bid you, dearest brother and earnestly desired, ever heartily farewell, and remember us. Greet all who are with you. Farewell.

NOTES

650. This Lucius is an African Bishop, not to be confused with the Lucius who was briefly Bishop of Rome from 253-254.
651. Cyprian had been warned in a vision about his impending martyrdom. See Pontius' *Life and Passion of Cyprian*, 12-13.
652. This "sacrifice" is a sum of money; see Letter 79.

LETTER 79[653]

FELIX, JADER, POLIANUS, AND THE REST OF THE MARTYRS TO CYPRIAN

To our dearest and best beloved Cyprian, Felix, Jader, Polianus, together with the presbyters and all who are abiding with us at the mine of Sigua, eternal health in the Lord. We reply to your salutation, dearest brother, by Herennianus the sub-deacon, Lucian and Maximus our brethren, strong and safe by the aid of your prayers, from whom we have received a sum under the name of an offering, together with your letter which you wrote, and in which you have condescended to comfort us as if we were sons, out of the heavenly words. And we have given and do give thanks to God the Father Almighty through His Christ, that we have been thus comforted and strengthened by your address, asking from the candor of your mind that you would deign to have us in mind in your constant prayers, that the Lord would supply what is wanting in your confession and ours, which He has condescended to confer on us. Greet all who abide with you. We bid you, dearest brother, ever heartily farewell in God. I Felix wrote this; I Jader subscribed it; I Polianus read it. I greet my lord Eutychianus.

NOTE

653. This letter is a response to Cyrpian's Letter 76.

LETTER 80

CYPRIAN TO SERGIUS AND THE CONFESSORS
IN PRISON

1. Cyprian to Sergius and Rogatianus, and the rest of the confessors in the Lord, everlasting health. I salute you, dearest and most blessed brethren, myself also desiring to enjoy the sight of you, if the state in which I am placed would permit me to come to you. For what could happen to me more desirable and more joyful than to be now close to you, that you might embrace me with those hands, which, pure and innocent, and maintaining the faith of the Lord, have rejected the profane obedience?[654] What more pleasant and sublime than now to kiss your lips, which with a glorious voice have confessed the Lord, to be looked upon even in presence by your eyes, which, despising the world, have become worthy of looking upon God? But since opportunity is not afforded me to share in this joy, I send this letter in my stead to your ears and to your eyes, by which I congratulate and exhort you that you persevere strongly and steadily in the confession of the heavenly glory; and having entered on the way of the Lord's condescension, that you go on in the strength of the Spirit, to receive the crown, having the Lord as your protector and guide, who said, "Lo, I am with you always, even unto the end of the world."[655] O blessed prison, which your presence has enlightened! O blessed prison, which sends the men of God to heaven! O darkness, more bright than the sun itself, and clearer than the light of this world, where now are placed temples of God, and your members are to be sanctified by divine confessions!

2. Nor let anything now be revolved in your hearts and minds besides the divine precepts and heavenly commands, with which the Holy Spirit has ever animated you to the endurance of suffering. Let no one think of death, but of immortality; nor of temporary punishment, but of eternal glory; since it is written, "Precious in the sight of the Lord is the death of His saints;" and again, "A broken spirit is a sacrifice to God, a contrite and humble heart God does not despise."[656] And again, where the sacred Scripture speaks of the tortures which consecrate God's martyrs, and sanctify them in the very trial of suffering: "And if they have suffered torments in the sight of men, yet is their hope full of immortality; and having been a little chastised, they shall be greatly rewarded: for God proved them, and found them worthy of Himself. As gold in the furnace has He tried them, and received them as a sacrifice of a burnt-offering, and in due time regard shall be had unto them. The righteous shall shine, and shall run to and fro like sparks among the stubble. They shall judge the nations, and have dominion over the people; and their Lord shall reign for ever."[657] When, therefore, you reflect that you shall judge and reign with Christ the Lord, you must needs exult and tread under foot present

531

sufferings, in the joy of what is to come; knowing that from the beginning of the world it has been so appointed that righteousness should suffer there in the conflict of the world, since in the beginning, even at the first, the righteous Abel was slain, and thereafter all righteous men, and prophets, and apostles who were sent. To all of whom the Lord also in Himself has appointed an example, teaching that none shall attain to His kingdom but those who have followed Him in His own way, saying, "He that loves his life in this world shall lose it; and he that hates his life in this world shall keep it unto life eternal."[658] And again: "Fear not them which kill the body, but are not able to kill the soul: but rather fear Him who is able to destroy both soul and body in hell."[659] Paul also exhorts us that we who desire to attain to the Lord's promises ought to imitate the Lord in all things. "We are," says he, "the sons of God: but if sons, then heirs; heirs of God, and joint-heirs with Christ; if so be that we suffer with Him, that we may also be glorified together."[660] Moreover, he added the comparison of the present time and of the future glory, saying, "The sufferings of this present time are not worthy to be compared with the coming glory which shall be revealed in us."[661] Of which brightness, when we consider the glory, it behooves us to bear all afflictions and persecutions; because, although many are the afflictions of the righteous, yet those are delivered from them all who trust in God.[662]

3. Blessed women also, who are established with you in the same glory of confession, who, maintaining the Lord's faith, and braver than their sex, not only themselves are near to the crown of glory, but have afforded an example to other women by their constancy! And lest anything should be wanting to the glory of your number, that each sex and every age also might be with you in honor, the divine condescension has also associated with you boys in a glorious confession; representing to us something of the same kind as once did Ananias, Azarias, and Misael, the illustrious youths to whom, when shut up in the furnace, the fires gave way, and the flames gave refreshment, the Lord being present with them, and proving that against His confessors and martyrs the heat of hell could have no power, but that they who trusted in God should always continue unhurt and safe in all dangers. And I beg you to consider more carefully, in accordance with your religion, what must have been the faith in these youths which could deserve such full acknowledgment from the Lord. For, prepared for every fate, as we ought all to be, they say to the king, "O king Nebuchadnezzar, we are not careful to answer you in this matter; for our God whom we serve is able to deliver us from the burning fiery furnace; and He will deliver us out of your hand, O king! But if not, be it known unto you, O king, that we will not serve your gods, nor worship the golden image which you have set up."[663] Although they believed, and, in accordance with their faith, knew that they might even be delivered from their present punishment, they still would not boast of this, nor claim it for themselves, saying, "But if not." Lest the virtue of their confession should be less without the testimony of their suffering, they added that God could do all things; but yet they would not trust in this, so as to wish to be delivered at the moment; but they thought on that glory of eternal liberty and security.

4. And you also, retaining this faith, and meditating day and night, with your whole heart prepared for God, think of the future only, with contempt for the present, that you may be able to come to the fruit of the eternal kingdom, and to the embrace and kiss, and the sight of the Lord, that you may follow in all things Rogatianus the presbyter, the glorious old man who, to the glory of our time, makes a way for you by his religious courage and divine condescension, who, with Felicissimus our brother, ever quiet and temperate, receiving the attack of a ferocious people, first prepared for you a dwelling in the prison, and, marking out the way for you in some measure, now also goes before you. That this may be consummated in you, we beseech the Lord in constant prayers, that from beginnings going on to the highest results, He may cause those whom He has made to confess, also to be crowned. I bid you, dearest and most beloved brethren, ever heartily farewell in the Lord; and may you attain to the crown of heavenly glory. Victor the deacon, and those who are with me, greet you.

NOTES

654. Meaning that Sergius and Rogatianus were brought before the proconsul and refused to offer sacrifices to Caesar.
655. Matt. 28:20.
656. Ps. 116:15, Ps. 51:17.
657. Wis. 3:4-8, referred to as "sacred Scripture" by Cyprian.
658. John 12:28.
659. Matt. 10:28.
660. Rom. 8:16-17.
661. Rom. 8:18.
662. Ps. 34:19.
663. Dan. 3:16-18.

LETTER 81

CYPRIAN TO SUCCESSUS ON THE PERSECUTION AT ROME

1. Cyprian to his brother Successus, greeting. The reason why I could not write to you immediately, dearest brother, was that all the clergy, being placed in the very heat of the contest, were unable in any way to depart hence, all of them being prepared in accordance with the devotion of their mind for divine and heavenly glory. But know that those have come whom I had sent to the City for this purpose, that they might find out and bring back to us the truth, in whatever manner it had been decreed respecting us. For many various and uncertain things are current in men's opinions. But the truth concerning them is as follows, that Valerian had sent a rescript to the Senate, to the effect that bishops and presbyters and deacons should immediately be punished; but that senators, and men of importance, and Roman knights, should lose their dignity, and moreover be deprived of their property; and if, when their means were taken away, they should persist in being Christians, then they should also lose their heads; but that matrons should be deprived of their property, and sent into banishment. Moreover, people of Caesar's household, whoever of them had either confessed before, or should now confess, should have their property confiscated, and should be sent in chains by assignment to Caesar's estates. The Emperor Valerian also added to this address a copy of the letters which he sent to the presidents of the provinces concerning us; which letters we are daily hoping will come, waiting according to the strength of our faith for the endurance of suffering, and expecting from the help and mercy of the Lord the crown of eternal life. But know that Xistus[664] was martyred in the cemetery on the eighth day of the Ides of August, and with him four deacons. Moreover, the prefects in the City are daily urging on this persecution; so that, if any are presented to them, they are martyred, and their property claimed by the treasury.

2. I beg that these things may be made known by your means to the rest of our colleagues, that everywhere, by their exhortation, the brotherhood may be strengthened and prepared for the spiritual conflict, that every one of us may think less of death than of immortality; and, dedicated to the Lord, with full faith and entire courage, may rejoice rather than fear in this confession, wherein they know that the soldiers of God and Christ are not slain, but crowned. I bid you, dearest brother, ever heartily farewell in the Lord.

NOTE

664. Pope Sixtus II (Greek: Xystus) succeeded Pope Stephen, who was beheaded in August, 257. Sixtus, as Cyprian relates, was subsequently martyred on August 6th, 258. Cyprian himself would suffer the following month. The Feast of St. Sixtus and companions is celebrated on August 7th and he is mentioned in the Canon of the Mass ("Sixtus, Cornelius, Cyprian...").

LETTER 82[665]

TO THE CLERGY AND PEOPLE CONCERNING HIS RETIREMENT BEFORE HIS MARTYRDOM

1. Cyprian to the presbyters and deacons, and all the people, greeting. When it had been told to us, dearest brethren, that the jailers had been sent to bring me to Utica, and I had been persuaded by the counsel of those dearest to me to withdraw for a time from my gardens, as a just reason was afforded I consented. For the reason that it is fit for a bishop, in that city in which he presides over the Church of the Lord, there to confess the Lord, and that the whole people should be glorified by the confession of their prelate in their presence. For whatever, in that moment of confession, the confessor-bishop speaks, he speaks in the mouth of all, by inspiration of God. But the honor of our Church, glorious as it is, will be mutilated if I, a bishop placed over another church, receiving my sentence or my confession at Utica, should go thence as a martyr to the Lord, when indeed, both for my own sake and yours, I pray with continual supplications, and with all my desires entreat, that I may confess among you, and there suffer, and thence depart to the Lord even as I ought. Therefore here in a hidden retreat I await the arrival of the proconsul returning to Carthage, that I may hear from him what the emperors have commanded upon the subject of Christian laymen and bishops, and may say what the Lord will wish to be said at that hour.

2. But do you, dearest brethren, according to the discipline which you have ever received from me out of the Lord's commands, and according to what you have so very often learned from my discourse, keep peace and tranquility; nor let any of you stir up any tumult for the brethren, or voluntarily offer himself to the Gentiles. For when apprehended and delivered up, he ought to speak, inasmuch as the Lord abiding in us speaks in that hour, who willed that we should rather confess than profess. But for the rest, what it is fitting that we should observe before the proconsul passes sentence on me for the confession of the name of God, we will with the instruction of the Lord arrange in common. May our Lord make you, dearest brethren, to remain safe in His Church, and condescend to keep you. So be it through His mercy.

NOTE

665. This is Cyprian's last letter, written only a few weeks before his martyrdom on September 14th, 258.

THE SEVENTH COUNCIL OF CARTHAGE UNDER CYPRIAN[1]

CONCERNING THE BAPTISM OF HERETICS.
THE JUDGMENT OF EIGHTY-SEVEN BISHOPS

When, in the kalends of September, a great many bishops from the provinces of Africa, Numidia, and Mauritania, had met together at Carthage, together with the presbyters and deacons, and a considerable part of the congregation who were also present; and when the letter of Jubaianus written to Cyprian had been read, as also the reply of Cyprian to Jubaianus,[2] about baptizing heretics, and what the same Jubaianus had subsequently rejoined to Cyprian.

Cyprian said: "You have heard, my dearly beloved colleagues, what Jubaianus our co-bishop has written to me, taking counsel of my poor intelligence concerning the unlawful and profane baptism of heretics, as well as what I wrote in answer to him, decreeing, to wit, what we have once and again and frequently determined, that heretics who come to the Church must be baptized and sanctified by the baptism of the Church. Moreover, another letter of Jubaianus has also been read to you, wherein, replying, in accordance with his sincere and religious devotion, to my letter, he not only acquiesced in what I had said, but, confessing that he had been instructed thereby, he returned thanks for it. It remains, that upon this same matter each of us should bring forward what we think, judging no man, nor rejecting any one from the right of communion, if he should think differently from us. For neither does any of us set himself up as a bishop of bishops,[3] nor by tyrannical terror does any compel his colleague to the necessity of obedience; since every bishop, according to the allowance of his liberty and power, has his own proper right of judgment, and can no more be judged by another than he himself can judge another.[4] But let us all wait for the judgment of our Lord Jesus Christ, who is the only one that has the power both of preferring us in the government of His Church, and of judging us in our conduct there.

Caecilius of Bilta[5] said: "I know only one baptism in the Church, and none out of the Church. This one will be here, where there is the true hope and the certain faith. For thus it is written: 'One faith, one hope, one baptism;'[6] not among heretics, where there is no hope, and the faith is false, where all things are carried on by lying; where a demoniac exorcises; where one whose mouth and words send forth a cancer puts the sacramental interrogation; the faithless gives faith; the wicked bestows pardon of sins; and Antichrist baptizes in the name of Christ; he who is cursed of God blesses; he who is dead promises life; he who is unpeaceful gives peace; the blasphemer calls upon God; the profane person administers the office of the priesthood; the sacrilegious person establishes an altar. In addition to all these things, there is also this evil, that the priests of the devil dare to celebrate the Eucharist; or else let those who stand by them say that all these things concerning heretics are false. Behold to what kind of things the Church is compelled to consent, and is constrained without baptism, without pardon of sins, to hold communion. And this thing, brethren, we ought to flee from and avoid, and to separate ourselves from so great a wickedness, and to hold one baptism, which is granted by the Lord to the Church alone."[7]

Primus of Misgirpa said: "I decide, that every man who comes to us from heresy must be baptized. For in vain does he think that he has been baptized there, seeing that there is no baptism save the one and true baptism in the Church; because not only is God one, but the faith is one, and the Church is one, wherein stands the one baptism, and holiness, and the rest. For whatever is done without, has no effect of salvation."[8]

Polycarp from Adrumetum said: "They who approve the baptism of heretics make void our baptism."

Novatus of Thamugada said: "Although we know that all the Scriptures give witness concerning the saving baptism, still we ought to declare our faith, that heretics and schismatics who come to the Church, and appear to have been falsely baptized, ought to be baptized in the everlasting fountain; and therefore, according to the testimony of the Scriptures, and according to the decree of our colleagues, men of most holy memory,[9] that all schismatics and heretics who are converted to the Church must be baptized; and moreover, that those who appeared to have been ordained must be received among lay people."

Nemesianus of Thubunae[10] said: "That the baptism which heretics and schismatics bestow is not the true one, is everywhere declared in the Holy Scriptures, since their very leading men are false Christs and false prophets, as the Lord says by Solomon: "He who trusts in that which is false, he feeds the winds; and the very same, moreover, follows the flight of birds. For he forsakes the ways of his own vineyard, he has wandered from the paths of his own little field. But he walks through pathless places, and dry, and a land destined for thirst; moreover, he gathers together fruitless things in his hands." And again: "Abstain from strange water, and from the fountain of another do not drink, that you may live a long time; also that the years of life may be added to you."[11] And in the Gospel our Lord Jesus Christ spoke with His divine voice, saying, "Unless a man be born again of water and the Spirit, he cannot enter the kingdom of God."[12] This is the Spirit which from the beginning was borne over the waters; for neither can the Spirit operate without the water, nor the water without the Spirit. Certain people therefore interpret for themselves ill, when they say that by imposition of the hand they receive the Holy Ghost, and are thus received, when it is manifest that they ought to be born again in the Catholic Church by both sacraments. Then indeed they will be able to be sons of God, as says the apostle:

"Taking care to keep the unity of the Spirit in the bond of peace. There is one body, and one Spirit, as you have been called in one hope of your calling; one Lord, one faith, one baptism, one God."[13] All these things speaks the Catholic Church. And again, in the Gospel the Lord says: "That which is born of the flesh is flesh, and that which is born of the Spirit is spirit; because God is a Spirit, and he is born of God."[14] Therefore, whatsoever things all heretics and schismatics do are carnal, as the apostle says: "For the works of the flesh are manifest, which are, fornications, uncleannesses, incest, idolatries, witchcrafts, hatreds, contentions, jealousy, anger, divisions, heresies, and the like to these; concerning which have told you before, as I also foretell you now, that whoever do such things shall not inherit the kingdom of God."[15] And thus the apostle condemns, with all the wicked, those also who cause division, that is, schismatics and heretics. Unless therefore they receive saving baptism in the Catholic Church, which is one, they cannot be saved, but will be condemned with the carnal in the judgment of the Lord Christ.[16]

Januarius of Lambesis said: "According to the authority of the Holy Scriptures, I decree that all heretics must be baptized, and so admitted into the holy Church."

Lucius of Castra Galbae[17] said: "Since the Lord in His Gospel said, 'You are the salt of the earth: but if the salt should have lost its savor, wherewith shall it be salted? It is thenceforth good for nothing, but to be cast out of doors, and to be trodden under foot of men.'"[18] And again, after His resurrection, sending His apostles, He gave them charge, saying, "All power is given unto me, in heaven and in earth. Go and teach all nations, baptizing them in the name of the Father, and of the Son, and of the Holy Ghost."[19] Since, therefore, it is manifest that heretics—that is, the enemies of Christ—have not the sound confession of the sacrament; moreover, that schismatics cannot season others with spiritual wisdom, since they themselves, by departing from the Church, which is one, having lost the savor, have become contrary to it—let it be done as it is written, "The house of those that are contrary to the law owes a cleansing."[20] And it is a consequence that those who, having been baptized by people who are contrary to the Church, are polluted, must first be cleansed, and then at length be baptized.

Crescens of Cirta said: "In such an assembly of most holy fellow priests, as the letters of our most beloved Cyprian to Jubaianus and also to Stephen have been read, containing in them so much of the holy testimonies which descend from the divinely made Scriptures, that with reason we ought, all being made one by the grace of God, to consent to them; I judge that all heretics and schismatics who wish to come to the Catholic Church, shall not be allowed to enter without they have first been exorcised and baptized; with the exception of those indeed who may previously have been baptized in the Catholic Church, and these in such a way that they may be reconciled to the penitence of the Church by the imposition of hands."

Nicomedes of Segermae said: "My opinion is this, that heretics coming to the Church should be baptized, for the reason that among sinners without they can obtain no remission of sins."[21]

Munnulus of Girba said: "The truth of our Mother the Catholic Church, brethren, has always remained and still remains with us, and even especially in the Trinity of baptism, as our Lord says, "Go and baptize the nations, in the name of the Father, of the Son, and of the Holy Spirit."[22] Since, then, we manifestly know that heretics have not either Father, or Son, or Holy Spirit, they ought, when they come to the Church our Mother, truly to be born again and to be baptized;[23] that the cancer which they had, and the anger of damnation, and the witchery of error, may be sanctified by the holy and heavenly laver.

Secundinus of Cedias said: Since our Lord Christ says, "He who is not with me is against me;"[24] and John the apostle calls those who depart from the Church Antichrists[25]—undoubtedly enemies of Christ—any such as are called Antichrists cannot minister the grace of saving baptism. And therefore I think that those who flee from the snares of the heretics to the Church must be baptized by us, who are called friends of God, of His condescension."

Felix of Bagai said: "As, when the blind leads the blind, they fall together into the ditch; so, when the heretic baptizes a heretic, they fall together into death. And therefore a heretic must be baptized and made alive, lest we who are alive should hold communion with the dead."

Polianus of Mileum[26] said: "It is right that a heretic be baptized in the holy Church."

Theogenes of Hippo Regius said: "According to the sacrament of God's heavenly grace which we have received, we believe one baptism which is in the holy Church."

Dativus of Badis said: "We, as far as in us lies, do not hold communion with heretics, unless they have been baptized in the Church, and have received remission of their sins."

Successus of Abbir Germaniciana[27] said: "Heretics can either do nothing, or they can do all. If they can baptize, they can also bestow the Holy Spirit. But if they cannot give the Holy Spirit, because they have not the Holy Spirit, neither can they spiritually baptize. Therefore we judge that heretics must be baptized."

Fortunatus of Tuccaboris said: "Jesus Christ our Lord and God, Son of God the Father and Creator, built His Church upon a rock, not upon heresy; and gave the power of baptizing to bishops, not to heretics. Wherefore they who are without the Church, and, standing in opposition to Christ, disperse His sheep and flock, cannot baptize, being without."

Sedatus of Tuburbo said: "In the degree in which water sanctified in the Church by the prayer of the priest, washes away sins; in that degree, if infected with heretical discourse as with a cancer, it heaps up sins. Wherefore we must endeavor with all peaceful powers, that no one infected and stained with heretical error refuse to receive the single and true baptism of the Church, by which whosoever is not baptized, shall become an alien from the kingdom of heaven."

Privatianus of Sufetula said: Let him who says that heretics have the power of baptizing, say first who rounded heresy. For if heresy is of God, it also may have the divine indulgence. But if it is not from God, how can it either have the grace of God, or confer it upon any one?"[28]

Privatus of Sufes said: He who approves the baptism of heretics, what else does he do than communicate with heretics?[29]

Hortensianus of Lares said: "Let either these presumptuous ones, or those who favor heretics, consider how many baptisms there are. We claim for the Church one baptism, which we know not except in the Church. Or how can they baptize any one in the name of Christ, whom Christ Himself declares to be His adversaries?"

Cassius of Macomadae said: "Since there cannot be two baptisms, he who yields baptism to the heretics takes it away from himself. I judge therefore that heretics, lamentable and corrupt, must be baptized when they begin to come to the Church; and that when washed by the sacred and divine washing, and illuminated by the light of life, they may be received into the Church, not as enemies, but as made peaceful; not as foreigners, but as of the household of the faith of the Lord; not as children of adultery, but as sons of God; not of error, but of salvation; except those who once faithful have been supplanted, and have passed over from the Church to the darkness of heresy, but that these must be restored by the imposition of hands."

Another, **Januarius of Vicus Caesaris**, said: "If error does not obey truth, much more truth does not consent to error; and therefore we stand by the Church in which we preside, that, claiming her baptism for herself alone, we should baptize those whom the Church has not baptized."

Another, **Secundinus of Carpi**, said: "Are heretics Christians or not? If they are Christians, why are they not in the Church of God? If they are not Christians, how come they to make Christians? Or whither will tend the Lord's discourse, when He says, "He that is not with me is against me, and he who gathers not with me scatters?"[30] Whence it appears plain that upon strange children, and on the offspring of Antichrist, the Holy Ghost cannot descend only by imposition of hands, since it is manifest that heretics have not baptism."

Victoricus of Thabraca said: "If heretics are allowed to baptize and to give remission of sins, wherefore do we brand them with infamy and call them heretics?"

Another, **Felix of Uthina,** said: "Nobody doubts, most holy fellow priests, that human presumption is not able to do so much as the adorable and venerable majesty of our Lord Jesus Christ. Therefore, remembering the danger, we ought not only to observe this also, but moreover to confirm it by the voice of all of us, that all heretics who come to the bosom of Mother Church should be baptized, that thus the heretical mind that has been polluted by a long decay, purged by the sanctification of the laver, may be reformed for the better."

Quietus of Baruch said: "We who live by faith ought to obey with careful observance those things which before have been foretold for our instruction. For it is written in Solomon: "He that is baptized from the dead, (and again touches the dead) what avails his washing?"[31] which certainly speaks of those who are washed by heretics, and of those that wash them. For if those who are baptized among them obtain by remission of their sins life eternal, why do they come to the Church? But if from a dead person no salvation is received, and therefore, acknowledging their previous error, they return to the truth with penitence, they ought to be sanctified with the one vital baptism which is in the Catholic Church."

Castus of Sicca said: "He who with contempt of the truth presumes to follow custom, is either envious and malignant in respect of his brethren to whom the truth is revealed, or is ungrateful in respect of God, by whose inspiration His Church is instructed."[32]

Euchratius of Thenae said: "God and our Lord Jesus Christ, teaching the apostles with His own mouth, has entirely completed our faith, and the grace of baptism, and the rule of the ecclesiastical law, saying: "Go and teach all nations, baptizing them in the name of the Father, and of the Son, and of the Holy Ghost."[33] Thus the false and wicked baptism of heretics must be rejected by us, and refuted with all detestation, from whose mouth is expressed poison, not life, not celestial grace, but blasphemy of the Trinity. And therefore it is manifest that heretics who come to the Church ought to be baptized with the sound and Catholic baptism, in order that, being purified from the blasphemy of their presumption, they may be reformed by the grace of the Holy Spirit."

Libosus of Vaga said: "In the Gospel the Lord says, 'I am the truth.'[34] He said not, 'I am the custom.' Therefore the truth being manifest, let custom yield to truth; so that, although for the past any one was not in the habit of baptizing heretics in the Church, let him now begin to baptize them."

Lucius of Thebeste said: "I determine that blasphemous and unrighteous heretics, who with various words tear asunder the holy and adorable words of the Scriptures, are to be accursed, and therefore that they must be exorcised and baptized."

Eugenius of Ammedera said: "And I determine the same—that heretics must be baptized."

Also another **Felix of Amaccora** said: "And I myself, following the authority of the divine Scriptures, judge that heretics must be baptized; and, moreover, those also who contend that they have been baptized among the schismatics. For if, according to Christ's warning, our font is private to us, let all the adversaries of our Church understand that it cannot be for another. Nor can He who is the Shepherd of the one flock give the saving water to two peoples. And therefore it is plain that neither heretics nor schismatics can receive anything heavenly, seeing that they dare to receive from men who are sinners, and from those who are external to the Church. When there is no place for the giver, assuredly there is no profit for the receiver."

Also another **Januarius of Muzzuli** said: "I am surprised, since all confess that there is one baptism, that all do not perceive the unity of the same baptism. For the Church and heresy are two things, and different things. If heretics have baptism, we have it not; but if we have it, heretics cannot have it. But there is no doubt that the Church alone possesses the baptism of Christ, since she alone possesses both the grace and the truth of Christ."

Adelphius of Thasvalte said: "Certain persons without reason impugn the truth by false and envious words, in saying that we rebaptize, when the Church does not rebaptize heretics, but baptizes them."

Demetrius of Leptiminus said: "We maintain one baptism, because we demand for the Church Catholic alone her own property. But they who say that heretics truly and legitimately baptize, are themselves the people who make not one, but many baptisms. For since heresies are many, according to their number will be reckoned baptisms."

Vincentius of Thibaris said: "We know that heretics are worse than Gentiles. If, therefore, being converted, they should wish to come to the Lord, we have assuredly the rule of truth which the Lord by His divine precept commanded to His apostles, saying, "Go, lay on hands in my name, expel demons. And in another place: Go and teach the nations, baptizing them in the name of the Father, of the Son, and of the Holy Ghost."[35] Therefore first of all by imposition of hands in exorcism, secondly by the regeneration of baptism, they may then come to the promise of Christ. Otherwise I think it ought not to be done."

Marcus of Mactaris said: "It is not to be wondered at if heretics, enemies, and impugners of the truth claim to themselves a matter in the power and condescension of others. But it is to be wondered at, that some of us, prevaricators of the truth, support heretics and oppose themselves to Christians. Therefore we decree that heretics must be baptized."

Sattius of Sicilibba said: "If to heretics in baptism their sins are remitted, they come to the Church without reason. For since, in the day of judgment, there are sins which are punished, there is nothing which the heretics can fear from Christ's judgment, if they have already obtained remission of their sins."

Victor of Gor said: "Since sins are not remitted save in the baptism of the Church, he who admits a heretic to communion without baptism does two things against reason: he does not cleanse the heretics, and he befouls the Christians."

Aurelius of Utica said: "Since the apostle says that we are not to communicate with other people's sins, what else does he do but communicate with other

543

people's sins, who holds communion with heretics without the Church's baptism? And therefore I judge that heretics must be baptized, that they may receive forgiveness of their sins; and thus communion may be had with them."

Iambus of Germaniciana said: "They who approve of the baptism of heretics, disapprove of ours, in denying that they who are, I will not say washed, but befouled, outside the Church, ought to be baptized in the Church."

Lucianus of Rucuma said: "It is written, "And God saw the light, that it was good, and divided between the light and the darkness."[36] If there can be agreement between light and darkness, there may be something in common between us and heretics. Therefore I determine that heretics must be baptized."

Pelagianus of Luperciana said: "It is written, "Either the Lord is God, or Baal is God."[37] Therefore in the present case also, either the Church is the Church, or heresy is the Church. On the other hand, if heresy is not the Church, how can the Church's baptism be among heretics?"[38]

Jader of Midila said: "We know that there is but one baptism in the Catholic Church, and therefore we ought not to receive a heretic unless he has been baptized among us; lest he should think that he has been baptized out of the Catholic Church."

Also another **Felix of Marazana** said: "There is one faith, one baptism, that of the Catholic Church, which alone has the right to baptize."

Paulus of Obba said: "It does not disturb me if any man does not assert the faith and truth of the Church, since the apostle says, "For what if some of them have fallen away from the faith? Has their unbelief made the faith of God of no effect? By no means. For God is true, but every man a liar."[39] But if God is true, how can the truth of baptism be among the heretics, among whom God is not?"

Pomponius of Dionysiana said: "It is evident that heretics cannot baptize and give remission of sins, seeing that they have not power to be able to loose or to bind anything on earth."

Venantius of Timisa said: "If a husband, going into foreign parts, had commended his wife to the guardianship of his friend, that friend would take care of her who was commended to him with all possible diligence, that her chastity and holiness should not be corrupted by any one. Christ the Lord and our God, going to His Father, has commended to us His bride. Shall we guard her incorrupt and inviolate, or shall we betray her integrity and chastity to adulterers and corrupters? For he who makes the Church's baptism common to heretics, betrays the spouse of Christ to adulterers."

Ahymnus of Ausvaga said: "We have received one baptism, and that same we maintain and practice. But he who says that heretics also may lawfully baptize, makes two baptisms."

Saturninus of Victoriana said: "If heretics may baptize, they who do unlawful things are excused and defended; nor do I see why either Christ should have called them adversaries, or the apostle should have called them Antichrists."[40]

Saturninus of Thucca said: "The Gentiles, although they worship idols, do yet know and confess a supreme God as Father and Creator. Against Him Marcion blasphemes, and some persons do not blush to approve the baptism of Marcion. How do such priests either observe or vindicate God's priesthood, who do not baptize God's enemies, and hold communion with them as they are!"

Marcellus of Zama said: "Since sins are not remitted save in the baptism of the Church, he who does not baptize a heretic holds communion with a sinner."

Irenaeus of Ululi said: "If the Church does not baptize a heretic, for the reason that he is said to be already baptized, it is the greater heresy."

Donatus of Cibaliana said: "I know one Church and her one baptism. If there is any who says that the grace of baptism is with heretics, he must first show and prove that the Church is among them."[41]

Zosimus of Tharassa said: "When a revelation of the truth is made, let error give place to truth; because Peter also, who previously circumcised, yielded to Paul when he preached the truth."

Julianus of Telepte said: "It is written, 'No man can receive anything unless it have been given him from heaven.' If heresy is from heaven, it can also give baptism."

Faustus of Timida Regia said: "Let not them who are in favor of heretics flatter themselves. He who interferes with the baptism of the Church on behalf of heretics, makes them Christians, and us heretics."

Geminius of Furni said: "Some of our colleagues may prefer heretics to themselves, they cannot to us: and therefore what we have once determined we maintain—that we baptize those who come to us from the heretics."

Rogatianus of Nova said: "Christ instituted the Church; the devil, heresy. How can the synagogue of Satan have the baptism of Christ?"

Therapius of Bulla said: "He who concedes and betrays the Church's baptism to heretics, what else has he been to the spouse of Christ than a Judas?"

Also another **Lucius of Membresa** said: "It is written, God hears not a sinner. How can a heretic who is a sinner be heard in baptism?"

Also another, **Felix of Bussacene**, said: "In the matter of receiving heretics without the baptism of the Church, let no one prefer custom to reason and truth, because reason and truth always exclude custom."[42]

Another **Saturninus of Avitini** said: "If Antichrist can give to any one the grace of Christ, heretics also are able to baptize, for they are called antichrists."

Quintus of Aggya: "He can give something who has something. But what can heretics give, who, it is plain, have nothing?"

Another, **Julianus of Marcelliana**, said: "If a man can serve two masters, God and mammon, baptism also can serve two masters, the Christian and the heretic."

Tenax of Horrea Caeliae said: "Baptism is one, but it is the Church's. Where the Church is not there, there can be no baptism."

Another **Victor of Assuri** said: "It is written, that God is one, and Christ is one, and the Church is one, and baptism is one. How, therefore, can any one be baptized there, where God, and Christ, and the one Church is not?"

Donatulus of Capse said: "And I also have always thought this, that heretics, who can obtain nothing without the Church, when they are converted to the Church, must be baptized."

Verulus of Rusiccada said: "A man who is a heretic cannot give what he has not; much more a schismatic, who has lost what he once had."

Pudentianus of Cuiculis said: "The novelty of my episcopal office,[43] beloved brethren, has caused me to await what my elders should judge. For it is manifest that heresies have nothing, nor can have any thing. And thus, if any one comes from them, it is most justly decreed that they must be baptized."

Peter of Hippo Diarrhytus said: "Since there is one baptism in the Catholic Church, it is manifest that one cannot be baptized outside the Church. And therefore I judge that those who have been dipped in heresy or in schism, when they come to the Church, should be baptized."

Also another **Lucius of Ausafa** said: "According to the direction of my mind, and of the Holy Spirit, as there is one God and Father of our Lord Jesus Christ, and one Christ, and one hope, and one Spirit, and one Church, there ought also to be one baptism. And therefore I say, that if any thing had been set on foot or accomplished by heretics, it ought to be rescinded, and that those who come thence must be baptized in the Church."

Also another **Felix of Gurgites** said: "I judge that, according to the precepts of the holy Scriptures, he who is unlawfully baptized by heretics outside the Church, when he wishes to take refuge in the Church, should obtain the grace of baptism where it is lawfully given."

Pusillus of Lamasba said: "I believe that there is no saving baptism except in the Catholic Church. Whatsoever is apart from the Catholic Church is a pretence."

Salvianus of Gazaufala said: "It is certain that heretics have nothing, and therefore they come to us that they may receive what they have not."

Honoratus of Thucca said: "Since Christ is the Truth, we ought rather to follow truth than custom; so that we should sanctify heretics with the Church's baptism, seeing that they come to us for the reason that they could receive nothing without."

Victor of Octavum said: "As yourselves also know, I have not long been appointed a bishop, and I therefore waited for the decision of my predecessors. I therefore think this, that as many as come from heresy should undoubtedly be baptized."

Clarus of Mascula said: "The sentence of our Lord Jesus Christ is plain, when He sent His apostles, and accorded to them alone the power given to Him by His

Father; and to them we have succeeded, governing the Lord's Church with the same power, and baptizing the faith of believers. And therefore heretics, who neither have power without, nor have the Church of Christ, are able to baptize no one with His baptism."

Secundianus of Thambei said: "We ought not to deceive heretics by our presumption; so that they who have not been baptized in the Church of our Lord Jesus Christ, and have not obtained by this means remissions of their sins, when the day of judgment shall come, should impute to us that through us they were not baptized, and did not obtain the indulgence of divine grace. On which account, since there is one Church and one baptism, when they are converted to us they should obtain, together with the Church, the Church's baptism also."

Also another **Aurelius of Chullabi** said: "John the apostle laid it down in his epistle, saying: "If any one come unto you, and have not the doctrine of Christ, receive him not into your house, and say not to him, 'Hail.' For he that says to him, 'Hail,' partakes with his evil deeds."[44] How can such be rashly admitted into God's house, who are prohibited from being admitted into our private dwelling? Or how can we hold communion with them without the Church's baptism, to whom, if we should only say 'Hail,' we are partakers of their evil deeds?"

Litteus of Gemelli said: "If the blind lead the blind, both fall into the ditch, Since, then, it is manifest that heretics cannot give light to any, as being themselves blind, their baptism does not avail."

Natalis of Oëa said: "As well I who am present, as Pompey of Sabrata, as also Dioga of Leptis Magna—who, absent indeed in body, but present in spirit, have given me charge—judge the same as our colleagues, that heretics cannot hold communion with us, unless they shall be baptized with ecclesiastical baptism."

Junius of Neapolis said: "From the judgment which we once determined on I do not recede, that we should baptize heretics who come to the Church."

Cyprian of Carthage said: "The letter which was written to our colleague Jubaianus very fully expresses my opinion, that, according to evangelical and apostolic testimony, heretics, who are called adversaries of Christ and Antichrists, when they come to the Church, must be baptized with the one baptism of the Church, that they may be made of adversaries, friends, and of Antichrists, Christians."

NOTES

1. This was not an ecumenical council but a regional gathering of bishops, more properly termed a Synod. This Synod was convened over the issue of rebaptism of heretics, in which Cyprian and a large number of African bishops took issue with the teaching of Pope Stephen I. Previous Carthaginian Synods included the Synod of Agrippinus about AD 220; the long Synod of 236-248, which condemned Privatus of Lambesa (mentioned in Cyprian's Letter 54); further Carthaginian synods in 251 (dealing with the *lapsi* and convened under St. Cyprian), 252, 254, 255. The Seventh Synod of Carthage was called by Cyprian in Spring of 256 and convened in September of the same year. The African Church's position in favor of rebaptism of heretics was laid down by Agrippinus at the First Synod and subsequently supported by Cyprian. After Cyprian's death the African Church would fall in line with Roman custom; St. Augustine writes a lengthy rebuttal of the arguments in favor of rebaptism in his work *De Baptismo,* some of which are quoted below.

2. Letter 72.

3. This renunciation of the title Bishop of Bishops (*Episcopus Episcoporum*) demonstrates that the title was already claimed by the Roman pontiffs as early as 256; Tertullian, in his work *On Modesty* (c. 215), also attests that the Bishops of Rome had already claimed the titles of *Episcopus Episcoporum* as well as *Pontifex Maximus* even in his own day (see *On Modesty* [*De Pudicitia*], 1).

4. St. Cyprian had already taught that the Roman Church, in the person of Peter, was the visible source of the Church's unity (*On the Unity of the Church*, 4) and was always solicitous to keep the See of Rome informed of all his actions (Letter 28); he also implicitly teaches the impossibility of the Roman See falling into error when he expressed disbelief that the Roman Church could ever "overthrow the majesty of faith" (Letter 30:3). In the amended version of his treatise on Church unity, he had said, "[T]hough to all His Apostles He gave an equal power yet did He set up one chair, and disposed the origin and manner of unity by his authority. The other Apostles were indeed what Peter was, but the primacy is given to Peter, and the Church and the chair is shown to be one. And all are pastors, but the flock is shown to be one, which is fed by all the Apostles with one mind and heart. He that holds not this unity of the Church, does he think that he holds the faith? He who deserts the chair of Peter, upon whom the Church is founded, is he confident that he is in the Church?" (*On the Unity of the Church*, 4—see footnote 11). Given all these statements, one can only assume that Cyprian has here changed his opinion in the heat of the rebaptism controversy or else was being disingenuous in his statements to the Roman See in 250. Given what we know of Cyrpian's personality and of the rigorist tendencies of the African Church in general, the former is more probable.

5. Bilta (Biltha, Vilta) was in Africa Proconsularis. This Caecilius is probably the same bishop as the one addressed by Cyprian in Letter 63.

6. Eph. 4:5. This passage from St. Paul on the unity of the Church will be the most often cited verse in support of the rigorist position of the council.

7. Caecilius here errs in attributing the efficacy of the sacraments to the relative holiness of the minister and not to the power of Christ working through the minister of the sacrament, thus making the sacraments a work of man and not of Christ. "Since it is ultimately Christ who acts and effects salvation through the ordained minister, the unworthiness of the latter does not prevent Christ from acting" (*Catechism of the Catholic Church*, 1584); St. Augustine says: "As for the proud minister, he is to be ranked with the devil. Christ's gift is not thereby profaned: what flows through him keeps its purity, and what passes through him remains clear and reaches the fertile earth...The spiritual power of the sacrament is indeed comparable to light: those to be enlightened receive it in its purity, and if it should pass through defiled beings, it is not itself defiled" (*Tractates in the Gospel of John*, 5:15); see also the Canons of the Council of Trent, Session VII, "On the Sacraments," Canon XII and "On Baptism," Canon XI.

8. Primus restricts the grace of God solely to the confines of the institutional Church. This teaching is opposed by Pope Stephen, and later by Peter Lombard and St. Thomas Aquinas. Aquinas, following the Church's teaching on the efficacy of validly conferred baptism outside of the physical confines of the Church, says that the reason these baptisms are valid is found in will of God that the means of salvation be extended to as many as possible and with the greatest ease: "It is due to the mercy of Him 'Who will have all men to be saved' (1 Timothy 2:4) that in those things which are necessary for salvation, man can easily find the remedy. Now the most necessary among all the sacraments is Baptism, which is man's regeneration unto spiritual life: since for children there is no substitute, while adults cannot otherwise than by Baptism receive a full remission both of guilt and of its punishment. Consequently, lest man should have to go without so necessary a remedy, it was ordained, both that the matter of Baptism should be something common that is easily obtainable by all, i.e. water; and that the minister of Baptism should be anyone, even not in orders, lest from lack of being baptized, man should suffer loss of his salvation" (*STh*, III. Q. 67 Art. 3).

9. A reference to the first Carthaginian synod of 220 under Agrippinus.

10. This Nemesianus was later condemned to the mines under the persecution of Valerian (see Letters 76 & 77).

11. Prov. 9:19.

12. John 3:5.

13. Eph. 4:3-6.

14. John 3:6.

15. Gal. 5:19-21.

16. Again, Nemesianus makes the error of confounding the sanctity of the minister with the validity of the sacrament. St. Augustine reminds us that the power of baptism comes from Christ, not from the minister: "[W]hen they baptize, it is not themselves that baptize, but He of whom John says, 'The same is He which baptizes'" (*On Baptism, Against the Donatists*, Book VI, Chap. 28).

17. Mentioned in the greeting to Cyrpian's Letter 67.

18. Matt. 5:13.

19. Matt. 28:18-19.

20. A paraphrase of the Septuagint translation of Prov. 14:9: "The houses of transgressors will need purification; but the houses of the just are acceptable."

21. The principle argued by Nicomedes is that "you cannot give what you do not have" (see the comment of Bishop Successus below). If the schismatic or heretical priests are deprived of God's grace, how can they confer it upon others? The error in this thinking is in ascribing the giving of grace to the priest himself as a man rather than as an *alter Christus*, in whom Christ always acts through the sacraments (provided they are carried out in the manner and with the intention willed by the Church), regardless of the personal piety of the mnister.

22. Matt. 28:19.

23. An indirect testimony to the belief in the early Church that the phrase "born again" used in John 3:3 refers to baptism.

24. Matt, 12:30.

25. 1 John 2:18-19.

26. Addressed in Cyprian's Letters 76 and 79.

27. Cyprian addressed the very important Letter 81 to this Bishop Successus, in which we learn most of what we know about the persecution of Valerian and the Church of Carthage.

28. St. Augustine answers Privatianus' objection: "This man may thus be answered word for word: He who says that malicious and envious persons have the power of baptizing, should first say who was the founder of malice and envy. For if malice and envy are of God, they may have the divine favor; but if they are not of God, how can they either have or confer on any one the grace of God? But as these words are in the same way most manifestly false, so are also those which these were uttered to confute. For the malicious and envious baptize, as even

Cyprian himself allows, because he bears testimony that they also are within [the Church]. So therefore even heretics may baptize, because baptism is the sacrament of Christ; but envy and heresy are the works of the devil. Yet though a man possesses them, he does not thereby cause that if he have the sacrament of Christ, lest it also should itself be reckoned in the number of the devil's works" (*On Baptism, Against the Donatists*, Book VI, Chap. 26).

29. Again, St. Augustine responds: "It is not the baptism of heretics which we approve in heretics, as it is not the baptism of the covetous, or the treacherous, or deceitful, or of robbers, or of envious men which we approve in them; for all of these are unjust, but Christ is just, whose sacrament existing in them, they do not in its essence violate. Otherwise another man might say: What can be said of the man who approves the baptism of the unjust, save that he communicates with the unjust. And if this objection were brought against the Catholic Church herself, it would be answered just as I have answered the above" (ibid., Chap. 27).

30. Matt. 12:30.

31. Sir. 34:25.

32. It is interesting that in this, and in following arguments against "custom" (see the statement of Libosus of Vaga below), it becomes evident that it had been the Tradition of the Church to not rebaptize heretics. This exposes the position of the Council as novel and against apostolic custom.

33. Matt. 28:18.

34. John 14:6.

35. Matt. 28:19.

36. Gen. 1:4.

37. 1 Kings 18:21.

38. St. Augustine answers this objection by pointing out that the grace of Christ extends out and is able to reach even the unrighteous and the sinners. "To him we may answer as follows: Either Paradise is Paradise, or Egypt is Paradise. Further, if Egypt be not Paradise, how can the water of Paradise be in Egypt? But it will be said to us that it extends even there by flowing forth from Paradise. In like manner, therefore, baptism extends to heretics. Also we say: Either the rock is the Church, or the sand is the Church. Further, since the sand is not the Church, how can baptism exist with those who build upon the sand by hearing the words of Christ and doing them not? And yet it does exist with them; and in like manner also it exists among the heretics" (*On Baptism, Against the Donatists*, Book VII, Chap. 8).

39. Rom. 3:3-4.

40. St. Augustine rightly points out that admitting the ability of heretics to validly administer baptism is not to say they are excused from their heresy or other sins. See *On Baptism, Against the Donatists*, Book VII, Chap. 15.

41. "To him we answer: If you say that the grace of baptism is identical with baptism, then it exists among heretics; but if baptism is the sacrament or outward sign of grace, while the grace itself is the abolition of sins, then the grace of baptism does not exist with heretics. But so there is one baptism and one Church, just as there is one faith. As therefore the good and bad, not having one hope, can yet have one baptism, so those who have not one common Church can have one common baptism" (ibid., Chap. 19). Augustine here makes an important distinction between the external, sacramental signs (*sacramentum tantum*) and the reality of the grace conferred by the sacrament (*res tantum*).

42. This Felix thus admits the apostolic custom of not rebaptizing heretics and sets the Church of Carthage against the Tradition.

43. From this, and similar comments by Victor of Octavum below, it appears the bishosp under Cyprian were speaking in order of seniority.

44. 2 John 1:10

APPENDICES

INTRODUCTION TO THE APPENDIX

In the process of tracking down the sources of the 1,490 scriptural quotes made by Cyprian throughout his writings, the thought struck me of categorizing all his citations so that we could get a look at what books had the most influence on the great Bishop of Carthage. A year a half and countless hours of labor later, I am proud to present the results of this work in this appendix. The graphs on the following pages break down Cyprian's 1,490 direct citations into eight different categories in order to visually represent them and show where he was most influenced.

By far, the most frequently cited books are the Gospel of Matthew with 175 citations, followed by the Psalms (127), the Gospel of John (121) Isaiah (109) and 1 Corinthians (80); other frequently cited books are Jeremiah, Revelation, the Gospel of Luke, Proverbs, Romans and Exodus. Out of the entire seventy-three books of the Bible, quotes from Matthew make up 12% of Cyprian's total citations. Matthew, Psalms, John and Isaiah together comprise 36% of his total citations.

It is interesting to note that citations from the Deuterocanonicals (the "Apocrypha" of the Protestants) make up 12% of Cyprian's total citations from the Old Testament (by comparison, the Minor Prophets only make up 8% of the total Old Testament citations; the historical books are only 5%). Cyprian frequently calls these books "Holy Scripture" and cites them freely alongside the rest of the Old Testament books. This is very damaging to the Protestant argument that the Catholic Church "added" these books at a much later date. Cyprian accepts them as canonical and draws heavily from them.

There are thirteen books of the Bible that are never cited anywhere in the Cyprianic corpus. In the Old Testament these are Ruth, Ezra, 1 Chronicles, Judith, Esther, Lamentations, Obadiah, Jonah; in the New Testament, Philemon, James, 2 John, 3 John, and Jude. It is not surprising that Obadiah and Philemon are omitted; they are both extremely brief and their exclusion may mean nothing other than that Cyprian never had an appropriate occasion to cite them. 1 Chronicles is basically repeated in 2 Chronicles, which Cyprian does cite. The absence of Ruth, Ezra and Lamentations is more interesting; Ruth's modesty and humility would have presented an excellent source to draw upon in Cyprian's *On the Dress of Virgins*, which was written to encourage Christian women to avoid worldly attire; the same thing could be said for Esther.

In the New Testament, the absence of Jude is somewhat strange, since the book had been accepted in North Africa since the time of Tertullian and was also accepted in Rome. While Cyprian quotes copiously from 1 John (thirty-seven times), he never quotes 2 John or 3 John, probably due to the fact that these epistles were disputed in the west for a long time to come. In Eusebius' day they were still considered *antilegomena* (questionable) and their canonicity would not be settled until the close of the 4th century.

More surprising is the absence of James, a much larger epistle with more doctrinal content. The canonicity of James was contested in the ancient Church down to Eusebius' day, but it was accepted by St. Clement, St. Irenaeus and Tertullian, so it is inconceivable the Cyprian's omission of James is due to lack of knowledge about its existence. Why Cyprian omits it is unknown, especially with its passages on patient endurance of trials that would have been very relevant during the Decian persecution. The only plausible answer is that Cyprian may have rejected the book's canonicity.

When looking at the prevalence of the Psalms in Cyprian's Old Testament citations, it ought to be pointed out that these are very heavily concentrated in a single treatise: *Testimonies Against the Jews*, which is probably responsible for 75% of all of Cyprian's quotes from the Psalms. The Book of Hebrews, though traditionally ascribed to Paul, is counted among the Catholic Epistles because it is addressed to Jewish Christians in general and not to any specific community.

Both books of the Maccabees are counted with the historical books, as are Tobit and Judith.

In compiling and sorting these citations, the following criteria have been followed:

- Unattributable citations were not used. For example, Cyprian states he is citing Baruch in *Testimonies Against the Jews*, Book III:29, yet what he cites is not found anywhere in any codex of the Book of Baruch and is of unknown origin. Such quotes were not counted.
- When Cyprian makes an errant citation (for example, quoting Sirach but saying it is from Ecclesiastes), we have categorized the quote correctly, not according to Cyprian's error.
- Paraphrased quotes are included so long as the paraphrase is readily recognizable. If the paraphrase is uncertain, in such a way that it is unclear where it came from, the quote was not counted.
- Citations not by Cyprian are omitted; for example, quotes from the letters of the Roman clergy to Cyprian, or quotes from other bishops that are typically included in the Cyprianic corpus.
- Sometimes Cyprian cites a phrase from the Gospels that is found in more than one of the Synoptics. If it is not certain which Gospel he is quoting from, each possible source is attributed. For example, the phrase "Render unto Caesar what is Caesar's" could come from Matt. 22, Luke 20, or Mark

12, if no other information is provided. In these cases, rather than arbitrarily choose one Gospel to attribute the phrase to, each Gospel is counted. It is thus possible that one quote gets counted multiple times, although this does not affect the ratio since it is attributed equally to each possible source.

- Cyprian sometimes merges citations together within a single sentence. For example, John 6:35 ("I am the bread of life") and John 6:51 ("I am the living bread that came down from heaven") are both merged together into a single quote within one sentence. In such cases, even though Cyprian is drawing from two passages, the citation is treated as a single quote and counted once, since he is intending to use the citation as a single quotation. Thus, in above example, the merged sentence would be counted as one quote from the Gospel of John.

- It also happens that Cyprian will put multiple quotations from a single book in a row without merging them; this happens frequently in *Testimonies Against the Jews*. For example, he will say, "In the Gospel according to John: 'Unless a man be born again of water and the Spirit, he cannot enter into the kingdom of God. For that which is born of the flesh is flesh; and that which is born of the Spirit is spirit.' Also in the same place: 'Unless you eat the flesh of the Son of man, and drink His blood, you shall not have life in you.'" Since his usage of the quotations them separate, they are counted as two different quotes.

- Allusions to Scripture passages are counted if they are specific and being used to make a point; for example, if Cyprian, in his own words, relates the story of Hannah's conception of Samuel in order to encourage confidence in prayer, then 1 Samuel is cited. However, an allusion is not counted if it is vague or not being used to make a point; for example, Cyprian mentioning casually that "our Lord rose for us" does not mean that the Gospel passages pertaining to the Resurrection are cited.

- There are certain books that, while they are cited by Cyprian, are done so with such infrequency as to make them statistically irrelevant. For example, in Cyprian's entire corpus he cites the prophet Nahum only one time, which means Nahum represents a meager .0040% of all Cyprian's citations from the prophets. Thus, on the following charts, Nahum is said to be referenced zero times. The same is true for 2 Peter in the New Testament.

Despite these guidelines, there was a small deree of subjectivity in deciding what was a specific allusion versus a vague allusion, or too what degree a paraphrase was truly recognizable. Thus, the data presented here should not be taken as absolutely error-free. I am not a statitician, and I admit that other, more scientific inquiries into this question may produce somewhat different results.

Even so, this data is basically sound and should provide a good jump-off point for anyone interested in further study of the writings of St. Cyprian.

CITATIONS OF ST. CYPRIAN

Matthew	175	Tobit	14
Psalms	127	1 Samuel	13
John	121	Job	13
Isaiah	109	Philippians	13
1 Corinthians	80	2 Timothy	11
Luke	78	Colossians	11
Revelation	51	1 Kings	8
Romans	51	2 Thessalonians	6
Proverbs	48	Joshua	6
Jeremiah	45	1 Thessalonians	4
Exodus	40	2 Chronicles	3
1 John	37	2 Samuel	3
Sirach	34	2 Kings	2
Acts	31	Hebrews	2
Deuteronomy	30	Judges	2
Ephesians	26	2 Peter	1
Galatians	25	Nahum	1
Genesis	25	1 Chronicles	0
Mark	22	2 John	0
2 Corinthians	21	3 John	0
Daniel	18	Esther	0
Wisdom	18	James	0
1 Timothy	16	Jude	0
Leviticus	16	Judith	0
Numbers	16	Philemon	0
1 Peter	14	Ruth	0

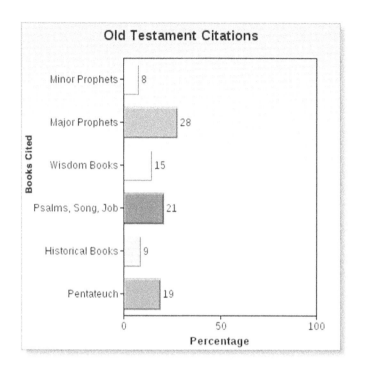

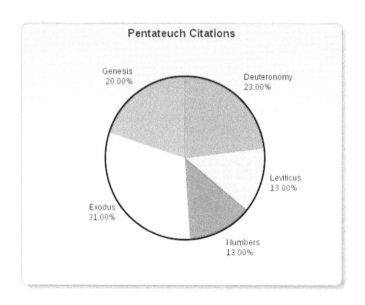

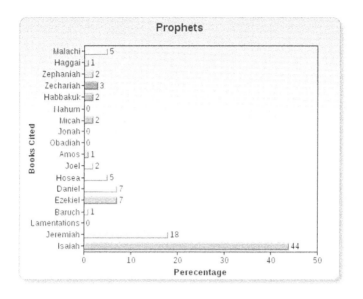

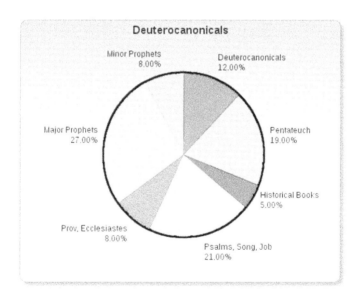

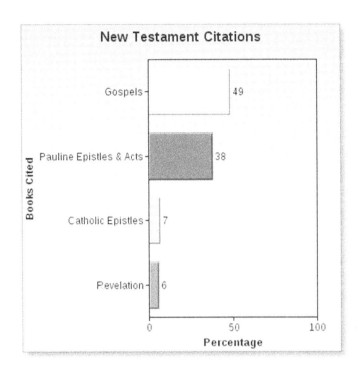

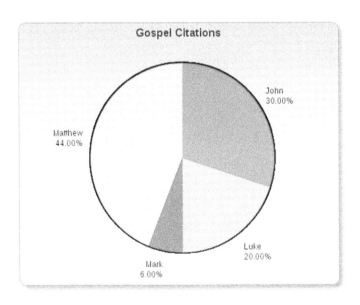

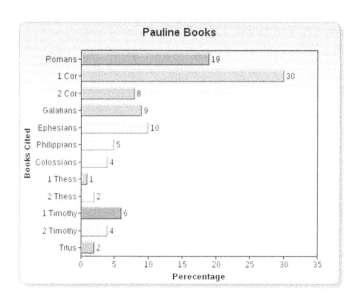

THE QUOTABLE CYPRIAN

CHRISTIAN LIFE

"But if you keep the way of innocence, the way of righteousness, if you walk with a firm and steady step, if, depending on God with your whole strength and with your whole heart, you only be what you have begun to be, liberty and power to do is given you in proportion to the increase of your spiritual grace." (Letter 1:5)

"For the crown of sorrows and sufferings cannot be received unless patience in sorrow and suffering precede it." (*On the Advantage of Patience*, 10)

"It is a persistent evil to persecute a man who belongs to the grace of God. It is a calamity without remedy to hate the happy." (*On Jealousy and Envy*, 9)

"Nothing distinguishes between the unrighteous and the righteous more than that in affliction the unrighteous man impatiently complains and blasphemes, while the righteous is proved by his patience." (*On the Advantage of Patience*, 17)

"We are constrained to have more love for what we shall be, by being allowed to know and to condemn what we were....When the soul, in its gaze into heaven, has recognized its Author, it rises higher than the sun, and far transcends all this earthly power, and begins to be that which it believes itself to be." (Letter 1:14)

"But nevertheless it disturbs some that the power of this disease attacks our people equally with the heathens, as if the Christian believed for this purpose, that he might have the enjoyment of the world and this life free from the contact of ills; and not as one who undergoes all adverse things here and is reserved for future joy." (*On Mortality*, 8)

"We had renounced the world when we were baptized; but we have now indeed renounced the world when tried and approved by God, we leave all that we have, and have followed the Lord, and stand and live in His faith and fear." (Letter 6:5)

"[W]e feel the rods and the stripes, because we neither please God with good deeds nor atone for our sins." (Letter 7:2)

"There is no advantage in setting forth virtue by our words, and destroying the truth by our deeds." (*On Mortality*, 20)

"[U]ndoubtedly God, who rebukes whom He loves, when He rebukes, rebukes that He may amend, amends that He may preserve." (Letter 7:5)

"Continence and modesty consist not alone in purity of the flesh, but also in seemliness, as well as in modesty of dress and adornment." (*On the Dress of Virgins*, 5)

"[He who,] remembering the divine precept, with meekness and patience, and obeying the priests of God, deserves well of the Lord by his obedience and his righteous works." (Letter 13:1)

"But how can they follow Christ, who are held back by the chain of their wealth? Or how can they seek heaven, and climb to sublime and lofty heights, who are weighed down by earthly desires? They think that they possess, when they are rather possessed; as slaves of their profit, and not lords with respect to their own money, but rather the bond-slaves of their money." (*On the Lapsed*, 12)

"Let us turn to the Lord with our whole heart, and, expressing our repentance for our sin with true grief, let us entreat God's mercy. Let our soul lie low before Him. Let our mourning atone to Him. Let all our hope lean upon Him." (*On the Lapsed*, 29)

"What now must be the mind in you, how elevated, how large the heart, when such and so great things are resolved, when nothing but the precepts of God and the rewards of Christ are considered! The will is then only God's will; and although you are still placed in the flesh, it is the life not of the present world, but of the future, that you now live." (Letter 15:3)

"We ask that the will of God may be done both in heaven and in earth, each of which things pertains to the fulfillment of our safety and salvation. For since we possess the body from the earth and the spirit from heaven, we ourselves are earth and heaven; and in both—that is, both in body and spirit—we pray that God's will may be done. For between the flesh and spirit there is a struggle; and there is a daily strife as they disagree one with the other, so that we cannot do those very things that we would, in that the spirit seeks heavenly and divine things, while the flesh lusts after earthly and temporal things; and therefore we ask that, by the help and assistance of God, agreement may be made between these two natures, so that while the will of God is done both in the spirit and in the flesh, the soul which is new-born by Him may be preserved." (*On the Lord's Prayer*, 16)

"An illustrious and divine thing, dearest brethren, is the saving labor of charity; a great comfort of believers, a wholesome guard of our security, a protection of hope, a safeguard of faith, a remedy for sin, a thing placed in the power of the doer, a thing both great and easy, a crown of peace without the risk of persecution; the true and greatest gift of God, needful for the weak, glorious for the strong, assisted by which the Christian accomplishes spiritual grace, deserves well of Christ the Judge, accounts God his debtor." (*On Works and Alms*, 26)

"[T]he Lord has condescended to teach and instruct us by the Holy Scriptures, that, being led away from the darkness of error, and enlightened by His pure and shining light, we may keep the way of life through the saving sacraments." (*Three Books of Testimonies Against the Jews*, Book I, Preface)

THE CHURCH

"The Church also is one, which is spread abroad far and wide into a multitude by an increase of fruitfulness. As there are many rays of the sun, but one light; and many branches of a tree, but one strength based in its tenacious root; and since from one spring flow many streams, although the multiplicity seems diffused in the liberality of an overflowing abundance, yet the unity is still preserved in the source." (*On the Unity of the Church*, 5)

"To [the schismatics] we have once given this reply, nor shall we cease to command them to lay aside their pernicious dissensions and disputes, and to be aware that it is an impiety to forsake their Mother." (Letter 40:2)

"[T]he house of God is one, and there can be no salvation to any except in the Church." (Letter 61:4)

"There is one God, and Christ is one, and there is one Church, and one chair founded upon the rock by the word of the Lord. Another altar cannot be constituted nor a new priesthood be made, except the one altar and the one priesthood. Whosoever gathers elsewhere, scatters." (Letter 39:5)

"He can no longer have God for his Father, who has not the Church for his mother. If any one could escape who was outside the ark of Noah, then he also may escape who shall be outside of the Church." (*On the Unity of the Church*, 6)

"For it weighs me down and saddens me, and the intolerable grief of a smitten, almost prostrate, spirit seizes me, when I find that you there, contrary to ecclesiastical order, contrary to evangelical law, contrary to the unity of the Catholic institution, had consented that another bishop should be made. That is what is neither right nor allowable to be done; that another church should be set up; that Christ's members should be torn asunder; that the one mind and body of the Lord's flock should be lacerated by a divided emulation." (Letter 43)

"Does he think that he has Christ, who acts in opposition to Christ's priests, who separates himself from the company of His clergy and people?" (*On the Unity of the Church*, 17)

"God is one, and Christ is one, and His Church is one, and the faith is one, and the people are joined into a substantial unity of body by the cement of concord. Unity cannot be severed; nor can one body be separated by a division of its structure, nor torn into pieces, with its entrails wrenched asunder by laceration. Whatever has proceeded from the womb cannot live and breathe in its detached condition, but loses the substance of health." (*On the Unity of the Church*, 23)

"O blessed Church of ours, which the honor of the divine condescension illuminates, Which in our own times the glorious blood of martyrs renders illustrious! She was white before in the works of the brethren; now she has become purple in the blood of the martyrs. Among her flowers are wanting neither roses nor lilies. Now let each one strive for the largest dignity of either honor. Let them receive crowns, either white, as of labors, or of purple, as of suffering. In the heavenly camp both peace and strife have their own flowers, with which the soldier of Christ may be crowned for glory." (Letter 8)

"Nor can a sinful people be a son; but the name of sons is attributed to those to whom remission of sins is granted, and to them immortality is promised anew, in the words of our Lord Himself: 'Whosoever commits sin is the servant of sin. And the servant abides not in the house for ever, but the son abides ever.'" (*On the Lord's Prayer*, 10)

"[T]he Apostle Paul says, 'For this cause shall a man leave his father and mother, and shall cleave unto his wife; and they two shall be one flesh. This is a great mystery; but I speak concerning Christ and the Church;'—when, I say, the blessed apostle says this, and with his sacred voice testifies to the unity of Christ with the Church, cleaving to one another with indivisible links, how can he be with Christ who is not with the spouse of Christ, and in His Church? (Letter 48:1)

"For although there seem to be tares in the Church, yet neither our faith nor our charity ought to be hindered, so that because we see that there are tares in the Church we ourselves should withdraw from the Church: we ought only to labor that we may be wheat, that when the wheat shall begin to be gathered into the Lord's barns, we may receive fruit for our labor and work." (Letter 50:3)

"He who is not in the Church of Christ is not a Christian." (Letter 51:24)

"I entreat all to return into the Church. I beg all our fellow-soldiers to be included within the camp of Christ, and the dwelling-place of God the Father. I remit everything. I shut my eyes to many things, with the desire and the wish to gather together the brotherhood." (Letter 54:16)

"[T]he very interrogation which is put in baptism is a witness of the truth. For when we say, 'Do you believe in eternal life and remission of sins through the holy Church?' we mean that remission of sins is not granted except in the Church." (Letter 69:2)

"The Church, setting forth the likeness of paradise, includes within her walls fruit-bearing trees, whereof that which does not bring forth good fruit is cut off and is cast into the fire. These trees she waters with four rivers, that is, with the four Gospels, wherewith, by a celestial inundation, she bestows the grace of saving baptism. Can any one water from the Church's fountains who is not within the Church?" (Letter 72:10)

"Where and of whom and to whom is he born, who is not a son of the Church, so as that he should have God as his Father, before he has had the Church for his Mother?" (Letter 73:7)

"[T]he spouse of Christ is one, which is the Catholic Church [and] it is she herself who alone bears sons of God." (Letter 74:14, Firmilian to Cyprian)

"For they who are baptized, doubtless, fill up the number of the Church." (Letter 74:17, Firmilian to Cyprian)

CONFESSION OF SIN AND PENANCE

"I entreat you, beloved brethren, that each one should confess his own sin, while he who has sinned is still in this world, while his confession may be received, while the satisfaction and remission made by the priests are pleasing to the Lord." (*On the Lapsed*, 29)

"And how necessarily, how providently and salutarily, are we admonished that we are sinners, since we are compelled to entreat for our sins, and while pardon is asked for from God, the soul recalls its own consciousness of sin! Lest any one should flatter himself that he is innocent, and by exalting himself should more deeply perish, he is instructed and taught that he sins daily, in that he is bidden to entreat daily for his sins." (*On the Lord's Prayer*, 22)

"[The schismatics teach] that the Lord should not be appeased through bishops and priests, but that the Lord's priests being, forsaken, a new tradition of a sacrilegious appointment should arise, contrary to the evangelical discipline." (Letter 39:3)

"[W]e do not prejudge when the Lord is to be the judge; save that if He shall find the repentance of the sinners full and sound, He will then ratify what shall have been here determined by us. If, however, any one should delude us with the pretence of repentance, God, who is not mocked, and who looks into man's heart, will judge of those things which we have imperfectly looked into, and the Lord will amend the sentence of His servants." (Letter 51:18)

"The Lord exhorts [the lapsed] to rise up again by his works, because it is written, 'Alms do deliver from death,' and not, assuredly, from that death which once the blood of Christ extinguished, and from which the saving grace of baptism and of our Redeemer has delivered us, but from that which subsequently creeps in through sins." (Letter 51:22)

"Efforts are used [by the heretics] that the sins may not be atoned for with just satisfactions and lamentations, that the wounds may not be washed away with tears." (Letter 54:13)

"[O]nly they who are set over the Church and established in the Gospel law, and in the ordinance of the Lord, are allowed to baptize and to give remission of sins; but that without, nothing can either be bound or loosed, where there is none who can either bind or loose anything." (Letter 72:7)

"[I]n the Gospel, when Christ breathed on the apostles alone, saying, 'Receive the Holy Ghost: whose soever sins you remit they are remitted unto them, and whose soever sins you retain they are retained.' Therefore the power of remitting sins was given to the apostles, and to the churches which they, sent by Christ, established, and to the bishops who succeeded to them by vicarious ordination." (Letter 74:16, Firmilian to Cyprian)

EPISCOPACY

"[T]he glory of the Church is the glory of the bishop." (Letter 6:1)

"[T]hrough the changes of times and successions, the ordering of bishops and the plan of the Church flow onwards; so that the Church is founded upon the bishops, and every act of the Church is controlled by these same rulers...[t]his, then, is founded on the divine law..." (Letter 26:1)

[That the bishops have the authority to determine on what terms Christians may be said to be in communion with the Church] "If any unrestrained and impetuous person, whether of our presbyters or deacons or of strangers, should dare, before our decree, to communicate with the lapsed, let him be expelled from our communion, and plead the cause of his rashness before all of us when, by the Lord's permission, we shall assemble together again." (Letter 27:3)

"The sentence of our Lord Jesus Christ is plain, when He sent His apostles, and accorded to them alone the power given to Him by His Father; and to them we [bishops] have succeeded, governing the Lord's Church with the same power." (Seventh Council of Carthage)

"When a bishop is once made and approved by the testimony and judgment of his colleagues and the people, another can by no means be appointed." (Letter 40:2)

"[T]here is one person for the time priest in the Church, and for the time judge in the stead of Christ; whom, if, according to divine teaching, the whole fraternity should obey, no one would stir up anything against the college of priests; no one, after the divine judgment, after the suffrage of the people, after the consent of the co-bishops, would make himself a judge, not now of the bishop, but of God." (Letter 54:5)

"The chief rulers [bishops], who by vicarious ordination succeed to the apostles." (Letter 68:4)

"And the Lord also in the Gospel, when disciples forsook Him as He spoke, turning to the twelve, said, 'Will you also go away?' Then Peter answered Him, 'Lord, to whom shall we go? You have the word of eternal life; and we believe, and are sure, that You are the Son of the living God.' Peter speaks there, on whom the Church was to be built, teaching and showing in the name of the

Church, that although a rebellious and arrogant multitude of those who will not hear and obey may depart, yet the Church does not depart from Christ; and they are the Church who are a people united to the priest, and the flock which adheres to its pastor. Whence you ought to know that the bishop is in the Church, and the Church in the bishop; and if any one be not with the bishop, that he is not in the Church, and that those flatter themselves in vain who creep in, not having peace with God's priests, and think that they communicate secretly with some; while the Church, which is Catholic and one, is not cut nor divided, but is indeed connected and bound together by the cement of priests who cohere with one another." (Letter 68:8)

"Novatian is not in the Church; nor can he be reckoned as a bishop, who, succeeding to no one, and despising the evangelical and apostolic tradition, sprang from himself." (Letter 75:3)

HERESY AND SCHISM

"Hence heresies not only have frequently been originated, but continue to be so; while the perverted mind has no peace—while a discordant faithlessness does not maintain unity. But the Lord permits and suffers these things to be, while the choice of one's own liberty remains, so that while the discrimination of truth is testing our hearts and our minds, the sound faith of those that are approved may shine forth with manifest light." (*On the Unity of the Church*, 10)

"These are they who of their own accord, without any divine arrangement, set themselves to preside among the daring strangers assembled, who appoint themselves prelates without any law of ordination, who assume to themselves the name of bishop, although no one gives them the episcopate." (*On the Unity of the Church*, 10)

"God had not respect unto Cain's offerings; for he could not have God at peace with him, who through envious discord had not peace with his brother. What peace, then, do the enemies of the brethren promise to themselves? What sacrifices do those who are rivals of the priests think that they celebrate? Do they deem that they have Christ with them when they are collected together, who are gathered together outside the Church of Christ?" (*On the Unity of the Church*, 13)

"The quarrelsome and disunited, and he who has not peace with his brethren, in accordance with what the blessed apostle and the Holy Scripture testifies, even if he have been slain for the name of Christ, shall not be able to escape the crime of fraternal dissension, because, as it is written, 'He who hates his brother is a murderer,' and no murderer attains to the kingdom of heaven, nor does he live with God. He cannot be with Christ, who had rather be an imitator of Judas than of Christ. How great is the sin which cannot even be washed away by a baptism of blood—how heinous the crime which cannot be expiated by martyrdom!" (*On the Lord's Prayer*, 24)

"Think not that you are thus maintaining the Gospel of Christ when you separate yourselves from the flock of Christ." (Letter 43)

"Neither can those remain in God's Church, who have not maintained its divine and ecclesiastical discipline, either in the conversation of their life or the peace of their character." (Letter 48:2)

"He alone who has not been planted in the precepts and warnings of God the Father, can depart from the Church: he alone can forsake the bishops and abide in his madness with schismatics and heretics." (Letter 48:4)

"[I]f rejected by the Church, [one] should pass over to heretics and schismatics; where, although he should afterwards be put to death on account of the name, still, being placed outside the Church, and divided from unity and from charity, he could not in his death be crowned." (Letter 51:17)

"Know that, in the first place, we ought not even to be inquisitive as to what [a heretic] teaches, so long as he teaches out of the pale of unity. Whoever he may be, and whatever he may be, he who is not in the Church of Christ is not a Christian." (Letter 51:24)

"For neither have heresies arisen, nor have schisms originated, from any other source than from this, that God's priest is not obeyed." (Letter 54:5)

INFANT BAPTISM

"But in respect of the case of the infants, which you say ought not to be baptized within the second or third day after their birth, and that the law of ancient circumcision should be regarded, so that you think that one who is just born should not be baptized and sanctified within the eighth day, we all thought very differently in our council. For in this course which you thought was to be taken, no one agreed; but we all rather judge that the mercy and grace of God is not to be refused to any one born of man. For as the Lord says in His Gospel, 'The Son of man is not come to destroy men's lives, but to save them.' As far as we can we must strive that, if possible, no soul be lost. For what is wanting to him who has once been formed in the womb by the hand of God? To us, indeed, and to our eyes, according to the worldly course of days, they who are born appear to receive an increase. But whatever things are made by God, are completed by the majesty and work of God their Maker. Moreover, belief in divine Scripture declares to us, that among all, whether infants or those who are older, there is the same equality of the divine gift." (Letter 58:2-3)

"If anything could hinder men from obtaining grace, their more heinous sins might rather hinder those who are mature and grown up and older. But again, if even to the greatest sinners, and to those who had sinned much against God, when they subsequently believed, remission of sins is granted—and nobody is hindered from baptism and from grace—how much rather ought we to shrink from hindering an infant, who, being lately born, has not sinned, except in that, being born after the flesh according to Adam, he has contracted the contagion of the ancient death at its earliest birth, who approaches the more easily on this very account to the reception of the forgiveness of sins—that to him are remitted, not his own sins, but the sins of another?" (Letter 58:5)

INTERCESSION/MERITS OF THE SAINTS

"We believe, indeed, that the merits of martyrs and the works of the righteous are of great avail with the Judge." (*On the Lapsed*, 18)

"We regard paradise as our country—we already begin to consider the patriarchs as our parents: why do we not hasten and run, that we may behold our country, that we may greet our parents? There a great number of our dear ones is awaiting us, and a dense crowd of parents, brothers, children, is longing for us, already assured of their own safety, and still solicitous for our salvation." (*On Mortality*, 26)

"[Celerinus'] grandmother, Celerina, was some time since crowned with martyrdom. Moreover, his paternal and maternal uncles, Laurentius and Egnatius, who themselves also were once warring in the camps of the world, but were true and spiritual soldiers of God, casting down the devil by the confession of Christ, merited palms and crowns from the Lord by their illustrious passion. We always offer sacrifices for them, as you remember, as often as we celebrate the passions and days of the martyrs in the annual commemoration." (Letter 33:3)

JESUS CHRIST

"For if Jesus Christ, our Lord and God, is Himself the chief priest of God the Father, and has first offered Himself a sacrifice to the Father, and has commanded this to be done in commemoration of Himself, certainly that priest truly discharges the office of Christ, who imitates that which Christ did; and he then offers a true and full sacrifice in the Church to God the Father, when he proceeds to offer it according to what he sees Christ Himself to have offered." (Letter 62:14)

"The Lord's passion is the sacrifice which we offer." (Letter 62:17)

"For whereas in the Gospels, and in the epistles of the apostles, the name of Christ is alleged for the remission of sins; it is not in such a way as that the Son alone, without the Father, or against the Father, can be of advantage to anybody; but that it might be shown to the Jews, who boasted as to their having the Father, that the Father would profit them nothing, unless they believed on the Son whom He had sent." (Letter 72:17)

"He is the power of God, He is the reason, He is His wisdom and glory; He enters into a virgin; being the holy Spirit, He is endued with flesh; God is mingled with man. This is our God, this is Christ, who, as the mediator of the two, puts on man that He may lead them to the Father. What man is, Christ was willing to be, that man also may be what Christ is...What Christ is, we Christians shall be, if we imitate Christ." (*On the Vanity of Idols*, 11, 15)

"But he follows Christ who stands in His precepts, who walks in the way of His teaching, who follows His footsteps and His ways, who imitates that which Christ both did and taught." (*On Jealousy and Envy*, 11)

JEWS/JUDAISM

"Nor ought we, beloved brethren, only to observe and understand that we should call Him Father who is in heaven; but we add to it, and say our Father, that is, the Father of those who believe—of those who, being sanctified by Him, and restored by the nativity of spiritual grace, have begun to be sons of God. This is a word, moreover, which rebukes and condemns the Jews, who not only unbelievingly despised Christ, who had been announced to them by the prophets, and sent first to them, but also cruelly put Him to death; and these cannot now call God their Father, since the Lord confounds and confutes them, saying, "You are born of your father the devil, and the lusts of your father you will do. For he was a murderer from the beginning, and abode not in the truth, because there is no truth in him." (*On the Lord's Prayer*, 10)

"But there is need of continual prayer and supplication, that we fall not away from the heavenly kingdom, as the Jews, to whom this promise had first been given, fell away; even as the Lord sets forth and proves: 'Many,' says He, 'shall come from the east and from the west, and shall recline with Abraham, and Isaac, and Jacob in the kingdom of heaven. But the children of the kingdom shall be cast out into outer darkness: there shall be weeping and gnashing of teeth.' He shows that the Jews were previously children of the kingdom, so long as they continued also to be children of God; but after the name of Father ceased to be recognized among them, the kingdom also ceased; and therefore we Christians, who in our prayer begin to call God our Father, pray also that God's kingdom may come to us." (*On the Lord's Prayer*, 13)

"[T]he Jews...have remained in darkness by having forsaken the light." (*On the Lord's Prayer*, 36)

"First of all, favor with God was given to the Jews. Thus they of old were righteous; thus their ancestors were obedient to their religious engagements. Thence with them both the loftiness of their rule flourished, and the greatness of their race advanced. But subsequently becoming neglectful of discipline, proud, and puffed up with confidence in their fathers, they despised the divine precepts, and lost the favor conferred upon them. But how profane became their life, what offense to their violated religion was contracted, even they themselves bear witness, since, although they are silent with their voice, they confess it by their end. Scattered and straggling, they wander about; outcasts from their own soil and climate, they are thrown upon the hospitality of strangers." (*On the Vanity of Idols*, 10)

"Did not the Jews perish for this reason, that they chose rather to envy Christ than to believe Him? Disparaging those great works which He did, they were deceived by blinding jealousy, and could not open the eyes of their heart to the knowledge of divine things." (*On Jealousy and Envy*, 5)

"For because among the Jews there was a want of spiritual grace, wine also was wanting. For the vineyard of the Lord of hosts was the house of Israel; but Christ, when teaching and showing that the people of the Gentiles should succeed them, and that by the merit of faith we should subsequently attain to the place which the Jews had lost, of water made wine; that is, He showed that at the marriage of Christ and the Church, as the Jews failed, the people of the nations should rather flow together and assemble." (Letter 62:12)

MASS & EUCHARIST

"[A] woman who in advanced life and of more mature age secretly crept in among us when we were sacrificing, received not food, but a sword for herself;

and as if taking some deadly poison into her jaws and body, began presently to be tortured, and to become stiffened with frenzy; and suffering the misery no longer of persecution, but of her crime, shivering and trembling, she fell down. The crime of her dissimulated conscience was not long unpunished or concealed. She who had deceived man felt that God was taking vengeance." (*On the Lapsed*, 26)

"[W]hen one, who himself was defiled, dared with the rest to receive secretly a part of the sacrifice celebrated by the priest; he could not eat nor handle the holy of the Lord, but found in his hands when opened that he had a cinder." (*On the Lapsed*, 26)

"Christ is the bread of those who are in union with His body. And we ask that this bread should be given to us daily, that we who are in Christ, and daily receive the Eucharist for the food of salvation, may not, by the interposition of some heinous sin, by being prevented, as withheld and not communicating, from partaking of the heavenly bread, be separated from Christ's body, as He Himself predicts, and warns, 'I am the bread of life which came down from heaven. If any man eat of my bread, he shall live for ever: and the bread which I will give is my flesh, for the life of the world.' When, therefore, He says, that whoever shall eat of His bread shall live for ever; as it is manifest that those who partake of His body and receive the Eucharist by the right of communion are living, so, on the other hand, we must fear and pray lest any one who, being withheld from communion, is separate from Christ's body should remain at a distance from salvation; as He Himself threatens, and says, 'Unless you eat the flesh of the Son of man, and drink His blood, you shall have no life in you.' And therefore we ask that our bread—that is, Christ—may be given to us daily, that we who abide and live in Christ may not depart from His sanctification and body." (*On the Lord's Prayer*, 18)

"But now indeed peace is necessary, not for the sick, but for the strong; nor is communion to he granted by us to the dying, but to the living, that we may not leave those whom we stir up and exhort to the battle unarmed and naked, but may fortify them with the protection of Christ's body and blood. And, as the Eucharist is appointed for this very purpose that it may be a safeguard to the receivers, it is needful that we may arm those whom we wish to be safe against the adversary with the protection of the Lord's abundance. For how do we teach or provoke them to shed their blood in confession of His name if we deny to those who are about to enter on the warfare the blood of Christ? Or how do we make them fit for the cup of martyrdom, if we do not first admit them to drink, in the Church, the cup of the Lord by the right of communion?" (Letter 53:2)

"Yea, it is the great honor and glory of our episcopate to have granted peace to martyrs, so that we, as priests, who daily celebrate the sacrifices of God, may prepare offerings and victims for God." (Letter 52:3)

"[T]he soldiers of Christ ought to prepare themselves with uncorrupted faith and robust courage, considering that they drink the cup of Christ's blood daily, for the reason that they themselves also may be able to shed their blood for Christ." (Letter 55:1)

"Let us also arm the right hand with the sword of the Spirit, that it may bravely reject the deadly sacrifices; that, mindful of the Eucharist, the hand which has received the Lord's body may embrace the Lord Himself, hereafter to receive from the Lord the reward of heavenly crowns." (Letter 55:9)

"For when Christ says, 'I am the true vine,' the blood of Christ is assuredly not water, but wine; neither can His blood by which we are redeemed and quickened appear to be in the cup, when in the cup there is no wine whereby the blood of Christ is shown forth, which is declared by the sacrament and testimony of all the Scriptures." (Letter 62:2)

"When the blood of the Lord and the cup of salvation have been drunk, the memory of the old man is laid aside, and there arises an oblivion of the former worldly conversation, and the sorrowful and sad breast which before was oppressed by tormenting sins is eased by the joy of the divine mercy; because that only is able to rejoice him who drinks in the Church which, when it is drunk, retains the Lord's truth." (Letter 62:11)

"[W]e ought in the ordinations of priests to choose none but unstained and upright ministers, who, holily and worthily offering sacrifices to God, may be heard in the prayers which they make for the safety of the Lord's people." (Letter 67:2)

PAGANISM

"Men imitate the gods whom they adore, and to such miserable beings their crimes become their religion." (Letter 1:8)

"Certainly when those things [plagues, wars, famines] occur which show the anger of an offended God, they happen not on account of us by whom God is worshipped, but they are called down by your sins and deservings, by whom God is neither in any way sought nor feared, because your vain superstitions are not forsaken, nor the true religion known in such wise that He who is the one God over all might alone be worshipped and petitioned." (*To Demetrianus*, 5)

"Oh, would you but hear and see them when they are adjured by us, and tortured with spiritual scourges, and are ejected from the possessed bodies with tortures of words, when howling and groaning at the voice of man and the power of God, feeling the stripes and blows, they confess the judgment to come!...You will see that under our hands they stand bound, and tremble as captives, whom you took up to and venerate as lords: assuredly even thus you might be confounded in those errors of yours, when you see and hear your gods, at once upon our interrogation betraying what they are, and even in your presence unable to conceal those deceits and trickeries of theirs." (*To Demetrianus*, 15)

"They are impure and wandering spirits, who, after having been steeped in earthly vices, have departed from their celestial vigor by the contagion of earth, and do not cease, when ruined themselves, to seek the ruin of others; and when degraded themselves, to infuse into others the error of their own degradation." (*On the Vanity of Idols*, 6)

PRAYER

"It is a loving and friendly prayer to beseech God with His own word, to come up to His ears in the prayer of Christ." (*On the Lord's Prayer*, 3)

"[L]et our speech and petition when we pray be under discipline, observing quietness and modesty. Let us consider that we are standing in God's sight. We must please the divine eyes both with the habit of body and with the measure of voice. For as it is characteristic of a shameless man to be noisy with his cries, so, on the other hand, it is fitting to the modest man to pray with moderated petitions." (*On the Lord's Prayer*, 4)

"Teacher of peace and the Master of unity would not have prayer to be made singly and individually, as for one who prays to pray for himself alone....Our prayer is public and common; and when we pray, we pray not for one, but for the whole people, because we the whole people are one." (*On the Lord's Prayer*, 8)

PURGATORY

"It is one thing, tortured by long suffering for sins, to be cleansed and long purged by fire; another to have purged all sins by suffering." (Letter 50:20)

SEE OF ROME/PETER

"The Lord speaks to Peter, saying, 'I say unto you, that you are Peter; and upon this rock I will build my Church, and the gates of hell shall not prevail against it. And I will give unto you the keys of the kingdom of heaven; and whatsoever you shall bind on earth shall be bound also in heaven, and whatsoever you shall loose on earth shall be loosed in heaven.' And again to the same He says, after His resurrection, 'Feed my sheep.' And although to all the apostles, after His resurrection, He gives an equal power, and says, 'As the Father has sent me, even so send I you: Receive the Holy Ghost: Whose soever sins you remit, they shall be remitted unto him; and whosesoever sins you retain, they shall be retained;' yet, that He might set forth unity, He arranged by His authority the origin of that unity, as beginning from one." (*On the Unity of the Church*, 4)

"Upon one He builds His Church, and to the same He says after His resurrection, 'feed My sheep.' And though to all His Apostles He gave an equal power yet did He set up one chair, and disposed the origin and manner of unity by his authority. The other Apostles were indeed what Peter was, but the primacy is given to Peter, and the Church and the chair is shown to be one. And all are pastors, but the flock is shown to be one, which is fed by all the Apostles with one mind and heart. He that holds not this unity of the Church, does he think that he holds the faith? He who deserts the chair of Peter, upon whom the Church is founded, is he confident that he is in the Church?" (*On the Unity of the Church*, 4)

"I had read your letter which you lately wrote hither to my clergy by Crementius the sub-deacon, to the effect that assistance should be given to those who might, after their lapse, be seized with sickness, and might penitently desire communion; I judged it well to stand by your judgment, lest our proceedings, which ought to be united and to agree in all things, should in any respect be different." (Letter 14:3)

"Both our common love and the reason of the thing demand, beloved brethren, that I should keep back from your knowledge nothing of those matters which are transacted among us, that so we may have a common plan for the advantage of the administration of the Church." (Letter 28)

"Far be it from the Roman Church to slacken her vigor with so profane a facility, and to loosen the nerves of her severity by overthrowing the majesty of faith." (Letter 30:3)

"There is one God, and Christ is one, and there is one Church, and one chair founded upon the rock by the word of the Lord. Another altar cannot be constituted nor a new priesthood be made, except the one altar and the one priesthood. Whosoever gathers elsewhere, scatters." (Letter 39:5)

"For we, who furnish every person who sails [to Rome] with a plan that they may sail without any offense, know that we have exhorted them to acknowledge and hold the root and matrix of the Catholic Church." (Letter 44:3)

"Since Rome from her greatness plainly ought to take precedence over Carthage, [Novatian] there committed still greater and graver crimes." (Letter 48:2)

"Cornelius was made bishop by the judgment of God and of His Christ, by the testimony of almost all the clergy, by the suffrage of the people who were then present, and by the assembly of ancient priests and good men, when no one had been made so before him, when the place of Fabian, that is, when the place of Peter and the degree of the sacerdotal throne was vacant; which being occupied by the will of God, and established by the consent of all of us, whosoever now wishes to become a bishop, must needs be made from without; and he cannot have the ordination of the Church who does not hold the unity of the Church." (Letter 51:8)

"Peter, upon whom by the same Lord the Church had been built, speaking one for all, and answering with the voice of the Church, says, 'Lord, to whom shall we go? You have the words of eternal life; and we believe, and are sure that You are the Christ, the Son of the living God'." (Letter 54:7)

"After such things as these, moreover, they still dare—a false bishop having been appointed for them by heretics—to set sail and to bear letters from schismatic and profane persons to the throne of Peter, and to the chief church whence priestly unity takes its source." (Letter 54:14)

"The faith, dearest brethren, which the blessed apostle commended in [the Church of Rome] has shone brightly. He even then in the spirit foresaw this praise of courage and firmness of strength; and, attesting your merits by the commendation of your future doings, in praising the parents he provokes the children." (Letter 55:2, see footnote in text)

"Cyprian, with his colleagues, to Lucius his brother, greeting. We had lately also congratulated you indeed, dearest brother, when the divine condescension, by a double honor, appointed you in the administration of God's Church." (Letter 57:1)

"Basilides, after the detection of his crimes, and the baring of his conscience even by his own confession, went to Rome and deceived Stephen our colleague, placed at a distance, and ignorant of what had been done, and of the truth, to canvass that he might be replaced unjustly in the episcopate from which he had been righteously deposed." (Letter 67:5)

"And the Lord also in the Gospel, when disciples forsook Him as He spoke, turning to the twelve, said, 'Will you also go away?' Then Peter answered Him, 'Lord, to whom shall we go? You have the word of eternal life; and we believe, and are sure, that You are the Son of the living God.' Peter speaks there, on whom the Church was to be built, teaching and showing in the name of the Church, that although a rebellious and arrogant multitude of those who will not hear and obey may depart, yet the Church does not depart from Christ; and they are the Church who are a people united to the priest, and the flock which adheres to its pastor." (Letter 68:8)

"[B]oth baptism is one and the Holy Spirit is one, and the Church founded by Christ the Lord upon Peter, by a source and principle of unity, is one also." (Letter 69:3)

"Peter, whom first the Lord chose, and upon whom He built His Church..." (Letter 70:3)

"But it is manifest where and by whom remission of sins can be given; to wit, that which is given in baptism. For first of all the Lord gave that power to Peter, upon whom He built the Church, and whence He appointed and showed the source of unity—the power, namely, that whatsoever he loosed on earth should be loosed in heaven." (Letter 72:7)

"Whither is he to come who thirsts? Shall he come to the heretics, where there is no fountain and river of living water at all; or to the Church which is one, and is founded upon one who has received the keys of it by the Lord's voice?" (Letter 72:11)

"But what is the greatness of his error, and what the depth of his blindness, who says that remission of sins can be granted in the synagogues of heretics, and does not abide on the foundation of the one Church which was once based by Christ upon the rock, may be perceived from this, that Christ said to Peter alone, 'Whatsoever you shall bind on earth shall be bound in heaven, and whatsoever you shall loose on earth shall be loosed in heaven.'" (Letter 74:16, Firmilian to Cyprian)

"Stephen...contends that he holds the succession from Peter, on whom the foundations of the Church were laid." (Letter 74:17, Firmilian to Cyprian)

MISCELLANEOUS

"The whole world is wet with mutual blood; and murder, which in the case of an individual is admitted to be a crime, is called a virtue when it is committed wholesale." (Letter 1:6)

"Avoid the envenomed tongue of the devil, who from the beginning of the world, always deceitful and lying, lies that he may deceive, cajoles that he may injure, promises good that he may give evil, promises life that he may put to death. Now also his words are evident, and his poisons are plain. He promises peace, in order that peace may not possibly be attained; he promises salvation, that he who has sinned may not come to salvation; he promises a Church, when he so contrives that he who believes him may utterly perish apart from the Church." (Letter 39:6)

"Nor would the infirmity and weakness of human frailty have any resource, unless the divine mercy, coming once more in aid, should open some way of securing salvation by pointing out works of justice and mercy, so that by almsgiving we may wash away whatever foulness we subsequently contract." (*On Works and Alms*, 1)

"Let those beware, who, obeying either their own rage or lust, and unmindful of the divine law and holiness, rejoice to throw abroad in the meantime things which they cannot prove; and although they may not be successful in destroying and ruining innocence, are satisfied with scattering stains upon it with lying reports and false rumors." (Letter 41:2)

"Not even an enemy has so much power as to prevent us, who love the Lord with our whole heart, and life, and strength, from declaring His blessings and praises always and everywhere with glory." (*On the Lapsed*, 1)

"For when one has pity on the poor, he lends to God; and he who gives to the least gives to God—sacrifices spiritually to God an odor of a sweet smell." (*On the Lord's Prayer*, 33)

"[The demons] however, when adjured by us through the true God, at once yield and confess, and are constrained to go out from the bodies possessed. You may see them at our voice, and by the operation of the hidden majesty, smitten with stripes, burnt with fire, stretched out with the increase of a growing punishment, howling, groaning, entreating, confessing whence they came and when depart, even in the hearing of those very persons who worship them, and either springing forth at once or vanishing gradually, even as the faith of the sufferer comes in aid, or the grace of the healer effects. Hence they urge the common people to detest our name, so that men begin to hate us before they know us, lest they should either imitate us if known, or not be able to condemn us." (*On the Vanity of Idols*, 7)

"God does not ask for our blood, but for our faith." (*On Mortality*, 17)

"He is not worthy to receive consolation in death who has not reflected that he was about to die." (Letter 51:23)

"The bishops our predecessors religiously considering this, and wholesomely providing for it, decided that no brother departing should name a cleric for executor or guardian; and if any one should do this, no offering should be made for him, nor any sacrifice be celebrated for his repose. For he does not deserve to be named at the altar of God in the prayer of the priests, who has wished to call away the priests and ministers from the altar." (Letter 65:2)

"For unity and peace and concord afford the greatest pleasure not only to men who believe and know the truth, but also to heavenly angels themselves, to whom the divine word says it is a joy when one sinner repents and returns to the bond of unity. But assuredly this would not be said of the angels, who have their conversation in heaven, unless they themselves also were united to us, who rejoice at our unity; even as, on the other hand, they are assuredly saddened when they see the diverse minds and the divided wills of some, as if not only they do not together invoke one and the same God, but as if, separated and divided from one another, they can neither have a common conversation nor discourse." (Firmilian to Cyprian, Letter 74:2)

"[T]he obstinate wickedness of the devil prevails even up to the saving water, but that in baptism it loses all the poison of his wickedness." (Letter 75:15)

Also available in the Christian Roman Empire Series

The Life of Belisarius
  by Lord Mahon (1848)

The Gothic History of Jordanes:
In English Version with an Introduction and a Commentary
  Translated by Charles Christopher Mierow (1915)

The Book of the Popes (Liber Pontificalis):
To the Pontificate of Gregory I
  Translated by Louise Ropes Loomis (1916)

The Chronicle of John, Bishop of Nikiu:
Translated from Zotenberg's Ethiopic Text
  Translated by R. H. Charles (1916)

The Ecclesiastical Annals of Evagrius:
A History of the Church from AD 431 to AD 594
  by Edward Walford (1846)

The Life of Saint Augustine:
A Translation of the Sancti Augustini Vita *by Possidius, Bishop of Calama*
  by Herbert T. Weiskotten (1919)

The Life of Saint Simeon Stylites:
A Translation of the Syriac in Bedjan's Acta Martyrum et Sanctorum
  by Rev. Frederick Lent (1915)

The Life of the Blessed Emperor Constantine:
In Four Books from 306 to 337 AD
  by Eusebius Pamphilus (1845)

The Dialogues of Saint Gregory the Great
  edited by Edmund G. Gardner (1911)

For more information on this series, see our website at:
http://www.evolpub.com/CRE/CREseries.html

CPSIA information can be obtained
at www.ICGtesting.com
Printed in the USA
FFHW022307080919
54787532-60481FF